STUDENT EDITION

Automated Accounting
8.0 Windows® 95, 98, NT, 2000, Me, and XP

Warren W. Allen, M.A. & Dale H. Klooster, Ed.D.

THOMSON

SOUTH-WESTERN

Australia · Canada · Mexico · Singapore · Spain · United Kingdom · United States

Automated Accounting 8.0
By Warren Allen & Dale Klooster

Editor-in-Chief:
Jack Calhoun

Vice President/Executive Publisher:
Dave Shaut

Team Leader:
Karen Schmohe

Acquisitions Editor:
Marilyn Hornsby

Project Manager:
Carol Sturzenburger

Production Editor:
Darrell E. Frye

Production Manager:
Patricia Matthews Boies

Manufacturing Coordinator:
Kevin Kluck

Consulting Editor:
Bill Lee

Compositor:
Argosy

Senior Marketing Manager:
Nancy A. Long

Marketing Coordinator:
Yvonne Patton-Beard

Internal Designer:
Graphica and Tippy McIntosh

Cover Designer:
Tippy McIntosh

Printer:
RR Donnelley & Sons
Willard, OH

COPYRIGHT © 2003 by South-Western, a division of Thomson Learning. Thomson Learning™ is a trademark used herein under license.

Printed in the United States of America
3 4 5 DW 06 05 04

For more information,
contact South-Western,
5191 Natorp Boulevard,
Mason, Ohio 45040.
Or you can visit our Internet site at:
http://www.swep.com

ALL RIGHTS RESERVED.
No part of this work covered by the copyright hereon may be reproduced or used in any form or by any means—graphic, electronic, or mechanical, including photocopying, recording, taping, Web distribution, or information storage and retrieval systems—without the written permission of the publisher.

For permission to use material from this text or product, contact us by
Tel (800) 730-2214
Fax (800) 730-2215
http://www.thomsonrights.com

ISBN: 0-538-43505-4

About the Authors

Warren Allen, M.A., is an author and developer of software for numerous educational courseware products. He has taught accounting and computer programming and is the author of computer-related products. He has also designed, developed, and installed numerous computerized accounting systems for businesses and governmental organizations.

Dale Klooster, Ed.D., is an author of educational courseware products. He has worked with various computer systems in business and industry and has been an educator in the field of computer information processing. He has also been a consultant to many businesses and educational institutions.

YOUR COURSE PLANNING JUST GOT EASIER!

★ **NEW! Automated Accounting 8.0**
by Allen and Klooster
This Windows software package takes the functionality of commercial accounting software and incorporated educational features so that students are prepared for the workplace.

Student Text	0-538-43505-4
Windows Program Disk (site license)	0-538-43517-8
Working Papers	0-538-43509-7

★ **NEW! Century 21 Accounting Anniversary Edition**
by Ross, Gilbertson, Lehman, and Hanson
Here is the fundamental accounting content you've come to trust from South-Western. 100 years of accounting excellence!

Multicolumn Journal Student Text	0-538-43524-0
General Journal Student Text	0-538-43529-1
Advanced Student Text	0-538-43534-8

★ **NEW! Managerial Accounting (Business 2000 Series)**
by Lee
Business 2000 is an exciting new modular instructional program that allows you to create customized courses or enhance already existing curriculum.

Learner Guide	0-538-43168-7
Instructional Module*	0-538-43169-5

*Each module includes one Learner Guide, Video, Annotated Instructor's Edition, Instructor's Resource CD, and ExamView® Pro CD.

★ **Keeping Financial Records for Business 9E**
by Schultheis, Kaliski, and Passalacqua
This package gives students a broad knowledge of business operations and the basic skills they need to keep better financial records.

Student Text	0-538-69151-4
Working Papers	0-538-69174-3

★ **NEW! Business Math 15E**
by Schultheis and Kazmarski
The 15th edition of this market-leading text provides the foundation for basic business math skills.

Student Text	0-538-43235-5
Student Activities and Study Guide	0-538-43254-3

★ **NEW! Banking and Financial Systems**
by Center for Financial Training
This text provides an overview of banking and financial services, including career opportunities.

Student Text	0-538-43241-1
Multimedia Module	0-538-43242-X

★ **NEW! Security First Bank 4E**
by Sargent and Ward
This popular simulation empowers students by providing a sound foundation in banking procedures from a consumer standpoint. Students learn by doing!

Simulation (one per student)	0-538-43187-3

Instructor support material available for all titles.

THOMSON ★ **SOUTH-WESTERN**

Join us on the Internet at www.swep.com

How to Use This Book

PRESENTATION ENGAGES STUDENT INTEREST

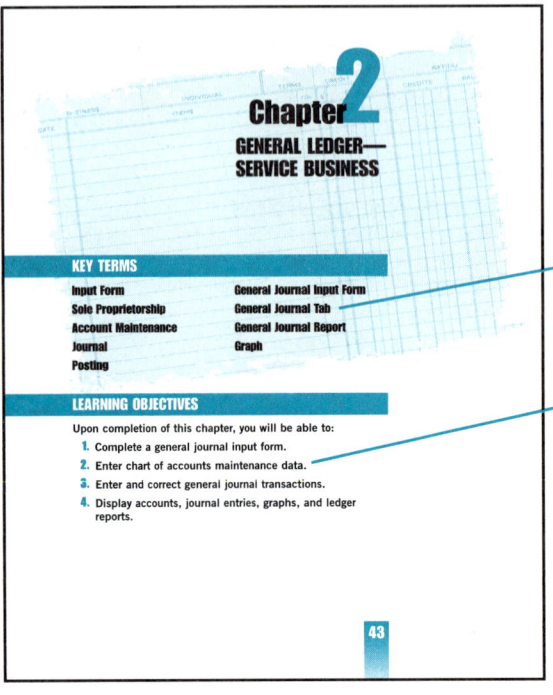

Key Terms are vocabulary words defined within the chapter.

Learning Objectives are clearly stated goals, which represent sections of the chapter.

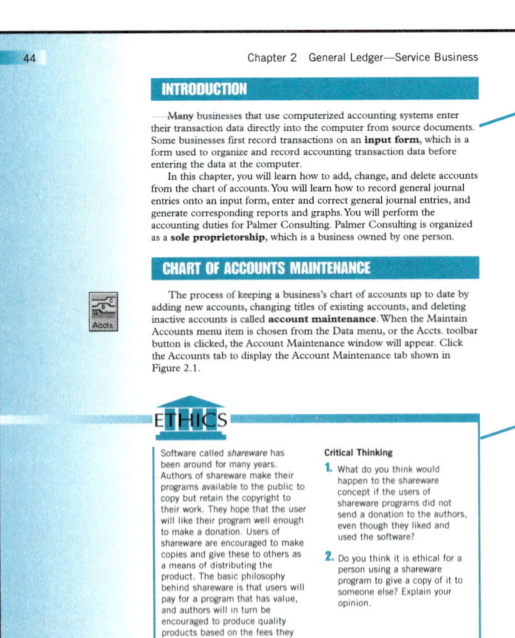

Introduction describes the chapter topics to be covered.

Ethics presents a computer-related situation that requires you to use critical thinking skills.

SPECIAL FEATURES ENHANCE LEARNING

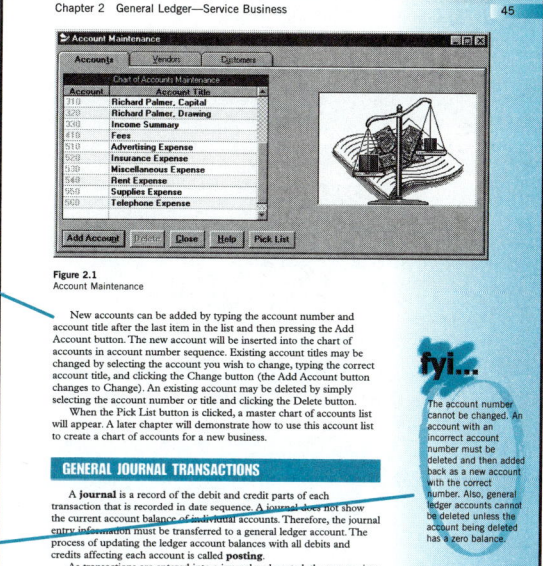

Operating procedures are presented with the illustrations and notes needed for you to process the text material.

FYI features provide tips about the accounting software and procedures.

Accounting Careers in Depth describes the career options open to students who specialize in accounting.

Internet features contain interesting facts about the World Wide Web.

ACTIVITIES AND PROBLEMS PROVIDE REVIEW AND ASSESSMENT

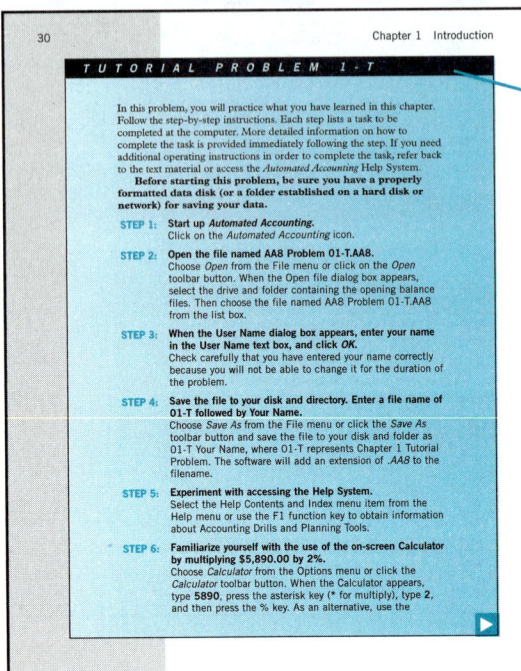

The computer **Tutorial Problem** contains step-by-step instructions for solving a problem that covers the chapter material.

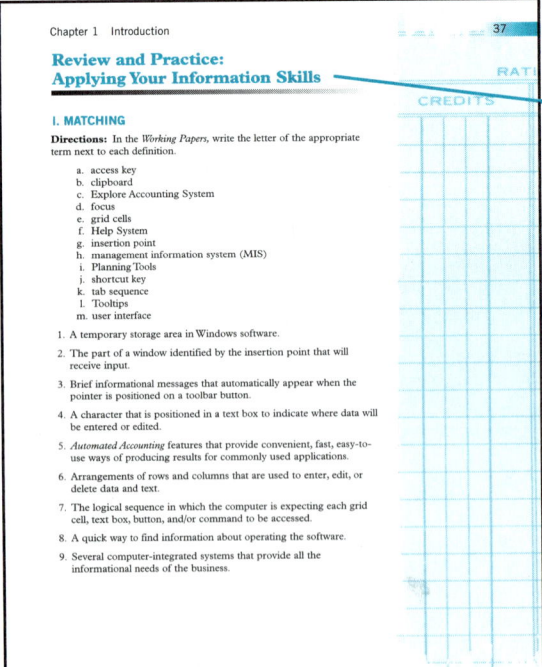

Applying Your Information Skills tests your recall of the chapter's main points and presents an optional Internet Activity.

A computer **Practice Problem** includes detailed instructions but no solution.

Independent Practice Problem 1-P

In the following problem, you will practice what you have learned in this chapter. *Note:* As you complete this problem, access the browser for helpful check figures to audit your work.

STEP 1: Complete the Applying Your Technology Skills 1-P questions at the end of this section as you work through the following steps.

STEP 2: Start up *Automated Accounting*.

STEP 3: Open and load the file named AA8 Problem 01-P.AA8.

STEP 4: Enter your name in the User Name dialog box.

STEP 5: Choose *Save As* and save the file to your disk and folder with a file name of 01-P Your Name.

STEP 6: Access the Help System to obtain information about using the Web Browser to search the Internet.

STEP 7: Use the on-screen Calculator to multiply $3,275.00 by 5%.

STEP 8: Calculate the annual cost of college based upon savings using the College Planner. With the Annual College Cost option set on, enter the data provided below. Then display the schedule of college savings and payments reports.

Beginning College Savings $1,950.00
Annual Yield (Percent) 7.75
Years Until College 8
Number of Years of College 4
Annual Contribution $3,750.00

STEP 9: Use the Accounting Equation tab in the Drills window to enter the following transactions.

Sept. 1 Received cash from owner as an investment, $8,500.00.
2 Paid cash for supplies, $210.00.
3 Paid cash for insurance, $405.00.
4 Paid cash for advertising, $500.00.
5 Bought supplies on account, $1,250.00.
6 Owner withdrew cash for personal use, $1,500.00.
6 Paid cash on account, $750.00.

Mastery Problem 1-M

In the following problem, you will practice what you have learned in this chapter.

STEP 1: Complete the Applying Your Technology Skills 1-M questions at the end of this section as you work through the following steps.

STEP 2: Start up *Automated Accounting*.

STEP 3: Open and load the file named AA8 Problem 01-M.

STEP 4: Enter your name in the User Name dialog box.

STEP 5: Choose *Save As* and save the file to your disk and folder with a file name of 01-M Your Name.

STEP 6: Access the Help System to obtain information about using the Internet feature of the software to download accounting files.

STEP 7: Use the on-screen Calculator to divide $42,360.00 by 12.

STEP 8: Calculate the annual cost of college based upon savings by using the College Planner. With the Annual College Cost option set on, enter the data provided below. Then display the schedule of college savings and payments reports.

Beginning College Savings $3,500.00
Annual Yield (Percent) 8.00
Years Until College 12
Number of Years of College 4
Annual Contribution $2,400.00

STEP 9: Use the Accounting Equation tab in the Drills window to enter the following transactions.

Sept. 1 Received cash from owner as an investment, $10,500.00.
2 Paid cash for supplies, $435.00.
2 Paid cash for insurance, $750.00.
3 Bought supplies on account, $2,550.00.
4 Paid cash for utility bills, $176.32.
5 Owner withdrew cash for personal use, $2,000.00.
6 Paid cash on account, $1,200.00.

A computer **Mastery Problem** will challenge you with only brief, general instructions.

STEP 10: Display the Accounting Equation Report.

STEP 11: Use the Classify Accounts tab in the Drills window to identify the account classification, normal account balance, and debit or credit increase for each of the following accounts:

Supplies
Accounts Payable
Advertising Expense
Utilities Expense
Heather Payne, Drawing
Rent Expense

STEP 12: Display the Classify Accounts Report.

STEP 13: Use the Explorer to display the Accounts Payable account activity.

STEP 14: Save the data file.

STEP 15: End the *Automated Accounting* session.

Applying Your Technology Skills 1-M

Directions: Write the answers to the following questions in the *Working Papers*.

1. From the Help System, note the procedure to use the Internet to download accounting files.
2. What is the result of using the Calculator to find the quotient of $42,360 divided by 12?
3. From the College Planner, what is the calculated annual college payment?
4. What is the total amount of assets shown on the accounting equation report?
5. What account number is assigned to Utilities Expense?
6. From the Explorer, note the transaction activity for Accounts Payable.

Applying Your Technology Skills contains audit questions for the Practice and Mastery problems, in which you must interpret your computer-generated output.

Preface

We live in an era in which powerful, low-cost personal computers are meeting a wide variety of business recordkeeping and accounting needs. During the past two decades, we have seen, and will continue to see, an expansion of personal computers that now use powerful graphical user interface operating systems such as Microsoft, Windows,[1] and OS/2 from IBM[2]. The *Automated Accounting 8.0* software that accompanies this textbook enables students to learn how computers are used for accounting applications with today's powerful computer systems.

MAJOR FEATURES

The major feature of *Automated Accounting 8.0* is its seamless integration within the *Automated Accounting 8.0* software applications of general ledger, accounts payable, accounts receivable, bank reconciliation, plant assets, budgeting, payroll, purchase order processing, and sales order processing. For example, as payroll transactions are entered, the resulting journal entry is immediately placed into the general ledger. In addition, menu options are available to generate periodic journal entries such as depreciation adjusting entries and employer's payroll taxes. The *Automated Accounting 8.0* software also offers integration with other applications, such as spreadsheets and word processors, via copy and paste capabilities.

HIGHLIGHTS OF AUTOMATED ACCOUNTING 8.0

This version of *Automated Accounting 8.0* retains and expands upon the features that made the previous Windows and DOS versions successful, while taking full advantage of the innovations of the respective graphical user interface operating systems. It will run in the Windows 95, 98, NT, Me, XP and 2000 environments. The design and development of the software follows the standard conventions of each of these graphical user interface operating systems. This standardization has been tremendously helpful to users. When you have learned to use one application, you have learned the essentials for using most other applications that run in the same environment. The authors have taken great care in the development of the software to follow the standard interface to ensure that operating procedures learned while running other applications are immediately transferable to *Automated Accounting 8.0*. Likewise, the operating procedures learned while running *Automated Accounting 8.0* are immediately transferable to other applications.

---

[1] Microsoft and Windows are registered trademarks of Microsoft Corporation. Any reference to Microsoft or Windows refers to this footnote.
[2] IBM is a registered trademark of International Business Machines Corporation. Any reference to IBM refers to this footnote.

Preface

Among the major features found in this version of *Automated Accounting 8.0* are the following:

- All of the frequently used options are accessible by clicking on a **toolbar button**, which takes the user to a window containing multiple tabs. The tabs access various grid-based data-entry screens that facilitate efficient entry of multiple transactions.

- A **comprehensive setup/customization** capability permits customization to be centralized in one window with six tabs.

- A **features selection** is provided that allows the user to select which systems are active. The accounting system is always active. Plant assets, payroll, inventory, budgeting, and accounting drills are optional. If a system is not selected, all traces of it disappear from the software. For example, if payroll is inactive, the Employee Maintenance and Payroll Transaction tabs disappear from the respective input windows, all menu options pertaining to payroll disappear, and all payroll reports disappear from the report selection.

- The **setup process** is very intuitive. For example, the software automatically classifies accounts to the most likely possibility, so keying is rarely needed. The required accounts needed for system integration are automatically determined by examining account titles based upon the type of business and business organization.

- A **Journal Wizard** is provided that allows users to create their own special journals and to tailor journals to the many varieties of problems in this textbook, as well as most other accounting texts and applications.

- **Accounting review** textual material with accompanying computer drills have been provided as a review of the basic accounting principles associated with (1) the accounting equation, (2) classifying accounts, and (3) analyzing transactions.

- An **Explorer** feature has been provided that enables the user to access data stored by the software in order to perform audit checks, check account activity, isolate errors, and perform other tasks that are helpful in managing account information.

- A **Web Browser** feature is available that uses the computer system's default browser to access the Internet to complete the optional **Internet activities** provided at the end of each chapter. Also, this feature can be used to access and display check figures (while off-line) that are available for student reference during solution of all "P" designated computer problems.

- **Bank reconciliation** software has been provided that simplifies the reconciliation process by automatically bringing the Cash account balance forward, displaying all checks stored by the computer from which outstanding checks can be selected, and performing all bank reconciliation computations.

- A **tax table** allows the user to change federal and state tax tables, as well as tax rates and limits for social security, Medicare, unemployment, and city tax rates.

- Five **Planning Tools** are provided for personal use as well as for problems in the textbook. The Planning Tools are the (1) College Planner, (2) Savings Planner, (3) Retirement Planner, (4) Loan Planner, and (5) Notes and Interest Planner.

- The software automatically generates **closing entries**. Journal entries are retained after closing so that errors discovered after closing can be corrected easily.

- A powerful **application integration** capability is available that permits all the accounting reports to be copied to the clipboard for pasting to spreadsheet or word processor application software.

- A **check writing** feature is available that will prepare checks when a cash-payment transaction involving a vendor is posted or when an employee's payroll information is entered.

- A menu option to automatically generate the **depreciation adjusting entries** for plant assets is provided.

- Menu options are available that automatically generate the **current payroll journal entry** and the **employer's payroll taxes journal entry**.

- A **purchase order processing** capability has been integrated with inventory to process purchase orders, purchases, and purchase returns on the computer. When a purchase order transaction is entered, the system automatically generates a purchase order form, updates inventory, and stores the information for later retrieval. When the merchandise is received and entered, the system automatically generates a purchase invoice form and updates inventory, the purchases journal, the vendor account, and the general ledger accounts.

- A **sales order processing** capability has been integrated with inventory to process sales and sales return transactions on the computer. As the invoice is processed, the system automatically generates a sales invoice form and updates inventory, the sales journal, the customer account, and the general ledger accounts.

- A **budgeting system** has been provided for income statement accounts. A budget report can be generated that shows an income statement with account balances, budgets, and variances.

- The software has a **user-selectable font**, font size, etc., allowing users to exploit the capabilities of their particular printers.

- A **graphing feature** automatically generates the following graphs: (1) income statement bar graph; (2) expense distribution pie graph; (3) actual-versus-budgeted income statement bar graph; (4) balance sheet bar graph; (5) sales line graph; (6) top five customers bar graph; (7) labor distribution by expense account graph; (8) depreciation comparison line graph comparing asset depreciation by several methods; (9) five most profitable inventory items graph; and (10) five least profitable inventory items graph.

- **Run dates** (which appear on all reports) are automatically determined by the software. When a report is selected, the default run date appears as editable text so it can be accepted or changed. All dates used by the computer can be changed by clicking a calendar icon button and selecting the desired date, by striking the + and – keys, or by keying the desired date.

- An extensive, comprehensive, **context-sensitive Help System** has been provided that offers a quick way to find information about operating the software.

ORGANIZATIONAL FEATURES

The textbook consists of thirteen chapters and three comprehensive problems. Each chapter begins with an introduction that describes the topics to be covered. The operating procedures are presented with ample illustrations and notes required to process the accounting material. A chapter summary follows the presentation. A computer tutorial problem comes next and contains detailed step-by-step instructions for completing a problem that covers the material presented in the chapter. Following the tutorial problem is a student exercise, an optional Internet activity, a computer practice problem, and a computer mastery problem. The computer practice and mastery problems have accompanying audit questions designed to interpret the computer-generated output. The audit questions can also be used to check student work when it is not practical to print reports. Also, most computer problems contain optional spreadsheet and word processing activities that utilize the information generated by the accounting system. These optional activities are not required to complete the problems; however, if access to a spreadsheet or word processor is available, it is highly recommended that these activities be completed.

LEARNING OBJECTIVES

This courseware package is intended for students who want to learn about computerized accounting principles. Therefore, the major objectives of this book and its associated software are: (1) to present and integrate accounting principles in such a way that no prior knowledge of computers or computerized accounting is required; (2) to provide a hands-on approach to learning how modern computerized automated accounting systems function; and (3) to provide knowledge and hands-on experience in integrating accounting with other business applications such as spreadsheets and word processors. Each chapter identifies the learning objectives to be mastered for that chapter.

Additional flexibility has been designed into the computer software to permit its use with most traditional accounting textbooks. The computer can be used to solve manual accounting problems in these textbooks.

MESSAGE TO THE STUDENT

The *Automated Accounting 8.0* software is designed so that computer-generated output and the accounting procedures are very similar to those currently used in business and industry. The significant difference between the software used in this package and an actual business system is the simplicity of computer operation.

When a business uses a computerized system to control such valuable assets as cash, inventory, and accounts receivable, very tight controls are maintained on security, data entry, and audit trail procedures. These controls often complicate the operation of a computerized system. Some of these restrictions have been intentionally omitted from this package to simplify the operations and provide a usable, relevant educational tool.

MESSAGE TO THE INSTRUCTOR

This package has been designed so that the material and the computer problems presented in this textbook can be introduced gradually through the use of template (opening balances) files that permit the processing of ongoing accounting systems. In this way, students can concentrate on learning accounting topics while they gain experience with the various features of the software.

Each chapter contains a tutorial problem. Each chapter also contains a student exercise, an optional Internet activity, and two computer challenge problems (with audit questions) to ensure that the students comprehend the material presented. This approach permits the students to work independently and at their own speed.

An *Instructor's Manual* is provided to assist you while using *Automated Accounting 8.0*. In addition, a solution checker called the *Electronic Auditor* is available to automatically check your students' solutions against the solutions that are installed to your hard disk along with the *Auditor* software. These solution files contain the same data provided in print in the *Instructor's Manual*.

Preface

REQUIRED HARDWARE

The *Automated Accounting 8.0* package can be installed and executed on computers capable of running the Microsoft Windows 95, 98, NT, Me, XP and 2000 operating systems. A hard drive with at least 15 megabytes of available disk space and a CD drive are required for installation. Access to a printer is optional but recommended.

ACKNOWLEDGMENTS

We would like to express our appreciation to all who have provided helpful comments and suggestions. Many useful comments from instructors and students have resulted in significant improvements in the textbook and software. We would also like to acknowledge the excellent support received from the sales, editorial, and production staffs at South-Western Educational Publishing. Their expertise, professionalism, and commitment to quality have made our association with them a rewarding working experience.

DEMONSTRATION PROBLEM

A demonstration problem is provided with the files for *Automated Accounting 8.0*. The demonstration problem is started by opening file AA8 Demonstration.

The activities in this demonstration problem will assist you in becoming familiar with *Automated Accounting 8.0*. Step-by-step instructions are provided and can be viewed and/or printed by clicking the Browser button once the file has been opened. The problem showcases many of the major features of the *Automated Accounting 8.0* software in accounting, bank reconciliation, plant assets, payroll, sales order processing and inventory control, budgeting, planning tools, spreadsheet integration, and period-end closing activities.

You may also explore on your own by choosing menu items, displaying reports and graphs, entering your own data, etc., or you can pick and choose from the activities included to learn more about the specific features of the software.

Because you may choose to practice only selected portions of this problem or add additional transactions and activities, no solution has been provided in the *Electronic Auditor* for the Demonstration Problem.

Warren W. Allen
Dale H. Klooster

Contents

CHAPTER 1 Introduction — 1

Introduction	2
Installation and Memory Requirements	4
Automated Accounting Startup	4
Operating Procedures	5
Help System	15
On-Screen Calculator	17
Planning Tools	17
Accounting Review	18
Explore Accounting System	25
Internet Web Browser	26
Review and Practice: Applying Your Information Skills	37
Independent Practice Problem 1-P	39
Mastery Problem 1-M	41

CHAPTER 2 General Ledger—Service Business — 43

Introduction	44
Chart of Accounts Maintenance	44
General Journal Transactions	45
General Journal Report	49
Graphing	52
Review and Practice: Applying Your Information Skills	64
Independent Practice Problem 2-P	66
Mastery Problem 2-M	69

CHAPTER 3 General Ledger—End-of-Fiscal-Period for a Service Business and Bank Reconciliation — 71

Introduction	73
Adjusting Entries	73
Financial Statements	75
Bank Reconciliation	78
Period-End Closing	80
Review and Practice: Applying Your Information Skills	97
Independent Practice Problem 3-P	98
Mastery Problem 3-M	102

Table of Contents

Reinforcement Activity R-1   106

CHAPTER 4   Purchases and Cash Payments   113

Introduction	114
Maintain Vendors	115
Purchases	115
Cash Payments	118
Journal Reports	120
Ledger Reports	121
Review and Practice: Applying Your Information Skills	138
Independent Practice Problem 4-P	139
Mastery Problem 4-M	143

CHAPTER 5   Sales and Cash Receipts   147

Introduction	148
Maintain Customers	149
Sales	150
Cash Receipts	152
Journal Reports	155
Ledger Reports	156
Statements of Account	158
Review and Practice: Applying Your Information Skills	174
Independent Practice Problem 5-P	175
Mastery Problem 5-M	178

CHAPTER 6   End of Fiscal Period for a Partnership (Merchandising Business)   182

Introduction	183
Adjusting Entries	183
Financial Statements	185
Period-End Closing for a Partnership	186
Review and Practice: Applying Your Information Skills	201
Independent Practice Problem 6-P	201
Mastery Problem 6-M	206

Reinforcement Activity R-2   210

CHAPTER 7   Discounts, Debit Memorandums, and Credit Memorandums   216

Introduction	217
Purchases Discounts	218
Sales Discounts	219
Debit Memorandums	219
Credit Memorandums	220
Review and Practice: Applying Your Information Skills	234
Independent Practice Problem 7-P	235
Mastery Problem 7-M	239

CHAPTER 8   Plant Assets   243

Introduction	244
Plant Assets Input Form	245
Maintain Plant Assets Data	247
Displaying Plant Assets Reports	247
Generating and Posting Depreciation Adjusting Entries	250
Review and Practice: Applying Your Information Skills	262
Independent Practice Problem 8-P	264
Mastery Problem 8-M	266

CHAPTER 9   Corporations   269

Introduction	270
Journal Entries	270
Checks	275
Income Statement By Month and Year	275
Review and Practice: Applying Your Information Skills	301
Independent Practice Problem 9-P	302
Mastery Problem 9-M	307

Reinforcement Activity R-3	313

CHAPTER 10 Payroll — 320

Introduction	321
Employee Input Form	321
Employee Maintenance	324
Payroll Transactions Input Form	325
Payroll Transactions	325
Payroll Journal Entries	328
Payroll Reports	330
Review and Practice: Applying Your Information Skills	350
Independent Practice Problem 10-P	351
Mastery Problem 10-M	356

CHAPTER 11 Accounts Payable: Purchase Order Processing and Inventory Control — 360

Introduction	361
Inventory	361
Purchase Orders	364
Purchase Invoices and Receiving Reports	368
Purchase Invoice and Purchase Return Transactions	369
Transactions	369
Purge Invoices and Purchase Orders	372
Reports	373
Review and Practice: Applying Your Information Skills	399
Independent Practice Problem 11-P	401
Mastery Problem 11-M	406

CHAPTER 12 Accounts Receivable: Sales Order Processing and Inventory Control — 411

Introduction	412
Sales Invoices Input Form	414
Sales and Sales Return Transactions	415
Purge Sales Invoices	417
Review and Practice: Applying Your Information Skills	438
Independent Practice Problem 12-P	439
Mastery Problem 12-M	444

CHAPTER 13 Accounting System Setup — 450

Introduction	451
System Setup Specifications	451
System Setup Data	460
Review and Practice: Applying Your Information Skills	488
Independent Practice Problem 13-P	489
Mastery Problem 13-M	493

Glossary	**500**
Index	**506**

Chapter 1
Introduction

KEY TERMS

Management Information System (MIS)
User Interface
Tooltips
Title Bar
Current User Name
File Name
Menu Bar
Toolbar Buttons
Menu Title
Shortcut Key
Menu Item
Drop-Down Menu
Access Key
Focus
Insertion Point
Grid Cells
Clipboard
Tab Sequence
Help System
Planning Tools
Explore Accounting System

LEARNING OBJECTIVES

Upon completion of this chapter, you will be able to:

1. Identify and define the features of the *Automated Accounting 8.0* software and textbook.
2. Perform startup procedures.
3. Make menu and toolbar selections.
4. Use window controls.
5. Perform file-handling tasks (e.g., loading data from disk and saving data to disk).
6. Use Planning Tools.
7. Access Help System information.
8. Use the on-screen Calculator.
9. Apply basic principles of accounting concepts.
10. Use the Explorer feature of the software.
11. Use the Internet Web Browser feature of the software.

INTRODUCTION

Everyone uses accounting to some extent. For example, we use accounting when we purchase or sell goods and services, pay our bills, balance our checkbooks, budget our money, and prepare our tax returns. Businesses also use accounting to prepare reports for individuals, other businesses, and various government agencies regarding their financial activities. *Accounting* is an informational system that plans, analyzes, records, and reports financial information. An *accountant* is someone who summarizes detailed accounting information and then analyzes and interprets that information to assist owners and managers in making financial decisions. In many businesses, personnel called *bookkeepers* and *accounting clerks* assist the accountant and do the general accounting work of recording, reporting, and filing that are required on a routine basis.

A *business* is an economic entity that endeavors to sell goods and services to customers at prices that will pay all the costs of doing business and return a profit to the owners. To help achieve this objective, many businesses have turned to the use of the computer as a tool to help them collect, organize, and report large amounts of information. Today's modern businesses' informational needs are stored and managed by what is called a management information system (MIS). A typical **management information system (MIS)** consists of several computer-integrated systems that supply all the informational needs of the business. The accounting system is one of the most important of all these systems because it is used to manage the internal and external flow of the business's financial data.

Business owners, managers, accountants, bookkeepers, and accounting clerks need to know how to use modern MIS computerized

Using a computer to access another computer user's data can actually be a criminal activity. This activity is commonly referred to as *hacking*. The term hacking is often used by computer enthusiasts to describe the challenge of breaking codes or other protection schemes that prohibit unauthorized access. Hackers who break codes to access other users' confidential information, records, computer time, and so on are committing a crime.

Critical Thinking

1. Do you think that most hackers realize they are committing a criminal act?

2. What can be done to deter hacking?

Chapter 1 Introduction

accounting systems in order to efficiently perform accounting tasks. This text will teach you about computerized accounting, accounting spreadsheet applications, and word processing applications using a hands-on approach. You will learn to operate the software by entering realistic accounting transactions for a variety of business applications and by generating financial statements, spreadsheets, and other management information reports.

In software, a **user interface** is the way the user communicates with the software through images on the monitor. The *Automated Accounting* software uses a standard Windows user interface that includes drop-down menus, a toolbar, movable overlapping windows, on-screen help, and other operational conventions. Because this software uses the standard Windows interface, the techniques and terminology you learn from this text and accompanying software can be applied to many other software application packages. This facilitates the learning process and greatly reduces the need to retrain for each new application you use in the future.

The *Automated Accounting* software that accompanies this textbook is designed to handle general ledger, accounts payable, accounts receivable, financial statement analysis, bank reconciliation, plant assets, order processing, inventory, and payroll. In addition, data from the *Automated Accounting* software may be passed into most spreadsheet programs, such as Lotus 1-2-3, Quattro® Pro, and Excel, for further analysis. Report contents may be passed into most word processing programs, including Word, Works, and WordPerfect®, for use in formal reporting or presentations. You will learn several of these applications in the following chapters. You are not required to have access to spreadsheet or word processing software in order to use *Automated Accounting*. However, each of the end-of-chapter problems in this textbook contains optional steps for further spreadsheet and word processing analysis and reporting. It is recommended that you complete these optional applications if you have the software available.

Opening Balances Data

The installation disks include files that contain opening balance data for each problem in this textbook. When *Automated Accounting* is installed on your hard disk drive or network server, the opening balance files will automatically be included in the same folder as the software. Before a problem can be solved, the opening balances file must be loaded from this folder.

You may change the default folder from which opening balance files are loaded. The default folder should be changed only if the opening balance problems you need in order to complete your work have been stored in a folder other than the folder in which the software has been stored. To change the opening balance file default: (1) right-click on the Start button; (2) choose the Open menu item; (3) double-click Programs in the Start window; (4) double-click *Automated Accounting 8* in the Programs window;

(5) right-click *Automated Accounting 8.0*; (6) when the menu appears, click on the Properties menu item; (7) edit the pathname for the name of the default folder in the "Start in" text box; and (8) click OK.

User Data Files

Automated Accounting permits you to store data on a separate data disk, hard disk, or network file server. This feature enables you to save your work for completion at a later time. If you are using a floppy disk to save your data, make sure that it is properly formatted before use. For information on formatting a disk, refer to your computer system's operations manual or Help System.

INSTALLATION AND MEMORY REQUIREMENTS

Automated Accounting comes complete on a standard CD (compact disk). To use the software you need a processor running in the Windows 95, Windows 98, Windows NT, Windows 2000, Windows Me, or Windows XP, environment. In addition, a hard disk drive with at least 15 megabytes of available disk space and a CD drive are required for installation. A printer is optional but highly recommended.

The installation CD included in the software package contains compressed *Automated Accounting* program files, opening balance files, and the optional spreadsheet and word processing files required to complete all of the problems in this textbook. During the installation process, all of these compressed files are expanded into an executable format onto your computer's hard disk. The installation is a common procedure. Detailed step-by-step instructions are provided on the installation disk's label. Your instructor or computer center technician has probably already completed this one-time installation procedure.

Note: It is possible, in rare cases, that the colors chosen by the user within the computer's color control panel may conflict with the colors used by *Automated Accounting* in such a way that images and/or text may appear invisible. If you experience any problems with colors, go to the Control Panel that controls the colors and change colors. Choose the default colors provided by your user interface system software to prevent this conflict.

AUTOMATED ACCOUNTING STARTUP

To begin working with *Automated Accounting* (after the installation has been completed): (1) click the Windows Start button, (2) position the pointer on Programs, (3) position the pointer on *Automated Accounting 8*, and (4) when the sub-menu appears, click on *Automated Accounting 8.0*.

Automated Accounting contains several components that you will use to perform accounting tasks. Review Figure 1.1 to acquaint yourself with

Chapter 1 Introduction

terminology and location of the items on the toolbar. Notice the information message dialog "End the accounting program." This is called a Tooltip. **Tooltips** are brief informational messages that automatically appear when the pointer is positioned on a toolbar button. As shown in Figure 1.1, the "End accounting system" message appears when the pointer is positioned on the Exit toolbar button.

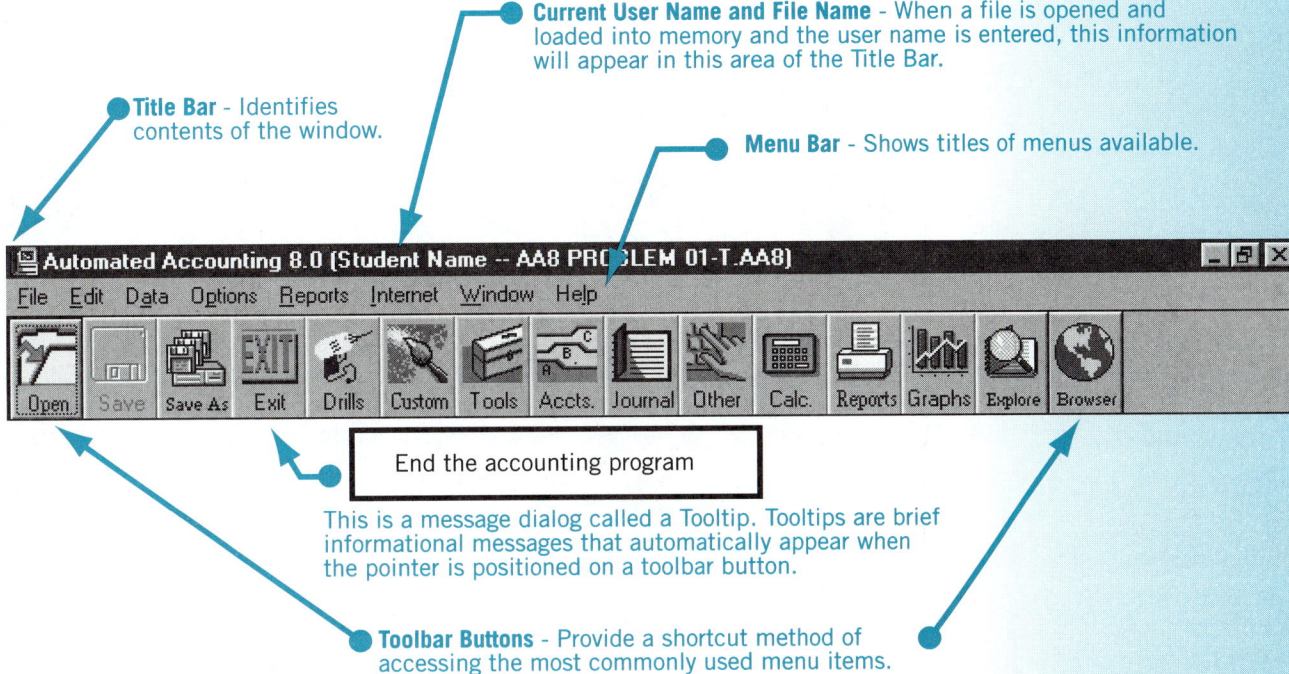

Figure 1.1
Automated Accounting Application Window

OPERATING PROCEDURES

The following topics cover the use of the menu bar, menu item selection, window controls, text selection, and other special features that have been provided to make the operation of the software easy to learn and efficient to use. Following the operating procedures, the Help System, on-screen Calculator, Planning Tools, Accounting Review Drills, Explorer, Web Browser, and Internet FTP features of the software will be covered.

The Menu Bar

One of the ways in which you communicate with the computer is to use the menu bar. As shown in Figure 1.1, the menu bar used by *Automated Accounting* contains eight menu titles—File, Edit, Data,

Options, Reports, Internet, Window, and Help. Each title contains menu items that instruct the computer to perform its processing tasks. The type of menu used in *Automated Accounting* is called a *drop-down menu*, because once it is selected via a mouse or keyboard (using the Alt key), a list of menu items displays immediately below the menu title selected. Figure 1.2 illustrates the parts of the *Automated Accounting* File drop-down menu. You may use the mouse or keyboard to select drop-down menus and choose menu items. If an item is "dimmed," it is not available for selection.

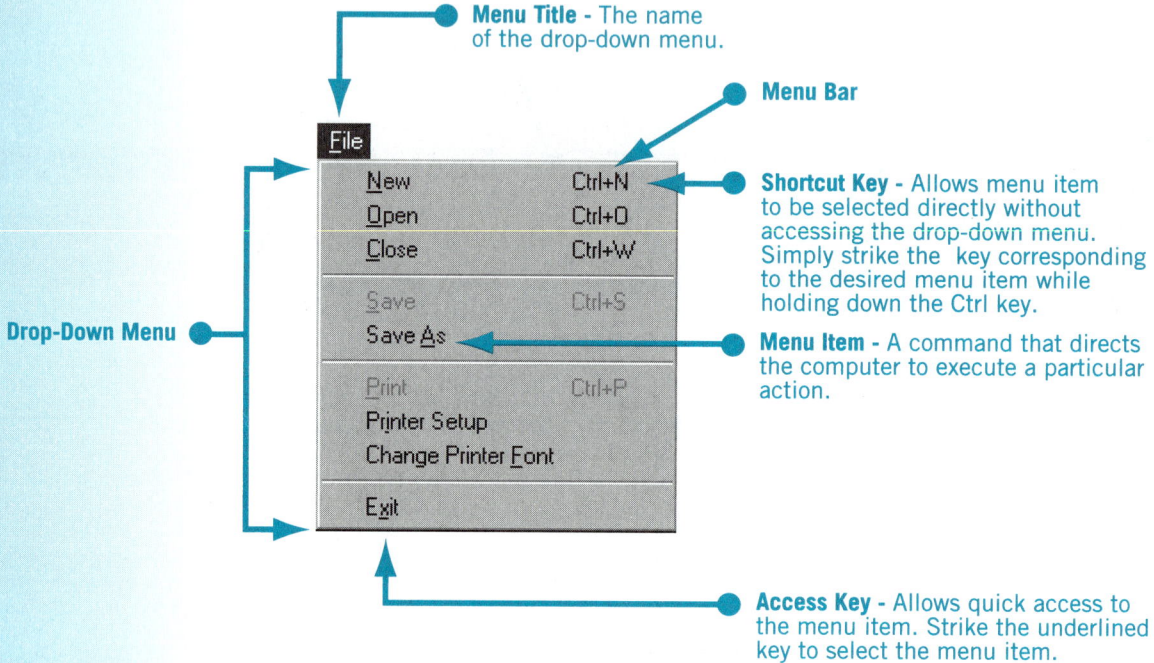

Figure 1.2
File Drop-Down Menu

Selecting and Choosing Menu Titles and Menu Items

In this textbook, the terms *select* and *choose* have different meanings. When menu titles on the menu bar or menu items are selected, they are highlighted. When a highlighted (or *selected*) menu title or item is *chosen*, the software will take the appropriate action. *Dimmed items* are not available for selection; you may need to select another item or perform a processing task before a dimmed item is activated.

Window Controls

You interact with the computer to perform *Automated Accounting* procedures through windows. A *window* is a rectangular area of the screen in which the software communicates with the user. Often the display screen contains only one window. At times, two or more overlapping windows may appear on the screen. However, only one window is active at a time. *Automated Accounting* uses several different windows to perform its accounting activities. For example, some windows contain tabs consisting of text boxes and grid cells used to enter data from the keyboard, some contain lists and reports, and others may display dialog box messages and operational information. Regardless of the activity, the part of the window that will receive input is said to have the **focus**. For example, a data field that has the focus is identified by the **insertion point**, which is a character that is positioned in a text box to indicate where data will be entered or edited. The insertion point usually appears as a vertical bar (|). A decision or choice of several options that has the focus is identified by a dotted rectangular box.

Many of the windows that appear may be moved, resized, and made inactive/active. For example, to move a window, point to the window's title bar (located at the top of the window) and drag the mouse. The pointer and an outline of the window will move as you drag. For specific information regarding moving a window, changing its size, making it inactive/active, etc., reference your computer's user interface operational manual.

It is important to understand how the operational controls contained in the windows and discussed below enable you to enter and edit data, select items from lists, and navigate the grids and controls. Refer to this section of the text for reference purposes as you encounter these controls later in this textbook. The following paragraphs identify the controls used by this software and describe how to use these controls.

Be sure you understand the meaning of the following terms that refer to the operations of most Windows software:

Check Boxes
Command Buttons
Dimmed Items
Double-Click
Drop-Down List
Drop-Down Menu
List Box
Menu Bar
Menu Item
Option Buttons
Text Box
Title Bar
Toolbar

Tabs *Automated Accounting* has been designed to use the visual image of folders to clarify and simplify operation. Several menu items (or toolbar selections) contain windows that include multiple folders with identifying tabs. These tabs provide for additional entry of data, options, and processing. For example, the Account Maintenance folder that appears when the Maintain Accounts menu item is chosen from the Data menu (or the Accts. Toolbar button is clicked) is shown in Figure 1.3. Notice that the window contains six different tabs: Accounts, Vendors, Customers, Plant Assets, Employees, and Inventory. The first tab (Accounts) appears as the active tab and is used to maintain accounts in the *chart of accounts*. To switch to another account maintenance function within the window, simply click on the desired tab. For example, to perform vendor maintenance, click on the tab labeled Vendors. The number of tabs that appear may vary depending on options set in the problem being worked.

Text Boxes A *text box* is an area into which the user types information, as shown in Figure 1.4. The user can accept the current text, edit it, or delete it. When a text box receives the focus, existing text

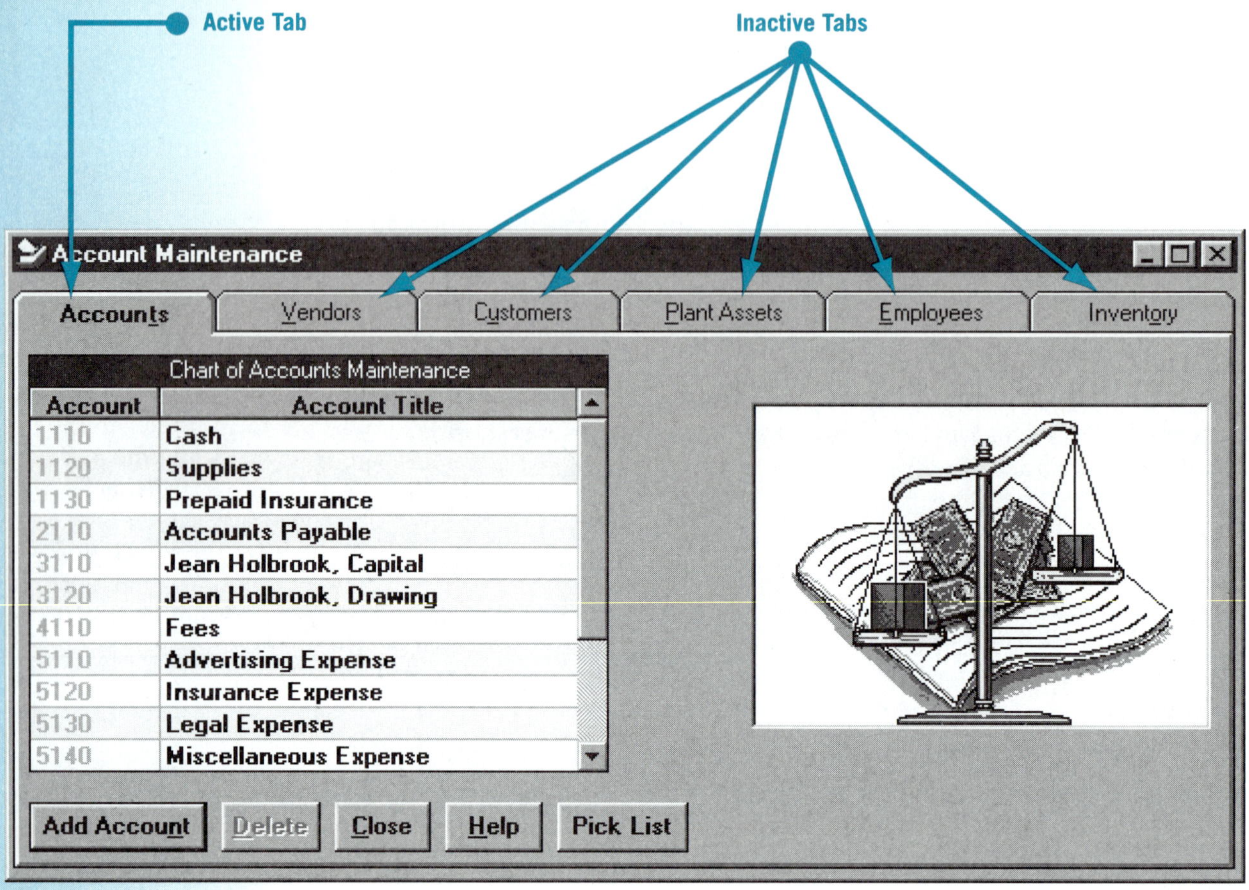

Figure 1.3
Tabs in the Account Maintenance Window

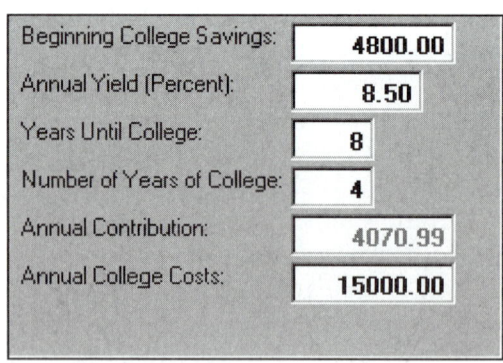

Figure 1.4
A Text Box

is selected and the insertion point appears to the right of the last character of text. Selected text is highlighted (indicated with light text on a dark background). An example of selected text is shown in Figure 1.5. If the insertion point is moved, the text is unselected. If the user types when text is selected, the selected text is discarded and replaced with the newly typed data.

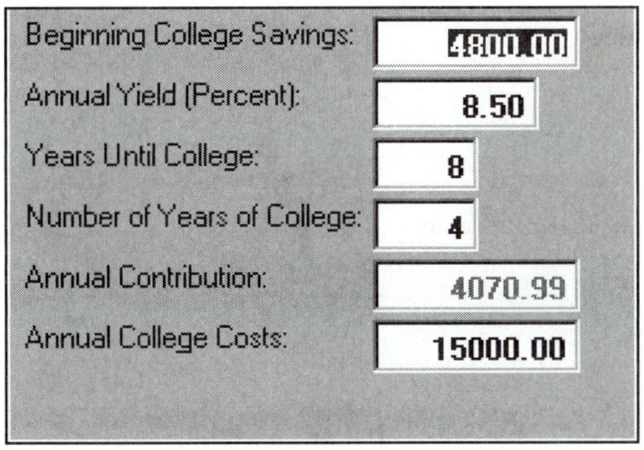

Chapter 1 Introduction

Figure 1.5
Text Box with Selected Text

Grid Cells Most of the data you will enter into the *Automated Accounting* software will be entered into windows that contain grid cells. **Grid cells** are arrangements of rows and columns that, like text boxes, are used to enter, edit, or delete data and text. When a grid cell receives the focus, any existing data or text within it is selected (highlighted) and the insertion point appears to the right of the last character within the cell. Figure 1.6 shows an example of how data that has been entered into grid cells appears. Notice that the amount of $10,000.00 under the Jean Holbrook, Capital column has been selected. If the insertion point is moved within the cell, the text is unselected and the contents may be edited. If the user types data with text selected, the selected text within the cell is discarded and replaced with the newly entered data.

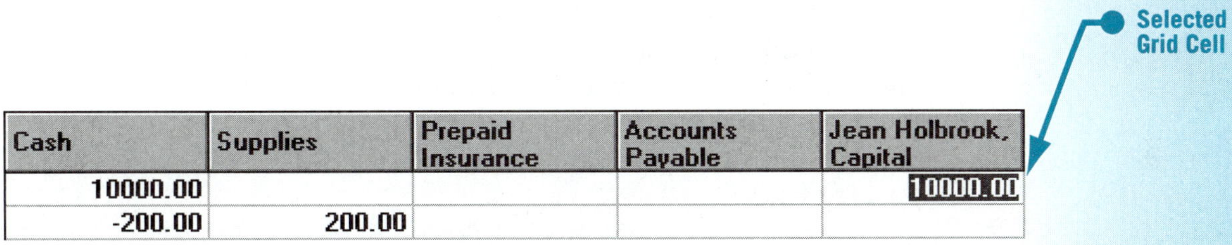

Selected Grid Cell

Cash	Supplies	Prepaid Insurance	Accounts Payable	Jean Holbrook, Capital
10000.00				10000.00
-200.00	200.00			

Figure 1.6
Example of Grid Cells

List Boxes A *list box* is used to display choices for the user. A list box and a drop-down list are similar in that each allows the user to select a single entry from a list of items. Figure 1.7 shows a chart of accounts list box. A highlight bar (or underline) identifies the currently selected item. Both the mouse and keyboard can be used to scroll through the list and choose items from the list. To select an item from the list, simply click on the desired item and then click OK (or double-click on the desired item).

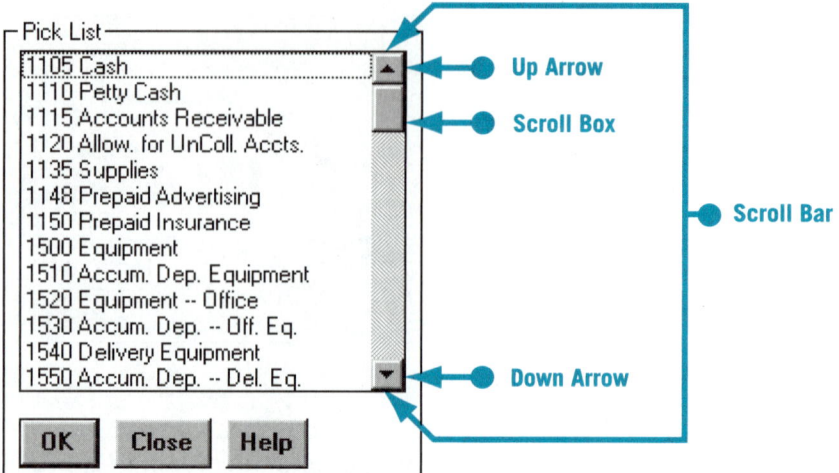

Figure 1.7
List Box

Drop-Down List The *drop-down list* consists of a text box with a drop-down arrow button immediately to the right. The text must be selected from among the items in the drop-down list. The drop-down list does not allow the user to enter new data that is not in the existing list into the text box. However, the user may enter an item that *is* in the drop-down list into the text box. Upon typing the first one or more characters, the computer will search the list and place the first occurrence of the matching item from the list in the text box.

A drop-down list, shown in Figure 1.8 before it has been opened, is used to control the customizing of a report. The same drop-down list is shown in Figure 1.9 after it has been opened. If the drop-down list contains more items than will fit, a scroll bar will be included. To toggle a drop-down list between open and closed, click on the drop-down arrow or press Alt+Down Arrow (while holding down the Alt key, press the Down Arrow key).

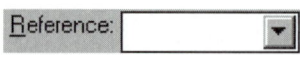

Figure 1.8
Drop-Down List
(Closed)

Note: While the drop-down list has the focus, an easy way to select an item from the list is to type the first character of the desired item. The first occurrence will appear in the text box. Later occurrences of items starting with the same character can be accessed by subsequent striking of the key corresponding to the first character. As an alternative, you may use the Up Arrow and Down Arrow keys to scroll through the items until the desired item is displayed in the text box.

Figure 1.9
Drop-Down List (Open)

Chapter 1 Introduction

Option Buttons *Option buttons* (sometimes referred to as *radio buttons*) represent a single choice within a set of mutually exclusive choices. You can select only one button from the choices provided. Empty circles represent option buttons. When an option is selected, the circle is filled (⊙). When an option is not selected, the circle is empty. (See Figure 1.10.)

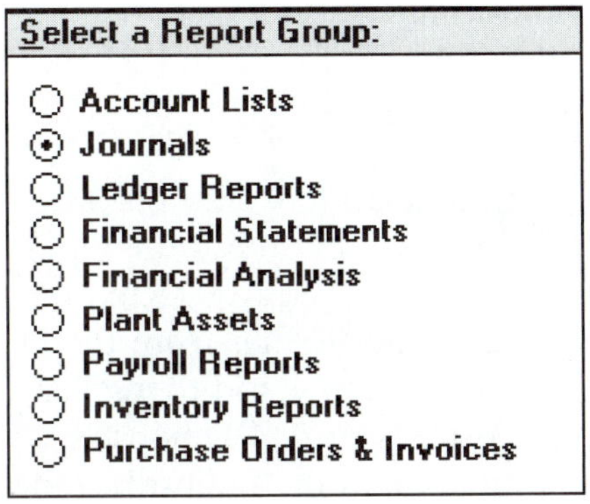

```
Select a Report Group:
  ○ Account Lists
  ⊙ Journals
  ○ Ledger Reports
  ○ Financial Statements
  ○ Financial Analysis
  ○ Plant Assets
  ○ Payroll Reports
  ○ Inventory Reports
  ○ Purchase Orders & Invoices
```

Figure 1.10
Option Buttons within a Group Box

Check Boxes *Check boxes* are used to control the selection of individual choices. When a task requiring multiple choices is selected, a group section will appear containing check boxes (☐) to the left of each choice. The check boxes are turned On or Off in any combination. When a check box is selected, it contains a check mark (☑) inside it. Figure 1.11 shows the check boxes that allow the user to select the Fixed Assets and Inventory features of the software.

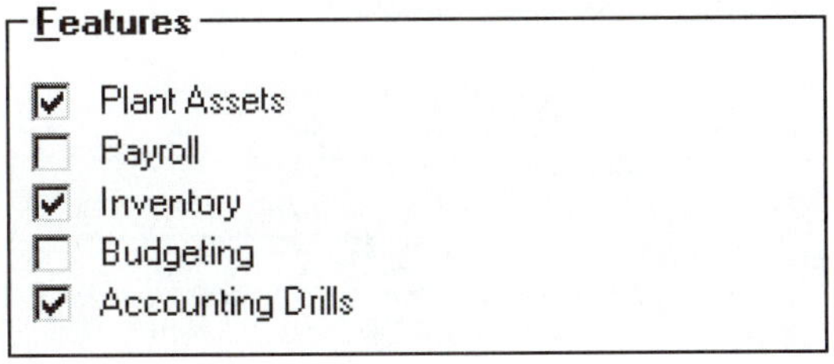

```
┌─ Features ──────────────┐
│  ☑  Plant Assets        │
│  ☐  Payroll             │
│  ☑  Inventory           │
│  ☐  Budgeting           │
│  ☑  Accounting Drills   │
└─────────────────────────┘
```

Figure 1.11
Check Boxes

Command Buttons A *command button* is a rectangular shaped figure containing a label that specifies an immediate action or response that will be taken by the computer when it is chosen. When a command button has a dotted line and/or dark shadow around the button (see the OK button in Figure 1.12), it is said to be the default button. The default

Figure 1.12
Command Buttons

command button can be chosen from anywhere in the window by pressing the Enter key.

File Menu

When the File menu is selected from the menu bar, the drop-down menu shown in Figure 1.2 appears. We will examine several of the menu items you will need in order to complete the problems at the end of this chapter.

Open The Open menu item is used to load a data file stored on disk into the computer's memory for processing. Figure 1.13 shows the Open dialog box. The highlighted file name identifies the currently selected file. Either the mouse or the keyboard can be used to choose files from the list. To choose a file, simply click on the desired file name and then click on the Open button (or double-click on the desired item). To choose a file using the keyboard, press the Tab key until a file in the file list has the focus, press the Up and Down Arrow keys to highlight the desired file, and then press the Enter key.

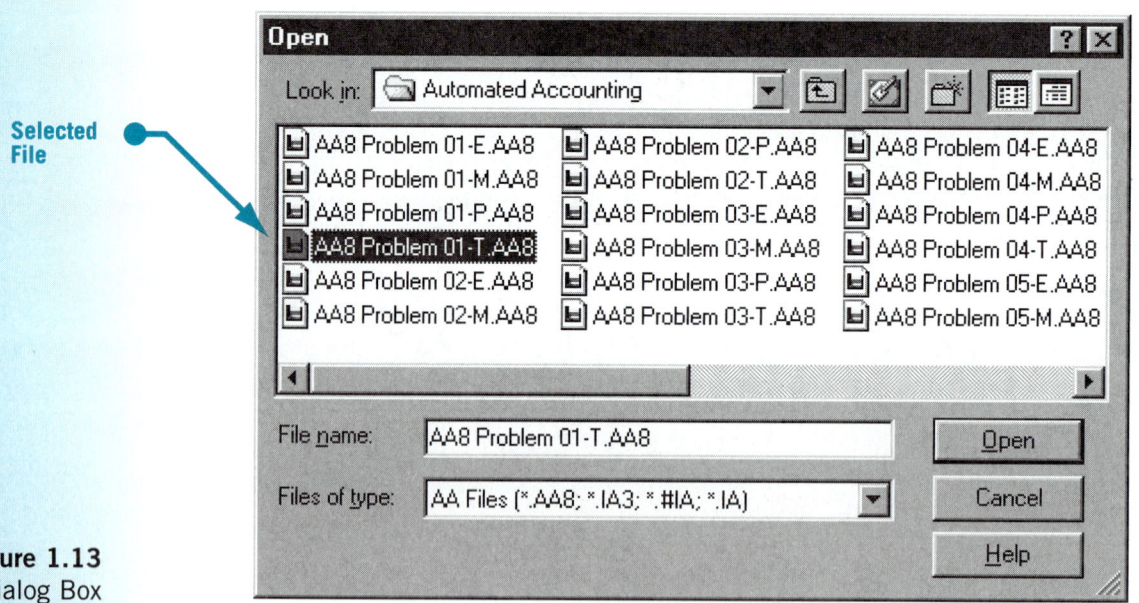

Figure 1.13
Open Dialog Box

Close Use the Close menu item in the File menu to close the current file displayed in the active window (removes the data from the computer's memory). When Close is chosen, the active window and all other windows containing data from the same file are closed. Close does *not* remove any data from disk.

Chapter 1   Introduction

Save   Use the Save menu item in the File menu to store your data to disk so that you can continue a problem in a later session. The data will be saved to disk with the current path (disk drive and folder) with the file name displayed in the title bar located at the top of the *Automated Accounting* application window. If you wish to save your data with a path (disk drive and/or folder) or file name different from the current path and file name, use Save As (described below).

Save As   This menu item is the same as Save except that the data can be saved with a path and/or file name different from the current path and file name. Save As is useful for making a backup copy of a data file. For example, you may want to make a backup of your data file before entering adjusting entries or before generating period-end closing entries. To make a backup copy, open the data file you wish to back up and use Save As to save it under a different name.

You *cannot* save a file to disk with the same file name as an opening balance file.

Print   The purpose of Print is to create a printed version of any report or graphic currently displayed in a report or graphic window. The entire contents of the displayed data windows will be printed when Print is chosen.

Print Setup   When the Print button is clicked while a report is displayed or when the Print Setup menu item is chosen from the File menu, a Print Setup dialog box will appear. The Print Setup dialog box is used to provide choices about the printer(s) connected to your computer, the paper size, the printing enhancements, etc. You will not need to use Print Setup unless you are having trouble printing. Check with your instructor for the proper information before making changes to your print setup. *Automated Accounting* uses the current printer information specified in your computer's user interface when processing a print command.

Change Printer Font   When reports are printed to an attached printer, *Automated Accounting* uses the font, font style, and size specified in the printer's Font dialog box. You may want to change the printer font, style, and/or size to make reports more attractive or to make the size smaller if fields are overflowing or wrapping incorrectly. Also, changing the font to one that is native to the printer you are using (e.g., Courier) will often increase the print speed.

Exit   This menu item is used to quit *Automated Accounting*. When Exit is chosen, the computer checks to see if the current data in its memory has been saved. If not, a dialog box will appear asking if you wish to save your data to disk.

Edit Menu

The Edit menu (shown in Figure 1.14) contains several menu items that can be used to remove and copy data from one location within *Automated Accounting* to another location in *Automated Accounting* or another application program. There are five menu items that will help you locate data. Each of these features will be discussed in detail as they are used throughout the text. The Cut, Copy, and Paste menu items are discussed below so that you may use them as desired at any time while working with the software.

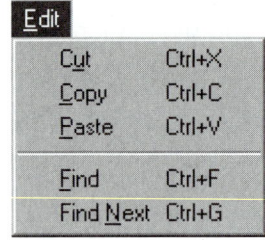

Figure 1.14
Edit Menu

Cut, Copy, and Paste The Cut and Copy menu items in the Edit menu may be used to place copies of the current selection (data that is highlighted in text or cell grid boxes) to the **clipboard**, a temporary storage area, in preparation for being pasted elsewhere. Copy leaves the source intact, whereas Cut erases it. The Cut, Copy, and Paste menu items in *Automated Accounting* work as in other applications.

Caution: If the destination already contains data, you may overwrite it when you choose Paste. Be careful that you allow enough space for the complete source to be pasted.

Navigation

Grid cells, text boxes, option buttons, check boxes, and command buttons should be filled in or selected in the normal tab sequence. The **tab sequence** is the logical sequence in which the computer is expecting each grid cell, text box, button, and/or command to be accessed. The sequence is usually left to right and top to bottom.

As you have already learned, the focus identifies the location within a window, tab, list, or dialog box in which the computer will receive the next input. For example, as the Tab key is pressed, the focus moves to the next item in the tab sequence. Pressing Shift+Tab moves the focus to the previous item in the tab sequence. When a grid cell or text box has the focus, an insertion point character (|) will appear to mark the current position where data will be entered or edited. When data is typed, the insertion point moves one character to the right for each character typed, and new characters appear to the left of the insertion point. Press the Enter key to choose the action or response of the default command button or command button that currently has the focus. Use the Esc key to choose Cancel or Close within the active window, tab, list, or dialog box.

Chapter 1 Introduction

HELP SYSTEM

Automated Accounting's on-screen **Help System** offers a quick way to find information about operating the software. To access Help, you can: (1) choose the Help Contents and Index menu item from the Help menu; (2) press the F1 function key at any time; or (3) choose the Help command button that appears at the bottom of various windows. The Help window shown in Figure 1.15 appears when the Help Contents and Index menu item is chosen from the Help menu. This initial display provides instructions for the basic operation of the Help system.

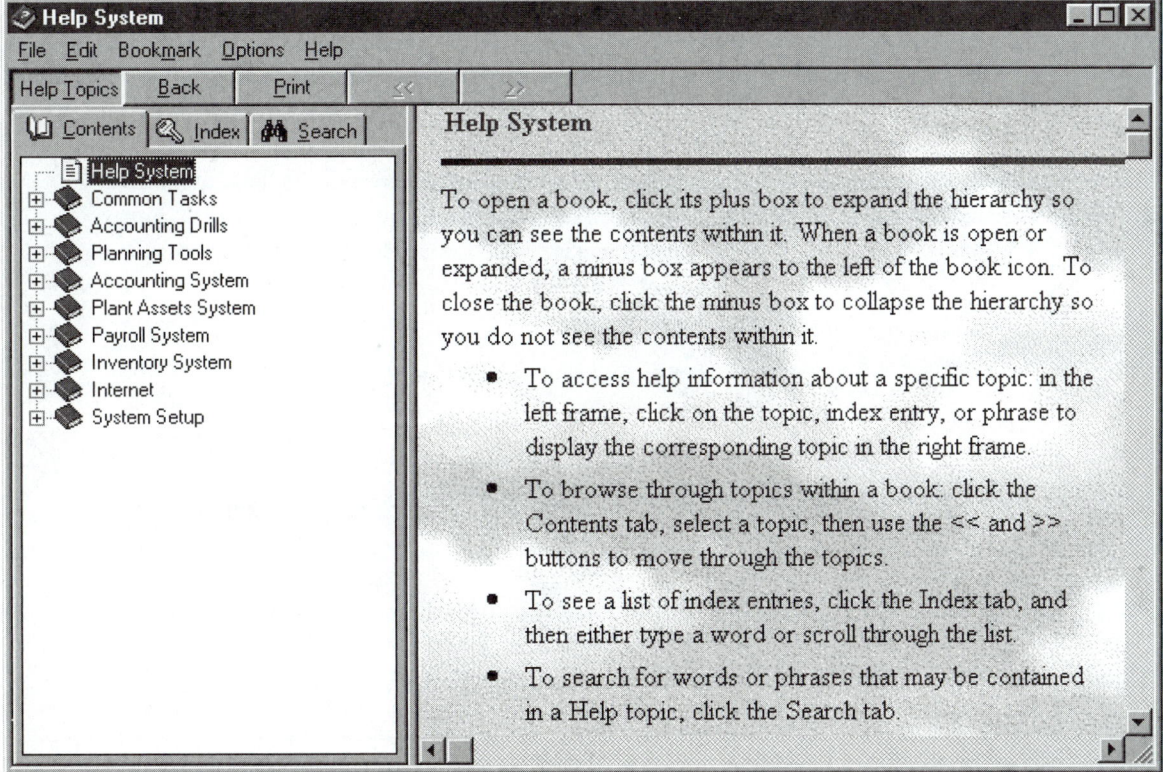

Figure 1.15
Help Window (Left Contents Frame and Right Topics Frame)

The Help window consists of two frames. The frame on the left contains tabs that display the contents, an index, and a search argument. This frame is used to select, or help find, a specific topic. The frame on the right displays the detailed information about the corresponding topic selected in the left frame.

When using the F1 key or the Help command button, the topic that is selected and displayed depends on which Help menu item you choose or which window you were using when you chose the Help button. Within a Help topic, there may be one or more *jumps*, which you can click on to display additional information about a term or a new Help topic. The Help window shown in Figure 1.16 automatically was displayed when the F1 key was pressed while the Save menu item in the File menu was highlighted.

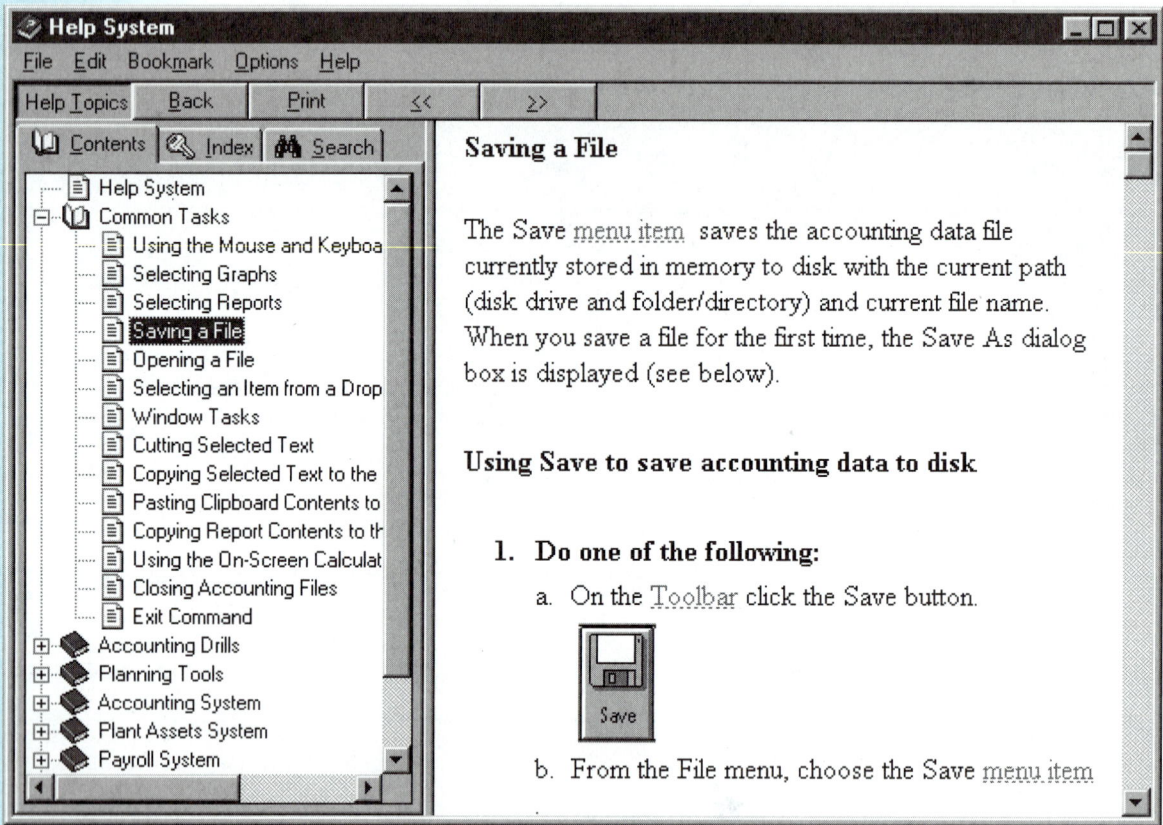

Figure 1.16
Help Window (Saving a File)

You can use the Index and Search tabs to find words or topics quickly. The Help window shown in Figure 1.17 appeared when "save" was keyed into the text box at the top of the Index tab. The Search tab can also be used to find information about "save."

Chapter 1   Introduction

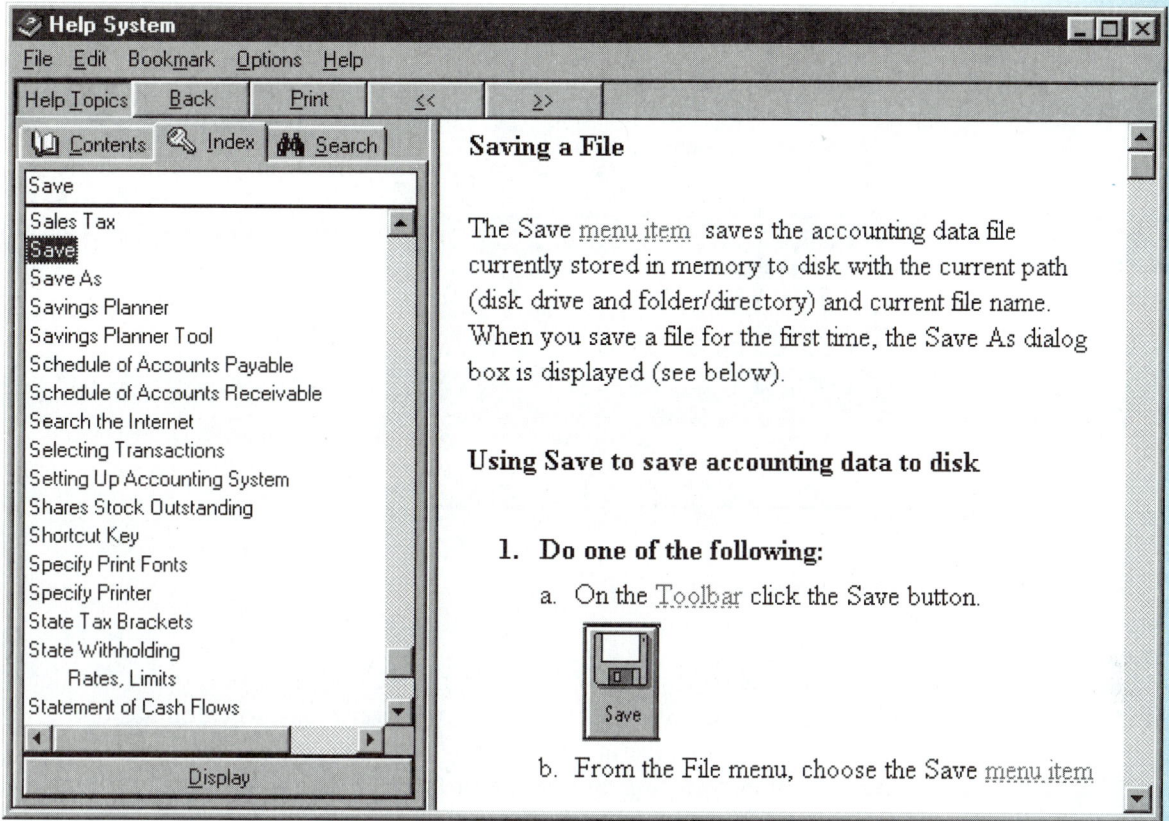

Figure 1.17
Help Window (Using Index Tab)

ON-SCREEN CALCULATOR

The on-screen Calculator is operated like a hand-held calculator. Your computer's standard Calculator can perform all the calculations required in this textbook. The results can be pasted into the text box that has the focus. Once the Calculator appears (as shown in Figure 1.18), a Help menu is available from the Calculator, providing a detailed explanation of the Calculator operation.

PLANNING TOOLS

Planning Tools are convenient, fast, easy-to-use ways of producing results for commonly used applications. These applications may be for your personal or business use. Five different planners are provided: college, savings, loan, retirement, and notes and interest. Each of these planners contains options that direct the computer to calculate different

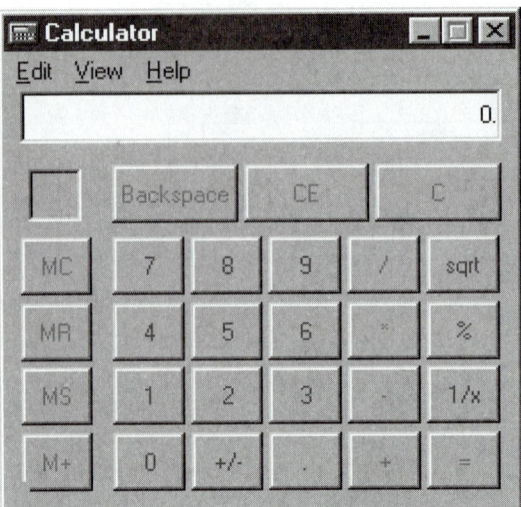

Figure 1.18
Standard On-Screen Calculator

information. Select the tab identifying the desired planner, enter the data required, and click on Report to cause the computer to calculate the desired result(s) and display a report.

Note: An accounting file does not have to be loaded into memory in order to use any of the Planning Tools.

The College Planner is used in this chapter as an example to show you how to select calculation options, enter data, and generate a report showing the results using any of the Planning Tools provided. The operational procedure for each planning tool is the same and will not be covered again in this text. The College Planner is used to calculate the amount of an annual contribution required to reach a particular savings amount and calculate the amount saved for each year of college. A completed College Planner is illustrated in Figure 1.19. The figure shows the Calculate option set to Annual Contribution and the data entered into the appropriate text boxes.

ACCOUNTING REVIEW

A *chart of accounts* is a listing of all the accounts used by a business. Each account consists of an account number and an account title. In a manual accounting system, each account is kept on a separate sheet of paper or on a legal-sized, cardboard-like card. Each of these sheets of paper, or cards, is placed together in a book or file drawer. Similarly, in modern computerized accounting systems, the data for each account are kept in a separate record that is stored on disk or tape. Each of these records, stored together in a file, is referred to by accountants as the *general ledger*.

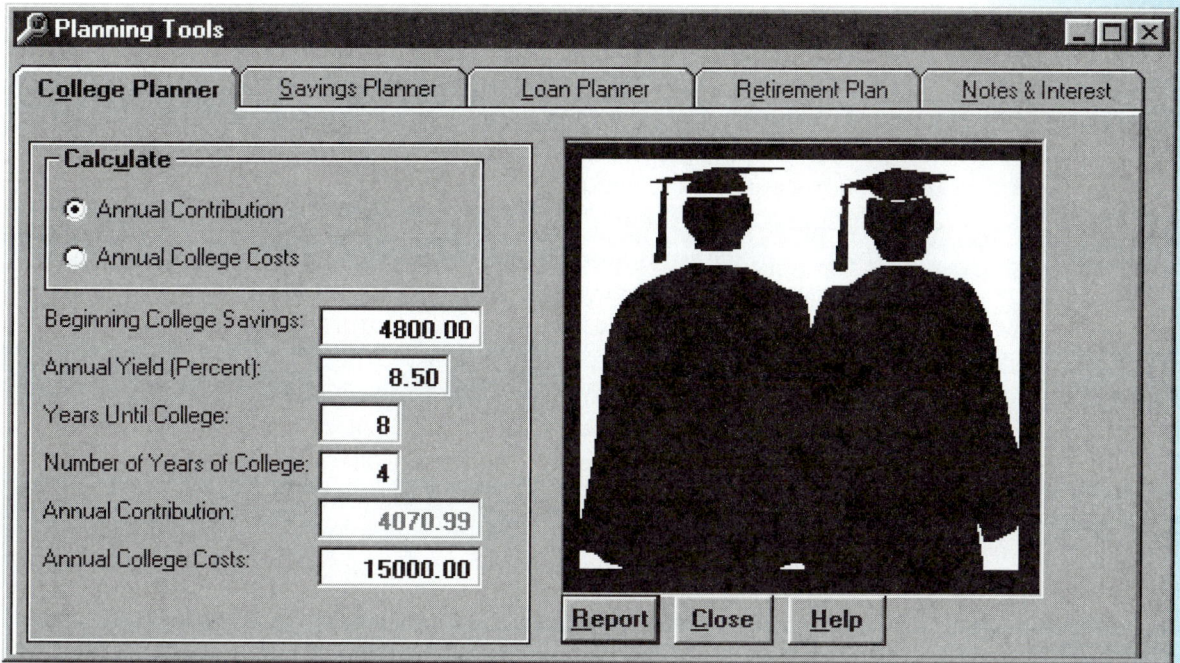

Figure 1.19
College Planner

In the following material, you will review basic accounting principles and how the application of these principles affects the chart of accounts and general ledger. At the end of this chapter, you will use computer drill problems to reinforce your knowledge of these basic accounting principles.

The Accounting Equation

Most accounting systems, whether computerized or manual, use similar accounting practices and procedures regardless of the size of an organization, its type of business, or its complexity. All accounting systems have assets, liabilities, and equity. *Assets* are things a business owns, such as cash, supplies, insurance, buildings, and land. *Liabilities* are amounts owed by a business. The difference between the total amount of assets minus the total amount of liabilities is the *owner's equity*. The relationship among assets, liabilities, and owner's equity is shown in the *accounting equation*, which is stated as follows:

Assets = Liabilities + Owner's Equity

The accounting equation must always be equal. That is, the total of the amounts on the left side must equal the total of the amounts on the right side.

Be sure you understand the meaning of the following accounting terms:

Account Classification
Accountant
Accounting
Accounting Clerks
Accounting Equation
Assets
Bookkeepers
Business
Chart of Accounts
Credit
Debit
Expense Accounts
General Ledger
Liabilities
Owner's Equity

Transactions and the Accounting Equation

Transactions completed by an organization during a specific period of time may number from a few to thousands, depending upon the size and complexity of the organization and its accounting system. Each transaction causes increases and/or decreases in assets, liabilities, and/or owner's equity. Accountants must be careful to record transactions in a systematic manner so that the accounting equation is always in balance after each transaction is recorded. Increases and decreases that are caused by a transaction are recorded in specific accounts. Each account has an account balance and an account title. For example, the asset account Cash is used to record and store the amount of money available to the business. The computer stores each account title and balance used by the business.

As transactions are entered, the appropriate account balance is updated. After all transactions have been entered, the account information can be further processed and displayed or printed in various report formats and stored to disk for recall at a later time. To see how this process works, consider the following transactions:

Sept. 1 Received cash from owner as an investment, $10,000.00.
2 Paid cash for supplies, $220.00.
3 Paid cash for insurance, $875.00.
4 Bought supplies on account, $1,200.00.
6 Paid cash on account, $625.00.

The transactions entered into the accounting equation are shown in Figure 1.20. Notice that each transaction affects at least two accounts

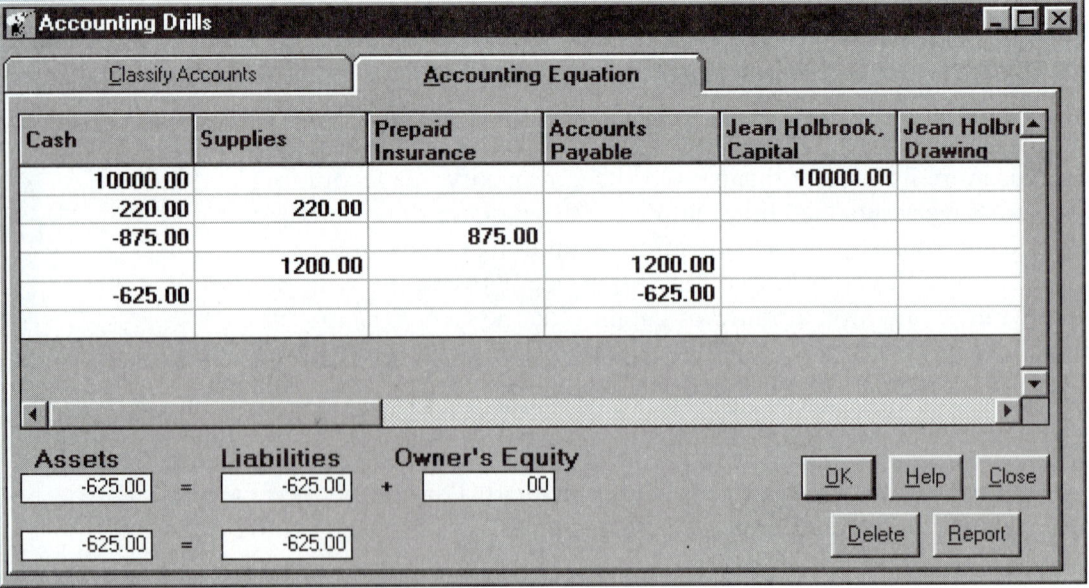

Figure 1.20
Transactions Entered into the Accounting Equation

Chapter 1   Introduction

and has been entered on separate lines in the order in which it occurred by date. Also, notice how the equation at the bottom of the figure shows that the last transaction entered is in balance.

After all the transactions have been entered into the accounting equation and stored by the computer, an Accounting Equation Report can be generated. Figure 1.21 shows the Accounting Equation Report listing each account's beginning balance, transaction activity, and new balance. Notice that the accounts are grouped by assets, liabilities, and owner's equity, just as they are in the accounting equation. At the end of the report, the computer prints the total of all the asset accounts ($10,575.00), and the total of all liability plus owner's equity account balances ($10,575.00) to prove that it is in balance.

```
                      Holbrook Ad Agency
                   Accounting Equation Report
                          09/01/--
```

Account	Classification	Description	Amount
Cash	Asset	Balance Forward	.00
		Transaction	10000.00
		Transaction	-220.00
		Transaction	-875.00
		Transaction	-625.00
		New Balance	8280.00
Supplies	Asset	Balance Forward	.00
		Transaction	220.00
		Transaction	1200.00
		New Balance	1420.00
Prepaid Insurance	Asset	Balance Forward	.00
		Transaction	875.00
		New Balance	875.00
Accounts Payable	Liability	Balance Forward	.00
		Transaction	1200.00
		Transaction	-625.00
		New Balance	575.00
Jean Holbrook, Capital	Owner's Equity	Balance Forward	.00
		Transaction	10000.00
		New Balance	10000.00
Jean Holbrook, Drawing	Owner's Equity	Balance Forward	.00
		New Balance	.00
		Assets =	10575.00
		Liabilities + Equity =	10575.00

Equation in Balance

Figure 1.21
Accounting Equation Report

Classifying Accounts and Analyzing Transactions

Transactions that occur as a result of a business's operation must be recorded into the accounting system to update the appropriate accounts. But before transactions can be recorded, they must be analyzed and assigned to their appropriate accounts. For example, a transaction for the purchase of supplies for cash affects the assets of the company. In this case, the Cash and Supplies accounts, which are classified as asset accounts, are used to record this transaction in the accounting system.

All accounts that are used by a business and stored in the general ledger are grouped into categories. A category for similar accounts in a general ledger is called an *account classification*. As shown in Figure 1.22, each account is assigned an account number that is used to identify the account as well as the category or group to which it belongs. Notice that the business assigns a four-digit account number to each account. The first digit of the account number is the account classification that is used to identify the category within the general ledger. The remaining three digits indicate the location of each account within the category and may be used to further group the accounts. Holbrook Ad Agency assigns account numbers in increments of ten so that new accounts can be easily added between existing accounts.

In the chart of accounts in Figure 1.22, account numbers that begin with the digit 1 are classified as Asset accounts. Account numbers that begin with the digit 2 are Liabilities, and those that begin with the digit 3 are Owner's Equity accounts. Notice that two additional account classifications have been added: Revenue and Expenses. The account number that begins with the digit 4 is Revenue, and account numbers that begin with the digit 5 are classified as Expense accounts. *Revenue accounts* are used to record the sale of goods or services, have a normal credit balance, and result in an increase in owner's equity. *Expense accounts* are used to record transactions for goods or services needed to operate the business, have normal debit balances, and result in a decrease in the asset account Cash (therefore, a decrease in owner's equity).

The Double-Entry Accounting System The double-entry accounting system is based on recording debit and credit parts of a transaction so that the total dollar amount of debits equals the total dollar amount of credits. Each transaction affects at least two general ledger accounts. At least one debit or credit is recorded in each of these accounts in such a way that the entire system is always in balance. For example, a transaction in which $220.00 in cash is paid for supplies affects the Cash and Supplies general ledger accounts. The Cash account is decreased by $220.00, and the Supplies account is increased by $220.00, ensuring that the accounting system remains in balance. A *T account* is a useful tool to help analyze transactions and to visualize their effect on accounts in the double-entry accounting system.

Chapter 1   Introduction

```
               Holbrook Ad Agency
               Chart of Accounts
                   09/01/—

Assets
1110         Cash
1120         Supplies
1130         Prepaid Insurance

Liabilities
2110         Accounts Payable

Owner's Equity
3110         Jean Holbrook, Capital
3120         Jean Holbrook, Drawing

Revenue
4110         Fees

Expenses
5110         Advertising Expense
5120         Insurance Expense
5130         Legal Expense
5140         Miscellaneous Expense
5150         Rent Expense
5160         Supplies Expense
5170         Utilities Expense
```

Figure 1.22
Chart of Accounts

The T Account   In its simplest form, each account in the general ledger can be portrayed as consisting of three parts: (1) an account title; (2) a debit side, located on the left side; and (3) a credit side, located on the right side. This illustrative format of an account, shown in Figure 1.23, is called a T account because it resembles the letter T.

An entry made on the left side is called a *debit* (or debit entry), and an entry made on the right side is called a *credit* (or credit entry). Accounts are increased and decreased based upon their normal account balance. To illustrate how this works, note how the accounting equation you worked with earlier (which includes revenue and expense classifications) has been formatted into T accounts in Figure 1.24, with debit and credit sides for each account classification.

```
              Account Title
    ─────────────────────────────
    Debit Side    │   Credit Side
    (Left Side)   │   (Right Side)
```

Figure 1.23
T Account

Notice that accounts classified as assets and expenses have a normal debit balance, but accounts classified as liabilities, owner's equity, and revenue have normal credit balances. The basic rule that regulates increases and decreases in account balances is: *Account balances increase on the normal balance side of an account and decrease on the side opposite the*

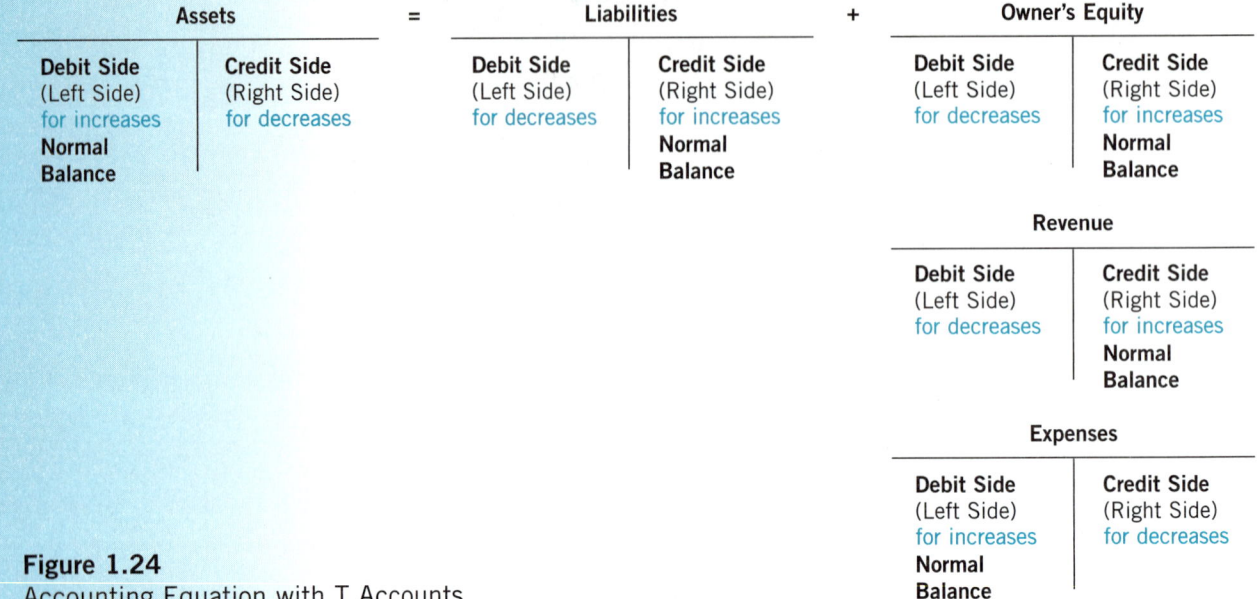

Figure 1.24
Accounting Equation with T Accounts

normal balance side. Therefore, a debit amount would increase an asset and expense account, and a credit would increase a liability, owner's equity, and revenue account. Similarly, a credit amount would decrease an asset and expense account, and a debit amount would decrease a liability, owner's equity, and revenue account. Stated another way: (1) Increases to accounts classified as assets and expenses are debited and decreases are credited. (2) Increases to accounts classified as liabilities, owner's equity, and revenue are credited and decreases are debited.

Three Analytical Questions When you record a transaction, it is helpful to answer the following three questions in the order stated:

1. **What general ledger accounts are affected?**
   To obtain a list of the general ledger accounts, refer to the chart of accounts.

2. **How is each of the affected accounts classified?**
   Gilbert Advertising classifies its accounts as assets, liabilities, owner's equity, revenue, and expenses.

3. **How is each amount entered in the affected accounts?**
   The amount is either debited or credited to increase or decrease the affected accounts' normal account balance.

Figure 1.25 illustrates the use of the above three questions, using the example in which $220.00 in cash is paid for supplies. Notice that (1) the Cash and Supplies general ledger accounts are affected; (2) both the Cash and Supplies accounts are classified as asset accounts; and (3) the Supplies account is debited $220.00 (increased since it has a normal

Chapter 1 Introduction

Supplies	
Debit Side Normal Balance	Credit Side
Increase $220.00	

Cash	
Debit Side Normal Balance	Credit Side
	Decrease $220.00

Figure 1.25
Transaction Analysis

debit balance) and the Cash account is credited $220.00 (decreased since it has a normal debit balance).

Notice that the total amount of debits equals the total amount of credits. Therefore, the accounting system remains in balance after recording this transaction.

EXPLORE ACCOUNTING SYSTEM

When the Explore Accounting System menu item is chosen from the Data menu or when the Explore toolbar button is clicked, the Explore Accounting System window will appear. **Explore Accounting System** is used to access data stored by the software in order to perform audit checks, check account activity, isolate errors, and perform other tasks that are helpful to managing account information. An example of the Explore Accounting System window, showing all the Cash account data activity, is shown in Figure 1.26.

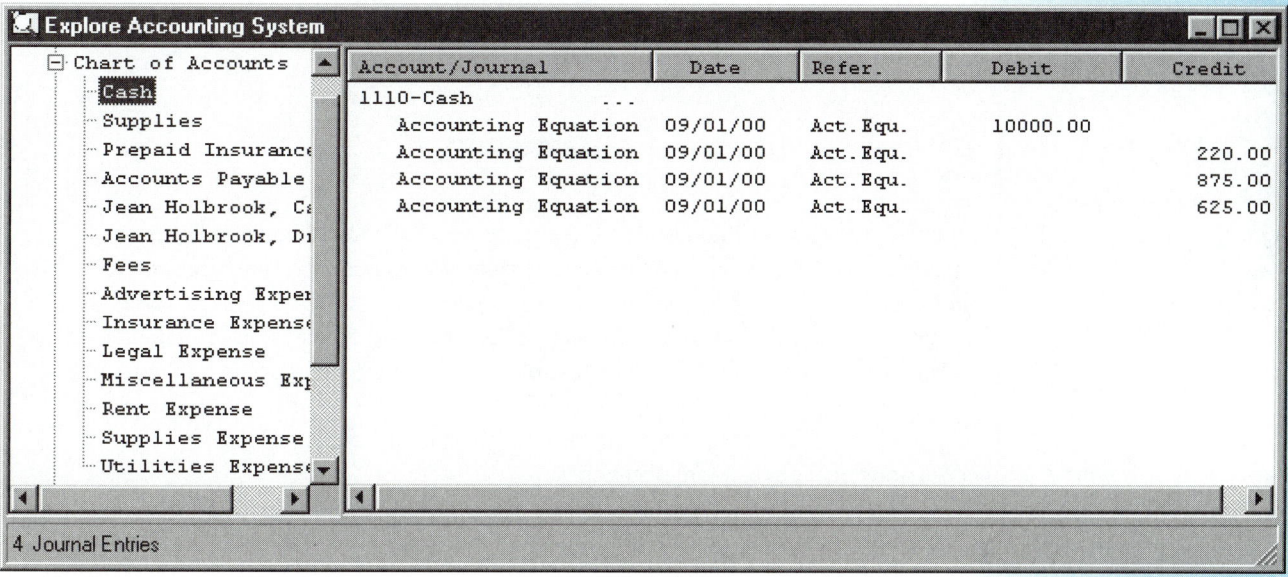

Figure 1.26
Explore Accounting System Window

To use the Explore Accounting System, select the plus box of the desired accounting system in the left frame, and then click on the desired account. A detailed report will appear in the right frame, showing the selected account's activity.

INTERNET WEB BROWSER

The Internet Web browser used with *Automated Accounting* is your computer system's default browser. If your computer has been set up on a local area network (LAN), or an Internet service provider's (ISP) program has been installed, then you're most likely ready to connect to the Internet. Even if you do not have Internet capability, you will be able to use your browser to obtain check figures for all the computer problems in this text. Figure 1.27 shows a Browser window that appears when the Browser toolbar button is clicked or when the Web Browser menu item is chosen from the Internet menu (and an Internet connection

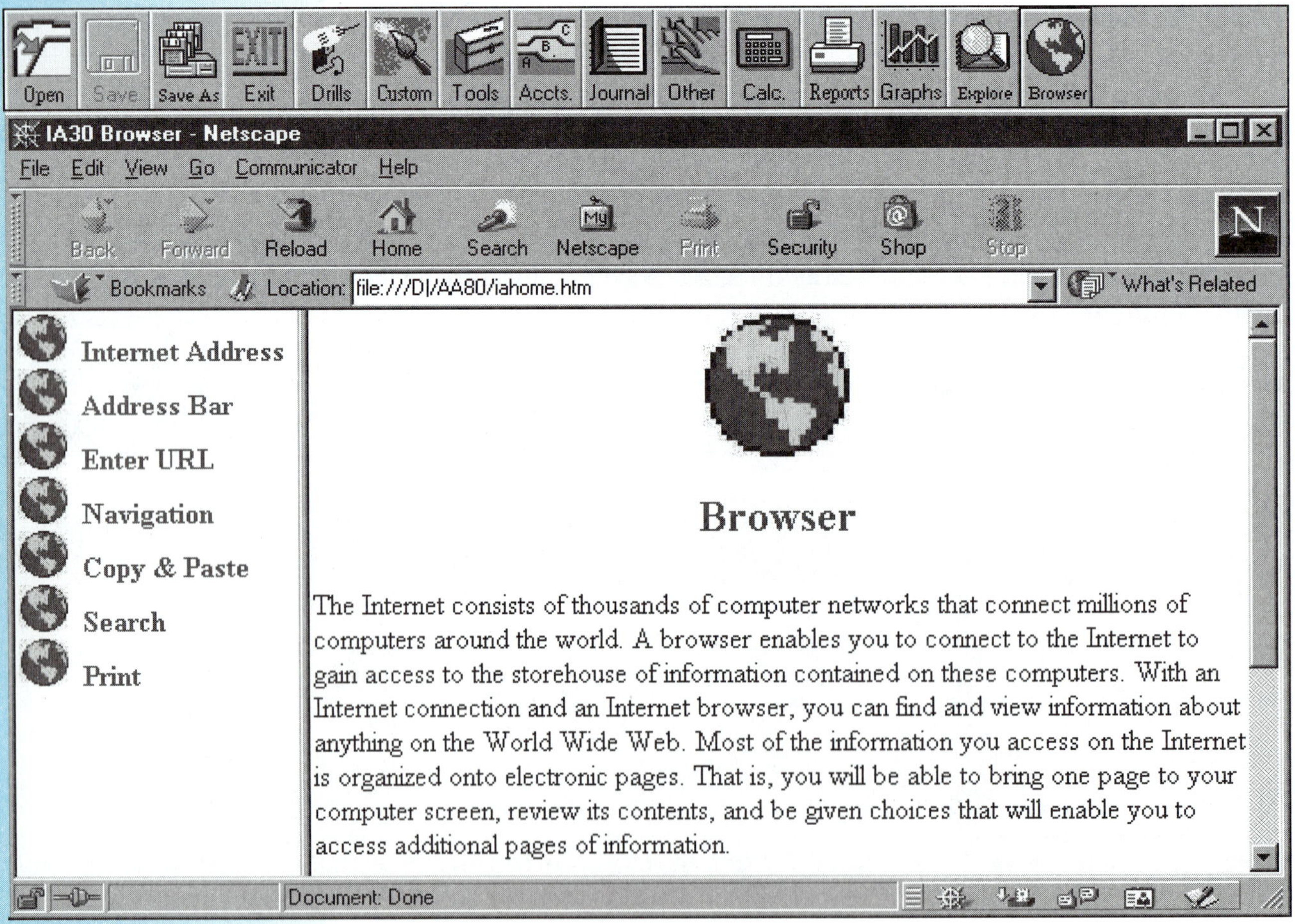

Figure 1.27
Web Browser

Chapter 1   Introduction

has not been established). Notice that the Browser application window has been sized to fit within the *Automated Accounting* window for ease of operation. Also note that an Internet Web browser is not required to complete the problems in this textbook.

To learn how to use the basic operational features of your browser, click on the Browser toolbar button immediately after *Automated Accounting* loads and before you open an accounting problem file. Then, simply click on the desired Earth icon next to a topic in the left frame. Detailed instructional information about the selected topic will appear in the right frame.

Chapter Review

1. Accounting can be defined as an informational system that plans, analyzes, records, and reports financial information.

2. A business is an economic entity that endeavors to sell goods and services to customers at prices that will pay all the costs of doing business and return a profit to the owners. Today's modern businesses store and manage their informational needs by what is called a *management information system* (MIS).

3. A user interface uses drop-down menus, a toolbar, movable overlapping windows, on-screen help, and other operational conventions.

4. *Automated Accounting* contains integrated features designed to handle general ledger, accounts payable, accounts receivable, financial statement analysis, bank reconciliation, plant assets, order processing, inventory, and payroll. In addition, data may be transferred to spreadsheet and word processing applications for a variety of other accounting-related uses.

5. Opening balance files must be opened and loaded before the end-of-chapter problems can be solved.

6. *Automated Accounting* permits you to store data on a separate data disk, hard disk, or network file server for future reference or completion.

7. One of the ways you communicate with the computer is to use the menu bar. When a menu is chosen from the menu bar, a list of

menu items that instruct the computer to perform its processing tasks displays immediately below the menu title.

8. A window is a rectangular area of the screen in which the software communicates with the user. At times, two or more overlapping windows may appear on the screen. However, only one window is active at a time. *Automated Accounting* uses several different windows to perform its accounting activities. Some windows contain tabs consisting of text boxes and grid cells used to enter data from the keyboard, some contain lists and reports, and others may display dialog box messages and operational information.

9. The File menu contains menu items used to handle files and print related input and output operations.

10. Navigation, or tab sequence, is the logical sequence in which the computer is expecting each grid cell, text box, button, and/or command to be accessed. The sequence is usually left to right and top to bottom. The focus identifies the location within a window in which the computer will receive the next piece of input.

11. The Help System provides a quick way to find information about operating the software. Information may be accessed by: (1) choosing either the Help Contents and Index menu item from the Help menu; (2) pressing the F1 key at any time; or (3) choosing the Help button that appears at the bottom of various windows.

12. The on-screen Calculator can be accessed at any time and is operated like a hand-held calculator. Results from the Calculator can be copied and pasted into the text box that has the focus.

13. Planning Tools are convenient, fast, easy-to-use ways of producing results for commonly used personal or business applications. The five Planning Tools provided in Automated Accounting are: college, savings, loan, retirement, and notes and interest planners.

14. The relationship among assets, liabilities, and owner's equity is stated in the accounting equation: Assets = Liabilities + Owner's Equity.

15. Each account used by a business and stored in the general ledger is assigned an account number that is used to identify the account as well as the account classification to which it belongs.

Chapter 1   Introduction

16. The Explore Accounting System feature of the software is used to access data stored by the computer in order to perform audit checks, check account activity, isolate errors, and perform other tasks that are helpful in managing account information.

17. The Web Browser enables you to connect to the Internet and access information about problems in this text.

ACCOUNTING CAREERS IN DEPTH

Just what are the career options open to those students who specialize in accounting?

Accounting education provides many career paths. Some accounting careers are more challenging than others. It all depends on your interest, ambition, and perseverance. Ask yourself how you like spending your workday and what kind of lifestyle you want to have.

There are different levels of education and skill required of accountants. For example, you may want to become a Certified Public Accountant (C.P.A.). To accomplish this goal, you must receive your high school diploma. Next, you will need to get a college education and then pass the C.P.A. examination.

Every type of business needs accountants. Therefore, students have a unique opportunity to combine other interests with accounting by finding employment in a business area most appealing to them.

Accounting Careers in Depth will present you with a view of different careers in accounting and various industries that would allow you to use your skills. It is important to remember that if college is not a choice for you, there are still many job opportunities available. In many cases, these accounting jobs provide career advancement and continuing education courses in areas related to your accounting position.

Accounting Careers in Depth may be your window to a future in accounting.

TUTORIAL PROBLEM 1-T

In this problem, you will practice what you have learned in this chapter. Follow the step-by-step instructions. Each step lists a task to be completed at the computer. More detailed information on how to complete the task is provided immediately following the step. If you need additional operating instructions in order to complete the task, refer back to the text material or access the *Automated Accounting* Help System.

Before starting this problem, be sure you have a properly formatted data disk (or a folder established on a hard disk or network) for saving your data.

STEP 1: **Start up *Automated Accounting*.**
Click on the *Automated Accounting* icon.

STEP 2: **Open the file named AA8 Problem 01-T.AA8.**
Choose *Open* from the File menu or click on the *Open* toolbar button. When the Open file dialog box appears, select the drive and folder containing the opening balance files. Then choose the file named AA8 Problem 01-T.AA8 from the list box.

STEP 3: **When the User Name dialog box appears, enter your name in the User Name text box, and click *OK*.**
Check carefully that you have entered your name correctly because you will not be able to change it for the duration of the problem.

STEP 4: **Save the file to your disk and directory. Enter a file name of 01-T followed by Your Name.**
Choose *Save As* from the File menu or click the *Save As* toolbar button and save the file to your disk and folder as 01-T Your Name, where 01-T represents Chapter 1 Tutorial Problem. The software will add an extension of *.AA8* to the filename.

STEP 5: **Experiment with accessing the Help System.**
Select the Help Contents and Index menu item from the Help menu or use the F1 function key to obtain information about Accounting Drills and Planning Tools.

STEP 6: **Familiarize yourself with the use of the on-screen Calculator by multiplying $5,890.00 by 2%.**
Choose *Calculator* from the Options menu or click the *Calculator* toolbar button. When the Calculator appears, type **5890**, press the asterisk key (* for multiply), type **2**, and then press the % key. As an alternative, use the

Chapter 1 Introduction

TUTORIAL PROBLEM 1-T

mouse to click on each of the appropriate keys to perform the calculation. The result should be **117.8**.

STEP 7: **Calculate the annual contribution toward the cost of college by using the College Planner.**

Choose *Planning Tools* from the Data menu or click the *Tools* toolbar button. When the Planning Tools window appears, click the *College Planner* tab (if not already selected). Click the *Annual Contribution* option in the Calculate section. Then enter the information provided below:

Beginning College Savings	4800.00
Annual Yield (Percent)	8.50
Years Until College	8
Number of Years of College	4
Annual College Costs	15000.00

Press *Tab* after entering Annual College Costs and the calculated Annual Contribution will appear.

The College Savings Plan Schedules (Annual Contribution) are shown in Figure 1.28. Click the *Report* button in the College Planner window to display the report in the Report window.

The report consists of two schedules based on the data in the college planner. The first schedule shows the annual contribution, annual yield, and the total amount saved each year until college. The second schedule shows the effect of the $15,000.00 per year payments. Note that the amount of savings continues to generate interest. The calculated annual contribution is $4,070.99, which is the annual amount of savings required to provide $15,000.00 per year for four years of college expenses (given the other data provided). When you are finished, close the Report and Planning Tools windows.

STEP 8: **Enter the following transactions into the accounting equation and display the Accounting Equation Report.**

Sept. 1 Received cash from owner as an investment, $10,000.00.
     2 Paid cash for supplies, $220.00.
     3 Paid cash for insurance, $875.00.

TUTORIAL PROBLEM 1-T

```
                    College Savings Plan
                         10/23/--

Schedule of College Savings

                    Annual          Annual          College
Year                Contribution    Yield           Savings

(Beginning Balance)                                 4800.00
1                   4070.99         408.00          9278.99
2                   4070.99         788.71          14138.69
3                   4070.99         1201.79         19411.47
4                   4070.99         1649.98         25132.44
5                   4070.99         2136.26         31339.69
6                   4070.99         2663.87         38074.55
7                   4070.99         3236.34         45381.88
8                   4070.99         3857.46         53310.33

Schedule of College Payments

College             Annual          Annual          Savings
Year                Payments        Yield           Balance

(College Savings)                                   53310.33
1                   15000.00        3256.38         41566.71
2                   15000.00        2258.17         28824.88
3                   15000.00        1175.11         14999.99
4                   14999.99                             .00
```

Figure 1.28
College Savings Plan Schedules for Annual Contribution

4   Paid cash for a legal expense, $400.00.
5   Bought supplies on account, $1,200.00.
6   Owner withdrew cash for personal use, $1,500.00.
    Jean Holbrook, Drawing is a Contra account. Contra accounts always reduce a related account. In this case, the Owner's Drawing account is a Contra account (with a normal debit balance) to its related Owner's Capital account (with a normal credit balance).
7   Paid cash on account, $625.00.

TUTORIAL PROBLEM 1-T

a. Choose *Accounting Drills*.
b. Select the *Accounting Equation* tab.
c. Enter the accounting transactions (your entered transactions should match Figure 1.29).
   - Use the *Tab* key to move to the next grid cell or reposition the insertion point using the mouse.
   - Press *Enter* when a line is complete to display a new line of grid cells.
   - Use a minus sign to show a decrease in an account.
d. Click the *Report* button to obtain a display of your work (your report should match Figure 1.30). Click the *Close Report* button.

Cash	Supplies	Prepaid Insurance	Accounts Payable	Jean Holbrook, Capital	Jean Holbrook, Drawing	Fees	Advertising Expense	Insurance Expense	Legal Expense
10000.00				10000.00					
-220.00	220.00								
-875.00		875.00							
-400.00									400.00
	1200.00		1200.00						
-1500.00					1500.00				
-625.00			-625.00						

Figure 1.29
Accounting Equation Tab

Holbrook Ad Agency
Accounting Equation Report
09/01/—

Account	Classification	Description	Amount
Cash	Asset	Balance Forward	.00
		Transaction	10000.00
		Transaction	-220.00
		Transaction	-875.00
		Transaction	-400.00
		Transaction	-1500.00
		Transaction	-625.00
		New Balance	6380.00

continued

TUTORIAL PROBLEM 1-T

Supplies	Asset	Balance Forward	.00
		Transaction	220.00
		Transaction	1200.00
		New Balance	1420.00
Prepaid Insurance	Asset	Balance Forward	.00
		Transaction	875.00
		New Balance	875.00
Accounts Payable	Liability	Balance Forward	.00
		Transaction	1200.00
		Transaction	-625.00
		New Balance	575.00
Jean Holbrook, Capital	Owner's Equity	Balance Forward	.00
		Transaction	10000.00
		New Balance	10000.00
Jean Holbrook, Drawing	Owner's Equity	Balance Forward	.00
		Transaction	1500.00
		New Balance	1500.00
Fees	Revenue	Balance Forward	.00
		New Balance	.00
Advertising Expense	Expense	Balance Forward	.00
		New Balance	.00
Insurance Expense	Expense	Balance Forward	.00
		New Balance	.00
Legal Expense	Expense	Balance Forward	.00
		Transaction	400.00
		New Balance	400.00
Miscellaneous Expense	Expense	Balance Forward	.00
		New Balance	.00
Rent Expense	Expense	Balance Forward	.00
		New Balance	.00
Supplies Expense	Expense	Balance Forward	.00
		New Balance	.00
Utilities Expense	Expense	Balance Forward	.00
		New Balance	.00
		Assets =	8675.00
		Liabilities + Equity =	8675.00
Equation in Balance			

Figure 1.30
Accounting Equation Report

Chapter 1 Introduction

TUTORIAL PROBLEM 1-T

STEP 9: **Identify account classifications, normal account balances, and debit or credit increases for each account in the general ledger.**

   a. Choose *Accounting Drills* by clicking the *Drill* toolbar button. Then click the *Classify Accounts* tab.
   b. Select the desired account from the drop-down list by clicking the drop-down arrow button and selecting one of the accounts listed above. Click the *Next* button to proceed.
   c. Select the account classification by clicking the drop-down arrow button and selecting the appropriate account classification. Click the *Next* button to proceed.
   d. Select the appropriate normal balance. Click the *Next* button to proceed.
   e. Select whether the account is increased with a debit or credit. Click the *Finish* button.
   f. Repeat Steps b-e for each of the remaining accounts listed above.
   g. Click the *Report* button to obtain a display of your work (items that are incorrect are displayed in the color red). Click the *Close Report* button.

STEP 10: **Use the Explorer to display the Cash account's activity and current balance.**

   a. Choose the Explorer by clicking the *Explore Accounting System* menu item in the Reports menu or by clicking the *Explore* toolbar button.
   b. Click the plus sign (+) in front of Chart of Accounts in the left frame. (A listing of all accounts will appear.) Note that clicking the Chart of Accounts title will cause the software to display a list of all the accounts in the chart of accounts.
   c. Click *Cash*. The Cash account's activity and current balance will appear in the right frame. (It should match Figure 1.25.)
   d. Click the *Close* box (X) in the upper-right corner of the window to exit the Explorer.

TUTORIAL PROBLEM 1-T

STEP 11: Access the Web Browser to obtain information about how to find information on the World Wide Web.

  a. Choose the Browser by clicking the *Web Browser* menu item in the Internet menu or by clicking the *Browser* toolbar button.
  b. Click the earth icon in front of Search in the left frame. The corresponding information will appear in the right frame.
  c. Click the Close box (X) in the upper-right corner of the window to exit the Browser.

STEP 12: Save the data file.
Click the *Save* toolbar button. The file will be saved to disk with the current path and file name (note the file name in the Title Bar of the *Automated Accounting* application window).

STEP 13: End the *Automated Accounting* session.
Click the *Exit* toolbar button.

Evidence of the growth of e-mail is the great decline in messages previously sent through the U.S. Postal System. Yearly, over a trillion e-mail messages replace what otherwise would be paper correspondence.

An *Internet address* is a set of numbers or words that identifies a unique computer user. Every user and computer on the Internet must have a different address so that the system knows where to send electronic mail and other data.

A *host* is a computer that is attached directly to the Internet and that provides services to users. Host computers are called *servers*.

Chapter 1 Introduction

Review and Practice: Applying Your Information Skills

I. MATCHING

Directions: In the *Working Papers,* write the letter of the appropriate term next to each definition.

a. access key
b. clipboard
c. Explore Accounting System
d. focus
e. grid cells
f. Help System
g. insertion point
h. management information system (MIS)
i. Planning Tools
j. shortcut key
k. tab sequence
l. Tooltips
m. user interface

1. A temporary storage area in Windows software.

2. The part of a window identified by the insertion point that will receive input.

3. Brief informational messages that automatically appear when the pointer is positioned on a toolbar button.

4. A character that is positioned in a text box to indicate where data will be entered or edited.

5. *Automated Accounting* features that provide convenient, fast, easy-to-use ways of producing results for commonly used applications.

6. Arrangements of rows and columns that are used to enter, edit, or delete data and text.

7. The logical sequence in which the computer is expecting each grid cell, text box, button, and/or command to be accessed.

8. A quick way to find information about operating the software.

9. Several computer-integrated systems that provide all the informational needs of the business.

10. An *Automated Accounting* feature used to access data stored by the software in order to perform audit checks, check account activity, isolate errors, and perform other tasks that are helpful to managing account information.

11. A key that is pressed while holding down the Ctrl key that allows a menu item to be selected directly without accessing the drop-down menu.

12. The way the user communicates with the software through images on the monitor.

13. An underlined letter in a menu item; the key may be pressed to select the menu item.

II. REVIEW QUESTIONS

Directions: Write the answers to each of the following questions in the *Working Papers*.

1. What is the definition of accounting?
2. What is the name of the job occupation of a person who summarizes detailed accounting information and then analyzes and interprets the information to assist owners and managers in making financial decisions?
3. What is a business?
4. State the accounting equation.
5. What is an account classification?
6. What is a double-entry accounting system?
7. What is the purpose of the Web Browser?
8. Identify the five Planning Tools provided in *Automated Accounting*.

III. INTERNET ACTIVITY

Directions: If you have access to the Internet, use the Browser to find information about careers in the accounting field. **Hint:** Use a search argument of *accounting careers* to narrow your search. Select one of the careers and report your findings. Be sure to include the source and the URL (Internet address) of your search.

Chapter 1 Introduction

Independent Practice Problem 1-P

In the following problem, you will practice what you have learned in this chapter. *Note:* As you complete this problem, access the Browser for helpful check figures to audit your work.

STEP 1: Complete the Applying Your Technology Skills 1-P questions at the end of this section as you work through the following steps.

STEP 2: Start up *Automated Accounting*.

STEP 3: Open and load the file named AA8 Problem 01-P.AA8.

STEP 4: Enter your name in the User Name dialog box.

STEP 5: Choose *Save As* and save the file to your disk and folder with a file name of 01-P Your Name.

STEP 6: Access the Help System to obtain information about using the Web Browser to search the Internet.

STEP 7: Use the on-screen Calculator to multiply $3,275.00 by 5%.

STEP 8: Calculate the annual cost of college based upon savings using the College Planner. With the Annual College Cost option set on, enter the data provided below. Then display the schedule of college savings and payments reports.

Beginning College Savings $1,950.00
Annual Yield (Percent) 7.75
Years Until College 8
Number of Years of College 4
Annual Contribution $3,750.00

STEP 9: Use the Accounting Equation tab in the Drills window to enter the following transactions.

Sept. 1 Received cash from owner as an investment, $8,500.00.
     2 Paid cash for supplies, $210.00.
     3 Paid cash for insurance, $405.00.
     4 Paid cash for advertising, $500.00.
     5 Bought supplies on account, $1,250.00.
     6 Owner withdrew cash for personal use, $1,500.00.
     6 Paid cash on account, $750.00.

STEP 10: Display the Accounting Equation Report.

STEP 11: Use the Classify Accounts tab in the Drill window to identify the account classification, normal account balance, and debit or credit increase for each of the following accounts:

Cash
Roger Browne, Capital
Prepaid Insurance
Legal Expense
Miscellaneous Expense
Accounts Payable

STEP 12: Display the Classify Accounts Report.

STEP 13: Use the Explorer to display the Supplies account activity and current balance.

STEP 14: Save the data file.

STEP 15: End the *Automated Accounting* session.

Applying Your Technology Skills 1-P

Directions: Write the answers to the following questions in the *Working Papers*.

1. From the Help System, note the procedure used in order to have the browser search the Internet.

2. What is the result of using the Calculator to find 5% of $3,275.00?

3. From the College Planner, what are the calculated annual college payments?

4. What is the total amount of assets shown on the accounting equation report?

5. What account number is assigned to Fees?

6. From the Explorer, note the transaction activity for the Supplies account.

Chapter 1 Introduction

Mastery Problem 1-M

In the following problem, you will practice what you have learned in this chapter.

STEP 1: Complete the Applying Your Technology Skills 1-M questions at the end of this section as you work through the following steps.

STEP 2: Start up *Automated Accounting*.

STEP 3: Open and load the file named AA8 Problem 01-M.

STEP 4: Enter your name in the User Name dialog box.

STEP 5: Choose *Save As* and save the file to your disk and folder with a file name of 01-M Your Name.

STEP 6: Access the Help System to obtain information about using the Internet feature of the software to download accounting files.

STEP 7: Use the on-screen Calculator to divide $42,360.00 by 12.

STEP 8: Calculate the annual cost of college based upon savings by using the College Planner. With the Annual College Cost option set on, enter the data provided below. Then display the schedule of college savings and payments reports.

Beginning College Savings $3,500.00
Annual Yield (Percent) 8.00
Years Until College 12
Number of Years of College 4
Annual Contribution $2,400.00

STEP 9: Use the Accounting Equation tab in the Drills window to enter the following transactions.

Sept. 1 Received cash from owner as an investment, $10,500.00.
     2 Paid cash for supplies, $435.00.
     2 Paid cash for insurance, $750.00.
     3 Bought supplies on account, $2,550.00.
     4 Paid cash for utility bills, $176.32.
     5 Owner withdrew cash for personal use, $2,000.00.
     6 Paid cash on account, $1,200.00.

STEP 10: Display the Accounting Equation Report.

STEP 11: Use the Classify Accounts tab in the Drills window to identify the account classification, normal account balance, and debit or credit increase for each of the following accounts:

Supplies
Accounts Payable
Advertising Expense
Utilities Expense
Heather Payne, Drawing
Rent Expense

STEP 12: Display the Classify Accounts Report.

STEP 13: Use the Explorer to display the Accounts Payable account activity.

STEP 14: Save the data file.

STEP 15: End the *Automated Accounting* session.

Applying Your Technology Skills 1-M

Directions: Write the answers to the following questions in the *Working Papers*.

1. From the Help System, note the procedure to use the Internet to download accounting files.
2. What is the result of using the Calculator to find the quotient of $42,360 divided by 12?
3. From the College Planner, what is the calculated annual college payment?
4. What is the total amount of assets shown on the accounting equation report?
5. What account number is assigned to Utilities Expense?
6. From the Explorer, note the transaction activity for Accounts Payable.

Chapter 2
GENERAL LEDGER—SERVICE BUSINESS

KEY TERMS

Input Form
Sole Proprietorship
Account Maintenance
Journal
Posting

General Journal Input Form
General Journal Tab
General Journal Report
Graph

LEARNING OBJECTIVES

Upon completion of this chapter, you will be able to:

1. Complete a general journal input form.
2. Enter chart of accounts maintenance data.
3. Enter and correct general journal transactions.
4. Display accounts, journal entries, graphs, and ledger reports.

INTRODUCTION

Many businesses that use computerized accounting systems enter their transaction data directly into the computer from source documents. Some businesses first record transactions on an **input form**, which is a form used to organize and record accounting transaction data before entering the data at the computer.

In this chapter, you will learn how to add, change, and delete accounts from the chart of accounts. You will learn how to record general journal entries onto an input form, enter and correct general journal entries, and generate corresponding reports and graphs. You will perform the accounting duties for Palmer Consulting. Palmer Consulting is organized as a **sole proprietorship**, which is a business owned by one person.

CHART OF ACCOUNTS MAINTENANCE

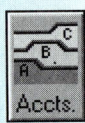

The process of keeping a business's chart of accounts up to date by adding new accounts, changing titles of existing accounts, and deleting inactive accounts is called **account maintenance**. When the Maintain Accounts menu item is chosen from the Data menu, or the Accts. toolbar button is clicked, the Account Maintenance window will appear. Click the Accounts tab to display the Account Maintenance tab shown in Figure 2.1.

Software called *shareware* has been around for many years. Authors of shareware make their programs available to the public to copy but retain the copyright to their work. They hope that the user will like their program well enough to make a donation. Users of shareware are encouraged to make copies and give these to others as a means of distributing the product. The basic philosophy behind shareware is that users will pay for a program that has value, and authors will in turn be encouraged to produce quality products based on the fees they receive.

Critical Thinking

1. What do you think would happen to the shareware concept if the users of shareware programs did not send a donation to the authors, even though they liked and used the software?

2. Do you think it is ethical for a person using a shareware program to give a copy of it to someone else? Explain your opinion.

Chapter 2 General Ledger—Service Business

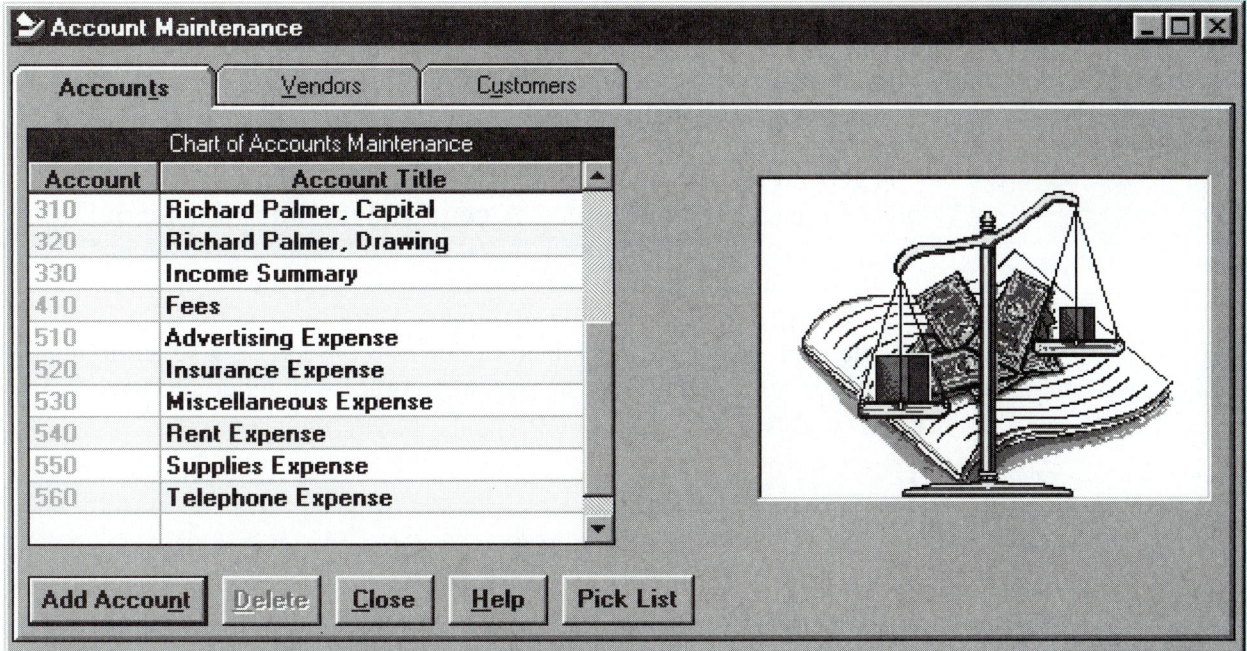

Figure 2.1
Account Maintenance

New accounts can be added by typing the account number and account title after the last item in the list and then pressing the Add Account button. The new account will be inserted into the chart of accounts in account number sequence. Existing account titles may be changed by selecting the account you wish to change, typing the correct account title, and clicking the Change button (the Add Account button changes to Change). An existing account may be deleted by simply selecting the account number or title and clicking the Delete button.

When the Pick List button is clicked, a master chart of accounts list will appear. A later chapter will demonstrate how to use this account list to create a chart of accounts for a new business.

GENERAL JOURNAL TRANSACTIONS

A **journal** is a record of the debit and credit parts of each transaction that is recorded in date sequence. A journal does not show the current account balance of individual accounts. Therefore, the journal entry information must be transferred to a general ledger account. The process of updating the ledger account balances with all debits and credits affecting each account is called **posting**.

As transactions are entered into a journal and posted, the appropriate ledger account balance is updated. After all transactions have been entered and posted, the account information can be further processed

The account number cannot be changed. An account with an incorrect account number must be deleted and then added back as a new account with the correct number. Also, general ledger accounts cannot be deleted unless the account being deleted has a zero balance.

(totals accumulated, and so on), displayed, or printed in various report formats. The data can also be stored to disk for recall at a later time.

General Journal Input Form

A general journal is a journal with two amount columns in which all kinds of entries can be recorded. A **general journal input form** is a form with two amount columns that is used to organize and record accounting transaction data before entering data at the computer. It is similar to a general journal in a manual accounting system. Each debit part and each credit part of a transaction is recorded on a separate line of the input form, as shown in the partially completed general journal input form in Figure 2.2.

GENERAL JOURNAL INPUT FORM

Date 10/10/--   Problem No. 2-T

Date	Reference	Account Number	Debit Amount	Credit Amount	Vendor/Customer
10/01/--	C811	540	935.00		
		110		935.00	
10/01/--	C812	560	245.63		
		110		245.63	
10/03/--	T356	110	2105.20		
		410		2105.20	
		Totals	3285.83	3285.83	

Figure 2.2
General Journal Input Form

The bottom of the form contains totals for the Debit and Credit columns. To prove the equality of debits and credits, these totals must be equal.

    Oct. 01   Paid cash for office rent, $935.00. C811.
          01   Paid cash for telephone bill, $245.63. C812.
          03   Received cash from sales, $2,105.20. T356.

Each line represents one part of a transaction, and each column on the form matches one of the columns in the General Journal window in which the data will be keyed. (The Vendor/Customer column will be discussed in the next chapter.) Notice that the Date and Reference columns are completed only for the first line of each journal entry. The field names and a description of each column are illustrated in the General Journal window shown in Figure 2.3.

General Journal Tab

Journal

The **General Journal tab** is a set of grid cells within the Journal Entries window that is used to enter and post general journal entries and to make corrections to or delete existing journal entries. In Chapters 4 and 5, you will learn how to use the other tabs in this window to enter purchases, cash payments, sales, and cash receipts journal transactions. When the Journal Entries menu item is chosen from the Data menu or the Journal toolbar button is clicked, the Journal Entries window shown in Figure 2.3 will appear.

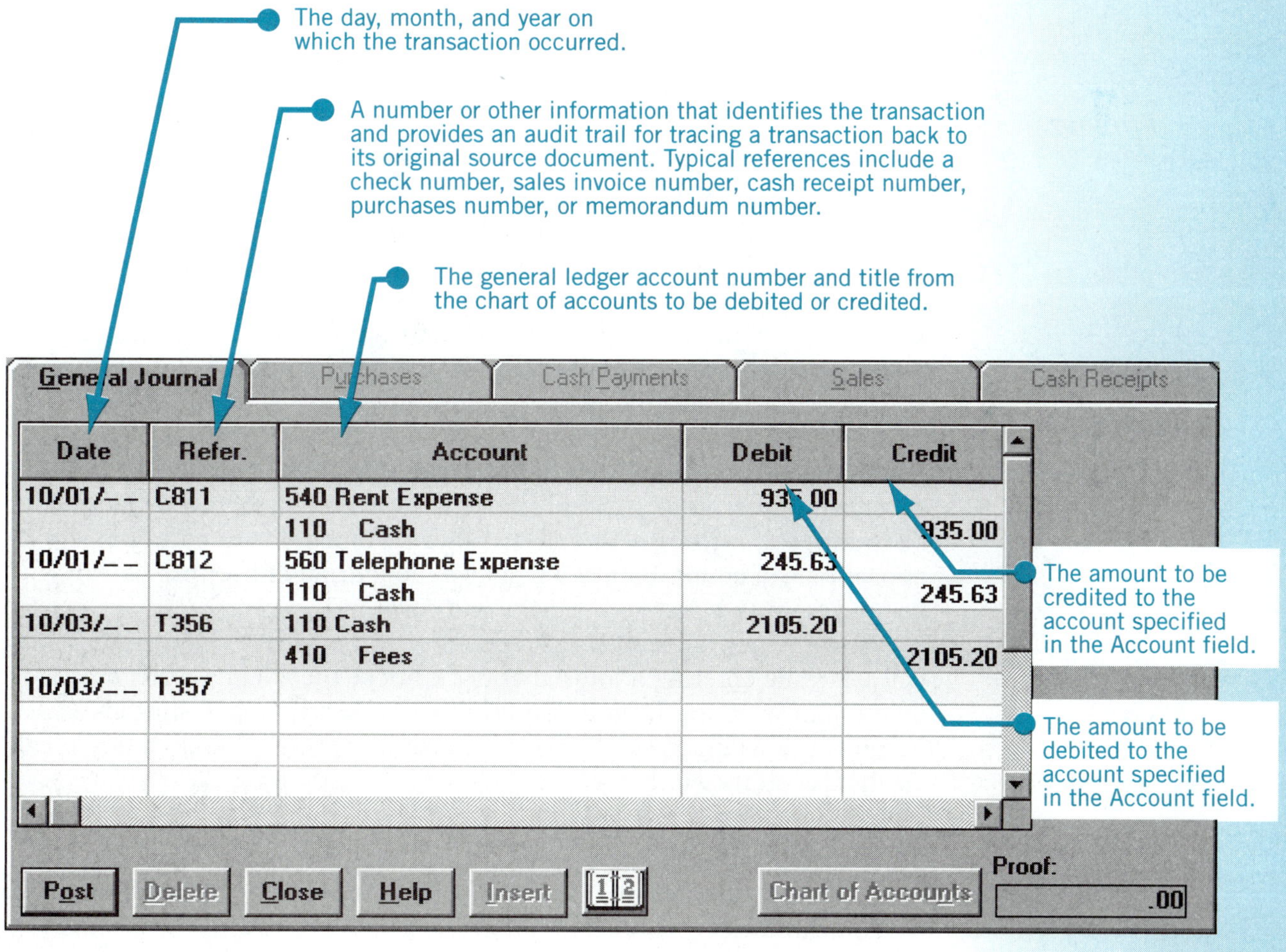
The day, month, and year on which the transaction occurred.
A number or other information that identifies the transaction and provides an audit trail for tracing a transaction back to its original source document. Typical references include a check number, sales invoice number, cash receipt number, purchases number, or memorandum number.
The general ledger account number and title from the chart of accounts to be debited or credited.
General Journal
Purchases
Cash Payments
Sales
Cash Receipts
Date
Refer.
Account
Debit
Credit
10/01/-- C811 540 Rent Expense 935.00
110 Cash 935.00
10/01/-- C812 560 Telephone Expense 245.63
110 Cash 245.63
10/03/-- T356 110 Cash 2105.20
410 Fees 2105.20
10/03/-- T357
The amount to be credited to the account specified in the Account field.
The amount to be debited to the account specified in the Account field.
Post
Delete
Close
Help
Insert
Chart of Accounts
Proof:
.00

Figure 2.3
General Journal Window

Date When the General Journal tab is chosen, the general journal shown in Figure 2.3 appears. When the general journal first appears, the Date column contains the date of the last transaction that was entered, even if it was entered in an earlier session. Press the + key to increase the date or the - key to decrease the date. Continue to press either key until the appropriate date appears. You could also key the day of the month. As an alternative, you can click the Calendar icon and select the desired date when the Calendar appears.

Reference Tab to the Reference column. This column contains the next number in sequence for the last transaction that was entered. During the entering of journal entry transactions, the computer will attempt to intuitively anticipate the correct reference even if different, multiple references have been entered. If no transactions have been entered, the Date column will contain a default date and the Reference column will be blank. Enter a new reference number if the one generated by the software is not correct.

Account Tab to the Account column. This column contains the account number and title of the account to be debited or credited. There are three ways to enter the account number and title when the Account column has the focus: (1) key the appropriate account number and press the Tab key; (2) click the Chart of Accounts button to display the chart of accounts selection list, select an account, and then click OK; or (3) key the account title and press the Tab key. If a complete account title is keyed and the Tab key is pressed, the software will attempt to find a matching title in the chart of accounts and put it and its account number in the Account field. If a partial account title is keyed and the Tab key is pressed, the software will attempt to find the first occurrence of that partial matching account title in the chart of accounts and put it and its account number in the Account field. If no matching account titles can be found, you must use one of the other two methods to enter the appropriate account. Figure 2.3 shows the journal entries previously entered from the general journal input form in Figure 2.2.

Note: A new general ledger account can be added, changed, or deleted while entering a journal entry. Choose the Maintain Accounts menu item from the Data menu or click the Accts. toolbar button. When the Account Maintenance window appears, click the Accounts tab to call up the Accounts window.

Debit and Credit Amounts Tab to the Debit or Credit column and key the amount. Press the Tab key at the end of the line to advance to the next line.

Posting After the last line of a journal entry is completed, click Post or press Enter to post the entry. This will also generate a new line with a date and the next reference number. A warning will display if your entries are not in balance.

Changing or Deleting General Journal Transactions

Existing general journal transactions can be changed or deleted. Simply select the transaction that you wish to change, enter the corrections to the transaction, and click the Post button. If you wish to delete the transaction, click the Delete button.

Adding Lines to a Transaction

To add lines to an existing transaction, select the transaction and click the Insert button. A blank line will be inserted under the selected transaction, upon which you can enter the additional debit or credit part.

Note: If you accidentally insert a blank line, leave it. It will be removed when the journal is posted.

Finding a Journal Entry

While a journal is displayed, you can use the Find item from the Edit menu to locate and display any previously entered transaction. The Find Journal Entry dialog box is shown in Figure 2.4.

Figure 2.4
Find Journal Entry Dialog Box

Enter the date, reference, amount, or any other data from the transaction you want to find in the Find What text box and click the OK button. If a matching transaction is found, it will be displayed in the journal where it can be changed or deleted. By choosing the Find Next item in the Edit menu, you will locate the next occurrence of the search criteria.

GENERAL JOURNAL REPORT

In this chapter, you will learn how to select journal reports and to specify which journal entries are to appear in the report. The **General Journal Report** is a display or printout of the general journal that is

useful in detecting errors and verifying the equality of debits and credits. The totals of debits and credits on the General Journal Report must match the totals of debits and credits on the general journal input form. This report becomes a permanent accounting document and provides an audit trail so that transactions can be traced to their original source document.

To display a General Journal Report, choose the Report Selection menu item from the Reports menu or click the Reports toolbar button. The Report selection dialog box shown in Figure 2.5 will appear.

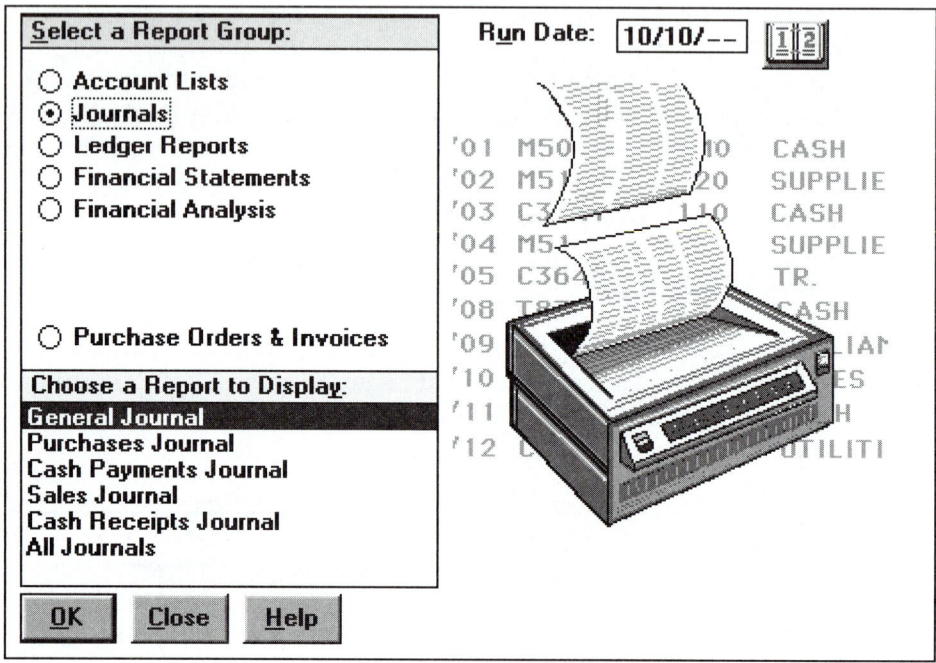

Figure 2.5
Report Selection Dialog Box

Figure 2.6
Journal Report Selection Dialog Box

Choose the Journals option from Select a Report Group. Select the General Journal report from Choose a Report to Display, and click OK. The Journal Report Selection dialog box shown in Figure 2.6 will appear, allowing you to display all the general journal entries or customize your General Journal Report.

Choose the Customize Journal Report option to control the data to be included on the report. If you want to include *all* journal transactions on the report, choose the Include All Journal Entries option. When the

Chapter 2   General Ledger—Service Business

Customize Journal Report option is chosen, the dialog box shown in Figure 2.7 will appear.

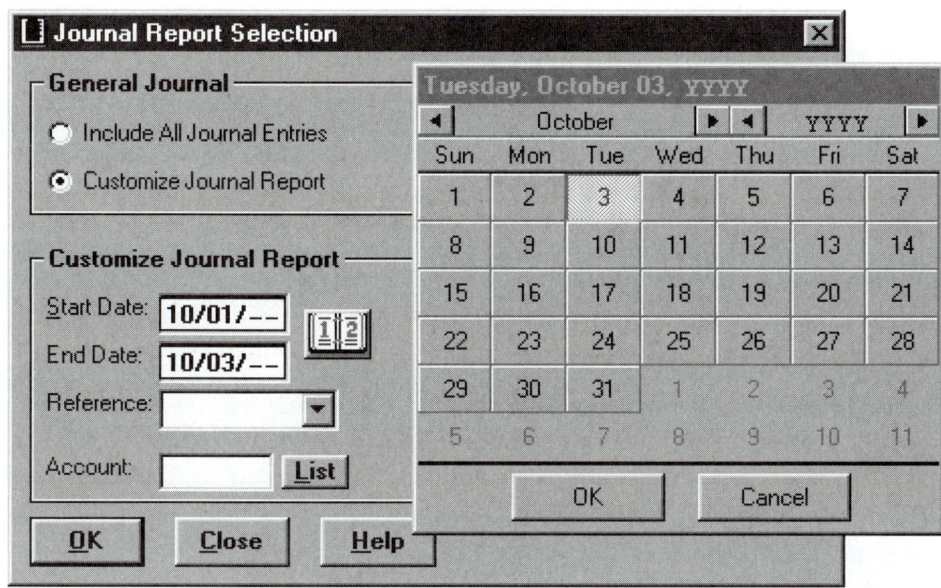

Figure 2.7
Customize Journal Report Dialog Box

Notice that the Calendar appears on the right side of the dialog box if the Calendar icon (located next to the start and end dates) is clicked.

Enter the desired start and end dates. As an alternative, select either the Start Date or End Date text box and then click the Calendar icon. When the Calendar appears, as shown in Figure 2.7, select the desired date and click OK. The selected date will be placed in the text box that has the focus.

Enter an identifying reference in the Reference text box if you wish to restrict the report to a particular reference by clicking the drop-down arrow to obtain a list of all the references available. Use the Up and Down Arrow keys to browse through the entries. For example, you might want to display only adjusting entries, or only a certain invoice. As an alternative, you can type the first character of the reference in the text box. The first entry that begins with that character will automatically be displayed in the text box.

Enter an account number in the Account Number text box if you wish to restrict the report to a particular account by clicking the List button to obtain a chart of accounts selection list window from which you can select the desired account number.

An example of the General Journal Report for the transactions recorded on the general journal input form shown in Figure 2.2 and entered in the general journal in Figure 2.3 is shown in Figure 2.8.

```
                Palmer Consulting
                  General Journal
                    10/10/--

Date      Refer.    Acct.   Title              Debit       Credit

10/01     C811      540     Rent Expense       935.00
10/01     C811      110     Cash                           935.00

10/01     C812      560     Telephone Expense  245.63
10/01     C812      110     Cash                           245.63

10/03     T356      110     Cash               2105.20
10/03     T356      410     Fees                           2105.20

                            Totals             3285.83     3285.83
                                               =======     =======
```

Figure 2.8
General Journal Report

GRAPHING

Many new accounting packages are capable of producing graphs of data contained within their files. A **graph** is a pictorial representation of data that can be depicted on a computer screen or printed. Computer-generated graphs are used to clarify the meaning of the words and numbers that appear. Graphs are commonly used to enhance presentations, track sales, monitor expenses, identify trends, and make forecasts. To generate graphs, simply choose the Graph Selection menu item from the Reports menu, or click the Graphs toolbar button. The Graph Selection dialog box shown in Figure 2.9 will appear.

When the desired graph button is clicked, a three-dimensional graph illustrating the appropriate data will appear. Figure 2.10 shows an expense distribution graph generated by the *Automated Accounting 8.0* software. This pie chart illustrates the relative account balances in each of the expense accounts. In addition, it clearly shows that Rent Expense is the largest expense, followed by Telephone Expense.

Chapter 2   General Ledger—Service Business

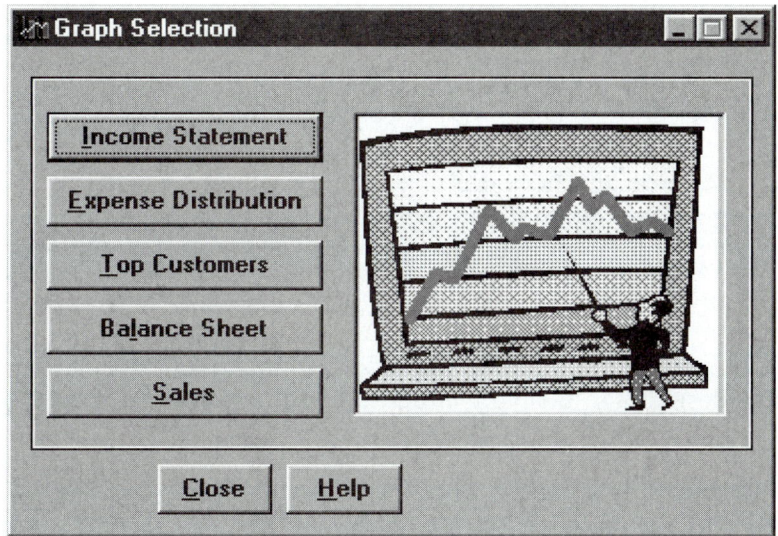

Figure 2.9
Graph Selection Dialog Box

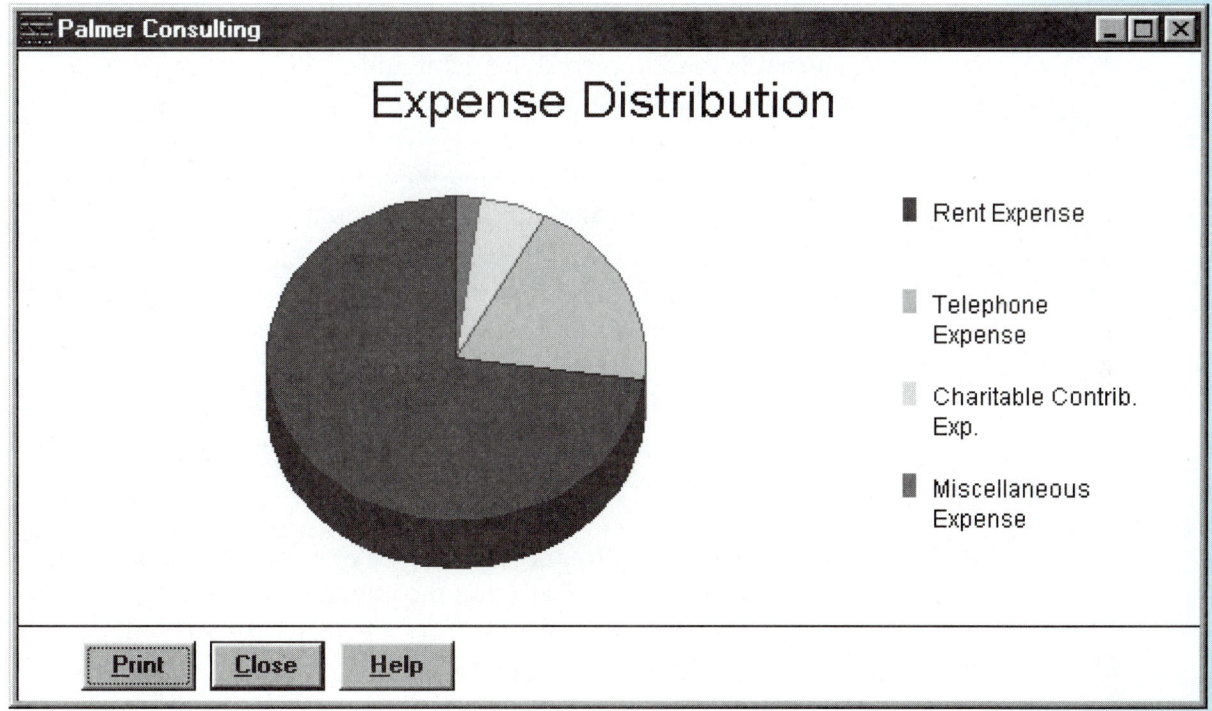

Figure 2.10
Three-Dimensional Expense Distribution Pie Graph

Chapter Review

1. Input forms that correspond to the computer journal windows can save computer time and help you organize your data prior to commencing an *Automated Accounting* computer session.

2. To complete the problems in this text, you can first complete the input forms in the *Working Papers* or enter transactions directly from the narrative provided. *Automated Accounting 8.0* has been specifically designed to facilitate either mode of entry.

3. The general journal input form is used for recording transactions in a general journal.

4. The Accounts tab within the Account Maintenance window is used to add new accounts to the chart of accounts, change account titles, and delete inactive accounts.

5. A journal is used to record the debit and credit parts of each transaction in date sequence.

6. Posting is the process of updating the ledger account balances with all debits and credits that affect each account.

7. As transactions are entered and posted into a computer's journal, the appropriate ledger account balance is updated.

8. The General Journal tab within the Journal Entries window is used to enter and post general journal entries and to make corrections to or delete existing journal entries.

9. The General Journal Report is a display or printout that is useful for detecting errors and verifying the equality of debits and credits.

10. Graphs are pictorial representations of data produced by the computer that is used to clarify the meaning of the words and numbers, enhance presentations, track sales, monitor expenses, identify trends, and make forecasts.

ACCOUNTING CAREERS IN DEPTH

Accounting Clerk

An accounting clerk performs any combination of the following duties:

- Calculating, posting, and verifying to obtain financial data for use in maintaining accounting records.
- Compiling and sorting documents such as invoices and checks to substantiate business transactions.
- Verifying and posting details of business transactions, such as funds received and disbursed, and totaling accounts, using a calculator or a computer.
- Computing and recording charges, refunds, cost of lost or damaged goods, freight charges, rentals, and similar items.

An accounting clerk may also be responsible for the following:

- Typing vouchers, invoices, check account statements, reports, and other records by using a typewriter or a computer.
- Reconciling bank statements.

The accounting clerk job is an entry-level position in most businesses. Taking accounting courses prior to working in this type of position is usually a requirement. In some companies, you must pass a test in order to be considered for the position. This should not be difficult if you have already studied accounting.

Accounting clerk positions can be found in most companies. Sometimes a different title might be used, but the work responsibilities are the same. An accounting clerk might be designated according to the type of accounting performed, such as Accounts-Payable Clerk and Accounts-Receivable Clerk.

There are usually many opportunities to be found in this career choice. Depending on your drive and plans for the future, a position as an accounting clerk can open doors to professional advancement.

TUTORIAL PROBLEM 2-T

The general journal entries for Palmer Consulting are illustrated in Figure 2.11.

STEP 1: **Start up *Automated Accounting 8.0*.**

STEP 2: **Load the opening balances problem file named AA8 Problem 02-T.AA8.**

STEP 3: **Enter your name in the User Name text box and click *OK*.**

STEP 4: **Save the file to your disk and folder with a file name of 02-T followed by Your Name.**

STEP 5: **Add Charitable Contrib. Exp. to the chart of accounts with an account number of 512 so that it will be positioned immediately following Advertising Expense.**

Click the *Accts.* toolbar button. Then click the *Accounts* tab and add the Charitable Contrib. Exp. account.

STEP 6: **Enter the general journal transactions shown in Figure 2.11.**

Click the *Journal* toolbar button. When the Journal Entries window appears, click the *General Journals* tab (if not already chosen) and enter the journal entries. The following transactions for Palmer Consulting occurred during the period of October 1 through October 10 of the current year. The transaction reference numbers are abbreviated as follows: Check no., C; Memorandum, M; Calculator tape, T.

Oct. 01 Paid cash for office rent, $935.00. C811.
01 Paid cash for telephone bill, $245.63. C812.
03 Received cash from sales, $2,105.20. T356.
06 Paid cash for charitable contribution, $75.00. C813.
07 Paid cash on account to Weston Office Supply, $80.00. C814.
08 Bought supplies on account from Weston Office Supply, $210.95. M314.
09 Paid cash for miscellaneous expense, $25.00. C815.
10 Paid cash for supplies, $50.00. C816.
10 Paid cash for insurance, $325.00. C817.
Note: Insurance coverage is paid in advance and is considered an asset because it is something of

TUTORIAL PROBLEM 2-T

Date	Refer.	Account	Debit	Credit
10/01/--	C811	540 Rent Expense	935.00	
		110　Cash		935.00
10/01/--	C812	560 Telephone Expense	245.63	
		110　Cash		245.63
10/03/--	T356	110 Cash	2105.20	
		410　Fees		2105.20
10/06/--	C813	512 Charitable Contrib. Exp.	75.00	
		110　Cash		75.00
10/07/--	C814	250 Weston Office Supply	80.00	
		110　Cash		80.00
10/08/--	M314	120 Supplies	210.95	
		250　Weston Office Supply		210.95
10/09/--	C815	530 Miscellaneous Expense	25.00	
		110　Cash		25.00
10/10/--	C816	120 Supplies	50.00	
		110　Cash		50.00
10/10/--	C817	130 Prepaid Insurance	325.00	
		110　Cash		325.00

Figure 2.11
Completed General Journal Window

value owned by Palmer Consulting. Therefore, the premium is recorded in *Prepaid Insurance,* account number 130, which is an asset account.

STEP 7: **Display the chart of accounts.**

Click the *Reports* toolbar button. When the Report Selection window appears, choose the *Account Lists* option from Select a Report Group. Select the *Chart of Accounts Report* from the Choose a Report to Display list (if not already highlighted), and click *OK*. Examine the report in Figure 2.12 and verify that the account you entered in Step 5 is correct.

Note: Use the Page Up and Page Down keys or click the arrows at either end of the scroll bar to scroll the report data.

To print the report currently displayed in the report window, click the *Print* button. To close the report viewer window, click the *Close* button in the lower portion of the window.

TUTORIAL PROBLEM 2-T

```
          Palmer Consulting
          Chart of Accounts
              10/10/--
Assets

110    Cash
120    Supplies
130    Prepaid Insurance

Liabilities

210    Abbe Business Supplies
220    Barnes Advertising, Inc.
230    Computer Center
240    Gibson Graphics, Inc.
250    Weston Office Supply

Owner's Equity

310    Richard Palmer, Capital
320    Richard Palmer, Drawing
330    Income Summary

Revenue

410    Fees

Expenses

510    Advertising Expense
512    Charitable Contrib. Exp.
520    Insurance Expense
530    Miscellaneous Expense
540    Rent Expense
550    Supplies Expense
560    Telephone Expense
```

Figure 2.12
Chart of Accounts Report

STEP 8: **Display the General Journal report.**

From the Report Selection window, select the *Journals* option and the *General Journal* report. Then click *OK*. When the Journal Report Selection window appears, choose the *Customize Journal Report* option. Set the Start Date to 10/01/-- and the End Date to 10/10/-- (where -- is the current year). Then click *OK*. The General Journal Report is shown in Figure 2.13.

Chapter 2 General Ledger—Service Business

TUTORIAL PROBLEM 2-T

Palmer Consulting
General Journal
10/10/--

Date	Refer.	Acct.	Title	Debit	Credit
10/01	C811	540	Rent Expense	935.00	
10/01	C811	110	Cash		935.00
10/01	C812	560	Telephone Expense	245.63	
10/01	C812	110	Cash		245.63
10/03	T356	110	Cash	2105.20	
10/03	T356	410	Fees		2105.20
10/06	C813	512	Charitable Contrib. Exp.	75.00	
10/06	C813	110	Cash		75.00
10/07	C814	250	Weston Office Supply	80.00	
10/07	C814	110	Cash		80.00
10/08	M314	120	Supplies	210.95	
10/08	M314	250	Weston Office Supply		210.95
10/09	C815	530	Miscellaneous Expense	25.00	
10/09	C815	110	Cash		25.00
10/10	C816	120	Supplies	50.00	
10/10	C816	110	Cash		50.00
10/10	C817	130	Prepaid Insurance	325.00	
10/10	C817	110	Cash		325.00
			Totals	4051.78	4051.78

Figure 2.13
General Journal Entries Report

Note: If the transactions were entered correctly, the Start and End Dates will be the default dates set automatically by the computer. The software uses the first day of the month as the Start Date and the latest date of the general journal transactions as the End Date.

TUTORIAL PROBLEM 2-T

STEP 9: **Display a trial balance.**

Choose *Ledger Reports* in the Report Selection window, select the *Trial Balance* report, and then click *OK*. The report appears in Figure 2.14.

```
                    Palmer Consulting
                      Trial Balance
                        10/10/--

Acct.         Account
Number        Title                       Debit         Credit

110           Cash                     14256.48
120           Supplies                  1110.04
130           Prepaid Insurance          487.00
220           Barnes Advertising, Inc.                   276.90
240           Gibson Graphics, Inc.                      245.10
250           Weston Office Supply                       210.95
310           Richard Palmer, Capital                  14296.00
410           Fees                                       2105.20
512           Charitable Contrib. Exp.    75.00
530           Miscellaneous Expense       25.00
540           Rent Expense               935.00
560           Telephone Expense          245.63
                                       ------------   ------------
              Totals                    17134.15        17134.15
                                       ============   ============
```

Figure 2.14
Trial Balance Report

STEP 10: **Generate a 3D expense distribution pie chart.**

Click the *Graphs* toolbar button. When the Graph Selection window appears, click the *Expense Distribution* button. The 3D Expense Distribution pie chart is shown in Figure 2.15.

STEP 11: **Save the data file.**

Click the *Save* toolbar button.

Chapter 2 General Ledger—Service Business

TUTORIAL PROBLEM 2-T

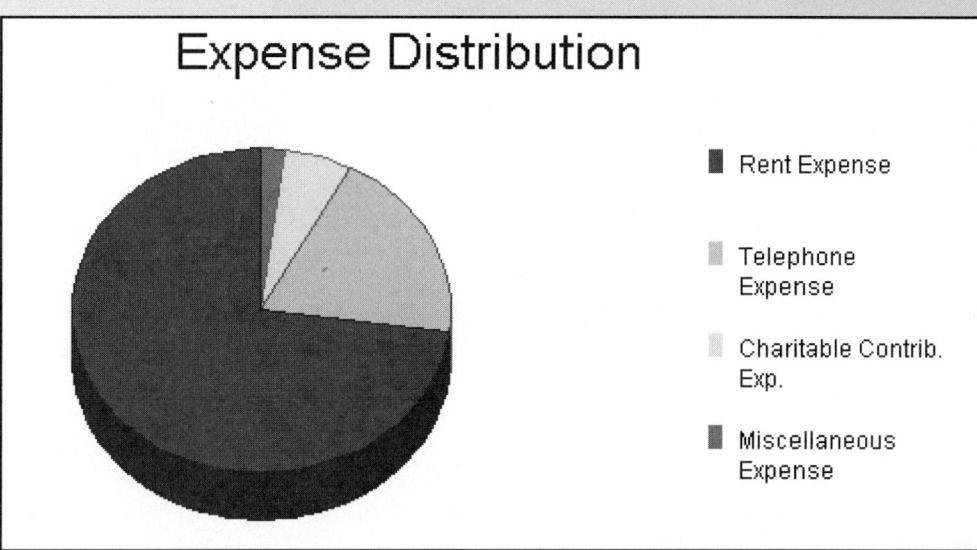

Figure 2.15
Expense Distribution Pie Chart

STEP 12: Optional Spreadsheet Activity.

You will create a spreadsheet report showing only the cash paid during the period October 1–10 from the accounting system data.

a. Follow the procedure in Step 8 to display the General Journal Report for October 1–10. When the General Journal Report appears, click the *Copy* button and select the *Spreadsheet Format* option to copy the report to the clipboard.
b. Start up your spreadsheet software.
c. Open the spreadsheet template file named AA8 Spreadsheet 02-T.WK1. The file is in the same folder as the AA8.0 problem template files.
d. Save your spreadsheet file to your disk and folder with a file name of 02-T Your Name.
e. Select cell A1 as the current cell (if not already selected).
f. Select *Paste* from the Edit menu and paste the General Journal Report (copied to the clipboard in Step a) into the spreadsheet.

TUTORIAL PROBLEM 2-T

g. Delete all rows of data that are not a cash-payment transaction (all rows with a reference other than C). Leave one blank row between each journal entry.
h. Change the title of the report from General Journal to Cash Paid.
i. Replace the old totals with the Sum of the debit [@SUM(F9..F28)] and credit [@SUM (G9..G28)] columns.
j. Format the spreadsheet to match the completed spreadsheet shown in Figure 2.16.

Student Name

Palmer Consulting
Cash Paid
As Of 10/10/--

Date	Refer.	Acct.	Title	Debit	Credit
01-Oct	C811	540	Rent Expense	$935.00	
01-Oct	C811	110	Cash		$935.00
01-Oct	C812	560	Telephone Expense	$245.63	
01-Oct	C812	110	Cash		$245.63
06-Oct	C813	512	Charitable Contrib. Exp.	$75.00	
06-Oct	C813	110	Cash		$75.00
07-Oct	C814	250	Weston Office Supply	$80.00	
07-Oct	C814	110	Cash		$80.00
09-Oct	C815	530	Miscellaneous Expense	$25.00	
09-Oct	C815	110	Cash		$25.00
10-Oct	C816	120	Supplies	$50.00	
10-Oct	C816	110	Cash		$50.00
10-Oct	C817	130	Prepaid Insurance	$325.00	
10-Oct	C817	110	Cash		$325.00
			Totals	$1,735.63	$1,735.63

Figure 2.16
Spreadsheet Cash Paid Report (October 1–10)

Chapter 2   General Ledger—Service Business   63

TUTORIAL PROBLEM 2-T

k. Print the completed Cash Payments Report (cells A1–C31).
l. Save your spreadsheet file.
m. End your spreadsheet session and return to the *Automated Accounting* application.

STEP 13: End your *Automated Accounting* session.

Click the *Exit* toolbar button.

A bookmark or hotlist is a special file used to save addresses and locations. By saving and recalling addresses, it is easy for you to visit your favorite sites repeatedly.

Cyberspace is the electronic world of the Internet that exists only on computers. Cyberspace is sometimes called *virtual reality*.

A Uniform Resource Locator (URL) is an address code for finding hypertext or hypermedia documents on World Wide Web (WWW) servers around the world. URLs can be accessed by WWW browsers.

Spam is unsolicited advertising that finds its way into e-mailboxes. It usually isn't necessary to read this mail.

Chapter 2 General Ledger—Service Business

Review and Practice: Applying Your Information Skills

I. MATCHING

Directions: In the *Working Papers*, write the letter of the appropriate term next to each definition.

a. account maintenance
b. General Journal input form
c. General Journal Report
d. General Journal tab
e. graph
f. input form
g. journal
h. posting
i. sole proprietorship

1. A pictorial representation of data that can be displayed on a computer screen or printed.

2. A form with two amount columns that is used to organize and record accounting transaction data before entering data at the computer.

3. A form used to organize and record accounting transactions before entering data at the computer.

4. A record of the debit and credit parts of each transaction, recorded in date sequence.

5. A set of grid cells within the Journal Entries window that is used to enter and post general journal entries and to make corrections to or delete existing journal entries.

6. The process of updating the ledger account balances with all debits and credits affecting each account.

7. A display or printout of the general journal that is useful in detecting errors and verifying the equality of debits and credits.

8. The process of keeping a business's chart of accounts up to date by adding new accounts, changing titles of existing accounts, and deleting inactive accounts.

9. A business that is owned by one person.

Chapter 2 General Ledger—Service Business

II. TRUE/FALSE

Directions: Write the answers to each of the following questions in the *Working Papers*.

1. An entry to add a new account is entered in the General Journal window.
2. Only transactions that do not involve cash can be recorded in the General Journal window.
3. General ledger accounts cannot be deleted unless the account balance is zero.
4. The Find menu item in the Edit menu can be used to find a transaction that contains a specified debit or credit amount.
5. The Chart of Accounts button in the General Journal window displays a Chart of Accounts selection list.
6. A new general ledger account can be added or changed while entering a journal entry.
7. Instead of keying an account number in the General Journal, you can select the account from the Chart of Accounts selection list window.

III. REVIEW QUESTIONS

Directions: Write the answers to each of the following questions in the *Working Papers*.

1. Describe the process for adding an account to the chart of accounts.
2. Describe the process for changing the title of an existing account in the chart of accounts.
3. Describe the process for deleting an account that has a zero balance from the chart of accounts.
4. What kind of transaction(s) can be entered in the general journal?
5. Describe the process for correcting a general journal entry.
6. Describe the process for deleting a general journal entry.
7. Explain how the Chart of Accounts button can be used while entering general journal transactions.
8. Complete the date range section of the Journal Report Selection window in Figure 2.17 to display all general journal entries from July 1 through July 31 of the current year.

9. Complete the Journal Report Selection window in Figure 2.17 to display all general journal entries from August 1 through August 10 of the current year with a reference of C412.

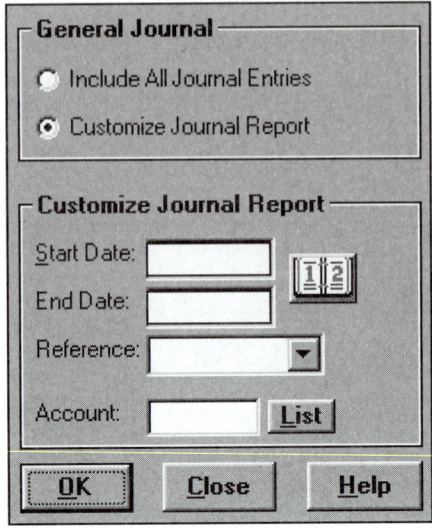

Figure 2.17
Journal Report Selection Window

IV. INTERNET ACTIVITY

Directions: If you have access to the Internet, use the Browser to find information about a national accounting association. *Hint:* Use a search argument of *accounting organizations* or *national accounting associations* to narrow your search. Select one of the associations and report your findings. Be sure to include the source and the URL (Internet address) of your search.

Independent Practice Problem 2-P

In this problem, you will process any additions, changes, and deletions to the chart of accounts as well as the general journal entries for the period October 11 through October 20 of the current year. A general journal input form is provided in the working papers.

STEP 1: Start up *Automated Accounting 8.0*.

STEP 2: Open the opening balances file named AA8 Problem 02-P.

STEP 3: Enter your name in the User Name text box.

Chapter 2 General Ledger—Service Business

STEP 4: Save the file to your drive and folder with a file name of 02-P Your Name.

STEP 5: Enter the following account maintenance and October 14–20 general journal transactions. The transaction reference numbers are abbreviated as follows: Check no., C; Memorandum, M; Calculator tape, T.

Oct. 14 Received cash from sales, $2,815.50. T357.
Note: Delete Computer Center from the chart of accounts.

14 Bought a subscription on account from Bates Journals, Inc., $165.35. M315.
Note: Add Dues & Subscriptions Exp. to the chart of accounts with account number 515, and add Bates Journals, Inc. to the chart of accounts with account number 225.

15 Paid cash for miscellaneous expense, $80.00. C818.

15 Paid cash on account to Barnes Advertising, Inc. $276.90. C819.

15 Received cash from sales, $2,950.00. T358.

16 Bought advertising on account from Barnes Advertising, Inc., $585.00. M316.

17 Paid cash on account to Gibson Graphics & Design, $245.10. C820.
Note: Change the account title of Gibson Graphics, Inc. to Gibson Graphics & Design.

20 Paid cash for travel expense, $164.23. C821.
Note: Add Travel & Entertain. Exp. to the chart of accounts with account number 570.

STEP 6: Display a Chart of Accounts Report.

STEP 7: Display the General Journal Report for the period October 11 to October 20. Make corrections, if necessary.

STEP 8: Display a trial balance.

STEP 9: Generate an expense distribution graph.

STEP 10: Save your data to disk.

STEP 11: Optional Spreadsheet and Word Processing Integration Activity.

Use a spreadsheet to create a report showing only the fees entered into the accounting system for the period October 11–20. Then prepare an interoffice memorandum to Mr. Palmer that contains this information.

a. Display and copy the General Journal Report for October 11–20 to the clipboard in spreadsheet format.
b. Start up your spreadsheet software and load the spreadsheet template file named AA8 Spreadsheet 02-T.
c. Select cell *A1* as the current cell and paste the General Journal Report into the spreadsheet.
d. Delete all rows of data that are not fee-received transactions. Keep only those rows with a reference starting with T. Change the title of the report from General Journal to Fees, and replace the old totals with the Sum of the debit and credit columns. Format the spreadsheet similar to Figure 2.16.
e. Save your spreadsheet file with a file name of 02-P Your Name.
f. Select and copy the spreadsheet report to the clipboard.
g. End your spreadsheet application.
h. Start up your word processing application software and load the template file named AA8 Wordprocessing 02-P (load as a text file).
i. Replace *FROM: Student Name* with your name.
j. Position the insertion point at the end of the document and paste the spreadsheet report. Format your document as necessary.
k. Print the completed document.
l. Save your document with a file name of 02-P Your Name.
m. End your word processing application and return to the *Automated Accounting* application.

STEP 12: End the *Automated Accounting* session.

Applying Your Technology Skills 2-P

Directions: Write the answers to the following questions in the *Working Papers*.

1. Why do you think account number 515 was assigned to Dues & Subscriptions Exp.?

2. What is the amount of check number 819 shown on the General Journal Report?

3. What is the balance in the Rent Expense account?

4. What is the balance in the Dues & Subscriptions Expense account?

Chapter 2   General Ledger—Service Business

5. What are the debit and credit totals on the Trial Balance Report?
6. From the Expense Distribution graph, what are the three highest expenses?

Mastery Problem 2-M

In this problem, you will process any additions, changes, and deletions to the chart of accounts as well as the general journal entries for the period October 21 through October 31 of the current year. A general journal input form is provided in the *Working Papers*.

STEP 1: Open the opening balances file named AA8 Problem 02-M.AA8. Save the file to your drive and folder with a file name of 02-M Your Name.

STEP 2: Enter the following account maintenance and October 21–31 general journal transactions.

Oct. 21   Bought supplies on account from Weston Office Supply, $228.10. M317.
Note: Delete Abbe Business Supplies from the chart of accounts.
  23   Paid cash for insurance, $350.00. C822.
  23   Received cash from sales, $2,700.00. T359.
  27   Paid cash on account to Weston Office Supply, $210.95. C823.
  28   Bought supplies on account from Gibson Graphics & Design, 405.75. M318.
  29   Received cash from sales, $2,637.15. T360.
  30   Paid cash for electric bill, $507.41. C824.
Note: Add Utilities Expense to the chart of accounts with account number 580 so that it will be positioned immediately following Travel & Entertain. Exp.
  30   Paid cash for charitable contribution, $120.00. C825.
  31   Paid cash for miscellaneous expense, $205.00. C826.
  31   Paid cash to owner for personal use, $4,750.00. C827.

STEP 3: Display the following reports and graph: Chart of Accounts, General Journal Report (October 21–31), Trial Balance, and Expense Distribution Graph.

STEP 4: Save your file.

STEP 5: Display reports as necessary to answer the questions in Applying Your Technology Skills 2-M.

STEP 6: Optional Spreadsheet Activity.

Create a spreadsheet report showing the cash that was received for the period October 21–31 from the accounting system data.

a. Start up your spreadsheet software and load the spreadsheet template file named AA8 Spreadsheet 02-T.
b. Copy and paste the October 21–31 General Journal Report into the spreadsheet.
c. Delete all rows of data that are not cash-paid transactions. Change the title of the report, replace the old totals with the sum of the debit and credit columns, and format the spreadsheet similar to Figure 2.16.
d. Save your spreadsheet file with a file name of 02-M Your Name.
e. Print the completed report.

Applying Your Technology Skills 2-M

Directions: Write the answers to the following questions in the *Working Papers*.

1. Why was account number 580 assigned to Utilities Expense?
2. What are the debit and credit totals on the General Journal Report?
3. What is the amount of check number 824 shown on the General Journal Report?
4. What is the balance in the Advertising Expense account?
5. What is the balance in the Miscellaneous Expense account?
6. From the expense distribution graph, what are the two highest expenses?

Chapter 3

GENERAL LEDGER—END-OF-FISCAL-PERIOD FOR A SERVICE BUSINESS AND BANK RECONCILIATION

KEY TERMS

Adjusting Entries
Income Statement
Component Percentage
Balance Sheet
Statement of Owner's Equity

Bank Reconciliation
Period-End Closing
Temporary Accounts
Income Summary Account
Post-Closing Trial Balance

LEARNING OBJECTIVES

Upon completion of this chapter, you will be able to:

1. Record and display adjusting entries.
2. Display financial statements.
3. Complete bank reconciliation procedures.
4. Perform period-end closing.

ETHICS

Copyright is the right to prohibit other people from making copies. This is known as an exclusive right to reproduce the work. Copyright involves five exclusive rights: (1) the exclusive right to make copies; (2) the exclusive right to distribute copies to the public; (3) the exclusive right to prepare derivative works; (4) the exclusive right to perform the work in public (applies mainly to plays, dances, etc.); and (5) the exclusive right to display the work in public.

The Software Act of 1980 made programs copyrightable as long as they had a minimal amount of creativity. As a matter of fact, a program is also copyrightable if it is stored in the computer's memory rather than on paper.

Ideas cannot be copyrighted. Copyright law protects only words, images, sounds, etc., that an author uses to express ideas. Authors are free to express the same ideas in their own way. That is why there are many different word processors, databases, and spreadsheets on the market. The idea of a word processor, database, and spreadsheet cannot be copyrighted. However, the courts have found the following elements to be copyrightable expressions of ideas: (1) source code and object code; (2) flowcharts; (3) sequence, structure, and organization of a program; (4) structure of a program's audiovisual displays; and (5) menu structure, including what appears in the menu.

The Software Act allows the person who purchases a software product to make a backup copy, as long as it is for archival purposes only. The archive copy cannot be given to another person for his or her use. The original and backup can be given away, sold, lent or rented to others only if the original purchaser does not retain a copy. Although the copyright owner has the exclusive right to distribute copies of the software, that right applies only to the first sale of any particular copy. That is, if you buy a copyrighted book, you may give your book to a friend or sell it to someone else. The copyright owner does not have the right to control resales of the first copy.

Any program that comes into existence in a tangible medium (i.e, source and object code, flowchart, stored on a disk, etc.) is copyright protected. Programs do not have to be registered to be copyright protected, although it is a good idea. The reason that programs are registered is for protection *before* infringements take place. The court can award up to $100,000.00 per infringed work, called statutory damages, and impose other actions to stop the illegal copyright activities.

Critical Thinking

1. How can the copyright owner of computer software prevent someone from making an unauthorized copy of the work?

2. Do you agree that software copyright should be enforced by law? Explain your position.

3. What is the major effect of the copyright law on: (1) the person (or business) who sells a software product; and (2) the person who buys the software product?

Chapter 3 General Ledger—End-of-Fiscal-Period and Bank Reconciliation

INTRODUCTION

In the previous chapter, you learned how to maintain the chart of accounts and process transactions. In this chapter, you will learn how to complete the end-of-fiscal-period processing for a service business. To complete the accounting cycle, adjusting entries are recorded on the general journal input form, entered into the computer, and verified for accuracy. The financial statements are then generated. Finally, closing journal entries are generated and posted by the software, and a post-closing trial balance is prepared. In this chapter, you will also learn how to use the software to complete a bank reconciliation.

ADJUSTING ENTRIES

Journal entries recorded to update general ledger accounts at the end of a fiscal period are called **adjusting entries**. Portions of assets, such as supplies and prepaid insurance, are consumed during the fiscal period and become expenses of the business. For example, the supplies that have been consumed must be deducted from the asset account Supplies and recorded in the expense account Supplies Expense. The amount of prepaid insurance that has expired must be deducted from the asset account Prepaid Insurance and recorded in the expense account Insurance Expense.

Adjusting entries are not entered in the general journal until after all other transactions for the accounting period have been entered into the computer and posted. The trial balance is then displayed or printed. This trial balance and the period-end adjustment data are the basis for the adjusting entries. The adjusting entries may then be analyzed, recorded on the general journal input form, entered into the computer, and posted. A Journal Entries Report is then displayed to prove the equality of the debits and credits.

All the adjusting entries are for the same date and use *Adj.Ent.* as the reference. The trial balance before adjustments is shown in Figure 3.1. The following adjustment data is for Frentz Consulting. The adjusting entries have been entered into the general journal shown in Figure 3.2.

Supplies inventory $1,100.00
Value of insurance policies on October 31 . . . . . .   500.00

The adjustment amounts are calculated as follows:

Supplies account balance, Oct. 31
   (from trial balance) $1,743.64
Less supplies inventory, Oct. 31 . . . . 1,100.00
Equals supplies used during October
   (adjusting entry) $643.64

Prepaid Insurance account balance, Oct. 31
(from trial balance) $772.00
Less current value of insurance polices 500.00
Equals insurance used during October
(adjusting entry) $272.00

```
                    Frentz Consulting
                      Trial Balance
                       10/31/--
```

Acct. Number	Account Title	Debit	Credit
110	Cash	18319.89	
120	Supplies	1743.64	
130	Prepaid Insurance	772.00	
220	Bauer Advertising, Inc.		595.00
225	Burton Journals, Inc.		155.65
240	Gordon Graphics & Design		425.50
250	Weber Office Supply		218.10
310	Michael Frentz, Capital		14296.00
320	Michael Frentz, Drawing	4500.00	
410	Fees		12751.45
510	Advertising Expense	595.00	
512	Charitable Contrib. Exp.	190.00	
515	Dues & Subscriptions Exp.	155.65	
530	Miscellaneous Expense	285.00	
540	Rent Expense	950.00	
560	Telephone Expense	263.45	
570	Travel & Entertain. Exp.	173.73	
580	Utilities Expense	493.34	
	Totals	28441.70	28441.70

Figure 3.1
Trial Balance (Before Adjusting Entries)

Date	Refer.	Account	Debit	Credit
10/31/--	Adj.Ent.	550 Supplies Expense	643.64	
		120 Supplies		643.64
10/31/--	Adj.Ent.	520 Insurance Expense	272.00	
		130 Prepaid Insurance		272.00

Figure 3.2
Adjusting Entries Entered in the General Journal Window

In a manual accounting system, a worksheet is used as a tool for analyzing the adjusting entries and preparing the financial statements.

Chapter 3 General Ledger—End-of-Fiscal-Period and Bank Reconciliation

Since the computer generates the financial statements directly from the general ledger data, a worksheet is not required for an automated accounting system. Therefore, once the adjusting entries have been entered in a journal, posted, and verified, the financial statements can be displayed.

FINANCIAL STATEMENTS

The financial statements available for a nondepartmentalized business organized as a sole proprietorship are the income statement, the balance sheet, and the statement of owner's equity. A performance report is available only if budgeting data is available.

To display financial statements, choose the Report Selection menu item from the Reports menu or click the Reports toolbar button. When the Report Selection dialog box appears, choose the Financial Statements option button from the Select a Report Group list. A list of all the reports within the chosen Financial Statements option will appear, as shown in Figure 3.3.

The date that appears in the upper-right corner will be used to date the selected report(s). To change this date, select it and then enter the desired date, or press "+" to increase and "−" to decrease the date, or click the calendar icon and use the calendar.

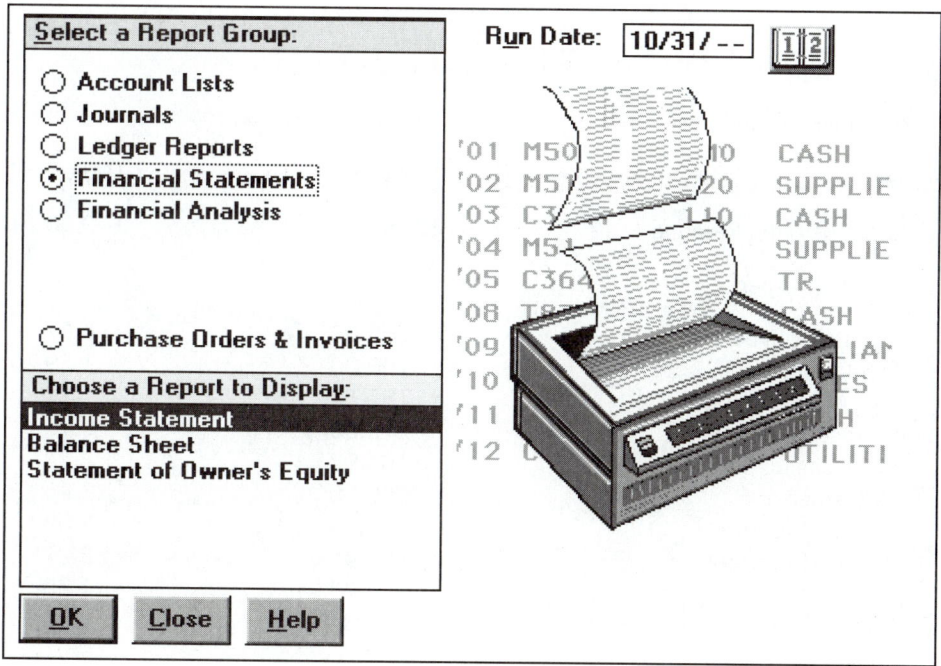

Figure 3.3
Report Selection (Financial Statements)

Choose the financial statement report you would like to display from the Choose a Report to Display list. Then click the OK button.

Income Statement

The **income statement** is a financial statement that provides information about the net income or net loss of a business over a specific period of time. The up-to-date account balances stored by the software are used to calculate and display the revenue earned and the expenses incurred during a fiscal period. Total revenue minus total expenses equals net income. If this difference is negative, it is the net loss.

Automated Accounting offers two formats for the income statement—Report by Month and Year and Report by Fiscal Period. This option is set in the Customize Accounting System window, which will be covered in a later chapter. This chapter uses the Report by Fiscal Period option shown in Figure 3.4. With this format, the profitability of the business is shown from the beginning of the fiscal period until the time when the income statement is displayed.

Also included for each amount is a component percentage. A **component percentage** shows the percentage relationship between one financial statement item and the total that includes that item. Component

```
                        Frentz Consulting
                        Income Statement
                      For Period Ended 10/31/--

Operating Revenue

  Fees                                       12751.45              100.00
                                             ----------
  Total Operating Revenue                    12751.45              100.00

Operating Expenses

  Advertising Expense                          595.00                4.67
  Charitable Contrib. Exp.                     190.00                1.49
  Dues & Subscriptions Exp.                    155.65                1.22
  Insurance Expense                            272.00                2.13
  Miscellaneous Expense                        285.00                2.24
  Rent Expense                                 950.00                7.45
  Supplies Expense                             643.64                5.05
  Telephone Expense                            263.45                2.07
  Travel & Entertain. Exp.                     173.73                1.36
  Utilities Expense                            493.34                3.87
                                             ----------
  Total Operating Expenses                    4021.81               31.54
                                             ----------
Net Income                                    8729.64               68.46
                                             ==========
```

Figure 3.4
Income Statement by Fiscal Period

percentages calculated on an income statement show the relationship of items to total operating revenue or sales.

The Balance Sheet

The **balance sheet** is a financial statement that reports assets, liabilities, and owner's equities on a specific date. The balance sheet can help financial statement users evaluate the overall financial strength of a business. Many factors determine the financial strength of a business, one factor being an adequate ratio of assets to liabilities.

Although the balance sheet may be displayed at any time, it is typically displayed at the end of a fiscal period. The balance sheet is illustrated in Figure 3.5. Note that total owner's equity equals the owner's capital account balance less the owner's drawing account balance plus the net income.

```
                    Frentz Consulting
                      Balance Sheet
                        10/31/--

Assets

Cash                                  18319.89
Supplies                               1100.00
Prepaid Insurance                       500.00
                                      ---------
Total Assets                                              19919.89
                                                          ========

Liabilities

Bauer Advertising, Inc.                 595.00
Burton Journals, Inc.                   155.65
Gordon Graphics & Design                425.50
Weber Office Supply                     218.10
                                      ---------
Total Liabilities                                          1394.25

Owner's Equity

Michael Frentz, Capital               14296.00
Michael Frentz, Drawing               -4500.00
Net Income                             8729.64
                                      ---------
Total Owner's Equity                                      18525.64
                                                          ---------
Total Liabilities & Equity                                19919.89
                                                          ========
```

Figure 3.5
Balance Sheet

Statement of Owner's Equity

The **statement of owner's equity** is a financial statement that shows the changes to owner's equity during the fiscal period. The statement shows the capital at the beginning of the period, additions and subtractions to capital, and capital at the end of the fiscal period. Business owners can review this report to determine if their equity is increasing or decreasing and what is causing the change. Changes to owner's equity result from additional investments, withdrawals, and net income or net loss. A sample owner's equity statement is shown in Figure 3.6.

```
                    Frentz Consulting
                 Statement of Owner's Equity
                 For Period Ended 10/31/--

Michael Frentz, Capital (Beg. of Period)          14296.00
Michael Frentz, Drawing                           -4500.00
Net Income                                         8729.64
                                                 ----------
Michael Frentz, Capital (End of Period)           18525.64
                                                 ==========
```

Figure 3.6
Owner's Equity Statement

BANK RECONCILIATION

A **bank reconciliation** is the process of verifying that the bank statement and the checkbook balance are in agreement. The Bank Reconciliation option is accessed via the Other Activities menu item in the Data menu or the Other toolbar button. Information maintained by the software, such as the checkbook balance and checks that were written during the period, will be automatically provided to make the reconciliation process simpler and more accurate.

To complete a bank reconciliation, choose the Other Activities menu item from the Data menu, or click the Other toolbar button. When the Other Activities window appears, click the Clear button. This will cause the software to erase any previous transaction data. Enter any bank credits, bank charges, the bank statement balance, and outstanding deposit amounts. Figure 3.7 shows a partially completed bank reconciliation. Use the Tab key to move between fields or double-click a new field with the mouse. Note that the Enter key is the equivalent of clicking OK, which registers the bank reconciliation and closes the window. The Cash account balance automatically appears in the Checkbook Balance text box, and the checks written during the period are displayed in a list box. If necessary, you can key a different Checkbook balance amount.

Chapter 3 General Ledger—End-of-Fiscal-Period and Bank Reconciliation

Select the outstanding checks by moving the pointer to the Checks from the Journals list, selecting the desired check (point and click to highlight), and clicking the Select button (or double-clicking the desired check). The selected check will be moved to the Outstanding Checks list, and the Adjusted Bank Balance will be automatically updated. Repeat this procedure for each outstanding check. If you move the wrong check to Outstanding Checks by mistake, select it and click Remove, or double-click it to return it to the Checks from the Journals list. Notice that the bank reconciliation is out of balance. It will be in balance when the remaining two checks from the journal are selected.

If you press the Enter key and the bank reconciliation closes, simply click the Other tool to reopen it.

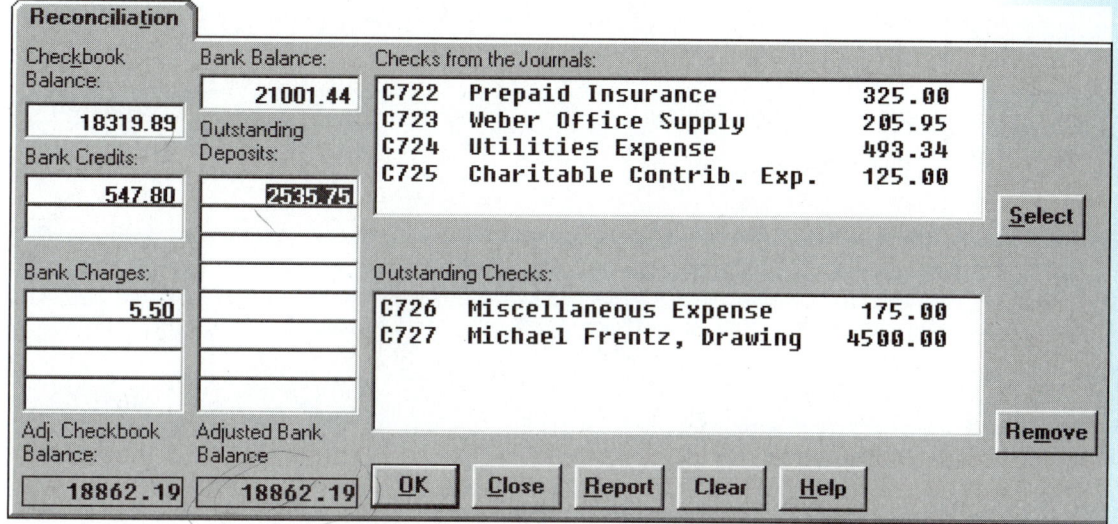

Figure 3.7
Bank Reconciliation

Note: Click the OK command button to record your data and dismiss the bank reconciliation. Click the Clear button if you want to erase all the data that has been keyed and/or selected in the bank reconciliation.

Click the Report command button at the bottom of the Reconciliation window to display the Bank Reconciliation Report. The completed Bank Reconciliation Report is shown in Figure 3.8. Notice that the adjusted checkbook balance is equal to the adjusted bank balance. If the two balances are not equal, the errors must be found and corrected by checking the following items:

1. The bank reconciliation may be incomplete or have errors.

2. The checkbook records may have incorrect or missing entries or calculation errors.

3. The bank statement may have errors. Errors in bank statements are relatively rare, but they can occur.

```
                    Frentz Consulting
                    Bank Reconciliation
                         10/31/--

Checkbook Balance                                      18319.89

Plus Bank Credits:
                              547.80
                          ------------
                                                         547.80

Less Bank Charges:
                                5.50
                          ------------
                                                           5.50
                                                      ----------
Adjusted Checkbook Balance                             18862.19
                                                      ==========
Bank Statement Balance                                 21001.44

Plus Outstanding Deposits:
                             2535.75
                          ------------
                                                        2535.75

Less Outstanding Checks:
              C726            175.00
              C727           4500.00
                          ------------
                                                        4675.00
                                                      ----------
Adjusted Bank Balance                                  18862.19
                                                      ==========
```

Figure 3.8
Bank Reconciliation Report

PERIOD-END CLOSING

Period-end closing is the process of recording and posting closing entries to the general ledger to prepare temporary accounts for a new fiscal period. **Temporary accounts** are accounts that accumulate information until it is transferred to the owner's capital account. The **Income Summary account** is an account used to summarize the closing entries for the revenue and expense accounts.

In a manual accounting system, closing entries are recorded in the journal and posted to the general ledger to close all of the temporary income statement accounts to the Income Summary account, close the Income Summary account to the capital account, and close the drawing account to the capital account. In an automated accounting system, the software generates and records the closing journal entries in the general. When these closing entries are posted to the general ledger, the software updates the account balances and stores them as the last fiscal period's account balances for use with financial statement analysis.

Chapter 3 General Ledger—End-of-Fiscal-Period and Bank Reconciliation

In this system, the closing journal entries remain stored by the computer after they are posted. This allows corrections to be made for the previous year if necessary.

After the period-end closing procedure is completed, a post-closing trial balance report is displayed. A **post-closing trial balance** is a trial balance that verifies that debits equal credits in the general ledger accounts after closing entries have been posted. The only difference between a regular trial balance and a post-closing trial balance is *when* it is displayed.

To generate, display, and post the closing journal entries, choose the Generate Closing Journal Entries menu item from the Options menu. (The dialog box shown in Figure 3.9 will appear.)

Click the Yes button to proceed. A dialog box showing the closing entries automatically generated by the computer will appear. (Figure 3.10 shows the closing entries that were generated after all the transactions and adjusting entries were entered and posted.)

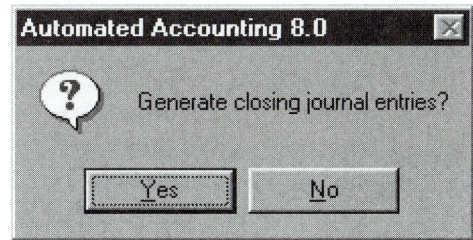

Figure 3.9
Generate Closing Journal Entries

Click the Post button to instruct the computer to post the closing entries and to store the last fiscal period's account balances for future use. The general journal will appear to show that the closing entries were posted with a reference of Clo.Ent.

The post-closing trial balance for Frentz Consulting is shown in Figure 3.11.

fyi...

A regular trial balance and a post-closing trial balance are the same except that the latter is displayed after closing. On the Report Selection dialog box, choose Ledger Reports and then choose Trial Balance.

Acct. #	Account Title	Debit	Credit
410	Fees	12751.45	
330	Income Summary		12751.45
330	Income Summary	4021.81	
510	Advertising Expense		595.00
512	Charitable Contrib. Exp.		190.00
515	Dues & Subscriptions Exp.		155.65
520	Insurance Expense		272.00
530	Miscellaneous Expense		285.00
540	Rent Expense		950.00
550	Supplies Expense		643.64
560	Telephone Expense		263.45
570	Travel & Entertain. Exp.		173.73
580	Utilities Expense		493.34
330	Income Summary	8729.64	
310	Michael Frentz, Capital		8729.64
310	Michael Frentz, Capital	4500.00	
320	Michael Frentz, Drawing		4500.00

Figure 3.10
Closing Entries

```
                        Fentz Consulting
                         Trial Balance
                           10/31/--

Acct.    Account
Number   Title                          Debit           Credit

110      Cash                        18319.89
120      Supplies                     1100.00
130      Prepaid Insurance             500.00
220      Bauer Advertising, Inc.                         595.00
225      Burton Journals, Inc.                           155.65
240      Gordon Graphics & Design                        425.50
250      Weber Office Supply                             218.10
310      Michael Frentz, Capital                       18525.64
                                     ---------        ---------
         Totals                      19919.89         19919.89
                                     =========        =========
```

Figure 3.11
Post-Closing Trial Balance

If an error is detected after closing, complete the following steps: (1) correct the erroneous journal entry; (2) delete the closing entries; and (3) again generate, display, and post the closing journal entries. If the closing entry is in error, correct the entry and post. Be sure to print another post-closing trial balance.

Journal entries can be purged (removed) from the system at any time or when the maximum capacity of 600 journal entries has been reached. (This will not occur for any of the problems in this textbook.) Since the account balances are updated as journal entries are posted, all account balances will be correct after the journal entries are purged. Therefore, no information will be lost. The Purge Journal Entries menu item is located in the Options menu.

Chapter Review

1. Adjusting entries are not entered into the general journal until all other transactions for the accounting period have been entered into the computer and posted. The trial balance is then displayed or printed. This trial balance and the period-end adjustment data are the basis for the adjusting entries.

2. The income statement provides information on the net income or net loss of a business over a specific period of time. Up-to-date account balances stored by the computer are used to calculate and display the revenue earned and the expenses incurred during a fiscal period. Total revenue minus total expenses equals the net income or net loss. A component percentage is included for each amount on the income statement, indicating each amount's percentage of total operating revenue.

3. The balance sheet reports assets, liabilities, and owner's equities on a specific date. The balance sheet can help financial statement users evaluate the overall financial strength of a business.

4. The statement of owner's equity shows the changes to owner's equity during the fiscal period. The statement shows the capital at the beginning of the period, additions and subtractions to capital, and capital at the end of the fiscal period.

5. Each month, after the bank statement is received, the bank statement is reconciled to the checkbook balance. The checkbook balance is the same as the Cash account balance in the general ledger.

6. Closing journal entries generated by the software close all of the temporary income statement accounts to the income summary account, close the income summary account to the capital account, and close the drawing account to the capital account. When the closing entries are posted to the general ledger, the software updates the account balances and stores them as the last fiscal period's account balances for use with financial statement analysis.

7. A post-closing trial balance report is displayed to verify that debits equal credits in the general ledger accounts after closing entries are posted.

ACCOUNTING CAREERS IN DEPTH

Self-Employed C.P.A.

A C.P.A. is a Certified Public Accountant. Establishing a business as a C.P.A. would be a good career choice for those accountants who prefer to work for themselves. They can provide tax services, accounting services, auditing services, and investment services. A C.P.A.'s preparation of corporate and personal income tax statements helps provide suggestions and formulate tax strategies to assist a client in saving money.

A self-employed C.P.A. can provide many types of services to individuals as well as corporations. Although it is a big responsibility to work for yourself, it can be very rewarding. Some persons feel confined, working a standard eight-hour day; however, when you are self-employed, you can schedule your own hours. Be aware that you may have to work more hours in a day when you work for yourself. Although you must generate your own business, the work offers close customer contact, a high degree of independence, and potential financial rewards.

It is very important for an accountant to have a positive image with the public. This is especially important when you work for yourself because your name and the services you provide are what will bring you new clients.

The preparation for becoming a C.P.A. involves completing a four-year college degree in accounting, passing the C.P.A. exam, and gaining acceptable work experience. For a C.P.A., it is necessary to complete continuing education in order to keep one's certification. This can be done by participating in workshops, seminars, and short courses of study. Continuing education is required because of changes in laws that affect how companies can operate.

Persons who choose to become self-employed C.P.A.s will enjoy a rewarding experience, will work hard, and most likely will become an integral part of the community where they have set up their business.

TUTORIAL PROBLEM 3-T

In this tutorial problem, you will complete the end-of-fiscal-period processing for a service business by keying the adjusting entries, displaying the financial statements, displaying charts and graphs, and performing period-end closing for Frentz Consulting. In addition, you will reconcile the bank statement balance to the checkbook balance and complete a spreadsheet activity (optional).

The adjusting entries for Frentz Consulting are for the month of October of the current year and are illustrated in Figure 3.12.

STEP 1: **Start up *Automated Accounting 8.0*.**

STEP 2: **Load the opening balances problem file named AA8 Problem 03-T.**

STEP 3: **Enter your name in the User Name text box and click the *OK* button.**

STEP 4: **Save the file to your disk and folder with a file name of 03-T followed by Your Name.**

STEP 5: **Enter the adjusting entries shown in Figure 3.12.**
Click the *Journal* toolbar button, and then click the *General Journal* tab and enter the adjusting entries. The following adjustment data is for the month of October for Frentz Consulting:

Supplies inventory, October 31 . . . . $1,100.00
Value of insurance policies on October 31 . . . .   500.00

Calculate the amounts for the adjusting entries by first displaying a trial balance to obtain the current balances of the accounts affected.

Date	Refer.	Account	Debit	Credit
10/31/--	Adj.Ent.	550 Supplies Expense	643.64	
		120 Supplies		643.64
10/31/--	Adj.Ent.	520 Insurance Expense	272.00	
		130 Prepaid Insurance		272.00

Figure 3.12
General Journal (Adjusting Entries)

TUTORIAL PROBLEM 3-T

STEP 6: **Display the adjusting entries.**
Click the *Reports* toolbar button. When the Report Selection dialog box appears, choose the *Journals* option button. Choose the *General Journal* report, and click the *OK* button. When the Journal Report Selection dialog box appears (Figure 3.13), choose the *Customize Journal Report* option and enter a Reference restriction of *Adj.Ent.* so that only the adjusting entries are reported. The General Journal Report appears in Figure 3.14.

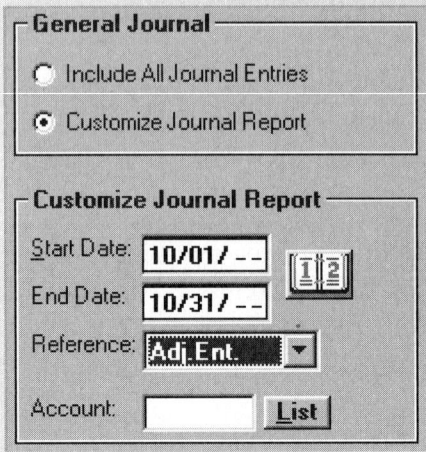

Figure 3.13
Journal Report Selection Dialog Box

```
                    Frentz Consulting
                     General Journal
                        10/31/--

Date     Refer.      Acct.    Title                    Debit       Credit

10/31    Adj.Ent.    550      Supplies Expense         643.64
10/31    Adj.Ent.    120      Supplies                             643.64
10/31    Adj.Ent.    520      Insurance Expense        272.00
10/31    Adj.Ent.    130      Prepaid Insurance                    272.00

                              Totals                   915.64      915.64
                                                       ======      ======
```

Figure 3.14
General Journal Report (Adjusting Entries)

TUTORIAL PROBLEM 3-T

STEP 7: **Display the income statement.**
Choose the *Financial Statements* option button from the Report Selection dialog box, choose the *Income Statement* report, and then click *OK*. The income statement is shown in Figure 3.15.

```
                    Frentz Consulting
                    Income Statement
                 For Period Ended 10/31/--

Operating Revenue

Fees                              12751.45            100.00
                                  --------
Total Operating Revenue           12751.45            100.00

Operating Expenses

Advertising Expense                  595.00             4.67
Charitable Contrib. Exp.             190.00             1.49
Dues & Subscriptions Exp.            155.65             1.22
Insurance Expense                    272.00             2.13
Miscellaneous Expense                285.00             2.24
Rent Expense                         950.00             7.45
Supplies Expense                     643.64             5.05
Telephone Expense                    263.45             2.07
Travel & Entertain. Exp.             173.73             1.36
Utilities Expense                    493.34             3.87
                                  --------
Total Operating Expenses            4021.81            31.54
                                  --------
Net Income                          8729.64            68.46
                                  ========
```

Figure 3.15
Income Statement

STEP 8: **Display the balance sheet.**
Select the *Balance Sheet* report, and then click the *OK* button. The balance sheet is shown in Figure 3.16.

TUTORIAL PROBLEM 3-T

```
                    Frentz Consulting
                      Balance Sheet
                        10/31/--

Assets

Cash                             18319.89
Supplies                          1100.00
Prepaid Insurance                  500.00
                                ---------
Total Assets                                    19919.89
                                                ========

Liabilities

Bauer Advertising, Inc.            595.00
Burton Journals, Inc.              155.65
Gordon Graphics & Design           425.50
Weber Office Supply                218.10
                                ---------
Total Liabilities                                1394.25

Owner's Equity

Michael Frentz, Capital          14296.00
Michael Frentz, Drawing          -4500.00
Net Income                        8729.64
                                ---------
Total Owner's Equity                            18525.64
                                                ---------
Total Liabilities & Equity                      19919.89
                                                ========
```

Figure 3.16
Balance Sheet

STEP 9: **Display the statement of owner's equity.**
Select the *Statement of Owner's Equity* report, and then click the *OK* button. The statement of owner's equity is shown in Figure 3.17.

STEP 10: **Generate an income statement graph.**
Click the *Graphs* toolbar button. When the Graph Selection dialog box appears, click the *Income Statement* button. The 3-D income statement graph that results is shown in Figure 3.18.

Chapter 3 General Ledger—End-of-Fiscal-Period and Bank Reconciliation

TUTORIAL PROBLEM 3-T

```
                   Frentz Consulting
               Statement of Owner's Equity
                For Period Ended 10/31/--

Michael Frentz, Capital (Beg. of Period)         14296.00
Michael Frentz, Drawing                          -4500.00
Net Income                                        8729.64
                                                 --------
Michael Frentz, Capital (End of Period)          18525.64
                                                 ========
```

Figure 3.17
Statement of Owner's Equity

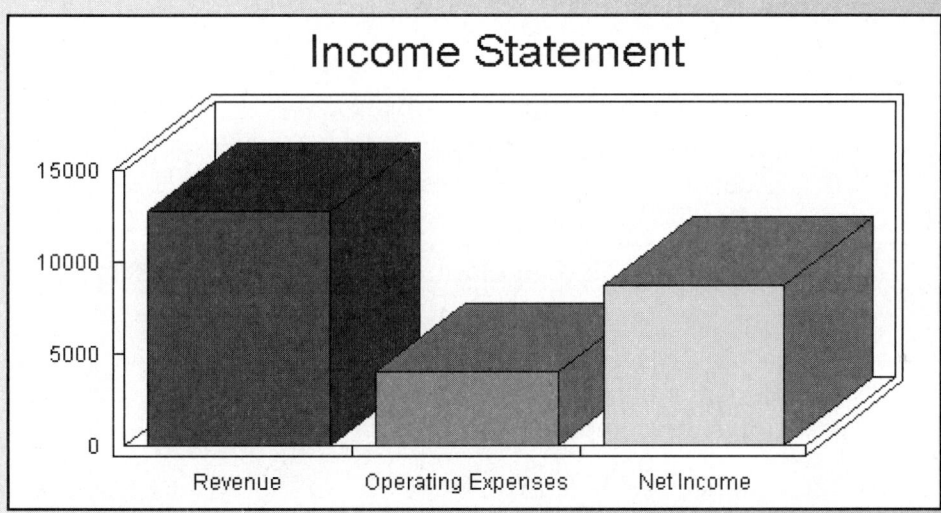

Figure 3.18
Income Statement Graph

STEP 11: Process the bank reconciliation data listed below.
Click the *Other* toolbar button. When the Reconciliation tab appears, enter the bank credit, bank charge, balance shown on bank statement, and outstanding deposit amounts. (The Checkbook balance will be provided by the computer.) To enter the outstanding checks, move the pointer to the *Checks from the Journals* list, select the desired check (point and click to highlight), and click the *Select* button. The selected check will appear in the Outstanding Checks

TUTORIAL PROBLEM 3-T

list, and the Adjusted Bank Balance will automatically be updated. Repeat this procedure for each outstanding check.

Checkbook balance	$18,319.99
Bank credit	547.80
Bank charge	5.50
Balance shown on bank statement	22,150.73
Outstanding deposit	2,535.75

Outstanding checks as follows:

Check No.	Amount
722	$325.00
723	$205.95
724	$493.34
725	$125.00
726	$175.00
727	$4,500.00

STEP 12: **Display the Bank Reconciliation Report.**
Click the *Report* button located at the bottom of Bank Reconciliation. The report is shown in Figure 3.19.

STEP 13: **Save your data file to disk with a file name of 03-TBC (where BC is "Before Closing") followed by Your Name.**

STEP 14: **Optional Spreadsheet Integration Activity.**
Frentz Consulting has asked you to use a spreadsheet to prepare a balance sheet for the month of October that shows the component percentage of total assets.

a. Display and copy the balance sheet to the clipboard in spreadsheet format.
b. Start up your spreadsheet software and load the template file named AA8 Spreadsheet 03-T.WK1.
c. Select cell A1 as the current cell (if not already selected).
d. Paste the balance sheet that was copied to the clipboard in Step a into the spreadsheet. Select the *Paste* item from the Edit menu.
e. Enter the heading *Component %* in cell D8.
Enter the formula to calculate the component % in cell D10. For example, @ABS(B10-C10)/+$C$14.
Copy and paste the formula in cell D10 to cells D11, D12, D14, D19, D20, D21, D22, D24, D32, and D34.

Chapter 3 General Ledger—End-of-Fiscal-Period and Bank Reconciliation

TUTORIAL PROBLEM 3-T

f. Format the amounts in currency format ($X,XXX.XX) and the component calculations in percentage format (XXX.XX%), if necessary.
g. Print the spreadsheet (cells A1–D35). The completed spreadsheet report is shown in Figure 3.20.
h. Save your spreadsheet file with a file name of 03-T Your Name.
i. End your spreadsheet session.

```
                    Frentz Consulting
                    Bank Reconciliation
                         10/31/--

Checkbook Balance                                        18319.89

Plus Bank Credits:
                                       547.80
                                     ---------
                                                           547.80
Less Bank Charges:
                                         5.50
                                     ---------
                                                             5.50
                                                         ---------
Adjusted Checkbook Balance                               18862.19
                                                         =========

Bank Statement Balance                                   22150.73

Plus Outstanding Deposits:
                                      2535.75
                                     ---------
                                                          2535.75
Less Outstanding Checks:
                    C722               325.00
                    C723               205.95
                    C724               493.34
                    C725               125.00
                    C726               175.00
                    C727              4500.00
                                     ---------
                                                          5824.29
                                                         ---------
Adjusted Bank Balance                                    18862.19
                                                         =========
```

Figure 3.19
Bank Reconciliation Report

TUTORIAL PROBLEM 3-T

Student Name

Frentz Consulting
Balance Sheet
As Of 10/31/--

Assets

			Component %
Cash	$18,319.89		91.97%
Supplies	$1,100.00		5.52%
Prepaid Insurance	$500.00		2.51%
Total Assets		$19,919.89	100.00%

Liabilities

Bauer Advertising, Inc.	$595.00		2.99%
Burton Journals, Inc.	$155.65		0.78%
Gordon Graphics & Design	$425.50		2.14%
Weber Office Supply	$218.10		1.09%
Total Liabilities		$1,394.25	7.00%

Owner's Equity

Michael Frentz, Capital	$14,296.00		
Michael Frentz, Drawing	($4,500.00)		
Net Income	$8,729.64		
Total Owner's Equity		$18,525.64	93.00%
Total Liabilities & Equity		$19,919.89	100.00%

Figure 3.20
Balance Sheet Spreadsheet with Component Percentages

- **STEP 15:** **Optional Word Processing Integration Activity.**
  You have been asked to provide Mr. Frentz, President of Frentz Consulting, with the income statement for the period ended October 31 of the current year. Copy and paste the income statement from the accounting system into your word processor so you can enhance its appearance.

  a. Display and copy the income statement to the clipboard in word processor format.
  b. Start up your word processing software application and create a new document.

Chapter 3 General Ledger—End-of-Fiscal-Period and Bank Reconciliation

TUTORIAL PROBLEM 3-T

c. Paste the income statement into your word processing document.
d. Format the income statement to enhance its appearance (the recommended font is Courier, size 10). Notice that the completed document shown in Figure 3.21 has the main heading bold and centered and the classification headings are also in bold. Experiment by adding further enhancements. For example, if your word processor has graphic capabilities, a company logo could be added.
e. Print your document.
f. Save your document with a file name of 03-T Your Name.
g. End your word processing application.

```
                    Frentz Consulting
                    Income Statement
                  For Period Ended 10/31/--

Operating Revenue

Fees                                  12751.45              100.00
                                      ----------
Total Operating Revenue               12751.45              100.00

Operating Expenses

Advertising Expense                     595.00                4.67
Charitable Contrib. Exp.                190.00                1.49
Dues & Subscriptions Exp.               155.65                1.22
Insurance Expense                       272.00                2.13
Miscellaneous Expense                   285.00                2.24
Rent Expense                            950.00                7.45
Supplies Expense                        643.64                5.05
Telephone Expense                       263.45                2.07
Travel & Entertain. Exp.                173.73                1.36
Utilities Expense                       493.34                3.87
                                      ----------
Total Operating Expenses               4021.81               31.54
                                      ----------
Net Income                             8729.64               68.46
                                      ==========
```

Figure 3.21
Completed Word Processing Integrated Document

TUTORIAL PROBLEM 3-T

STEP 16: Generate and post the closing journal entries.

Choose the *Generate Closing Journal Entries* menu item from the Options menu. When the dialog box appears asking if you want to generate closing journal entries, click the *Yes* button. The closing entries automatically generated by the computer are shown in the Closing Entries window in Figure 3.22. Click *Post*.

Acct. #	Account Title	Debit	Credit
410	Fees	12751.45	
330	Income Summary		12751.45
330	Income Summary	4021.81	
510	Advertising Expense		595.00
512	Charitable Contrib. Exp.		190.00
515	Dues & Subscriptions Exp.		155.65
520	Insurance Expense		272.00
530	Miscellaneous Expense		285.00
540	Rent Expense		950.00
550	Supplies Expense		643.64
560	Telephone Expense		263.45
570	Travel & Entertain. Exp.		173.73
580	Utilities Expense		493.34
330	Income Summary	8729.64	
310	Michael Frentz, Capital		8729.64
310	Michael Frentz, Capital	4500.00	
320	Michael Frentz, Drawing		4500.00

Figure 3.22
Closing Entries Window

STEP 17: Display the closing entries.

Click the *Reports* toolbar button. When the Reports Selection dialog box appears, choose the *Journals* option button, and then select the *General Journal* report and click the *OK* button. When the Journal Report Selection dialog box appears, choose the *Customize Journal Report* option and enter a Reference restriction of *Clo.Ent.* so that only the closing entries are reported. Then click *OK*. The report appears in Figure 3.23.

Chapter 3 General Ledger—End-of-Fiscal-Period and Bank Reconciliation

TUTORIAL PROBLEM 3-T

```
                        Frentz Consulting
                         General Journal
                            10/31/--

Date     Refer.     Acct.   Title                      Debit       Credit

10/31    Clo.Ent.   410     Fees                       12751.45
10/31    Clo.Ent.   330     Income Summary                         12751.45
10/31    Clo.Ent.   330     Income Summary             4021.81
10/31    Clo.Ent.   510     Advertising Expense                       595.00
10/31    Clo.Ent.   512     Charitable Contrib. Exp.                  190.00
10/31    Clo.Ent.   515     Dues & Subscriptions Exp.                 155.65
10/31    Clo.Ent.   520     Insurance Expense                         272.00
10/31    Clo.Ent.   530     Miscellaneous Expense                     285.00
10/31    Clo.Ent.   540     Rent Expense                              950.00
10/31    Clo.Ent.   550     Supplies Expense                          643.64
10/31    Clo.Ent.   560     Telephone Expense                         263.45
10/31    Clo.Ent.   570     Travel & Entertain. Exp.                  173.73
10/31    Clo.Ent.   580     Utilities Expense                         493.34

10/31    Clo.Ent.   330     Income Summary             8729.64
10/31    Clo.Ent.   310     Michael Frentz, Capital                  8729.64

10/31    Clo.Ent.   310     Michael Frentz, Capital    4500.00
10/31    Clo.Ent.   320     Michael Frentz, Drawing                  4500.00
                                                      ---------    ---------
                            Totals                    30002.90     30002.90
                                                      =========    =========
```

Figure 3.23
Closing Entries Report

STEP 18: **Display a post-closing trial balance.**
Choose the *Ledger Reports* option button, select the *Trial Balance* Report, and click *OK*. The Post-Closing Trial Balance Report in Figure 3.24 appears.

TUTORIAL PROBLEM 3-T

```
                     Frentz Consulting
                      Trial Balance
                        10/31/--

Acct.      Account
Number     Title                    Debit            Credit

110        Cash                     18319.89
120        Supplies                  1100.00
130        Prepaid Insurance          500.00
220        Bauer Advertising, Inc.                     595.00
225        Burton Journals, Inc.                       155.65
240        Gordon Graphics & Design                    425.50
250        Weber Office Supply                         218.10
310        Michael Frentz, Capital                   18525.64
                                    ----------      ----------
           Totals                   19919.89         19919.89
                                    ==========      ==========
```

Figure 3.24
Post-Closing Trial Balance

STEP 19: Use the Save As menu item to save your data with a file name of 03-TAC (where AC is "after closing") followed by Your Name.

STEP 20: End your *Automated Accounting* session.

The World Wide Web is a sub-network of computers that displays multimedia information, including text, graphics, sound, and video clips. Web documents also contain special connections that allow users to switch to other documents that could be on computers anywhere in the world.

Netiquette is an Internet phrase that refers to the rules of conduct and behavior on the Net. For example, don't send unwanted advertising, do keep your messages brief and to the point, and don't use ALL CAPS unless you mean to shout.

Chapter 3 General Ledger—End-of-Fiscal-Period and Bank Reconciliation

Review and Practice: Applying Your Information Skills

I. MATCHING

Directions: In the *Working Papers*, write the letter of the appropriate term next to each definition.

    a. adjusting entries
    b. balance sheet
    c. bank reconciliation
    d. component percentage
    e. income statement
    f. Income Summary account
    g. period-end closing
    h. post-closing trial balance
    i. statement of owner's equity
    j. temporary accounts

1. A financial statement that shows the changes to owner's equity during the fiscal period.

2. A financial statement that provides information on the net income or net loss of a business over a specific period of time.

3. A financial statement that reports assets, liabilities, and owner's equities on a specific date.

4. The process of verifying that the bank statement and the checkbook are in agreement.

5. The percentage relationship between one financial statement item and the total that includes that item.

6. Journal entries recorded to update general ledger accounts at the end of a fiscal period.

7. A trial balance that verifies that debits equal credits in the general ledger accounts after closing entries have been posted.

8. The process of recording and posting closing entries to the general ledger to prepare temporary accounts for a new fiscal period.

9. An account used to summarize the closing entries for the revenue and expense accounts.

10. Accounts that accumulate information until it is transferred to the owner's capital account.

II. REVIEW QUESTIONS

Directions: Write the answers to each of the following questions in the *Working Papers*.

1. If the balance in the Supplies account after all transactions for the fiscal period have been processed and before adjusting entries is $1,500.00 and the current supplies inventory is $1,200.00, what is the amount of the supplies adjusting entry?

2. What financial statements are available for a nondepartmentalized business organized as a sole proprietorship?

3. How do you know when the bank statement reconciles to the checkbook on the Bank Reconciliation Report?

4. Briefly describe the closing entries generated by the computer.

5. Describe the procedure to correct an error discovered after closing.

III. INTERNET ACTIVITY

Directions: If you have access to the Internet, use the browser to find accounting software services that are available via the Internet. For example, use the term *Internet Accounting Software* to narrow your search. Report on the services provided from one of the sites you found. Be sure to include the source and the URL (Internet address) of your search.

Independent Practice Problem 3-P

In Practice Problem 3-P, you will process any additions, changes, and deletions to the chart of accounts. You will also process the monthly transactions for November, complete the end of fiscal period processing, reconcile the bank statement, and complete a spreadsheet activity (optional).

STEP 1: Start up *Automated Accounting 8.0*.

STEP 2: Open the opening balances file named AA8 Problem 03-P.

STEP 3: Enter your name in the User Name text box.

STEP 4: Save the opening balances file with a file name of 03-P Your Name.

STEP 5: Enter the following account maintenance activities and transactions for November:

   Nov. 03   Record the October bank service charge, $6.50. Charge Miscellaneous Expense. M219.

03 Record the October bank interest income, $148.23. M220.
   Note: Add Interest Income (account number 710) to the chart of accounts. Cash is increased by this transaction.
03 Paid cash for rent, $925.00. C728.
04 Paid cash for telephone bill, $315.17. C729.
06 Bought repairs on account from Wenkel Heating, $425.50. M221.
   Note: Add Repairs Expense (account number 545), and add Wenkel Heating (account number 260) to the chart of accounts.
07 Paid cash for insurance, $120.00. C730.
10 Paid cash on account to Burton Journals, Inc., $155.65. C731.
14 Paid cash on account to Bauer Advertising, Inc., $595.00. C732.
17 Received cash from fees, $3,200.00. T261.
18 Bought supplies on account from Gordon Graphics & Design, $210.45. M222.
19 Paid cash on account to Weber Office Products, $218.10. C733.
   Note: Change the account title of Weber Office Supply to Weber Office Products in the chart of accounts.
20 Bought advertising on account from Bauer Advertising, Inc., $280.00. M223.
21 Received cash from fees, $3,850.00. T262.
21 Paid cash for travel expense, $72.35. C734.
24 Paid cash on account to Gordon Graphics & Design, $425.50. C735.
25 Paid cash for electric bill, $447.24. C736.
26 Received cash from fees, $2,918.00. T263.
27 Paid cash to owner for personal use, $4,750.00. C737.
28 Paid cash for charitable contribution, $125.00. C738.
30 Paid cash for professional dues, $210.00. C739.

STEP 6: Display a Chart of Accounts Report.

STEP 7: Display the General Journal Report for the period November 1 through November 30 of the current year. Make corrections, if necessary.

STEP 8: Display a Trial Balance Report.

STEP 9: Enter the November adjusting entries from the following data. Use the trial balance from Step 8 as the basis for making the adjusting entries. Use Adj.Ent. as the reference.

Supplies inventory on November 30 . . . . $665.00
Value of insurance policies on November 30 . . . . 270.00

STEP 10: Display the General Journal Report for the adjusting entries. Use a reference restriction of Adj.Ent. so that only adjusting entries will be included on the report.

STEP 11: Display the financial statements.

STEP 12: Display a balance sheet graph.

STEP 13: Process the bank reconciliation data based on the following information:

Checkbook balance $20,070.61
Bank credit $721.00
Bank charge 6.50
Bank statement balance 24,042.95
Outstanding deposit 2,918.00
Outstanding checks:

Check No.	Amount
733	$218.10
735	$425.50
736	$447.24
737	$4,750.00
738	$125.00
739	$210.00

STEP 14: Display the Bank Reconciliation Report.

STEP 15: Use the Save As menu item to save your data with a file name of 03-PBC Your Name.

STEP 16: Optional Spreadsheet Integration Activity.
Prepare a balance sheet for the month of November that shows the component percentage of total assets.

a. Display and copy the balance sheet to the clipboard in spreadsheet format.
b. Start up your spreadsheet software and load the template file named AA8 Spreadsheet 03-T.
c. Select cell A1 as the current cell (if not already selected) and paste the balance sheet into the spreadsheet.

Chapter 3 General Ledger—End-of-Fiscal-Period and Bank Reconciliation

d. Enter the heading *Component %* in cell D8.
   Enter the formula to calculate component % in cell D10. Then copy and paste it into the appropriate cells using the format illustrated in Figure 3.20.
e. Format the amounts in currency format ($X,XXX.XX) and the component calculations in percentage format (XXX.XX%), if necessary.
f. Save your spreadsheet file with a file name of 03-P Your Name.
g. Print the spreadsheet.
h. End your spreadsheet session and return to the *Automated Accounting* application.

STEP 17: **Optional Word Processing Integration Activity.**
Copy and paste the income statement ended November 30 of the current year from the accounting system into your word processor and enhance its appearance.

a. Display and copy the income statement to the clipboard in word processor format.
b. Start up your word processing software application and create a new document.
c. Paste the income statement into your word processing document.
d. Format the income statement to enhance its appearance. The recommended font is Courier, size 10.
e. Print your document.
f. Save your document with a file name of 03-P Your Name.
g. End your word processing application.

STEP 18: Generate and post the closing journal entries.

STEP 19: Display the General Journal Report for Closing Entries.
Use a reference restriction of Clo.Ent. so that only closing entries will be included on the report.

STEP 20: Display a post-closing trial balance.

STEP 21: Save your data to disk with a file name of 03-PAC Your Name where AC is "After Closing."

STEP 22: End your *Automated Accounting* session.

Applying Your Technology Skills 3-P

Directions: Write the answers to the following questions in the *Working Papers*.

1. Based on the General Journal Report, what is the amount of Check No. C737?
2. What is the balance in the Cash account at the end of the month?
3. What are the totals of the Debit and Credit columns of the adjusting entries shown on the General Journal Report for adjusting entries?
4. What is the total operating revenue?
5. What are the total operating expenses?
6. What are the total operating expenses for the month as a percentage of total operating revenue?
7. What is the net income?
8. What is the net income for the month as a percentage of total operating revenue?
9. What are the total assets?
10. What are the total liabilities?
11. What is the owner's equity at the end of the fiscal period?
12. What is the adjusted bank balance amount on the Bank Reconciliation Report?

Mastery Problem 3-M

In this problem, you will process any additions, changes, and deletions to the chart of accounts. You will also process the monthly transactions for December, complete the end-of-fiscal-period processing, reconcile the bank statement, and complete a spreadsheet activity (optional).

STEP 1: Open and load the opening balance file named AA8 Problem 03-M.

STEP 2: Enter your name in the User Name text box.

STEP 3: Save the opening balances file with a file name of 03-M Your Name.

Chapter 3 General Ledger—End-of-Fiscal-Period and Bank Reconciliation

STEP 4: **Enter the following December account maintenance activities and general journal transactions:**

Dec. 01 Record the November bank charges, $6.50. M224.
Charge Miscellaneous Expense.
01 Record the November bank interest income, $721.00. M225.
02 Paid cash for rent, $925.00. C740.
03 Paid cash for telephone bill, $302.59. C741.
04 Bought supplies on account from Weber Office Products, $381.46. M226.
05 Paid cash for travel expense, $50.00. C742.
08 Received cash from fees, $3,345.00. T264.
09 Paid cash on account to Gordon Graphics & Design, $210.45. C743.
10 Paid cash for charitable contribution, $150.00. C744.
11 Paid cash for a subscription, $200.00. C745.
Note: Change the account Burton Journals, Inc., to Burton Periodicals.
15 Paid cash for insurance, $500.00. C746.
16 Paid cash on account to Wenkel Heating, $425.50. C747.
17 Received cash from fees, $3,735.00. T265.
18 Bought advertising on account from Bauer Advertising, Inc., $350.00. M227.
19 Paid cash on account to Bauer Advertising, Inc., $280.00. C748.
22 Paid cash for miscellaneous expense, $95.50. C749.
26 Paid cash for electric bill, $437.20. C750.
26 Received cash from fees, $3,500.00. T266.
29 Bought repairs on account from Yeager Plumbing, Inc., $264.25. M228.
Note: Add Yeager Plumbing, Inc., to the chart of accounts. Assign account number 270 so that it will be positioned immediately following Wenkel Heating.
30 Paid cash to owner for personal use, $4,500.00. C751.

STEP 5: **Display a chart of accounts, a General Journal Report of December transactions, and a trial balance.**

STEP 6: **Enter the adjusting entries.**

Supplies inventory on December 31 . . . . $572.26
Value of insurance policies on December 31. . . . . 500.00

STEP 7: Display the adjusting entries.

STEP 8: Display the financial statements.

STEP 9: Display an expense distribution graph.

STEP 10: Process the bank reconciliation data.

Bank Statement Data:
Checkbook balance $23,288.87
Bank statement balance.. .... 26,783.05
Bank credit. 827.53
Bank charge 6.50
Outstanding deposit 3,350.00
Outstanding checks:

Check No.	Amount
743	$210.45
746	$500.00
748	$280.00
749	$95.50
750	$437.20
751	$4,500.00

STEP 11: Display a Bank Reconciliation Report.

STEP 12: Optional Spreadsheet Integration Activity.
Prepare a balance sheet for the month of December that shows the component percentage of total assets.

a. Display and copy the balance sheet to the clipboard in spreadsheet format.
b. Start up your spreadsheet software and load the template file named AA8 Spreadsheet 03-T.
c. Select cell A1 and paste the balance sheet into the spreadsheet.
d. Enter the labels and formulas required to report and calculate the component percentage of total assets, using the format illustrated in Figure 3.20.
e. Print the spreadsheet.
f. Save your spreadsheet file with a file name of 03-M Your Name.
g. End your spreadsheet session and return to the *Automated Accounting* application.

STEP 13: Save your data with a file name of 03-MBC Your Name.

STEP 14: Generate and post the closing entries.

STEP 15: Display the General Journal Report for Closing Entries.

STEP 16: Display a post-closing trial balance.

Chapter 3 General Ledger—End-of-Fiscal-Period and Bank Reconciliation

STEP 17: Save your data with a file name of 03-MAC Your Name.

STEP 18: End your *Automated Accounting* session.

Applying Your Technology Skills 3-M

Directions: Write the answers to the following questions in the *Working Papers*.

1. Based on the General Journal Report, what is the amount of Check No. C748?
2. What is the balance in the Cash account at the end of the month?
3. What are the totals of the Debit and Credit columns shown on the General Journal Report for adjusting entries?
4. What are the total fees for the period?
5. What is the total amount of telephone expense?
6. What are the total operating expenses for the month as a percentage of total operating revenue?
7. What is the net income?
8. What is the net income for the month as a percentage of total operating revenue?
9. What is the ending balance for Supplies?
10. What are the total liabilities?
11. What is the owner's equity at the end of the fiscal period?
12. What is the total of outstanding checks on the Bank Reconciliation Report?

Reinforcement Activity R-1

AKW Carpet Cleaning, Inc., is a small service business that cleans commercial and residential carpets. In Reinforcement Activity R-1, you will process the account maintenance activities and transactions for April, complete the end-of-fiscal-period processing, reconcile the bank statement, and complete a spreadsheet activity (optional). Separate fee accounts are maintained for commercial and residential sales. As you are recording the fees-received transactions, if the fee received is for commercial cleaning, record the account number for Fees—Commercial. If the fee received is for residential cleaning, record the account number for Fees—Residential.

STEP 1: Start up the *Automated Accounting 8.0* software.

STEP 2: Open and load the opening balances file named AA8 Problem R-1.

STEP 3: Enter your name in the User Name text box.

STEP 4: Save the opening balances file with a file name of R-1 Your Name.

STEP 5: Enter the following account maintenance and general journal transactions:

Apr. 01 Received bank statement showing March bank service charge, $6.75. Charge miscellaneous expense. M52.

01 Paid cash on account to Elco Office Supplies, $442.54. C745.

01 Paid cash for rent, $1,150.00. C746.
Note: Change the account named Lane Advertising Co. to Lane Promotions.

02 Paid cash for water bill, $87.46. C747.

02 Received cash from commercial cleaning, $935.00. T232.

02 Received cash from residential cleaning, $500.00. T233.

05 Bought supplies on account from Phelps Supply Co., $498.50. M53.
Note: Add Phelps Supply Co. to the chart of accounts. Assign account number 250 so that it will be positioned immediately following Lane Promotions in the chart of accounts.

05 Paid cash to owner for personal use, $325.00. C748.

06 Bought advertising on account from Lane Promotions, $400.00. M54.

Reinforcement Activity R-1

Note: Add Advertising Expense to the chart of accounts. Assign account number 505 so that it will be positioned immediately following Fees—Residential in the chart of accounts.

06   Paid cash for miscellaneous expense, $75.00. C749.

07   Paid cash for repairs, $314.80. C750.
Note: Add Repairs Expense to the chart of accounts. Assign account number 535 so that it will be positioned immediately following Rent Expense in the chart of accounts.

07   Paid cash for telephone bill, $173.95. C751.

08   Paid cash for miscellaneous expense, $15.00. C752.

09   Received cash from commercial cleaning, $1,100.00. T234.

09   Received cash from residential cleaning, $525.00. T235.

12   Paid cash on account to Cody Supply Co., $792.99. C753.

12   Paid cash on account to Burnell Chemicals, Inc., $1,003.07. C754.

12   Paid cash to owner for personal use, $325.00. C755.

13   Paid cash for electric bill, $378.14. C756.

13   Paid cash for miscellaneous expense, $25.00. C757.

14   Paid cash for repairs, $74.83. C758.

15   Bought supplies on account from Burnell Chemicals, Inc., $410.30. M55.

15   Paid cash for advertising, $75.00. C759.

16   Received cash from commercial cleaning, $1,250.00. T236.

16   Received cash from residential cleaning, $650.00. T237.

19   Paid cash to owner for personal use, $325.00. C760.

19   Bought supplies on account from Elco Office Supplies, $402.07. M56.

19   Paid cash for professional dues, $150.00. C761.
Note: Add Dues & Subscriptions Exp. to the chart of accounts. Assign account number 507 so that it will be positioned immediately following Advertising Expense in the chart of accounts.

20   Paid cash for insurance, $315.00. C762.

20   Paid cash for miscellaneous expense, $20.00. C763.

21	Paid cash on account to Lane Promotions, $400.00. C764.
21	Bought supplies on account from Cody Supply Co., $224.65. M57.
21	Paid cash for advertising, $50.00. C765.
22	Paid cash on account to Phelps Supply Co., $498.50. C766.
23	Received cash from commercial cleaning, $1,050.00. T238.
23	Received cash from residential cleaning, $520.00. T239.
26	Paid cash to owner for personal use, $325.00. C767.
26	Paid cash for miscellaneous expense, $35.00. C768.
26	Bought supplies on account from Phelps Supply Co., $217.30. M58.
27	Paid cash on account to Cody Supply Co., $224.65. C769.
27	Paid cash for miscellaneous expense, $19.75. C770.
28	Paid cash for advertising, $200.00. C771.
28	Bought a subscription on account from Lane Promotions, $75.00. M59.
28	Paid cash for repairs, $69.45. C772.
29	Paid cash for insurance, $180.00. C773.
29	Bought supplies on account from Sather Chemicals, Inc., $365.00. M60. **Note:** Add Sather Chemicals, Inc., to the chart of accounts. Assign account number 260 so that it will be positioned immediately following Phelps Supply Co. in the chart of accounts.
29	Paid cash on account to Burnell Chemicals, Inc., $410.30. C774.
30	Received cash from commercial cleaning, $1,225.00. T240.
30	Received cash from residential cleaning, $780.00. T241.
30	Paid cash on account to Elco Office Supplies, $402.07. C775.

STEP 6: Display a Chart of Accounts Report.

STEP 7: Display the General Journal Report for the period April 1 through April 30 of the current year. Make corrections if errors are detected.

STEP 8: Display a Trial Balance Report.

Reinforcement Activity R-1

STEP 9: Enter the adjusting entries for the month of April. The adjustment data are shown below. Use the trial balance printed in the previous step as the basis for making the adjusting entries. Record Adj.Ent. as the reference.

Supplies inventory on April 30. . . . . $2,570.50
Value of insurance policies on April 30 . . . .   465.00

STEP 10: Display the General Journal Report for the adjusting entries. Use a reference restriction of Adj.Ent. so that only adjusting entries will be included on the report.

STEP 11: Display the financial statements.

STEP 12: Display an income statement graph.

STEP 13: Process the bank reconciliation based on the information provided below:

Bank credit. $315.37
Bank charge 6.75
Bank statement balance 8,778.36

Outstanding deposits are:
$1,050.00
$520.00
$1,225.00
$780.00

Outstanding checks are:

Check No.	Amount
768	$35.00
769	$224.65
770	$19.75
771	$200.00
772	$69.45
773	$180.00
774	$410.30
775	$402.07

STEP 14: Display the Bank Reconciliation Report.

STEP 15: Optional Spreadsheet Activity.
Create a business summary report for the month of April that shows the cash balance, total liabilities, total fees, and total expenses.

    a. Display and copy the trial balance to the clipboard in spreadsheet format.
    b. Start up your spreadsheet software and load the template file named AA8 Spreadsheet R-1.

c. Select cell A1 as the current cell (if not already selected) and paste the trial balance into the spreadsheet.
d. Center the contents of cell B1 and the headings in cells B3–B5. Center the column headings in rows 7 and 8. Center the contents of cells A1–A29.
e. Copy and paste cell B3 to cell B34.
f. Enter Business Summary Report in cell B35.
g. Copy and paste cell B5 to cell B36.
h. If necessary, center the contents of cells B3–B36.
i. Enter Cash Balance in cell A38, Total Liabilities in cell A39, Total Fees in cell A40, and Total Expenses in cell A41.
j. Use a cell reference to put the amount from cell C10 in cell C38.
k. Enter the formula to sum the total liabilities in cell C39 [@SUM(D14..D16)].
l. Enter the formula to sum the fees in cell C40 (+D19+D20).
m. Enter the formula to sum the total expenses in cell C41 [@SUM(C21..C29)].
n. Format columns C and D in currency format if necessary.
o. Print the entire spreadsheet (cells A1–D41).
p. Save your spreadsheet file with a file name of R-1 Your Name.
q. End your spreadsheet session and return to the *Automated Accounting* application.

STEP 16: Use Save As to save your data with a file name of R-1BC Your Name.

STEP 17: Generate and post the closing journal entries.

STEP 18: Display the General Journal Report for the closing entries. Use a reference restriction of Clo.Ent. so that only closing entries will be included on the report.

STEP 19: Display a post-closing trial balance.

STEP 20: Save your data with a file name of R-1AC Your Name.

STEP 21: End the *Automated Accounting* session.

Reinforcement Activity R-1

Applying Your Technology Skills R-1

Directions: Write the answers to the following questions in the *Working Papers*.

1. Based on the General Journal Report, what is the amount of Check No. 774?
2. What are the totals of the debit and credit columns of the General Journal Report of the monthly transactions?
3. What is the balance in the Cash account at the end of the month?
4. What are the totals of the Debit and Credit columns shown on the General Journal Report for adjusting entries?
5. What are the total fees for commercial?
6. What is the total operating revenue?
7. What are the total operating expenses?
8. What are the total operating expenses for the month as a percentage of total operating revenue?
9. What is the net income?
10. What is the net income for the month as a percentage of total operating revenue?
11. What are the total assets?
12. What are the total liabilities?
13. What is the owner's equity at the end of the fiscal period?
14. What is the adjusted bank balance amount on the Bank Reconciliation Report?

Use your online Help options to learn more about your browser. The more features you learn and use, the more helpful your browser will be to you.

A modem is a hardware device that allows two computers to communicate over a telephone line or cable. A modem turns internal computer information into sound and reconverts sound into computer data.

A Web-hosting service is a private business that maintains the web sites of individuals and organizations on its computers for a fee. The service provides the hardware, software, and technical personnel to make sure the web sites operate effectively.

ACCOUNTING CAREERS IN DEPTH

Payroll Clerk

A payroll clerk compiles payroll data; enters data or computes and posts wages; and reconciles errors. This person maintains payroll records by using a computer or a calculator. A payroll clerk performs the following duties:

- Compiling payroll data, such as hours worked; sales or piecework; taxes, insurance, and union dues to be withheld; and employee identification numbers, from time sheets and other records.
- Preparing computer input forms, entering data into computer files or computing wages and deductions, using a calculator, and posting to payroll records.
- Reviewing wages computed and correcting errors to ensure the accuracy of the payroll.
- Recording changes affecting net wages, such as exemptions, insurance coverage, and loan payments for each employee to update the master payroll records.
- Recording data concerning the transfer of employees between departments.

The payroll clerk may also do the following:

- Prorating expenses to be debited or credited to each department for cost accounting.
- Preparing periodic reports of earnings, taxes, and deductions.
- Keeping records of leave pay and nontaxable wages.
- Preparing and issuing paychecks.

Attention to detail is very important for a payroll clerk. Entering incorrect information in computer systems or payroll documentation could directly affect an employee's paycheck. If you have ever experienced an error in your paycheck, you can understand how important it is to make as few errors as possible, if any at all.

A career as a payroll clerk can be very interesting. The data to be processed gives you the opportunity to see confidential information, which would need to be handled very carefully. Also, you gain a better understanding of how employee and payroll figures are processed. The knowledge gained in accounting courses could provide a good background to a payroll clerk position and could give you a competitive edge when looking toward advancement opportunities.

The experience gained in a payroll clerk job is transferable in all industries because all companies have payroll departments. Therefore, if you are particularly interested in a specific industry, a career as a payroll clerk in that industry would be even more enjoyable.

Chapter 4
PURCHASES AND CASH PAYMENTS

KEY TERMS

Partnership
Merchandising Business
Merchandise
Merchandise Inventory
  Account
Purchases Account
Purchases Journal
Cash Payments Journal
Vendor
Purchase on Account
Purchases Journal Input Form

Cash Payment
Cash Payments Journal Input
  Form
Direct Payment
Cash Payment on Account
General Ledger Report
Schedule of Accounts Payable
  Report
Accounts Payable Ledger
  Report

LEARNING OBJECTIVES

Upon completion of this chapter, you will be able to:

1. Enter vendor maintenance data.
2. Enter purchases-on-account transactions.
3. Enter cash-payments transactions.
4. Correct journal entries.
5. Generate journal reports.
6. Generate ledger reports.

INTRODUCTION

In previous chapters, you learned about accounting activities for a service business. In this chapter, you will work with a merchandising business organized as a partnership as you learn to add, change, or delete vendors and to enter and correct purchases and cash payments journal entries. A **partnership** is a business that is owned by two or more persons. A **merchandising business** is a business that purchases and resells goods. The goods purchased for resale are called **merchandise**. The **Merchandise Inventory account** is an asset account that shows the value of goods on hand for sale to customers. A merchandising business also has an account titled Purchases. The **Purchases account** is an account used to record the cost of the merchandise purchased for resale.

A merchandising business has many frequently occurring transactions that affect single accounts. A number of these transactions would require many entries in the general journal's debit and credit columns. Therefore, special journals are used to simplify keeping records for these types of transactions. The special journal used to record the purchase of merchandise on account is called the **purchases journal**. The special journal used to record all payments of cash is called the **cash payments journal**.

ETHICS

The widespread use of CD-ROMs and online services using the Internet have made it very easy to obtain graphics images of almost any subject. With this easy access comes the temptation to use any graphic, regardless of its source and the intended use, for personal and commercial use.

To protect their rights, many photographers and artists copyright their images. Copyrighting makes it illegal to use an image without permission from the copyright owner. In addition, the ways in which copyrighted images can be used are strictly limited, according to the wishes of the owner. Typically, a publisher will give permission to use the copyrighted image in newsletters and flyers but place restrictions on selling the image in any form to other people.

Critical Thinking

1. Suppose you created a masterpiece image using a drawing or painting program. After toiling over it for untold hours, would you want someone else to sell it and profit from your work? Explain.

2. How can photographers and artists protect their work from unauthorized copy or use?

3. What punishment do you believe should be given to people who violate copyright laws?

Chapter 4 Purchases and Cash Payments

MAINTAIN VENDORS

A business from which merchandise is purchased or supplies and other assets are bought is called a **vendor**. Accounts for vendors can be added, changed, or deleted from the accounting system, using a procedure similar to maintaining the general ledger chart of accounts.

When the Maintain Accounts menu item is chosen from the Data menu, or the Accts. toolbar button is clicked, the Account Maintenance window will appear. Choose the Vendors tab to display the Vendor Maintenance list shown in Figure 4.1.

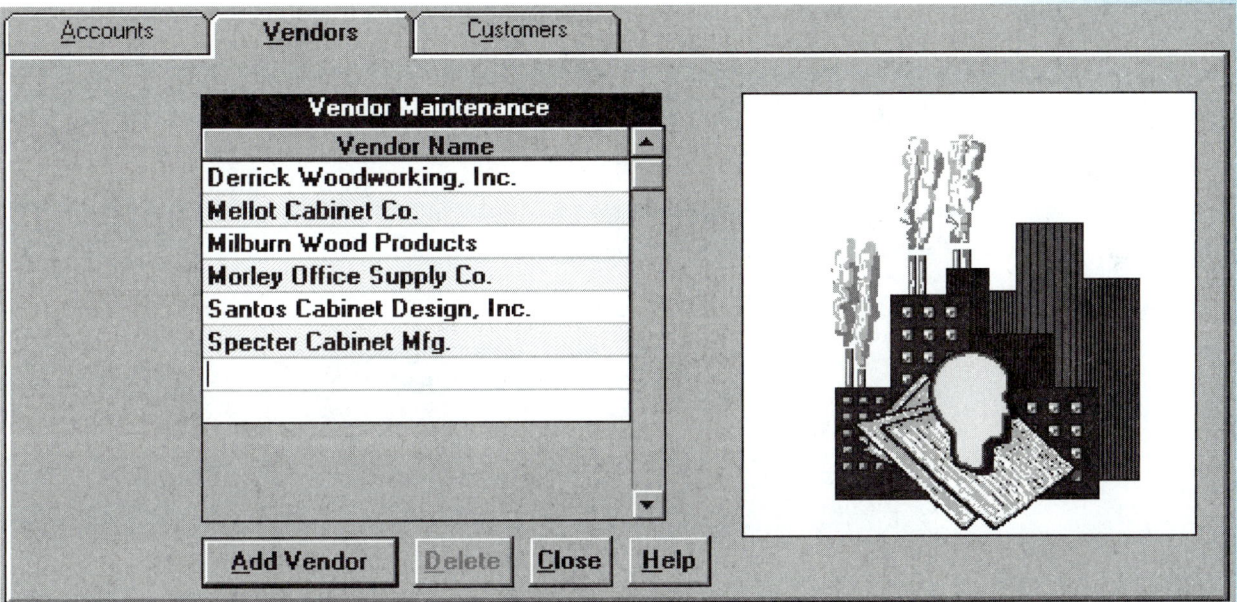

Figure 4.1
Vendor Maintenance List

New vendors can be added by entering a vendor name after the last item in the list and pressing the Add Vendor button. The new vendor will be inserted into the vendor list in alphabetical order. Existing vendor names can be changed by selecting the vendor you wish to change, keying in the correct vendor name, and clicking the Change Vendor button. (The Add Vendor button changes to Change Vendor.) An existing vendor can be deleted by simply selecting the vendor that you wish to delete and clicking the Delete button.

A vendor cannot be deleted if the account has a balance.

PURCHASES

A **purchase on account** is a transaction in which merchandise that is purchased is paid for at a later date. Businesses that purchase merchandise on account from many vendors maintain a separate vendor file in order to avoid creating a bulky general ledger. The total owed to all vendors maintained in the vendor file is summarized in a single general ledger liability account titled Accounts Payable.

Purchases Journal Input Form

Purchases transactions can be entered directly into the computer from the transaction statement or document or recorded on an input form. Figure 4.2 shows a **purchases journal input form**, which is an input form used to record only purchases of merchandise on account. The transactions are then entered into the computer from the data recorded on the form. Each line on the input form is used to record a purchase invoice. A company may have more than one purchases account if different types of merchandise are accounted for separately. In this case, a single invoice may require more than one line on the purchases journal input form. When the debit portion of a purchase-on-account transaction is entered, the computer will automatically make the credit to Accounts Payable. Therefore, the credit to the Accounts Payable account need not be recorded on the input form.

PURCHASES JOURNAL INPUT FORM

Date 02/10/--   Problem No. Example

Date	Refer.	Purch. Debit	Vendor
02/01/--	P220	1415.20	Spence Cabinet Mfg.
02/03/--	P221	647.30	Mellen Cabinet Co.

Figure 4.2
Purchases Journal Input Form

D & K Cabinet Tree, a wholesale business, purchases merchandise directly from manufacturers and then sells merchandise wholesale to cabinet retailers. The following transactions for D & K Cabinet Tree are recorded on the purchases journal input form shown in Figure 4.2. Each transaction is an example of a purchase of merchandise on account. Transactions for buying items other than merchandise inventory on account (i.e., office supplies, rent, utilities, insurance, etc.) are entered via the general journal. Purchases of merchandise inventory for cash are entered on a cash payments journal input form, as shown later in this chapter.

fyi...

Only purchases of merchandise inventory on account are entered in the purchases journal.

Chapter 4 Purchases and Cash Payments

Feb. 01 Purchased merchandise on account from Spence Cabinet Mfg., $1,415.20. P220.
03 Purchased merchandise on account from Mellen Cabinet Co., $647.30. P221.

Purchases Journal

The purchases journal is used for entering purchases transactions, for making corrections, and for deleting existing purchases transactions. Recall that only merchandise that is purchased on account is recorded in this journal. When the Journal Entries menu item is chosen from the Data menu or the Journal toolbar button is clicked, the Journal Entries window will appear. When the Purchases tab is clicked, the purchases journal shown in Figure 4.3 will appear. The two purchases transactions recorded on the purchases journal input form in Figure 4.2 have already been entered as an example. Notice that the computer automatically calculated and displayed the Accounts Payable Credit amount (after the Purchases Debit amount was entered).

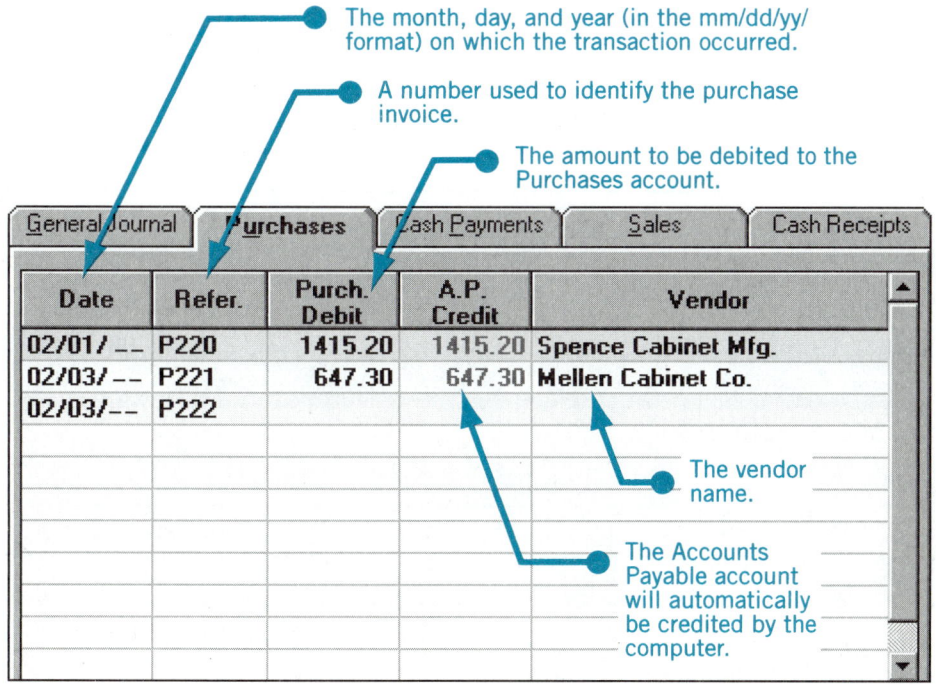

Figure 4.3
Purchases Journal

You can choose a vendor name from the drop-down list by typing the first letter of the vendor's name. The first vendor in the list whose name begins with that letter will appear in the grid cell. Pressing the letter again will cause the next name beginning with that letter to appear.

Transactions entered into the purchases journal (as well as the other special journals described in the following material) can be changed or deleted, and additional lines can be added using the same procedure you used in Chapter 2 for the general journal.

CASH PAYMENTS

Any type of transaction involving the payment of cash is called a **cash payment**. Cash payment transactions are recorded for expenses, cash purchases of merchandise inventory, payments to vendors, and payments not involving a check, such as a direct withdrawal from a checking account by the bank for a service charge.

Cash Payments Journal Input Form

All cash disbursements can be recorded on the same input form. An input form on which all cash payments can be recorded is a **cash payments journal input form**. Figure 4.4 illustrates a completed cash payments journal input form. Each line on the form can be used to record a cash payment or one part of a cash payment. The three transactions listed below are recorded on the form. Additional examples of the various types of cash payment transactions that may be recorded on this form are illustrated in Tutorial Problem 4-T.

Feb. 02 Paid cash for store supplies, $107.35. Check No. 136.
03 Paid cash for insurance, $180.00. Check No. 137.
04 Paid cash on account to Salas Cabinet Design, $1,955.82, covering P214. Check No. 138.

CASH PAYMENTS JOURNAL INPUT FORM

Date 02/10/-- Problem No. Example

Date	Refer.	Acct. No.	Debit	Credit	A.P. Debit	Vendor
02/02/--	C136	1150	107.35			
02/03/--	C137	1160	180.00			
02/04/--	C138				1955.82	Salas Cabinet Design

Figure 4.4
Cash Payments Journal Input Form

Cash Payments

The Cash Payments journal is used to enter all cash payment transactions and to correct or delete existing cash payment journal entries. It is not necessary to enter the credit to Cash because it is automatically calculated and displayed by the computer.

---

fyi...

It is not necessary to record the credit to the Cash account on the input form, since the computer automatically records this credit. Therefore, a Cash Credit column is not provided.

Chapter 4   Purchases and Cash Payments

There are two types of cash payments: (1) direct payments; and (2) cash payments on account. A **direct payment** is a cash disbursement that does *not* affect Accounts Payable. Examples of direct payments are checks written to pay expenses or buy assets. A **cash payment on account** is a cash disbursement that *does* affect Accounts Payable.

Direct Payment   A cash payments journal with sample data for two direct cash payments is shown in Figure 4.5. Notice that the Vendor text box column is left blank. The vendor is needed only for transactions that affect Accounts Payable or if the computer is to generate the check, as described in Chapter 9. The account debited reflects why the cash was disbursed, such as miscellaneous expense, rent, etc. The Cash credit amount is automatically calculated and displayed by the computer.

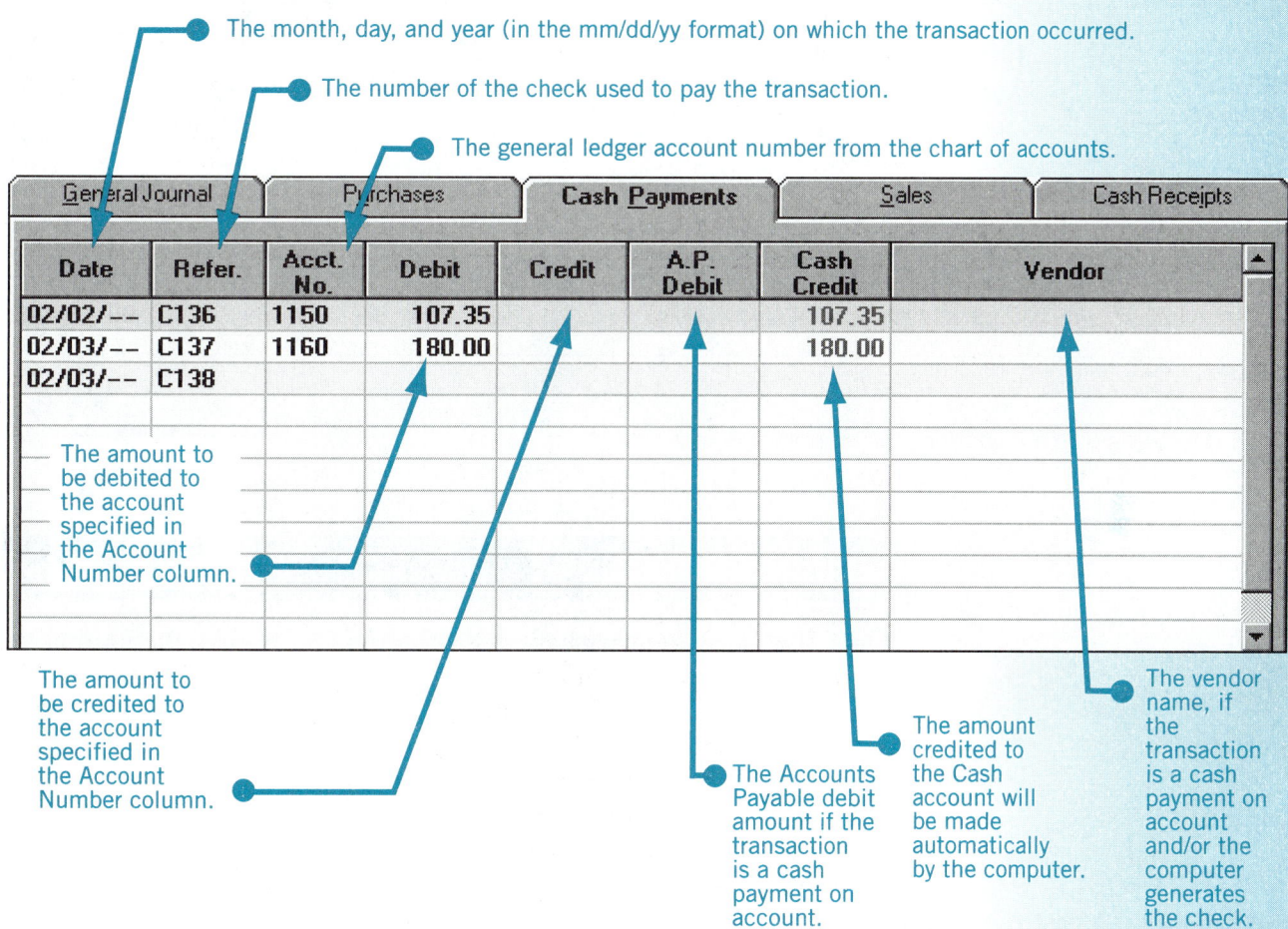

Figure 4.5
Cash Payments (Direct Payment)

Cash Payments on Account A cash payment on account is illustrated in Figure 4.6. A vendor account is required because the Accounts Payable account is affected. The amount of the invoice is entered in the Accounts Payable Debit (A.P. Debit) text box column. The Cash credit amount is automatically calculated and displayed by the computer.

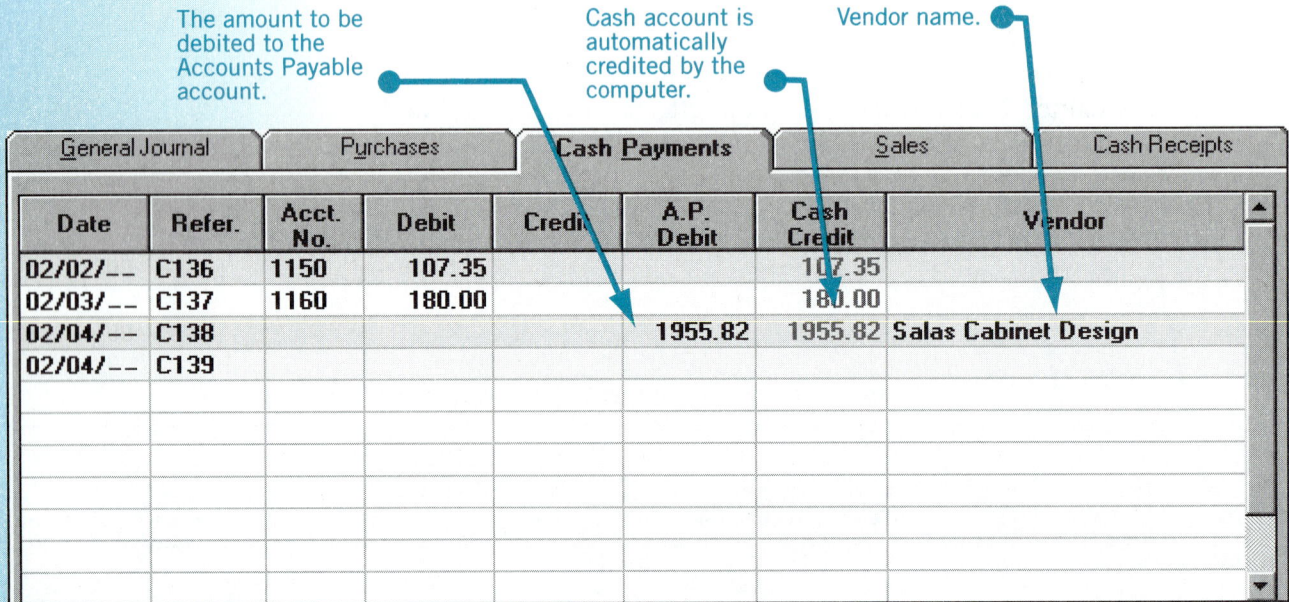

Figure 4.6
Cash Payments (Cash Payment on Account)

JOURNAL REPORTS

Once the journal entries have been entered and posted, the journal reports can be displayed. Click the Reports toolbar button. When the Report Selection dialog box appears, choose the Journals option button from the Select a Report Group list. A list of all the reports within the chosen Journals option will appear, as shown in Figure 4.7.

Choose the desired journal report from the Choose a Report to Display list. Then click OK. The Journal Report Selection dialog box shown in Figure 4.8 will appear, allowing you to display all the journal entries for the chosen journal or to customize your journal report. The operational procedures to customize all the journal reports listed are identical to the procedures you used for the General Journal Reports in Chapters 2 and 3.

Chapter 4 Purchases and Cash Payments

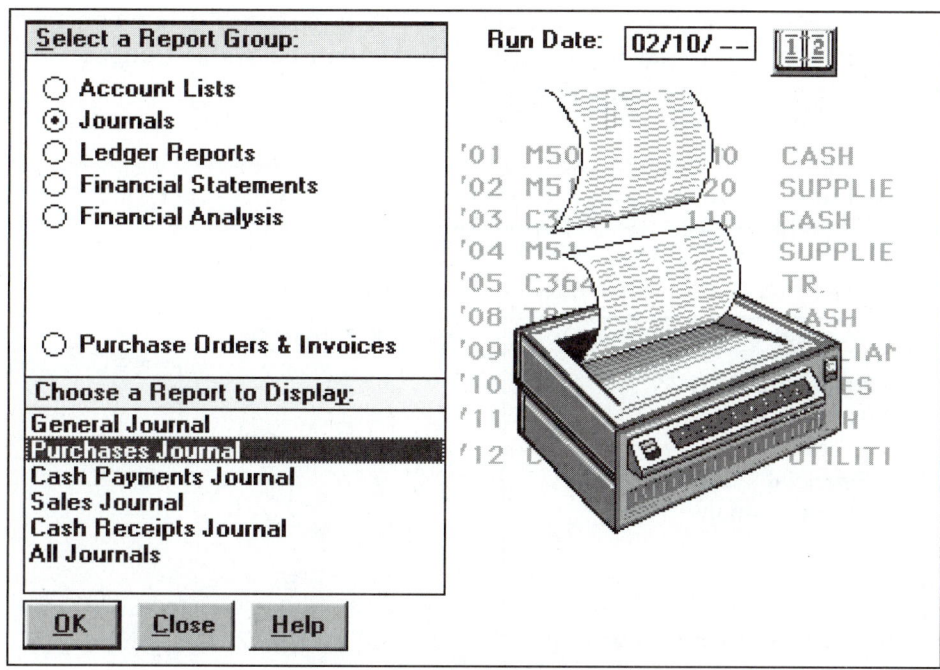

Figure 4.7
Report Selection Dialog Box

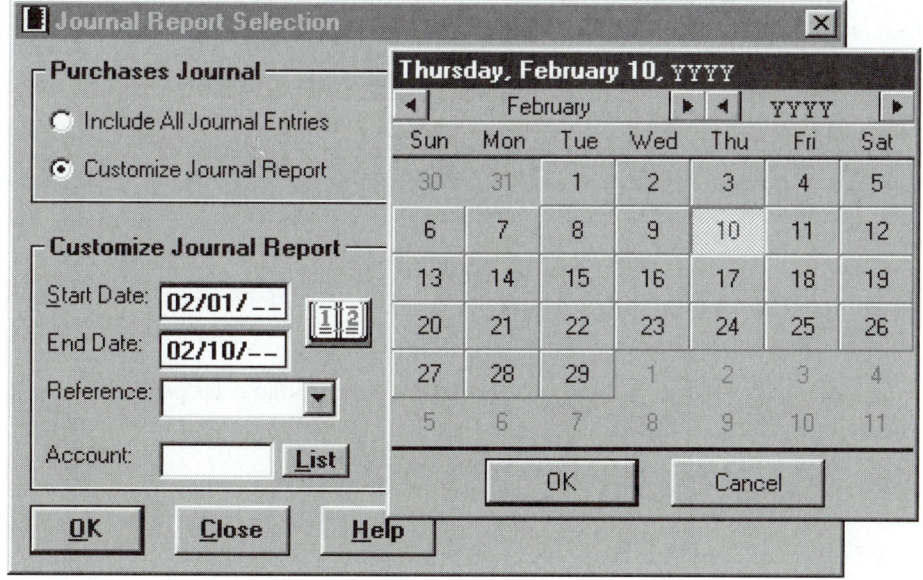

Figure 4.8
Journal Report Selection Dialog Box

LEDGER REPORTS

Automated Accounting 8.0 uses three ledgers: (1) general ledger; (2) accounts payable ledger; and (3) accounts receivable ledger. There are two reports available for each. The General Ledger Reports are the Trial Balance and the General Ledger. The two reports available for the

Accounts Payable Ledger are the Schedule of Accounts Payable and the Accounts Payable Ledger Report. The Accounts Receivable Ledger Reports will be covered in Chapter 5.

To display the ledger reports, click the Reports toolbar button. When the Report Selection dialog box appears, choose the Ledger Reports option button from the Select a Report Group list. A list of all the reports within the chosen Ledger option will appear, as shown in Figure 4.9.

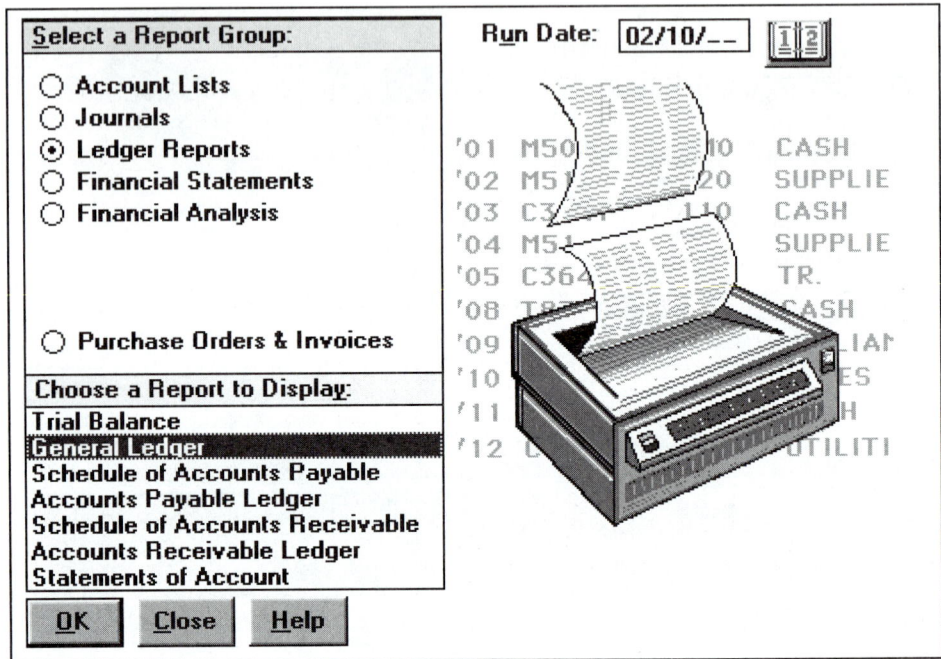

Figure 4.9
Ledger Report Selection Dialog Box

Choose the desired ledger report from the Choose a Report to Display list. Then click OK.

General Ledger Report

A **General Ledger Report** is a report that shows detailed journal entry activity by account. Any range of accounts can be displayed, from one account to all accounts. If you have determined that a particular account balance is incorrect, displaying all journal activity for that account can be very useful in locating the error.

When the General Ledger Report is chosen, the Account Range dialog box shown in Figure 4.10 will appear. Enter the range of accounts to be included in the General Ledger Report. You can use the drop-down list buttons at the end of the From: and To: text boxes to select accounts from an account list, rather than key the account numbers. You can also key the first digit of an account number to go directly to that part of the

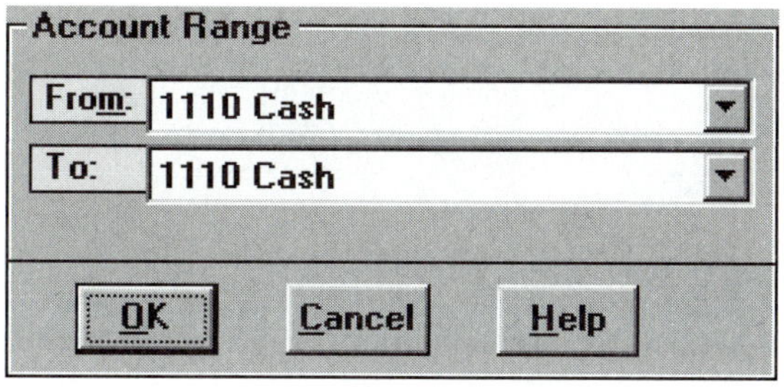

Chapter 4 Purchases and Cash Payments

Figure 4.10
Account Range Dialog Box

selection list. You can then scroll down by pressing the keyboard's Down Arrow key or by keying the digit again.

If only one account is to be displayed, the From: and To: text boxes can be the same. In Figure 4.10, account number 1110 is for the Cash account. Since the account number range is from 1110 to 1110, only activity for the Cash account will be displayed. Click the OK button. A General Ledger Report showing the Cash account activity is shown in Figure 4.11.

```
                        D & K Cabinet Tree
                          General Ledger
                            02/10/--
```

Account	Journal	Date	Refer.	Debit	Credit	Balance
1110-Cash						
	Balance Forward					37370.82Dr
	Cash Payments	02/01	C135		7.50	37363.32Dr
	Cash Payments	02/02	C136		107.35	37255.97Dr
	Cash Payments	02/03	C137		180.00	37075.97Dr
	Cash Payments	02/04	C138		1955.82	35120.15Dr
	Cash Payments	02/05	C139		800.00	34320.15Dr
	Cash Payments	02/08	C140		1022.57	33297.58Dr
	Cash Payments	02/09	C141		1389.41	31908.17Dr
	Cash Payments	02/10	C142		142.15	31766.02Dr
	Cash Payments	02/10	C143		550.00	31216.02Dr

Figure 4.11
General Ledger Report for the Cash Account

Schedule of Accounts Payable

A **Schedule of Accounts Payable Report** is a report that lists each vendor account balance and the total balance due all vendors. The total due all vendors must equal the balance in the Accounts Payable account in the general ledger. A sample report is shown in Figure 4.12.

```
              D & K Cabinet Tree
          Schedule of Accounts Payable
                   02/10/--

Name                                    Balance

Decko Woodworking, Inc.                 1636.50
Mellen Cabinet Co.                       647.30
Milton Wood Products                    2070.35
Morgan Office Supply Co.                 920.16
Spence Cabinet Mfg.                     1415.20
Ultra Cabinets                           905.00

Total                                   7594.51
                                       ========
```

Figure 4.12
Schedule of Accounts Payable

Accounts Payable Ledger Report

An **Accounts Payable Ledger Report** is a report that shows detailed journal entry activity by vendor. All the journal entries for the current fiscal period that affect each vendor are listed. This information is useful in locating errors within a single account, in obtaining status information about a specific vendor's activity, or in identifying transactions posted to the wrong vendor.

When the Accounts Payable Ledger Report is chosen in the Report Selection dialog box, the Vendor Range dialog box shown in Figure 4.13 will appear. Select the range of vendors you wish to appear on the report.

If only one vendor is to be displayed, the From: and To: portions of the vendor range should be the same. The Accounts Payable Ledger Report for the range of vendors selected in Figure 4.13 is shown in Figure 4.14.

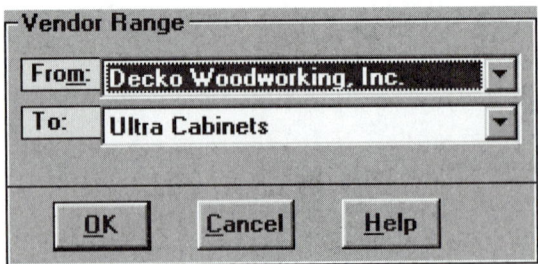

Figure 4.13
Vendor Range Dialog Box

Chapter 4 Purchases and Cash Payments

D & K Cabinet Tree
Accounts Payable Ledger
02/10/--

Account	Journal	Date	Refer.	Debit	Credit	Balance
Decko Woodworking, Inc.						
	Balance Forward					1636.50Cr
Mellen Cabinet Co.						
	Balance Forward					1022.57Cr
	Purchases	02/03	P221		647.30	1669.87Cr
	Cash Payments	02/08	C140	1022.57		647.30Cr
Milton Wood Products						
	Balance Forward					1174.40Cr
	Purchases	02/08	P222		895.95	2070.35Cr
Morgan Office Supply Co.						
	Balance Forward					471.60Cr
	General	02/03	M47		110.00	581.60Cr
	General	02/10	M50		338.56	920.16Cr
Salas Cabinet Design						
	Balance Forward					1955.82Cr
	Cash Payments	02/04	C138	1955.82		.00
Spence Cabinet Mfg.						
	Balance Forward					1389.41Cr
	Purchases	02/01	P220		1415.20	2804.61Cr
	Cash Payments	02/09	C141	1389.41		1415.20Cr
Ultra Cabinets						
	Purchases	02/09	P223		905.00	905.00Cr

Figure 4.14
Accounts Payable Ledger Report

Chapter Review

1. Vendors can be added, changed, or deleted from the accounting system by using a procedure similar to maintaining the chart of accounts.

2. The cost of merchandise purchased for resale is recorded in the Purchases account. Purchases-on-account transactions can be entered directly into the computer. However, purchase transactions can also be recorded on a purchases journal input form before entering them into the computer.

3. Only purchases of merchandise on account are entered into the purchases journal.

4. Businesses from which merchandise is purchased or supplies and other assets are bought are called vendors.

5. Cash-payments transactions are recorded for expenses, cash purchases of merchandise, payments to vendors, and payments not involving a check, such as a direct withdrawal by the bank for a service charge.

6. There are two types of cash payments: (1) direct payments; and (2) cash payments on account. A direct payment is a cash disbursement that does *not* affect accounts payable. Cash payments on account are cash disbursements that *do* affect accounts payable.

7. *Automated Accounting 8.0* generates General Ledger Reports, Schedule of Accounts Payable Reports, and Accounts Payable Ledger Reports to obtain detailed information. The Schedule of Accounts Payable Report lists each vendor that currently has a balance.

ACCOUNTING CAREERS IN DEPTH

Teller

A teller receives and pays out money and keeps records of money and negotiable instruments involved in financial transactions. A teller performs the following duties:

- Receiving checks and cash for deposit, verifying amounts, and examining checks for endorsements.
- Cashing checks and paying out money after the verification of signatures and customer balances.
- Entering customers' transactions in a computer to record transactions and issuing computer-generated receipts.
- Placing holds on accounts for uncollected funds.
- Ordering a daily supply of cash and counting incoming cash.
- Balancing currency, coins, and checks in the cash drawer at the end of the shift, using a calculator, and comparing totaled amounts with data displayed on the computer screen.
- Explaining, promoting, or selling products or services, such as traveler's checks, savings bonds, money orders, and cashier's checks.

A teller may also do the following:

- Open new accounts.
- Remove deposits from, and count and balance cash in, automated teller machines and the night depository.
- Accept utility bill and loan payments.
- Use a computer, a typewriter, a photocopier, and a check protector to prepare checks and financial documents.

There is a great deal of customer contact in teller positions. Therefore, excellent customer service is necessary when representing a financial institution. This involves clear communication, a pleasant personality, and a helpful attitude toward the customer.

Studying accounting in high school could be a good way to start out your career as a teller. The background knowledge gained in accounting would provide a job applicant with a competitive advantage. If you are interested in applying for positions at a higher level, there are always opportunities for advancement. Also, financial institutions offer courses that can help new employees learn about the banking and securities industries and prepare them for future assignments.

A career as a teller can open the door for many opportunities. It can be a great start, especially if you enjoy working with customers.

TUTORIAL PROBLEM 4-T

In this tutorial problem, you will maintain vendor accounts, enter purchases and cash payments journal entries, and display the related reports. You will enter the February 1–10 purchases and cash payments transactions for D & K Cabinet Tree.

STEP 1: Start up *Automated Accounting 8.0*.

STEP 2: Open and load the opening balances file named AA8 Problem 04-T.

STEP 3: Enter your name in the User Name text box and click *OK*.

STEP 4: Save the file with a file name of 04-T Your Name.

STEP 5: Add Ultra Cabinets to the vendor list.
Click the *Accts.* toolbar button, and then choose the *Vendors* tab. Enter *Ultra Cabinets,* and click the *Add Vendor* button.

STEP 6: Enter the journal entries from the general, purchases, and cash payments journals shown in Figures 4.15 through 4.17.
Key the following information from the transaction statements or refer to Figures 4.15 through 4.17 for input data. The reference numbers have been abbreviated as follows: Check, C; Purchase Invoice, P; Memorandum, M.

Feb. 01 Paid cash for miscellaneous expense, $7.50. C135.
01 Purchased merchandise on account from Spence Cabinet Mfg., $1,415.20. P220.
02 Paid cash for store supplies, $107.35. C136.
03 Purchased merchandise on account from Mellen Cabinet Co., $647.30. P221.
03 Bought office supplies on account from Morgan Office Supply Co., $110.00. M47.
Note: This is not a purchase of merchandise; therefore, this transaction must be recorded in the general journal.
03 Paid cash for insurance, $180.00. C137.
04 James Doring, partner, withdrew merchandise for personal use, $225.00. M48. Record this transaction in the general journal.
Note: The Purchases account is credited because this deduction decreases the amount of merchandise purchases.
04 Paid cash on account to Salas Cabinet Design, $1,955.82, covering P214, C138.

TUTORIAL PROBLEM 4-T

05 Discovered that a transaction for office supplies bought for cash in January was journalized and posted in error as a debit to Purchases instead of Supplies—Office, $75.00. M49. Record this transaction in the general journal.
05 Robert Kremer, partner, withdrew cash for personal use, $800.00. C139.
08 Purchased merchandise on account from Milton Wood Products, $895.95. P222.
08 Paid cash on account to Mellen Cabinet Co., $1,022.57, covering P215. C140.
09 Purchased merchandise on account from Ultra Cabinets, $905.00. P223.
09 Paid cash on account to Spence Cabinet Mfg., $1,389.41, covering P216. C141.
10 Paid cash for office supplies, $142.15. C142.
10 James Doring, partner, withdrew cash for personal use, $550.00. C143.
10 Bought store supplies on account from Morgan Office Supply Co., $338.56. M50.

Date	Refer.	Account	Debit	Credit	Vendor/Customer
02/03/--	M47	1145 Supplies--Office	110.00		
		2110 Accounts Payable		110.00	Morgan Office Supply Co.
02/04/--	M48	3120 James Doring, Drawing	225.00		
		5110 Purchases		225.00	
02/05/--	M49	1145 Supplies--Office	75.00		
		5110 Purchases		75.00	
02/10/--	M50	1150 Supplies--Store	338.56		
		2110 Accounts Payable		338.56	Morgan Office Supply Co.

Figure 4.15
General Journal (February 1–10)

Date	Refer.	Purch. Debit	A.P. Credit	Vendor
02/01/ --	P220	1415.20	1415.20	Spence Cabinet Mfg.
02/03/ --	P221	647.30	647.30	Mellen Cabinet Co.
02/08/ --	P222	895.95	895.95	Milton Wood Products
02/09/ --	P223	905.00	905.00	Ultra Cabinets

Figure 4.16
Purchases Journal (February 1–10)

Chapter 4 Purchases and Cash Payments

TUTORIAL PROBLEM 4-T

Date	Refer.	Acct. No.	Debit	Credit	A.P. Debit	Cash Credit	Vendor
02/01/__	C135	6120	7.50			7.50	
02/02/__	C136	1150	107.35			107.35	
02/03/__	C137	1160	180.00			180.00	
02/04/__	C138				1955.82	1955.82	Salas Cabinet Design
02/05/__	C139	3140	800.00			800.00	
02/08/__	C140				1022.57	1022.57	Mellen Cabinet Co.
02/09/__	C141				1389.41	1389.41	Spence Cabinet Mfg.
02/10/__	C142	1145	142.15			142.15	
02/10/__	C143	3120	550.00			550.00	

Figure 4.17
Cash Payments Journal (February 1–10)

STEP 7: **Display the vendor list.**
Click the *Reports* toolbar button. Choose the *Accounts List* option button and choose *Vendor List*. Click *OK*. Examine the vendor report in Figure 4.18 and verify that the vendor you keyed in Step 5 is correct.

```
D & K Cabinet Tree
Vendor List
02/10/--

Vendor Name

Decko Woodworking, Inc.
Mellen Cabinet Co.
Milton Wood Products
Morgan Office Supply Co.
Salas Cabinet Design
Spence Cabinet Mfg.
Ultra Cabinets
```

Figure 4.18
Vendor List

STEP 8: **Display the General Journal, Purchases Journal, and Cash Payments Journal Reports.**
Select *Journals* from the Select a Report Group list. Choose the desired journal report and click *OK*. When the Journal Report Selection dialog box appears, click *OK* to select *Include All Journal Entries*. The General Journal, Purchases Journal, and Cash Payments Journal Reports appear in Figures 4.19 through 4.21.

TUTORIAL PROBLEM 4-T

```
                    D & K Cabinet Tree
                     General Journal
                       02/10/--

Date     Refer.  Acct.   Title                        Debit      Credit

02/03    M47     1145    Supplies--Office             110.00
02/03    M47     2110    AP/Morgan Office Supply Co.             110.00

02/04    M48     3120    James Doring, Drawing        225.00
02/04    M48     5110    Purchases                                225.00

02/05    M49     1145    Supplies--Office              75.00
02/05    M49     5110    Purchases                                 75.00

02/10    M50     1150    Supplies--Store              338.56
02/10    M50     2110    AP/Morgan Office Supply Co.             338.56
                                                      -------    -------
                        Totals                        748.56     748.56
                                                      =======    =======
```

Figure 4.19
General Journal Report

```
                    D & K Cabinet Tree
                     Purchases Journal
                       02/10/--

Date     Inv. No. Acct.  Title                        Debit      Credit

02/01    P220    5110    Purchases                   1415.20
02/01    P220    2110    AP/Spence Cabinet Mfg.                 1415.20

02/03    P221    5110    Purchases                    647.30
02/03    P221    2110    AP/Mellen Cabinet Co.                   647.30

02/08    P222    5110    Purchases                    895.95
02/08    P222    2110    AP/Milton Wood Products                 895.95

02/09    P223    5110    Purchases                    905.00
02/09    P223    2110    AP/Ultra Cabinets                       905.00
                                                      -------    -------
                        Totals                       3863.45    3863.45
                                                      =======    =======
```

Figure 4.20
Purchases Journal Report

Chapter 4 Purchases and Cash Payments

TUTORIAL PROBLEM 4-T

```
                    D & K Cabinet Tree
                    Cash Payments Journal
                         02/10/--

Date      Ck. No.  Acct.  Title                       Debit     Credit

02/01     C135     6120   Miscellaneous Expense        7.50
02/01     C135     1110   Cash                                    7.50

02/02     C136     1150   Supplies--Store            107.35
02/02     C136     1110   Cash                                  107.35

02/03     C137     1160   Prepaid Insurance          180.00
02/03     C137     1110   Cash                                  180.00

02/04     C138     2110   AP/Salas Cabinet Design   1955.82
02/04     C138     1110   Cash                                 1955.82

02/05     C139     3140   Robert Kremer, Drawing     800.00
02/05     C139     1110   Cash                                  800.00

02/08     C140     2110   AP/Mellen Cabinet Co.     1022.57
02/08     C140     1110   Cash                                 1022.57

02/09     C141     2110   AP/Spence Cabinet Mfg.    1389.41
02/09     C141     1110   Cash                                 1389.41

02/10     C142     1145   Supplies--Office           142.15
02/10     C142     1110   Cash                                  142.15

02/10     C143     3120   James Doring, Drawing      550.00
02/10     C143     1110   Cash                                  550.00
                                                    --------   --------
                         Totals                     6154.80    6154.80
                                                    ========   ========
```

Figure 4.21
Cash Payments Journal Report

STEP 9: **Display a Trial Balance Report, a General Ledger Report for the Accounts Payable account, a Schedule of Accounts Payable Report, and an Accounts Payable Ledger Report for all vendors.**

Select *Ledger Reports*, choose the desired ledger report, and then click the *OK* button. When displaying the general ledger report, be sure to enter the Accounts Payable account (2110) number in both the From: and To: text

TUTORIAL PROBLEM 4-T

boxes in the Account Range dialog box. When displaying the Accounts Payable Ledger Report, make sure the first vendor appears in the From: text box and the last vendor appears in the To: text box in the Vendor Range dialog box. The reports appear in Figures 4.22 through 4.25.

```
                    D & K Cabinet Tree
                      Trial Balance
                        02/10/--

Acct.         Account
Number        Title                          Debit          Credit

1110          Cash                        31216.02
1120          Petty Cash                    100.00
1130          Accounts Receivable          1598.80
1140          Merchandise Inventory      131278.14
1145          Supplies--Office              889.04
1150          Supplies--Store               900.18
1160          Prepaid Insurance            1122.04
2110          Accounts Payable                             7594.51
2120          Sales Tax Payable                            1051.06
3110          James Doring, Capital                       81802.30
3120          James Doring, Drawing         775.00
3130          Robert Kremer, Capital                      81802.30
3140          Robert Kremer, Drawing        800.00
5110          Purchases                    3563.45
6120          Miscellaneous Expense           7.50
                                         ----------     ----------
              Totals                      172250.17      172250.17
                                         ==========     ==========
```

Figure 4.22
Trial Balance

STEP 10: **Save your data file to disk.**
Click the *Save* toolbar button.

STEP 11: **Optional Spreadsheet Activity.**
D & K Cabinet Tree has asked you to use a spreadsheet to calculate the component percent owed each vendor as of February 10. Prepare a report showing this information and generate a pie chart depicting the same data.

a. Display and copy the Schedule of Accounts Payable Report to the clipboard in spreadsheet format.

Chapter 4 Purchases and Cash Payments

TUTORIAL PROBLEM 4-T

```
                    D & K Cabinet Tree
                      General Ledger
                        02/10/--
```

Account	Journal	Date	Refer.	Debit	Credit	Balance
2110-Accounts Payable						
	Balance Forward					7650.30Cr
	Purchases	02/01	P220		1415.20	9065.50Cr
	General	02/03	M47		110.00	9175.50Cr
	Purchases	02/03	P221		647.30	9822.80Cr
	Cash Payments	02/04	C138	1955.82		7866.98Cr
	Purchases	02/08	P222		895.95	8762.93Cr
	Cash Payments	02/08	C140	1022.57		7740.36Cr
	Purchases	02/09	P223		905.00	8645.36Cr
	Cash Payments	02/09	C141	1389.41		7255.95Cr
	General	02/10	M50		338.56	7594.51Cr

Figure 4.23
General Ledger Report

```
              D & K Cabinet Tree
           Schedule of Accounts Payable
                    02/10/--

  Name                           Balance

  Decko Woodworking, Inc.        1636.50
  Mellen Cabinet Co.              647.30
  Milton Wood Products           2070.35
  Morgan Office Supply Co.        920.16
  Spence Cabinet Mfg.            1415.20
  Ultra Cabinets                  905.00
                                 -------
  Total                          7594.51
                                 =======
```

Figure 4.24
Schedule of Accounts Payable

b. Start up your spreadsheet software and load the template file named AA8 Spreadsheet 04-T. A blank, formatted worksheet will appear.
c. Select cell B1 as the current cell, if not already selected.

TUTORIAL PROBLEM 4-T

```
                    D & K Cabinet Tree
                    Accounts Payable Ledger
                         02/10/--
```

Account Journal	Date	Refer.	Debit	Credit	Balance
Decko Woodworking, Inc.					
Balance Forward					1636.50Cr
Mellen Cabinet Co.					
Balance Forward					1022.57Cr
Purchases	02/03	P221		647.30	1669.87Cr
Cash Payments	02/08	C140	1022.57		647.30Cr
Milton Wood Products					
Balance Forward					1174.40Cr
Purchases	02/08	P222		895.95	2070.35Cr
Morgan Office Supply Co.					
Balance Forward					471.60Cr
General	02/03	M47		110.00	581.60Cr
General	02/10	M50		338.56	920.16Cr
Salas Cabinet Design					
Balance Forward					1955.82Cr
Cash Payments	02/04	C138	1955.82		.00
Spence Cabinet Mfg.					
Balance Forward					1389.41Cr
Purchases	02/01	P220		1415.20	2804.61Cr
Cash Payments	02/09	C141	1389.41		1415.20Cr
Ultra Cabinets					
Purchases	02/09	P223		905.00	905.00Cr

Figure 4.25
Accounts Payable Ledger

    d. Paste the Schedule of Accounts Payable Report (copied to the clipboard in Step 11a) into the spreadsheet.
    e. Enter the word *Percent* in cell D7.
Enter the formula to calculate the component percentage in cell D9. For example, (+C9/+$C$16). Copy and paste the formula in cell D9 to cells D10, D11, D12, D13, and D14.

TUTORIAL PROBLEM 4-T

f. Format the amounts in currency format and the calculated percentages in percentage format, if necessary.
g. Generate a pie chart.
Select the range of cells B9 through C14, and then choose the Chart or Graph menu item from the spreadsheet program you are using. If the computer asks for a graph name, use *Vendors*. Choose *Pie Chart* if the graph that appears is not a pie chart. Finally, if the spreadsheet you are using permits copying and pasting the graph into the worksheet, copy and paste the graph into cells A22 through D40. Alternatively, insert the graph into the spreadsheet and drag it to begin in cell A22; then click the bottom corner and drag to enlarge the graph to fill cells D22 to D40.
h. Save your spreadsheet data with a file name of 04-T Your Name.
i. Print the spreadsheet and pie chart. The completed spreadsheet and pie chart are shown in Figure 4.26.
j. What if Milton Wood Products' balance amount is now $3,500.00? Enter this change and the formula to compute the Total. Notice the effects of the change on the component percentages and pie chart.
k. End your spreadsheet session without saving your changes made in Step 11j.

STEP 12: Optional Word Processing Integration Activity.
D & K Cabinet Tree consults with Hicks & Associates, a local accounting firm, for financial advice. As part of the information needed, Sara Hicks, owner and C.P.A. of the accounting firm, has asked that you fax her a list of the vendors and their account balances at the end of each week. You are to use the word processing fax template used by D & K Cabinet Tree for most of its facsimile transmittals to prepare this document for the week ended February 10 of the current year.

a. Display and copy the Schedule of Accounts Payable Report to the clipboard in word processing format.
b. Start up your word processing application software and load the template file named AA8 Wordprocessing 04-T as a text file.

TUTORIAL PROBLEM 4-T

Student Name

D & K Cabinet Tree
Schedule of Accounts Payable
As Of 02/10/--

Name	Balance	Percent
Decko Woodworking, Inc.	$1,636.50	21.55%
Mellen Cabinet Co.	$647.30	8.52%
Milton Wood Products	$2,070.35	27.26%
Morgan Office Supply Co.	$920.16	12.12%
Spence Cabinet Mfg.	$1,415.20	18.63%
Ultra Cabinets	$905.00	11.92%
Total	$7,594.51	

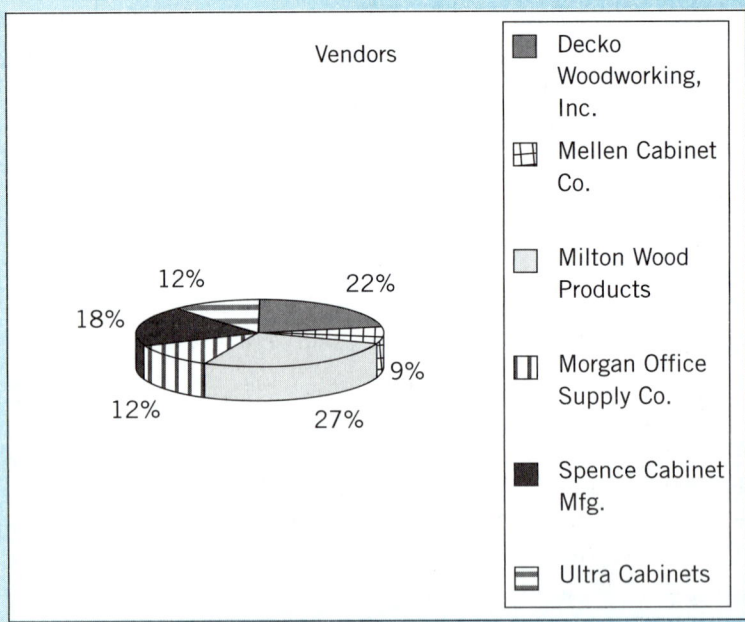

Figure 4.26
Vendor Component Percentage Report and Pie Chart

c. Enter your name in the FROM field and complete the remainder of the top portion of the facsimile, as shown in Figure 4.27.
d. Position the insertion point one line after the Notes/Comments section and paste the report. Delete

Chapter 4 Purchases and Cash Payments 137

TUTORIAL PROBLEM 4-T

```
                    D & K Cabinet Tree
                      65 Maple Lane
                 Minneapolis, MN 55435-1282
                      (503) 555-8511

                        FACSIMILE

           TO:  Sara Hicks
      COMPANY:  Hicks & Associates
         DATE:  February 10, Current Year
 PHONE NUMBER:  (612) 555-7460
   FAX NUMBER:  (612) 555-7497
         FROM:  Your Name
      SUBJECT:  END-OF-THE-WEEK VENDOR ACCOUNT BALANCES
```

Notes/Comments:

As per your request, our vendors and their account balances as of February 10 are:

Decko Woodworking, Inc.	$1,636.50
Mellen Cabinet Co.	647.30
Milton Wood Products	2,070.35
Morgan Office Supply Co.	920.16
Spence Cabinet Mfg.	1,415.20
Ultra Cabinets	905.00

Figure 4.27
February 10 Facsimile

        the report headings and format the document to match Figure 4.27. Experiment adding further enhancements to the appearance of the fax.
    e. Save the document with a file name of 04-T Your Name.
    f. Print the completed document. Many computers have the capability to fax documents electronically directly from the word processor so that a hard copy may not be necessary.
    g. End your word processing session.

STEP 13: End your *Automated Accounting* session.

Review and Practice: Applying Your Information Skills

I. MATCHING

Directions: In the *Working Papers*, write the letter of the appropriate term next to each definition.

   a. Accounts Payable Ledger Report
   b. cash payment
   c. cash payment on account
   d. cash payments journal
   e. cash payments journal input form
   f. direct payment
   g. General Ledger Report
   h. merchandise
   i. Merchandise Inventory account
   j. merchandising business
   k. partnership
   l. purchase on account
   m. Purchases account
   n. purchases journal
   o. purchases journal input form
   p. Schedule of Accounts Payable Report
   q. vendor

1. A report that shows detailed journal entry activity by vendor.
2. A business that purchases and resells goods.
3. The special journal used to record the purchase of merchandise on account.
4. The special journal used to record all payments of cash.
5. An account that shows the value of goods on hand for sale to customers.
6. An account used to record the cost of merchandise purchased for resale.
7. A cash disbursement that does *not* affect Accounts Payable.
8. A cash disbursement that *does* affect Accounts Payable.
9. A report that lists each vendor account balance and total balance due all vendors.
10. Goods purchased for resale.
11. A report that shows detailed journal entry activity by account.

Chapter 4   Purchases and Cash Payments

12. A business from which merchandise is purchased or supplies and other assets are bought.

13. A transaction in which merchandise that is purchased is paid for at a later date.

14. Any type of transaction involving the payment of cash.

15. An input form on which all purchases of merchandise on account can be recorded.

16. An input form on which all cash payments can be recorded.

17. A business that is owned by two or more persons.

II. REVIEW QUESTIONS

Directions: Write the answers to each of the following questions in the *Working Papers*.

1. How are vendors added to the accounting system?

2. What type of transaction is recorded in the purchases journal?

3. What are the two types of cash payments?

4. What are three journal reports that can be displayed once the journal entries have been entered?

5. What are the reports available for the general ledger and the accounts payable ledger?

III. INTERNET ACTIVITY

Directions: If you have access to the Internet, use the browser to find the 12 U.S. Federal Reserve Banks. Use *Federal Reserve Banks* for your search. Identify the location of each of the 12 Federal Reserve Banks from your findings. Note the address and phone number of the U.S. Federal Reserve Bank nearest to where you live. Be sure to include the source and the URL (Internet address) of your search.

Independent Practice Problem 4-P

In this problem, you will process any additions, changes, or deletions to vendors' accounts. You will also process purchases and cash payments transactions for the period February 11 through February 20 of the current year.

STEP 1: Start up *Automated Accounting 8.0*.

STEP 2: Open and load the opening balances template file named AA8 Problem 04-P.

Chapter 4 Purchases and Cash Payments

STEP 3: Enter your name in the User Name text box.

STEP 4: Save your file as 04-P Your Name.

STEP 5: Enter the following transactions:

Feb. 11 Paid cash for rent, $2,500.00. C144.
11 Paid cash on account to Decko Woodworking, Inc., $1,636.50, covering P217. C145.
11 Paid cash for store supplies, $278.60. C146.
12 Robert Kremer, partner, withdrew merchandise for personal use, $385.00. M51. Record this transaction in the general journal.
12 Purchased merchandise on account from Salas Cabinet Design, $2,110.50. P224.
12 Paid cash for miscellaneous expense, $105.00. C147.
15 Paid cash on account to Milton Wood Products, $1,174.40, covering P218. C148.
15 Paid cash for office supplies, $147.35. C149.
15 Robert Kremer, partner, withdrew cash for personal use, $800.00. C150.
16 Discovered that a transaction for office supplies bought for cash in January was journalized and posted in error as a debit to Prepaid Insurance instead of Supplies—Office, $145.12. M52.
16 Bought store supplies on account from Morgan Office Supply Co., $234.25 M53.
17 Paid cash on account to Morgan Office Supply Co., $471.60, covering M45. C151.
17 Purchased merchandise on account from Spence Cabinet Mfg., $2,067.58. P225.
17 Purchased merchandise on account from Decko Woodworking, Inc., $1,695.95. P226.
18 Paid cash on account to Mellen Cabinet Co., $647.30, covering P221. C152.
18 Purchased merchandise for cash, $2,589.73. C153.
18 Paid cash for miscellaneous expense, $15.00. C154.
18 Paid cash for insurance, $535.00. C155.
19 Paid cash for electric bill, $296.80. C156.
19 Paid cash on account to Spence Cabinet Mfg., $1,415.20, covering P220. C157.
19 Paid cash on account to Morgan Office Supply Co., $110.00, covering M47. C158.
19 Bought store supplies on account from Suncoast Supply Co., $637.45. M54.
Note: Add Suncoast Supply Co. to the vendor list.

Chapter 4 Purchases and Cash Payments

           20   Purchased merchandise on account from Mellen Cabinet Co., $340.00. P227.

STEP 6: Display the following reports: General Journal, Purchases Journal, and Cash Payments Journal for the period February 11 through February 20 of the current year. If errors are detected, make corrections.

STEP 7: Display the following ledger reports: Trial Balance, General Ledger Report for the Cash account, Schedule of Accounts Payable, and Accounts Payable Ledger (all vendors).

STEP 8: Save your data.

STEP 9: **Optional Spreadsheet Integration Activity.**
D & K Cabinet Tree has asked you to use a spreadsheet to calculate the component percent owed each vendor as of February 20. Prepare a report showing this information and generate a pie chart depicting the same data.

   a. Display and copy the Schedule of Accounts Payable Report to the clipboard in spreadsheet format.
   b. Start up your spreadsheet software and load the template file named AA8 Spreadsheet 04-T. A blank, formatted worksheet will appear.
   c. Select cell B1 as the current cell (if not already selected) and paste the Schedule of Accounts Payable Report into the spreadsheet.
   d. Enter the word *Percent* in cell D7.
      Enter the formula to calculate the component percentage in cell D9.
      Copy and paste the formula in cell D9 to the appropriate cells.
   e. Format the amounts in currency format and the calculated percentages in percentage format, if necessary.
   f. Generate a pie chart depicting the data in the report. Use *Vendors* as the title.
   g. Save your spreadsheet data with a file name of 04-P Your Name.
   h. Print the spreadsheet and pie chart.
   i. What if Mellen Cabinet Co.'s balance is now $700.00 and Salas Cabinet Design's balance is now $3,150.00? Enter these changes and the formula to compute the total. Notice the effects of these changes on the component percentages and pie chart.
   j. End your spreadsheet session without saving your changes from Step 9i and return to *Automated Accounting*.

STEP 10: **Optional Word Processing Integration Activity.**
You are to use the company's word processing fax template to prepare the vendor account balance information for the accounting firm, covering the week ended February 20.

a. Display and copy the Schedule of Accounts Payable Report to the clipboard in word processing format.
b. Start up your word processing application software and load the template file named AA8 Wordprocessing 04-T as a text file.
   Note: As an alternative, load the solution word processing file from Tutorial Problem 4-T and modify it as necessary to complete this activity.
c. Enter your name in the FROM field and complete the remainder of the top portion of the facsimile, as shown in Figure 4.27.
d. Paste the report, delete report headings, totals, etc., and format the document to match Figure 4.27.
e. Save the document with a file name of 04-P Your Name.
f. Print the completed document.
g. End your word processing session.

STEP 11: End your *Automated Accounting* session.

Applying Your Technology Skills 4-P

Directions: Using Independent Practice Problem 4-P, write the answers to the following questions in the *Working Papers*.

1. What are the totals of the debit and credit columns in the General Journal Report?
2. From the Purchases Journal Report, what is the amount of Invoice No. 225?
3. What is the amount of Check No. 151 to Morgan Office Supply Co.?
4. What is the current balance in Accounts Payable?
5. What is the current balance in the Office Supplies account?
6. What was the balance at the beginning of the period in the Cash account?
7. What is the current balance owed to Spence Cabinet Mfg.?
8. What is the total owed to all vendors on February 20?

Chapter 4 Purchases and Cash Payments

9. What was the balance owed to Mellen Cabinet Co., at the beginning of the period?

10. What is the total amount purchased from Mellen Cabinet Co., during February?

Mastery Problem 4-M

In this problem, you will process any additions, changes, or deletions to vendors' accounts. You will also process the purchases and cash-payments transactions for the period February 21 through February 28 of the current year.

STEP 1: **Open and load the opening balances file named AA8 Problem 04-M.**

STEP 2: **Enter your name in the User Name text box.**

STEP 3: **Save the opening balance data as 04-M Your Name.**

STEP 4: **Enter the following transactions:**

Feb. 22 Purchased merchandise for cash, $582.09. C159.
22 Paid cash on account to Milton Wood Products, $895.95, covering P222. C160.
22 Paid cash for miscellaneous expense, $20.00. C161.
23 Paid cash for store supplies, $105.17. C162.
23 Purchased merchandise on account from Salas Cabinet Design, $645.70. P228.
23 Paid cash on account to Ultra Cabinets, $905.00, covering P223. C163.
24 Paid cash for insurance, $150.00. C164.
24 Discovered that a payment for a miscellaneous expense was journalized and posted in error as a debit to Rent Expense instead of Miscellaneous Expense, $25.00. M55.
24 Purchased merchandise for cash, $295.99. C165.
24 Paid cash for office supplies, $146.95. C166.
24 Bought office supplies on account from Suncoast Supply Co., $148.62. M56.
25 Paid cash on account to Morgan Office Supply Co., Inc., $338.56, covering M50. C167.
25 Purchased merchandise on account from Ashley Interiors, $798.00. P229.

Note: Add Ashley Interiors to the vendor list.

25 James Doring, partner, withdrew cash for personal use, $850.00. C168.

25 Purchased merchandise on account from Milton Wood Products, $623.50. P230.

26 Paid cash to replenish the petty cash fund, $100.00: miscellaneous, $48.00; office supplies, $15.00; store supplies, $37.00. C169.

Note: Each of the items (miscellaneous expense, office supplies, etc.) is entered on separate grid cell lines in the cash payments journal.

28 Purchased merchandise on account from Mellen Cabinet Co., $350.00. P231.

STEP 5: **Display the following reports: Journal Reports, Trial Balance, General Ledger Report for Office and Store Supply accounts, Schedule of Accounts Payable, and Accounts Payable Ledger (all vendors) for the period February 21 through February 28 of the current year.**

STEP 6: **Save your data.**

STEP 7: **Optional Spreadsheet Integration Activity.**

Prepare a report showing the component percent owed each vendor, and generate a pie chart depicting this data as of February 28.

a. Display and copy the Schedule of Accounts Payable Report to the clipboard in spreadsheet format.

b. Start up your spreadsheet software and load the template file named AA8 Spreadsheet 04-T.

c. Select cell B1 as the current cell and paste the Schedule of Accounts Payable Report into the spreadsheet.

d. Enter the labels and formulas required to report and compute the component percentages, using the format illustrated in Figure 4.26.

e. Generate a pie chart depicting the data in the report.

f. Save your spreadsheet data with a file name of 04-M Your Name.

g. Print the spreadsheet and pie chart.

h. What if Ashley Interiors' balance is now $605.00 and Spence Cabinet Mfg.'s balance is now $1,150.00? Enter these changes and the formula to compute the Total. Notice the effects of the changes on the component percentages and pie chart.

i. End your spreadsheet without saving your changes from Step 7h.

Chapter 4 Purchases and Cash Payments

STEP 8: **Optional Word Processing Integration Activity.**
  a. Display and copy the Schedule of Accounts Payable Report to the clipboard in word processing format.
  b. Start up your word processing application software and load the template file named AA8 Wordprocessing 04-T (load as a text file).
  Note: As an alternative, and if completed, load your solution word processing file from either Tutorial Problem 4-T or Practice Problem 4-P and modify it as necessary to complete this activity.
  c. Enter your name in the FROM: field and complete the remainder of the top portion of the facsimile, as shown in Figure 4.27. Paste the report, delete report headings, totals, etc., and format the document as necessary.
  d. Save the document with a file name of 04-M Your Name.
  e. Print the completed document.
  f. End your word processing session.

STEP 9: End your *Automated Accounting* session.

Applying Your Technology Skills 4-M

Directions: Using Mastery Problem 4-M, write the answers to the following questions in the *Working Papers*.

1. On the Purchases Journal Report, what is the amount credited to Milton Wood Products for Invoice No. 230?
2. What is the amount of Check No. 161 in the cash payments journal?
3. What is the balance in Robert Kremer's Drawing account?
4. What is the balance in the Miscellaneous Expense account?
5. From the General Ledger Report, what is the amount of the office supplies bought on Memorandum No. 56?
6. From the General Ledger Report, was the amount of the office supplies bought on Memorandum No. 56 (mentioned in Question 5) debited or credited to Office Supplies?
7. What is the balance owed to Ashley Interiors on February 28?
8. What is the total amount owed to all vendors as of February 28?

9. From the Accounts Payable Ledger Report, what is the amount of the cash payment to Morgan Office Supply Co. on February 25, Check No. C167?

10. From the Accounts Payable Ledger Report, what is the amount on Memorandum No. 56 to Suncoast Supply Co.?

Listserv is a mailing list program designed to copy and distribute electronic mail to everyone who has subscribed to it.

A firewall uses special software that screens people who enter and/or exit a network by requesting specific information such as passwords.

The Internet is not a single network but rather a super network made up of thousands of smaller subnetworks. The Internet is often referred to as the network of networks.

FTP stands for File Transfer Protocol. FTP software transfers files of data from one computer to another.

A "hit" is recorded every time someone connects to an Internet home page. A popular home page can take many hits. When traffic is too great on the Internet, you may not be able to reach a favorite site.

The most important person on a network is the network administrator. The administrator manages all the hardware and software issues on a network and keeps things running.

Chapter 5
SALES AND CASH RECEIPTS

KEY TERMS

Customer
Sales Transaction
Sales Journal
Sales Journal Input Form
Sales Invoice
Cash Receipt
Cash Receipts Journal
Cash Receipts Journal Input Form

Direct Receipt
Cash Receipt on Account
Schedule of Accounts Receivable Report
Accounts Receivable Ledger Report
Statement of Account

LEARNING OBJECTIVES

Upon completion of this chapter, you will be able to:

1. Enter customer maintenance data.
2. Enter sales transactions.
3. Enter cash-receipt transactions.
4. Display reports that summarize activities for the time period.

Chapter 5 Sales and Cash Receipts

INTRODUCTION

In this chapter, you will again work with a sample company, D & K Cabinet Tree, as you learn to add, change, and delete customers and to enter and correct sales and cash receipts journal entries. D & K Cabinet Tree is a wholesale merchandising business. This company sells merchandise on account to retail stores at wholesale prices. Retailers do not pay sales tax since sales of merchandise for resale are not subject to sales tax. Occasionally, D & K Cabinet Tree sells on account to individuals. Sales on account to individuals are subject to sales tax. The

One of the tasks that can be performed by computers is the coding and decoding of sensitive information. The coding of data is known as *encryption*. The reverse procedure—decoding—is known as *decryption*. In the encryption phase, readable data is turned into unreadable code; "Hello" might become "&W$Qd." Readable data means that it is readable to the computer, but not necessarily to a human. In the decryption phase, unreadable code is turned back into readable data. In the coding and decoding of data, an element known as an *encryption key* is used. The key is composed of alphabetic characters and/or numeric values that are used by a mathematic formula that does all the work of encryption and decryption.

Coded data has played a major role in the military for many years. The outcome of wars has been determined by successfully breaking codes, and military advantage has been maintained by keeping secret codes secret. In fact, much of the research that has contributed to today's sophisticated encryption techniques has come from the military. However, coding is not limited to only the military. Encryption is a technique used frequently by businesses. Much data, especially data in transit electronically from one location to another, is subject to piracy by electronic interception. By preventing unauthorized eyes from spying on this information, companies can maintain confidentially and a competitive edge.

Critical Thinking

1. Do you believe that breaking an encryption code and using (or selling) the information is ethical or unethical? Is it a violation of law? Explain.

2. Identify at least two reasons why businesses may want to use encryption when transmitting financial information from one location to another.

3. In general, do you think that the use of encryption is ethical or unethical? Explain.

Chapter 5 Sales and Cash Receipts

company also sells merchandise at retail prices to individuals for cash. The cash sales to individuals are also subject to sales tax.

MAINTAIN CUSTOMERS

A business or individual to whom merchandise or services are sold is called a **customer**. Businesses that sell merchandise on account maintain a separate file for each customer. The total owed by all customers in the customer file is summarized in a single general ledger asset account titled Accounts Receivable.

Customers can be added, changed, or deleted from the accounting system using a procedure similar to maintaining the chart of accounts and vendor lists. When the Maintain Accounts menu item is chosen from the Data menu, or the Accts. toolbar button is clicked, the Account Maintenance window will appear. Choose the Customers tab to display the Customers Maintenance window shown in Figure 5.1.

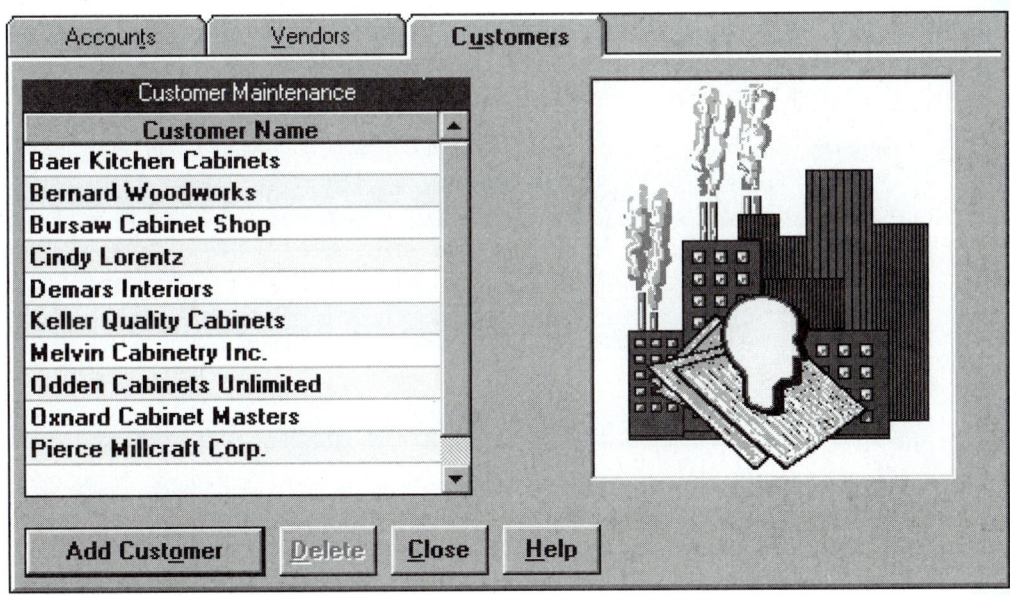

Figure 5.1
Customers Maintenance Window

New customers can be added by entering a customer name after the last item in the list and clicking the Add Customer button. The new customer will be inserted into the customer list in alphabetical order. Existing customer names can be changed by selecting the customer you wish to change, keying in the correct customer name, and clicking the Change Customer button. (The Add Customer button changes to Change Customer.) An existing customer can be deleted by simply selecting the customer that you wish to delete and clicking the Delete button.

A customer cannot be deleted if it has a balance.

SALES

A transaction in which merchandise is sold in exchange for another asset, usually money, is called a **sales transaction**. A sales transaction of merchandise may be (1) on account or (2) for cash.

Sales Journal Input Form

The **sales journal** is a special journal used to enter only sales-of-merchandise-on-account transactions. Sales on account can be entered directly into the computer from the transaction statement. Sales-on-account-transactions can also be recorded on the **sales journal input form,** which is an input form used to record only sales-on-account transactions, and then entered into the computer. A sales journal input form is shown in Figure 5.2. Each line of the input form can be used to record a sales invoice or one part of a sales invoice that is charged to multiple revenue accounts.

SALES JOURNAL INPUT FORM

Date 02/10/-- Problem No. Example

Date	Refer.	Sales Credit	Sales Tax Credit	Customer
02/02/--	S622	1560.00		Baer Kitchen Cabinets
02/10/--	S629	435.40	26.12	Cindy Lorentz

Figure 5.2
Sales Journal Input Form

A **sales invoice** is a form used to describe the goods sold, the quantity, and the price. It is used as a source document for recording sales-on-account transactions. When the credit portion of a sales transaction is entered, the computer automatically calculates and displays the debit to the Accounts Receivable account. Therefore, the debit amount to the Accounts Receivable account need not be recorded on the input form. The field names and a description of each column of the input form are illustrated in the sales journal shown in Figure 5.3.

Transactions are recorded on the sales journal input form illustrated in Figure 5.2. The first transaction is a sale of merchandise to a wholesale company that does *not* involve sales tax. The second transaction is a sale of merchandise to an individual that *does* involve sales tax.

Chapter 5 Sales and Cash Receipts

Feb. 02 Sold merchandise on account to Baer Kitchen Cabinets, $1,560.00. Sales invoice no. S622.

10 Sold merchandise on account to Cindy Lorentz, $435.40; plus sales tax, $26.12; total, $461.52. Sales invoice no. S629.

Sales Journal

The sales journal is shown in Figure 5.3. Only sales-on-account transactions are entered into the sales journal.

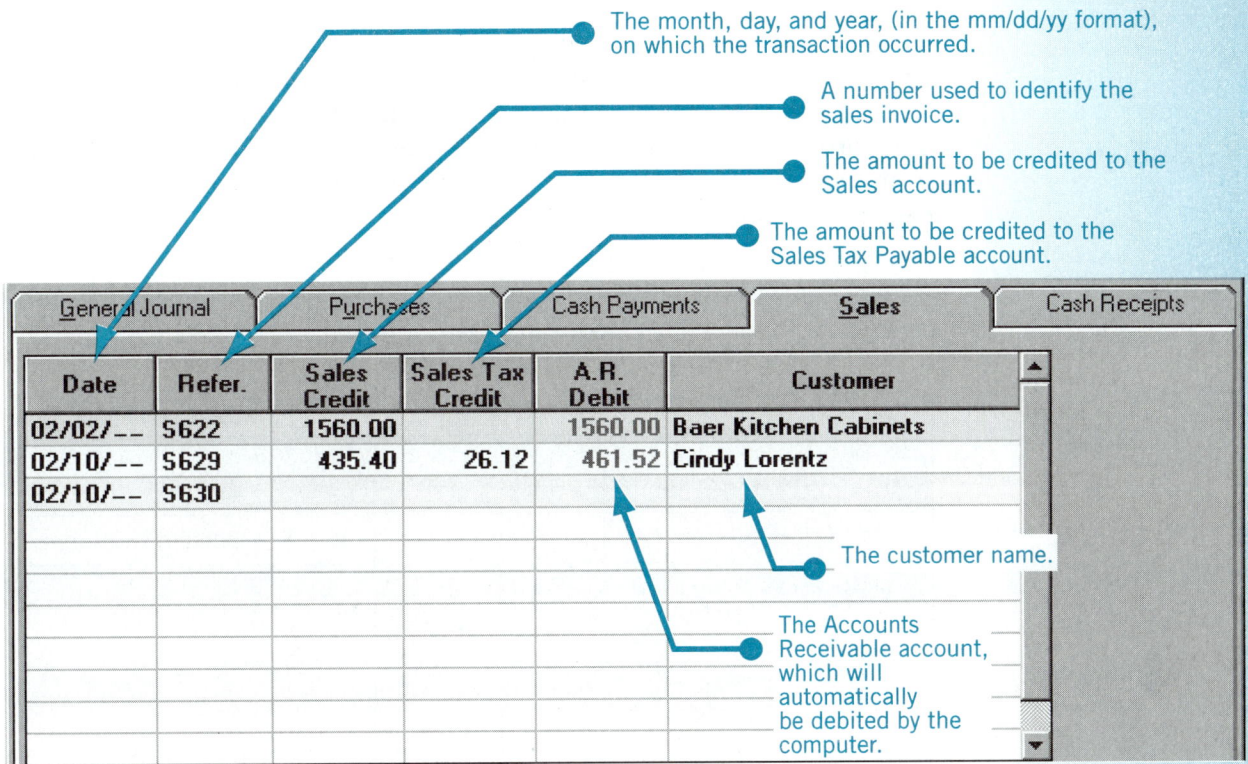

Figure 5.3
Sales Journal

To enter sales journal transactions, click the Journal toolbar button. When the Journal Entries window appears, click the Sales tab. Enter the date, reference number, invoice amount (in the Sales Credit field), sales tax (in the Sales Tax Credit field), and the customer name. The computer automatically calculates and displays the Accounts Receivable Debit amount. The sales transactions listed earlier, and recorded on the sales journal input form shown in Figure 5.2, have been entered and posted in the sales journal shown in Figure 5.3.

Transactions entered into the sales journal can be changed or deleted, and additional lines can be added using the same procedure you used in previous chapters for the general, purchases, and cash payments journals.

CASH RECEIPTS

Any type of transaction involving the receipt of cash is called a **cash receipt**. Cash-receipt transactions must be entered and posted for all cash that is received. Cash receipts may be from customers paying on account or from other sources such as sales made for cash or interest earned on a bank account.

Cash Receipts Journal Input Form

A **cash receipts journal** is a special journal used to enter all cash-receipt transactions. Cash receipts can be entered directly into the computer from a source document. Cash receipts can also be recorded on the **cash receipts journal input form,** which is an input form used to record all cash receipts. They can then be entered into the computer from the data recorded on the form. Figure 5.4 illustrates a completed cash receipts journal input form.

CASH RECEIPTS JOURNAL INPUT FORM

Date 02/10/--   Problem No. Example

Date	Refer	Acct. No.	Debit	Credit	A.R. Credit	Customer
02/01/--	R756				461.08	Bernard Woodworks
02/01/--	T5	4110		3502.87		
		2120		210.17		

Figure 5.4
Cash Receipts Journal Input Form

Each line of the form can be used to record a cash-receipt transaction or one part of a cash-receipt transaction involving multiple parts. When the credit portion of a cash-receipt transaction is entered, the computer automatically calculates and displays the debit to the Cash account. Therefore, the debit amount to the Cash account need not be recorded on the input form. The field names and a description of each field in the input form are illustrated in the cash receipts journal shown in Figure 5.5.

The transactions listed below are recorded on the cash receipts journal input form. Additional examples of the various types of cash-receipt transactions that can be recorded on this form are illustrated in Tutorial Problem 5-T. The first transaction is an example of a cash

Chapter 5 Sales and Cash Receipts

receipt on account that *does* involve Accounts Receivable. The second transaction is an example of a direct receipt that does *not* involve Accounts Receivable.

> Feb. 01 Received cash on account from Bernard Woodworks, $461.08, covering sales invoice no. S617. Cash Receipt No. R756.
> 01 Recorded cash and credit card sales, $3,502.87, plus sales tax, $210.17; total, $3,713.04. Calculator Tape No. 5.

Cash Receipts Journal

The cash receipts journal is shown in Figure 5.5. As the data is entered, the computer automatically calculates and displays the debit to Cash.

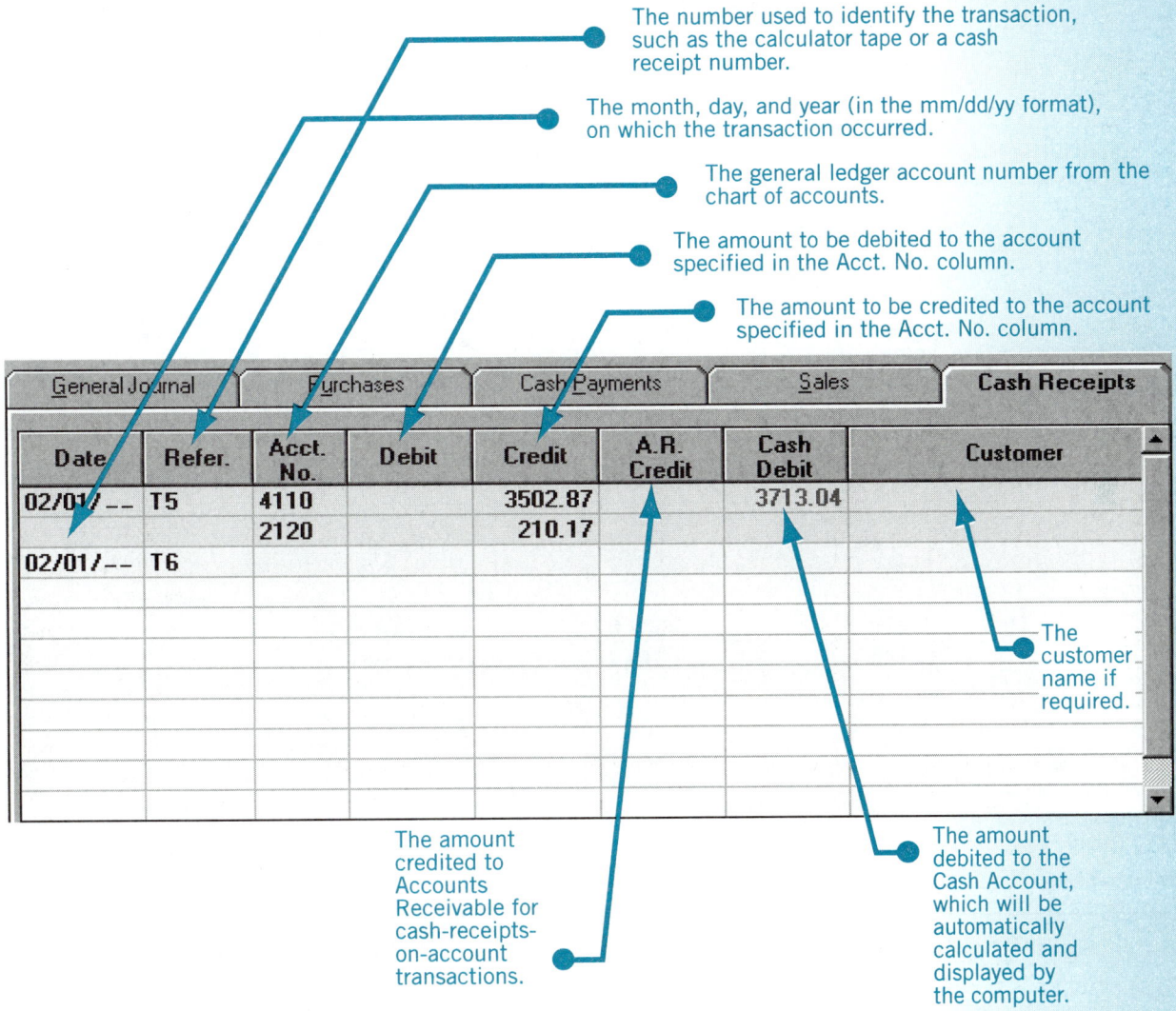

Figure 5.5
Cash Receipts Journal (Direct Receipt)

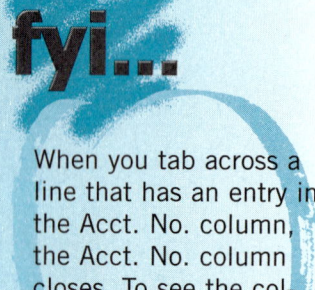

fyi...

When you tab across a line that has an entry in the Acct. No. column, the Acct. No. column closes. To see the column again, click in the Date column and press the Tab key.

There are two types of cash receipts: (1) direct receipt and (2) receipt on account. A **direct receipt** is a cash-receipt transaction that does *not* affect Accounts Receivable. Examples of direct receipts are cash sales, cash received from the sale of an asset, or cash received when money is borrowed. A **cash receipt on account** is a cash-receipt transaction that *does* affect Accounts Receivable. It involves a receipt of cash from a customer on account.

Direct Receipt A cash receipts journal with sample data for a direct cash-receipt transaction is shown in Figure 5.5. Notice that the Customer text box column is left blank. A customer is needed only for transactions that affect Accounts Receivable. The Cash Credit amount is automatically calculated and displayed by the computer. The account(s) credited will vary, depending on why the cash was received. A typical transaction is shown in Figure 5.5, with credits to Sales (account number 4110) and Sales Tax Payable (account number 2120).

Cash Receipt on Account A cash-receipt-on-account transaction is shown in the cash receipts journal illustrated in Figure 5.6. A customer name is required because the Accounts Receivable account is affected. The accounts receivable amount is entered in the Accounts Receivable Credit (A.R. Credit) text box column. The Cash Debit amount is automatically calculated and displayed by the computer.

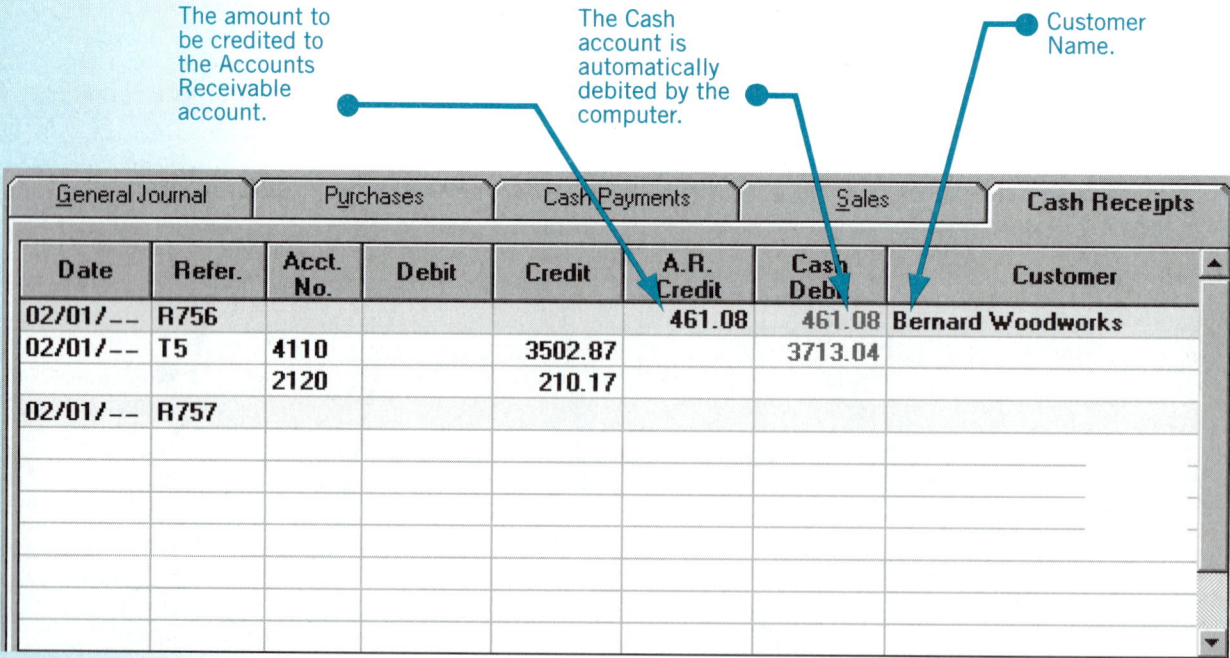

Figure 5.6
Cash Receipts Journal (Receipt on Account)

Chapter 5 Sales and Cash Receipts

JOURNAL REPORTS

After transactions have been entered, the journal reports can be displayed. Click the Reports toolbar button. When the Report Selection dialog box appears, choose the Journals option button from the Select a Report Group list. A list of all the reports within the chosen Journal option will appear, as shown in Figure 5.7.

Choose the desired journal report from the Choose a Report to Display list. Then click OK. The Journal Report Selection dialog box shown in Figure 5.8 will appear, allowing you to display all the journal entries for the chosen journal or customize your journal report. The operational procedures to customize all the journal reports listed are identical to the procedures you used for other journal reports in Chapters 2–4.

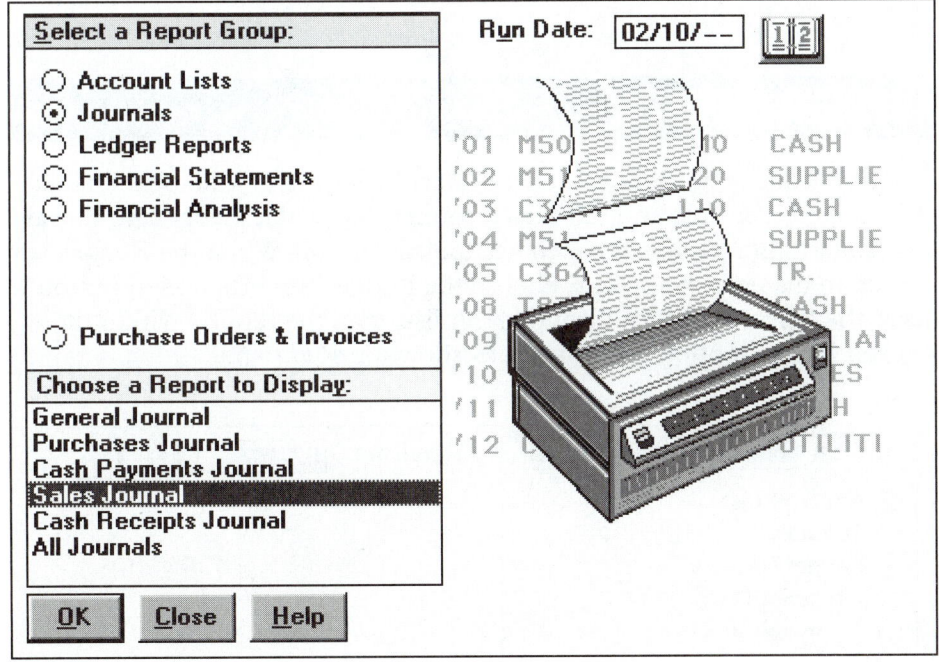

Figure 5.7
Report Selection Dialog Box

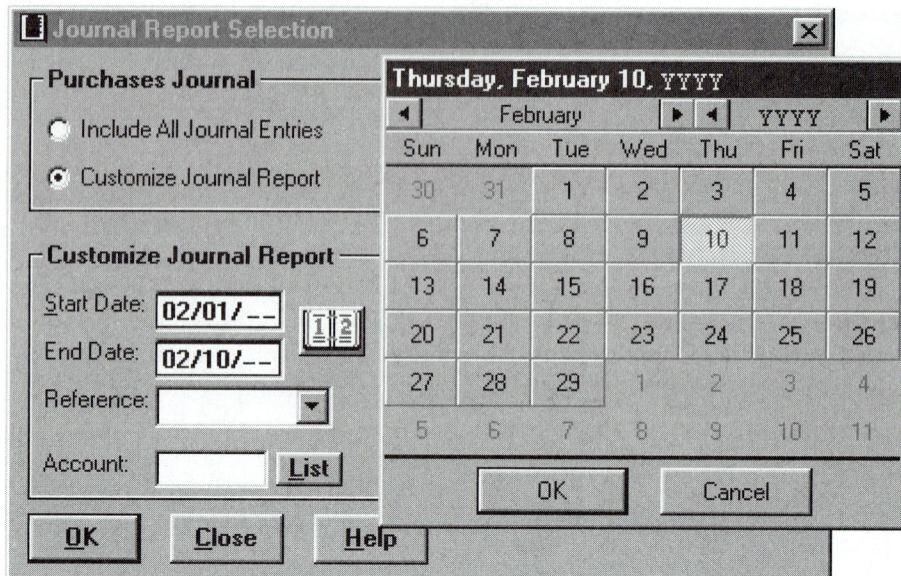

Figure 5.8
Journal Report Selection Dialog Box

LEDGER REPORTS

Two ledger reports for Accounts Receivable are (1) the Schedule of Accounts Receivable and (2) the Accounts Receivable Ledger. To display the ledger reports, click the Reports toolbar button. When the Report Selection dialog box appears, choose the Ledger Reports option button from the Select a Report Group list. A list of all the reports within the chosen Ledger option will appear, as shown in Figure 5.9.

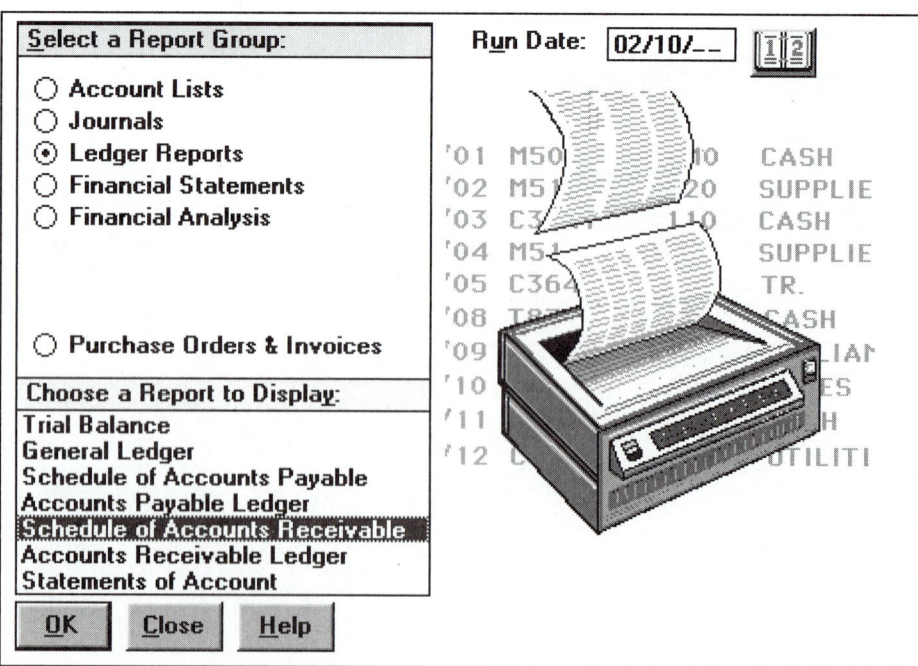

Figure 5.9
Ledger Report Selection Dialog Box

Chapter 5   Sales and Cash Receipts

Schedule of Accounts Receivable

The **Schedule of Accounts Receivable Report** is a report that lists each customer account balance and the total due from all customers. The total due from all customers must equal the balance in the Accounts Receivable account in the general ledger. A sample report is shown in Figure 5.10.

```
                    D & K Cabinet Tree
                Schedule of Accounts Receivable
                          02/10/--

Name                                              Balance

Bernard Woodworks                                 2000.00
Bursaw Cabinet Shop                                685.10
Cindy Lorentz                                      461.52
Demars Interiors                                  1325.00
Melvin Cabinetry Inc.                             1750.00
Oxnard Cabinet Masters                            1827.18

Total                                             8048.80
                                                 ========
```

Figure 5.10
Schedule of Accounts Receivable

Accounts Receivable Ledger Report

The **Accounts Receivable Ledger Report** is a report that shows detailed journal entry activity by customer. All the journal entries for the current fiscal period that affect each customer are listed. This information can be used to locate errors within a single account, in obtaining status information about a specific customer's activity, or in identifying transactions posted to the wrong customer.

When the Accounts Receivable Ledger Report is chosen, the Customer Range dialog box shown in Figure 5.11 will appear. Select the range of customers you wish to appear on the report.

Figure 5.11
Customer Range Dialog Box

The Accounts Receivable Ledger Report displaying customers Baer Kitchen Cabinets through Cindy Lorentz is shown in Figure 5.12.

```
                              D & K Cabinet Tree
                           Accounts Receivable Ledger
                                   02/10/--
```

Account	Journal	Date	Refer.	Debit	Credit	Balance
Baer Kitchen Cabinets						
	Balance Forward					340.63Dr
	Sales	02/02	S622	1560.00		1900.63Dr
	Cash Receipts	02/04	R760		340.63	1560.00Dr
	Cash Receipts	02/09	R762		1560.00	.00
Bernard Woodworks						
	Balance Forward					461.08Dr
	Cash Receipts	02/01	R756		461.08	.00
	Sales	02/03	S623	2000.00		2000.00Dr
Bursaw Cabinet Shop						
	Sales	02/03	S624	685.10		685.10Dr
Cindy Lorentz						
	Sales	02/10	S629	461.52		461.52Dr

Figure 5.12
Accounts Receivable Ledger Report

STATEMENTS OF ACCOUNT

A report that shows the customer name and date, description and amount of each sales invoice, payments on account, and total amount due for that customer is called a **statement of account**. Statements of account are mailed to customers to solicit payment.

Choose the Statements of Account Report from the Choose a Report to Display and click OK. The first statement of account will appear, as illustrated in Figure 5.13. Click Print to obtain a printed copy of the statement. Click the << and >> command buttons to scroll through the statements.

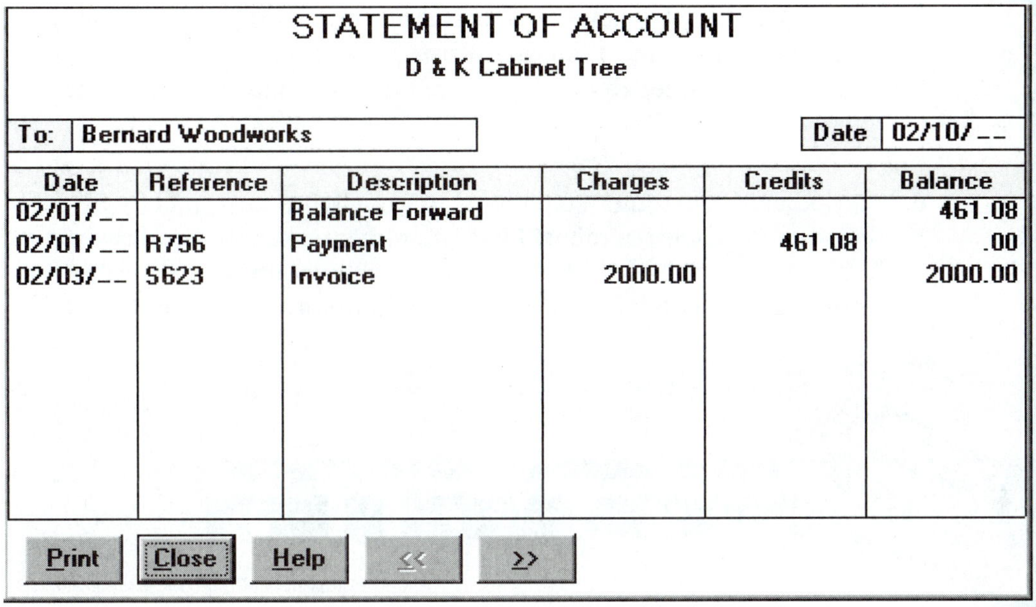

Chapter 5 Sales and Cash Receipts

STATEMENT OF ACCOUNT
D & K Cabinet Tree

To: Bernard Woodworks Date 02/10/__

Date	Reference	Description	Charges	Credits	Balance
02/01/__		Balance Forward			461.08
02/01/__	R756	Payment		461.08	.00
02/03/__	S623	Invoice	2000.00		2000.00

Print   Close   Help   <<   >>

Figure 5.13
Statement of Account

Chapter Review

1. Businesses or individuals to whom merchandise or services are sold are called customers. Customers must be added, changed, and deleted as necessary to maintain an up-to-date customer file.

2. Sales transactions may be for cash or on account. Sales-on-account transactions can be recorded on the sales journal input form or entered directly into the sales journal from the transaction.

3. A direct-receipt transaction does not affect Accounts Receivable. A cash-receipt-on-account transaction does affect Accounts Receivable. Both direct receipts and cash receipts on account can be recorded on the cash receipts journal input form or entered directly into the cash receipts journal.

4. Once all journal entries have been entered, the journal reports can be displayed. Sales and Cash Receipts Journal Reports can be customized by a date, reference, or account number restriction.

5. The Schedule of Accounts Receivable Report lists each customer account balance and total due from all customers. The Accounts Receivable Ledger Report shows detailed journal entry activity by customer.

6. Periodically, customer statements are mailed to customers with a balance to solicit payment. These statements of account show the customer name and date, description and amount of each sales invoice, payments on account, and total due for each customer.

ACCOUNTING CAREERS IN DEPTH

Tax Accountant

A tax accountant's job duties include:

- Preparing federal, state, or local tax returns for an individual, a business establishment, or another organization.
- Using a computer to examine accounts and records and compute taxes owed according to prescribed rates, laws, and regulations.
- Advising management regarding the effects of business activities on taxes and regarding strategies for minimizing tax liability.
- Ensuring that the business complies with periodic tax payment, information reporting, and other taxing authority requirements.
- Representing the business principal before taxing bodies.

Tax accountants also formulate tax strategies, involving issues such as financial choice, how to best treat a merger or acquisition, deferral of taxes, and when it is best to expense items. This work requires a thorough understanding of economics and the tax code.

Preparation for a career as a tax accountant includes completing a four-year college degree in accounting and, ideally, a cooperative experience within a business practicing tax accounting. Increasingly, large corporations are looking for persons with both an accounting and a legal background in tax. For example, a person with a J.D. (law) degree and a C.P.A. designation (Certified Public Accountant) would be especially desirable to many accounting firms. Students who pursue this route are also able to later set up self-employment and provide tax services to the public for a fee.

A career choice as a self-employed tax accountant is ideal for persons who prefer to work for themselves. This choice comes with a great responsibility. Many who choose this career path prefer to be certified as a Certified Public Accountant in order to eliminate accountability to others and to experience more autonomy in their work.

The skills required in addition to a college education include people skills, sales skills, communication skills, analytical skills, creative ability, initiative, computer skills, and a willingness to work 40–70 hours per week.

Tax accountants meet many people and can enjoy varied rewards when choosing to be self-employed. This form of work requires you to generate your own business, but it has the benefits of offering close customer contact, a high degree of independence and, depending on how good you are, considerable financial compensation.

TUTORIAL PROBLEM 5-T

In this tutorial problem, you will maintain customer accounts, enter sales and cash receipts journal entries, and display reports and graphs. You will enter sales and cash-receipt transactions that occurred for D & K Cabinet Tree during the period February 1 through 10 of the current year. These journal entries are illustrated in Figures 5.14 and 5.15. Any additions, changes, or deletions to customers have been provided.

Date	Refer.	Sales Credit	Sales Tax Credit	A.R. Debit	Customer
02/01/--	S621	410.50		410.50	Keller Quality Cabinets
02/02/--	S622	1560.00		1560.00	Baer Kitchen Cabinets
02/03/--	S623	2000.00		2000.00	Bernard Woodworks
02/03/--	S624	685.10		685.10	Bursaw Cabinet Shop
02/04/--	S625	621.54		621.54	Oxnard Cabinet Masters
02/05/--	S626	1750.00		1750.00	Melvin Cabinetry Inc.
02/10/--	S627	1325.00		1325.00	Demars Interiors
02/10/--	S628	1205.64		1205.64	Oxnard Cabinet Masters
02/10/--	S629	435.40	26.12	461.52	Cindy Lorentz

Figure 5.14
Sales Journal

Date	Refer.	Acct. No.	Debit	Credit	A.R. Credit	Cash Debit	Customer
02/01/--	R756				461.08	461.08	Bernard Woodworks
02/01/--	T5	4110		3502.87		3713.04	
		2120		210.17			
02/02/--	R757				302.96	302.96	Oxnard Cabinet Masters
02/03/--	R758				183.58	183.58	Keller Quality Cabinets
02/03/--	R759				310.55	310.55	Melvin Cabinetry Inc.
02/04/--	R760				340.63	340.63	Baer Kitchen Cabinets
02/08/--	T13	4110		2980.50		3159.33	
		2120		178.83			
02/08/--	R761				410.50	410.50	Keller Quality Cabinets
02/09/--	R762				1560.00	1560.00	Baer Kitchen Cabinets

Figure 5.15
Cash Receipts

STEP 1: **Start up *Automated Accounting 8.0*.**

STEP 2: **Load the opening balances template file named Problem 05-T.**

TUTORIAL PROBLEM 5-T

STEP 3: Enter your name in the User Name text box and click *OK*.

STEP 4: Save the file as 05-T Your Name.

STEP 5: Add Bursaw Cabinet Shop and Demars Interiors to the customer list. Change the name of the customer Melvin Wood Products to Melvin Cabinetry Inc., and delete J & M Fine Cabinetry from the customer list.

Click the *Accts.* toolbar icon and then click the *Customers* tab. Enter the customer maintenance.

STEP 6: Enter the journal entries from the sales and cash receipts journals shown in Figures 5.14 and 5.15.

Key the following information from the transaction statements or refer to Figures 5.16 and 5.17 for input data. The reference numbers have been abbreviated as follows: sales invoice, S; cash receipt, R; calculator tape, T.

Feb. 01 Sold merchandise on account to Keller Quality Cabinets, $410.50. S621.
   01 Received cash on account from Bernard Woodworks, $461.08, covering S617. R756.
   01 Recorded cash and credit card sales, $3,502.87, plus sales tax, $210.17 total, $3,713.04. T5.
   02 Sold merchandise on account to Baer Kitchen Cabinets, $1,560.00. S622.
   02 Received cash on account from Oxnard Cabinet Masters, $302.96, covering S620. R757.
   03 Received cash on account from Keller Quality Cabinets, $183.58, covering S616. R758.
   03 Received cash on account from Melvin Cabinetry Inc., $310.55, covering S618. R759.
   03 Sold merchandise on account to Bernard Woodworks, $2,000.00. S623.
   03 Sold merchandise on account to Bursaw Cabinet Shop, $685.10. S624.
   04 Received cash on account from Baer Kitchen Cabinets, $340.63, covering S617. R760.
   04 Sold merchandise on account to Oxnard Cabinet Masters, $621.54. S625.
   05 Sold merchandise on account to Melvin Cabinetry Inc., $1,750.00. S626.
   08 Recorded cash and credit card sales, $2,980.50, plus sales tax, $178.83; total, $3,159.33. T13.

Chapter 5 Sales and Cash Receipts

TUTORIAL PROBLEM 5-T

08 Received cash on account from Keller Quality Cabinets, $410.50, covering S621. R761.
09 Received cash on account from Baer Kitchen Cabinets, $1,560.00, covering S622. R762.
10 Sold merchandise on account to Demars Interiors, $1,325.00. S627.
10 Sold merchandise on account to Oxnard Cabinet Masters, $1,205.64. S628.
10 Sold merchandise on account to Cindy Lorentz, $435.40, plus sales tax, $26.12; total, $461.52. S629.

STEP 7: Display the customer list.
Click the *Reports* toolbar button. Select the *Account Lists* option button and choose *Customer List*. Click *OK*. Examine the customer report in Figure 5.16 and verify that the maintenance data you keyed in Step 5 is correct.

```
              D & K Cabinet Tree
                Customer List
                  02/10/--

Customer Name

Baer Kitchen Cabinets
Bernard Woodworks
Bursaw Cabinet Shop
Cindy Lorentz
Demars Interiors
Keller Quality Cabinets
Melvin Cabinetry Inc.
Odden Cabinets Unlimited
Oxnard Cabinet Masters
Pierce Millcraft Corp.
```

Figure 5.16
Customer List

STEP 8: Display the Sales Journal and Cash Receipts Journal Reports.
Select *Journals* from the Select a Report Group list. Choose the desired journal report from the Choose a Report to Display list and then click *OK*. Click *OK* to select *Include All Journal Entries*. The reports appear in Figures 5.17 and 5.18.

TUTORIAL PROBLEM 5-T

D & K Cabinet Tree
Sales Journal
02/10/--

Date	Inv. No.	Acct.	Title	Debit	Credit
02/01	S621	1130	AR/Keller Quality Cabinets	410.50	
02/01	S621	4110	Sales		410.50
02/02	S622	1130	AR/Baer Kitchen Cabinets	1560.00	
02/02	S622	4110	Sales		1560.00
02/03	S623	1130	AR/Bernard Woodworks	2000.00	
02/03	S623	4110	Sales		2000.00
02/03	S624	1130	AR/Bursaw Cabinet Shop	685.10	
02/03	S624	4110	Sales		685.10
02/04	S625	1130	AR/Oxnard Cabinet Masters	621.54	
02/04	S625	4110	Sales		621.54
02/05	S626	1130	AR/Melvin Cabinetry Inc.	1750.00	
02/05	S626	4110	Sales		1750.00
02/10	S627	1130	AR/Demars Interiors	1325.00	
02/10	S627	4110	Sales		1325.00
02/10	S628	1130	AR/Oxnard Cabinet Masters	1205.64	
02/10	S628	4110	Sales		1205.64
02/10	S629	1130	AR/Cindy Lorentz	461.52	
02/10	S629	4110	Sales		435.40
02/10	S629	2120	Sales Tax Payable		26.12
			Totals	10019.30	10019.30

Figure 5.17
Sales Journal Report

Since the Internet contains opinions as well as facts, don't be too quick to believe everything you read.

Chapter 5 Sales and Cash Receipts

TUTORIAL PROBLEM 5-T

D & K Cabinet Tree
Cash Receipts Journal
02/10/--

Date	Refer.	Acct.	Title	Debit	Credit
02/01	R756	1110	Cash	461.08	
02/01	R756	1130	AR/Bernard Woodworks		461.08
02/01	T5	1110	Cash	3713.04	
02/01	T5	4110	Sales		3502.87
02/01	T5	2120	Sales Tax Payable		210.17
02/02	R757	1110	Cash	302.96	
02/02	R757	1130	AR/Oxnard Cabinet Masters		302.96
02/03	R758	1110	Cash	183.58	
02/03	R758	1130	AR/Keller Quality Cabinets		183.58
02/03	R759	1110	Cash	310.55	
02/03	R759	1130	AR/Melvin Cabinetry Inc.		310.55
02/04	R760	1110	Cash	340.63	
02/04	R760	1130	AR/Baer Kitchen Cabinets		340.63
02/08	T13	1110	Cash	3159.33	
02/08	T13	4110	Sales		2980.50
02/08	T13	2120	Sales Tax Payable		178.83
02/08	R761	1110	Cash	410.50	
02/08	R761	1130	AR/Keller Quality Cabinets		410.50
02/09	R762	1110	Cash	1560.00	
02/09	R762	1130	AR/Baer Kitchen Cabinets		1560.00
			Totals	10441.67	10441.67

Figure 5.18
Cash Receipts Journal Report

TUTORIAL PROBLEM 5-T

STEP 9: Display a Trial Balance Report, a Schedule of Accounts Receivable Report, an Accounts Receivable Ledger Report for all customers, and a Statement of Account for Bernard Woodworks.

Select *Ledger Reports* from the Select a Report Group list. Choose the desired ledger report and then click *OK*. When displaying the Accounts Receivable Ledger Report, select the first customer in the From: text box and the last customer in the To: text box in the Customer Range dialog box. The reports appear in Figures 5.19 through 5.22.

```
                     D & K Cabinet Tree
                       Trial Balance
                         02/10/--

Acct.      Account
Number     Title                    Debit          Credit

1110       Cash                     24545.50
1120       Petty Cash                 100.00
1130       Accounts Receivable      8048.80
1140       Merchandise Inventory  131278.14
1145       Supplies--Office          1492.08
1150       Supplies--Store           2192.65
1160       Prepaid Insurance         1661.92
2110       Accounts Payable                         9651.55
2120       Sales Tax Payable                        1466.18
3110       James Doring, Capital                   81802.30
3120       James Doring, Drawing    1625.00
3130       Robert Kremer, Capital                  81802.30
3140       Robert Kremer, Drawing   1985.00
4110       Sales                                   16476.55
5110       Purchases               15277.49
6120       Miscellaneous Expense     220.50
6130       Rent Expense             2475.00
6160       Utilities Expense         296.80
                                   ----------      ----------
           Totals                  191198.88       191198.88
                                   ==========      ==========
```

Figure 5.19
Trial Balance Report

Chapter 5 Sales and Cash Receipts

TUTORIAL PROBLEM 5-T

```
                D & K Cabinet Tree
             Schedule of Accounts Receivable
                     02/10/--

Name                                          Balance

Bernard Woodworks                             2000.00
Bursaw Cabinet Shop                            685.10
Cindy Lorentz                                  461.52
Demars Interiors                              1325.00
Melvin Cabinetry Inc.                         1750.00
Oxnard Cabinet Masters                        1827.18
                                             --------
Total                                         8048.80
                                             ========
```

Figure 5.20
Schedule of Accounts Receivable Report

```
                        D & K Cabinet Tree
                     Accounts Receivable Ledger
                             02/10/--

Account     Journal         Date      Refer.    Debit      Credit     Balance

Baer Kitchen Cabinets
            Balance Forward                                            340.63Dr
            Sales            02/02    S622    1560.00                 1900.63Dr
            Cash Receipts    02/04    R760                  340.63    1560.00Dr
            Cash Receipts    02/09    R762                 1560.00         .00

Bernard Woodworks
            Balance Forward                                            461.08Dr
            Cash Receipts    02/01    R756                  461.08         .00
            Sales            02/03    S623    2000.00                 2000.00Dr

Bursaw Cabinet Shop
            Sales            02/03    S624     685.10                  685.10Dr

                                                                     (continued)
```

Figure 5.21
Accounts Receivable Ledger Report

TUTORIAL PROBLEM 5-T

Account	Journal	Date	Refer.	Debit	Credit	Balance
Cindy Lorentz						
	Sales	02/10	S629	461.52		461.52Dr
Demars Interiors						
	Sales	02/10	S627	1325.00		1325.00Dr
Keller Quality Cabinets						
	Balance Forward					183.58Dr
	Sales	02/01	S621	410.50		594.08Dr
	Cash Receipts	02/03	R758		183.58	410.50Dr
	Cash Receipts	02/08	R761		410.50	.00
Melvin Cabinetry Inc.						
	Balance Forward					310.55Dr
	Cash Receipts	02/03	R759		310.55	.00
	Sales	02/05	S626	1750.00		1750.00Dr
Odden Cabinets Unlimited						
	*** No Activity ***					.00
Oxnard Cabinet Masters						
	Balance Forward					302.96Dr
	Cash Receipts	02/02	R757		302.96	.00
	Sales	02/04	S625	621.54		621.54Dr
	Sales	02/10	S628	1205.64		1827.18Dr
Pierce Millcraft Corp.						
	*** No Activity ***					.00

Figure 5.21
Continued

STEP 10: Generate a sales graph.
Click the *Graphs* toolbar button. Click the *Sales* button. The sales graph illustrating the daily sales for February 1 through February 10 is shown in Figure 5.23.

STEP 11: Save your data file.

TUTORIAL PROBLEM 5-T

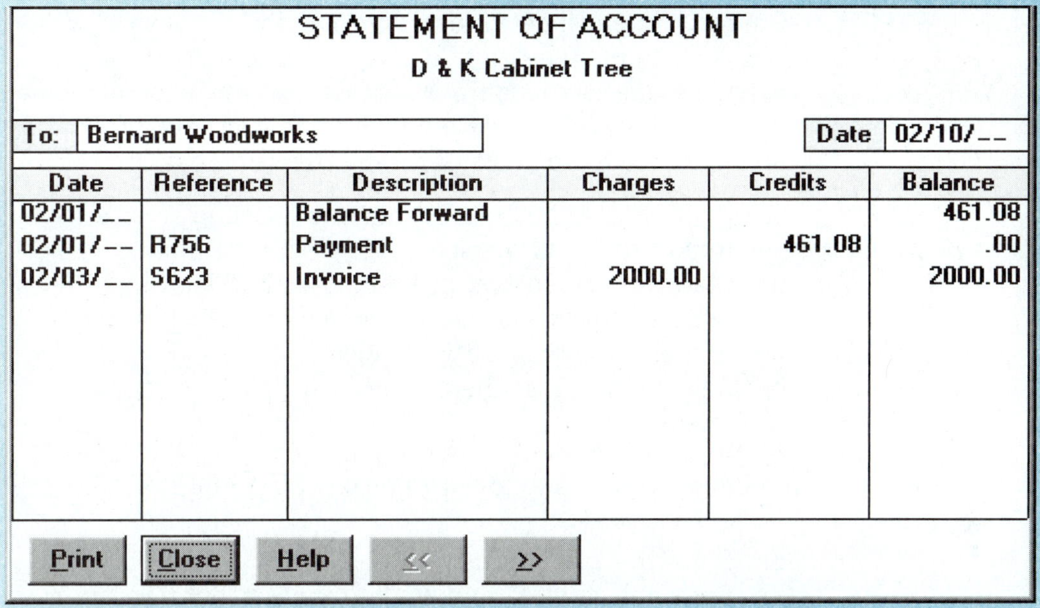

STATEMENT OF ACCOUNT
D & K Cabinet Tree

To: Bernard Woodworks   Date: 02/10/__

Date	Reference	Description	Charges	Credits	Balance
02/01/__		Balance Forward			461.08
02/01/__	R756	Payment		461.08	.00
02/03/__	S623	Invoice	2000.00		2000.00

[Print] [Close] [Help] [<<] [>>]

Figure 5.22
Statement of Account—Bernard Woodworks

Figure 5.23
Sales Bar Graph

TUTORIAL PROBLEM 5-T

STEP 12: Optional Spreadsheet Integration Activity.
D & K Cabinet Tree has asked you to use a spreadsheet to calculate the component percentage owed by each customer as of February 10. Prepare a report showing this information and generate a pie chart depicting the same data.

a. Display and copy the Schedule of Accounts Receivable Report to the clipboard in spreadsheet format.
b. Start up your spreadsheet software and load the template file named AA8 Spreadsheet 05-T. A blank, formatted worksheet will appear.
c. Select cell B1 as the current cell, if not already selected.
d. Paste the Schedule of Accounts Receivable Report (copied to the clipboard in Step 12a) into the spreadsheet.
e. Enter the word *Percent* in cell D7.
Enter the formula to calculate the percent owed in cell D9. For example, (+C9/+$C$16).
Copy and paste the formula in cell D9 to cells D10, D11, D12, D13, and D14.
f. Format the amounts in currency format and the calculated percentages in percentage format, if necessary.
g. Generate a pie chart. Select the range of cells B9 through C14, and then choose the Chart or Graph menu item from the spreadsheet program you are using. Choose Pie Chart if the graph that appears is not a pie chart. If the computer asks for a graph name, etc., use *Customers*. Finally, if the spreadsheet you are using permits copying and pasting the graph into the worksheet, copy and paste the graph into cells A22 through E40.
h. Save your spreadsheet data with a file name of 05-T Your Name.
i. Print the spreadsheet and pie chart. The completed spreadsheet and pie chart are shown in Figure 5.24.
j. What if Bursaw Cabinet Shop's balance is $1,200.00 and Melvin Cabinetry Inc.'s balance is now $2,950.00? Enter these changes and the formula to compute a new Total. Observe the affect of the changes on the component percentages and pie chart.
k. End your spreadsheet session without saving your changes made in step 12j.

TUTORIAL PROBLEM 5-T

Student Name
D & K Cabinet Tree
Schedule of Accounts Receivable
As of 02/10/--

Name	Balance	Percent
Bernard Woodworks	$2,000.00	24.85%
Bursaw Cabinet Shop	$685.10	8.51%
Cindy Lorentz	$461.52	5.73%
Demars Interiors	$1,325.00	16.46%
Melvin Cabinetry Inc.	$1,750.00	21.74%
Oxnard Cabinet Masters	$1,827.18	22.70%
Total	$8,048.80	

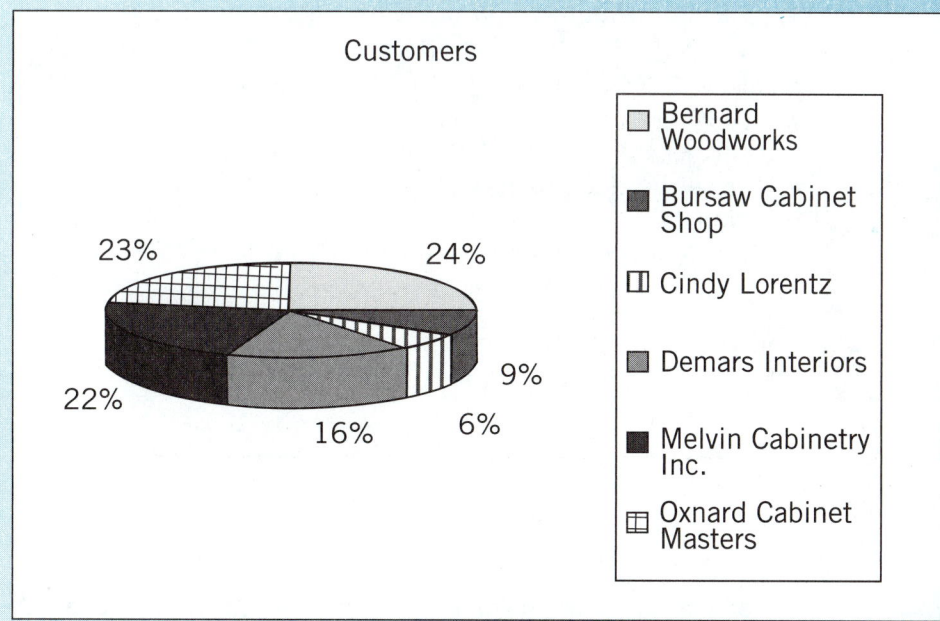

Figure 5.24
Customer Component Percentage Report and Pie Chart

TUTORIAL PROBLEM 5-T

STEP 13: **Optional Word Processing Integration Activity.**
D & K Cabinet Tree consults with Hicks & Associates, a local accounting firm, for financial advice. As part of the information needed, Sara Hicks, owner and CPA of the accounting firm, has asked that you fax her a list of the customers with their account balances at the end of each week. You are to use the word processing fax template used by D & K Cabinet Tree to prepare this document for the week ended February 10.

a. Display and copy the Schedule of Accounts Receivable to the clipboard in word processing format.
b. Start up your word processing application software and load the template file named AA8 Wordprocessing 05-T as a text file.
c. Enter your name in the FROM: field and complete the remainder of the top portion of the facsimile, as shown in Figure 5.25.
d. Position the insertion point two lines after the text in the Notes/Comments section and paste the report. Delete report headings, totals, etc., and format the document to match Figure 5.25. Experiment adding further enhancement to the appearance of the fax.
e. Save the document with a file name of 05-T Your Name.
f. Print the completed document.
g. End your word processing session.

STEP 14: **End your *Automated Accounting* session.**

Telnet is a computer program that permits you to connect to another computer system.

Remember that e-mail can be traced to the source, so whatever you write in an e-mail message should be considered seriously. Inappropriate activities can and will be pursued by legal authorities.

Chapter 5 Sales and Cash Receipts

TUTORIAL PROBLEM 5-T

D & K Cabinet Tree
65 Maple Lane
Minneapolis, MN 55435-1282
(503) 555-8511

FACSIMILE

TO: Sara Hicks, CPA
COMPANY: Hicks & Associates
DATE: February 10, Current Year
PHONE NUMBER: (612) 555-7460
FAX NUMBER: (612) 555-7497
FROM: Your Name
SUBJECT: END-OF-THE-WEEK CUSTOMER ACCOUNT BALANCES

Notes/Comments:

As per your request, our customers and their account balances as of February 10 are:

Bernard Woodworks	$ 2,000.00
Bursaw Cabinet Shop	685.10
Cindy Lorentz	461.52
Demars Interiors	1,325.00
Melvin Cabinetry Inc.	1,750.00
Oxnard Cabinet Masters	1,827.18

Figure 5.25
Completed Facsimile

Webmasters are the people who create, organize, and manage Websites for schools, businesses, and governmental organizations.

Use caution on the Internet! Think carefully before ever giving out your password, name, personal address, phone number, or credit card numbers.

Review And Practice: Applying Your Information Skills

I. MATCHING

Directions: In the *Working Papers*, write the letter of the appropriate term next to each definition.

    a. Accounts Receivable Ledger Report
    b. cash receipt
    c. cash receipt on account
    d. cash receipts journal
    e. cash receipts journal input form
    f. customer
    g. direct receipt
    h. sales invoice
    i. sales journal
    j. sales journal input form
    k. sales transaction
    l. Schedule of Accounts Receivable Report
    m. statement of account

1. A transaction in which merchandise is sold in exchange for another asset, usually money.
2. An input form used to record only sales-on-account transactions.
3. A report that shows the customer name and date, description and amount of each sales invoice, payments on account, and total amount due for that customer.
4. A report that shows detailed journal entry activity by customer.
5. An input form used to record all cash-receipt transactions.
6. Any type of transaction involving the receipt of cash.
7. A cash-receipt transaction that does *not* affect Accounts Receivable.
8. A cash-receipt transaction that *does* affect Accounts Receivable.
9. A business or individual to whom merchandise or services are sold.
10. A report that lists each customer account balance and total due from all customers.
11. A special journal used to enter only sales-of-merchandise-on-account transactions.
12. A special journal used to enter all cash-receipt transactions.
13. A form used to describe the goods sold, the quantity, and the price.

Chapter 5   Sales and Cash Receipts

II. REVIEW QUESTIONS

Directions: Write the answers to the following questions in the *Working Papers*.

1. How are customers added to the accounting system?
2. List the two types of sales transactions.
3. List the two types of cash receipts.
4. List the two accounts receivable ledger reports.
5. Why are statements of account generated?

III. INTERNET ACTIVITY

Directions: If you have access to the Internet, use the browser to locate your state's Web page or link (use the name of your state and *US* as your search terms, such as *Minneapolis US*). Find the link to your state government's Department of Finance. Report on your state's taxes, tax incentives for new businesses, or any other information regarding the business climate of your state. Be sure to include the source and the URL (Internet address) of your search.

Independent Practice Problem 5-P

In this problem, you will process any additions, changes, or deletions to customers. You will also process the sales and cash-receipt transactions for the period February 11 through February 20 of the current year.

STEP 1: Start up *Automated Accounting 8.0*.

STEP 2: Load the file named AA8 Problem 05-P.

STEP 3: Enter your name in the User Name text box.

STEP 4: Save the file as 05-P Your Name.

STEP 5: Enter the following transactions:

Feb. 11   Received cash on account from Oxnard Cabinet Masters, $621.54, covering S625. R763.

11   Sold merchandise on account to Ritter Cabinet Company, $565.00. S630. Add Ritter Cabinet Company to the customer list. Delete customer Pierce Millcraft Corp.

12   Sold merchandise on account to Baer Kitchen Cabinets, $325.43. S631.

12 Sold merchandise on account to Melvin Cabinetry Inc., $899.95. S632.
15 Recorded cash and credit card sales, $2,685.50, plus sales tax, $161.13; total, $2,846.63. T20.
15 Received cash on account from Melvin Cabinetry Inc., $1,750.00, covering S626. R764.
15 Received cash on account from Bursaw Cabinet Co., $685.10, covering S624. R765. Change the customer name of Bursaw Cabinet Shop to Bursaw Cabinet Co.
16 Sold merchandise on account to Keller Quality Cabinets, $518.64. S633.
16 Sold merchandise on account to Bernard Woodworks, $500.00. S634.
16 Received cash on account from Oxnard Cabinet Masters, $1,205.64, covering S628. R766.
17 Sold merchandise on account to Demars Interiors, $665.35. S635.
17 Sold merchandise on account to Bursaw Cabinet Co., $538.00. S636.
18 Recorded cash and credit card sales, $2,240.18, plus sales tax, $134.41; total, $2,374.59. T23.
18 Sold merchandise on account to Oxnard Cabinet Masters, $311.47. S637.
18 Sold merchandise on account to Cindy Lorentz, $225.00, plus sales tax, $13.50; total, $238.50. S638.
19 Received cash on account from Demars Interiors, $1,325.00, covering S627. R767.
19 Received cash on account from Ritter Cabinet Company, $565.00, covering S630. R768.
19 Sold merchandise on account to Marso Cabinet Works, $492.15. S639. Add Marso Cabinet Works to the customer list.
20 Received cash on account from Cindy Lorentz, $461.52, covering S629. R769.

STEP 6: Display a customer list.

STEP 7: Display the sales and cash receipts journals for the period February 11 through February 20 of the current year. If errors are detected, make corrections.

STEP 8: Display the following ledger reports: Trial Balance, Schedule of Accounts Receivable, Accounts Receivable Ledger (all customers), and Statement of Account (first customer).

STEP 9: Generate a sales graph.

Chapter 5   Sales and Cash Receipts

STEP 10: **Save your data file.**

STEP 11: **Optional Spreadsheet Integration Activity.**
D & K Cabinet Tree has asked you to use a spreadsheet to calculate the component percentage owed by each customer as of February 20. Prepare a report showing this information and generate a pie chart depicting the same data.

  a. Display and copy the Schedule of Accounts Receivable Report to the clipboard in spreadsheet format.
  b. Start up your spreadsheet software and load the template file named AA8 Spreadsheet 05-T.
  c. Select cell B1 as the current cell and paste the Schedule of Accounts Receivable Report into the spreadsheet.
  d. Enter the word *Percent* in cell D7.
     Enter the formula to calculate the percent owed in cell D9.
     Copy and paste the formula in cell D9 to the appropriate cells.
  e. Format the amounts in currency format and the calculated percentages in percentage format, if necessary.
  f. Generate a pie chart depicting the data in the report.
  g. Save your spreadsheet data with a file name of 05-P Your Name.
  h. Print the spreadsheet and pie chart.
  i. What if Baer Kitchen Cabinets' balance is $995.25 and Melvin Cabinetry Inc.'s balance is now $1,369.95? Enter these changes and the formula to compute a new total. Observe the effect of the changes on the component percentages and pie chart.
  j. End your spreadsheet session without saving your changes made in Step 11i, and return to the *Automated Accounting* application.

STEP 12: **Optional Word Processing Integration Activity.**
You are to use the company's word processing fax template to prepare the customer account balance information for the accounting firm covering the week ended February 20.

  a. Display and copy the Schedule of Accounts Receivable Report to the clipboard in word processing format.
  b. Start up your word processing application software and load the template file named AA8 Wordprocessing 05-T as a text file. *Note:* As an alternative, and if completed, load the solution word processing file from Tutorial Problem 5-T and modify it as necessary to complete this activity.

c. Enter your name in the FROM: field and complete the remainder of the top portion of the facsimile, as shown in Figure 5.25.
d. Paste the report, delete report headings, totals, etc., and format the document to match Figure 5.25.
e. Save the document with a file name of 05-P Your Name.
f. Print the completed document.
g. End your word processing session.

STEP 13: End the *Automated Accounting* session.

Applying Your Technology Skills 5-P

Directions: Using Independent Practice Problem 5-P, write the answers to the following questions in the *Working Papers*.

1. What are the totals of the debit and credit columns in the Sales Journal Report?

2. From the Sales Journal Report, what is the amount of Invoice No. 635?

3. What is the amount of cash received from Ritter Cabinet Company on Cash Receipt No. 768?

4. What is the current balance in Accounts Receivable?

5. What is the current balance in the Sales Tax Payable account?

6. What is the current balance for Oxnard Cabinet Masters?

7. What is the total due from customers as of February 20?

8. List the amounts of the cash receipts transactions for Oxnard Cabinet Masters for the period February 11 through February 20.

9. How many sales were made to Melvin Cabinetry Inc., during the period February 11 through February 20?

Mastery Problem 5-M

In this problem, you will process any additions, changes, or deletions to customers. You will also process sales and cash-receipt transactions for the period February 21 through February 28 of the current year.

Directions: Abbreviate the reference numbers as follows: Sales invoice no., S; Cash receipt no., C; Calculator tape, T.

Chapter 5 Sales and Cash Receipts

STEP 1: Start up *Automated Accounting 8.0* and load the file named AA8 Problem 05-M.

STEP 2: Enter your name in the User Name text box.

STEP 3: Save the file as 05-M Your Name.

STEP 4: Enter the customer maintenance and transactions.

Feb. 22 Sold merchandise on account to Baer Kitchen Cabinets, $331.05. S640.

22 Sold merchandise on account to Ritter Cabinet Company, $410.12. S641.

23 Received cash on account from Bernard Woodworks, $2,000.00, covering S623. R770.

23 Sold merchandise on account to Melvin Cabinetry Inc., $362.95. S642.

23 Recorded cash and credit card sales, $1,853.17, plus sales tax, $111.19; total, $1,964.36. T28.

24 Sold merchandise on account to Bursaw Cabinet Co., $498.73. S643.

24 Sold merchandise on account to Cindy Lorentz, $124.50, plus sales tax, $7.47; total, $131.97. S644.

24 Received cash on account from Baer Kitchen Cabinets, $325.43, covering S631. R771.

25 Received cash on account from Melvin Cabinetry Inc., $899.95, covering S632. R772.

25 Received cash on account from Demars Interiors, $665.35, covering S635. R773.

25 Sold merchandise on account to Slater Finished Cabinets, $326.43. S645. Add Slater Finished Cabinets to the customer list. Delete customer Odden Cabinets Unlimited.

25 Sold merchandise on account to Demars Interiors, $98.95. S646.

26 Recorded cash and credit card sales, $1,572.68, plus sales tax, $94.36; total, $1,667.04. T31.

26 Received cash on account from Bernard Woodworks, $500.00, covering S634. R774.

26 Received cash on account from Bursaw Cabinet Co., $538.00, covering S636. R775.

26 Sold merchandise on account to Keller Quality Cabinets, $65.00. S647.

27 Received cash on account from Oxnard Cabinet Masters, $311.47, covering S637. R776.

28 Sold merchandise on account to Marso Millcraft, Inc., $336.50. S648. Change the customer name of Marso Cabinet Works to Marso Millcraft, Inc.

STEP 5: Display the following reports for the period February 21 through February 28 of the current year: Customer List, Sales and Cash Receipts Journal Reports, Trial Balance, Schedule of Accounts Receivable, Accounts Receivable Ledger (all customers), and Statement of Account (first customer).

STEP 6: Generate a sales graph.

STEP 7: Save your data.

STEP 8: Optional Spreadsheet Integration Activity.
Prepare a report showing the component percentage owed by each customer and generate a pie chart depicting this data as of February 28.

a. Display and copy the Schedule of Accounts Receivable Report to the clipboard in spreadsheet format.
b. Start up your spreadsheet software and load the template file named AA8 Spreadsheet 05-T.
c. Select cell B1 as the current cell and paste the Schedule of Accounts Receivable Report into the spreadsheet.
d. Enter the labels and formulas required to report and compute the customer component percentages, using the format illustrated in Figure 5.24.
e. Generate a pie chart depicting the data in the report.
f. Save your spreadsheet data with a file name of 05-M Your Name.
g. Print the spreadsheet and pie chart.
h. What if Demars Interiors' balance is $265.00 and Ritter Cabinet Company's balance is now $1,680.00? Enter these changes and the formula to compute a new total. Observe the effect of the changes on the component percentages and pie chart.
i. End your spreadsheet session without saving your changes from Step 8h, and return to the *Automated Accounting* application.

STEP 9: Optional Word Processing Integration Activity.

a. Display and copy the Schedule of Accounts Receivable Report to the clipboard in word processing format.
b. Start up your word processing application software and load the template file named AA8 Wordprocessing 05-T as a text file. *Note:* As an alternative, and if completed, load your solution word processing file from either Tutorial Problem 5-T or Independent Practice Problem 5-P and modify it as necessary to complete this activity.

Chapter 5 Sales and Cash Receipts

c. Enter your name in the FROM: field and complete the remainder of the top portion of the facsimile, as shown in Figure 5.25. Paste the report, delete report headings, totals, etc., and format the document as necessary.
d. Save the document with a file name of 05-M Your Name.
e. Print the completed document.
f. End your word processing session.

STEP 10: **End your *Automated Accounting* session.**

Applying Your Technology Skills 5-M

Directions: Using Mastery Problem 5-M, write the answers to the following questions in the *Working Papers*.

1. In the Sales Journal Report, what is the amount debited to Slater Finished Cabinets for Invoice No. 645?

2. In the Sales Journal Report, what is the amount of sales tax for Invoice No. 644 to Cindy Lorentz?

3. What is the total of the debit column in the cash receipts journal?

4. What is the balance in the Sales Tax Payable account?

5. What is the balance in the Sales account?

6. What is the balance due from Bursaw Cabinet Co. on February 28?

7. What is the total amount due from all customers as of February 28?

8. From the Trial Balance, what is the balance in the Accounts Receivable account?

9. From the Accounts Receivable Ledger Report, what is the amount of Invoice No. 647 to Keller Quality Cabinets?

Chapter 6

END OF FISCAL PERIOD FOR A PARTNERSHIP (MERCHANDISING BUSINESS)

LEARNING OBJECTIVES

Upon completion of this chapter, you will be able to:

1. Process the adjusting entries for a merchandising business.
2. Generate the financial statements for a merchandising business organized as a partnership.
3. Complete the period-end closing process for a partnership.

Chapter 6 End of Fiscal Period for a Partnership (Merchandising Business)

INTRODUCTION

In previous chapters, you performed computerized accounting activities for businesses that were organized as sole proprietorships. In this chapter, you will learn how to complete the end-of-fiscal-period processing for a merchandising business that is organized as a partnership. A partnership is a business that is owned by two or more persons. Many small businesses are organized as partnerships in an effort to take advantage of the combined capital, managerial experience, and expertise of two or more individuals.

To complete the accounting cycle for a partnership, adjusting entries can be recorded on the general journal input form, entered into the computer, and verified for accuracy. Financial statements are then generated. After the financial statements have been produced, period-end closing can be completed.

ADJUSTING ENTRIES

Adjusting entries are entered after all other transactions for the accounting period have been processed and posted. A Trial Balance and the period-end adjustment data are the basis for the adjusting entries. A

Although the term "ethics" may seem theoretical or abstract, sometimes employees must make decisions about ethics in the workplace.

Consider the following case: An executive responsible for a business's finances gives a computer programmer in the company some detailed formulas in order to develop a program that will produce a report for investors showing the business's financial condition. While writing the program, the programmer discovers that the financial reports that will be generated by the new program will incorrectly show that the finances of the company are better than they really are. When the programmer tells the executive of this discovery, the programmer is told to follow the specifications or be fired.

Critical Thinking

1. What would you do if you were the programmer?

2. Do you think that what the programmer was asked to do was ethical or unethical?

3. Could the programmer be considered to have committed a computer crime if he or she knowingly participated in producing a report that deceived investors? Explain your response.

Trial Balance for D & K Cabinet Tree is shown in Figure 6.1. Recall that in Chapter 4, the purchases and cash-payments transactions were processed, and in Chapter 5, the sales and cash-receipt transactions were processed for the month of February. Therefore, D & K Cabinet Tree's transactions for the accounting period have already been processed and posted. The period-end adjustment data for D & K Cabinet Tree are as follows:

Balances on February 28:
Merchandise inventory $124,050.00
Office supplies inventory $560.00
Store supplies inventory $845.00
Value of insurance policies on February 28 . . . . . . $485.00

D & K Cabinet Tree
Trial Balance
02/28/--

Acct. Number	Account Title	Debit	Credit
1110	Cash	45252.12	
1120	Petty Cash	100.00	
1130	Accounts Receivable	3810.99	
1140	Merchandise Inventory	131278.14	
1145	Supplies--Office	1492.08	
1150	Supplies--Store	2192.65	
1160	Prepaid Insurance	1661.92	
2110	Accounts Payable		9651.55
2120	Sales Tax Payable		1988.24
3110	James Doring, Capital		81802.30
3120	James Doring, Drawing	1625.00	
3130	Robert Kremer, Capital		81802.30
3140	Robert Kremer, Drawing	1985.00	
4110	Sales		32423.30
5110	Purchases	15277.49	
6120	Miscellaneous Expense	220.50	
6130	Rent Expense	2475.00	
6160	Utilities Expense	296.80	
	Totals	207667.69	207667.69

Figure 6.1
Trial Balance Before Adjusting Entries

The adjusting entries are entered into the general journal. All adjusting entries occur on the same date and have the same reference, Adj.Ent. Each adjusting entry should be entered and posted separately.

Chapter 6 End of Fiscal Period for a Partnership (Merchandising Business)

The adjusting entries shown in the general journal illustrated in Figure 6.2 were derived from the period-end adjustment data and Trial Balance shown in Figure 6.1.

Just as in a manual accounting system, the changes in inventory resulting from purchases and sales transactions are not reflected in the Merchandise Inventory account of the automated accounting system. Therefore, the Merchandise Inventory account balance must be adjusted to reflect the changes resulting from purchases and sales during the fiscal period. Two accounts are used to adjust the merchandise inventory: Merchandise Inventory and Income Summary.

Notice in Figure 6.1 that before the adjustment, the Merchandise Inventory account has a debit balance of $131,278.14. The actual count of merchandise on February 28 shows that the inventory is valued at $124,050.00. The first adjusting entry in Figure 6.2 shows that Merchandise Inventory, account number 1140, is credited for $7,228.14, which is the difference between the current account balance of $131,278.14 and actual inventory on hand of $124,050.00. Income Summary, account number 3150, is debited for $7,228.14. If the current account balance of merchandise inventory is less than the actual amount of merchandise on hand, opposite entries would be made—that is, Merchandise Inventory would be debited and Income Summary would be credited.

Date	Refer.	Account	Debit	Credit	Vendor/Customer
02/28/--	Adj.Ent.	3150 Income Summary	7228.14		
		1140 Merchandise Inventory		7228.14	
02/28/--	Adj.Ent.	6140 Supplies Expense--Office	932.08		
		1145 Supplies--Office		932.08	
02/28/--	Adj.Ent.	6150 Supplies Expense--Store	1347.65		
		1150 Supplies--Store		1347.65	
02/28/--	Adj.Ent.	6110 Insurance Expense	1176.92		
		1160 Prepaid Insurance		1176.92	

Figure 6.2
General Journal (Adjusting Entries)

Adjustments that are made to Office Supplies, Store Supplies, and Insurance use their related temporary expense account. For example, in the second adjusting entry in Figure 6.2, when Supplies—Office, account number 1145, is adjusted, Supplies Expense—Office, account number 6140, is the related temporary expense account that is used.

FINANCIAL STATEMENTS

The financial statements generated by *Automated Accounting 8.0* for a nondepartmentalized merchandising business organized as a partnership are the income statement and the balance sheet. The Report Selection dialog box is shown in Figure 6.3. For businesses that account for budget data, a Performance Report will be available. Performance Reports will be discussed in a later chapter.

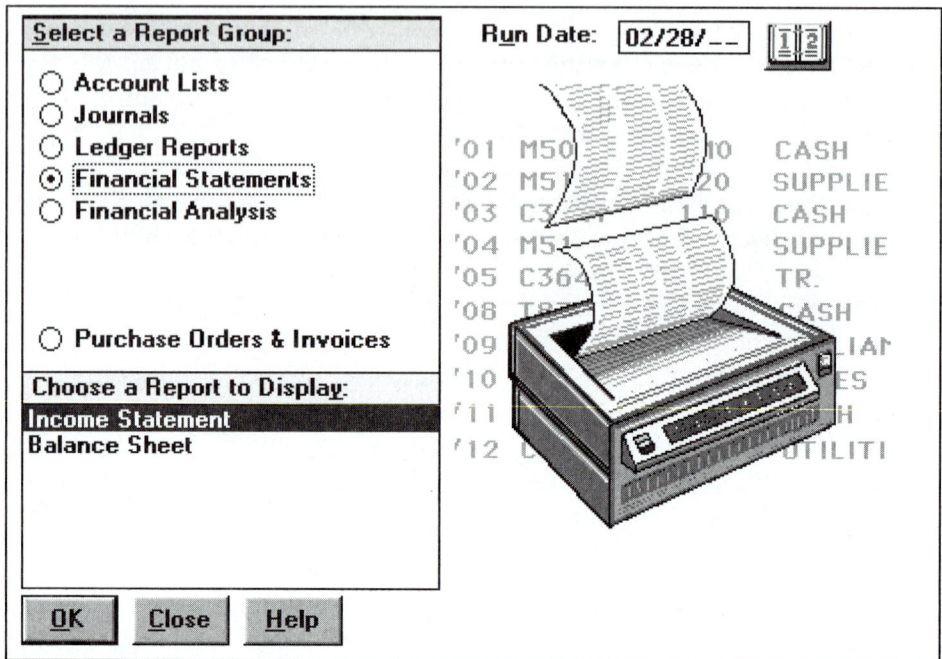

Figure 6.3
Report Selection Dialog Box

PERIOD-END CLOSING FOR A PARTNERSHIP

At the end of the fiscal period in a manual accounting system, closing entries are recorded in the general journal and posted to the general ledger. In an automated accounting system, the software generates and posts the entries to close the temporary accounts to the Income Summary account. An Income Summary account is used to summarize the closing entries for the revenue and expense accounts.

Partnerships have many different methods of distributing income, including allocating income on the basis of service rendered and on the basis of capital invested. The software automatically closes net income to the partners' capital accounts when income or loss is to be distributed equally among all partners. For a partnership with equal distribution of income or loss, the software generates and posts the entries to close out the revenue and expense accounts in the Income Summary account, distributes the balance in the Income Summary account to the partners'

Chapter 6 End of Fiscal Period for a Partnership (Merchandising Business)

capital accounts, and closes the partners' drawing accounts. Also, during the posting process, the software copies the current account balances and stores them as last fiscal period's account balances.

If the partnership has an unequal distribution of income or loss, closing entries will be generated and posted that will close out the revenue and expense accounts to the Income Summary account. The difference between revenue and expenses will be the partnership's net income or loss. Journal entries must then be made to distribute the net income or loss from the Income Summary account to the partners' capital accounts and to close the partners' drawing accounts to their respective capital accounts.

When the Generate Closing Journal Entries menu item is chosen from the Options menu, a dialog box will appear, asking if you want to generate closing journal entries. Click the Yes command button to proceed. A second dialog box showing the closing journal entries generated by the software will appear, as illustrated in Figure 6.4. Click the Post command button to proceed with the closing.

The distribution of net income to partners is set up when a business creates its opening balances file. If distribution is set as equal, the closing entry to distribute net income to partners is made automatically. If the distribution is not equal, the closing entries to distribute net income to partners are not made automatically. In this case, the closing entries must be entered in the general journal and posted.

Acct. #	Account Title	Debit	Credit
4110	Sales	32423.30	
3150	Income Summary		32423.30
3150	Income Summary	21726.44	
5110	Purchases		15277.49
6110	Insurance Expense		1176.92
6120	Miscellaneous Expense		220.50
6130	Rent Expense		2475.00
6140	Supplies Expense--Office		932.08
6150	Supplies Expense--Store		1347.65
6160	Utilities Expense		296.80
3150	Income Summary	3468.72	
3110	James Doring, Capital		1734.36
3130	Robert Kremer, Capital		1734.36
3110	James Doring, Capital	1625.00	
3120	James Doring, Drawing		1625.00
3130	Robert Kremer, Capital	1985.00	
3140	Robert Kremer, Drawing		1985.00

Figure 6.4
Closing Journal Entries Window

As the last step of the accounting cycle for a merchandising business organized as a partnership, a post-closing trial balance is generated. A post-closing Trial Balance is displayed to verify that debits equal credits in the general ledger accounts after closing entries are posted.

Chapter Review

1. To complete the accounting cycle for a partnership, adjusting entries can be recorded on the general journal input form, entered into the computer, and verified for accuracy. The financial statements are then generated. After the financial statements have been generated, the period-end closing is performed.

2. A Trial Balance and the period-end adjustment data are the basis for the adjusting entries. The changes in inventory resulting from purchases and sales transactions are not reflected in the Merchandise Inventory account. Therefore, the Merchandise Inventory account balance must be adjusted to reflect the changes resulting from purchases and sales during the fiscal period.

3. The income statement, balance sheet, and Performance Report (which is not discussed in this chapter) are available for a nondepartmentalized business organized as a partnership.

4. The software generates and posts all the journal entries to close all the temporary accounts to the Income Summary account. For a partnership with equal distribution of income or loss, the software generates and posts the entries to close out the revenue and expense accounts in the Income Summary account, distribute the balance in the Income Summary account to the partners' capital accounts, and close the partners' drawing accounts. If the distribution is unequal, entries will be generated and posted that will close the net income or loss to the Income Summary account. Journal entries must then be made to distribute the income or loss from the Income Summary account to the partners' capital accounts and to close the partners' drawing accounts to their respective capital accounts. After posting the closing entries, a post-closing Trial Balance is generated to prove the equality of debits and credits.

ACCOUNTING CAREERS IN DEPTH

Auditor

An auditor examines and analyzes accounting records to determine the financial status of a business and prepares financial reports related to operating procedures. An auditor performs the following duties:

- Reviewing records concerning assets, net worth, liabilities, capital stock, income, and expenditures.
- Inspecting accounting records to determine if accepted accounting procedure was followed in recording transactions.
- Counting cash on hand and inspecting notes receivable and payable, securities, and canceled checks.
- Verifying journal and ledger entries of cash and check payments, purchases, expenses, and trial balances by examining and authenticating inventory items.
- Preparing reports for management concerning the scope of the audit and financial condition of the business.

Auditing is considered the bread-and-butter work of accounting. An auditor comes to really understand how money is being made in the company that is being audited.

The work of an auditor can be done in any type of organization such as a small business, corporation, or government agency. The educational requirement for an auditor is completion of a college degree. If possible, an internship or co-op with a company is ideal in order to get work experience while the student is still in college. There are usually many travel opportunities available to offices in various locations.

One of the main requirements of working as an auditor, as with other accounting careers, is the need to pay close attention to detail. It is one of the most important prerequisites in accounting, and especially in auditing, because you are checking and verifying the work of others.

Auditing in any environment can be a rewarding experience and can build a solid foundation and accounting background.

TUTORIAL PROBLEM 6-T

In this tutorial problem, you will complete the end-of-fiscal-period processing for a merchandising business organized as a partnership. You will enter the adjusting entries, display the financial statements, generate and post closing journal entries, and use the Savings Planner tool. Since the partnership consists of two partners with an equal distribution of income or loss, the software will generate the entries to distribute the income or loss to the partners' capital accounts during the closing process.

STEP 1: Start up *Automated Accounting 8.0*.

STEP 2: Load the opening balances file named AA8 Problem 06-T.

STEP 3: Enter your name in the User Name text box and click *OK*.

STEP 4: Save with a file name of 06-T Your Name.

STEP 5: Enter the adjusting entries in the general journal, as shown in Figure 6.5.
These adjusting entries were derived from the period-end adjustment data and trial balance shown in Figure 6.1.

Date	Refer.	Account	Debit	Credit	Vendor/Customer
02/28/--	Adj.Ent.	3150 Income Summary	7228.14		
		1140 Merchandise Inventory		7228.14	
02/28/--	Adj.Ent.	6140 Supplies Expense--Office	932.08		
		1145 Supplies--Office		932.08	
02/28/--	Adj.Ent.	6150 Supplies Expense--Store	1347.65		
		1150 Supplies--Store		1347.65	
02/28/--	Adj.Ent.	6110 Insurance Expense	1176.92		
		1160 Prepaid Insurance		1176.92	

Figure 6.5
General Journal (Adjusting Entries)

STEP 6: Display the adjusting entries.
Click the *Reports* toolbar button and choose *Journals* from the Select a Report Group list. Select the *General Journal* Report. Select *Include All Journal Entries* and click *OK*. The report appears in Figure 6.6.

Chapter 6 End of Fiscal Period for a Partnership (Merchandising Business)

TUTORIAL PROBLEM 6-T

D & K Cabinet Tree
General Journal
02/28/--

Date	Refer.	Acct.	Title	Debit	Credit
02/28	Adj.Ent.	3150	Income Summary	7228.14	
02/28	Adj.Ent.	1140	Merchandise Inventory		7228.14
02/28	Adj.Ent.	6140	Supplies Expense--Office	932.08	
02/28	Adj.Ent.	1145	Supplies--Office		932.08
02/28	Adj.Ent.	6150	Supplies Expense--Store	1347.65	
02/28	Adj.Ent.	1150	Supplies--Store		1347.65
02/28	Adj.Ent.	6110	Insurance Expense	1176.92	
02/28	Adj.Ent.	1160	Prepaid Insurance		1176.92
			Totals	10684.79	10684.79

Figure 6.6
General Journal Report (Adjusting Entries)

STEP 7: **Display the financial statements.**
Choose *Financial Statements* and select the desired financial statement reports. Click *OK*. The income statement and balance sheet are shown in Figures 6.7 and 6.8, respectively.

STEP 8: **Generate an income statement graph.**
The income statement graph is illustrated in Figure 6.9 (page 194).

STEP 9: **Save your data file as 06-TBC Your Name.**
06-T is the problem number, and BC is "Before Closing."

TUTORIAL PROBLEM 6-T

D & K Cabinet Tree
Income Statement
For Period Ended 02/28/--

Operating Revenue

Sales	32423.30	100.00
Total Operating Revenue	32423.30	100.00

Cost of Merchandise Sold

Beginning Inventory	131278.14	404.89
Purchases	15277.49	47.12
Merchandise Available for Sale	146555.63	452.01
Less Ending Inventory	−124050.00	−382.60
Cost of Merchandise Sold	22505.63	69.41
Gross Profit	9917.67	30.59

Operating Expenses

Insurance Expense	1176.92	3.63
Miscellaneous Expense	220.50	0.68
Rent Expense	2475.00	7.63
Supplies Expense--Office	932.08	2.87
Supplies Expense--Store	1347.65	4.16
Utilities Expense	296.80	0.92
Total Operating Expenses	6448.95	19.89
Net Income	3468.72	10.70

Figure 6.7
Income Statement Report

The number of senior citizens who are avid computer users is growing and is bound to increase as the baby boomers get older. Many seniors find the Internet a rich source of friends, support, and information.

TUTORIAL PROBLEM 6-T

```
                    D & K Cabinet Tree
                      Balance Sheet
                        02/28/--
Assets

Cash                              45252.12
Petty Cash                          100.00
Accounts Receivable                3810.99
Merchandise Inventory            124050.00
Supplies--Office                    560.00
Supplies--Store                     845.00
Prepaid Insurance                   485.00
                                 ----------
Total Assets                                    175103.11
                                                =========

Liabilities

Accounts Payable                   9651.55
Sales Tax Payable                  1988.24
                                 ----------
Total Liabilities                                11639.79

Owners' Equity

James Doring, Capital             81802.30
James Doring, Drawing             -1625.00
Robert Kremer, Capital            81802.30
Robert Kremer, Drawing            -1985.00
Net Income                         3468.72
                                 ----------
Total Owners' Equity                            163463.32
                                                ----------
Total Liabilities & Equity                      175103.11
                                                =========
```

Figure 6.8
Balance Sheet Report

A *search engine* is a software program available on the Internet that allows users to find and retrieve specific information based on selected keywords.

TUTORIAL PROBLEM 6-T

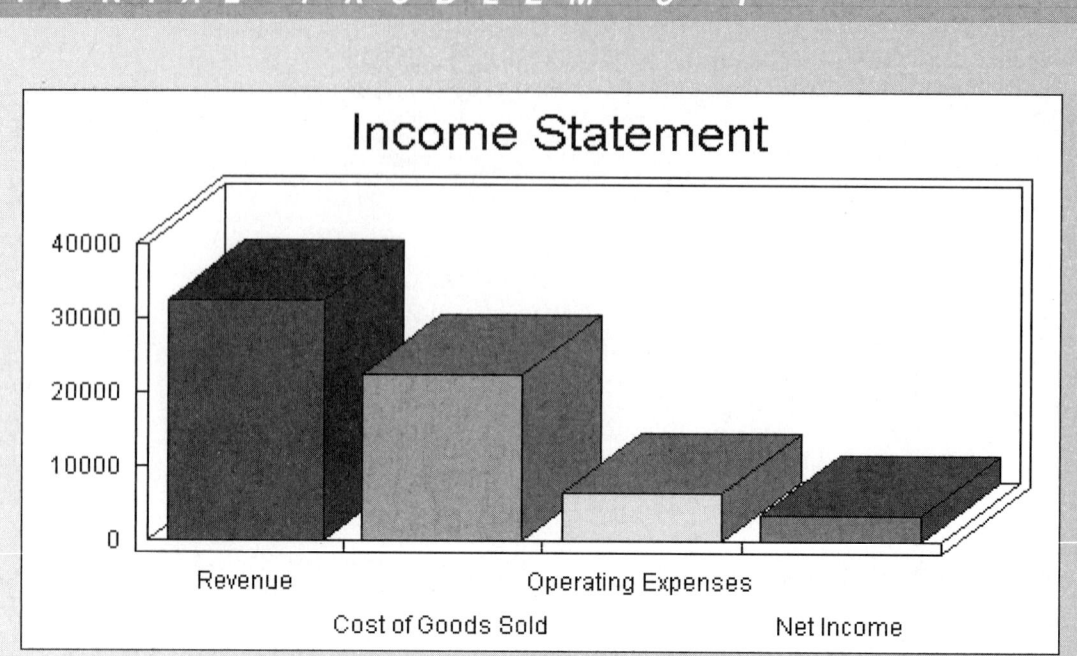

Figure 6.9
Income Statement Graph

STEP 10: Optional Spreadsheet Integration Activity.
D & K Cabinet Tree has asked you to use a spreadsheet to prepare a Distribution of Net Income Statement for the period ended 2/28. A spreadsheet template file has been partially completed.

a. Display and copy the income statement to the clipboard in spreadsheet format.
b. Start up your spreadsheet software and load the template file named AA8 Spreadsheet 06-T.
c. Select cell A1 as the current cell, and paste the income statement into the spreadsheet.
d. Enter the formula to calculate the distribution of net income for each partner and the formula to obtain a sum of the two partners' distribution.
e. Format the amounts in currency format, if necessary. Format the percentage amounts in number format with two decimal places.
f. Save your spreadsheet data with a file name of 06-T Your Name.
g. Print the spreadsheet. The completed spreadsheet is shown in Figure 6.10.

Chapter 6 End of Fiscal Period for a Partnership (Merchandising Business)

TUTORIAL PROBLEM 6-T

Student Name

D & K Cabinet Tree
Income Statement
For Period Ended 02/28/--

Operating Revenue

Sales	$32,423.30	100.00
Total Operating Revenue	$32,423.30	100.00

Cost of Merchandise Sold

Beginning Inventory	$131,278.14	404.89
Purchases	$15,277.49	47.12
Merchandise Available for Sale	$146,555.63	452.01
Less Ending Inventory	($124,050.00)	-382.60
Cost of Merchandise Sold	$22,505.63	69.41
Gross Profit	$9,917.67	30.59

Operating Expenses

Insurance Expense	$1,176.92	3.63
Miscellaneous Expense	$220.50	0.68
Rent Expense	$2,475.00	7.63
Supplies Expense--Office	$932.08	2.87
Supplies Expense--Store	$1,347.65	4.16
Utilities Expense	$296.80	0.92
Total Operating Expenses	$6,448.95	19.89
Net Income	$3,468.72	10.70

D & K Cabinet Tree
Distribution of Net Income Statement
For Period Ended 02/28/--

James Doring	
50.0% of Net Income	$1,734.36
Robert Kremer	
50.0% of Net Income	$1,734.36
Net Income	$3,468.72

Figure 6.10
Distribution of Net Income Statement Spreadsheet

TUTORIAL PROBLEM 6-T

h. What if the distribution of net income were changed as follows: James Doring, 70%; Robert Kremer, 30%? Change the Distribution of Net Income Statement to reflect this change.
i. End your spreadsheet session without saving your changes made in Step 10h.

STEP 11: Optional Word Processing Integration Activity.
You have been asked to prepare a memo addressed to each partner of D & K Cabinet Tree showing their distribution of net income for the period ended February 28.

a. Start up your word processing software application and create a new document.
b. Enter the memo to James Doring and Robert Kremer shown in Figure 6.11. If you completed the optional spreadsheet activity in Step 10, copy and paste the Distribution of Net Income from your spreadsheet into your document.
c. Save the memo with a file name of 06-T Your Name.
d. Print the memo.
e. End your word processing session.

MEMORANDUM

TO: James Doring, Partner
     Robert Kremer, Partner
DATE: February 28 of the Current Year
FROM: Student Name
SUBJECT: Distribution of Net Income

For your information, the distribution of net income for the period ended February 28 is as follows:

James Doring
    50.0% of Net Income $1,734.36
Robert Kremer
    50.0% of Net Income $1,734.36

Net Income $3,468.72
                                 =========

Figure 6.11
Completed Distribution of Net Income Document

TUTORIAL PROBLEM 6-T

STEP 12: Generate and post the closing journal entries.
Choose *Generate Closing Entries* from the Options menu. When the dialog box appears asking if you want to generate closing journal entries, click the *Yes* button. When the closing entries have been generated, the Closing Entries shown in Figure 6.12 will appear. Click the *Post* button.

Acct. #	Account Title	Debit	Credit
4110	Sales	32423.30	
3150	Income Summary		32423.30
3150	Income Summary	21726.44	
5110	Purchases		15277.49
6110	Insurance Expense		1176.92
6120	Miscellaneous Expense		220.50
6130	Rent Expense		2475.00
6140	Supplies Expense--Office		932.08
6150	Supplies Expense--Store		1347.65
6160	Utilities Expense		296.80
3150	Income Summary	3468.72	
3110	James Doring, Capital		1734.36
3130	Robert Kremer, Capital		1734.36
3110	James Doring, Capital	1625.00	
3120	James Doring, Drawing		1625.00
3130	Robert Kremer, Capital	1985.00	
3140	Robert Kremer, Drawing		1985.00

Figure 6.12
Closing Entries

STEP 13: Display the closing entries.
Click the *Reports* toolbar button and choose *Journals* from the Select a Report Group list. Select the *General Journal* Report. Select *Customize Journal Report*, then choose *Clo.Ent.* from the Reference drop-down list, and click *OK*. The report appears in Figure 6.13.

STEP 14: Display a post-closing Trial Balance.
Click the *Reports* toolbar button and choose *Ledger Reports*; then select *Trial Balance* and click *OK*. The post-closing Trial Balance Report appears in Figure 6.14.

TUTORIAL PROBLEM 6-T

D & K Cabinet Tree
General Journal
02/28/--

Date	Refer.	Acct.	Title	Debit	Credit
02/28	Clo.Ent.	4110	Sales	32423.30	
02/28	Clo.Ent.	3150	Income Summary		32423.30
02/28	Clo.Ent.	3150	Income Summary	21726.44	
02/28	Clo.Ent.	5110	Purchases		15277.49
02/28	Clo.Ent.	6110	Insurance Expense		1176.92
02/28	Clo.Ent.	6120	Miscellaneous Expense		220.50
02/28	Clo.Ent.	6130	Rent Expense		2475.00
02/28	Clo.Ent.	6140	Supplies Expense--Office		932.08
02/28	Clo.Ent.	6150	Supplies Expense--Store		1347.65
02/28	Clo.Ent.	6160	Utilities Expense		296.80
02/28	Clo.Ent.	3150	Income Summary	3468.72	
02/28	Clo.Ent.	3110	James Doring, Capital		1734.36
02/28	Clo.Ent.	3130	Robert Kremer, Capital		1734.36
02/28	Clo.Ent.	3110	James Doring, Capital	1625.00	
02/28	Clo.Ent.	3120	James Doring, Drawing		1625.00
02/28	Clo.Ent.	3130	Robert Kremer, Capital	1985.00	
02/28	Clo.Ent.	3140	Robert Kremer, Drawing		1985.00
			Totals	61228.46	61228.46

Figure 6.13
Closing Entries Report

STEP 15: **Save your data with a file name of 06-TAC Your Name.**
06-T is the problem number, and AC is "After Closing."

STEP 16: **Calculate the amount of savings over a given period of time using the Savings Planner.**
D & K Cabinet Trees' partners, James Doring and Robert Kremer, are considering purchasing land and a building. Based upon their financial condition, they can transfer

Chapter 6 End of Fiscal Period for a Partnership (Merchandising Business)

TUTORIAL PROBLEM 6-T

```
                    D & K Cabinet Tree
                      Trial Balance
                        02/28/--

Acct.      Account
Number     Title                      Debit           Credit

1110       Cash                      45252.12
1120       Petty Cash                  100.00
1130       Accounts Receivable        3810.99
1140       Merchandise Inventory    124050.00
1145       Supplies--Office            560.00
1150       Supplies--Store             845.00
1160       Prepaid Insurance           485.00
2110       Accounts Payable                           9651.55
2120       Sales Tax Payable                          1988.24
3110       James Doring, Capital                     81911.66
3130       Robert Kremer, Capital                    81551.66
                                    ----------      ----------
           Totals                   175103.11       175103.11
                                    ==========      ==========
```

Figure 6.14
Post-Closing Trial Balance Report

$5,000.00 from their checking account to a savings account and contribute $1,200.00 into the account monthly. This investment will earn interest of 8.5% over the next 5 years (60 months).

Click the *Tools* toolbar button. When the Planning Tools window appears, click the *Savings Planner* tab. With the *Ending Savings Balance* option in the Calculate grouping selected, enter the following savings information and generate the Savings Planner Schedule shown in Figure 6.15.

Beginning Savings $5,000.00
Annual Yield (Percent) 8.50
Number of Months   60
Monthly Contribution $1,200.00

TUTORIAL PROBLEM 6-T

```
                    Savings Plan
                    02/28/--

Savings Planner Schedule

Month           Monthly            Monthly        Cumulative
Number          Contribution       Yield          Total

(Beginning Balance)                               5000.00
1               1200.00            35.42          6235.42
2               1200.00            44.17          7479.59
3               1200.00            52.98          8732.57
4               1200.00            61.86          9994.43
5               1200.00            70.79          11265.22
6               1200.00            79.80          12545.02
7               1200.00            88.86          13833.88
8               1200.00            97.99          15131.87
9               1200.00            107.18         16439.05
10              1200.00            116.44         17755.49
11              1200.00            125.77         19081.26
12              1200.00            135.16         20416.42
/\/\/\/\/\/\/\/\/\/\/\/\/\/\/\/\/\/\/\/\/\/\/\/\/\/\/\/\/\/\
55              1200.00            608.61         87730.37
56              1200.00            621.42         89551.79
57              1200.00            634.33         91386.12
58              1200.00            647.32         93233.44
59              1200.00            660.40         95093.84
60              1200.00            673.59         96967.43
```

Figure 6.15
Savings Planner Schedule Report

STEP 17: End the *Automated Accounting* session.

A Website owner's unique Internet address is called its *domain name*.

A company that does almost all of its business activities through the Internet is often referred to as a *dot-com business*. However, most businesses use the Internet for only a portion of their activities.

Chapter 6 End of Fiscal Period for a Partnership (Merchandising Business)

Review and Practice: Applying Your Information Skills

I. REVIEW QUESTIONS

Directions: Write the answers to the following questions in the *Working Papers*.

1. What is the amount of the office supplies adjusting entry if the current account balance shown in the trial balance is $1,685.50 and the actual amount is $736.25?

2. What is the amount of the prepaid insurance adjusting entry if the current account balance shown in the trial balance is $1,895.00 and the actual amount is $645.00?

3. List three reasons why small businesses are sometimes organized as partnerships.

4. Explain how the partners' capital accounts are affected by the period-end closing process for a partnership with a 50/50 split of income or loss.

5. List four things that happen during the posting of closing journal entries.

II. INTERNET ACTIVITY

Directions: If you have access to the Internet, use your browser to find information about international entrepreneur business trends and opportunities. ***Note:*** Use *business opportunities* and *entrepreneur* as your search arguments. Report on your findings. Be sure to include the source and the URL (Internet address) of your search.

Independent Practice Problem 6-P

In this problem, you will process the monthly transactions for the month of March and complete the end-of-fiscal-period processing for D & K Cabinet Tree. In this partnership, the net income or loss is divided equally among partners.

STEP 1: Start up *Automated Accounting 8.0*.

STEP 2: Load the opening balance file named AA8 Problem 06-P.

STEP 3: Enter your name in the User Name text box.

STEP 4: Save the opening balances file with a file name of 06-P Your Name.

STEP 5: Enter the March transactions.

Mar. 01 Sold merchandise on account to Bernard Woodworks, $4,736.80. S649.

03 Sold merchandise on account to Oxnard Cabinet Masters, $5,095.00. S650.

04 Purchased merchandise for cash, $159.95. C170.

05 Purchased merchandise on account from Ultra Cabinets, $5,145.00. P232

05 Paid cash for miscellaneous expense, $50.00. C171.

08 Purchased merchandise on account from Milton Wood Products, $1,050.00. P233.

09 Paid cash on account to Salas Cabinet Design, $2,110.50, covering P224. C172.

10 Paid cash on account to Suncoast Supply Co., $637.45, covering M54. C173.

11 Paid cash for rent, $2,500.00. C174.

11 Received cash on account from Keller Quality Cabinets, $518.64, covering S633. R777.

12 Received cash on account from Cindy Lorentz, $238.50, covering S638. R778.

15 Add Riverhills Cabinetry to the customer list. Sold merchandise on account to Riverhills Cabinetry, $4,450.00. S651.

16 Bought store supplies on account from Morgan Office Supply Co., $343.65. M57.

17 Paid cash for insurance, $810.00. C175.

18 Sold merchandise on account to Baer Kitchen Cabinets, $5,200.00. S652.

19 Paid cash for electric bill, $389.72. C176.

23 Bought office supplies on account from Suncoast Supply Co., $105.00. M58.

24 Received cash on account from Melvin Cabinetry Inc., $362.95, covering S642. R779.

25 James Doring, partner, withdrew merchandise for personal use, $122.45. M59.

26 Purchased merchandise on account from Spence Cabinet Mfg., $2,238.61. P234.

29 Discovered that a transaction for store supplies bought for cash in January was journalized and posted in error as a debit to Purchases instead of Supplies—Store, $142.76. M60.

Chapter 6 End of Fiscal Period for a Partnership (Merchandising Business)

29 Paid cash on account to Decko Woodworking, Inc., $1,695.95, covering P226. C177.
30 Paid cash on account to Ashley Interiors, $798.00, covering P229. C178.
31 Recorded cash and credit card sales, $5,205.36, plus sales tax, $312.32; total, $5,517.68. T36.
31 Robert Kremer, partner, withdrew cash for personal use, $1,100.00. C179.
31 James Doring, partner, withdrew cash for personal use, $850.00. C180.
31 Paid cash to replenish the petty cash fund, $90.00: office supplies, $38.10; store supplies, $51.90. C181.

STEP 6: Display the General, Purchases, Cash Payments, Sales, and Cash Receipts Journal Reports for the period March 1 through March 31 of the current year. If errors are detected, make corrections.

STEP 7: Display a Trial Balance, Schedule of Accounts Payable, and Schedule of Accounts Receivable.

STEP 8: Enter the adjusting entries using the following adjustment. Use the Trial Balance generated in Step 7 as the basis for making the adjusting entries. Use Adj.Ent. as the reference.

Balance on March 31
Merchandise inventory $118,890.00
Office supplies inventory 350.00
Store supplies inventory 950.00
Value of insurance policies 965.00

STEP 9: Display the General Journal Report for the adjusting entries. Use a reference restriction of Adj.Ent. so that only adjusting entries will be included on the report.

STEP 10: Display the income statement and balance sheet.

STEP 11: Generate an income statement graph.

STEP 12: Save your data with a file name of 06-PBC Your Name, where 06-P is the problem number, and BC is "Before Closing."

STEP 13: Optional Spreadsheet and Word Processing Integration Activities.
D & K Cabinet Tree has asked you to use a spreadsheet to prepare an Owners' Equity Statement for the period ended March 31. Next, prepare a memo addressed to each partner

of D & K Cabinet Tree, containing their statement of Owners' Equity.

Spreadsheet Activity:

a. Display and copy the Trial Balance to the clipboard in spreadsheet format.
b. Start up your spreadsheet software and load the template file named AA8 Spreadsheet 06-P.
c. Select cell A1 as the current cell and paste the Trial Balance into the spreadsheet.
d. Enter the respective partner's capital and drawing accounts cell references from the Trial Balance to the Owner's Equity Statement. Enter the amount $3,571.84 in cells C43 and C51. This is the share of net income. Enter the formulas where indicated in the Owners' Equity Statement.
e. Format the amounts in currency format if necessary.
f. Save your spreadsheet data with a file name of 06-P Your Name.
g. Print the entire spreadsheet, including the Trial Balance and Owners' Equity Statement.

Word Processing Activity:

a. Start up your word processing software application and create a new document. If you completed the optional word processing activity in Tutorial Problem 6-T, load and use that memo template.
b. Enter the memo information. Use the memo format shown in Figure 6.11. Two lines below the subject line, type *For your information, the statement of owner's equity for the period ended March 31 is as follows:*. Copy and paste the body of the Owners' Equity Statement from your spreadsheet into your memo.
c. Save the document with a file name of 06-P Your Name.
d. Print the memo.
e. End your spreadsheet and word processing sessions.

STEP 14: Generate and post the closing general journal entries.

STEP 15: Display the closing entries. Use a reference restriction of Clo.Ent. so that only closing entries will be included on the report.

STEP 16: Display a post-closing Trial Balance.

STEP 17: Save your data as 06-PAC Your Name.

Chapter 6 End of Fiscal Period for a Partnership (Merchandising Business)

STEP 18: Calculate the monthly savings contribution over a given period of time using the Savings Planner. D & K Cabinet Tree wants to save $100,000.00 over the next five years toward the purchase of land and a building.
Note: Select the *Monthly Contribution* option in the Calculate grouping, and then enter the following savings information:

Beginning Savings	$5,000.00
Annual Yield (Percent)	8.5
Number of Months	60
Ending Savings Balance	$100,000.00

STEP 19: End the *Automated Accounting* session.

Applying Your Technology Skills 6-P

Directions: Using Independent Practice Problem 6-P, write the answers to the following questions in the *Working Papers*.

1. From the Purchases Journal Report, what is the amount of the credit to Spence Cabinet Mfg.?
2. In the Cash Payments Journal Report, what are the total debits and total credits?
3. From the Sales Journal Report, what is the amount of Sales Invoice No. 651?
4. From the Cash Receipts Journal Report, what is the amount of cash received from Cindy Lorentz for Cash Receipt No. 778?
5. From the Schedule of Accounts Payable, what is the amount currently owed to Milton Wood Products?
6. From the Schedule of Accounts Receivable, what is the amount currently due from Riverhills Cabinetry?
7. What is the gross profit for the period?
8. What are the total operating expenses?
9. What is the net income?
10. What are the total assets?
11. How much must D & K Cabinet Tree contribute to savings each month over the next five years to accumulate $100,000.00 toward the purchase of land and a building?

Mastery Problem 6-M

In this problem, you will process the monthly transactions for the month of April and complete the end-of-fiscal-period processing for D & K Cabinet Tree. In this partnership, the net income or loss is divided equally among partners.

STEP 1: Load the file named AA8 Problem 06-M.

STEP 2: Enter your name in the User Name text box.

STEP 3: Save the opening balances file as 06-M Your Name.

STEP 4: Enter the April maintenance and transactions.

Apr. 03 Paid cash for quarterly sales tax, $2,300.56. C182.
03 Sold merchandise on account to Ritter Cabinet Company, $4,527.48. S653.
04 Sold merchandise on account to Bursaw Cabinet Co., $4,075.25. S654.
05 Purchased merchandise on account from Mellen Cabinet Co., $5,245.00. P235.
06 Purchased merchandise for cash, $637.45. C183.
06 Paid cash for office supplies, $82.16. C184.
07 Purchased merchandise on account from Salas Cabinet Design, $3,795.00. P236.
07 Paid cash for miscellaneous expense, $35.00. C185.
07 Paid cash on account to Morgan Office Supply Co., $577.90, covering M53 and M57. C186.
10 Paid cash on account to Mellen Cabinet Co., $690.00, covering P227 and P231. C187.
10 Paid cash for rent, $2,500.00. C188.
10 Received cash on account from Marso Millcraft, Inc., $828.65, covering S639 and S648. R780.
11 Received cash on account from Bursaw Cabinet Co., $498.73, covering S643. R781.
11 Purchased merchandise on account from Sana Fine Millwork, $2,389.50. P237.
Add Sana Fine Millwork to the vendor list.
12 Bought office supplies on account from Suncoast Supply Co., $92.00. M61.
13 Sold merchandise on account to Melvin Cabinetry Inc., $3,800.00. S655.
13 Paid cash for electric bill, $402.68. C189.
14 Paid cash for insurance, $625.00. C190.

Chapter 6 End of Fiscal Period for a Partnership (Merchandising Business)

	15	Sold merchandise on account to Demars Interiors, $4,805.10. S656.
	15	Received cash on account from Keller Quality Cabinets, $65.00, covering S647. R782.
	16	Received cash on account from Baer Kitchen Cabinets, $331.05, covering S640. R783.
	17	Robert Kremer, partner, withdrew merchandise for personal use, $342.20. M62.
	24	Purchased merchandise on account from Decko Woodworking, Inc., $3,872.45. P238.
	25	Discovered that a withdrawal of cash by James Doring, partner, was journalized and posted in error as a credit to Purchases instead of Cash, $500.00. M63.
	26	Paid cash on account to Spence Cabinet Mfg., $4,306.19, covering P225 and P234. C191.
	27	Paid cash on account to Milton Wood Products, $1,673.50, covering P230 and P233. C192.
	28	Recorded cash and credit card sales, $5,804.00, plus sales tax, $348.24; total, $6,152.24. T37.
	28	Robert Kremer, partner, withdrew cash for personal use, $1,200.00. C193.
	28	James Doring, partner, withdrew cash for personal use, $1,500.00. C194.
	30	Paid cash to replenish the petty cash fund, $100.00: office supplies, $10.50; store supplies, $19.65; Robert Kremer, partner, $25.00; miscellaneous expense, $44.85. C195.

STEP 5: Display the journal reports.

STEP 6: Display a Trial Balance, Schedule of Accounts Payable, and Schedule of Accounts Receivable.

STEP 7: Enter the adjusting entries.

Balance on April 30
Merchandise Inventory $116,995.09
Office supplies inventory 410.00
Store supplies inventory 675.00
Value of insurance policies 1,250.00

STEP 8: Display the adjusting entries.

STEP 9: Display the financial statements.

STEP 10: Generate a sales graph.

STEP 11: Save your data with a file name of 06-MBC Your Name.

STEP 12: **Optional Spreadsheet and Word Processing Integration Activities.**

Prepare an owners' equity statement for the period ended April 30. Next, prepare a memo addressed to each partner of D & K Cabinet Tree showing their owners' equity.

Spreadsheet Activity:

a. Display and copy the Trial Balance to the clipboard in spreadsheet format.
b. Start up your spreadsheet software and load the template file named AA8 Spreadsheet 06-M.
c. Select cell A1 as the current cell and paste the income statement into the spreadsheet.
d. Enter the respective partner's capital and drawing accounts cell references from the trial balance into proper cells in the Owners' Equity Statement.
   Enter the amount of each partner's net income in the proper cells: James Doring, $638.94; Robert Kremer, $638.94. Enter the formulas where indicated in the Owners' Equity Statement.
e. Format the amounts in currency format, if necessary.
f. Save your spreadsheet data with a file name of 06-M Your Name.
g. Print the entire spreadsheet, including the Trial Balance and Owners' Equity Statement.

Word Processing Activity:

a. Start up your word processing software application and create a new document. If you completed the optional word processing activity in either Tutorial Problem 6-T or Independent Practice Problem 6-P, load and use that memo template.
b. Enter the necessary memo information. Use the memo format shown in Figure 6.11. Two lines below the subject line, type *For your information, the statement of owners' equity for the period ended April 30 is as follows:*. Copy and paste the body of the Owners' Equity Statement from the spreadsheet into your memo.
c. Save the document with a file name of 06-M Your Name.
d. Print the memo.
e. End your spreadsheet and word processing sessions.

STEP 13: **Generate and post the closing journal entries.**

STEP 14: **Display the closing entries.**

Chapter 6 End of Fiscal Period for a Partnership (Merchandising Business)

STEP 15: Display a post-closing Trial Balance.

STEP 16: Save your data with a file name of 06-MAC Your Name.

STEP 17: Use the Savings Planner to calculate the number of months needed to accumulate $100,000 given the following information:

Beginning Savings	$10,000.00
Annual Yield (Percent)	8.75
Monthly Contribution	$1,200.00
Ending Savings Balance	$100,000.00

STEP 18: End the *Automated Accounting* session.

Applying Your Technology Skills 6-M

Directions: Using Mastery Problem 6-M, write the answers to the following questions in the *Working Papers*.

1. From the Purchases Journal Report, what is the amount purchased from Salas Cabinet Design?

2. In the Cash Payments Journal Report, what are the total debits and total credits?

3. From the Sales Journal Report, what is the amount of Sales Invoice No. 655?

4. From the Cash Receipts Journal Report, what is the amount of cash received from Marso Millcraft, Inc. for Cash Receipt No. 780?

5. From the Schedule of Accounts Payable, what is the amount currently owed to all vendors?

6. From the Schedule of Accounts Receivable, what is the amount currently due from Ritter Cabinet Company?

7. What is the gross profit for the period?

8. What are the total operating expenses?

9. What is the net income?

10. What are the total assets?

11. From the Savings Planner, how many months will it take D & K Cabinet Tree to save $100,000 based on the data provided?

Reinforcement Activity R-2

A-Z Video & Electronics sells TVs, stereos, and VCRs to retail stores. In Reinforcement Activity R-2, you will process the monthly transactions for February and complete the end-of-fiscal-period processing for this business.

STEP 1: Start up the *Automated Accounting 8.0* software.

STEP 2: Open and load the opening balances template file named AA8 Problem R-2.

STEP 3: Enter your name in the User Name text box.

STEP 4: Save the opening balances file with a file name of R-2 Your Name.

STEP 5: Add Voss Video Mfg. to the vendor list. Delete Segar Electronics Co. and Massa Stereo Corp. from the vendor list.

STEP 6: Add Sara Nielsen and Linda Jaeger to the customer list. Delete Pahl Audio-Video Center from the customer list.

STEP 7: Enter the February transaction data. Abbreviate the reference numbers on the input forms as follows: Check No., C; Memorandum, M; Cash Receipts Tape, T; Cash Receipt No., R; Sales Invoice No., S; Purchase Invoice No., P.

Feb. 01 Paid cash for sales tax, $1,397.11. C511.
01 Sold merchandise on account to Murphy Television, $1,654.98. S904.
01 Sold merchandise on account to Barnes TV & VCR Repairs, $2,195.00. S905.
02 Sold merchandise on account to Cline Sound Systems, $1,800.00. S906.
02 Paid cash for rent, $2,700.00. C512.
02 Paid cash for electric bill, $501.63. C513.
03 Bought store supplies on account from Valis Office Supply Co., $120.47. M232.
03 Received cash on account from Anna Tischer, $441.05, covering S895. R756.
03 Purchased merchandise on account from Rossow VCR Products., $1,502.00. P416.
04 Purchased merchandise for cash, $810.00. C514.
04 Paid cash for miscellaneous expense, $286.34. C515.
05 Bought office supplies on account from Valis Office Supply Co., $406.95. M233.

Reinforcement Activity R-2

- 05 Sold merchandise on account to Murphy Television, $1,582.00. S907.
- 06 Sold merchandise on account to Mosher Video & Service, $2,015.00. S908.
- 06 Sold merchandise on account to Tilton Video Products, $1,775.00. S909.
- 06 Paid cash for insurance, $1,400.00. C516.
- 06 Recorded cash and credit card sales, $2,142.00, plus sales tax, $128.52; total, $2,270.52. T5.
- 06 Discovered that a purchase of merchandise for cash was journalized and posted in error as a debit to Supplies—Office instead of Purchases, $345.50. M234.
- 08 Purchased merchandise on account from Conrad Video Products, $1,144.21. P417.
- 08 Purchased merchandise on account from Duffee Electronics Inc., $1,550.00. P418.
- 09 Paid cash on account to Sieberg Video Systems, $1,465.88, covering P400. C517.
- 09 Received cash on account from Sloan Entertainment, $2,627.93, covering S896. R757.
- 10 Received cash on account from Scott TV Satellite Co., $1,158.26, covering S897. R758.
- 10 Purchased merchandise on account from Somers TV & Radio, $1,352.80. P419.
- 10 Paid cash for utilities expense, $396.05. C518.
- 11 Received cash on account from Cline Sound Systems, $3,025.55, covering S898. R759.
- 12 Sold merchandise on account to Sara Nielsen, $200.00, plus sales tax, $12.00; total, $212.00. S910.
- 12 Paid cash on account to Rossow VCR Products, $3,497.90, covering P415 and P416. C519.
- 13 Paid cash on account to Valis Office Supply Co., $472.08, covering M231. C520.
- 13 Paid cash on account to Somers TV & Radio, $1,456.25, covering P414. C521.
- 13 Purchased merchandise on account from Voss Video Mfg., $1,100.00. P420.
- 13 Recorded cash and credit card sales, $1,806.00, plus sales tax, $108.36; total, $1,914.36. T12.
- 15 Discovered that a payment for rent was journalized and posted in error as a debit to Purchases instead of Rent Expense, $2,700.00. M235.
- 15 Bought store supplies on account from Valis Office Supply Co., $95.00. M236.

16 Received cash on account from Barnes TV & VCR Repairs, $3,604.82, covering S899 and S905. R760.
16 Received cash on account from Tilton Video Products, $1,757.95, covering S902. R761.
16 Purchased merchandise for cash, $1,012.18. C522.
17 Gloria Romero, partner, withdrew merchandise for personal use, $230.00. M237.
17 Sold merchandise on account to Scott TV Satellite Co., $1,063.00. S911.
18 Purchased merchandise on account from Cray TransVideo Co., $995.00. P421.
18 Purchased merchandise on account from Somers TV & Radio, $1,399.95. P422.
19 Bought office supplies on account from Valis Office Supply Co., $331.60. M238.
20 Discovered that a withdrawal of merchandise by Gloria Romero for personal use was journalized and posted in error as a debit to Sergio Romero, Drawing instead of Gloria Romero, Drawing, $515.00. M239.
20 Purchased merchandise for cash, $678.00. C523.
20 Paid cash for miscellaneous expense, $250.00. C524.
20 Sergio Romero, partner, withdrew merchandise for personal use, $495.00. M240.
20 Paid cash for store supplies, $50.25. C525.
20 Recorded cash and credit card sales, $2,466.00, plus sales tax, $147.96; total, $2,613.96. T19.
22 Received cash on account from Murphy Television, $1,654.98, covering S904. R762.
22 Received cash on account from Mosher Video & Service, $1,977.70, covering S903. R763.
23 Sold merchandise on account to Linda Jaeger, $510.00, plus sales tax, $30.60; total, $540.60. S912.
23 Sold merchandise on account to Sloan Entertainment, $2,264.30. S913.
24 Paid cash for office supplies, $105.62. C526.
24 Discovered that a payment for a miscellaneous expense was journalized and posted in error as a debit to Rent Expense instead of Miscellaneous Expense, $90.00. M241.
25 Received cash on account from Murphy Television, $1,582.00, covering S907. R764.

Reinforcement Activity R-2

25 Received cash on account from Sara Nielsen, $212.00, covering S910. R765.
26 Sold merchandise on account to Barnes TV & VCR Repairs, $2,100.00. S914.
26 Sold merchandise on account to Mosher Video & Service, $1,785.30. S915.
26 Purchased merchandise on account from Duffee Electronics Inc., $1,164.10. P423.
26 Received cash on account from Boyd TV & Stereos, $685.41, covering S900. R766.
27 Paid cash on account to Valis Office Supply Co., $954.02, covering M232, M233, M236, and M238. C527.
27 Gloria Romero, partner, withdrew cash for personal use, $2,850.00. C528.
27 Sergio Romero, partner, withdrew cash for personal use, $2,850.00. C529.
27 Paid cash to replenish the petty cash fund, $100.00: office supplies, $16.50; store supplies, $36.50; Gloria Romero, partner, $32.50; miscellaneous expense, $14.50. C530.
28 Recorded cash and credit card sales, $1,640.00, plus sales tax, $98.40; total, $1,738.40. T26.

STEP 8: Display the journal reports (General, Purchases, Cash Payments, Sales, and Cash Receipts) for the period of February 1 to February 28 of the current year. If errors are detected, make corrections.

STEP 9: Display a Trial Balance, Schedule of Accounts Payable, and Schedule of Accounts Receivable.

STEP 10: Enter the adjusting entries using the following adjustment data. Use the Trial Balance generated in Step 9 as the basis for making the adjusting entries. Use Adj.Ent. as the reference.

Balance on February 28
Merchandise Inventory $86,950.27
Office supplies inventory $735.00
Store supplies inventory $615.00
Value of insurance policies $2,290.00

STEP 11: Display the General Journal Report for the adjusting entries. Use a reference restriction of Adj.Ent. so that only adjusting entries will be included on the report.

STEP 12: Display the income statement and balance sheet.

STEP 13: Generate income statement and balance sheet graphs.

STEP 14: Save your data with a file name of R-2BC Your Name, where BC indicates "Before Closing."

STEP 15: Optional Spreadsheet and Word Processing Integration Activities.

A-Z Video & Electronics has asked you to use a spreadsheet to prepare an Owners' Equity Statement for the period ended February 28. Next, prepare a memo addressed to each partner, containing their owners' equity information.

Spreadsheet Activity:

a. Display and copy the Trial Balance to the clipboard in spreadsheet format.
b. Start up your spreadsheet software and load the template file named AA8 Spreadsheet R-2.
c. Select cell A1 as the current cell and paste the Trial Balance into the spreadsheet.
d. Enter the cell references from the Trial Balance of the respective partner's capital and drawing accounts. Enter $2,228.52 in cell C43 and $2,228.52 in cell C51. This is each partner's share of net income. Enter the formulas where indicated in the Owners' Equity Statement.
e. Format the amounts in currency format, if necessary.
f. Save your spreadsheet data with a file name of R-2 Your Name.
g. Print the entire spreadsheet, including the Trial Balance and Owners' Equity Statement.

Word Processing Activity:

a. Start up your word processing software application and create a new document.
b. Enter a memo to Gloria and Sergio Romero. Copy and paste the Owners' Equity Statement from your spreadsheet into the memo.
c. Save the document with a file name of R-2 Your Name.
d. Print the memo.
e. End your spreadsheet and word processing sessions.

STEP 16: Generate and post the closing journal entries.

STEP 17: Display the closing entries. Use a reference restriction of Clo.Ent. so that only closing entries will be included on the report.

STEP 18: Display a post-closing Trial Balance.

Reinforcement Activity R-2

STEP 19: Save your data with a file name of R-2AC Your Name, where AC indicates "After Closing."

STEP 20: End the *Automated Accounting* session.

Applying Your Technology Skills R-2

Directions: Using Reinforcement Activity R-2, write the answers to the following questions in the *Working Papers*.

Journals

1. From the General Journal Report, what is the total of the credit column?
2. From the Purchases Journal Report, what is the amount of the credit to Conrad Video Products?
3. On the Cash Payments Journal Report, what are the total debits and total credits?
4. From the Sales Journal Report, what is the amount of Sales Invoice No. 906?
5. From the Cash Receipts Journal Report, what is the amount of cash received from Scott TV Satellite Co. for Cash Receipt No. 758?

Ledgers

6. From the Schedule of Accounts Payable, what is the amount currently owed to all vendors?
7. From the Schedule of Accounts Receivable, what is the amount currently due from Mosher Video & Service?

Financial Statements

8. What is the gross profit for the period?
9. What are the total operating expenses?
10. What is the net income?
11. What are the total liabilities?

Chapter 7

DISCOUNTS, DEBIT MEMORANDUMS, AND CREDIT MEMORANDUMS

KEY TERMS

Purchases Discount
Sales Discount
Debit Memorandum
Credit Memorandum
Discount Period

LEARNING OBJECTIVES

Upon completion of this chapter, you will be able to:

1. Process purchases discounts.
2. Process sales discounts.
3. Process debit memorandums.
4. Process credit memorandums.

Chapter 7 Discounts, Debit Memorandums, and Credit Memorandums

INTRODUCTION

In this chapter, you will learn how to process purchases discounts, sales discounts, debit memorandums, and credit memorandums. You will learn how to analyze, enter, and post these transactions at the computer. As an alternative, you can record the transactions on input forms before entering and posting the transactions at the computer.

ETHICS

The method of communication that conveys the most information is talking face to face with another person. Spoken words convey meaning, but meaning is also conveyed through voice inflection, posture, gestures, eye contact, and general demeanor. And all those elements can say as much—if not more—than words.

When communication is via e-mail (electronic mail), the words still have meaning; however, the meaning conveyed through other methods is lost. E-mail offers some advantages over letters and memos in that it is easy to compose and the message is delivered almost instantaneously to its recipients. But those advantages can lead to problems if e-mail is misused.

With e-mail, it is just as easy to send a message to a huge group of people as to one person. This capability leads some persons to use e-mail for non-business purposes, thus wasting the time required to screen "garbage" messages before deleting them.

A potentially more costly problem could be called "quick to anger." If an e-mail (or network) user gets mad at someone, it is tempting to immediately compose a nasty message and share it with everyone. Before e-mail, when thoughts had to be put on paper for delivery, at least there was an automatic "cooling-off period" enforced by the process itself. There is particular danger when supervisors transmit messages that have accusations that violate legal standards and open up potential employee lawsuits. Likewise, angry messages from employees can contain comments that lead to firing. A word of good advice is to never send an e-mail message that you would not want anyone else to see and to do unto others as you would like them to do unto you.

Critical Thinking

1. Do you think that e-mail should be used for private, confidential communication? Justify your belief.

2. Who, besides the sender and intended receiver, do you think can access e-mail communication?

3. Identify several policies that you think a company's employees should follow when using e-mail.

Buyers are often given a deduction on the sales invoice amount in order to encourage early payment. From the buyer's point of view, a deduction for early payment of an invoice is called a **purchases discount**. From the seller's point of view, a deduction for early payment of an invoice is referred to as a **sales discount**. If the invoice amount is paid within the time period specified on the invoice, the discount may be deducted from the payment.

Buyers are sometimes granted credit for returned or damaged merchandise. Credit given for damaged goods not returned is known as an *allowance*. From the buyer's point of view, returns and allowances result in a debit to the vendor's account, because the amount owed to the vendor is reduced. The form prepared by the customer showing the price deduction for returns and allowances is called a **debit memorandum**. From the seller's point of view, returns and allowances result in a credit to the customer's account, because the amount the customer owes is reduced. The form prepared by the vendor showing the amount deducted for returns and allowances is called a **credit memorandum**.

PURCHASES DISCOUNTS

A purchases discount is an incentive offered by the vendor to pay the invoice before the due date. If the invoice is paid within the specified time period, a discount amount may be deducted from the invoice amount. The specified time period within which a deduction from an invoice amount may be taken is called the **discount period**. The discount amount is usually based on a percentage of the invoice amount and is shown on the invoice. For example, "1/10, n/30" means that 1% of the invoice amount may be deducted if the invoice is paid within 10 days of the invoice date and that the total invoice amount must be paid within 30 days.

Purchases discounts are entered into the computer at the time the invoice is paid. The sample transaction shown below has been entered in the cash payments journal in Figure 7.1.

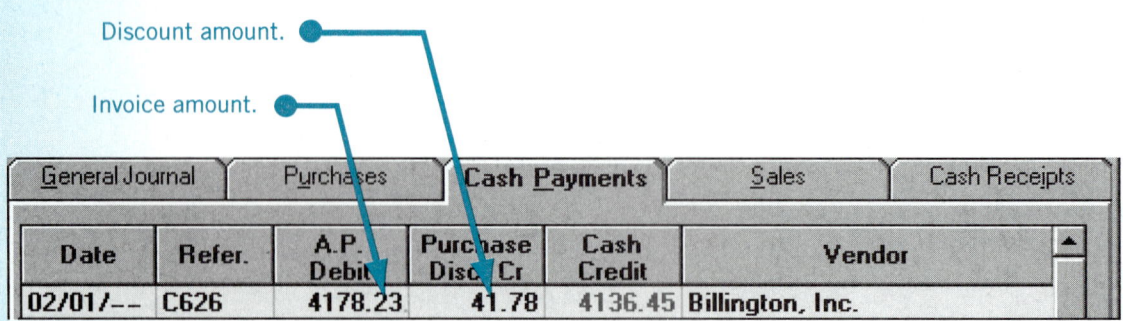

Figure 7.1
Cash Payments Journal (Purchases Discount)

Chapter 7 Discounts, Debit Memorandums, and Credit Memorandums

Feb. 01 Paid cash on account to Billington, Inc., $4,136.45, covering P300 for $4,178.23, less 1% discount, $41.78. C626.

SALES DISCOUNTS

In this accounting system, sales discounts are recorded in the cash receipts journal at the time the cash is received on account. The first sample transaction shown in Figure 7.2 is an example of a cash receipt on account with a sales discount. The second sample transaction is provided to show how cash and credit card sales are entered into the expanded cash receipts journal.

Feb. 02 Received cash on account from Blume Lighting Co., $5,356.12, covering S448 for $5,410.22, less 1% discount, $54.10. R217.

Feb. 10 Recorded cash and credit card sales, $3,680.72, plus sales tax, $257.65; total, $3,938.37. T17.

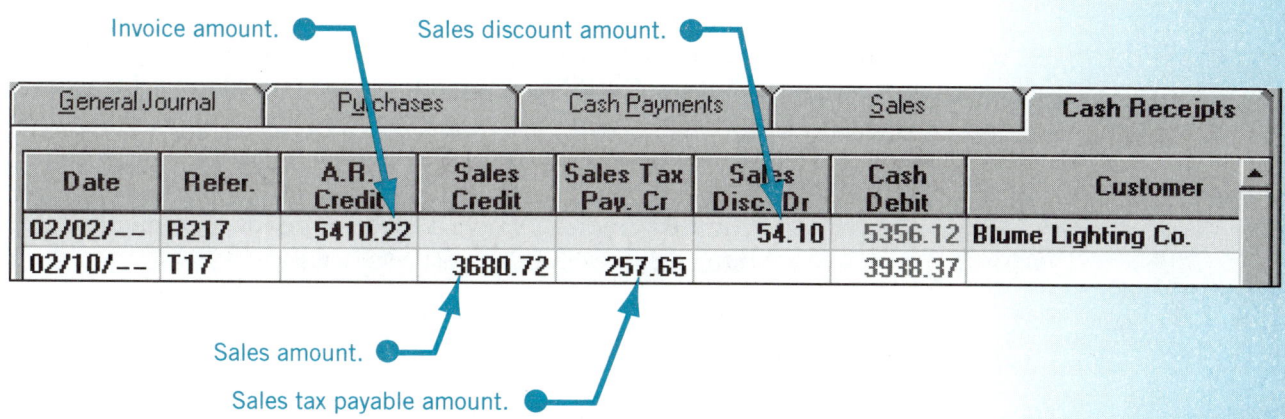

Figure 7.2
Cash Receipts Journal (Sales Discount and Cash Sales)

DEBIT MEMORANDUMS

A debit memorandum results when a buyer receives credit from a vendor for merchandise returned or receives an allowance for inferior or damaged merchandise. Debit memorandums are recorded in the general journal. A sample transaction involving a debit memorandum is listed below and shown entered into the general journal in Figure 7.3.

Feb. 02 Returned merchandise to Segar Lighting Corp., $1,285.28, against P298. DM32.

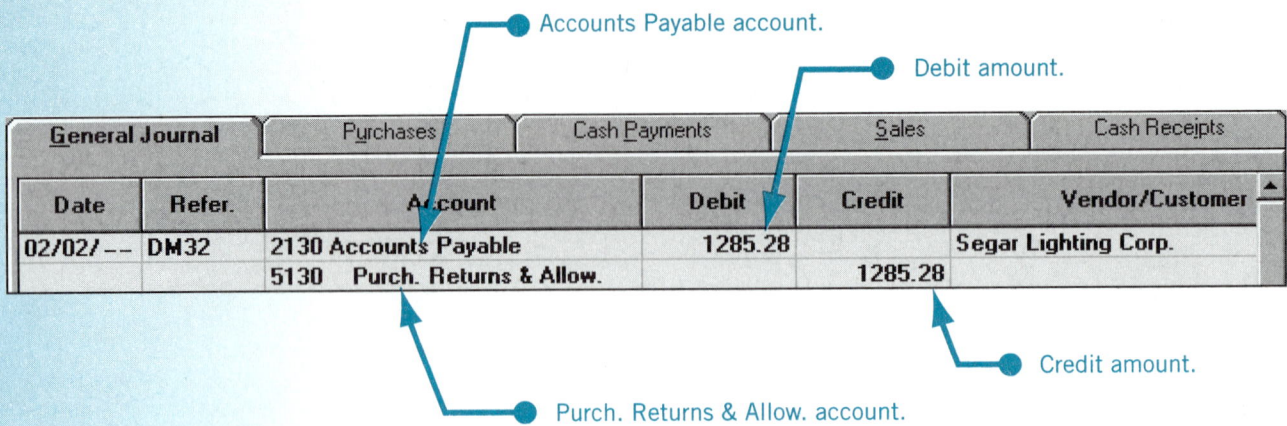

Figure 7.3
General Journal (Debit Memorandum)

CREDIT MEMORANDUMS

A credit memorandum results when a seller grants credit to a customer for merchandise returned or grants an allowance for inferior or damaged merchandise. Credit memorandums are recorded in the general journal. A sample transaction involving a credit memorandum is listed below and shown entered in the general journal in Figure 7.4.

Feb. 04   Granted credit to Weber Lite Shoppe for merchandise returned, $395.00, against S451. CM52.

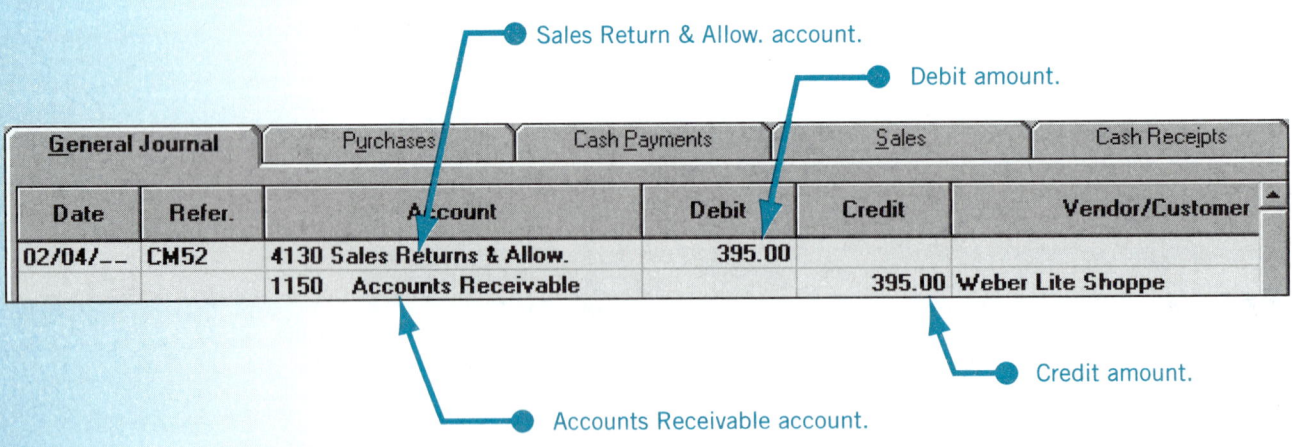

Figure 7.4
General Journal (Credit Memorandum)

Chapter 7 Discounts, Debit Memorandums, and Credit Memorandums

Chapter Review

1. A purchases discount is a deduction on the invoice amount of the purchase that is given a buyer in order to encourage early payment. Purchases discounts are recorded in the cash payments journal. A time period during which a deduction of the invoice amount may be taken is known as the discount period.

2. A sales discount is a deduction on the invoice amount of the sale that is given by the seller to a buyer in order to encourage early payment. Sales discounts are recorded in the cash receipts journal.

3. A debit memorandum is the form prepared by the customer showing the price deduction for returns and allowances.

4. A credit memorandum is the form prepared by the vendor showing the amount deducted for returned or damaged merchandise. Both credit and debit memorandums are recorded in the general journal.

ACCOUNTING CAREERS IN DEPTH

Audit Clerk

Audit clerks verify the accuracy of figures, calculations, and postings pertaining to business transactions recorded by other workers. An audit clerk performs the following duties:

- Examining expense accounts, commissions paid to employees, loans made on insurance policies, interest and account payments, cash receipts, sales tickets, bank records, inventory and stock-record sheets, and similar items to verify the accuracy of recorded data.
- Correcting errors or listing discrepancies for adjustment.
- Computing percentages and totals, using adding or calculating machines, and comparing results of recorded entries.

Audit clerks are also known by other titles, depending on the type of records to be audited. Some examples are: Cash-Sales Audit Clerk; Charge-Account Audit Clerk; C.O.D. Audit Clerk; Commission Auditor (insurance); Expense Clerk; Inventory-Audit Clerk; Journal-Entry Audit Clerk; and Medical-Records Auditor. As you can see, there are many opportunities to work as an audit clerk. The positions can be found in a variety of industries such as the medical, insurance, and retail fields.

A position as an audit clerk can be very detail-oriented because the work requires that the clerk check every detail of a transaction. In such a position, there are opportunities to learn many details of the organization in which you work. This will give you knowledge about different aspects of a company, which could give you a competitive advantage when seeking opportunities for advancement.

There is always the chance that if you enjoy being an audit clerk, you may choose to further your education and become an auditor. If not, job satisfaction is still possible, especially if you choose to become an audit clerk in an area in which you are interested.

TUTORIAL PROBLEM 7-T

In this tutorial problem, you will enter the journal entries for transactions involving sales discounts, purchases discounts, sales returns and allowances, and purchases returns and allowances. In addition, you will generate journal entries reports, a Trial Balance, and Schedules of Accounts Payable and Accounts Receivable.

STEP 1: **Start up *Automated Accounting 8.0*.**

STEP 2: **Load the file named AA8 Problem 07-T.**

STEP 3: **Enter your name in the User Name text box and click *OK*.**

STEP 4: **Save the file as 07-T Your Name.**
Key the following information from the transaction statements or refer to Figures 7.5 through 7.9. The reference numbers have been abbreviated as follows: purchase invoice no., P; check no., C; sales invoice no., S; cash receipt no., R; cash register tape, T; memorandum, M; credit memorandum, CM; debit memorandum, DM.

Feb. 01 Paid cash on account to Billington, Inc., $4,136.45, covering P300 for $4,178.23, less 1% discount, $41.78. C626.

01 Purchased merchandise on account from Wolf Electric Light Co., $2,995.00. P303.

02 Received cash on account from Blume Lighting Co., $5,356.12, covering S448 for $5,410.22, less 1% discount, $54.10. R217.

02 Sold merchandise on account to Anton Lite-House, $4,846.30. S454.

02 Returned merchandise to Segar Lighting Corp., $1,285.28, against P298. DM32.

03 Received cash on account from Oliver Electric Supply, $4,304.56, covering S449. No discount. R218.

03 Sold merchandise on account to Riley Lighting Systems, $6,000.00. S455.

04 Granted credit to Weber Lite Shoppe for merchandise returned, $395.00, against S451. CM52.

05 Sold merchandise on account to Moen Lighting Outlet, $4,510.00. S456.

05 Paid cash on account to Wolf Electric Light Co., $2,705.60, covering P296. No discount. C627.

Chapter 7 Discounts, Debit Memorandums, and Credit Memorandums

TUTORIAL PROBLEM 7-T

06 Purchased merchandise on account from Diamond Lighting, Inc., $3,480.20. P304.

06 Paid cash on account to Solberg Supplies, Inc., $514.25, covering M24 for $519.44, less 1% discount, $5.19. C628.

06 Received cash on account from Moen Lighting Outlet, $5,160.45, covering S452 for $5,212.58, less 1% discount, $52.13. R219.

08 Returned merchandise to Stein Light Fixture Co., $1,050.00, against P302. DM33.

08 Paid cash on account to Segar Lighting Corp., $2,088.12, covering P298 less DM32, no discount. C629.

09 Received cash on account from Weber Lite Shoppe, $4,329.70, covering S451 less CM52, no discount. R220.

10 Granted credit to Riley Lighting Systems for merchandise returned, $950.00, against S455. CM53.

10 Recorded cash and credit card sales, $3,680.72, plus sales tax, $257.65; total, $3,938.37. T17.

STEP 5: **Enter the data from the general journal shown in Figure 7.5.** Click the *Journal* toolbar button. Click the *General Journal* tab and enter the journal entries.

Date	Refer.	Account	Debit	Credit	Vendor/Customer
02/02/--	DM32	2130 Accounts Payable	1285.28		Segar Lighting Corp.
		5130 Purch. Returns & Allow.		1285.28	
02/04/--	CM52	4130 Sales Returns & Allow.	395.00		
		1150 Accounts Receivable		395.00	Weber Lite Shoppe
02/08/--	DM33	2130 Accounts Payable	1050.00		Stein Light Fixture Co.
		5130 Purch. Returns & Allow.		1050.00	
02/10/--	CM53	4130 Sales Returns & Allow.	950.00		
		1150 Accounts Receivable		950.00	Riley Lighting Systems

Figure 7.5
General Journal

What motivates consumers to shop on the Internet? Most Net shoppers cite the speed of the transaction, selection, convenience, and price.

TUTORIAL PROBLEM 7-T

STEP 6: Enter the data from the purchases journal shown in Figure 7.6.
Click the *Purchases* tab and enter the journal entries.

Date	Refer.	Purch. Debit	A.P. Credit	Vendor
02/03/--	P303	2995.00	2995.00	Wolf Electric Light Co.
02/06/--	P304	3480.20	3480.20	Diamond Lighting, Inc.

Figure 7.6
Purchases Journal

STEP 7: Enter the data from the cash payments journal shown in Figure 7.7.
Click the *Cash Payments* tab and enter the journal entries.

Date	Refer.	A.P. Debit	Purchase Disc. Cr	Cash Credit	Vendor
02/01/--	C626	4178.23	41.78	4136.45	Billington, Inc.
02/05/--	C627	2705.60		2705.60	Wolf Electric Light Co.
02/06/--	C628	519.44	5.19	514.25	Solberg Supplies, Inc.
02/08/--	C629	2088.12		2088.12	Segar Lighting Corp.

Figure 7.7
Cash Payments Journal

STEP 8: Enter the data from the sales journal shown in Figure 7.8.
Click the *Sales* tab and enter the journal entries.

Date	Refer.	Sales Credit	Sales Tax Credit	A.R. Debit	Customer
02/02/--	S454	4846.30		4846.30	Anton Lite-House
02/03/--	S455	6000.00		6000.00	Riley Lighting Systems
02/05/--	S456	4510.00		4510.00	Moen Lighting Outlet

Figure 7.8
Sales Journal

Chapter 7 Discounts, Debit Memorandums, and Credit Memorandums

TUTORIAL PROBLEM 7-T

STEP 9: **Enter the data from the Cash Receipts Journal window shown in Figure 7.9.**
Click the *Cash Receipts* tab and enter the journal entries.

Date	Refer.	A.R. Credit	Sales Credit	Sales Tax Pay. Cr	Sales Disc. Dr	Cash Debit	Customer
02/02/--	R217	5410.22			54.10	5356.12	Blume Lighting Co.
02/03/--	R218	4304.56				4304.56	Oliver Electric Supply
02/06/--	R219	5212.58			52.13	5160.45	Moen Lighting Outlet
02/09/--	R220	4329.70				4329.70	Weber Lite Shoppe
02/10/--	T17		3680.72	257.65		3938.37	

Figure 7.9
Cash Receipts Journal

STEP 10: **Display the journal reports.**
Click the *Reports* toolbar icon. Choose the *Journals* option button. Select the desired journal report, and then click *OK*. When the Journal Report Selection window appears, choose the *Customize Journal Report* option and click *OK*. Set the Start and End Dates to February 1 and February 10 of the current year and click *OK*. The reports appear in Figures 7.10 through 7.14.

```
                     Denco Lighting Corp.
                        General Journal
                           02/10/--

-----------------------------------------------------------------
Date   Refer.  Acct.  Title                    Debit      Credit
-----------------------------------------------------------------

02/02  DM32    2130   AP/Segar Lighting Corp.  1285.28
02/02  DM32    5130   Purch. Returns & Allow.             1285.28

02/04  CM52    4130   Sales Returns & Allow.    395.00
02/04  CM52    1150   AR/Weber Lite Shoppe                 395.00

02/08  DM33    2130   AP/Stein Light Fixture Co. 1050.00
02/08  DM33    5130   Purch. Returns & Allow.             1050.00

02/10  CM53    4130   Sales Returns & Allow.    950.00
02/10  CM53    1150   AR/Riley Lighting Systems            950.00
                                                --------  --------
                      Totals                    3680.28   3680.28
                                                ========  ========
```

Figure 7.10
General Journal Report

TUTORIAL PROBLEM 7-T

Denco Lighting Corp.
Purchases Journal
02/10/--

Date	Inv. No.	Acct.	Title	Debit	Credit
02/03	P303	5110	Purchases	2995.00	
02/03	P303	2130	AP/Wolf Electric Light Co.		2995.00
02/06	P304	5110	Purchases	3480.20	
02/06	P304	2130	AP/Diamond Lighting, Inc.		3480.20
			Totals	6475.20	6475.20

Figure 7.11
Purchases Journal Report

Denco Lighting Corp.
Cash Payments Journal
02/10/--

Date	Ck. No.	Acct.	Title	Debit	Credit
02/01	C626	2130	AP/Billington, Inc.	4178.23	
02/01	C626	1110	Cash		4136.45
02/01	C626	5120	Purchases Discount		41.78
02/05	C627	2130	AP/Wolf Electric Light Co.	2705.60	
02/05	C627	1110	Cash		2705.60
02/06	C628	2130	AP/Solberg Supplies, Inc.	519.44	
02/06	C628	1110	Cash		514.25
02/06	C628	5120	Purchases Discount		5.19
02/08	C629	2130	AP/Segar Lighting Corp.	2088.12	
02/08	C629	1110	Cash		2088.12
			Totals	9491.39	9491.39

Figure 7.12
Cash Payments Journal Report

Chapter 7 Discounts, Debit Memorandums, and Credit Memorandums

TUTORIAL PROBLEM 7-T

Denco Lighting Corp.
Sales Journal
02/10/--

Date	Inv. No.	Acct.	Title	Debit	Credit
02/02	S454	1150	AR/Anton Lite-House	4846.30	
02/02	S454	4110	Sales		4846.30
02/03	S455	1150	AR/Riley Lighting Systems	6000.00	
02/03	S455	4110	Sales		6000.00
02/05	S456	1150	AR/Moen Lighting Outlet	4510.00	
02/05	S456	4110	Sales		4510.00
			Totals	15356.30	15356.30

Figure 7.13 Sales Journal Report

Denco Lighting Corp.
Cash Receipts Journal
02/10/--

Date	Refer.	Acct.	Title	Debit	Credit
02/02	R217	1110	Cash	5356.12	
02/02	R217	4120	Sales Discount	54.10	
02/02	R217	1150	AR/Blume Lighting Co.		5410.22
02/03	R218	1110	Cash	4304.56	
02/03	R218	1150	AR/Oliver Electric Supply		4304.56
02/06	R219	1110	Cash	5160.45	
02/06	R219	4120	Sales Discount	52.13	
02/06	R219	1150	AR/Moen Lighting Outlet		5212.58
02/09	R220	1110	Cash	4329.70	
02/09	R220	1150	AR/Weber Lite Shoppe		4329.70
02/10	T17	1110	Cash	3938.37	
02/10	T17	4110	Sales		3680.72
02/10	T17	2150	Sales Tax Payable		257.65
			Totals	23195.43	23195.43

Figure 7.14 Cash Receipts Report

TUTORIAL PROBLEM 7-T

STEP 11: Display a Trial Balance, a Schedule of Accounts Payable, and a Schedule of Accounts Receivable.
Choose *Ledger Reports*. Select the desired ledger report and click *OK*. The reports are shown in Figures 7.15 through 7.17.

Denco Lighting Corp.
Trial Balance
02/10/--

Acct. Number	Account Title	Debit	Credit
1110	Cash	24640.87	
1120	Petty Cash	200.00	
1130	Notes Receivable	7800.00	
1150	Accounts Receivable	26550.24	
1160	Merchandise Inventory	79633.79	
1170	Supplies--Office	470.00	
1180	Supplies--Store	885.00	
1190	Prepaid Insurance	800.00	
1510	Office Equipment	13085.00	
1520	Accum. Depr.--Ofc. Eqpt.		3492.38
1530	Store Equipment	10295.00	
1540	Accum. Depr.--Store Eqpt.		2350.00
2110	Notes Payable		10500.00
2130	Accounts Payable		17565.61
2150	Sales Tax Payable		1313.47
3110	Capital Stock		99000.00
3120	Retained Earnings		16645.60
4110	Sales		19037.02
4120	Sales Discount	106.23	
4130	Sales Returns & Allow.	1345.00	
5110	Purchases	6475.20	
5120	Purchases Discount		46.97
5130	Purch. Returns & Allow.		2335.28
	Totals	172286.33	172286.33

Figure 7.15
Trial Balance

Chapter 7 Discounts, Debit Memorandums, and Credit Memorandums

TUTORIAL PROBLEM 7-T

Denco Lighting Corp.
Schedule of Accounts Payable
02/10/--

Name	Balance
Diamond Lighting, Inc.	7302.06
Fossen Manufacturing	4043.00
Stein Light Fixture Co.	3225.55
Wolf Electric Light Co.	2995.00
Total	17565.61

Figure 7.16
Schedule of Accounts Payable

Denco Lighting Corp.
Schedule of Accounts Receivable
02/10/--

Name	Balance
Anton Lite-House	10394.25
Moen Lighting Outlet	4510.00
Riley Lighting Systems	11645.99
Total	26550.24

Figure 7.17
Schedule of Accounts Receivable

STEP 12: **Generate a sales graph.**
Click the *Graphs* toolbar button. Choose the *Sales* graph, and then select the *Line* graph. Click *OK*. The sales graph is shown in Figure 7.18.

TUTORIAL PROBLEM 7-T

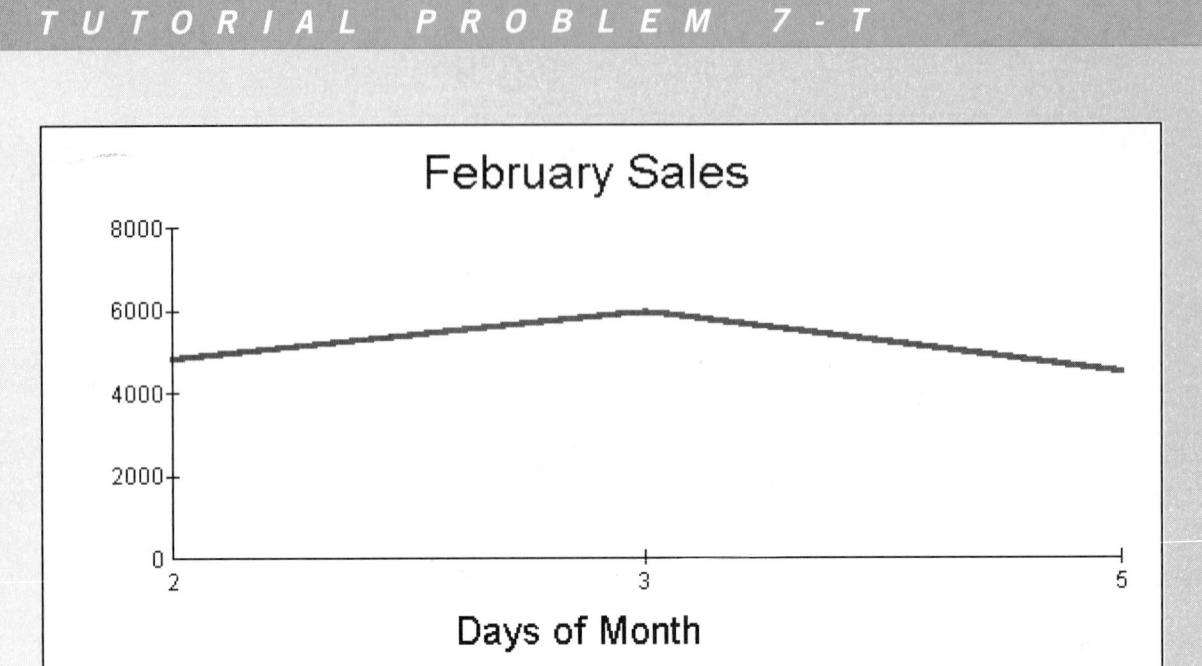

Figure 7.18
Sales Graph

STEP 13: Calculate a loan payment amount using the Loan Planner.
The management of Denco Lighting Corp. is considering acquiring a loan to purchase a conveyer system for its warehouse. Management has narrowed its choices to two local banks and has asked you to use the Loan Planner to furnish loan payment information based upon the data provided from each bank.

Click the *Tools* toolbar button. When the Planning Tools window appears, click the *Loan Planner* tab, enter the Bank 1 data, and display a loan amortization schedule. Repeat the procedure for Bank 2. The loan amortization schedule shown in Figure 7.19 is for Bank 1. The loan amortization schedule for Bank 2 will show a monthly payment amount of $730.29.

```
******** Bank 1 ********        ******** Bank 2 ********
Loan Amount       80000.00      Loan Amount       80000.00
Annual Interest       7.75      Annual Interest       7.25
Number of Payments    360       Number of Payments    180
```

Chapter 7 Discounts, Debit Memorandums, and Credit Memorandums

TUTORIAL PROBLEM 7-T

Denco Lighting Corp.
Loan Amortization Schedule
02/10/--

Payment Number	Payment Amount	Loan Principal	Interest	Balance
(Loan Amount)				80000.00
1	573.13	56.46	516.67	79943.54
2	573.13	56.83	516.30	79886.71
3	573.13	57.19	515.94	79829.52
4	573.13	57.56	515.57	79771.96
5	573.13	57.94	515.19	79714.02
6	573.13	58.31	514.82	79655.71
7	573.13	58.69	514.44	79597.02
8	573.13	59.07	514.06	79537.95
9	573.13	59.45	513.68	79478.50
10	573.13	59.83	513.30	79418.67
11	573.13	60.22	512.91	79358.45
12	573.13	60.61	512.52	79297.84
/\				
355	573.13	551.42	21.71	2810.85
356	573.13	554.98	18.15	2255.87
357	573.13	558.56	14.57	1697.31
358	573.13	562.17	10.96	1135.14
359	573.13	565.80	7.33	569.34
360	573.02	569.34	3.68	.00

Figure 7.19
Loan Amortization Schedule for Bank 1

STEP 14: Optional Spreadsheet and Word Processing Integration Activities.
Use a spreadsheet to create a Business Summary Report. Then use a word processor to format and enhance the appearance of the report for management. The report should contain the account balances for Cash, Accounts Receivable, Accounts Payable, net sales (Sales minus Sales Discounts and Sales Returns & Allowances), and net purchases (Purchases minus Purchases Discounts and Purchases Returns & Allowances) from the current Trial Balance.

TUTORIAL PROBLEM 7-T

Spreadsheet:

a. Display and copy the Trial Balance to the clipboard in spreadsheet format.
b. Start up your spreadsheet software and load the template file named AA8 Spreadsheet 07-T.
c. Select cell A1 as the current cell, and then paste the Trial Balance (copied to the clipboard in Step a) into the spreadsheet.
d. Enter the following labels, cell references, and formulas in the cells indicated:

	B	C
38	+B3	
39	Summary Report	
40	+B5	
41		
42	+B10	+C10
43	+B13	+C13
44	+B23	+D23
45	Net Sales	+D27-(C28+C29)
46	Net Purchases	+C30-(D31+D32)

e. Save the completed spreadsheet with a file name of 07-T Your Name. Subsequent Trial Balance reports for Denco Lighting Corp. that are saved in spreadsheet format can be merged into this template file whenever management requires an updated Summary Report.
f. Print the Summary Report (cells B38–C46). The completed Summary Report for February 10 is shown in Figure 7.20.

Denco Lighting Corp.
Summary Report
As of 02/10/--

Cash	24640.87
Accounts Receivable	26550.24
Accounts Payable	17565.61
Net Sales	17585.79
Net Purchases	4092.95

Figure 7.20
Spreadsheet Summary Report

Chapter 7 Discounts, Debit Memorandums, and Credit Memorandums

TUTORIAL PROBLEM 7-T

Word Processing:

a. Start up your word processing software and create a new document. Use a fixed font such as Courier.
b. Copy and paste the spreadsheet Summary Report into the new document.
c. Format and enhance the report's appearance.
d. Save the document with a file name of 07-T Your Name.
e. Print the report. The completed Summary Report is shown in Figure 7.21.
f. End your spreadsheet and word processing sessions.

Denco Lighting Corp.
Summary Report
As of 02/10/--

Cash	$ 24,640.87
Accounts Receivable	26,550.24
Accounts Payable	17,565.61
Net Sales	17,585.79
Net Purchases	4,092.95

Figure 7.21
Word Processed Summary Report

STEP 15: Save your data as 07-T Your Name.

STEP 16: End the *Automated Accounting* session.

Many car-related web sites allow you to search electronically for specific models, both new and used. Most will even get price quotes for you.

Humor on the Internet is one of its most popular features. However, the freedom to post any type of humor can result in material that people might find not funny or even offensive.

E-commerce is any transaction completed over a computer network that involves the transfer of ownership or rights to use goods and services.

Chapter 7 Discounts, Debit Memorandums, and Credit Memorandums

Review and Practice: Applying Your Information Skills

I. MATCHING

Directions: In the *Working Papers*, write the letter of the appropriate term next to each definition.

a. credit memorandum
b. debit memorandum
c. discount period
d. purchases discount
e. sales discount

1. The form prepared by the customer showing the price deduction for returns and allowances. From the buyer's point of view, returns and allowances result in a debit to the vendor's account.

2. From the seller's point of view, a deduction for early payment of an invoice.

3. From the buyer's point of view, a deduction for early payment of an invoice.

4. The specified time period within which a deduction from an invoice amount may be taken.

5. The form prepared by the vendor showing the amount deducted for returns and allowances. From the seller's point of view, returns result in a credit to the customer's account.

II. REVIEW QUESTIONS

Directions: Write the answers to the following questions in the *Working Papers*.

1. Which journal is used to enter a transaction involving a purchases discount?

2. When a transaction involving a purchases discount is entered, is the Purchases Discounts account debited or credited?

3. Which journal is used to enter a transaction involving a sales discount?

4. When a transaction involving a sales discount is entered, is the Sales Discounts account debited or credited?

5. In which journal is a debit memorandum entered?

Chapter 7 Discounts, Debit Memorandums, and Credit Memorandums

6. Does a debit memorandum affect a vendor's account or a customer's account?

7. When a debit memorandum is entered, which general ledger account is credited?

8. When a credit memorandum is entered, which general ledger account is debited?

III. INTERNET ACTIVITY

Directions: If you have access to the Internet, use your browser to obtain information about e-mail etiquette or e-mail abuse. Use *Computers Internet Etiquette* as your search argument. Report your findings. Be sure to note the source and the URL (Internet address) of your search.

Independent Practice Problem 7-P

In this problem, you will process selected transactions involving purchases discounts, sales discounts, debit memorandums, and credit memorandums for the period February 11 through February 20 of the current year.

STEP 1: Start up *Automated Accounting 8.0*.

STEP 2: Load the opening balances file named AA8 Problem 07-P.

STEP 3: Enter your name in the User Name text box.

STEP 4: Save the opening balances file as 07-P Your Name.

STEP 5: Enter the following transactions:

Feb. 11   Returned merchandise to Wolf Electric Light Co., $310.00, against P303. DM34.

11   Sold merchandise on account to Oliver Electric Supply, $2,448.00. S457.

11   Purchased merchandise on account from Fossen Manufacturing, $4,235.40. P305.

12   Paid cash on account to Stein Light Fixture Co., $3,225.55, covering P302, less DM33, no discount. C630.

12   Received cash on account from Anton Lite-House, $5,547.95, covering S450. No discount. R221.

12   Received cash on account from Anton Lite-House, $4,797.84, covering S454 for $4,846.30, less 1% discount, $48.46. R222.

13 Paid cash on account to Fossen Manufacturing, $4,043.00, covering P299. No discount. C631.
13 Paid cash on account to Diamond Lighting, Inc., $3,821.86, covering P297. No discount. C632.
13 Bought office supplies on account from Solberg Supplies, Inc., $825.00. M25.
15 Sold merchandise on account to Weber Lite Shoppe, $5,234.62. S458.
15 Sold merchandise on account to Blume Lighting Co., $4,210.00. S459.
15 Received cash on account from Moen Lighting Outlet, $4,464.90, covering S456 for $4,510.00 less 1% discount, $45.10. R223.
16 Received cash on account from Riley Lighting Systems, $6,595.99, covering S453. No discount. R224.
16 Paid cash on account to Diamond Lighting, Inc., $3,445.40, covering P304 for $3,480.20, less 1% discount, $34.80. C633.
16 Granted credit to Oliver Electric Supply for merchandise returned, $485.00, against S457. CM54.
17 Purchased merchandise on account from Segar Lighting Corp., $3,460.00. P306.
18 Sold merchandise on account to Anton Lite-House, $1,750.50. S460.
19 Returned merchandise to Wolf Electric Light Co., $60.00, against P303. DM35.
19 Paid cash on account to Fossen Manufacturing, $4,193.05, covering P305 for $4,235.40, less 1% discount, $42.35. C634.
19 Purchased merchandise on account from Stein Light Fixture Co., $3,175.95. P307.
20 Purchased merchandise on account from Billington, Inc., $3,713.28. P308.
20 Granted credit to Anton Lite-House for merchandise returned, $130.00, against S460. CM55.
20 Recorded cash and credit card sales, $3,254.72, plus sales tax, $227.83; total, $3,482.55. T30.

STEP 6: Display the General, Purchases, Cash Payments, Sales, and Cash Receipts Journal Reports for the period February 11 through February 20. If errors are detected, make corrections.

STEP 7: Display a Trial Balance, Schedule of Accounts Payable, and Schedule of Accounts Receivable.

Chapter 7 Discounts, Debit Memorandums, and Credit Memorandums

STEP 8: Generate a sales graph.

STEP 9: Save your data.

STEP 10: Calculate a loan amount using the Loan Planner.

Denco Lighting Corp. believes it can comfortably afford a loan payment of $1,250.00 per month over the next 7 years for a conveyer system for its warehouse. You have been asked to use the Loan Planner to find the loan amount, given the following information provided by two local banks.

Select the *Loan Amount* option in the Calculate grouping, and then enter the loan information provided below:

```
******** Bank 1 ********       ******** Bank 2 ********
Annual Interest      7.75      Annual Interest      7.25
Number of Payments    84       Number of Payments    84
Payment Amount   1250.00       Payment Amount   1250.00
```

STEP 11: Optional Spreadsheet and Word Processing Integration Activities.

Use a spreadsheet to create a Business Summary Report. Then use a word processor to format and enhance the appearance of the report for management. The report should contain the Cash balance, Accounts Receivable balance, Accounts Payable balance, net sales (Sales minus Sales Discounts and Sales Returns & Allowances), and net purchases (Purchases minus Purchases Discounts and Purchases Returns & Allowances) from the February 20 trial balance.

Spreadsheet:

a. Display and copy the Trial Balance to the clipboard in spreadsheet format.
b. Start up your spreadsheet software and load the template file named AA8 Spreadsheet 07-T. If you completed the optional spreadsheet activity in Tutorial Problem 7-T, load your solution spreadsheet template file and skip to Step 11-d.
c. Select cell A1 as the current cell, and then paste the Trial Balance (copied to the clipboard in Step a) into the spreadsheet.
d. Enter the appropriate label(s), cell references, and formulas (see Figure 7.20).
e. Save the completed spreadsheet with a file name of 07-P Your Name.
f. Print the Summary Report.

Word Processing:

a. Start up your word processing application software and create a new document. Use a fixed font such as Courier.
b. Copy and paste the spreadsheet Summary Report into the new document.
c. Format and enhance the report's appearance, similar to Figure 7.21.
d. Save the document with a file name of 07-P Your Name.
e. Print the report.
f. End your spreadsheet and word processing sessions.

STEP 12: End the *Automated Accounting* session.

Applying Your Technology Skills 7-P

Directions: Using Independent Practice Problem 7-P, write the answers to the following questions in the *Working Papers*.

Journal Reports

1. What is the amount of Debit Memorandum No. 34 for Wolf Electric Light Co.?
2. What is the amount of Credit Memorandum No. 55 for Anton Lite-House?
3. What is the amount of Purchase Invoice No. 305 for Fossen Manufacturing?
4. What are the total debits and total credits in the Purchases Journal Report?
5. What is the amount of Check No. 630 for Stein Light Fixture Co.?
6. What are the total debits and total credits in the Cash Payments Journal?
7. What is the amount of Sales Invoice No. 460 for Anton Lite-House?
8. What are the total debits and total credits in the Cash Receipts Journal?

Trial Balance

9. What is the balance in the Cash account?
10. What is the balance in the Accounts Payable account?

Chapter 7   Discounts, Debit Memorandums, and Credit Memorandums

Schedules of Accounts Payable and Accounts Receivable

11. What is the current balance due to the vendor Solberg Supplies, Inc.?

12. What is the total amount owed to all vendors?

13. What is the amount due from the customer Anton Lite-House?

14. What is the total amount due from all customers?

Loan Planner

15. What is the calculated loan amount for Bank 1?

16. What is the calculated loan amount for Bank 2?

Mastery Problem 7-M

In this problem, you will process selected transactions involving purchases discounts, sales discounts, debit memorandums, and credit memorandums for the period February 21 through February 28 of the current year.

STEP 1: Start up *Automated Accounting 8.0*.

STEP 2: Load the file named AA8 Problem 07-M.

STEP 3: Enter your name in the User Name text box.

STEP 4: Save the opening balances file as 07-M Your Name.

STEP 5: Enter the following transactions:

Feb. 22   Paid cash on account to Solberg Supplies, Inc., $816.75, covering M25 for $825.00, less 1% discount, $8.25. C635.

22   Received cash on account from Weber Lite Shoppe, $5,182.27, covering S458 for $5,234.62, less 1% discount, $52.35. R225.

22   Received cash on account from Blume Lighting Co., $4,167.90, covering S459 for $4,210.00, less 1% discount, $42.10. R226.

22   Sold merchandise on account to Moen Lighting Outlet, $5,345.25. S461.

22   Sold merchandise on account to Blume Lighting Co., $3,229.90. S462.

23   Purchased merchandise on account from Fossen Manufacturing, $3,000.00. P309.

23   Purchased merchandise on account from Diamond Lighting, Inc., $2,000.00. P310.

24 Received cash on account from Oliver Electric Supply, $1,963.00, covering S457, less CM54, no discount. R227.
24 Paid cash on account to Billington, Inc., $3,676.15, covering P308 for $3,713.28, less 1% discount, $37.13. C636.
24 Purchased merchandise on account from Stein Light Fixture Co., $2,999.00. P311.
24 Paid cash on account to Wolf Electric Light Co., $2,625.00, covering P303 less DM34 and DM35, no discount. C637.
25 Sold merchandise on account to Weber Lite Shoppe, $5,000.00. S463.
25 Received cash on account from Anton Lite-House, $1,620.50, covering S460 less CM55, no discount. R228.
25 Paid cash on account to Segar Lighting Corp., $3,425.40, covering P306 for $3,460.00, less 1% discount, $34.60. C638.
26 Sold merchandise on account to Oliver Electric Supply, $5,275.86. S464.
26 Received cash on account from Riley Lighting Systems, $5,050.00, covering S455 less CM53, no discount. R229.
26 Returned merchandise to Fossen Manufacturing, $120.00, against P309. DM36.
26 Granted credit to Moen Lighting Outlet for merchandise returned, $245.00, against S461. CM56.
26 Sold merchandise on account to Riley Lighting Systems, $2,325.00. S465.
27 Returned merchandise to Diamond Lighting, Inc., $105.00, against P310. DM37.
27 Granted credit to Blume Lighting Co. for merchandise returned, $125.40, against S462. CM57.
27 Purchased merchandise on account from Wolf Electric Light Co., $1,580.00. P312.
27 Paid cash on account to Stein Light Fixture Co., $3,144.19, covering P307 for $3,175.95, less 1% discount, $31.76. C639.
28 Recorded cash and credit card sales, $2,942.12, plus sales tax, $205.95; total, $3,148.07. T37.

STEP 6: Display the journal reports.

STEP 7: Display the Trial Balance, Schedule of Accounts Payable, and Schedule of Accounts Receivable.

Chapter 7 Discounts, Debit Memorandums, and Credit Memorandums

STEP 8: Generate a sales graph.

STEP 9: Save your data with a file name of 07-M Your Name.

STEP 10: Use the Loan Planner to calculate the number of payments, given the following information:

```
********* Bank 1 ********        ********* Bank 2 ********
Loan Amount    100000.00         Loan mount     100000.00
Annual Interest      7.25        Annual Interest      6.75
Payment Amount   1500.00         Payment Amount   2000.00
```

STEP 11: Optional Spreadsheet and Word Processing Integration Activities.

Create a spreadsheet Business Summary Report. Then use a word processor to format and enhance the appearance of the report for management. The report should contain the Cash balance, Accounts Receivable balance, Accounts Payable balance, net sales (Sales minus Sales Discounts and Sales Returns & Allowances), and net purchases (Purchases minus Purchases Discounts and Purchases Returns & Allowances) from the February 28 Trial Balance.

Spreadsheet:

a. Start up your spreadsheet software and load the file named AA8 Spreadsheet 07-T. If you completed Tutorial Problem 7-T or Independent Practice Problem 7-P, load your solution file.
b. Select cell A1, and then copy and paste the February 28 Trial Balance into the spreadsheet.
c. Enter the appropriate label(s), cell references, and formulas.
d. Save the completed spreadsheet with a file name of 07-M Your Name.
e. Print the report.

Word Processing:

a. Start up your word processor software and create a new document.
b. Copy and paste the spreadsheet Summary Report into the new document.
c. Format and enhance the report's appearance.
d. Save the document as 07-M Your Name.
e. Print the document.

STEP 12: End the *Automated Accounting* session.

Applying Your Technology Skills 7-M

Directions: Using Mastery Problem 7-M, write the answers to the following questions in the *Working Papers*.

Journal Reports

1. What is the amount of Debit Memorandum No. 37 for Diamond Lighting, Inc.?
2. What is the amount of Credit Memorandum No. 57 for Blume Lighting Co.?
3. What is the amount of Purchase Invoice No. 312 for Wolf Electric Light Co.?
4. What are the total debits and total credits in the Purchases Journal Report?
5. What is the amount of Check No. 636 for Billington, Inc.?
6. What are the total debits and total credits in the Cash Payments Journal?
7. What is the amount of Sales Invoice No. 463 for Weber Lite Shoppe?
8. What are the total debits and total credits in the Cash Receipts Journal?

Trial Balance

9. What is the balance in the Cash account?
10. What is the balance in the Accounts Payable account?

Schedules of Accounts Payable and Accounts Receivable

11. What is the current balance due to the vendor Fossen Manufacturing?
12. What is the total amount owed to all vendors?
13. What is the amount due from the customer Moen Lighting Outlet?
14. What is the total amount due from all customers?

Loan Planner

15. What is the number of payments, based on Bank 1's data?
16. What is the number of payments, based on Bank 2's data?

Chapter 8
PLANT ASSETS

KEY TERMS

Plant Assets
Depreciation
Asset Disposition
Useful Life
Original Cost
Salvage Value

Plant Assets Input Form
Plant Asset Maintenance
Plant Assets List Report
Depreciation Schedule
Depreciation Adjusting Entries

LEARNING OBJECTIVES

Upon completion of this chapter, you will be able to:

1. Record additions, changes, and deletions on the plant assets input form.
2. Enter and correct plant asset data.
3. Display plant assets reports.
4. Generate and post yearly depreciation adjusting entries.

INTRODUCTION

Plant assets are assets used for a number of years in the operation of a business. A computerized plant asset system can be used to maintain records for all plant assets. The information provided by the plant asset system is used by the business in several ways. Accounting uses plant asset information to show costs, to allocate an asset's cost as an expense, and to show asset disposition. The portion of a plant asset's cost that is transferred to an expense account in each fiscal period during its useful life is called **depreciation**. **Asset disposition** means removing an asset from use in the business.

When an asset is purchased, it must be added to the plant asset file. When adding a plant asset, the useful life, original cost, salvage value,

ETHICS

A new dilemma brought on by the ever-increasing speed and capability of computers and their decreasing price per unit of performance involves the revival of deceased movie stars. Computers now have the ability to reconstruct the stars' images and voices through simulations. This means that Clark Gable could come back to star in the sequel to *Gone with the Wind*, or Marilyn Monroe could extend her career by "appearing" in completely new films for a new generation of fans.

To-date, the expense of ultra-high-resolution computer animation, which is required to produce "human-quality" output, has prevented its use for anything other than brief scenarios. (Perhaps you have seen commercials or short movie scenes in which contemporary stars have "interacted" with departed actors.) With the cost of the computer hardware required to accomplish this task continually going down, the possibility of making entire movies using "reconstructed" screen stars is becoming technologically and financially feasible.

Critical Thinking

1. Who do you think owns the likeness of the departed? Is it the person's estate or the movie studio to which the person was under contract?

2. Who has the right to decide, years after a celebrity's death, whether he or she would have any interest in doing a particular movie? Could a simulated performance destroy the reputation of a star long after his or her demise?

3. Do you think this issue is something that today's living legends and their agents should consider now, or otherwise risk being haunted forever by the consequences of emerging computer technology?

Chapter 8 Plant Assets

and depreciation method must be determined. The **useful life** of an asset is the estimated amount of time an asset can be used in the business. The **original cost** of a plant asset is all costs that are paid to make the asset usable to a business. The amount an owner expects to receive when a plant asset is removed from use is known as an asset's **salvage value**. (Another name for salvage value is trade-in value.) There are several ways or methods to depreciate an asset. This chapter will use the straight-line method of depreciation. In the straight-line method of depreciation, the salvage value is subtracted from the original cost and then the difference is divided by the asset's useful life.

At the end of the accounting cycle, the plant asset depreciation adjusting entries are generated and posted to the general ledger. Changes, corrections, and deletions are made to the assets as needed.

Plant asset information is used beyond the accounting area. For example, plant assets reports are used for insurance purposes to ensure adequate coverage. In the case of an insurance claim, these reports are often used to determine the amount of the settlement. The information can also be used to estimate the worth of an asset for trade-in value. Trade-in value is considered as payment or partial payment toward another asset.

PLANT ASSETS INPUT FORM

A **plant assets input form** is an input form used to record additions, changes, and deletions to plant assets, as illustrated in Figure 8.1. The first entry shown is an example of an addition of a new plant asset. All data fields must be completed, including the appropriate accumulated depreciation and expense depreciation account numbers from the chart of accounts. The second entry demonstrates a change. Therefore, only the asset number and the fields that have changed need to be completed. The last entry is an example of a deletion. The asset number and (Delete) are recorded.

>   2002
> Mar. 01   Purchased a computer (P4-1.5GHz) for $3,149.50; salvage value, $300.00; useful life, 5 years; depreciation method, SL; Asset No. 115.
> June 10   Change the name of Asset No. 210 to Computer Organizer.
> July 21   Delete Asset No. 105, Computer (P-133).

Each line is used to maintain one asset. Each column on the input form matches one of the columns in the Plant Assets Account Maintenance window in which the data will be keyed. The field names and a description of each column are illustrated in the Plant Assets Account Maintenance Window shown in Figure 8.2.

PLANT ASSETS INPUT FORM

Run Date 12/31/02   Problem No. Example

Asset No.	Asset Name	Date Acquired	Useful Life	Original Cost	Salvage Value	Accum. Deprec.	Deprec. Exp.	Deprec. Method
115	Computer (P4-1.5GHz)	03/01/02	5	3149.50	300.00	1540	6130	SL
210	Computer Organizer							
105	(Delete)							

Figure 8.1
Plant Assets Input Form

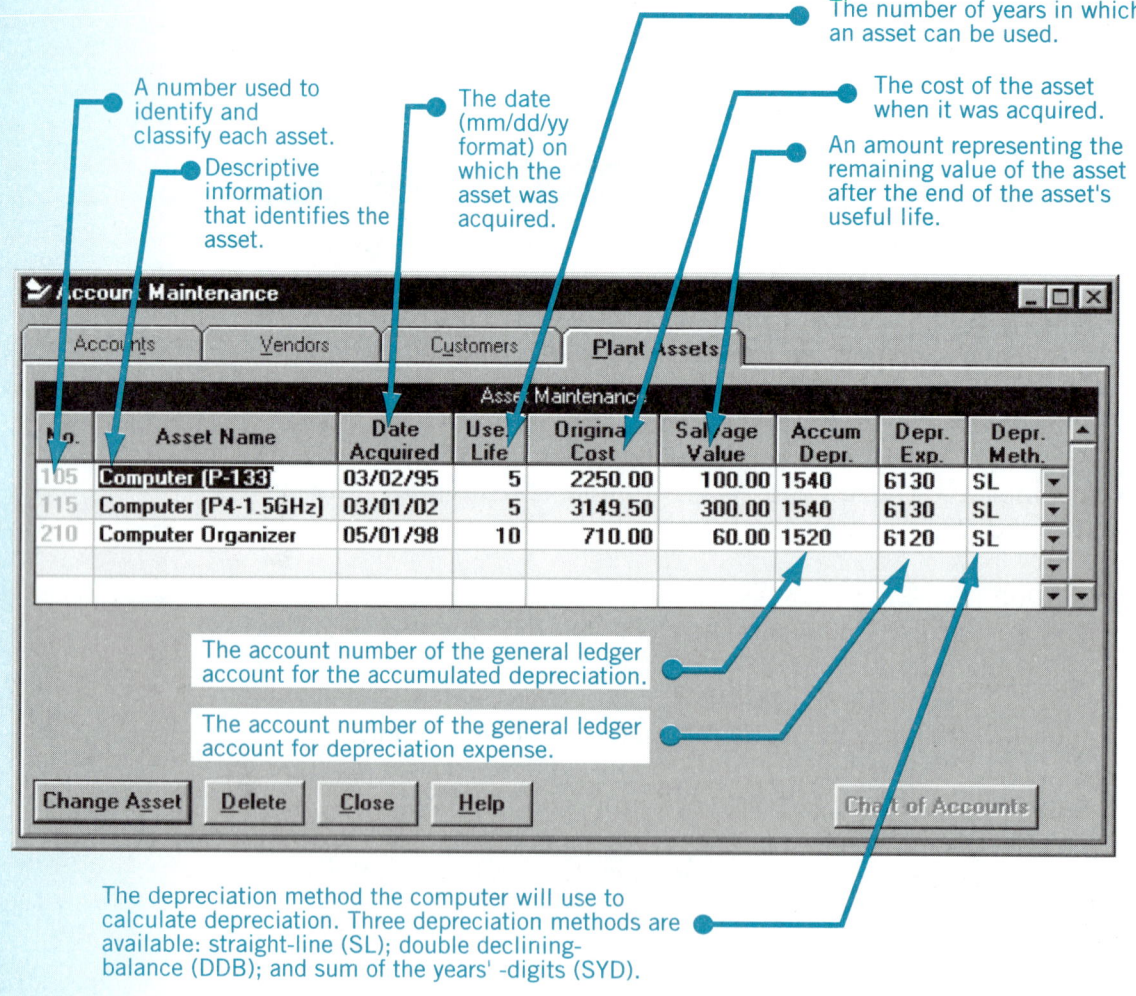

Figure 8.2
Plant Assets Maintenance Window

Chapter 8 Plant Assets

MAINTAIN PLANT ASSETS DATA

The process of adding, changing, and deleting plant assets is referred to as **plant asset maintenance**. When Maintain Accounts is chosen from the Data menu or the Accts. toolbar button is clicked, the Account Maintenance window will appear. Click the Plant Assets tab and enter the maintenance data. Figure 8.2 shows the maintenance data already entered from the plant assets input form in Figure 8.1. Asset no. 105 is shown selected and about to be deleted.

New assets can be added after the last plant asset in the list by keying the asset number, description, and each of the remaining columns of information shown in Figure 8.2 and then clicking the Add Asset button (the Change Asset button changes to Add Asset). The new asset will be inserted into the existing plant assets list in asset-number sequence. Existing plant assets can be changed by selecting the asset you wish to change, keying the correct data (or selecting a different depreciation method), and clicking the Change Asset button (the Add Asset button changes to Change Asset). An existing plant asset can be deleted by simply selecting the asset to be deleted and clicking the Delete button.

The asset number cannot be changed. A plant asset with an incorrect asset number must be deleted and then added back as a new plant asset with the correct number.

DISPLAYING PLANT ASSETS REPORTS

Once the asset data has been entered, the depreciation reports can be generated. Select Reports and choose the Plant Assets option button. (The Plant Assets List and Depreciation Schedules will appear as shown in Figure 8.3.) Select either of the two reports from the Choose a Report to Display list.

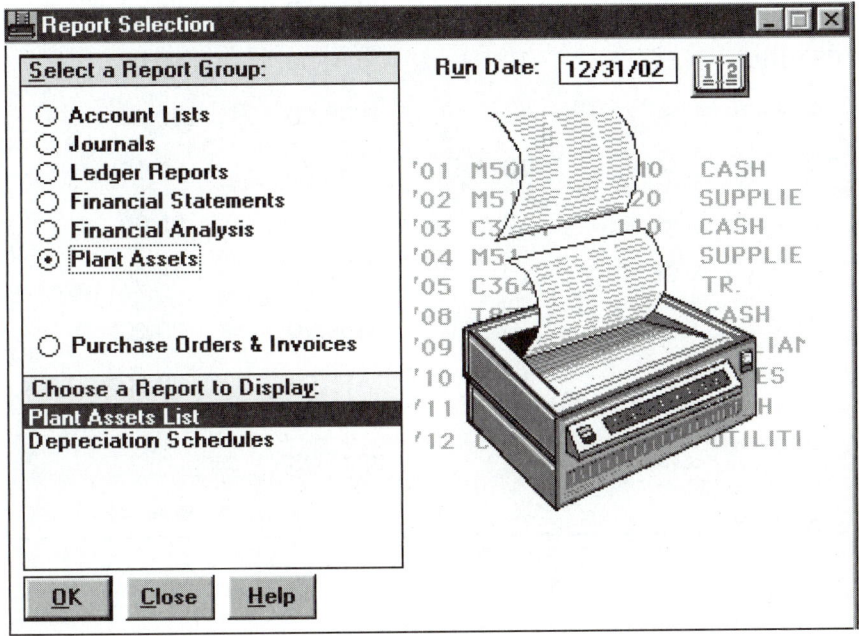

Figure 8.3
Report Selection
(Plant Asset Reports)

Plant Assets List Report

A report that provides a detailed list of all plant assets owned is called a **Plant Assets List Report**. The report provides information concerning the date acquired, depreciation method chosen, useful life, original cost, estimated salvage value, and depreciation accounts for each plant asset. The report is useful in detecting keying errors and verifying the accuracy of your input. An example of a Plant Assets List Report is shown in Figure 8.4.

Morales Jewelers
Plant Assets List
12/31/02

Asset	Date Acquired	Depr. Method	Useful Life	Original Cost	Salvage Value	Depr. Accts
110 Computer (P-800)	06/10/99	SL	5	2928.00	200.00	1540 6130
115 Computer (P4-1.5GHz)	03/01/02	SL	5	3149.50	300.00	1540 6130
120 Dot Matrix Printer	03/01/98	SL	5	320.00	50.00	1540 6130
130 File Server (598-32)	07/31/01	SL	5	1295.50	200.00	1540 6130
135 Hard Disk Drive	04/30/02	SL	5	499.95	40.00	1540 6130
140 Ink Jet Printer	07/20/01	SL	5	435.95	45.00	1540 6130
150 Notebook Computer	03/01/00	SL	5	1550.00	135.00	1540 6130
160 Copy Machine	02/20/00	SL	5	3875.00	425.00	1540 6130
170 Facsimile Machine	02/20/00	SL	5	549.00	25.00	1540 6130
180 Electronic Calculator	09/30/02	SL	5	125.50	20.00	1540 6130
210 Computer Organizer	05/01/98	SL	10	710.00	60.00	1520 6120
220 Display Case	05/01/98	SL	10	1800.00	150.00	1520 6120
230 Storage Credenza	05/01/98	SL	10	295.75	30.00	1520 6120
240 File Cabinet (6 Drawer)	09/02/99	SL	10	339.00	25.00	1520 6120
250 Book Case (5 Shelf)	10/03/98	SL	10	289.00	35.00	1520 6120
260 Copy Machine Stand	11/10/01	SL	10	169.90	20.00	1520 6120
270 File Cabinet (4 Drawer)	10/31/02	SL	10	485.00	50.00	1520 6120
Total Plant Assets				18817.05		

Figure 8.4
Plant Assets List Report

Chapter 8   Plant Assets

Depreciation Schedules

A report that provides annual depreciation for each year for the life of a plant asset is called a **Depreciation Schedule**. Depreciation Schedules can be generated for any range of assets.

When the Depreciation Schedules option is selected, the Depreciation Schedules window shown in Figure 8.5 appears, allowing you to select the range of assets for which Depreciation Schedules are to be generated. Figure 8.5 illustrates Asset Number 115, which was added earlier in the chapter.

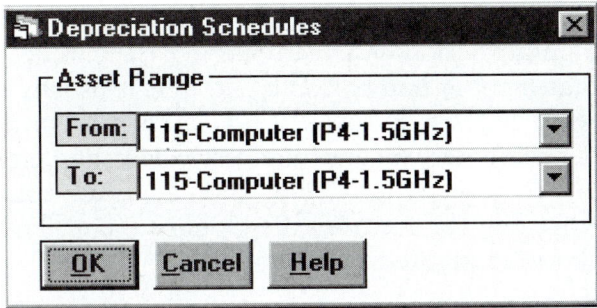

Figure 8.5
Depreciation Schedule Range Selection

Depreciation is calculated based on the date acquired, original cost, salvage value, and depreciation method. An asset purchased in any month other than January has first-year and last-year amounts that are prorated from the month the asset was purchased. In the example shown in Figure 8.6, which uses the straight-line method, the asset was purchased on March 1. Therefore, the first year's depreciation is for the period March through December, which is 10 months (or 10/12ths) of the annual depreciation of $569.90, or $474.92. The last 2 months in the last year are depreciated for 2/12ths of the annual depreciation of $569.90, or $94.98.

```
                    Morales Jewelers
                  Depreciation Schedules
                        12/31/02
```

	Year	Annual Deprec.	Accum. Deprec.	Book Value
(115) Computer (P4-1.5GHz	2002	474.92	474.92	2674.58
Acquired on 03/01/02	2003	569.90	1044.82	2104.68
Straight-Line	2004	569.90	1614.72	1534.78
Useful Life = 5	2005	569.90	2184.62	964.88
Original Cost = 3149.50	2006	569.90	2754.52	394.98
Salvage Value = 300.00	2007	94.98	2849.50	300.00

Figure 8.6
Depreciation Schedule

GENERATING AND POSTING DEPRECIATION ADJUSTING ENTRIES

Depreciation adjusting entries are the journal entries recorded to update the Depreciation Expense and Accumulated Depreciation accounts at the end of the fiscal period. When Depreciation Adjusting Entries is selected from the Options menu, the computer will analyze the plant assets records and determine the depreciation for the period, and then generate the depreciation adjusting entries. A dialog box containing the adjusting entries will appear.

The depreciation adjusting entries can be generated for either a monthly period or a yearly period, depending on how the Income Statement option button is set. This is usually selected during system setup and will be covered in Chapter 13. For the problems in this text, the computer will generate yearly adjusting entries.

To generate the depreciation adjusting entries, choose Depreciation Adjusting Entries from the Options menu. The confirmation dialog box shown in Figure 8.7 will appear.

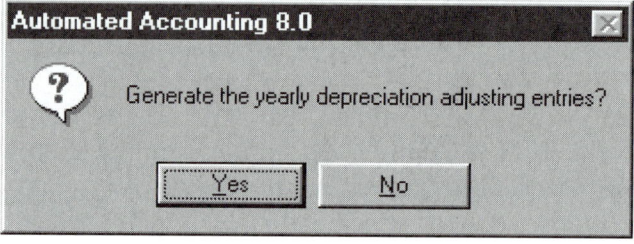

Figure 8.7
Confirmation Dialog Box

Click Yes. The computer-generated depreciation adjusting entry shown in Figure 8.8 will appear.

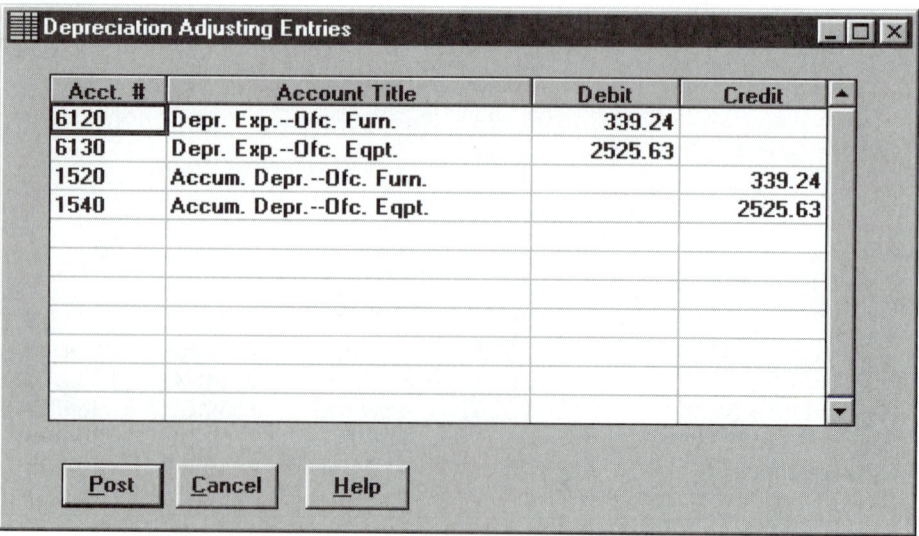

Figure 8.8
Depreciation Adjusting Entries Dialog Box

Chapter 8 Plant Assets

Click the Post button to post the entry to the general journal. The adjusting entry will then appear in the general journal, as illustrated in Figure 8.9. Verify the accuracy of the entry and click Post. If the adjusting entry is incorrect, return to the Plant Assets tab in the Account Maintenance window and make the necessary corrections. Then return to the general journal, delete the incorrect depreciation adjusting entry, and generate the new adjusting entries.

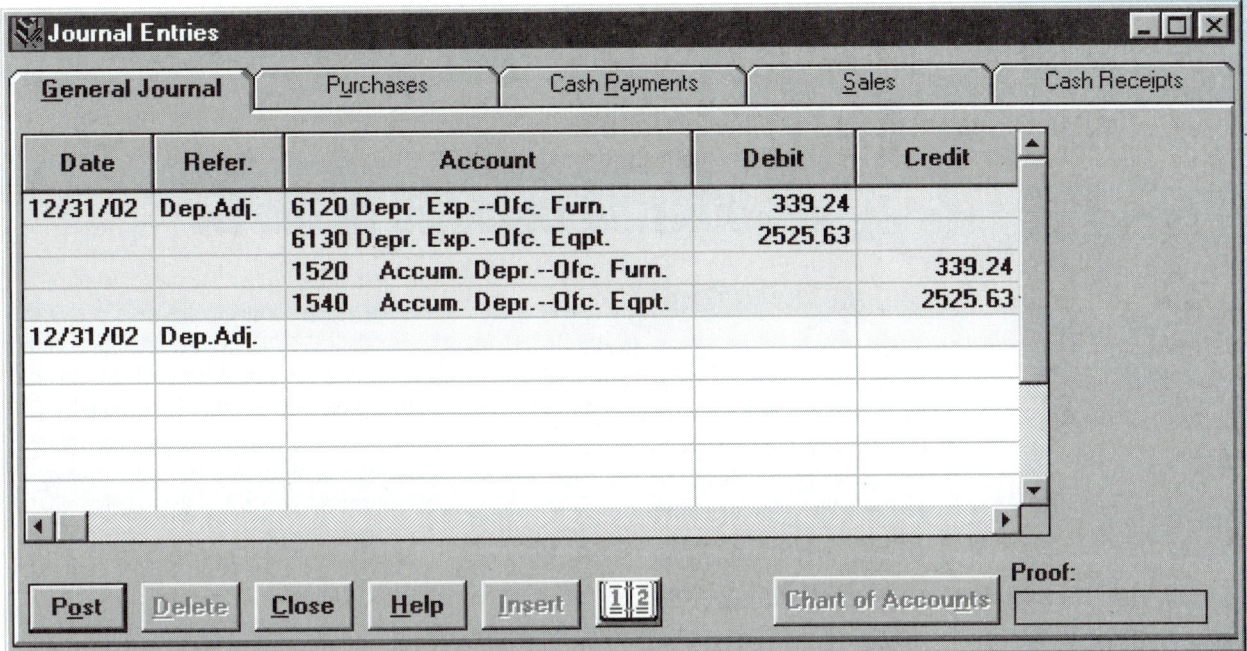

Figure 8.9
General Journal (Depreciation Adjusting Entries)

Chapter Review

1. Assets used for a number of years in the operation of a business are called plant assets. A computerized plant asset system is used to maintain records for all plant assets for a business. A plant assets input form is used to record all additions, changes, and deletions to plant assets.

2. Plant assets maintenance is the process of adding, changing, and deleting plant assets. Plant assets maintenance is performed by entering data in the Plant Assets tab within the Account Maintenance window.

3. The Plant Assets List Report provides information concerning the costs of assets and is useful in detecting keying errors and verifying the accuracy of input. Depreciation Schedules provide annual depreciation for each year for the life of the asset.

4. The software generates the depreciation adjusting entries by analyzing the plant asset records and determining the depreciation for the period.

ACCOUNTING CAREERS IN DEPTH

Budget Accountant

A budget accountant applies principles of accounting to analyze past and present financial operations and estimates future revenues and expenditures in order to prepare budgets. A budget accountant performs the following duties:

- Using a computer to analyze records of present and past operations, trends, and costs; estimated and realized revenues; administrative commitments; and obligations incurred in order to project future revenues and expenses.
- Maintaining budgeting systems that provide control of expenditures made to carry out activities—such as advertising and marketing, production, and maintenance—or to project activities such as the construction of buildings.

The educational requirements for a budget accountant include a college degree in accounting and preferably some work experience while in school. When students have acquired such work experience, they often have a competitive edge. Also, the internship or co-op experience may lead to the first job a student is offered when the college degree requirements have been met.

Analytical skills are very important in this career. It is necessary to be able to look at the "big picture" in order to accurately analyze reports or specific financial figures. Accountants must have the skills to create the financial reports and then analyze the figures used to prepare financial statements.

Choosing a career as a budget accountant can be as simple as balancing your checkbook and analyzing the trends of how you spend money; determining when you spend more for certain purchases; learning how much interest has accrued on your account; and then researching the possibility of transferring a portion of those funds in order to accrue a higher rate of return. Of course, doing this type of analysis for a corporation would involve many more factors and elements to consider.

Budget accountants are needed in all types of industries due to the nature of the work. You can choose the industry that interests you, and then assist a company in maintaining its budget while also being instrumental in keeping the company successful.

TUTORIAL PROBLEM 8-T

In this tutorial problem, you will add, change, and delete plant assets. In addition, you will generate the Plant Assets List Report and depreciation schedules.

STEP 1: **Start up *Automated Accounting 8.0*.**

STEP 2: **Load the opening balances template file named AA8 Problem 08-T.**

STEP 3: **Enter your name in the User Name text box and click *OK*.**

STEP 4: **Save the file as 08-T Your Name.**

STEP 5: **Enter the plant asset data.**
Click the *Accts.* toolbar button. When the Account Maintenance window appears, click the *Plant Assets* tab and enter the plant asset data described in the list of transactions. All transactions occurred in the year 2002. Figure 8.10 shows how the assets appear on the plant assets input form. Asset Number 105, Computer (P-133) is to be deleted. For Asset Number 210, only the name of the asset is to be changed.

Note: Asset numbers 100–199 are assigned to Office Equipment. Account number 1540 (Accum. Depr.—Ofc. Eqpt.) is used to accumulate office equipment depreciation, and account number 6130 (Depr. Exp.—Ofc. Eqpt.) is used to record the depreciation expense each fiscal period. Asset numbers 200–299 are assigned to Office Furniture. Account number 1520 (Accum. Depr.—Ofc. Furn.) is used to accumulate office furniture depreciation, and account number 6120 (Depr. Exp.—Ofc. Furn.) is used to record the depreciation expense each fiscal period.

It is very important that you enter the correct date acquired for each plant asset. Many of the calculated depreciation amounts are date sensitive and will display incorrectly if the dates are entered incorrectly.

2002
Mar. 01 Purchased a computer (P4-1.5GHz) for $3,149.50; salvage value, $300.00; useful life, 5 years; depreciation method, SL; Asset No. 115.

TUTORIAL PROBLEM 8-T

Apr. 30   Purchased a hard disk drive for $499.95; salvage value, $40.00; useful life, 5 years; depreciation method, SL; Asset No. 135.
June 10   Change the name of Asset No. 210 to Computer Organizer.
July 21   Delete Asset No. 105, Computer (P-133).
Sept. 30   Purchased an electronic calculator for $125.50; salvage value, $20.00; useful life, 5 years; depreciation method, SL; Asset No. 180.
Oct. 31   Purchased a file cabinet (4 drawer) for $485.00; salvage value, $50.00; useful life, 10 years; depreciation method, SL; Asset No. 270.

PLANT ASSETS INPUT FORM

Run Date 12/31/02   **Problem No.** 8-T

Asset No.	Asset Name	Date Acquired	Useful Life	Original Cost	Salvage Value	Accum. Deprec.	Deprec. Exp.	Deprec. Method
115	Computer (P4-1.5GHz)	03/01/02	5	3149.50	300.00	1540	6130	SL
135	Hard Disk Drive	04/30/02	5	499.95	40.00	1540	6130	SL
210	Computer Organizer							
105	(Delete)							
180	Electronic Calculator	09/30/02	5	125.50	20.00	1540	6130	SL
270	File Cabinet (4 Drawer)	10/31/02	10	485.00	50.00	1520	6120	SL

Figure 8.10
Completed Plant Assets

STEP 6:   **Display a Plant Assets List Report.**
Click the *Reports* toolbar button. Choose *Plant Assets* and select the *Plant Assets List* Report. Make sure the date on the Report Selection menu is set to 12/31/02. Click *OK*. The report is shown in Figure 8.11.

Chapter 8 Plant Assets

TUTORIAL PROBLEM 8-T

Morales Jewelers
Plant Assets List
12/31/02

Asset	Date Acquired	Depr. Method	Useful Life	Original Cost	Salvage Value	Depr. Accts
110 Computer (P-800)	06/10/99	SL	5	2928.00	200.00	1540 6130
115 Computer (P4-1.5GHz)	03/01/02	SL	5	3149.50	300.00	1540 6130
120 Dot Matrix Printer	03/01/98	SL	5	320.00	50.00	1540 6130
130 File Server (598-32)	07/31/01	SL	5	1295.50	200.00	1540 6130
135 Hard Disk Drive	04/30/02	SL	5	499.95	40.00	1540 6130
140 Ink Jet Printer	07/20/01	SL	5	435.95	45.00	1540 6130
150 Notebook Computer	03/01/00	SL	5	1550.00	135.00	1540 6130
160 Copy Machine	02/20/00	SL	5	3875.00	425.00	1540 6130
170 Facsimile Machine	02/20/00	SL	5	549.00	25.00	1540 6130
180 Electronic Calculator	09/30/02	SL	5	125.50	20.00	1540 6130
210 Computer Organizer	05/01/98	SL	10	710.00	60.00	1520 6120
220 Display Case	05/01/98	SL	10	1800.00	150.00	1520 6120
230 Storage Credenza	05/01/98	SL	10	295.75	30.00	1520 6120
240 File Cabinet (6 Drawer)	09/02/99	SL	10	339.00	25.00	1520 6120
250 Book Case (5 Shelf)	10/03/98	SL	10	289.00	35.00	1520 6120
260 Copy Machine Stand	11/10/01	SL	10	169.90	20.00	1520 6120
270 File Cabinet (4 Drawer)	10/31/02	SL	10	485.00	50.00	1520 6120
Total Plant Assets				18817.05		

Figure 8.11
Plant Assets List Report

TUTORIAL PROBLEM 8-T

STEP 7: **Display Depreciation Schedules for the new assets: 115, 135, 180, and 270.**

Choose the *Depreciation Schedules* option button from the Choose a Report to Display list, and then click the *OK* command button. When the Depreciation Schedules window shown in Figure 8.12 appears, select an asset range of 115-Computer (P4-1.5GHz) to 115-Computer (P4-1.5GHz)—the first asset—and then click the *OK* command button. Repeat this process for each of the assets for which Depreciation Schedules are to be generated. The first Depreciation Schedule is illustrated in Figure 8.13.

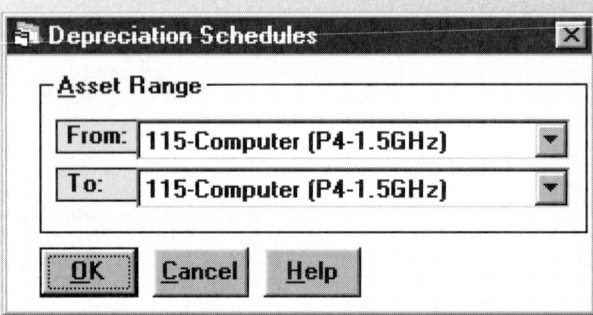

Figure 8.12
Selection Options (Depreciation Schedules)

Morales Jewelers
Depreciation Schedules
12/31/02

	Year	Annual Deprec.	Accum. Deprec.	Book Value
(115) Computer (P4-1.5GHz	2002	474.92	474.92	2674.58
Acquired on 03/01/02	2003	569.90	1044.82	2104.68
Straight-Line	2004	569.90	1614.72	1534.78
Useful Life = 5	2005	569.90	2184.62	964.88
Original Cost = 3149.50	2006	569.90	2754.52	394.98
Salvage Value = 300.00	2007	94.98	2849.50	300.00

Figure 8.13
Depreciation Schedule

TUTORIAL PROBLEM 8-T

STEP 8: **Generate the depreciation adjusting entries.**
Choose *Depreciation Adjusting Entries* from the Options menu. Click *Yes* when asked if you want to generate the depreciation adjusting entries. When the Depreciation Adjusting Entries are displayed, as shown in Figure 8.14, click the *Post* command button. The journal entry will reappear, posted, in the general journal. Click *Close*.

Acct. #	Account Title	Debit	Credit
6120	Depr. Exp.--Ofc. Furn.	339.24	
6130	Depr. Exp.--Ofc. Eqpt.	2525.63	
1520	Accum. Depr.--Ofc. Furn.		339.24
1540	Accum. Depr.--Ofc. Eqpt.		2525.63

Figure 8.14
Depreciation Adjusting Entries

Note: If your adjusting entry does not match Figure 8.14, check your Plant Assets List Report for keying errors and make the necessary corrections. Then return to the general journal window, delete the incorrect depreciation adjusting entry, and generate new adjusting entries.

STEP 9: **Display the adjusting entries.**
Click the *Reports* toolbar button. Choose the *Journals* option button, then select the *General Journal* Report, and click OK. When the Journal Report Selection window appears, choose *Customize Journal Report* and then select a date range of December 31, 2002 through December 31, 2002 and a Reference restriction of Dep.Ent. Click *OK*. The report appears in Figure 8.15.

STEP 10: **Display a Trial Balance.**
Choose the *Ledger Reports* option button from the Report Selection window, select the *Trial Balance* report, and then click the *OK* command button. The Trial Balance is shown in Figure 8.16.

STEP 11: **Save your data.**

TUTORIAL PROBLEM 8-T

```
                    Morales Jewelers
                    General Journal
                       12/31/02
---------------------------------------------------------------
Date    Refer.    Acct.   Title                  Debit    Credit
---------------------------------------------------------------
12/31   Dep.Adj.  6120   Depr. Exp.--Ofc. Furn.  339.24
12/31   Dep.Adj.  6130   Depr. Exp.--Ofc. Eqpt.  2525.63
12/31   Dep.Adj.  1520   Accum. Depr.--Ofc. Furn.         339.24
12/31   Dep.Adj.  1540   Accum. Depr.--Ofc. Eqpt.         2525.63
                                                 -------  -------
                        Totals                   2864.87  2864.87
                                                 =======  =======
```

Figure 8.15
General Journal Report (Adjusting Entries)

STEP 12: Optional Spreadsheet Integration Activity.
Since not all assets depreciate the same amount each year, the manager of the accounting department wants you to use a spreadsheet template to answer "what if" questions regarding the use of the declining-balance method of depreciation. Assets such as computers and other electronic equipment typically depreciate more in the early years of useful life than in later years. The declining-balance method results in a larger portion of an asset being depreciated in the early years. Therefore, you are to generate declining-balance schedules for each of the new assets. The manager will use this information to decide which assets should use this method of depreciation.

a. Display and copy the Plant Assets List Report to the clipboard in spreadsheet format.
b. Start up your spreadsheet software and load the template file named AA8 Spreadsheet 08-T.
c. Select cell A1 as the current cell and paste the Plant Asset List Report into the spreadsheet.
d. Enter the cell references and purchase month and year of the first asset added to the file: 115-Computer (P4-1.5GHz) in cells D51-D57. For example, in cell D51 enter +B12; in cell D53 enter 3; in cell D54 enter 2002; and so on.

TUTORIAL PROBLEM 8-T

Morales Jewelers
Trial Balance
12/31/02

Acct. Number	Account Title	Debit	Credit
1110	Cash	37709.17	
1120	Accounts Receivable	23984.30	
1130	Merchandise Inventory	163825.00	
1140	Prepaid Insurance	460.00	
1150	Supplies	875.00	
1510	Office Furniture	8590.39	
1520	Accum. Depr.--Ofc. Furn.		3739.03
1530	Office Equipment	13910.00	
1540	Accum. Depr.--Ofc. Eqpt.		5144.86
2110	Accounts Payable		10656.74
2120	Sales Tax Payable		370.77
3110	Carlota Gonzalez, Capital		225947.93
3120	Carlota Gonzalez, Drawing	9200.00	
4110	Sales		294195.57
4120	Sales Discounts	2630.65	
4130	Sales Returns & Allow.	14720.87	
5110	Purchases	171261.90	
5120	Purchases Discounts		1384.85
5130	Purch. Returns & Allow.		7331.21
6110	Advertising Expense	1064.32	
6120	Depr. Exp.--Ofc. Furn.	339.24	
6130	Depr. Exp.--Ofc. Eqpt.	2525.63	
6140	Insurance Expense	2955.05	
6150	Miscellaneous Expense	891.41	
6160	Office Salaries Expense	49358.03	
6170	Rent Expense	7720.00	
6180	Sales Salaries Expense	25032.42	
6190	Supplies Expense	6960.21	
6200	Telephone Expense	2995.70	
6210	Utilities Expense	1761.67	
	Totals	548770.96	548770.96

Figure 8.16
Trial Balance

Note: Compare the declining-balance spreadsheet schedule to the straight-line schedule in Figure 8.13. Notice that although the annual depreciation amounts differ, the total amount of accumulated depreciation at the end of the asset's useful life is the same.

TUTORIAL PROBLEM 8-T

e. Save the spreadsheet data with a file name of 08-T Your Name.
f. Print the declining-balance schedule (cells A60–A67). The completed schedule is shown in Figure 8.17.
g. What if the useful life is changed to 4 or 6 years? (It is not necessary to save this what-if data.) You have now created a template file that you can use for the remaining new assets (asset numbers 135, 180, and 270), if desired.

DECLINING-BALANCE METHOD

Description	=	Computer (P4-1.5GHz)
Date Purchased:		
Month	=	3
Year	=	2002
Useful Life	=	5
Original Cost	=	$3,149.50
Salvage Value	=	$300.00
Declining Bal. Rate	=	40.00%

Year	Description	Annual Deprec.	Accum. Deprec.	Book Value
2002	Computer (P4-1.5GHz)	$1,049.83	$1,049.83	$2,099.67
2003		$839.87	$1,889.70	$1,259.80
2004		$503.92	$2,393.62	$755.88
2005		$302.35	$2,695.97	$453.53
2006		$153.53	$2,849.50	$300.00

Figure 8.17
Declining-Balance Comparison (Computer P4-1.5GHz)

STEP 13: Optional Word Processing Integration Activity.
You have been asked to prepare a memo addressed to the manager of the accounting department. The memo is to show a comparison of asset 115 Computer (P4-1.5GHz) *Automated Accounting*-generated straight-line schedule and the spreadsheet declining-balance schedule.

a. Start up your word processing software application and create a new document. If your software has templates, load a memo format.
b. Enter the memo heading information shown in Figure 8.18. Copy and paste asset 115 Computer (P4-1.5GHz)

Chapter 8 Plant Assets

TUTORIAL PROBLEM 8-T

Automated Accounting-generated straight-line schedule and the spreadsheet declining-balance schedule you saved in the optional spreadsheet activity in Step 12 into the body of the memo. As an alternative, you may place the schedules vertically instead of using the horizontal arrangement shown in Figure 8.18 (placing the schedules horizontally requires a great deal of formatting).

c. Save the memo with a file name of 08-T Your Name.
d. Print the memo.
e. End your word processing and spreadsheet sessions.

Memorandum

To: Manager, Accounting Department

From: Student Name

Date: 12/31/02

Re: Depreciation Schedule Comparison

As per your request, the following table depicts a comparison of the straight-line and declining-balance methods of depreciation for Asset No. 115 Computer (P4-1.5GHz).

		------------ Declining-Balance ------------			------------- Straight-Line -------------		
Year	Description	Annual Deprec.	Accum. Deprec.	Book Value	Annual Deprec.	Accum. Deprec.	Book Value
2002	Computer (P4-1.5GHz)	$1,049.83	$1,049.83	$2,099.67	$474.92	$ 474.92	$2,674.58
2003		839.87	1,889.70	1,259.80	569.90	1,044.82	2,104.68
2004		503.92	2,393.62	755.88	569.90	1,614.72	1,534.78
2005		302.35	2,695.97	453.53	569.90	2,184.62	964.88
2006		153.53	2,849.50	300.00	569.90	2,754.52	394.98
2007					94.98	2,849.50	300.00

Figure 8.18
Depreciation Comparison Memo

STEP 14: End the *Automated Accounting* session.

Review and Practice: Applying Your Information Skills

I. MATCHING

Directions: In the *Working Papers*, write the letter of the appropriate term next to each definition.

a. asset disposition
b. depreciation
c. depreciation adjusting entries
d. Depreciation Schedule
e. original cost
f. plant asset maintenance
g. plant assets
h. plant assets input form
i. Plant Assets List Report
j. salvage value
k. useful life

1. A report that provides annual depreciation for each year for the life of a plant asset.

2. The process of adding, changing, and deleting plant assets.

3. The portion of a plant asset's cost that is transferred to an expense account in each fiscal period during its useful life.

4. The amount an owner expects to receive when a plant asset is removed from use.

5. The estimated amount of time an asset can be used in the business.

6. Removing an asset from use in the business.

7. Assets used for a number of years in the operation of a business.

8. All costs paid to make an asset usable to a business.

9. A report that provides a detailed list of all plant assets owned.

10. The journal entries recorded to update the depreciation expense and accumulated depreciation accounts at the end of the fiscal period.

11. An input used to record additions, changes, and deletions to plant assets.

Chapter 8 Plant Assets

II. TRUE/FALSE

Directions: In the *Working Papers*, write T or F next to each statement.

1. When recording changes on a plant assets input form, all data fields must be recorded.
2. The report most useful in verifying the accuracy of your input is the Depreciation Schedule Report.
3. Depreciation Schedules can be generated for any range of assets.
4. Depreciation adjusting entries must be generated after the general journal is displayed on the screen.
5. Depreciation adjusting entries do not need to be posted.

III. REVIEW QUESTIONS

Directions: Write the answers to the following questions in the *Working Papers*.

1. List three uses of the information provided by the plant asset system.
2. Briefly describe the procedure to generate the depreciation adjusting entries.
3. What report must be selected in order to obtain a listing of the depreciation adjusting entries?

IV. INTERNET ACTIVITY

Directions: If you have access to the Internet, use your browser to find financial wizard application software that includes various depreciation method calculations. **Hint:** Use *Depreciation* as a search argument. Report your findings. Be sure to include the source and the URL (Internet address) of your search on the form.

The most important element in encouraging consumers to try online buying is an inviting, easy-to-use Website with effective customer service.

Although the Internet can be a valuable research tool, in-depth inquiries can take time. Your message might even get lost the first time it is sent. So, for any important research, plan to spend a while.

Independent Practice Problem 8-P

In this problem, you will add, change, and delete plant assets. In addition, you will generate the Plant Assets Report, Depreciation Schedules, and depreciation adjusting entries.

Asset numbers 110–199 are assigned to Office Furniture, and asset numbers 210–299 are assigned to Office Equipment. Consult the chart of accounts stored with the file named AA8 Problem 08-P for the appropriate Accumulated Depreciation and Depreciation Expense account numbers.

STEP 1: Start up *Automated Accounting 8.0*.

STEP 2: Load the opening balances template file named AA8 Problem 08-P.

STEP 3: Enter your name in the User Name text box.

STEP 4: Save the file as 08-P Your Name.

STEP 5: Enter the following Plant Assets data:

2002
Jan. 03 Purchased a book shelf for $915.00; salvage value, $80.00; useful life, 10 years; depreciation method, SL; Asset No. 180.
Note: When recording the year acquired, be sure to use a year of 2002.
Jan. 03 Purchased an office chair (gray) for 429.00; salvage value, $45.00; useful life, 10 years, depreciation method, SL; Asset No. 145.
Mar. 01 Delete the Typewriter (Asset Number 200).
June 03 Purchased a Notebook Computer for $2,435.00; salvage value, 250.00; useful life, 5 years; depreciation method, SL; Asset No. 260.
Aug. 06 Change the asset description of Laser Printer (Asset Number 250) to Laser Printer NT.
Oct. 28 Purchased a CD-ROM drive for $350.00; salvage value, $35.00; useful life, 5 years, depreciation method, SL; Asset No. 270.
Dec. 02 Purchased a telephone system, $3,500.00; salvage value, $300.00; useful life, 8 years, depreciation method, SL; Asset No. 280.

STEP 6: Display a Plant Assets List Report. Use 12/31/02 as the run date for all reports.

STEP 7: Display Depreciation Schedules for the new assets.

STEP 8: Generate the depreciation adjusting entries.

Chapter 8 Plant Assets

STEP 9: **Display the adjusting entries.**

STEP 10: **Display a Trial Balance.**

STEP 11: **Save your data.**

STEP 12: **Optional Spreadsheet Integration Activity.**
Generate declining-balance schedules for each of the new assets.

a. Display and copy the Plant Assets List Report to the clipboard in spreadsheet format.
b. Start up your spreadsheet software and load the template file named AA8 Spreadsheet 08-T.
c. Select cell A1 as the current cell and paste the Plant Assets List Report into the spreadsheet.
d. Enter the cell references and purchase month and year of asset 280, Telephone System, in cells D51–D57.
e. Save the spreadsheet data with a file name of 08-P Your Name.
f. Print the declining-balance schedule.
g. What if the useful life is changed to 7 or 10 years? (It is not necessary to save this what-if data.) You may use this newly created template file for the remaining new assets, if desired.

STEP 13: **Optional Word Processing Integration Activity.**
Prepare a memo addressed to the manager of the accounting department, showing a comparison of the *Automated Accounting*-generated straight-line schedule and the spreadsheet declining-balance schedule for asset number 280, Telephone System. Use Figure 8.18 (page 261) as a guide.

a. Start up your word processing software and create a new document. If your software has templates, load a memo format.
b. Enter the memo heading information and copy and paste the *Automated Accounting*-generated straight-line schedule and the spreadsheet declining-balance schedule into the body of the memo. Paste the schedules vertically or horizontally with appropriate headings and format as necessary.
c. Save the memo with a file name of 08-P Your Name.
d. Print the memo.
e. End your word processing and spreadsheet sessions.

STEP 14: **End the *Automated Accounting* session.**

Applying Your Technology Skills 8-P

Directions: Using Independent Practice Problem 8-P, write the answers to the following questions in the *Working Papers*.

1. What is the total value of all assets based on original costs?
2. On what date was the Laser Printer NT acquired?
3. For Asset Number 180, Book Shelf, what will the accumulated depreciation be as of the end of 2005?
4. For Asset Number 145, Office Chair (Gray), what will the book value be as of the end of 2006?
5. For Asset Number 260, Notebook Computer, what is the annual depreciation for 2002?
6. For Asset Number 270, CD-ROM Drive, what will the book value be at the end of 2006?
7. For Asset Number 280, Telephone System, what will the annual depreciation be for the year 2010?
8. From the General Journal Report, what is the amount debited to Depr. Exp.—Ofc. Eqpt.?
9. From the General Journal Report, what is the amount debited to Depr. Exp.—Ofc. Furn.?
10. From the General Journal Report, what is the total amount of the debit column?

Mastery Problem 8-M

In this problem, you will add, change, and delete plant assets. In addition, you will generate the Plant Assets List Report, Depreciation Schedules, and depreciation adjusting entries.

Asset numbers 100–199 are assigned to Vehicles, asset numbers 200–299 are assigned to Office Equipment, and asset numbers 300–399 are assigned to Store Equipment. Consult the chart of accounts stored with the file named AA8 Problem 08-M for the appropriate Accumulated Depreciation and Depreciation Expense account numbers.

STEP 1: Load the opening balances template file named AA8 Problem 08-M.

STEP 2: Enter your name in the User Name text box.

Chapter 8 Plant Assets

STEP 3: Save the data as 08-M Your Name.

STEP 4: Enter the additions, changes, and deletions to plant assets.
2002
- Apr. 06 Purchased a Pentium Computer for $2,050.00; salvage value, $120.00; useful life, 5 years; depreciation method, SL; Asset No. 270.
- Apr. 06 Purchased an Ink Jet Printer for $498.00; salvage value, $50.00; useful life, 5 years; depreciation method, SL; Asset No. 280.
- Apr. 10 Purchased a copy machine for $3,595.85; salvage value, $200.00; useful life, 8 years; depreciation method, SL; Asset No. 260.
- June 10 Delete the word processor (Asset Number 220).
- Oct. 02 Purchased a cash register for $2,115.00; salvage value, $180.00; useful life, 8 years, depreciation method, SL; Asset No. 350.
- Nov. 01 Purchased a security display case for $3,000.00; salvage value, $120.00; useful life, 12 years, depreciation method, SL; Asset No. 360.

STEP 5: Display a Plant Assets List Report and Depreciation Schedules for each of the new assets. Use 12/31/02 as the run date for all reports.

STEP 6: Generate the depreciation adjusting entries.

STEP 7: Display the adjusting entries.

STEP 8: Display a Trial Balance.

STEP 9: Save your data.

STEP 10: Optional Spreadsheet Integration Activity.
Generate declining-balance schedules for each of the new assets.

  a. Copy and paste the Plant Assets List Report into the spreadsheet template file named AA8 Spreadsheet 08-T.
  b. Enter the cell references and purchase month and year of asset 270, Pentium Computer in cells D51-D57.
  c. Save the spreadsheet data with a file name of 08-M Your Name.
  d. Print the declining-balance schedule.
  e. What if the useful life is changed to 4 or 6 years? (It is not necessary to save this what-if data.) You may use this spreadsheet template file for the remaining new assets, if desired.

STEP 11: Optional Word Processing Integration Activity.
Prepare a memo addressed to the manager of the accounting department, showing a comparison of the

Automated Accounting-generated straight-line schedule and the spreadsheet declining-balance schedule for asset 270, Pentium Computer.

a. Create a new memorandum document. If your software has templates, load a memo format.
b. Enter the memo heading information, and copy and paste the Automated Accounting-generated straight-line schedule and the spreadsheet declining-balance schedule into the body of the memo. Format the memo as necessary.
c. Save the memo with a file name of 08-M Your Name.
d. Print the memo.

STEP 12: End the *Automated Accounting* session.

Applying Your Technology Skills 8-M

Directions: Using Mastery Problem 8-M, write the answers to the following questions in the *Working Papers*.

1. What is the total value of all assets based on original costs?
2. On what date was the Delivery Van (F100) acquired?
3. For Asset Number 260, Copy Machine, what will the accumulated depreciation be as of the end of 2005?
4. For Asset Number 270, Pentium Computer, what will the book value be as of the end of 2006?
5. For Asset Number 280, Ink Jet Printer, what is the annual depreciation for 2002?
6. For Asset Number 350, Cash Register, what will the book value be at the end of 2006?
7. For Asset Number 360, Security Display Case, what is the accumulated depreciation at the end of 2009?
8. From the General Journal Report, what is the amount debited to Depr. Exp.—Vehicles?
9. From the General Journal Report, what is the amount debited to Depr. Exp.—Ofc. Eqpt.?
10. From the General Journal Report, what is the amount credited to Accum. Depr.—Store Eqpt.?

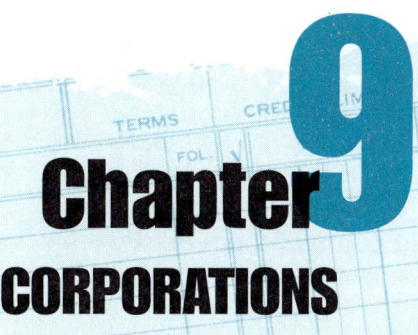

Chapter 9
CORPORATIONS

KEY TERMS

Corporation
Shares of Stock
Capital Stock
Shareholders
Board of Directors

Dividends
Retained Earnings
Declaring a Dividend
Corporate Income Tax

LEARNING OBJECTIVES

Upon completion of this chapter, you will be able to:

1. Identify the appropriate journals and use the proper procedures to enter and post transactions for a business organized as a corporation.
2. Generate checks.
3. Generate monthly financial statements.

INTRODUCTION

This chapter will identify the appropriate journals and proper procedures in order to enter and post transactions for a corporation. You will learn how to have the software generate checks for cash payments on account and direct payments. In addition, generating monthly financial statements will be covered.

A **corporation** is an organization that has many of the legal rights of an individual but is typically owned by many people. Corporations exist separately from their owners. The ownership of a corporation is divided into units. Units that represent ownership in a corporation are called **shares of stock**. The total shares of ownership in a corporation are called **capital stock**. Owners of the stock of a corporation are called **shareholders**. A group elected by shareholders to manage a corporation is called the **board of directors**.

In a sole proprietorship or partnership, assets withdrawn from the business are recorded in the owners' drawing accounts. Shareholders may not withdraw assets from the corporation. However, shareholders may receive **dividends**, which are earnings a corporation distributes to shareholders. Earnings not yet distributed to shareholders are referred to as **retained earnings**.

For sole proprietorships and partnerships, the income tax liability for net income rests with the owners. However, corporations must pay income tax on their earnings.

JOURNAL ENTRIES

Several journal entries related to corporations are introduced in this chapter. The cash payments journal entries are slightly different than in previous chapters, as the software will generate the vendor checks. A chart of accounts for American Cosmetic Corp. is shown in Figure 9.1.

A self-employed programmer was hired by a small company to develop the software for a payroll/personnel system the company had designed. After completing the project, the programmer sells the software, with minor modification, to other companies.

Critical Thinking

1. Who do you think owns the right to the programmer's code (program)?

2. Do you think that what the programmer did was ethical, unethical, or an act that could be considered computer crime? Justify your choice.

American Cosmetic Corp.
Chart of Accounts
04/30/--

Assets

1110	Cash
1120	Petty Cash
1130	Accounts Receivable
1140	Merchandise Inventory
1150	Supplies--Office
1160	Supplies--Store
1170	Prepaid Insurance
1510	Office Equipment
1520	Accum. Depr.--Ofc. Eqpt.
1530	Store Equipment
1540	Accum. Depr.--Store Eqpt.

Liabilities

2110	Accounts Payable
2120	Sales Tax Payable
2130	Employee Income Tax Pay.
2140	Federal Income Tax Pay.
2150	FICA Tax Payable
2160	Medicare Tax Payable
2170	Unemploy. Tax Pay.--Fed.
2180	Unemploy. Tax Pay.--State
2190	Health Ins. Premium Pay.
2200	Disability Insurance Pay.
2210	Dividends Payable

Stockholders' Equity

3110	Capital Stock
3120	Retained Earnings
3130	Dividends
3140	Income Summary

Revenue

4110	Sales
4120	Sales Discount
4130	Sales Returns & Allow.

Cost

5110	Purchases
5120	Purchases Discount
5130	Purch. Returns & Allow.

Expenses

6110	Advertising Expense
6120	Credit Card Fee Expense
6130	Depr. Exp.--Office Eqpt.
6140	Depr. Exp.--Store Eqpt.
6150	Insurance Expense
6160	Miscellaneous Expense
6170	Payroll Taxes Expense
6180	Rent Expense
6190	Salaries Expense
6200	Supplies Expense--Office
6210	Supplies Expense--Store
6220	Utilities Expense

Corporate Income Tax

9110	Federal Income Tax Exp.

Figure 9.1
Chart of Accounts

Making Cash Payments

This corporation does not write checks manually since all checks are generated by the computer. Each cash payment for which the computer is to generate a check must include the name of the vendor to whom the check is to be written. Therefore, the Vendors List must contain the names of both the vendors from whom merchandise and other items are bought on account and all other parties to whom direct cash payments are made. If the Vendor Name is left blank, a check will not be generated.

Two transactions are entered and posted in the cash payments journal shown in Figure 9.2. The first transaction is an example of a cash payment on account with a purchases discount. The second transaction is an example of a direct payment of an expense to a vendor. As an alternative, you can record the transactions on input forms before entering and posting the transactions at the computer.

Mar. 06   Paid cash on account to Anton Supply Depot, $878.80, covering M35 for $896.73, less 2% discount, $17.93. C1212.

06   Paid cash to Eastern Utilities Co. for electric bill, $518.68. C1213.

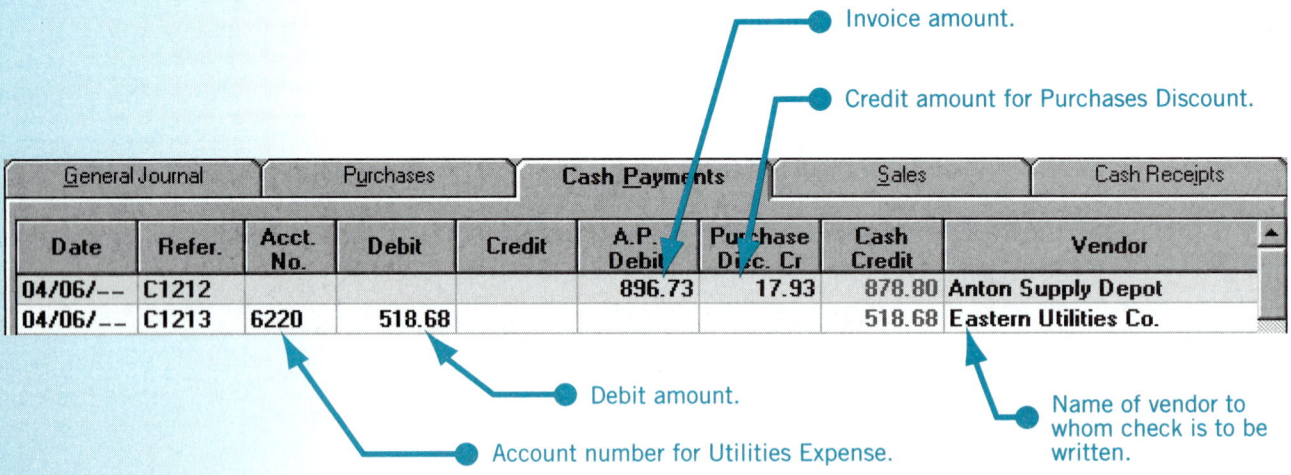

Figure 9.2
Cash Payments Journal

Declaring a Dividend

The decision by the board of directors to distribute earnings to the shareholders is called **declaring a dividend**. The dividend does not have to be distributed at the time it is declared. However, the declaration creates a liability to the corporation and requires a journal entry.

Chapter 9 Corporations

Mar. 10 American Cosmetic Corp.'s board of directors declared a dividend, $3,100.00. M31.

The above entry is entered and posted in the general journal, as illustrated in Figure 9.3.

General Journal		Purchases	Cash Payments	Sales	Cash Receipts
Date	Refer.	Account	Debit	Credit	Vendor/Customer
04/10/--	M31	3130 Dividends	3100.00		
		2210 Dividends Payable		3100.00	

To record this entry, debit the Dividends account (313) and credit the Dividends Payable account (2210).

Figure 9.3
General Journal (Declaring a Dividend)

Paying a Dividend

When the dividends are paid, a check is written and the transaction is recorded as a cash payment to the Shareholders Bank Account. The check is then deposited in a special bank account upon which the individual checks to the shareholders are drawn. The cash payments journal entry to record the payment of dividends is illustrated in Figure 9.4.

Apr. 12 Paid cash to Shareholders Bank Account for first quarter dividends declared in April, $3,100.00. C1219.

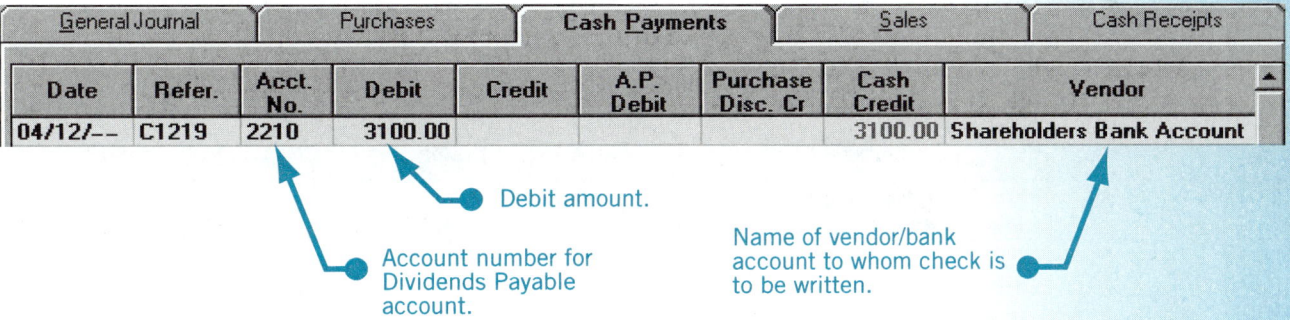

General Journal			Purchases		Cash Payments		Sales	Cash Receipts
Date	Refer.	Acct. No.	Debit	Credit	A.P. Debit	Purchase Disc. Cr	Cash Credit	Vendor
04/12/--	C1219	2210	3100.00				3100.00	Shareholders Bank Account

- Debit amount.
- Account number for Dividends Payable account.
- Name of vendor/bank account to whom check is to be written.

Figure 9.4
Cash Payments (Paying a Dividend)

Recording Corporate Income Tax

Corporate income tax is the tax that corporations are required to pay on their earnings. The corporation pays the taxes each quarter, based on an estimated tax liability. The estimated taxes are based on estimated net income. At the end of the year, the corporation must file a tax return with the Internal Revenue Service based on actual earnings. If additional tax is owed beyond the estimate, the additional tax must be paid when the return is filed. If the estimate exceeds the actual taxes, the corporation can request a refund of the difference or apply the excess to the estimated tax for the following year.

Because American Cosmetic Corp. completes the accounting cycle each month, an income tax adjustment is made each month. The corporation pays the estimated tax to the Internal Revenue Service on a quarterly basis. The payment of the quarterly estimated income tax is shown in Figure 9.5, and the monthly federal income tax adjustment is shown in Figure 9.6.

Apr. 13 Paid cash to Internal Revenue Service for quarterly estimated federal income tax, $1,020.00. C1222.
30 Adjustment for estimated federal income tax, 375.00.

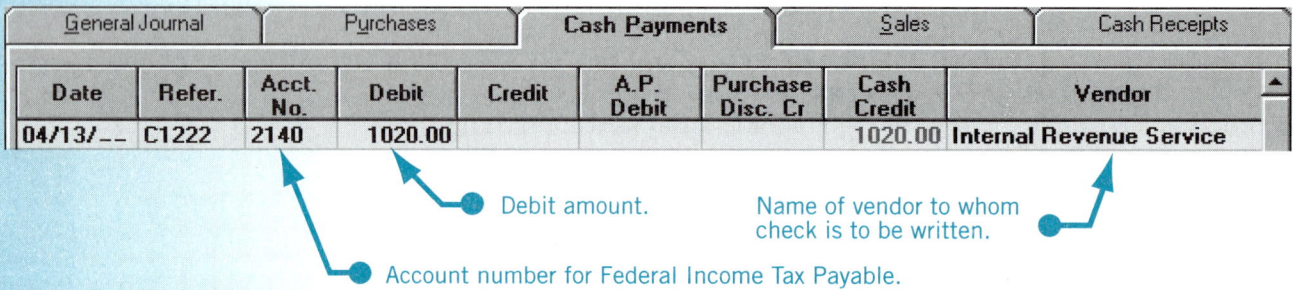

Figure 9.5
Cash Payments Journal (Payment of Quarterly Estimated Income Tax)

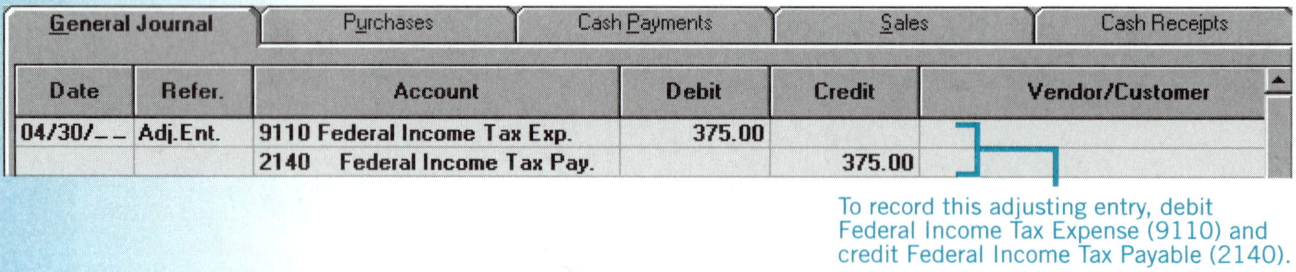

Figure 9.6
General Journal (Federal Income Tax Adjusting Entry)

Chapter 9 Corporations

CHECKS

If the Computer Checks option button is set to ON (this will be covered later in Chapter 13), a check will be generated each time a cash payment transaction involving a vendor is entered and posted. When the check appears on the display screen, it can be printed. A computer-generated check is shown in Figure 9.7.

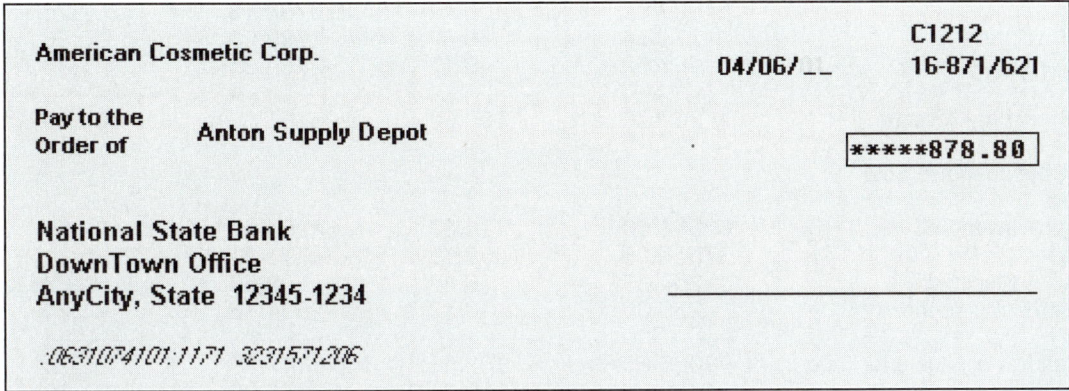

Figure 9.7
Check

INCOME STATEMENT BY MONTH AND YEAR

If the Income Statement option for Month and Year is set to ON (this will be covered in Chapter 13), the format of the income statement will be as shown in Figure 9.8. The report includes columns for the month and for the year. Also included for each column is a component percentage, indicating each amount's percentage of total operating revenue. When this format of the income statement is used, adjusting entries are entered and posted and financial statements are generated at the end of each month. The adjusting entries must be entered each month in order for the monthly column to be up-to-date and correct. Closing entries are not generated and posted until the end of the fiscal year.

Chapter Review

1. An organization that has many of the legal rights of a person, is owned by many people, and exists separately from its owners is called a corporation. Earnings that are distributed to shareholders are called dividends. The decision by the board of directors to distribute earnings to the shareholders is called declaring a dividend. Paying a dividend involves recording a cash-payment

American Cosmetic Corp.
Income Statement
For Period Ended 04/30/--

	Monthly Amount	Monthly Percent	Yearly Amount	Yearly Percent
Operating Revenue				
Sales	54507.00	100.44	210798.13	102.20
Sales Discount	−171.74	−0.32	−1783.98	−0.86
Sales Returns & Allow.	−67.50	−0.12	−2752.35	−1.33
Total Operating Revenue	54267.76	100.00	206261.80	100.00
Cost of Merchandise Sold				
Beginning Inventory	62064.00	114.37	62984.65	30.54
Purchases	37516.26	69.13	134711.21	65.31
Purchases Discount	−254.63	−0.47	−1793.53	−0.87
Purch. Returns & Allow.	−230.00	−0.42	−2554.78	−1.24
Merchandise Available for Sale	99095.63	182.61	193347.55	93.74
Less Ending Inventory	−64150.00	−118.21	−64150.00	−31.10
Cost of Merchandise Sold	34945.63	64.39	129197.55	62.64
Gross Profit	19322.13	35.61	77064.25	37.36
Operating Expenses				
Advertising Expense	500.00	0.92	2896.73	1.40
Credit Card Fee Expense	226.93	0.42	953.71	0.46
Depr. Exp.--Office Eqpt.	196.68	0.36	793.24	0.38
Depr. Exp.--Store Eqpt.	157.00	0.29	623.88	0.30
Insurance Expense	200.00	0.37	696.08	0.34
Miscellaneous Expense	125.42	0.23	422.29	0.20
Payroll Taxes Expense	777.27	1.43	3114.24	1.51
Rent Expense	2000.00	3.69	8000.00	3.88
Salaries Expense	9655.55	17.79	38686.36	18.76
Supplies Expense--Office	537.87	0.99	767.33	0.37
Supplies Expense--Store	346.95	0.64	550.89	0.27
Utilities Expense	518.68	0.96	2885.91	1.40
Total Operating Expenses	15242.35	28.09	60390.66	29.28
Net Income from Operations	4079.78	7.52	16673.59	8.08
Net Income before Income Tax	4079.78	7.52	16673.59	8.08
Income Tax				
Federal Income Tax Exp.	375.00	0.69	1402.12	0.68
Net Income after Income Tax	3704.78	6.83	15271.47	7.40

Figure 9.8
Income Statement by Month and Year

Chapter 9 Corporations

transaction for the amount of the dividends payable and then depositing the check generated in a special bank account on which the individual checks to the shareholders are drawn. Corporate income tax is a tax that the corporation pays each quarter, based on estimated tax liability. The estimated taxes are based on estimated net income.

2. Checks will be generated each time a cash-payment transaction involving a vendor is entered and posted. Checks may be displayed and printed, if desired.

3. Companies may choose to prepare financial statements monthly. In this case, an income statement with monthly and yearly figures would be generated.

ACCOUNTING CAREERS IN DEPTH

Cost Accountant

A cost accountant applies principles of cost accounting to conduct studies that provide detailed cost information not supplied by general accounting systems. A cost accountant's duties include:

- Planning, collecting, and studying data to determine costs of business activity, such as raw material purchases, inventory, and labor.
- Using a computer to analyze data obtained and record results.
- Analyzing changes in product design, raw materials, manufacturing methods, or services provided to determine effects on costs.
- Analyzing actual manufacturing costs and preparing periodic reports comparing standard costs to actual production costs.
- Providing management with reports specifying and comparing factors affecting prices and profitability of products or services.

Preparation for a career as a cost accountant in most cases requires a four-year college degree in accounting. A cooperative education experience in an environment using cost accounting techniques would be helpful in landing the first job after completing college.

For a cost accountant, career opportunities can be found in manufacturing and other corporate environments because all businesses deal with controlling costs. Some students choose to work in a particular business environment in which they are interested, such as insurance, entertainment, or manufacturing.

The skills that can be helpful to a cost accountant include the ability to install manual or computer-based cost accounting systems and to process information on these systems; a specialization in analyzing costs related to specific rate schedules; and a specialization in appraisal and evaluation of property or equipment.

If you enjoy analyzing costs and making decisions that assist you in providing alternatives that help to cut costs and increase profits in a business environment, this career could be a good choice for you.

TUTORIAL PROBLEM 9-T

In this tutorial problem, you will process the monthly transactions, generate checks, generate monthly statements of account, and complete the end-of-month processing for a corporation.

STEP 1: **Start up *Automated Accounting 8.0*.**

STEP 2: **Load the opening balance file named AA8 Problem 09-T.**

STEP 3: **Enter your name in the User Name text box and click *OK*.**

STEP 4: **Save the file with a file name of 09-T Your Name.**

STEP 5: **Add Anna Graham to the customer list.**
Click the *Accts.* toolbar icon, and then click the *Customers* tab. Enter Anna Graham as a new customer.

Note: The following transactions are illustrated in the appropriate journals shown in Figures 9.9 through 9.14. Source documents are abbreviated as follows: Purchase Invoice, P; Check, C; Sales Invoice, S; Cash Receipt, R; Cash Register Tape, T; Memorandums, M; Debit Memorandums, DM; Credit Memorandums, CM.

Apr. 02 Granted credit to Nolan's Beauty Shop for merchandise returned, $67.50, against S730. CM28.

02 Purchased merchandise on account from Hasher Chemical Co., $4,147.56. P501.

03 Sold merchandise on account to Tonya's Fashion Salon. $7,012.00. S733.

04 Bought advertising on account from Carley Marketing, $500.00. M36.

05 Received cash on account from Burnette Salon, $3,650.90, covering S726 for $3,687.78, less 1% discount, $36.88. R653.

05 Received cash on account from Patty's Hair Styles, $5,024.00, covering S731 for $5,074.75, less 1% discount, $50.75. R654.

 A quick way to close the check window if you do not wish to print the check is to press the keyboard *Enter* key.

06 Paid cash on account to Anton Supply Depot, $878.80, covering M35 for $896.73, less 2% discount, $17.93. C1212.

TUTORIAL PROBLEM 9-T

06 Paid cash to Eastern Utilities Co. for electric bill, $518.68. C1213.

07 Received cash on account from Nail & Hair Care, $4,116.93, covering S732 for $4,158.52, less 1% discount, $41.59. R655.

07 Purchased merchandise on account from Perrizo Salon Supplies, $5,875.00. P502.

07 Bought office supplies on account from Anton Supply Depot, $335.50. M37.

09 Paid cash on account to Hubin Manufacturing Co., $1,519.05, covering P495 for $1,534.39, less 1% discount, $15.34. C1214.

09 Returned merchandise to Perrizo Salon Supplies, $230.00, against P500. DM39.

09 Paid cash to Pagel Cosmetic Supplies for miscellaneous expense, $105.42. C1215.

10 Paid cash on account to Tipler & Rumkle Corp., $1,035.99, covering P494 for $1,046.45, less 1% discount, $10.46. C1216.

10 Purchased merchandise on account from Hubin Manufacturing Co., $5,000.00. P503.

11 Sold merchandise on account to Demars Hair Design, $7,205.00. S734.

12 Paid cash to Commissioner of Revenue for quarterly sales tax, $1,250.27. C1217.

12 Paid cash to Arndt Insurance Assoc. for liability for first quarter insurance premiums: health insurance, $2,975.98; disability insurance, $869.45; total, $3,845.43. C1218.
Note: The amounts for these premiums were recorded last month as credits to Health Ins. Premium Pay. and Disability Insurance Pay. This entry will debit these accounts.

12 Paid cash to Shareholders Bank Account for first quarter dividends declared in March, $3,100.00. C1219.
Note: Debit the Dividends Payable account.

13 Paid cash on account to Carley Marketing, $495.00, covering M36 for $500.00, less 1% discount, $5.00. C1220.

13 Paid cash to Internal Revenue Service for payroll taxes: employee income tax, $6,383.26;

TUTORIAL PROBLEM 9-T

FICA tax, $1,799.91; and Medicare tax, $420.94; total, $8,604.11. C1221.
Note: Debit the payroll tax liability accounts.

13 Paid cash to Internal Revenue Service for quarterly estimated federal income tax, $1,020.00. C1222.
Note: Debit Federal Income Tax Payable.

14 Paid cash on account to Mckee Beauty Supply, $2,593.27, covering P498 for $2,646.19, less 2% discount, $52.92. C1223.

14 Received cash on account from Douglas Boutique, $4,209.75, covering S728 for $4,252.27, less 1% discount, $42.52. R656.

16 Bought store supplies on account from Anton Supply Depot, $530.25. M38.

16 Sold merchandise on account to Sutter Tanning & Salon, $6,120.00. S735.

16 Paid cash on account to Kaplan Hair Products, $4,425.79, covering P496 for $4,470.50, less 1% discount, $44.71. C1224.

17 Purchased merchandise on account from Stapleton Corporation, $5,145.10. P504.

17 Sold merchandise on account to Burnette Salon, $6,250.00. S736.

18 Paid cash to Hammond Leasing, Inc. for monthly rent, $2,000.00. C1225.

19 Sold merchandise on account to Anna Graham, $105.00, plus sales tax, $7.35; total, $112.35. S737.

19 Purchased merchandise on account from Mckee Beauty Supply, $4,095.00. P505.

20 Received cash on account from Nolan's Beauty Shop, $5,750.62 (covering S730, less CM28), no discount. R657.

20 Paid cash on account to Anton Supply Depot, $848.43, covering M37 and M38 for $865.75, less 2% discount, $17.32. C1226.

21 Paid cash on account to Hubin Manufacturing Co., $4,950.00, covering P503 for $5,000.00, less 1% discount, $50.00. C1227.

21 Recorded cash and credit card sales, $22,720.00, plus sales tax, $1,590.40; total, $24,310.40. T40.

TUTORIAL PROBLEM 9-T

23 Bought office supplies on account from Anton Supply Depot, $805.32. M39.
25 Sold merchandise on account to Nail & Hair Care, $5,095.00 S738.
26 Purchased merchandise on account from Hubin Manufacturing Co., $5,200.00. P506.
26 Paid cash on account to Stapleton Corporation, $2,186.34, covering P497, no discount. C1228.
26 Recorded credit card fee expense for March, $226.93. M40.
Note: Record this entry in the cash payments journal. The bank deducts this amount from the checking account, so a memorandum is used instead of a check. Because no name is entered in the Vendor column, the system will not write a check.
27 Paid cash on account to Mckee Beauty Supply, $4,054.05, covering P505 for $4,095.00, less 1% discount, $40.95. C1229.
28 Purchased merchandise on account from Kaplan Hair Products, $3,595.00. P507.
28 Purchased merchandise on account from Tipler & Rumkle Corp., $4,458.60. P508.
30 Paid cash to Payroll Bank Account for monthly payroll, $5,530.40. Total payroll, $9,655.55, less deductions: employee income tax, $2,113.71; FICA tax, $598.64; Medicare tax, $140.01; health insurance premium, $985.00; disability insurance premium, $287.79. C1230.
Note: The net payroll amount of $5,530.40 is derived by subtracting the deductions from the total gross payroll. The computer automatically makes the $5,530.40 credit to Cash. Debit Salaries Expense and credit the appropriate liability accounts for the amounts withheld.
30 Recorded employer payroll taxes expense, $777.27 (FICA tax, $598.64; Medicare tax, $140.01; federal unemployment tax, $28.97; state unemployment tax, $9.65). M41. Record this transaction in the general journal.
30 Paid cash to Petty Cash Custodian to replenish petty cash fund, $98.75: office supplies, $37.05; store supplies, $41.70; miscellaneous expense, $20.00. C1231.

TUTORIAL PROBLEM 9-T

STEP 6: Enter the April general journal transaction data shown in Figure 9.9.

Click the *Journal* toolbar button. When the Journal Entries window appears, click the *General Journal* tab, and then enter the journal entries.

Date	Refer.	Account	Debit	Credit	Vendor/Customer
04/02/--	CM28	4130 Sales Returns & Allow.	67.50		
		1130 Accounts Receivable		67.50	Nolan's Beauty Shop
04/04/--	M36	6110 Advertising Expense	500.00		
		2110 Accounts Payable		500.00	Carley Marketing
04/07/--	M37	1150 Supplies--Office	335.50		
		2110 Accounts Payable		335.50	Anton Supply Depot
04/09/--	DM39	2110 Accounts Payable	230.00		Perrizo Salon Supplies
		5130 Purch. Returns & Allow.		230.00	
04/16/--	M38	1160 Supplies--Store	530.25		
		2110 Accounts Payable		530.25	Anton Supply Depot
04/23/--	M39	1150 Supplies--Office	805.32		
		2110 Accounts Payable		805.32	Anton Supply Depot
04/30/--	M41	6170 Payroll Taxes Expense	777.27		
		2150 FICA Tax Payable		598.64	
		2160 Medicare Tax Payable		140.01	
		2170 Unemploy. Tax Pay.--Fed.		28.97	
		2180 Unemploy. Tax Pay.--State		9.65	

Figure 9.9
General Journal

STEP 7: Enter the April purchases journal transaction data shown in Figure 9.10.

Click the *Purchases* tab, and then enter the journal entries.

Date	Refer.	Purch. Debit	A.P. Credit	Vendor
04/02/--	P501	4147.56	4147.56	Hasher Chemical Co.
04/07/--	P502	5875.00	5875.00	Perrizo Salon Supplies
04/10/--	P503	5000.00	5000.00	Hubin Manufacturing Co.
04/17/--	P504	5145.10	5145.10	Stapleton Corporation
04/19/--	P505	4095.00	4095.00	Mckee Beauty Supply
04/26/--	P506	5200.00	5200.00	Hubin Manufacturing Co.
04/28/--	P507	3595.00	3595.00	Kaplan Hair Products
04/28/--	P508	4458.60	4458.60	Tipler & Rumkle Corp.

Figure 9.10
Purchases Journal

Chapter 9 Corporations

TUTORIAL PROBLEM 9-T

STEP 8: Enter the April cash payments journal transaction data shown in Figure 9.11 and generate the vendor checks. The first check is shown in Figure 9.12.

Click the *Cash Payments* tab, and then enter the cash payments. The vendor checks will be displayed.

Date	Refer.	Acct. No.	Debit	Credit	A.P. Debit	Purchase Disc. Cr	Cash Credit	Vendor
04/06/--	C1212				896.73	17.93	878.80	Anton Supply Depot
04/06/--	C1213	6220	518.68				518.68	Eastern Utilities Co.
04/09/--	C1214				1534.39	15.34	1519.05	Hubin Manufacturing Co.
04/09/--	C1215	6160	105.42				105.42	Pagel Cosmetic Supplies
04/10/--	C1216				1046.45	10.46	1035.99	Tipler & Rumkle Corp.
04/12/--	C1217	2120	1250.27				1250.27	Commissioner of Revenue
04/12/--	C1218	2190	2975.98				3845.43	Arndt Insurance Assoc.
		2200	869.45					
04/12/--	C1219	2210	3100.00				3100.00	Shareholders Bank Account
04/13/--	C1220				500.00	5.00	495.00	Carley Marketing
04/13/--	C1221	2130	6383.26				8604.11	Internal Revenue Service
		2150	1799.91					
		2160	420.94					
04/13/--	C1222	2140	1020.00				1020.00	Internal Revenue Service
04/14/--	C1223				2646.19	52.92	2593.27	Mckee Beauty Supply
04/16/--	C1224				4470.50	44.71	4425.79	Kaplan Hair Products
04/18/--	C1225	6180	2000.00				2000.00	Hammond Leasing, Inc.
04/20/--	C1226				865.75	17.32	848.43	Anton Supply Depot
04/21/--	C1227				5000.00	50.00	4950.00	Hubin Manufacturing Co.
04/26/--	C1228				2186.34		2186.34	Stapleton Corporation
04/26/--	M40	6120	226.93				226.93	
04/27/--	C1229				4095.00	40.95	4054.05	Mckee Beauty Supply
04/30/--	C1230	6190	9655.55				5530.40	Payroll Bank Account
		2130		2113.71				
		2150		598.64				
		2160		140.01				
		2190		985.00				
		2200		287.79				
04/30/--	C1231	1150	37.05				98.75	Petty Cash Custodian
		1160	41.70					
		6160	20.00					

Figure 9.11
Cash Payments Journal

STEP 9: Enter the April sales journal transaction data shown in Figure 9.13.

Click the *Sales* tab, and then enter the journal entries.

TUTORIAL PROBLEM 9-T

```
American Cosmetic Corp.                      C1212
                                 04/06/--    16-871/621
Pay to the
Order of    Anton Supply Depot
                                             *****878.80

National State Bank
DownTown Office
AnyCity, State  12345-1234

.:063107410l:1171 323157206
```

Figure 9.12
First Check

Date	Refer.	Sales Credit	Sales Tax Credit	A.R. Debit	Customer
04/03/--	S733	7012.00		7012.00	Tonya's Fashion Salon
04/11/--	S734	7205.00		7205.00	Demars Hair Design
04/16/--	S735	6120.00		6120.00	Sutter Tanning & Salon
04/17/--	S736	6250.00		6250.00	Burnette Salon
04/19/--	S737	105.00	7.35	112.35	Anna Graham
04/25/--	S738	5095.00		5095.00	Nail & Hair Care

Figure 9.13
Sales Journal

STEP 10: Enter the April cash receipts journal transaction data shown in Figure 9.14.
Click the *Cash Receipts* tab, and then enter the journal entries.

Date	Refer.	A.R. Credit	Sales Credit	Sales Tax Pay. Cr	Sales Disc. Dr	Cash Debit	Customer
04/05/--	R653	3687.78			36.88	3650.90	Burnette Salon
04/05/--	R654	5074.75			50.75	5024.00	Patty's Hair Styles
04/07/--	R655	4158.52			41.59	4116.93	Nail & Hair Care
04/14/--	R656	4252.27			42.52	4209.75	Douglas Boutique
04/20/--	R657	5750.62				5750.62	Nolan's Beauty Shop
04/21/--	T40		22720.00	1590.40		24310.40	

Figure 9.14
Cash Receipts Journal

Chapter 9 Corporations

TUTORIAL PROBLEM 9-T

STEP 11: **Display the journal reports.**
Click the *Reports* toolbar button. Choose the Journals option, and then select and display each of the following journal reports: General Journal, Purchases Journal, Sales Journal, and Cash Receipts Journal. When the Journal Report Selection window appears, enter a date range of April 1 to April 30 of the current year. The reports appear in Figures 9.15 through 9.19.

American Cosmetic Corp.
General Journal
04/30/--

Date	Refer.	Acct.	Title	Debit	Credit
04/02	CM28	4130	Sales Returns & Allow.	67.50	
04/02	CM28	1130	AR/Nolan's Beauty Shop		67.50
04/04	M36	6110	Advertising Expense	500.00	
04/04	M36	2110	AP/Carley Marketing		500.00
04/07	M37	1150	Supplies--Office	335.50	
04/07	M37	2110	AP/Anton Supply Depot		335.50
04/09	DM39	2110	AP/Perrizo Salon Supplies	230.00	
04/09	DM39	5130	Purch. Returns & Allow.		230.00
04/16	M38	1160	Supplies--Store	530.25	
04/16	M38	2110	AP/Anton Supply Depot		530.25
04/23	M39	1150	Supplies--Office	805.32	
04/23	M39	2110	AP/Anton Supply Depot		805.32
04/30	M41	6170	Payroll Taxes Expense	777.27	
04/30	M41	2150	FICA Tax Payable		598.64
04/30	M41	2160	Medicare Tax Payable		140.01
04/30	M41	2170	Unemploy. Tax Pay.--Fed.		28.97
04/30	M41	2180	Unemploy. Tax Pay.--State		9.65
			Totals	3245.84	3245.84

Figure 9.15
General Journal Report

TUTORIAL PROBLEM 9-T

```
                American Cosmetic Corp.
                  Purchases Journal
                      04/30/--

-------------------------------------------------------------
Date    Inv. No.  Acct.  Title                    Debit     Credit
-------------------------------------------------------------

04/02   P501      5110   Purchases                4147.56
04/02   P501      2110   AP/Hasher Chemical Co.              4147.56

04/07   P502      5110   Purchases                5875.00
04/07   P502      2110   AP/Perrizo Salon Supplies           5875.00

04/10   P503      5110   Purchases                5000.00
04/10   P503      2110   AP/Hubin Manufacturing Co.          5000.00

04/17   P504      5110   Purchases                5145.10
04/17   P504      2110   AP/Stapleton Corporation            5145.10

04/19   P505      5110   Purchases                4095.00
04/19   P505      2110   AP/Mckee Beauty Supply              4095.00

04/26   P506      5110   Purchases                5200.00
04/26   P506      2110   AP/Hubin Manufacturing Co.          5200.00

04/28   P507      5110   Purchases                3595.00
04/28   P507      2110   AP/Kaplan Hair Products             3595.00

04/28   P508      5110   Purchases                4458.60
04/28   P508      2110   AP/Tipler & Rumkle Corp.            4458.60
                                                 ---------  ---------
                        Totals                   37516.26   37516.26
                                                 =========  =========
```

Figure 9.16
Purchases Journal Report

```
                American Cosmetic Corp.
                 Cash Payments Journal
                      04/30/--

-------------------------------------------------------------
Date    Ck. No.   Acct.  Title                    Debit     Credit
-------------------------------------------------------------

04/06   C1212     2110   AP/Anton Supply Depot    896.73
04/06   C1212     1110   Cash                                878.80
04/06   C1212     5120   Purchases Discount                   17.93
04/06   C1213     6220   Utilities Expense        518.68
04/06   C1213     1110   Cash                                518.68
04/09   C1214     2110   AP/Hubin Manufacturing Co. 1534.39
04/09   C1214     1110   Cash                               1519.05
04/09   C1214     5120   Purchases Discount                   15.34
04/09   C1215     6160   Miscellaneous Expense    105.42
04/09   C1215     1110   Cash                                105.42
04/10   C1216     2110   AP/Tipler & Rumkle Corp. 1046.45
04/10   C1216     1110   Cash                               1035.99
04/10   C1216     5120   Purchases Discount                   10.46
                                                         (continued)
```

Figure 9.17
Cash Payments Journal Report

Chapter 9 Corporations

TUTORIAL PROBLEM 9-T

American Cosmetic Corp.
Cash Payments Journal
04/30/--

Date	Ck. No.	Acct.	Title	Debit	Credit
04/12	C1217	2120	Sales Tax Payable	1250.27	
04/12	C1217	1110	Cash		1250.27
04/12	C1218	2190	Health Ins. Premium Pay.	2975.98	
04/12	C1218	2200	Disability Insurance Pay.	869.45	
04/12	C1218	1110	Cash		3845.43
04/12	C1219	2210	Dividends Payable	3100.00	
04/12	C1219	1110	Cash		3100.00
04/13	C1220	2110	AP/Carley Marketing	500.00	
04/13	C1220	1110	Cash		495.00
04/13	C1220	5120	Purchases Discount		5.00
04/13	C1221	2130	Employee Income Tax Pay.	6383.26	
04/13	C1221	2150	FICA Tax Payable	1799.91	
04/13	C1221	2160	Medicare Tax Payable	420.94	
04/13	C1221	1110	Cash		8604.11
04/13	C1222	2140	Federal Income Tax Pay.	1020.00	
04/13	C1222	1110	Cash		1020.00
04/14	C1223	2110	AP/Mckee Beauty Supply	2646.19	
04/14	C1223	1110	Cash		2593.27
04/14	C1223	5120	Purchases Discount		52.92
04/16	C1224	2110	AP/Kaplan Hair Products	4470.50	
04/16	C1224	1110	Cash		4425.79
04/16	C1224	5120	Purchases Discount		44.71
04/18	C1225	6180	Rent Expense	2000.00	
04/18	C1225	1110	Cash		2000.00
04/20	C1226	2110	AP/Anton Supply Depot	865.75	
04/20	C1226	1110	Cash		848.43
04/20	C1226	5120	Purchases Discount		17.32
04/21	C1227	2110	AP/Hubin Manufacturing Co.	5000.00	
04/21	C1227	1110	Cash		4950.00
04/21	C1227	5120	Purchases Discount		50.00
04/26	C1228	2110	AP/Stapleton Corporation	2186.34	
04/26	C1228	1110	Cash		2186.34
04/26	M40	6120	Credit Card Fee Expense	226.93	
04/26	M40	1110	Cash		226.93
04/27	C1229	2110	AP/Mckee Beauty Supply	4095.00	
04/27	C1229	1110	Cash		4054.05
04/27	C1229	5120	Purchases Discount		40.95
04/30	C1230	6190	Salaries Expense	9655.55	
04/30	C1230	1110	Cash		5530.40
04/30	C1230	2130	Employee Income Tax Pay.		2113.71
04/30	C1230	2150	FICA Tax Payable		598.64
04/30	C1230	2160	Medicare Tax Payable		140.01
04/30	C1230	2190	Health Ins. Premium Pay.		985.00
04/30	C1230	2200	Disability Insurance Pay.		287.79
04/30	C1231	1150	Supplies--Office	37.05	
04/30	C1231	1160	Supplies--Store	41.70	
04/30	C1231	6160	Miscellaneous Expense	20.00	
04/30	C1231	1110	Cash		98.75
			Totals	53666.49	53666.49

Figure 9.17
Continued

TUTORIAL PROBLEM 9-T

```
                American Cosmetic Corp.
                    Sales Journal
                      04/30/--

Date    Inv. No.  Acct.   Title                          Debit       Credit

04/03   S733      1130    AR/Tonya's Fashion Salon       7012.00
04/03   S733      4110    Sales                                       7012.00
04/11   S734      1130    AR/Demars Hair Design          7205.00
04/11   S734      4110    Sales                                       7205.00
04/16   S735      1130    AR/Sutter Tanning & Salon      6120.00
04/16   S735      4110    Sales                                       6120.00
04/17   S736      1130    AR/Burnette Salon              6250.00
04/17   S736      4110    Sales                                       6250.00
04/19   S737      1130    AR/Anna Graham                  112.35
04/19   S737      4110    Sales                                        105.00
04/19   S737      2120    Sales Tax Payable                              7.35
04/25   S738      1130    AR/Nail & Hair Care            5095.00
04/25   S738      4110    Sales                                       5095.00

                         Totals                         31794.35     31794.35
                                                        ========     ========
```

Figure 9.18
Sales Journal Report

```
               American Cosmetic Corp.
                 Cash Receipts Journal
                       04/30/--

Date    Refer.  Acct.   Title                      Debit       Credit

04/05   R653    1110    Cash                       3650.90
04/05   R653    4120    Sales Discount               36.88
04/05   R653    1130    AR/Burnette Salon                       3687.78
04/05   R654    1110    Cash                       5024.00
04/05   R654    4120    Sales Discount               50.75
04/05   R654    1130    AR/Patty's Hair Styles                  5074.75
04/07   R655    1110    Cash                       4116.93
04/07   R655    4120    Sales Discount               41.59
04/07   R655    1130    AR/Nail & Hair Care                     4158.52
04/14   R656    1110    Cash                       4209.75
04/14   R656    4120    Sales Discount               42.52
04/14   R656    1130    AR/Douglas Boutique                     4252.27
04/20   R657    1110    Cash                       5750.62
04/20   R657    1130    AR/Nolan's Beauty Shop                  5750.62
04/21   T40     1110    Cash                      24310.40
04/21   T40     4110    Sales                                  22720.00
04/21   T40     2120    Sales Tax Payable                       1590.40

                        Totals                    47234.34    47234.34
                                                  ========    ========
```

Figure 9.19
Cash Receipts Journal Report

TUTORIAL PROBLEM 9-T

STEP 12: Display a Trial Balance, a Schedule of Accounts Payable, a Schedule of Accounts Receivable, and the Statements of Account.

Choose the *Ledger Reports* option, and select and display each of the following reports: Trial Balance, Schedule of Accounts Payable, Schedule of Accounts Receivable, and Statements of Account. The reports are shown in Figures 9.20 through 9.22 (pages 290-291), and Figure 9.23 (page 292) shows the first statement of account.

STEP 13: Enter the adjusting entries from the general journal shown in Figure 9.24 (page 292).

Click the *Journal* toolbar button. When the Journal Entries window appears, click the *General Journal* tab and enter the adjusting entries. The adjustment data for the month of April for American Cosmetic Corp. are listed below.

April 30
Merchandise inventory $64,150.00
Office supplies inventory 1,650.00
Store supplies inventory 875.00
Value of insurance policies 950.00
Depreciation for the month:
    Office Equipment 196.68
    Store Equipment 157.00
Estimated federal income tax 375.00

STEP 14: Display the adjusting entries.

Click the *Reports* toolbar button. Choose the *Journals* option button, and then select the *General Journal* Report and click *OK*. When the Journal Report Selection window appears, choose the *Customize Journal Report* option and enter a Reference restriction of *Adj.Ent.* so that only the adjusting entries are reported. The report appears in Figure 9.25 (page 293).

Some web sites electronically record information about your visit to their site by depositing a piece of information called a *cookie* onto your computer. Some browsers will allow you to deactivate a cookie.

TUTORIAL PROBLEM 9-T

American Cosmetic Corp.
Trial Balance
04/30/--

Acct. Number	Account Title	Debit	Credit
1110	Cash	11931.62	
1120	Petty Cash	100.00	
1130	Accounts Receivable	47769.62	
1140	Merchandise Inventory	62064.00	
1150	Supplies--Office	2187.87	
1160	Supplies--Store	1221.95	
1170	Prepaid Insurance	1150.00	
1510	Office Equipment	14084.06	
1520	Accum. Depr.--Ofc. Eqpt.		2386.25
1530	Store Equipment	9104.06	
1540	Accum. Depr.--Store Eqpt.		1867.50
2110	Accounts Payable		34061.17
2120	Sales Tax Payable		1597.75
2130	Employee Income Tax Pay.		2116.71
2150	FICA Tax Payable		1197.28
2160	Medicare Tax Payable		280.02
2170	Unemploy. Tax Pay.--Fed.		116.06
2180	Unemploy. Tax Pay.--State		38.68
2190	Health Ins. Premium Pay.		985.00
2200	Disability Insurance Pay.		287.79
3110	Capital Stock		73000.00
3120	Retained Earnings		19780.00
3130	Dividends	3100.00	
3140	Income Summary	920.65	
4110	Sales		210798.13
4120	Sales Discount	1783.98	
4130	Sales Returns & Allow.	2752.35	
5110	Purchases	134711.21	
5120	Purchases Discount		1793.53
5130	Purch. Returns & Allow.		2554.78
6110	Advertising Expense	2896.73	
6120	Credit Card Fee Expense	953.71	
6130	Depr. Exp.--Office Eqpt.	596.56	
6140	Depr. Exp.--Store Eqpt.	466.88	
6150	Insurance Expense	496.08	
6160	Miscellaneous Expense	422.29	
6170	Payroll Taxes Expense	3114.24	
6180	Rent Expense	8000.00	
6190	Salaries Expense	38686.36	
6200	Supplies Expense--Office	229.46	
6210	Supplies Expense--Store	203.94	
6220	Utilities Expense	2885.91	
9110	Federal Income Tax Exp.	1027.12	
	Totals	352860.65	352860.65

Figure 9.20
Trial Balance

Chapter 9 Corporations

TUTORIAL PROBLEM 9-T

American Cosmetic Corp.
Schedule of Accounts Payable
04/30/--

Name	Balance
Anton Supply Depot	805.32
Hasher Chemical Co.	6091.02
Hubin Manufacturing Co.	5200.00
Kaplan Hair Products	3595.00
Perrizo Salon Supplies	8766.13
Stapleton Corporation	5145.10
Tipler & Rumkle Corp.	4458.60
Total	34061.17

Figure 9.21
Schedule of Accounts Payable

American Cosmetic Corp.
Schedule of Accounts Receivable
04/30/--

Name	Balance
Anna Graham	112.35
Burnette Salon	6250.00
Demars Hair Design	10008.06
Nail & Hair Care	5095.00
Studio 5 Styling Salon	3535.30
Sutter Tanning & Salon	9441.40
Tonya's Fashion Salon	13327.51
Total	47769.62

Figure 9.22
Schedule of Accounts Receivable

TUTORIAL PROBLEM 9-T

STATEMENT OF ACCOUNT
American Cosmetic Corp.

To: Anna Graham Date: 04/30/__

Date	Reference	Description	Charges	Credits	Balance
04/01/__		Balance Forward			.00
04/19/__	S737	Invoice	112.35		112.35

Figure 9.23
Statement of Account for Anna Graham

Date	Refer.	Account	Debit	Credit	Vendor/Customer
04/30/__	Adj.Ent.	1140 Merchandise Inventory	2086.00		
		3140 Income Summary		2086.00	
04/30/__	Adj.Ent.	6200 Supplies Expense--Office	537.87		
		1150 Supplies--Office		537.87	
04/30/__	Adj.Ent.	6210 Supplies Expense--Store	346.95		
		1160 Supplies--Store		346.95	
04/30/__	Adj.Ent.	6150 Insurance Expense	200.00		
		1170 Prepaid Insurance		200.00	
04/30/__	Adj.Ent.	6130 Depr. Exp.--Office Eqpt.	196.68		
		1520 Accum. Depr.--Ofc. Eqpt.		196.68	
04/30/__	Adj.Ent.	6140 Depr. Exp.--Store Eqpt.	157.00		
		1540 Accum. Depr.--Store Eqpt.		157.00	
04/30/__	Adj.Ent.	9110 Federal Income Tax Exp.	375.00		
		2140 Federal Income Tax Pay.		375.00	

Figure 9.24
Adjusting Entries

E-mail is probably the most widely used feature of the Internet. Although this communication method is much faster than using postal service, it doesn't provide the same level of interaction that a telephone conversation does.

Chapter 9 Corporations

TUTORIAL PROBLEM 9-T

American Cosmetic Corp.
General Journal
04/30/--

Date	Refer.	Acct.	Title	Debit	Credit
04/30	Adj.Ent.	1140	Merchandise Inventory	2086.00	
04/30	Adj.Ent.	3140	Income Summary		2086.00
04/30	Adj.Ent.	6200	Supplies Expense--Office	537.87	
04/30	Adj.Ent.	1150	Supplies--Office		537.87
04/30	Adj.Ent.	6210	Supplies Expense--Store	346.95	
04/30	Adj.Ent.	1160	Supplies--Store		346.95
04/30	Adj.Ent.	6150	Insurance Expense	200.00	
04/30	Adj.Ent.	1170	Prepaid Insurance		200.00
04/30	Adj.Ent.	6130	Depr. Exp.--Office Eqpt.	196.68	
04/30	Adj.Ent.	1520	Accum. Depr.--Ofc. Eqpt.		196.68
04/30	Adj.Ent.	6140	Depr. Exp.--Store Eqpt.	157.00	
04/30	Adj.Ent.	1540	Accum. Depr.--Store Eqpt.		157.00
04/30	Adj.Ent.	9110	Federal Income Tax Exp.	375.00	
04/30	Adj.Ent.	2140	Federal Income Tax Pay.		375.00
			Totals	3899.50	3899.50

Figure 9.25
General Journal Report (Adjusting Entries)

STEP 15: **Display a General Ledger Report for the Cash account.**
Choose the *Ledger Reports* option and select the *General Ledger* Report. When the General Ledger Account Range window appears, select an account number range of 1110 to 1110, and click *OK*. The report is shown in Figure 9.26.

Many companies, particularly those that sell computer hardware and software, offer customer service on the Internet. Among the services offered on World Wide Web pages or bulletin boards are free software upgrades and fixes.

TUTORIAL PROBLEM 9-T

American Cosmetic Corp.
General Ledger
04/30/--

Account Journal	Date	Refer.	Debit	Credit	Balance
1110-Cash					
Balance Forward					14155.73Dr
Cash Receipts	04/05	R653	3650.90		17806.63Dr
Cash Receipts	04/05	R654	5024.00		22830.63Dr
Cash Payments	04/06	C1212		878.80	21951.83Dr
Cash Payments	04/06	C1213		518.68	21433.15Dr
Cash Receipts	04/07	R655	4116.93		25550.08Dr
Cash Payments	04/09	C1214		1519.05	24031.03Dr
Cash Payments	04/09	C1215		105.42	23925.61Dr
Cash Payments	04/10	C1216		1035.99	22889.62Dr
Cash Payments	04/12	C1217		1250.27	21639.35Dr
Cash Payments	04/12	C1218		3845.43	17793.92Dr
Cash Payments	04/12	C1219		3100.00	14693.92Dr
Cash Payments	04/13	C1220		495.00	14198.92Dr
Cash Payments	04/13	C1221		8604.11	5594.81Dr
Cash Payments	04/13	C1222		1020.00	4574.81Dr
Cash Payments	04/14	C1223		2593.27	1981.54Dr
Cash Receipts	04/14	R656	4209.75		6191.29Dr
Cash Payments	04/16	C1224		4425.79	1765.50Dr
Cash Payments	04/18	C1225		2000.00	234.50Cr
Cash Payments	04/20	C1226		848.43	1082.93Cr
Cash Receipts	04/20	R657	5750.62		4667.69Dr
Cash Payments	04/21	C1227		4950.00	282.31Cr
Cash Receipts	04/21	T40	24310.40		24028.09Dr
Cash Payments	04/26	C1228		2186.34	21841.75Dr
Cash Payments	04/26	M40		226.93	21614.82Dr
Cash Payments	04/27	C1229		4054.05	17560.77Dr
Cash Payments	04/30	C1230		5530.40	12030.37Dr
Cash Payments	04/30	C1231		98.75	11931.62Dr

Figure 9.26
General Ledger Report

STEP 16: Display the financial statements.
Choose the *Financial Statements* option, and then select and display each of the following: income statement, balance sheet, and retained earnings statement. The reports are shown in Figure 9.27 (page 295-297).

Chapter 9 Corporations

TUTORIAL PROBLEM 9-T

American Cosmetic Corp.
Income Statement
For Period Ended 04/30/--

	Monthly Amount	Monthly Percent	Yearly Amount	Yearly Percent
Operating Revenue				
Sales	54507.00	100.44	210798.13	102.20
Sales Discount	-171.74	-0.32	-1783.98	-0.86
Sales Returns & Allow.	-67.50	-0.12	-2752.35	-1.33
Total Operating Revenue	54267.76	100.00	206261.80	100.00
Cost of Merchandise Sold				
Beginning Inventory	62064.00	114.37	62984.65	30.54
Purchases	37516.26	69.13	134711.21	65.31
Purchases Discount	-254.63	-0.47	-1793.53	-0.87
Purch. Returns & Allow.	-230.00	-0.42	-2554.78	-1.24
Merchandise Available for Sale	99095.63	182.61	193347.55	93.74
Less Ending Inventory	-64150.00	-118.21	-64150.00	-31.10
Cost of Merchandise Sold	34945.63	64.39	129197.55	62.64
Gross Profit	19322.13	35.61	77064.25	37.36
Operating Expenses				
Advertising Expense	500.00	0.92	2896.73	1.40
Credit Card Fee Expense	226.93	0.42	953.71	0.46
Depr. Exp.--Office Eqpt.	196.68	0.36	793.24	0.38
Depr. Exp.--Store Eqpt.	157.00	0.29	623.88	0.30
Insurance Expense	200.00	0.37	696.08	0.34
Miscellaneous Expense	125.42	0.23	422.29	0.20
Payroll Taxes Expense	777.27	1.43	3114.24	1.51
Rent Expense	2000.00	3.69	8000.00	3.88
Salaries Expense	9655.55	17.79	38686.36	18.76
Supplies Expense--Office	537.87	0.99	767.33	0.37
Supplies Expense--Store	346.95	0.64	550.89	0.27
Utilities Expense	518.68	0.96	2885.91	1.40
Total Operating Expenses	15242.35	28.09	60390.66	29.28
Net Income from Operations	4079.78	7.52	16673.59	8.08
Net Income before Income Tax	4079.78	7.52	16673.59	8.08
Income Tax				
Federal Income Tax Exp.	375.00	0.69	1402.12	0.68
Net Income after Income Tax	3704.78	6.83	15271.47	7.40

Figure 9.27
Financial Statements

TUTORIAL PROBLEM 9-T

American Cosmetic Corp.
Balance Sheet
04/30/--

Assets

Cash	11931.62	
Petty Cash	100.00	
Accounts Receivable	47769.62	
Merchandise Inventory	64150.00	
Supplies--Office	1650.00	
Supplies--Store	875.00	
Prepaid Insurance	950.00	
Office Equipment	14084.06	
Accum. Depr.--Ofc. Eqpt.	-2582.93	
Store Equipment	9104.06	
Accum. Depr.--Store Eqpt.	-2024.50	

Total Assets		146006.93
		=========

Liabilities

Accounts Payable	34061.17	
Sales Tax Payable	1597.75	
Employee Income Tax Pay.	2116.71	
Federal Income Tax Pay.	375.00	
FICA Tax Payable	1197.28	
Medicare Tax Payable	280.02	
Unemploy. Tax Pay.--Fed.	116.06	
Unemploy. Tax Pay.--State	38.68	
Health Ins. Premium Pay.	985.00	
Disability Insurance Pay.	287.79	

Total Liabilities		41055.46
		=========

Stockholders' Equity

Capital Stock	73000.00	
Retained Earnings	19780.00	
Dividends	-3100.00	
Net Income	15271.47	

Total Stockholders' Equity		104951.47

Total Liabilities & Equity		146006.93
		=========

Figure 9.27
Continued

Chapter 9 Corporations

TUTORIAL PROBLEM 9-T

```
                American Cosmetic Corp.
                Retained Earnings Statement
                For Period Ended 04/30/--

Retained Earnings (Beg. of Period)          19780.00
Dividends                                   -3100.00
Net Income                                  15271.47
                                          -----------
Retained Earnings (End of Period)           31951.47
                                          ===========
```

Figure 9.27
Continued

STEP 17: Generate an income statement and a balance sheet graph.
The graphs are shown in Figure 9.28.

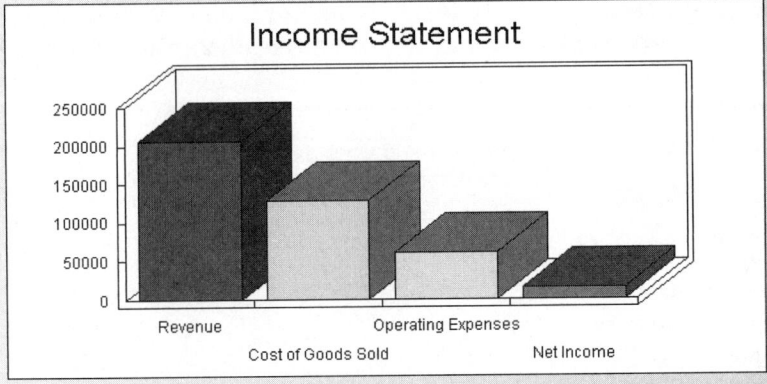

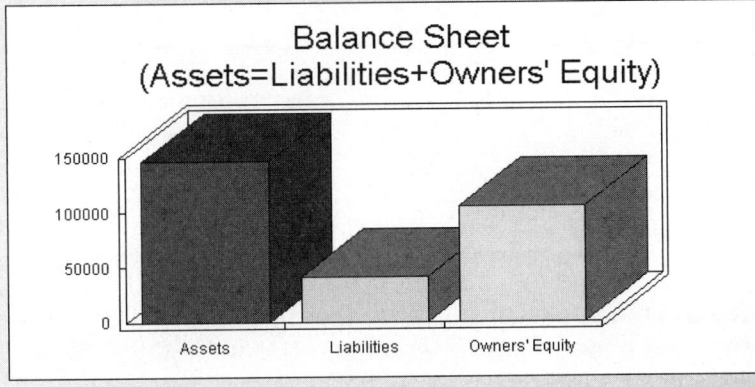

Figure 9.28
Income Statement and Balance Sheet Graphs

TUTORIAL PROBLEM 9-T

STEP 18: Use the Save menu command to save your data.

STEP 19: Calculate maturity dates and interest on notes.
Use the Notes & Interest Planner to calculate the maturity date, interest, and maturity value for each of the following notes. Use the current year for the date of each note.

Choose the *Planning Tools* menu item from the Data menu or click the *Tools* toolbar button. When the Planning Tools window appears, click the *Notes & Interest* tab, enter the data for Note 1, and display a Note Analysis Report. Repeat the procedure for Notes 2–5. The Note Analysis Report shown in Figure 9.29 is for Note 1.

Note	Date of Note	Principal of Note	Interest Rate	Time of Note	
1	Jan. 6	$5000.00	8.00	30 days	(based on 360 days)
2	Mar. 15	6500.00	9.50	1 year	(number of months)
3	May 1	2000.00	12.00	60 days	(based on 365 days)
4	July 12	1800.00	10.75	6 months	(number of months)
5	Sept. 21	4000.00	11.00	90 days	(based on 360 days)

```
                    American Cosmetic Corp.
                         Note Analysis
                           04/30/--

Date of the Note                                   01/06/--
Time of the Note                                   30 Days
Principal of the Note                              5000.00
Interest Rate of the Note                             8.00
Amount of Interest                                   33.33
Maturity Date of the Note                           2/5/--
Maturity Value of the Note                         5033.33
```

Figure 9.29
Note Analysis (Note 1)

STEP 20: Optional Spreadsheet and Word Processing Activities.
In addition to the income statement provided by the *Automated Accounting* software, the manager of the accounting department for American Cosmetic Corp. wants a condensed, single-step income statement. This income statement will be distributed to upper management as a

TUTORIAL PROBLEM 9-T

summary of the more detailed *Automated Accounting* income statement.

Spreadsheet:

a. Display and copy the income statement to the clipboard in spreadsheet format.
b. Start up your spreadsheet software and load the template file named AA8 Spreadsheet 09-T.
c. Select call A1 and paste the income statement into the spreadsheet.
d. Enter the cell references and formulas to complete the condensed, single-step income statement for the month in cells A61–D83.
   Note: Earnings per share is calculated by dividing the net income ($3,704.78) by the average number of shares of common stock outstanding (1300).
e. Save the entire spreadsheet with a file name of 09-T Your Name.
f. Print the condensed income statement (cell A61–D83). The completed condensed, single-step income statement is shown in Figure 9.30.

American Cosmetic Corp.
Income Statement
For Period Ended 04/30/--

REVENUE			
Net Sales			$54,267.76
COSTS AND EXPENSES			
Cost of Merchandise Sold		$34,945.63	
Operating Expenses		$15,242.35	

Total Costs and Expenses			$50,187.98

INCOME BEFORE TAXES			$4,079.78
Income Taxes			$375.00

NET INCOME			$3,704.78
			=========
Earnings Per Share			$2.85
			=========

Figure 9.30
Condensed, Single-Step Income Statement (Spreadsheet)

TUTORIAL PROBLEM 9-T

Word Processing:

a. Start up your word processing application and create a new document. Use a fixed font such as Courier.
b. Copy and paste the completed spreadsheet condensed, single-step income statement (cells A61-D83) into the new document.
c. Format and enhance the document's appearance.
d. Save the document with a file name of 09-T Your Name.
e. Print the document. The completed income statement is shown in Figure 9.31.
f. End your spreadsheet and word processing sessions.

```
                    American Cosmetic Corp.
                       Income Statement
                    For Period Ended 04/30/--

REVENUE
    Net Sales                                         $54,267.76

COSTS AND EXPENSES
    Cost of Merchandise Sold      $34,945.63
    Operating Expenses             15,242.35
                                  -----------
    Total Costs and Expenses                           50,187.98
                                                     -----------
INCOME BEFORE TAXES                                   $4,079.78
    Income Taxes                                         375.00
                                                     -----------
NET INCOME                                            $3,704.78
                                                     ===========
Earnings Per Share                                        $2.85
                                                     ===========
```

Figure 9.31
Condensed, Single-Step Income Statement (Word Processed)

STEP 21: End the *Automated Accounting* session.

Chapter 9 Corporations

Review and Practice: Applying Your Information Skills

I. MATCHING

Directions: In the *Working Papers*, write the letter of the appropriate term next to each definition.

a. board of directors
b. capital stock
c. corporate income tax
d. corporation
e. declaring a dividend
f. dividends
g. retained earnings
h. shareholders
i. shares of stock

1. Owners of the stock of a corporation.

2. Units that represent ownership of a corporation.

3. Earnings not yet distributed to shareholders.

4. The total shares of ownership in a corporation.

5. Earnings a corporation distributes to shareholders.

6. An organization that has many of the legal rights of an individual but is typically owned by many people.

7. A group elected by shareholders to manage a corporation.

8. The tax that corporations are required to pay on their earnings.

9. The decision by the board of directors to distribute earnings to the shareholders.

II. REVIEW QUESTIONS

Directions: Write the answers to the following questions in the *Working Papers*. Assume that the vendor checks and customer statements on account are being prepared by the computer.

1. What happens if you leave the Vendor field blank for a cash payment?

2. What is the decision by the board of directors of a corporation to distribute earnings to shareholders called?

3. Why is the check to pay dividends written to Shareholders Bank Account?

4. Which account is debited and which account is credited to record the adjusting entry for corporate income tax?

5. The income statement illustrated in this chapter has a percent column next to the monthly amount column and another percent column next to the yearly amount column. What do these percentages represent?

III. INTERNET ACTIVITY

Directions: If you have access to the Internet, use your browser to obtain an incorporation form from a state or city. Use *incorporation form* as your search argument. Print a copy of the form you find. Be sure to note the source and the URL (Internet address) of your search.

Independent Practice Problem 9-P

In this problem, you will process the monthly transactions, generate vendor checks, generate customer statements of account, and complete the end-of-month processing for American Cosmetic Corp. for the month of May of the current year. As you complete the problem, refer to the chart of accounts, vendor list, and customer list stored in problem AA8 Problem 09-P. Also, complete the Applying Your Technology Skills 9-P questions as you progress through the problem.

STEP 1: Start up *Automated Accounting 8.0*.

STEP 2: Load the opening balances file named AA8 Problem 09-P.

STEP 3: Enter your name in the User Name text box.

STEP 4: Use the Save As command to save the opening balances file with a file name of 09-P Your Name.

STEP 5: Enter the May transaction data.

May 01 Received cash on account from Nail & Hare Care, $5,044.05, covering S738 for $5,095.00, less 1% discount, $50.95. R658.
01 Purchased merchandise on account from Mckee Beauty Supply, $5,285.50. P509.
02 Received cash on account from Anna Graham, covering S737, $112.35, no discount. R659.
03 Paid cash on account to Hubin Manufacturing Co., $5,148.00, covering P506 for $5,200.00, less 1% discount, $52.00. C1232.

03 Received cash on account from Sutter Tanning & Salon, $9,441.40, covering S729 and S735, no discount. R660.
04 Purchased merchandise on account from Tipler & Rumkle Corp., $7,050.00. P510.
05 Paid cash on account to Kaplan Hair Products, $3,559.05, covering P507 for $3,595.00, less 1% discount, $35.95. C1233.
07 Purchased merchandise on account from Perrizo Salon Supplies, $260.25. P511.
08 Paid cash on account to Tipler & Rumkle Corp., $4,414.01, covering P508 for $4,458.60, less 1% discount, $44.59. C1234.
08 Paid cash to Eastern Utilities Co. for electric bill, $497.33. C1235.
09 Returned merchandise to Hasher Chemical Co., $1,600.00, against P501. DM40.
10 Paid cash on account to Mckee Beauty Supply, $5,179.79, covering P509 for $5,285.50, less 2% discount, $105.71. C1236.
11 Purchased merchandise on account from Hubin Manufacturing Co., $6,314.10. P512.
11 Received cash on account from Tonya's Fashion Salon, $13,327.51, covering S724 and S733, no discount. R661.
12 Paid cash to Arndt Insurance Assoc. for liability insurance, $500.00. C1237.
12 Paid cash on account to Tipler & Rumkle Corp., $6,979.50, covering P510 for $7,050.00, less 1% discount, $70.50. C1238.
14 Sold merchandise on account to Douglas Boutique, $3,342.20. S739.
15 Granted credit to Burnette Salon for merchandise returned, $2,660.00, against S736. CM29.
17 Paid cash on account to Perrizo Salon Supplies, $2,891.13, covering P499, less DM39. C1239.
18 Purchased merchandise on account from Mckee Beauty Supply, $4,995.99. P513.
19 Sold merchandise on account to Patty's Hair Styles, $2,200.00. S740.
19 Paid cash to Hammond Leasing, Inc. for monthly rent, $2,000.00. C1240.
21 Paid cash on account to Hubin Manufacturing Co., $6,250.96, covering P512 for $6,314.10, less 1% discount, $63.14. C1241.
22 Bought office supplies on account from Anton Supply Depot, $95.00. M42.

23 Received cash on account from Douglas Boutique, $3,308.78, covering S739 for $3,342.20, less 1% discount, $33.42. R662.
24 Bought store supplies on account from Anton Supply Depot, $215.35. M43.
25 Sold merchandise on account to Anna Graham, $75.00, plus sales tax, $5.25; total, $80.25. S741.
25 Received cash on account from Patty's Hair Styles, $2,178.00 covering S740 for $2,200.00, less 1% discount, $22.00. R663.
26 Paid cash on account to Mckee Beauty Supply, $4,896.07, covering P513 for $4,995.99, less 2% discount, $99.92. C1242.
28 Sold merchandise on account to Nolan's Beauty Shop, $8,950.00. S742.
28 Recorded credit card fee expense for April, $492.75. M44.
29 Sold merchandise on account to Sutter Tanning & Salon, $6,472.80. S743.
29 Recorded cash and credit card sales, $22,736.90, plus sales tax, $1,591.58; total, $24,328.48. T41.
30 Paid cash on account to Hasher Chemical Co., $1,943.46, covering P491, no discount. C1243.
30 Purchased merchandise on account from Kaplan Hair Products, $9,012.00. P514.
31 Sold merchandise on account to Tonya's Fashion Salon, $6,234.06. S744.
31 Paid cash to Payroll Bank Account for monthly payroll, $5,108.75. Total payroll, $9,018.10, less deductions: employee income tax, $1,949.58; FICA tax, $548.06; Medicare tax, $127.71; health insurance premium, $984.00; disability insurance premium, $300.00. C1244.
31 Recorded employee payroll taxes expense, $708.78 (FICA tax, $548.06; Medicare tax, $127.71; federal unemployment tax, $24.66; state unemployment tax, $8.35). M45.
31 Paid cash to Petty Cash Custodian to replenish petty cash fund, $84.05: office supplies, $6.20; store supplies, $22.85; miscellaneous expense, $55.00. C1245.

STEP 6: Display the General, Purchases, Cash Payments, Sales, and Cash Receipts Journal Reports for the month of May. If errors are detected, make corrections using the respective journal data entry window.

Chapter 9   Corporations

STEP 7: Display a Trial Balance, Schedule of Accounts Payable, Schedule of Accounts Receivable, and Statements of Account.

STEP 8: Enter the adjusting entries. Use a reference of Adj.Ent. The adjustment data for the month of May for American Cosmetic Corp. follow:

May 31
Merchandise inventory	65,100.00
Office supplies inventory	750.00
Store supplies inventory	715.00
Value of insurance policies	1,025.00
Depreciation for the month:	
Office Equipment	196.68
Store Equipment	157.00
Estimated federal income tax	375.00

STEP 9: Display the General Journal Report for the adjusting entries. Use a reference restriction of Adj.Ent. so that only adjusting entries will be included on the report.

STEP 10: Display a General Ledger Report for the Cash account.

STEP 11: Display the financial statements.

STEP 12: Generate a sales graph.

STEP 13: Save your data.

STEP 14: Calculate maturity dates and interest on notes. Use the Notes & Interest Planner to calculate the maturity date, interest, and maturity value for each of the following notes. Use the current year for the date of each note.

Note	Date of Note	Principal of Note	Interest Rate	Time of Note
1	Jan. 15	$3000.00	9.50	60 days (based on 360 days)
2	Mar. 15	1500.00	9.00	30 days (based on 365 days)
3	June 1	2200.00	10.35	1 year (number of months)
4	Aug. 21	900.00	10.75	6 months (number of months)
5	Nov. 11	3500.00	11.25	120 days (based on 360 days)

STEP 15: Optional Spreadsheet and Word Processing Activities.
Create a condensed, single-step income statement that can be distributed to upper management as a summary of the more detailed *Automated Accounting* income statement.

Spreadsheet:

a. Display and copy the income statement to the clipboard in spreadsheet format.

b. Start up your spreadsheet software and load the template file named AA8 Spreadsheet 09-T. If you completed the optional spreadsheet activity in Tutorial Problem 9-T, load your spreadsheet solution file instead.
c. Select cell A1 and paste the *Automated Accounting* income statement into the spreadsheet.
d. Enter the cell references and formulas to complete the condensed, single-step income statement in cells A61–D83. Use Figure 9.30 (page 299) as a guide.
   Note: Earnings per share is calculated by dividing the net income ($2,023.52) by the average number of shares of common stock outstanding (1350).
e. Save the entire spreadsheet with a file name of 09-P Your Name.
f. Print the completed condensed Income Statement.

Word Processing:

a. Start up your word processing software and create a new document. Use a fixed font such as Courier.
b. Copy and paste the completed spreadsheet condensed, single-step income statement into the new document.
c. Format and enhance the document's appearance. Use Figure 9.31 (page 300) as a guide.
d. Save the document with a file name of 09-P Your Name.
e. Print the document.
f. End your spreadsheet and word processing sessions.

STEP 16: End the *Automated Accounting* session.

Applying Your Technology Skills 9-P

Directions: Using Independent Practice Problem 9-P, write the answers to the following questions in the *Working Papers*.

Journals

1. What is the amount of the debit to Payroll Taxes Expense?
2. What is the amount of Purchase Invoice No. 509 to Mckee Beauty Supply?
3. What is the total of the debit column on the cash payments journal?
4. What is the amount of Sales Invoice No. 743 to Sutter Tanning & Salon?
5. What is the total of the credit column on the cash receipts journal?

Chapter 9   Corporations

Schedules of Accounts Payable and Receivable

6. What is the amount owed to Hasher Chemical Co.?
7. What is the amount due from all customers?

Checks and Statements of Account

8. What is the net amount paid to Hasher Chemical Co. with Check No. 1243?
9. What is the amount due from Tonya's Fashion Salon?

General Ledger Report

10. What was the Cash balance as of May 30?
11. What is the ending balance in the Cash account?

Financial Statements

12. What are the sales for the year?
13. What are the sales for the month?
14. What are the purchases for the year as a percent of total operating revenue?
15. What are the total operating expenses for the month as a percent of total operating revenue?
16. What are the total assets?
17. What is the total stockholders' equity?
18. What is the amount of retained earnings at the end of the month?

Notes & Interest

19. What are the maturity date, interest, and maturity value of Note 1?
20. What are the maturity date, interest, and maturity value of Note 2?
21. What are the maturity date, interest, and maturity value of Note 3?
22. What are the maturity date, interest, and maturity value of Note 4?
23. What are the maturity date, interest, and maturity value of Note 5?

Mastery Problem 9-M

In this problem, you will process the monthly transactions, generate vendor checks, generate customer monthly statements of account, and complete the end-of-month processing for American Cosmetic Corp. for the month of June of the current year. As you complete this problem,

refer to the chart of accounts, vendor list, and customer list stored with problem AA8 Problem 09-M when entering journal transactions. Also, complete the Applying Your Technology Skills 9-M questions as you progress through the problem.

STEP 1: Load the opening balances file named AA8 Problem 09-M.

STEP 2: Enter your name in the User Name text box.

STEP 3: Save the opening balances file with a file name of 09-M Your Name.

STEP 4: Enter the June transaction data.

June 01 Received cash on account from Anna Graham, from S741, $80.25, no discount. R664.
02 Sold merchandise on account to Patty's Hair Styles, $8,095.00. S745.
04 Granted credit to Demars Hair Design for merchandise returned, $1,500.00, against S737. CM30.
05 Purchased merchandise on account from Hubin Manufacturing Co., $7,868.50. P515.
06 Paid cash to Eastern Utilities Co., $528.04. C1246.
07 Paid cash to Arndt Insurance Assoc. for insurance premium, $950.00. C1247.
08 Received cash on account from Nolan's Beauty Shop, $8,860.50, covering S742 for $8,950.00, less 1% discount, $89.50. R665.
09 Received cash on account from Sutter Tanning & Salon, $6,408.07, covering S743 for $6,472.80, less 1% discount, $64.73. R666.
09 Received cash on account from Tonya's Fashion Salon, $6,171.72, covering S744 for $6,234.06, less 1% discount, $62.34. R667.
09 Paid cash on account to Kaplan Hair Products, $8,921.88, covering P514 for $9,012.00, less 1% discount, $90.12. C1248.
11 Purchased merchandise on account from Stapleton Corporation, $6,872.17. P516.
12 Paid cash to Pagel Cosmetic Supplies for miscellaneous expense, $145.00. C1249.
13 Bought office supplies on account from Anton Supply Depot, $210.50. M46.
15 Paid cash on account to Hubin Manufacturing Co., $7,789.81, covering P515 for $7,868.50, less 1% discount, $78.69. C1250.
16 Returned merchandise to Perrizo Salon Supplies, $1,150.00, against P503. DM41.

Chapter 9 Corporations

18 Sold merchandise on account to Studio 5 Styling Salon, $7,345.00. S746.
19 Paid cash to Hammond Leasing, Inc. for monthly rent, $2,000.00. C1251.
20 Recorded credit card fee expense for May, $524.89. M47.
21 Paid cash on account to Stapleton Corporation, $6,803.45, covering P516 for $6,872.17, less 1% discount, $68.72. C1252.
21 Received cash on account from Demars Hair Design, $1,303.06, covering S727 less CM30, no discount. R668.
22 Sold merchandise on account to Nail & Hair Care, $7,379.35. S747.
23 Purchased merchandise on account from Tipler & Rumkle Corp., $8,072.00. P517.
25 Bought advertising on account from Carley Marketing, $550.00. M48.
25 Sold merchandise on account to Anna Graham, $68.95, plus sales tax, $4.83; total, $73.78. S748.
26 Bought store equipment on account from Anton Supply Depot, $415.20. M49.
27 Paid cash on account to Hasher Chemical Co., $2,547.56, covering P501 less DM40, no discount. C1253.
28 Bought store supplies on account from Anton Supply Depot, $204.82. M50.
30 Paid cash on account to Payroll Bank Account for monthly payroll, $4,735.38. Total payroll, $8,380.15, less deductions: employee income tax, $1,844.38; FICA tax, $520.10; Medicare tax, $120.29; health insurance premium, $915.00; disability insurance premium, $245.00. C1254.
30 Recorded employee payroll taxes expense, $673.79 (FICA tax, $520.10; Medicare tax, $120.29; federal unemployment tax, $25.12; state unemployment tax, $8.28). M51.
30 Paid cash to Petty Cash Custodian to replenish petty cash fund, $91.45: office supplies, $74.15; store supplies, $17.30. C1255.
30 Recorded cash and credit card sales, $20,253.22, plus sales tax, $1,417.73; total, $21,670.95. T50.

STEP 5: Display the journal reports.

STEP 6: Display the Trial Balance, Schedule of Accounts Payable, Schedule of Accounts Receivable, and Statements of Account.

STEP 7: Enter the adjusting entries. The adjustment data for the month of June for American Cosmetic Corp. follows:

June 30
Merchandise inventory	$62,975.00
Office supplies inventory	850.00
Store supplies inventory	425.00
Value of insurance policies	995.00
Depreciation for the month:	
Office Equipment	196.00
Store Equipment	157.00
Estimated federal income tax	375.00

STEP 8: Display the adjusting entries.

STEP 9: Display a General Ledger Report for the Cash account.

STEP 10: Display the financial statements.

STEP 11: Generate an income statement and a sales graph.

STEP 12: Save your data.

STEP 13: Calculate maturity dates and interest on notes. Use the Notes & Interest Planner to calculate the maturity date, interest, and maturity value for each of the following notes. Use the current year for the date of each note.

Note	Date of Note	Principal of Note	Interest Rate	Time of Note
1	Feb 1	$1800.00	10.00	30 days (based on 365 days)
2	Apr. 15	3600.00	7.75	60 days based on 365 days)
3	Sept. 25	1950.00	12.00	120 days (based on 360 days)
4	Oct. 1	4200.00	11.75	1 year (number of months)

STEP 14: Optional Spreadsheet and Word Processing Activities.
Create a condensed, single-step income statement. Then use a word processor to format and enhance its appearance for management.

Spreadsheet:

a. Start up your spreadsheet software and load the template file named AA8 Spreadsheet 09-T. If you completed the optional spreadsheet activity in Tutorial Problem 9-T or Independent Practice Problem 9-P, load your spreadsheet solution file instead.
b. Select cell A1 and copy and paste the *Automated Accounting* income statement into the spreadsheet.
c. Enter the cell references and formulas to complete the condensed, single-step income statement in cells A61–D83. Use Figure 9.30 as a guide.

Chapter 9 Corporations

Note: Calculate the Earnings per share by dividing the net income by the number of shares outstanding (use 1350).

d. Save your file with a file name of 09-M Your Name.
e. Print the condensed income statement.

Word Processing:

a. Copy and paste the spreadsheet condensed income statement into a new document.
b. Format and enhance the document's appearance. Use Figure 9.31 (page 300) as a guide.
c. Save your document with a file name of 09-M Your Name.
d. Print the document.
e. End your spreadsheet and word processing sessions.

STEP 15: End the *Automated Accounting* session.

Applying Your Technology Skills 9-M

Directions: Using Mastery Problem 9-M, write the answers to the following questions in the *Working Papers*.

Journals

1. What is the amount of the credit to FICA Tax Payable?
2. What is the amount of Purchase Invoice No. 515 to Hubin Manufacturing Co.?
3. What is the total of the debit column on the cash payments journal?
4. What is the amount of Sales Invoice No. 746 to Studio 5 Styling Salon?
5. What is the total of the credit column on the cash receipts journal?

Schedules of Accounts Payable and Receivable

6. What is the amount owed to Anton Supply Depot?
7. What is the amount due from all customers?

Checks and Statements of Account

8. What is the net amount paid to Kaplan Products?
9. What is the amount of the Credit Memo No. 30 to Demars Hair Design?

General Ledger Report

10. What is the ending balance in the Cash account?

Financial Statements

11. What are the sales for the year?
12. What are the sales discounts for the month?
13. What are cost of goods sold for the year as a percent of total operating revenue?
14. What is the advertising expense for the month as a percent of total operating revenue?
15. What are the total assets?
16. What are the total liabilities?
17. What is the amount of retained earnings at the end of the month?

Notes & Interest

18. What are the maturity date, interest, and maturity value of Note 1?
19. What are the maturity date, interest, and maturity value of Note 2?
20. What are the maturity date, interest, and maturity value of Note 3?
21. What are the maturity date, interest, and maturity value of Note 4?

Reinforcement Activity R-3

In this problem, you will process the monthly transactions, generate vendor checks, generate monthly statements of account, and complete the end-of-month processing for Capital Mfg. Corporation.

STEP 1: Start up *Automated Accounting 8.0*.

STEP 2: Load the opening balances file named AA8 Problem R-3.

STEP 3: Enter your name in the User Name text box.

STEP 4: Save the opening balances file with a file name of R-3 Your Name.

STEP 5: Add Barbara Gibson to the customer list.

STEP 6: Enter the transactions data. Abbreviate the reference numbers as follows: Purchase Invoice, P; Check, C; Sales Invoice, S; Cash Receipt, R; Memorandums, M; Debit Memorandums, DM; Credit Memorandums, CM; Cash Register Tape, T. When entering the transactions, refer to the chart of accounts, vendor list, and customer list stored with the opening balances file named AA8 Problem R-3. Also, complete the Applying Your Technology Skills R-3 questions as you progress through the problem.

Apr. 01 Paid cash on account to Reid Fireplace Co., $34,521.19, covering P2244 for $34,869.89, less 1% discount, $348.70. C4073.

01 Purchased merchandise on account from Rathman Corporation, $57,500.00. P2249.

02 Paid cash to Salas & Salas, Inc. for miscellaneous expense, $342.86. C4074.

02 Received cash on account from Longworth Accessories, $50,687.44, covering S3811 for $51,199.43, less 1% discount, $511.99. R825.

03 Paid cash on account to Compton, Inc., $52,294.81, covering P2245 for $52,823.04, less 1% discount, $528.23. C4075.

04 Received cash on account from Elbers Fireplace Shop, $56,716.57, covering S3818 for $57,289.46, less 1% discount, $572.89. R826.

04 Paid cash on account to Rathman Corporation, $40,725.13, covering S2241 for $41,136.50 less 1% discount, $411.37. C4076.

06 Received cash on account from Volk Fireplaces & Mantels $39,687.38, covering S3820 for $40,088.26, less 1% discount, $400.88. R827.

07 Purchased merchandise on account from Wesely Manufacturing, Inc., $53,335.00. P2250.

07 Paid cash on account to Belmar Office Products, $7,091.78, covering P2247, no discount. C4077.

08 Received cash on account from Valley View Fireplaces, $31,117.07, covering S3816 for $31,431.38, less 1% discount, $314.31. R828.

09 Sold merchandise on account to Fireplace Plus, Inc., $121,375.00. S3821.

09 Paid cash on account to Scheidel Mfg., Inc., $66,899.80, covering P2246 for $68,265.10, less 2% discount, $1,365.30. C4078.

09 Returned merchandise to Timmerman Company, $10,950.00, against P2240. DM225.

10 Paid cash on account to Rathman Corporation, $56,925.00, covering P2249 for $57,500.00, less 1% discount, $575.00. C4079.

10 Granted credit to Alton Patio & Hearth for merchandise returned, $7,220.50, against S3812. CM211.

10 Bought office supplies on account from Belmar Office Products, $1,568.38. M266.

11 Purchased merchandise on account from Timmerman Company, $42,245.00. P2251.

11 Sold merchandise on account to Valley View Fireplaces, $117,410.00. S3822.

13 Paid cash to Commissioner of Revenue for March sales tax, $4,882.69. C4080.

14 Purchased merchandise on account from Scheidel Mfg., Inc., $61,250.00. P2252.

15 Granted credit to Fireplace Plus, Inc. for merchandise returned, $8,355.00, against S3814. CM212.

15 Paid cash to Porter Insurance Agency for liability for March insurance premiums: health insurance, $13,395.00; disability insurance, $5,390.00; total, $18,785.00. C4081.

15 Paid cash to Internal Revenue Service for payroll taxes: employee income tax, $37,671.28; FICA tax, $11,122.00; and Medicare tax, $2,601.11; total, $51,394.39. C4082.

15 Paid cash to Internal Revenue Service for quarterly estimated federal income tax, $15,600. C4083.

16 Bought store supplies on account from Belmar Office Products, $1,868.46. M267.

Reinforcement Activity R-3

16 Sold merchandise on account to Elbers Fireplace Shop, $133,575.00. S3823.
17 Received cash on account from Alton Patio & Hearth, $47,693.51, covering S3812 less CM211, no discount. R829.
17 Paid cash to Northern Utilities Co. for electric bill, $1,498.37. C4084.
17 Paid cash on account to Wesely Manufacturing, Inc., $52,801.65, covering P2250 for $53,335.00, less 1% discount, $533.35. C4085.
18 Received cash on account from Fireplace Plus, Inc., $120,161.25, covering S3821 for $121,375.00, less 1% discount, $1,213.75. R830.
18 Purchased merchandise on account from Compton, Inc., $62,415.00. P2253.
18 Paid cash to Sullivan Leasing Co. for monthly rent, $5,000.00. C4086.
18 Returned merchandise to Wesely Manufacturing, Inc., $5,332.00, against P2242. DM226.
20 Sold merchandise on account to Barbara Gibson, $16,700.00, plus sales tax, $1,169.00; total, $17,869.00. S3824.
20 Paid cash on account to Timmerman Company, $15,208.82, covering P2240 less DM225, no discount. C4087.
20 Purchased merchandise on account from Reid Fireplace Co., $41,795.95. P2254.
20 Bought advertising on account from Evans Marketing, Inc., $4,600.00. M268.
21 Received cash on account from Valley View Fireplaces, $116,235.90, covering S3822 for $117,410.00, less 1% discount, $1,174.10. R831.
21 Paid cash on account to Timmerman Company, $41,822.55, covering P2251 for $42,245.00, less 1% discount, $422.45. C4088.
22 Paid cash to Shareholders Bank Account for first quarter dividends declared in March, $94,000.00. C4089.
22 Received cash on account from Bernard Fireplace Co., $27,564.33, no discount. R832.
22 Granted credit to Wilder Hills Fireplaces for merchandise returned, $7,365.00, against S3813. CM213.

23 Bought store equipment on account from Belmar Office Products, $5,230.11. M269.
23 Sold merchandise on account to Volk Fireplaces & Mantels, $130,055.00. S3825.
24 Paid cash on account to Scheidel Mfg., Inc., $60,025.00, covering P2252 for $61,250.00, less 2% discount, $1,225.00. C4090.
24 Received cash on account from Fireplace Plus, Inc., $40,676.26, covering S3814 less CM212, no discount. R833.
25 Bought office equipment on account from Belmar Office Products, $6,332.00. M270.
25 Received cash on account from Elbers Fireplace Shop, $132,239.25, covering S3823 for $133,575.00, less 1% discount, $1,335.75. R834.
25 Sold merchandise on account to Bernard Fireplace Co., $125,795.00. S3826.
25 Purchased merchandise on account from Rathman Corporation, $79,118.45. P2255.
25 Recorded credit card fee expense for March, $635.19. M271.
27 Received cash on account from Bryan Dressler, $5,218.81, against S3819, no discount. R835.
27 Paid cash on account to Compton, Inc., $61,790.85, covering P2253 for $62,415.00, less 1% discount, $624.15. C4091.
27 Paid cash on account to Wesely Manufacturing, Inc., $34,522.39, covering P2242 less DM226, no discount. C4092.
27 Returned merchandise to Pulis Manufacturing, Co., $9,275.00, against P2248. DM227.
28 Purchased merchandise on account from Scheidel Mfg., Inc., $70,999.00. P2256.
28 Purchased merchandise on account from Compton, Inc., $87,475.50. P2257.
29 Paid cash on account to Reid Fireplace Co., $41,377.99, covering P2254 for $41,795.95, less 1% discount, $417.96. C4093.
29 Sold merchandise on account to Alton Patio & Hearth, $63,235.00. S3827.
29 Sold merchandise on account to Bryan Dressler, $6,275.00, plus sales tax, $439.25; total, $6,714.25. S3828.
30 Paid cash to Payroll Bank Account for monthly payroll, $109,156.98. Total payroll, $179,387.04, less deductions: employee income

Reinforcement Activity R-3

tax, $37,671.28; FICA tax, $11,122.00; Medicare tax, $2,601.11; health insurance premium, $13,454.05; disability insurance premium, $5,381.62. C4094.

30 Recorded employer payroll taxes expense, $19,284.11 (FICA tax, $11,122.00; Medicare tax, $2,601.11; federal unemployment tax, $717.55; state unemployment tax, $4,843.45). M272.

30 Paid cash to Petty Cash Account to replenish petty cash fund, $190.50: office supplies, $110.00; store supplies, $60.50; miscellaneous expense, $20.00. C4095.

30 Received cash on account from Bernard Fireplace Co., $124,537.05, covering S3826 for $125,795.00, less 1% discount, $1,257.95. R836.

30 Paid cash on account to Evans Marketing, Inc., $4,554.00, covering M268 for $4,600.00, less 1% discount, $46.00. C4096.

30 Recorded cash and credit card sales, $97,732.60, plus sales tax, $6,841.28; total, $104,573.88. T40.

STEP 7: Display the General, Purchases, Cash Payments, Sales, and Cash Receipts Journal Reports for the period April 1 to April 30 of the current year. If errors are detected, make corrections.

STEP 8: Display a Trial Balance, Schedule of Accounts Payable, Schedule of Accounts Receivable, and Statements of Accounts.

STEP 9: Enter the adjusting entries using the following adjustment data for the month of April. Use the Trial Balance generated in Step 8 as the basis for making the adjusting entries. Use Adj.Ent. as the reference.

April 30
Merchandise inventory $599,106.00
Office Supplies inventory 3,660.00
Store Supplies inventory 2,700.00
Value of insurance policies 5,200.00
Depreciation for the period:
   Office Equipment 2,091.92
   Store Equipment 1,564.35
Estimated federal income tax 5,250.00

STEP 10: Display the General Journal Report for the adjusting entries. Use a reference restriction of Adj.Ent. so that only adjusting entries will be included on the report.

STEP 11: Display a General Ledger Report for the Cash account.

STEP 12: Display the income statement, balance sheet, and retained earnings statement.

STEP 13: Generate a balance sheet graph.

STEP 14: Save your data.

STEP 15: Optional Spreadsheet and Word Processing Activities.
Create a condensed, multi-step income statement from the detailed income statement provided by the *Automated Accounting* system.

Spreadsheet:

a. Display and copy the income statement to the clipboard in spreadsheet format.
b. Start up your spreadsheet software and load the template file named AA8 Spreadsheet R-3.
c. Select cell A1 and paste the income statement into the spreadsheet.
d. Enter the cell references and formulas to complete the condensed, multi-step income statement for the month in cells A61–D79.
Note: Earnings per share is calculated by dividing the net income by the number of shares of capital stock issues, 5,000.
e. Save the entire spreadsheet with a file name of R-3 Your Name.
f. Print the completed income statement.

Word Processing:

a. Start up your word processing software and create a new document. Use a fixed font such as Courier.
b. Copy and paste the completed spreadsheet's condensed, multi-step income statement into the new document.
c. Format and enhance the document's appearance.
d. Save the document with a file name of R-3 Your Name.
e. Print the document.
f. End your spreadsheet and word processing sessions.

STEP 16: End the *Automated Accounting* session.

Reinforcement Activity R-3

Applying Your Technology Skills R-3

Directions: Using Reinforcement Activity R-3, write the answers to the following questions in the *Working Papers*.

Journals

1. In the general journal, what is the amount of the debit to Payroll Taxes Expense?
2. What is the amount of Purchase Invoice No. 2251 for Timmerman Company?
3. What is the total of the debit column on the cash payments journal?
4. What is the amount of Sales Invoice No. 3823 for Elbers Fireplace Shop?
5. What is the total of the credit column on the cash receipts journal?

Schedules of Accounts Payable and Receivable

6. What is the amount owed to Compton, Inc.?
7. What is the amount due from all customers?

Checks and Statements of Account

8. What is the net amount of the check paid to Reid Fireplace Co. on April 1?
9. What is the amount of the credit memo to Alton Patio & Hearth?

General Ledger Report

10. What is the Cash account balance as of April 29?
11. What is the ending balance in the Cash account?

Financial Statements

12. What are the sales for the year?
13. What is the sales discount amount for the month?
14. What is the cost of merchandise sold for the year as a percent of total operating revenue?
15. What is the amount of salaries expense for the month as a percent of total operating revenue?
16. What are the total current assets?
17. What are the total liabilities?
18. What is the amount of retained earnings at the end of the month?

Chapter 10
PAYROLL

KEY TERMS

Withholding Allowances
Number of Pay Periods
Marital Status
Salary Amount
Hourly Rate

Voluntary Deductions
Employee List Report
Payroll Report
Quarterly Report
W-2 Statement

LEARNING OBJECTIVES

Upon completion of this chapter, you will be able to:
1. Complete an employee input form.
2. Perform employee maintenance.
3. Complete a payroll transactions input form.
4. Enter and correct payroll transactions.
5. Generate and post payroll journal entries.
6. Display payroll reports.

Chapter 10 Payroll

INTRODUCTION

In a computerized payroll system, the computer stores data such as an employee's name, address, social security number, marital status, number of withholding allowances, pay rate, and voluntary deductions. At the end of each pay period, all payroll transaction data, such as gross pay and deductions, are entered into the computer. The computer can calculate the withholding taxes and create the resulting journal entries.

After the employee data is entered, an Employee List Report can be displayed to verify the accuracy of input data. A Payroll Report can be displayed that provides earnings and withholdings for the month, quarter, and year at any time. *Automated Accounting 8.0* can generate the current payroll and employer's payroll tax expenses journal entries. At the end of the quarter, the Quarterly Report is displayed, and at the end of the year, the W-2 Statements of earnings and withholdings are also produced.

It is important to note that the software uses the payroll transaction dates that are entered in order to accumulate totals and process the end-of-quarter and end-of-year reports. Therefore, *it is very important that the correct payroll transaction dates be entered each pay period.*

EMPLOYEE INPUT FORM

In this payroll system, the additions, changes, and deletions to employee data may be recorded on an employee input form, as illustrated in Figures 10.1 through 10.3. Figure 10.1 is an example of the addition of a new employee. Figure 10.2 shows a change in marital status and number of withholding allowances. Notice that only the employee number and the fields that have changed need to be completed. Figure 10.3 shows the deletion of an employee.

ETHICS

Midori works for a local business that uses personal computers. Her brother, who is taking a computer course in high school, asks Midori if she would use one of the personal computers at her place of employment to complete a homework assignment for him. Her brother assures her that his homework will not take more than 20 minutes of computer time and suggests that she do this work after normal office hours.

Critical Thinking

1. Do you think that what Midori's brother is proposing is ethical or unethical?

2. What do you think Midori should do? Justify your answer.

EMPLOYEE INPUT FORM

Run Date <u>12/31/--</u>   Problem No. <u>Example</u>

Employee Number	160
Name	Weston, Glen
Address	510 Fulton Pike
City, State, and Zip	Macon, GA 31208-8011
Social Security No.	482-70-8945
Withholding Allow.	2
Number Pay Periods	12
G.L. Account No.	545

Salary Amount	2000.00
Hourly Rate	
Piece Rate	
Commission %	

MARITAL STATUS
○ Single
● Married

Figure 10.1
Employee Input Form (New Employee)

EMPLOYEE INPUT FORM

Run Date <u>12/31/--</u>   Problem No. <u>Example</u>

Employee Number	110
Name	
Address	
City, State, and Zip	
Social Security No.	
Withholding Allow.	2
Number Pay Periods	
G.L. Account No.	

Salary Amount	
Hourly Rate	
Piece Rate	
Commission %	

MARITAL STATUS
○ Single
● Married

Figure 10.2
Employee Input Form (Changes to Employee)

Chapter 10 Payroll

```
                    EMPLOYEE
                   INPUT FORM
Run Date 12/31/--                    Problem No. Example

Employee Number    100
Name              (Delete)           Salary Amount
Address                              Hourly Rate
City, State, and Zip                 Piece Rate
Social Security No.                  Commission %
Withholding Allow.
Number Pay Periods                   MARITAL STATUS
G.L. Account No.                        ○ Single
                                        ○ Married
```

Figure 10.3
Employee Input Form (Deletion)

Each field in the form corresponds to a grid cell in the Employees Account Maintenance window. The field names and a description of each column are illustrated in the Employee Maintenance window shown in Figures 10.4a and 10.4b.

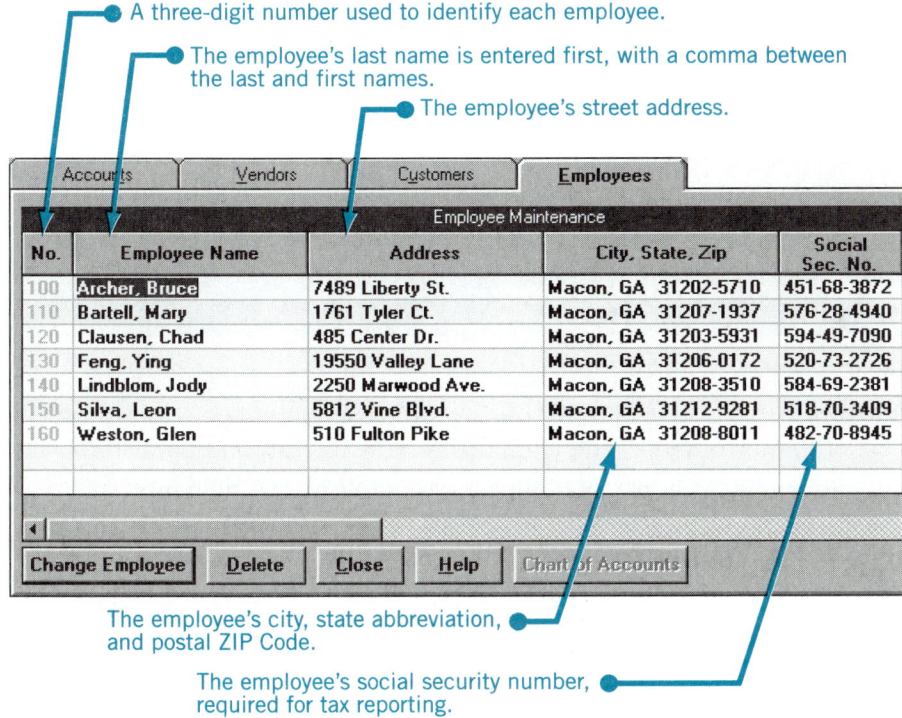

Figure 10.4a
Employee Maintenance Window

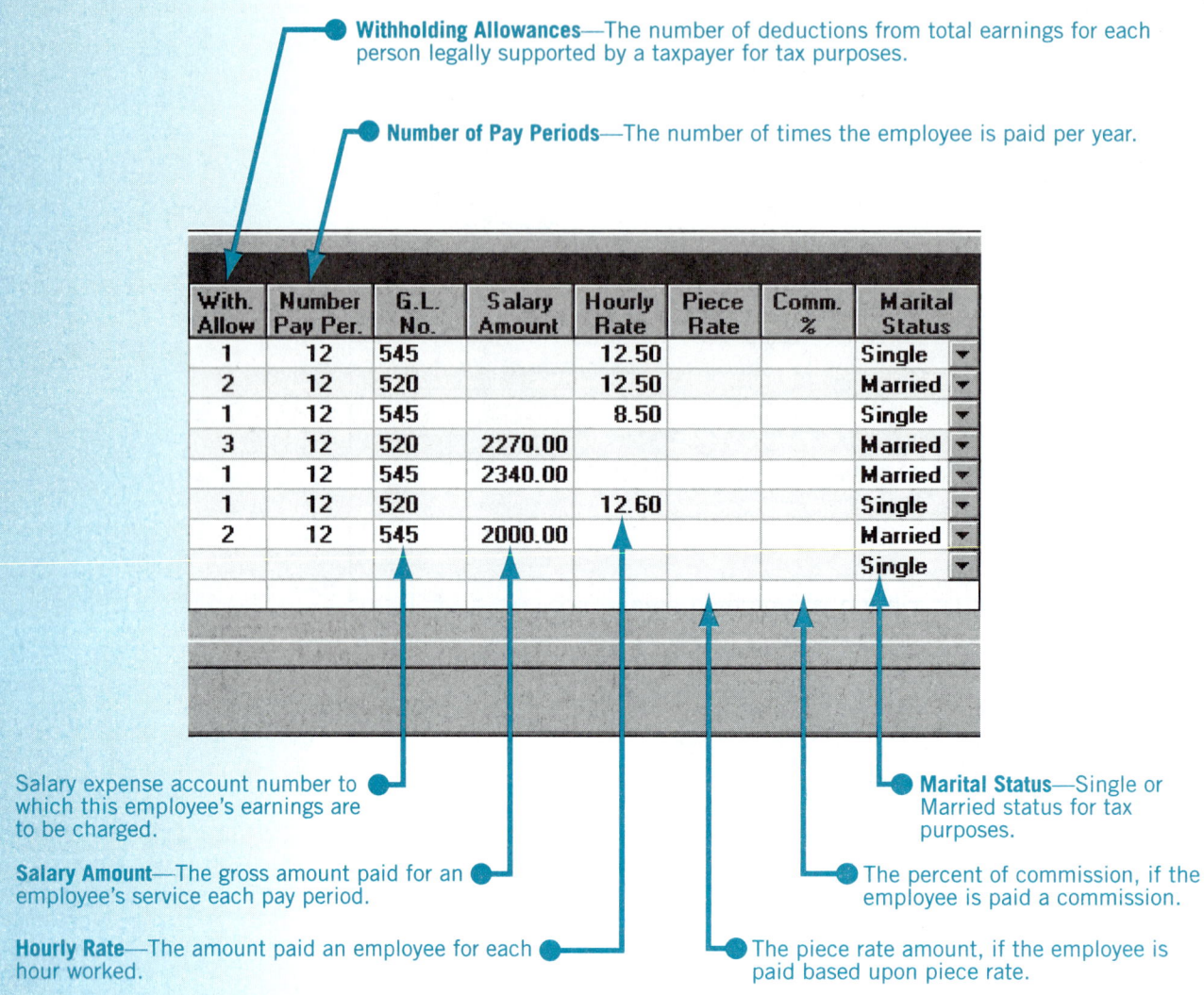

Figure 10.4b
Employee Maintenance Window (*continued*)

EMPLOYEE MAINTENANCE

When Maintain Accounts is chosen from the Data menu or the Accts. toolbar button is clicked, the Account Maintenance window will appear. To enter payroll data, click the Employees tab and enter the maintenance data. Figure 10.4 shows the maintenance data already entered from the Employee Input Forms in Figures 10.1 through 10.3. Employee No. 100 is shown selected and about to be deleted.

New employees can be added by keying the data fields in the grid cell boxes and choosing the employee's marital status. When the focus moves to the marital status, choose Single or Married from the drop-down list or type the first letter of the desired marital status (S or M). The new employee will be inserted into the existing employee list in employee-number sequence. Existing employee data can be changed by selecting the employee you wish to change, keying the correct data (or selecting a different marital status), and clicking the Change Employee button. (The Add Employee button changes to Change Employee.) An existing employee can be deleted by simply selecting the desired employee and clicking the Delete button.

PAYROLL TRANSACTIONS INPUT FORM

You will not be allowed to delete an employee with cumulative earnings for the current year until after the end of the calendar year.

To facilitate data input, you may wish to record the payroll transaction data on the payroll input form and then enter it into the computer. The input form illustrated in Figure 10.5 shows how the data for two employees are recorded. The first employee is paid hourly, and the second employee is salaried. Each has voluntary deductions. **Voluntary deductions** are employee-authorized withholdings from earnings for such options as health insurance, dental insurance, savings plans, and charitable contributions. The field names and a description of each column are illustrated in the Other Activities Payroll Tab shown in Figures 10.6a and 10.6b.

PAYROLL TRANSACTIONS INPUT FORM

Run Date 12/31/-- Problem No. Example

Employee Name	Salary Amount	Reg. Hours	O.T. Hours	Pieces	Sales	Health Insurance	Dental Insurance	Credit Union
Bartell, Mary		176	4.0			40.00	24.00	25.00
Feng, Ying						45.00	18.00	50.00

Figure 10.5
Payroll Transactions Input Form

PAYROLL TRANSACTIONS

Employee payroll transaction data for the pay period are entered into the Payroll tab in the Other Activities window. For each employee's payroll transaction, the payroll date, pay information, and employee deductions (if different from the previous pay period) are entered. The employee taxes can be either keyed or automatically calculated by the computer. The payroll problems in this textbook have the software to calculate employee taxes.

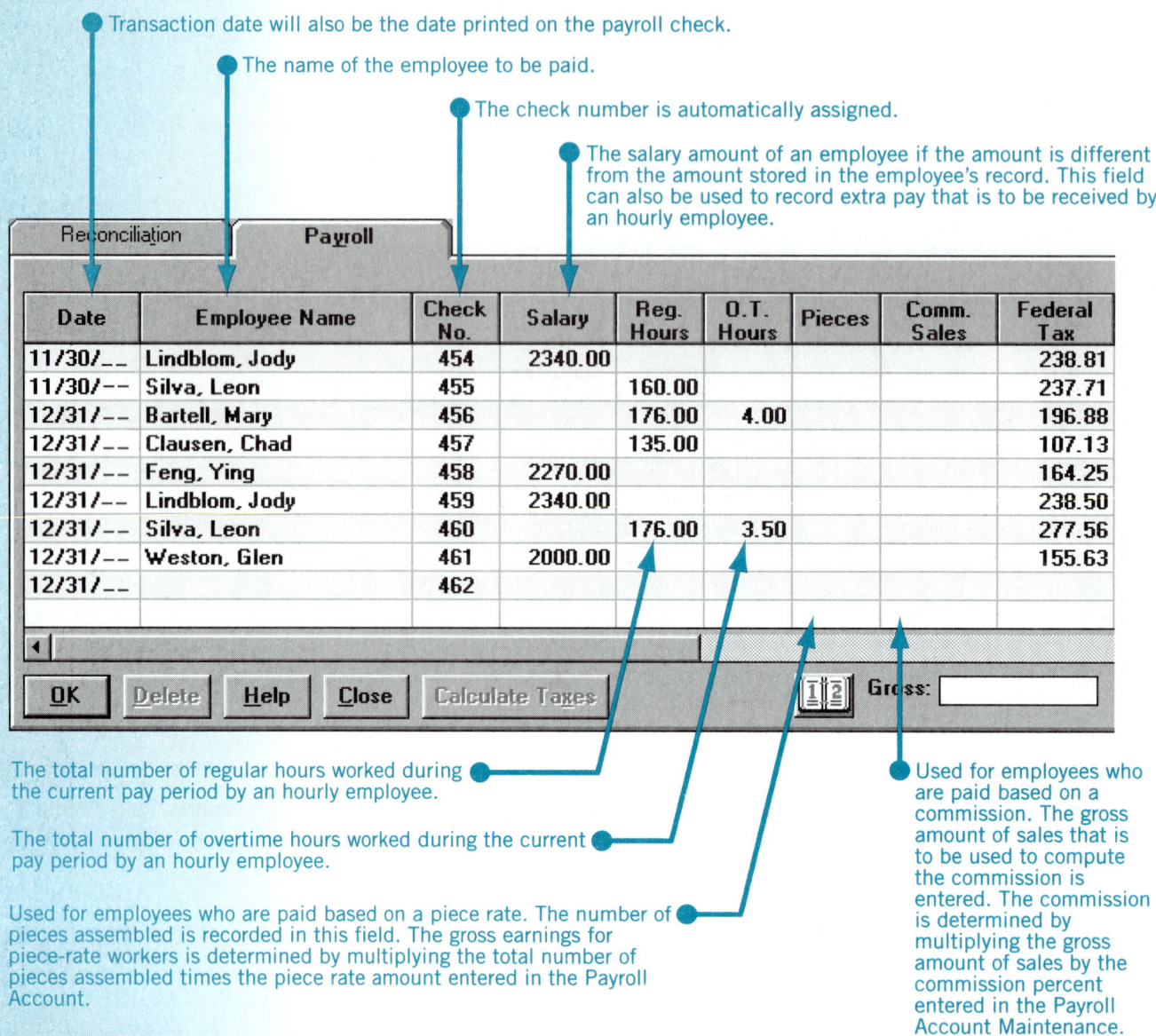

Figure 10.6a
Payroll Transactions Window

When the Other toolbar button is clicked, the Other Activities window will appear. Click the Payroll tab. The Payroll tab will appear as shown in Figures 10.6a and 10.6b. Note that the December 31 payroll transactions for Mary Bartell and Ying Feng are those recorded on the Payroll Transactions Input Form shown in Figure 10.5.

When entering the payroll transactions, be careful to enter the correct date of the check. Also, verify that the check number displayed by the computer is correct. Re-enter the correct check number if necessary.

If the employee is salaried, the salary amount will be displayed. You can enter a different salary amount that will override the amount already shown. If a salaried employee is to be paid a one-time bonus, the amount

Chapter 10   Payroll

State Tax	City Tax	Social Security	Medicare	Health Insurance	Dental Insurance	Credit Union	Net Pay
70.38	23.40	145.08	33.93	45.00	28.00	75.00	1680.40
54.68	20.16	124.99	29.23	40.00	24.00	30.00	1455.23
64.60	22.75	141.05	32.99	40.00	24.00	25.00	1727.73
18.49	11.48	71.15	16.64	40.00	24.00	35.00	823.61
61.74	22.70	140.74	32.92	45.00	18.00	50.00	1734.65
70.38	23.40	145.08	33.93	45.00	28.00	75.00	1680.71
67.65	22.84	141.59	33.11	40.00	24.00	30.00	1647.00
51.28	20.00	124.00	29.00	40.00	20.00	50.00	1510.09

These four fields (plus the Federal Tax field) contain the taxes withheld from an employee's pay. You may calculate and enter the amounts individually or have the software calculate the taxes.

These three fields contain voluntary deductions that are withheld from the employee's pay each period.

Figure 10.6b
Payroll Transactions Window (*continued*)

entered would be the employee's normal salary plus the bonus amount. Also, this grid cell can be used to enter extra pay earned by hourly employees. The software will add the amount entered to the hourly employees' earnings.

If the employee is paid hourly, enter the regular hours worked in the Reg. Hours grid cell. If the employee is paid hourly and is to be paid overtime at a rate of 1½ times his or her normal hourly rate, enter the overtime hours in the O.T. Hours grid cell.

Enter the employee voluntary deductions if different from those shown or if the employee is new, and then click the Calculate Taxes button to direct the software to calculate the employee taxes. The taxes will be calculated and displayed in the employee taxes grid cells.

Finally, after all the employee's data have been entered and taxes calculated, click OK. A payroll check will be generated and displayed. A payroll check generated by the computer shows the net amount of pay (earnings after payroll taxes and other deductions) earned by the employee during the pay period. The payroll check shown in Figure 10.7 was generated for Mary Bartell on 12/31/-- as recorded on the input form in Figure 10.5 and entered into the computer as shown in Figure 10.6.

A previously entered payroll transaction can be corrected by simply selecting the incorrect payroll transaction, keying in the correction, and clicking OK. The computer will update the employee's record and display a new check. The previously written check should be marked *Void* and filed as an audit trail document. Likewise, an existing payroll

The computer automatically sequences and generates the check number. However, if the check number (e.g., for a special check) or the check numbering sequence needs to be changed (e.g., switched banks or checking accounts), you can enter the desired check number in the Check No. grid cell.

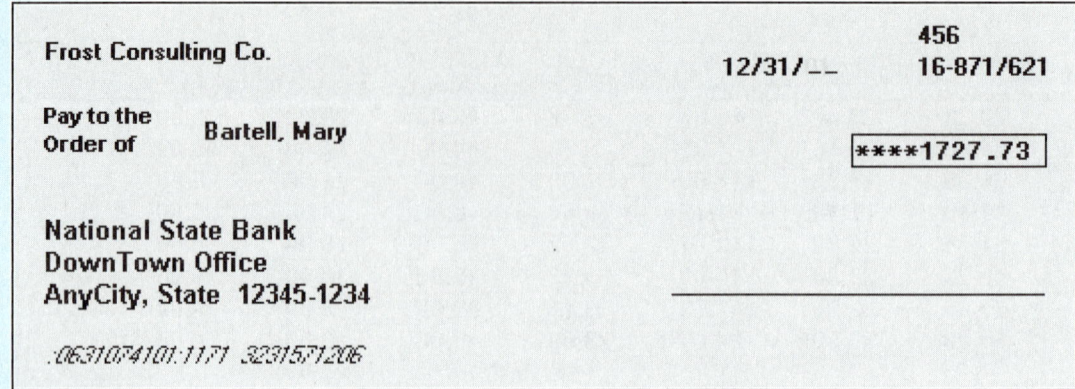

Figure 10.7
Payroll Check

transaction can be deleted by selecting the payroll transaction to be deleted and clicking the Delete button. Again, the previously written check should be marked *Void* and filed as an audit trail document.

PAYROLL JOURNAL ENTRIES

Automated Accounting 8.0 can generate the current payroll journal entry (that includes salary expenses, employee federal tax payable, employee state tax payable, employee city tax payable, Social Security tax payable, Medicare tax payable, and voluntary deductions). It can also generate the employer's payroll taxes journal entry, which includes Social Security, Medicare, federal unemployment, and state unemployment taxes.

The journal entry to record the current payroll can be generated by choosing the Current Payroll Journal Entry menu item from the Options menu. The journal entry to record the employer's payroll taxes can be generated by choosing the Employer's Payroll Taxes menu item from the Options menu. The journal entry will appear in a dialog box for your verification. When it is posted to the general ledger, the general journal appears showing the posted entry.

Generating the Current Payroll Journal Entries

Choose the Current Payroll Journal Entry menu item from the Options menu. When the confirmation dialog box shown in Figure 10.8 appears, click Yes. The generated journal entries for the current payroll will appear in a dialog box window, as illustrated in Figure 10.9. Click the Post button. When the current payroll journal entry is posted, the General Journal window will appear, showing that the entry has been automatically entered and posted. This entry is placed in the general journal in the event it must be changed or deleted at a later time.

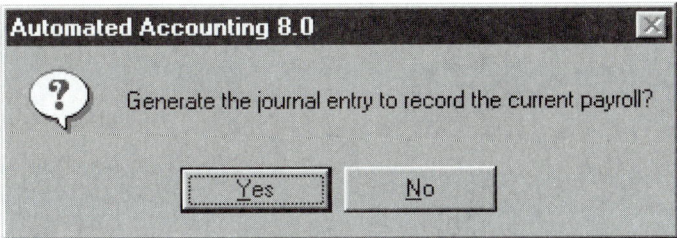

Figure 10.8
Current Payroll Journal Entry Confirmation Dialog Box

Acct. #	Account Title	Debit	Credit
520	Consultant Salaries Exp.	6828.75	
545	Office Salaries Exp.	5487.50	
265	Emp. Fed. Inc. Tax Pay.		1139.95
270	Emp. State Inc. Tax Pay.		334.14
275	Social Security Tax Pay.		763.61
280	Medicare Tax Payable		178.59
272	Emp. City Inc. Tax Pay.		123.17
297	Health Ins. Premiums Pay.		250.00
298	Dental Ins. Premiums Pay.		138.00
299	Credit Union Deduct. Pay.		265.00
285	Salaries Payable		9123.79

Figure 10.9
Current Payroll Journal Entries

If you must make a change or correction to a payroll transaction after the journal entry has been generated and posted, you must first delete the old journal entry and then generate the corrected journal entry.

Generating the Employer's Payroll Taxes Journal Entries

Choose Employer's Payroll Taxes from the Options menu. When the confirmation dialog box shown in Figure 10.10 appears, click Yes. The generated journal entries for the employer's payroll taxes will appear in a dialog window, as shown in Figure 10.11.

Figure 10.10
Employer's Payroll Taxes Confirmation Dialog Box

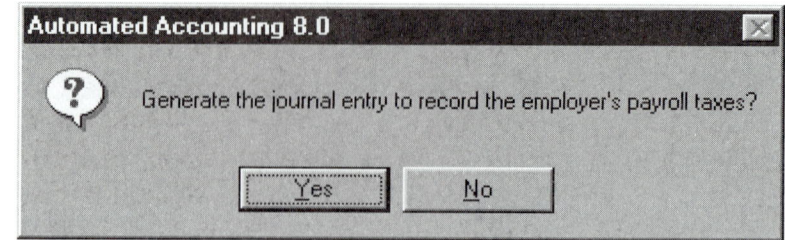

Figure 10.11
Employer's Payroll Taxes Journal Entries

If you discover an error in a payroll or payroll taxes journal entry after it has been posted, you must delete the journal entry, generate the journal entry again, and correct it before posting it.

PAYROLL REPORTS

After the payroll data for the period are recorded, the payroll reports are generated. There are four types of payroll reports available: Employee List Report, Payroll Report, Quarterly Report, and W-2 Statements.

After the payroll reports and other financial reports are generated, the period-end closing procedures can be completed. As you learned in earlier chapters, generating closing entries will prepare the temporary accounts for the next fiscal period. Likewise, generating closing entries will prepare the payroll system for the next fiscal period. Payroll transactions are purged and employee earnings and withholding accumulators are cleared.

To general the payroll reports, select Reports, and then choose the Payroll Reports option button. A list of payroll reports will appear, as shown in Figure 10.12. Select the desired report from the Choose a Report to Display list.

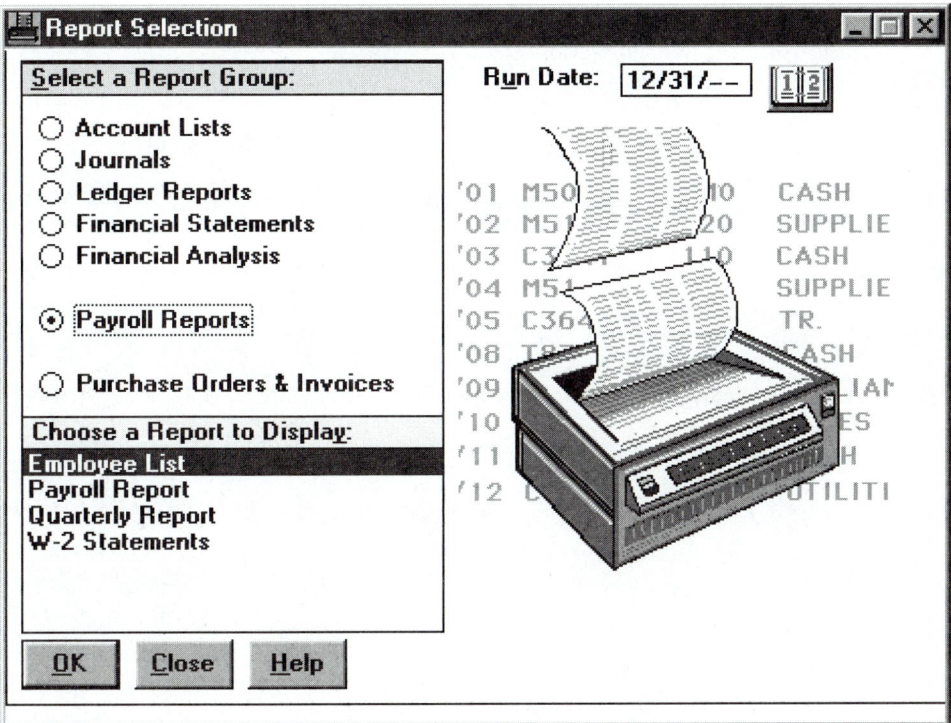

Figure 10.12
Report Selection (Payroll Reports)

Employee List Report

The **Employee List Report** is a complete listing of the employee payroll information. The information appearing in the Employee List Report was entered into the computer via the Employees tab in the Account Maintenance window. This report is useful in verifying the accuracy of data entered into the Employees window. An employee list report is shown in Figure 10.13.

Payroll Report

The **Payroll Report** is a list of earnings and withholding information for the month, quarter, and year. Earnings and withholding information for each employee appear at the beginning of the report. Summary information is included at the end of the report that provides information on earnings and withholdings for all employees. The Payroll Report should be generated each pay period. The first employee (Bartell, Mary) and the summary at the end of the Payroll Report are shown in Figure 10.14.

Emp. No.	Employee Name/Address	Soc. Sec./ Mar. Stat.	# Pay Periods	G.L. Acct.	Salary/ Rate	Piece Rate/ Commission
	Frost Consulting Co. Employee List 12/31/--					
110	Bartell, Mary 1761 Tyler Ct. Macon, GA 31207-1937	576-28-4940 Married W/H 2	12	520	12.50	
120	Clausen, Chad 485 Center Dr. Macon, GA 31203-5931	594-49-7090 Single W/H 1	12	545	8.50	
130	Feng, Ying 19550 Valley Lane Macon, GA 31206-0172	520-73-2726 Married W/H 3	12	520	2270.00	
140	Lindblom, Jody 2250 Marwood Ave. Macon, GA 31208-3510	584-69-2381 Married W/H 1	12	545	2340.00	
150	Silva, Leon 5812 Vine Blvd. Macon, GA 31212-9281	518-70-3409 Single W/H 1	12	520	12.60	
160	Weston, Glen 510 Fulton Pike Macon, GA 31208-8011	482-70-8945 Married W/H 2	12	545	2000.00	

Figure 10.13
Employee List Report

Quarterly Report

At the end of each quarter, the Quarterly Report must be generated. The **Quarterly Report** is a report used to disclose Social Security and Medicare taxable wages to the Internal Revenue Service. A Quarterly Report is shown in Figure 10.15.

W-2 Statements

A **W-2 Statement** is a report that summarizes an employee's taxable wages and various withholdings. At the end of the year, the company must provide a W-2 Statement to each employee paid during the past year, and must provide a copy to the Internal Revenue Service. The W-2 Statement is used for individual tax reporting purposes. A W-2 Statement for the first employee (Bartell, Mary) is shown in Figure 10.16.

Chapter 10 Payroll

```
                         Frost Consulting Co.
                            Payroll Report
                               12/31/--
```

		Current	Quarterly	Yearly
110-Bartell, Mary	Gross Pay	2275.00	6521.88	26128.14
520-Consultant	Federal W/H	196.88	704.53	3063.27
Married Acct. 520	State W/H	64.60	184.37	747.32
W/H 2 576-28-4940	Soc. Sec. W/H	141.05	404.36	1619.95
Pay Periods 12	Medicare W/H	32.99	94.57	378.86
Salary	City Tax W/H	22.75	65.22	261.29
Hourly Rate 12.50	Health Insurance	40.00	120.00	480.00
Piece Rate	Dental Insurance	24.00	72.00	288.00
Commission %	Credit Union	25.00	75.00	300.00
Check Number 456				
Check Date 12/31/--	Net Pay	1727.73	4801.83	18989.45
/\
Payroll Summary	Gross Pay	12316.25	32907.93	127087.47
	Federal W/H	1139.95	3264.30	13051.47
	State W/H	334.14	894.99	3493.00
	Soc. Sec. W/H	763.61	2040.29	7879.41
	Medicare W/H	178.59	477.17	1842.83
	City Tax W/H	123.17	329.09	1270.91
	Health Insurance	250.00	670.00	2560.00
	Dental Insurance	138.00	374.00	1436.00
	Credit Union	265.00	695.00	2630.00
	Net Pay	9123.79	24163.09	92923.85

Figure 10.14
Payroll Report

```
                      Frost Consulting Co.
                        Quarterly Report
                           12/31/--
```

Soc. Sec. Number	Employee Name	Taxable Soc. Sec.	Taxable Medicare
576-28-4940	Bartell, Mary	6521.88	6521.88
594-49-7090	Clausen, Chad	4139.50	4139.50
520-73-2726	Feng, Ying	6810.00	6810.00
584-69-2381	Lindblom, Jody	7020.00	7020.00
518-70-3409	Silva, Leon	6416.55	6416.55
482-70-8945	Weston, Glen	2000.00	2000.00
	Totals	32907.93	32907.93
	Total Employees 6		

Figure 10.15
Quarterly Report

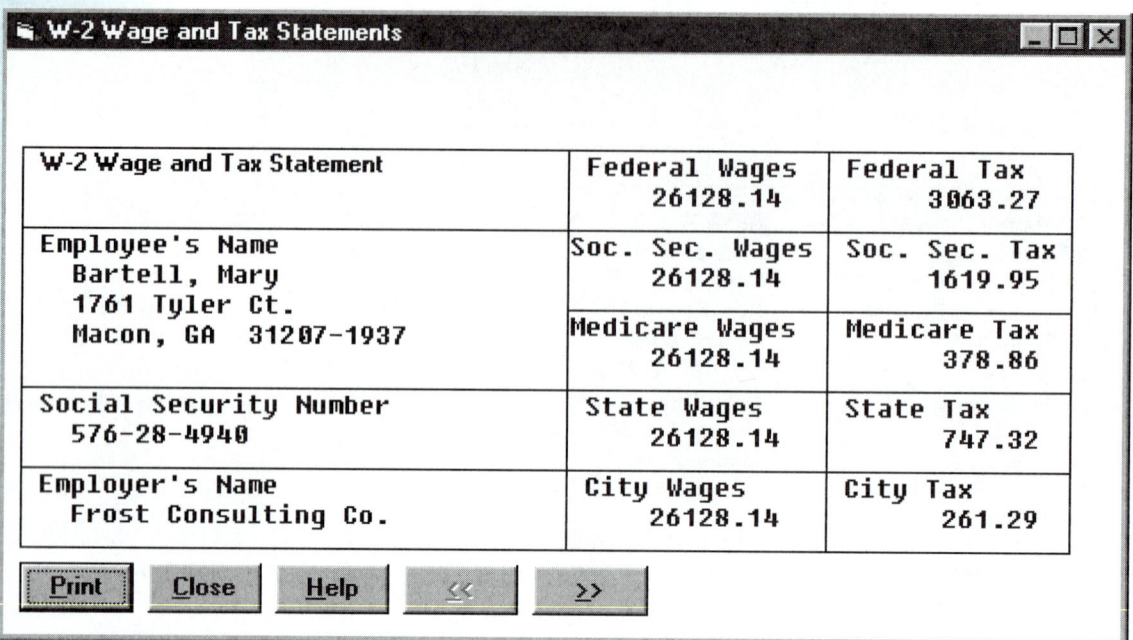

Figure 10.16
W-2 Statement

Click the Print button to print the currently displayed statement to an attached printer. Click the >> button to advance to the next statement or the << button to return to the previous statement.

Chapter Review

1. A computerized payroll system stores data for each employee, permits pay period transaction data to be entered, processes the data, and generates the required reports.

2. Employee input forms are completed when adding an employee to a payroll system, when making changes to employee information, or when deleting an employee from a payroll. To complete the input form, the following must be known: withholding allowances, number of pay periods, payroll general ledger account number, marital status, salary amount, and hourly rate.

3. To facilitate data input, a payroll transactions input form can be used to record the payroll transaction data.

4. Employee payroll transaction data are entered in the Payroll window. The purpose of entering the payroll transactions is to identify the employees to be paid for the current pay period and to enter the employees' pay-period transaction data.

5. The current payroll journal entry (salary expenses, employee federal, state, and city tax payable, Social Security, Medicare, and voluntary deductions) and employer's payroll taxes journal entry (Social Security, Medicare, federal unemployment, and state unemployment) can be generated by the *Automated Accounting* software after all payroll-related data have been entered.

6. The Employee List Report is useful in verifying the accuracy of data keyed into the computer via the Employee Account Maintenance window. The Payroll Report provides earnings and withholding information for each employee for the month, quarter, and year. The Quarterly Report is created at the end of each quarter and is used by the company to report Social Security and Medicare taxable wages to the Internal Revenue Service. W-2 Statements are used for individual tax reporting purposes and are provided to each employee at the end of the year.

ACCOUNTING CAREERS IN DEPTH

Investment Analyst

An investment analyst analyzes financial information in order to forecast business, industry, and economic conditions and to make investment decisions. An investment analyst performs the following duties:

- Gathering and analyzing company financial statements; industry, regulatory, and economic information; and financial periodicals and newspapers.
- Interpreting data concerning price, yield, stability, and future trends of investments.
- Summarizing data describing current and long-term trends in investments.
- Using a computer to draw charts and graphs to illustrate reports.
- Recommending investment timing and buy-and-sell orders to companies or to the staff of investment establishments that advise clients.

The educational requirements for a position in investment analysis include a college degree in accounting or finance. This level of education is a particular advantage because of the preparation that accountants receive throughout a college career. In most cases, accountants must prepare financial statements and gather other information for financial reporting. So, it is necessary to also know how to analyze the reports that have been prepared.

As with other careers in accounting, it is most helpful if future investment analysts get the opportunity to work while in college. A cooperative work experience makes a student more marketable to potential employers. Ultimately, this experience helps accounting students understand the environment that they would work in if they later become investment analysts.

A career as an investment analyst can be practiced in many industries. This enables accounting students to choose an environment that interests them while being able to use the skills they've acquired. Also, accountants who have a personal interest in the industry in which they are working will obtain more enjoyment in their careers.

TUTORIAL PROBLEM 10-T

In this tutorial problem, you will process the December payroll for Frost Consulting Co. You will perform the operating procedures necessary to add new employees, make changes to employee data, and delete employees. In addition, you will process the monthly payroll and generate the payroll journal entries. Since this is the last payroll of the year, it will include the end-of-quarter and end-of-year reports. The information given below is required to complete the December 31 payroll.

Addition of New Employee:
Weston, Glen
510 Fulton Pike
Macon, GA 31208-8011

Assign Employee No. 160; social security number, 482-70-8945; withholding allowances, 2; pay periods per year, 12; G.L. Account, 545 (Office Salaries Exp.); salaried, $2,000.00; married.

Changes to Current Employees:
Bartell, Mary: Change the number of withholding allowances to 2 and the marital status to married.
Lindblom, Jody: Change the street address to 2250 Marwood Ave.

Deletion of Employee:
Delete Employee No. 100 (Archer, Bruce)

Employees to Be Paid This Pay Period:

Employee Number	Employee Name	Regular Hours	Overtime Hours	Health Insurance	Dental Insurance	Credit Union
110	Bartell, Mary	176	4.0	40.00	24.00	25.00
120	Clausen, Chad	135		40.00	24.00	35.00
130	Feng, Ying			45.00	18.00	50.00
140	Lindblom, Jody			45.00	28.00	75.00
150	Silva, Leon	176	3.5	40.00	24.00	30.00
160	Weston, Glen			40.00	20.00	50.00

- **STEP 1:** Start up *Automated Accounting 8.0*.
- **STEP 2:** Load the file named **AA8 Problem 10-T**.
- **STEP 3:** Enter your name in the User Name text box and click *OK*.
- **STEP 4:** Save the file as 10-T Your Name.
- **STEP 5:** Enter the employee maintenance data from the Employee Input Forms in Figure 10.17.
  Click the *Accts.* toolbar button. Click the *Employees* tab and enter the employee maintenance data.

Chapter 10 Payroll

TUTORIAL PROBLEM 10-T

EMPLOYEE INPUT FORM

Run Date 12/31/--   Problem No. Example

Employee Number	160
Name	Weston, Glen
Address	510 Fulton Pike
City, State, and Zip	Macon, GA 31208-8011
Social Security No.	482-70-8945
Withholding Allow.	2
Number Pay Periods	12
G.L. Account No.	545

Salary Amount	2000.00
Hourly Rate	
Piece Rate	
Commission %	

MARITAL STATUS
○ Single
● Married

EMPLOYEE INPUT FORM

Run Date 12/31/--   Problem No. Example

Employee Number	110
Name	
Address	
City, State, and Zip	
Social Security No.	
Withholding Allow.	2
Number Pay Periods	
G.L. Account No.	

Salary Amount	
Hourly Rate	
Piece Rate	
Commission %	

MARITAL STATUS
○ Single
● Married

Figure 10.17
Completed Employee Input Forms

TUTORIAL PROBLEM 10-T

EMPLOYEE INPUT FORM

Run Date 12/31/-- Problem No. Example

Employee Number	140
Name	
Address	2250 Marwood Ave.
City, State, and Zip	
Social Security No.	
Withholding Allow.	
Number Pay Periods	
G.L. Account No.	

Salary Amount	
Hourly Rate	
Piece Rate	
Commission %	

MARITAL STATUS
○ Single
○ Married

EMPLOYEE INPUT FORM

Run Date 12/31/-- Problem No. Example

Employee Number	100
Name	(Delete)
Address	
City, State, and Zip	
Social Security No.	
Withholding Allow.	
Number Pay Periods	
G.L. Account No.	

Salary Amount	
Hourly Rate	
Piece Rate	
Commission %	

MARITAL STATUS
○ Single
○ Married

Figure 10.17
Continued

Chapter 10 Payroll

TUTORIAL PROBLEM 10-T

STEP 6: Enter the Payroll transactions and generate paychecks.
Click the *Other* toolbar button. Click the *Payroll* tab and enter the payroll transaction data provided in Figure 10.18. Have the computer calculate taxes. The first payroll check appears in Figure 10.19.

Note: It is very important that you enter the correct date (December 31 of the current year) when keying the payroll transactions. The current year should already be displayed for the transactions for the previous period. If the previous period's date is not visible, scroll up a line to see it. Payroll processing is date sensitive and will accumulate and display incorrectly if the dates are entered incorrectly.

Date	Employee Name	Check No.	Salary	Reg. Hours	O.T. Hours	Pieces	Comm. Sales	Federal Tax
12/31/--	Bartell, Mary	456		176.00	4.00			196.88
12/31/--	Clausen, Chad	457		135.00				107.13
12/31/--	Feng, Ying	458	2270.00					164.25
12/31/--	Lindblom, Jody	459	2340.00					238.50
12/31/--	Silva, Leon	460		176.00	3.50			277.56
12/31/--	Weston, Glen	461	2000.00					155.63

State Tax	City Tax	Social Security	Medicare	Health Insurance	Dental Insurance	Credit Union	Net Pay
64.60	22.75	141.05	32.99	40.00	24.00	25.00	1727.73
18.49	11.48	71.15	16.64	40.00	24.00	35.00	823.61
61.74	22.70	140.74	32.92	45.00	18.00	50.00	1734.65
70.38	23.40	145.08	33.93	45.00	28.00	75.00	1680.71
67.65	22.84	141.59	33.11	40.00	24.00	30.00	1647.00
51.28	20.00	124.00	29.00	40.00	20.00	50.00	1510.09

Figure 10.18
Completed Employee Transactions

Click the Calculate Taxes button after data cells for Salary, Reg. Hours, O.T. Hours, Pieces, and Comm. Sales have been entered. The software will calculate all the withholding taxes.

TUTORIAL PROBLEM 10-T

 Note that voluntary deductions for insurance and credit union are also automatically entered for most employees, using the same amounts from the previous period. Note that these amounts must be entered for Glen Weston. Because he is a new employee, there was no data in the previous period.

```
Frost Consulting Co.                                    456
                                       12/31/__     16-871/621
Pay to the
Order of    Bartell, Mary
                                                  |****1727.73|

National State Bank
DownTown Office
AnyCity, State  12345-1234

 .063107410111171 323157120B
```

Figure 10.19
First Paycheck

STEP 7: **Display the Employee List Report.**
Click the *Reports* toolbar button. Choose the *Payroll Reports* option. Select the *Employee List* Report, and then click *OK*. The report is shown in Figure 10.20. Verify the accuracy of the maintenance input, and make any corrections in the Employees tab in the Account Maintenance window.

STEP 8: **Display the Payroll Report.**
Make sure the Run Date is set to 12/31/--, choose the *Payroll Report* option, and click *OK*. The Payroll Report is shown in Figure 10.21. Verify the accuracy of the report and make any corrections via the Payroll tab in the Other Activities window.

STEP 9: **Generate and post the journal entry for the current payroll.**
Choose the *Current Payroll Journal Entry* menu item from the Options menu. Click *Yes* when asked if you want to generate the journal entries. When the entries appear in the Current Payroll Journal Entries dialog box, as shown in

▶

Chapter 10 Payroll

TUTORIAL PROBLEM 10-T

Figure 10.22, click *Post*. The journal entries will reappear and will be posted in the general journal.

If you make a change to an employee's data, either in the Account Maintenance Employees tab or the Other Activities Payroll tax to correct an error, you must also click the Calculate Taxes button to recalculate the withholding taxes. Then click OK to record the change.

Frost Consulting Co.
Employee List
12/31/--

Emp. No.	Employee Name/Address	Soc. Sec./ Mar. Stat.	# Pay Periods	G.L. Acct.	Salary/ Rate	Piece Rate/ Commission
110	Bartell, Mary 1761 Tyler Ct. Macon, GA 31207-1937	576-28-4940 Married W/H 2	12	520	12.50	
120	Clausen, Chad 485 Center Dr. Macon, GA 31203-5931	594-49-7090 Single W/H 1	12	545	8.50	
130	Feng, Ying 19550 Valley Lane Macon, GA 31206-0172	520-73-2726 Married W/H 3	12	520	2270.00	
140	Lindblom, Jody 2250 Marwood Ave. Macon, GA 31208-3510	584-69-2381 Married W/H 1	12	545	2340.00	
150	Silva, Leon 5812 Vine Blvd. Macon, GA 31212-9281	518-70-3409 Single W/H 1	12	520	12.60	
160	Weston, Glen 510 Fulton Pike Macon, GA 31208-8011	482-70-8945 Married W/H 2	12	545	2000.00	

Figure 10.20
Employee List

TUTORIAL PROBLEM 10-T

Frost Consulting Co.
Payroll Report
12/31/--

		Current	Quarterly	Yearly
110-Bartell, Mary	Gross Pay	2275.00	6521.88	26128.14
520-Consultant	Federal W/H	196.88	704.53	3063.27
Married Acct. 520	State W/H	64.60	184.37	747.32
W/H 2 576-28-4940	Soc. Sec. W/H	141.05	404.36	1619.95
Pay Periods 12	Medicare W/H	32.99	94.57	378.86
Salary	City Tax W/H	22.75	65.22	261.29
Hourly Rate 12.50	Health Insurance	40.00	120.00	480.00
Piece Rate	Dental Insurance	24.00	72.00	288.00
Commission %	Credit Union	25.00	75.00	300.00
Check Number 456				
Check Date 12/31/--	Net Pay	1727.73	4801.83	18989.45
120-Clausen, Chad	Gross Pay	1147.50	4139.50	17516.38
545-Office	Federal W/H	107.13	426.55	1850.89
Single Acct. 545	State W/H	18.49	81.09	359.26
W/H 1 594-49-7090	Soc. Sec. W/H	71.15	256.65	1086.01
Pay Periods 12	Medicare W/H	16.64	60.02	253.99
Salary	City Tax W/H	11.48	41.40	175.18
Hourly Rate 8.50	Health Insurance	40.00	120.00	480.00
Piece Rate	Dental Insurance	24.00	72.00	288.00
Commission %	Credit Union	35.00	105.00	420.00
Check Number 457				
Check Date 12/31/--	Net Pay	823.61	2976.79	12603.05
130-Feng, Ying	Gross Pay	2270.00	6810.00	27240.00
520-Consultant	Federal W/H	164.25	493.37	1974.41
Married Acct. 520	State W/H	61.74	185.22	740.88
W/H 3 520-73-2726	Soc. Sec. W/H	140.74	422.22	1688.88
Pay Periods 12	Medicare W/H	32.92	98.76	395.04
Salary 2270.00	City Tax W/H	22.70	68.10	272.40
Hourly Rate	Health Insurance	45.00	135.00	540.00
Piece Rate	Dental Insurance	18.00	54.00	216.00
Commission %	Credit Union	50.00	150.00	600.00
Check Number 458				
Check Date 12/31/--	Net Pay	1734.65	5203.33	20812.39
140-Lindblom, Jody	Gross Pay	2340.00	7020.00	28080.00
545-Office	Federal W/H	238.50	716.12	2865.41
Married Acct. 545	State W/H	70.38	211.14	844.56
W/H 1 584-69-2381	Soc. Sec. W/H	145.08	435.24	1740.96
Pay Periods 12	Medicare W/H	33.93	101.79	407.16
Salary 2340.00	City Tax W/H	23.40	70.20	280.80

(continued)

Figure 10.21
Payroll Report

Chapter 10 Payroll

TUTORIAL PROBLEM 10-T

Frost Consulting Co.
Payroll Report
12/31/--

		Current	Quarterly	Yearly
Hourly Rate	Health Insurance	45.00	135.00	540.00
Piece Rate	Dental Insurance	28.00	84.00	336.00
Commission %	Credit Union	75.00	225.00	900.00
Check Number 459				
Check Date 12/31/--	Net Pay	1680.71	5041.51	20165.11
150-Silva, Leon	Gross Pay	2283.75	6416.55	26122.95
520-Consultant	Federal W/H	277.56	768.10	3141.86
Single Acct. 520	State W/H	67.65	181.89	749.70
W/H 1 518-70-3409	Soc. Sec. W/H	141.59	397.82	1619.61
Pay Periods 12	Medicare W/H	33.11	93.03	378.78
Salary	City Tax W/H	22.84	64.17	261.24
Hourly Rate 12.60	Health Insurance	40.00	120.00	480.00
Piece Rate	Dental Insurance	24.00	72.00	288.00
Commission %	Credit Union	30.00	90.00	360.00
Check Number 460				
Check Date 12/31/--	Net Pay	1647.00	4629.54	18843.76
160-Weston, Glen	Gross Pay	2000.00	2000.00	2000.00
545-Office	Federal W/H	155.63	155.63	155.63
Married Acct. 545	State W/H	51.28	51.28	51.28
W/H 2 482-70-8945	Soc. Sec. W/H	124.00	124.00	124.00
Pay Periods 12	Medicare W/H	29.00	29.00	29.00
Salary 2000.00	City Tax W/H	20.00	20.00	20.00
Hourly Rate	Health Insurance	40.00	40.00	40.00
Piece Rate	Dental Insurance	20.00	20.00	20.00
Commission %	Credit Union	50.00	50.00	50.00
Check Number 461				
Check Date 12/31/--	Net Pay	1510.09	1510.09	1510.09
Payroll Summary	Gross Pay	12316.25	32907.93	127087.47
	Federal W/H	1139.95	3264.30	13051.47
	State W/H	334.14	894.99	3493.00
	Soc. Sec. W/H	763.61	2040.29	7879.41
	Medicare W/H	178.59	477.17	1842.83
	City Tax W/H	123.17	329.09	1270.91
	Health Insurance	250.00	670.00	2560.00
	Dental Insurance	138.00	374.00	1436.00
	Credit Union	265.00	695.00	2630.00
	Net Pay	9123.79	24163.09	92923.85

Figure 10.21
Continued

TUTORIAL PROBLEM 10-T

Acct. #	Account Title	Debit	Credit
520	Consultant Salaries Exp.	6828.75	
545	Office Salaries Exp.	5487.50	
265	Emp. Fed. Inc. Tax Pay.		1139.95
270	Emp. State Inc. Tax Pay.		334.14
275	Social Security Tax Pay.		763.61
280	Medicare Tax Payable		178.59
272	Emp. City Inc. Tax Pay.		123.17
297	Health Ins. Premiums Pay.		250.00
298	Dental Ins. Premiums Pay.		138.00
299	Credit Union Deduct. Pay.		265.00
285	Salaries Payable		9123.79

Figure 10.22
Current Payroll Journal Entry Dialog Box

If your journal entries do not match those shown in Figure 10.22, check your Employee List and Payroll Report for keying errors, and make the necessary corrections. Return to the General Journal window, delete the incorrect entries, and generate new entries.

STEP 10: Generate and post the employer's payroll taxes journal entry.
With the General Journal window still displayed, choose *Employer's Payroll Taxes* from the Options menu. Click *Yes* when asked if you want to generate the journal entry. When the entries appear in the Payroll Taxes Journal Entries dialog box, as shown in Figure 10.23, click *Post*. The journal entries will reappear and will be posted in the general journal.

STEP 11: Display the payroll journal entries.
Click the *Reports* toolbar button. Choose the *Journals* option. Select the *General Journal* report, and then click *OK*. When the Journal Report selection window appears, choose the *Customize Journal Report* option and click *OK*. If necessary, set the date range to 12/31/-- through 12/31/--. The report appears in Figure 10.24.

Chapter 10 Payroll

TUTORIAL PROBLEM 10-T

Acct. #	Account Title	Debit	Credit
550	Payroll Tax Expense	1066.20	
275	Social Security Tax Pay.		763.61
280	Medicare Tax Payable		178.59
290	State Unemp. Tax Payable		108.00
295	Federal Unemp. Tax Pay.		16.00

Figure 10.23
Employer's Payroll Taxes Journal Entry Dialog Box

```
                    Frost Consulting Co.
                       General Journal
                          12/31/--
```

Date	Refer.	Acct.	Title	Debit	Credit
12/31	Payroll	520	Consultant Salaries Exp.	6828.75	
12/31	Payroll	545	Office Salaries Exp.	5487.50	
12/31	Payroll	265	Emp. Fed. Inc. Tax Pay.		1139.95
12/31	Payroll	270	Emp. State Inc. Tax Pay.		334.14
12/31	Payroll	275	Social Security Tax Pay.		763.61
12/31	Payroll	280	Medicare Tax Payable		178.59
12/31	Payroll	272	Emp. City Inc. Tax Pay.		123.17
12/31	Payroll	297	Health Ins. Premiums Pay.		250.00
12/31	Payroll	298	Dental Ins. Premiums Pay.		138.00
12/31	Payroll	299	Credit Union Deduct. Pay.		265.00
12/31	Payroll	285	Salaries Payable		9123.79
12/31	Pay. Tax	550	Payroll Tax Expense	1066.20	
12/31	Pay. Tax	275	Social Security Tax Pay.		763.61
12/31	Pay. Tax	280	Medicare Tax Payable		178.59
12/31	Pay. Tax	290	State Unemp. Tax Payable		108.00
12/31	Pay. Tax	295	Federal Unemp. Tax Pay.		16.00
			Totals	13382.45	13382.45

Figure 10.24
General Journal Report (Payroll Journal Entries)

STEP 12: **Display the Quarterly Report.**
Choose the *Payroll Reports* option. Select the *Quarterly Report*, and then click *OK*. The quarterly report appears in Figure 10.25.

TUTORIAL PROBLEM 10-T

```
                    Frost Consulting Co.
                      Quarterly Report
                         12/31/--
----------------------------------------------------------------
Soc. Sec.                          Taxable          Taxable
Number        Employee Name        Soc. Sec.        Medicare
----------------------------------------------------------------
576-28-4940   Bartell, Mary        6521.88          6521.88
594-49-7090   Clausen, Chad        4139.50          4139.50
520-73-2726   Feng, Ying           6810.00          6810.00
584-69-2381   Lindblom, Jody       7020.00          7020.00
518-70-3409   Silva, Leon          6416.55          6416.55
482-70-8945   Weston, Glen         2000.00          2000.00
                                  ---------        ---------
              Totals              32907.93         32907.93
                                  =========        =========
              Total Employees 6
```

Figure 10.25
Quarterly Report

STEP 13: Display the W-2 Statements.
Select the *W-2 Statements,* and then click *OK*. The first statement is shown in Figure 10.26.

W-2 Wage and Tax Statement	Federal Wages 26128.14	Federal Tax 3063.27
Employee's Name Bartell, Mary 1761 Tyler Ct. Macon, GA 31207-1937	Soc. Sec. Wages 26128.14	Soc. Sec. Tax 1619.95
	Medicare Wages 26128.14	Medicare Tax 378.86
Social Security Number 576-28-4940	State Wages 26128.14	State Tax 747.32
Employer's Name Frost Consulting Co.	City Wages 26128.14	City Tax 261.29

Figure 10.26
W-2 Statement

Chapter 10 Payroll

TUTORIAL PROBLEM 10-T

STEP 14: Save your data.

STEP 15: Optional Spreadsheet Integration Activity.
Frost Consulting Co. has asked you to use a spreadsheet to provide them with an estimate of how much it would cost the company to give each employee a 3% raise next year.

a. Copy the Payroll Report to the clipboard in spreadsheet format.
b. Start up your spreadsheet software and load the template file named AA8 Spreadsheet 10-T.
c. Select cell A1 as the current cell and paste the report copied in Step 15a into the spreadsheet.
d. Enter 3% in cell C94 (percent of increase in gross pay).
Enter 6.2% in cell C95 (Social Security withholding rate).
Enter 1.45% in cell C96 (Medicare withholding rate).
Enter in cell C99 the formula to calculate the 3% increase amount of gross pay (+E81+(E81*C94)).
Enter in cell C100 the formula to calculate the amount of Social Security (+C99*C95).
Enter in cell C101 the formula to calculate the amount of Medicare (+C99*C96).
Enter in cell D99 the formula to calculate the difference between last year's gross pay and the 3% increased gross pay amount (+C99–E81).
Enter in cell D100 the formula to calculate the difference between last year's Social Security and the projected Social Security amount (+C100–E84).
Enter in cell D101 the formula to calculate the difference between last year's Medicare and the projected Medicare amount (+C101–E85).
Enter in cell D103 the formula to sum the total effect of a 3% increase in gross pay +D99+D100+D101.
e. The completed report section of the spreadsheet is shown in Figure 10.27. Format your spreadsheet to match Figure 10.27.
f. Save the spreadsheet with a file name of 10-T Your Name.
g. Print the results of a 3% increase in gross pay.

TUTORIAL PROBLEM 10-T

Pay Increase:	3.00%	
Soc. Sec. Rate:	6.20%	
Medicare Rate:	1.45%	

	Projections	Difference
Gross Pay	$130,900.09	$3,812.62
Soc. Sec. W/H	$8,115.81	$236.40
Medicare W/H	$1,898.05	$55.22
Total		$4,104.24

Figure 10.27
Estimated Cost of 3% Raise

    h. What would be the estimated cost to Frost Consulting Co. for a 4% raise? What if the Social Security rate increases to 6.5% or the Medicare rate increases to 1.75%? Adjust the spreadsheet to reflect these changes.

    i. End your spreadsheet session without saving your changes from Step 15h.

STEP 16: Optional Word Processing Activity.
Prepare an address list of the current, active employees for the personnel department.

    a. Display and copy the Employee List Report to the clipboard in word processing format.

    b. Start up your word processing application software and create a new document. Use a fixed type font such as Courier.

    c. Paste the Employee List Report into the document.

    d. Enter headings, delete unwanted data, etc., and format the document to match Figure 10.28.

    e. Save the document with a file name of 10-T Your Name.

    f. Print the completed address list.

    g. End your word processing session.

Chapter 10 Payroll

TUTORIAL PROBLEM 10-T

Frost Consulting Co.
Employee List
12/31/--

Emp. No.	Employee Name	Address	City, State, & Zip
110	Bartell, Mary	1761 Tyler Ct.	Macon, GA 31207-1937
120	Clausen, Chad	485 Center Dr.	Macon, GA 31203-5931
130	Feng, Ying	19550 Valley Lane	Macon, GA 31206-0172
140	Lindblom, Jody	2250 Marwood Ave.	Macon, GA 31208-3510
150	Silva, Leon	5812 Vine Blvd.	Macon, GA 31212-9281
160	Weston, Glen	510 Fulton Pike	Macon, GA 31208-8011

Figure 10.28
Employee Address List

STEP 17: End the *Automated Accounting* session.
Click the *Exit* toolbar button.

When making an online transaction, always look for your browser's symbol that indicates a secure site before entering your personal information. For example, a closed-lock symbol indicates a secure Web page.

Concerns about lost productivity are causing many companies to use devices that monitor employees' Internet use and even restrict the availability of certain Websites.

Review and Practice: Applying Your Information Skills

I. MATCHING

Directions: In the *Working Papers*, write the letter of the appropriate term next to each definition.

a. Employee List Report
b. hourly rate
c. marital status
d. number of pay periods
e. Payroll Report
f. Quarterly Report
g. salary amount
h. voluntary deductions
i. W-2 Statement
j. withholding allowances

1. A list of employee earnings and withholding information for the month, quarter, and year.

2. The gross amount paid for an employee's services each pay period.

3. A report that summarizes an employee's taxable wages and various withholdings that is used for individual tax reporting purposes.

4. Single or married status for tax purposes.

5. Employee-authorized withholdings from earnings for such options as health insurance, dental insurance, savings plans, and charitable contributions.

6. The amount paid an employee for each hour worked.

7. The number of deductions from total earnings for each person legally supported by a taxpayer for tax purposes.

8. A complete listing of the employee payroll information.

9. The number of times an employee is paid per year.

10. A report used to disclose Social Security and Medicare taxable wages to the Internal Revenue Service.

Chapter 10 Payroll

II. REVIEW QUESTIONS

Directions: Write the answers to each of the following questions in the *Working Papers*.

1. If an employee is paid biweekly (every two weeks), what would you record in the employee data field named Pay Periods Per Year?

2. Explain the difference between the Current Payroll Journal Entry and the Employer's Payroll Taxes menu items.

3. Explain the process for deleting a payroll transaction already entered and thus removing an employee from being paid.

4. How does the computer know what check numbers to assign to current payroll checks?

5. What is the purpose of the Quarterly Report?

III. INTERNET ACTIVITY

Directions: If you have access to the Internet, use your browser to access the U.S. Internal Revenue Internet site (use *U.S. Internal Revenue Service* as your search argument). Use the IRS Publications link to obtain the instructions and form for a W-2 Statement. Be sure to include the source (link) and the URL (Internet address) of your search on the instructions and form.

Independent Practice Problem 10-P

In this problem, you will process the September and October monthly payrolls for Eclipse Merchandising. You will perform the operating procedures necessary to add new employees, make changes to employee data, and delete employees. In addition, you will process the payroll for the months of September and October. Since September is the end of a quarter, the September payroll will include the end-of-quarter report.

September Payroll

Employees to Be Paid This Pay Period:

Employee Number	Employee Name	Regular Hours	Overtime Hours	Health Insurance	Dental Insurance	Credit Union
210	Faber, Jane			75.00	35.00	350.00
220	Fleming, Brian	176	1.0	65.00	25.00	75.00
240	Meier, Patricia	176	3.0	85.00	35.00	100.00
250	Mosher, Cathy	176	2.5	65.00	25.00	100.00
260	Shepherd, Dean			80.00	30.00	300.00
270	Willard, Deanne	176	2.0	65.00	25.00	50.00

STEP 1: Start up *Automated Accounting 8.0*.

STEP 2: Load the file named AA8 Problem 10-P.

STEP 3: Enter your name in the User Name text box.

STEP 4: Save the data with a file name of 10-P1 Your Name.

STEP 5: Enter the September payroll transactions. Use 09/30/-- as the transaction date and have the computer calculate taxes.

STEP 6: Display a Payroll Report.

STEP 7: Generate and post the journal entry for the current payroll.

STEP 8: Generate and post the employer's payroll taxes journal entry.

STEP 9: Display the September payroll journal entries.

STEP 10: Display a Quarterly Report.

STEP 11: Save your data as 10-P1 Your Name.

STEP 12: Optional Spreadsheet Integration Activity.
Eclipse Merchandising has asked you to use a spreadsheet to prepare a payroll distribution of gross earnings report for the quarter.

a. Copy the Payroll Report to the clipboard in spreadsheet format.
b. Start up your spreadsheet software and load the template file named AA8 Spreadsheet 10-P.
c. Select cell A1 as the current cell (if not already selected) and paste the report copied in Step 12a into the spreadsheet.
d. Enter +A3 in cell A106.
Enter *Payroll Distribution (Gross Earnings)* in cell A107.
Enter +A5 in cell A108.
Enter *Employee* in cell A110.
Enter *Gross Earnings* in cell B110.
Enter the cell references to each employee and their corresponding quarterly gross earnings in the columns under the respective headings.
Enter the formula to sum the gross earnings.
e. Generate a pie chart:
Select the range of cells containing the employee number/name and corresponding gross earnings, and then choose the Chart or Graph menu item from the spreadsheet program you are using. If the computer asks for a graph name, etc., enter *Payroll Distribution*. Choose Pie Chart from the toolbar if the graph that appears is not a pie chart. Finally, if the spreadsheet you

Chapter 10 Payroll

are using permits copying and pasting the chart into the worksheet, copy and paste the chart into blank cells.

f. Save the spreadsheet data with a file name of 10-P Your Name.

g. Print the payroll distribution report portion of the spreadsheet and pie chart.

h. End your spreadsheet session.

STEP 13: End the *Automated Accounting* session.

October Payroll

The step-by-step instructions for completing the October payroll for Eclipse Merchandising are listed below.

Addition of New Employee:
Young, Kevin
607 Hanover St.
Boston, MA 02160-7110

Assign Employee No. 280; social security number, 487-55-3613; withholding allowances, 2; pay periods per year, 12; G.L. Account No., 6170 (Office Salary Expense); salaried; married; salary amount, $2,850.00.

Changes to Current Employees:
Faber, Jane (Employee No. 210): Change the address to 9620 State St.

Mosher, Cathy (Employee No. 250): Change the social security number to 675-28-8744.

Deletion of Employee:
Delete Kinney, John (Employee No. 230) from the payroll file.

Employees to Be Paid This Pay Period:

Employee Number	Employee Name	Regular Hours	Overtime Hours	Health Insurance	Dental Insurance	Credit Union
210	Faber, Jane			75.00	35.00	350.00
220	Fleming, Brian	168	3.50	65.00	25.00	75.00
240	Meier, Patricia	168	85.00	35.00	100.00	
250	Mosher, Cathy	168	2.25	65.00	25.00	100.00
260	Shepherd, Dean			80.00	30.00	300.00
270	Willard, Deanne	168	65.00	25.00	50.00	
280	Young, Kevin			70.00	28.00	50.00

STEP 1: Start up *Automated Accounting 8.0*.

STEP 2: Load the September payroll data file saved in Step 11 on page 352 (10-P1 Your Name).

STEP 3: Save the data with a file name of 10-P2 Your Name.

STEP 4: Enter the employee maintenance data.

STEP 5: Enter the October payroll transactions. Use 10/31/-- as the transaction date and have the computer calculate taxes.

STEP 6: Display an Employee List Report.

STEP 7: Display a Payroll Report.

STEP 8: Generate and post the journal entry for the current payroll.

STEP 9: Generate and post the employer's payroll taxes journal entry.

STEP 10: Display the October payroll journal entries.

STEP 11: Save your data file (10-P2 Your Name).

STEP 12: Optional Word Processing Integration Activity.
The personnel department has asked you to prepare a report showing each employee's employee number, name, general ledger salary expense account number, and salary/hourly rate.

a. Display and copy the Employee List Report to the clipboard in word processing format.
b. Start up your word processing software and create a new document. Use a fixed type font such as Courier.
c. Paste the Employee List Report into the document.
d. Enter headings, delete unwanted data, etc., and format the report for the desired data.
e. Save the document with a file name of 10-P Your Name.
f. Print the completed report.
g. End your word processing session.

STEP 13: End the *Automated Accounting* session.

Applying Your Technology Skills 10-P

Directions: Using Independent Practice Problem 10-P, write the answers to the following questions in the *Working Papers*.

September Payroll:
Use the payroll file you saved under file name 10-P1 Your Name to answer the following questions for the September payroll.

Payroll Report

1. What is the number of withholding allowances for Jane Faber?

2. What is the current gross pay for Dean Shepherd?

3. What is the amount withheld for the quarter for Medicare for Deanne Willard?

Chapter 10 Payroll

4. What is the check number for the check written to Deanne Willard?
5. What is the total current net pay for all employees?
6. What is the total yearly gross pay for all employees?

Journal Entries Report

7. What is the amount of the debit to Sales Salaries Expense?
8. What is the amount of the debit to Payroll Taxes Expense?
9. What is the amount of the credit to Salaries Payable?

Quarterly Report

10. What is the Taxable Social Security (FICA) amount for Brian Fleming?
11. What is the total Taxable Medicare amount for all employees for the quarter?

October Payroll:
Use the payroll file you saved under file name 10-P2 Your Name to answer the following questions for the October payroll.

Employee List

1. What is the number of withholding allowances for Brian Fleming?
2. What is Patricia Meier's social security number?

Payroll Report

3. What is the salary amount for Kevin Young?
4. What is the current federal withholding amount for Cathy Mosher?
5. What is the Social Security (FICA) amount withheld for the year for Jane Faber?
6. What is the check number for the check written to Dean Shepherd?
7. What is the net amount of the check to Kevin Young?
8. What is the total amount withheld for Deduction 3 (credit union) for the year for all employees?
9. What is the total yearly gross pay for all employees?

Journal Entries Report

10. What is the amount of the debit to Office Salaries Expense?
11. What is the amount of the debit to Payroll Taxes Expense?
12. What is the amount of the credit to Salaries Payable?

Mastery Problem 10-M

In this problem, you will process the November and December payrolls for Eclipse Merchandising. Since December 31 is the end of the year, you will also display the quarterly report and W-2 statements.

November Payroll
The payroll data for the November payroll are given below.

Addition of New Employee:
Gregory, Bette
6768 Westwood Dr.
Boston, MA   02183-2410

Assign Employee No. 230; social security number, 583-67-1785; withholding allowances, 4; pay periods per year, 12; G.L. Account No., 6210 (Sales Salary Expense); salaried; married; salary, $2,850.00.

Change to Current Employee:
Young, Kevin (Employee No. 280): Change number of withholding allowances to 3.

Employees to Be Paid This Pay Period:

Employee Number	Employee Name	Regular Hours	Overtime Hours	Health Insurance	Dental Insurance	Credit Union
210	Faber, Jane			75.00	35.00	350.00
220	Fleming, Brian	168		65.00	25.00	75.00
230	Gregory, Bette			80.00	30.00	125.00
240	Meier, Patricia	168	4.0	85.00	35.00	100.00
250	Mosher, Cathy	168		65.00	25.00	100.00
260	Shepherd, Dean			80.00	30.00	300.00
270	Willard, Deanne	168		65.00	25.00	50.00
280	Young, Kevin			70.00	28.00	50.00

December Payroll
The payroll data for the December payroll is given next.

Employees to Be Paid This Pay Period:

Employee Number	Employee Name	Regular Hours	Overtime Hours	Health Insurance	Dental Insurance	Credit Union
210	Faber, Jane			75.00	35.00	350.00
220	Fleming, Brian	176		65.00	25.00	75.00
230	Gregory, Bette			80.00	30.00	125.00
240	Meier, Patricia	176		85.00	35.00	100.00
250	Mosher, Cathy	176		65.00	25.00	100.00
260	Shepherd, Dean			80.00	30.00	300.00
270	Willard, Deanne	176		65.00	25.00	50.00
280	Young, Kevin			70.00	28.00	50.00

Chapter 10 Payroll

STEP 1: Start up *Automated Accounting 8.0.*

STEP 2: Load the opening balances file named AA8 Problem 10-M.

STEP 3: Enter your name in the User Name text box.

STEP 4: Save the data with a name of 10-M1 Your Name.

STEP 5: Enter the November employee maintenance and payroll transactions. Use a transaction date of 11/30/-- and have the computer calculate taxes.

STEP 6: Display an Employee List Report.

STEP 7: Display the November Payroll Report.

STEP 8: Generate and post the journal entries for the current payroll and employer's payroll taxes for November.

STEP 9: Display the November payroll general journal entries.

STEP 10: Save your data with a file name of 10-M1 Your Name.

STEP 11: Use Save As to save the data with a name of 10-M2 Your Name.

STEP 12: Enter the December payroll transactions. Use a transaction date of 12/31/-- and have the computer calculate taxes.

STEP 13: Display a Payroll Report.

STEP 14: Generate and post the journal entries for the current payroll and employer's payroll taxes for December.

STEP 15: Display the December payroll general journal entries.

STEP 16: Display the Quarterly Report and W-2 Statements.

STEP 17: Save your data (as 10-M2 Your Name).

STEP 18: Optional Spreadsheet Integration Activity.
Use a spreadsheet to provide an estimate of how much it would cost the company to give each employee a 4% raise next year. Assume that the Social Security rate will be 6.20% and the Medicare rate will be 1.45%.

a. Copy the Payroll Report to the clipboard in spreadsheet format.
b. Start up your spreadsheet software and load the template file named AA8 Spreadsheet 10-M.
c. Select cell A1 as the current cell and paste the report copied in Step 18a into the spreadsheet.
d. Enter the percentages and formulas required to complete the spreadsheet in cells B120 through D129. Format the spreadsheet. Refer to Figure 10.27 (page 348) as a guide if necessary.

e. Save the spreadsheet with a file name of 10-M Your Name.
f. Print the results of a 4% increase in gross pay.
g. What would be the estimated cost if a 4.5% raise were given to the employees? What if the Social Security rate increased to 6.75% or the Medicare rate increased to 1.85%? Adjust the spreadsheet to reflect these changes.
h. End your spreadsheet session without saving your changes from Step 18g.

STEP 19: **Optional Word Processing Integration Activity.**
Prepare an address list of the current active employees.

a. Display and copy the Employee List Report to the clipboard in word processing format.
b. Start up your word processing software and create a new document. Use a fixed type font such as Courier.
c. Paste the Employee List Report into the document.
d. Enter headings, delete unwanted data, etc., and format the document as necessary. Use Figure 10.28 (page 349) as a guide.
e. Save the document with a file name of 10-M Your Name.
f. Print the completed address list.
g. End your word processing session.

STEP 20: End the *Automated Accounting* session.

Applying Your Technology Skills 10-M

Directions: Using Mastery Problem 10-M, write the answers to the following questions in the *Working Papers*.

November Payroll:
Use the payroll file you saved under file name 10-M1 Your Name to answer the following questions for the November payroll.

Employee List

1. What is the number of withholding allowances for Cathy Mosher?
2. What is Jane Faber's street address?

Payroll Report

3. What is Brian Fleming's hourly rate?
4. What is the current gross pay for Bette Gregory?
5. What is the Medicare amount withheld for the quarter for Cathy Mosher?

Chapter 10 Payroll

6. What is Kevin Young's gross pay for the quarter?
7. What is Dean Shepherd's current net pay?
8. What is the total current net pay for all employees?
9. What is the total yearly gross pay for all employees?

Journal Entries Report

10. What is the amount of the credit to Employee Federal Income Tax Payable?
11. What is the amount of the credit to Medicare Tax Payable?
12. What is the amount of the credit to Employee City Income Tax Payable?

December Payroll:
Use the payroll file you saved under file name 10-M2 Your Name to answer the following questions for the December payroll.

Payroll Report

1. What is the current net pay for Bette Gregory?
2. What is the current federal withholding amount for Jane Faber?
3. What is the Medicare amount withheld for the year for Dean Shepherd?
4. What is the check number for the check written to Deanne Willard?
5. What is the total current amount withheld for Deduction 2 (dental insurance) for all employees?
6. What is the total yearly Social Security (FICA) withheld for all employees?

Journal Entries Report

7. What is the amount of the credit to Medicare Tax Payable?
8. What is the amount of the debit to Payroll Taxes Expense?
9. What is the amount of the credit to Salaries Payable?

Quarterly Report

10. What is the Taxable FICA amount for Cathy Mosher?
11. What is the total Taxable Medicare amount for all employees for the quarter?

W-2 Statements

12. What is the amount of state tax shown for Jane Faber?
13. What is the Medicare tax shown for Brian Fleming?

Chapter 11

ACCOUNTS PAYABLE: PURCHASE ORDER PROCESSING AND INVENTORY CONTROL

KEY TERMS

Inventory Stock Items Input Form
Stock Number
Unit of Measure
Retail Price
Reorder Point
Computerized Purchase Order
   Processing System
Purchase Requisition
Purchase Order
Purchase Order Input Form
Purchase Invoice

Receiving Report
Purchase Invoice Input Form
Purchase Order Register
Purchase Invoice Register
Inventory List Report
Inventory Transactions Report
Inventory Exceptions Report
Inventory Valuation Report
Average Cost Method
LIFO Method
FIFO Method

LEARNING OBJECTIVES

Upon completion of this chapter, you will be able to:

1. Complete the inventory stock items, purchase order, and purchase invoice input forms.
2. Enter inventory stock item maintenance data.
3. Enter purchase order transactions.
4. Enter purchase invoice and purchase return transactions.
5. Purge purchase orders and purchase invoices.
6. Display reports reflecting purchase order processing and inventory integration.

Chapter 11 Accounts Payable: Purchase Order Processing and Inventory Control

INTRODUCTION

In this chapter, you will maintain the inventory stock items and enter purchase orders and purchase invoice transactions for Hughes Appliances. Hughes Appliances is a retail business that sells household appliances such as washers, dryers, refrigerators, freezers, ranges, dishwashers, and trash compactors.

INVENTORY

Merchandise inventory is often one of the costliest and most difficult to manage assets of a retail business. Successful control of merchandise inventory translates into greater profitability; however, managing merchandise inventory presents many challenges. Merchandise inventory can consist of thousands of different items that may be difficult to manage. The inventory is subject to pilferage and theft. Some inventory items may spoil or become obsolete. Inventory costs include the cost of storage space and the taxes and insurance premiums that must be paid on inventory. Businesses must often borrow money to purchase inventory, which results in interest payments and reduced profits.

Since the costs associated with merchandise inventory are high, a business must try to keep the stock levels as low as possible. While keeping low stock levels, the business must also maintain sufficient inventory to meet customer demand. Out-of-stock conditions may occur if the inventory is too low, resulting in lost sales, loss of customer confidence, and reduced profits. Therefore, the business must keep the inventory as low as possible while avoiding out-of-stock conditions.

A merchandising business is faced with other difficult decisions related to merchandise inventory. A business must decide when and how

ETHICS

A journalist, knowledgeable in the use of computer graphics, uses a paint and draw program to retouch a photograph of a suspected criminal to make the suspect appear mean and angry. The journalist then submits the altered photo to the editor to be included on the front page of the local newspaper.

Critical Thinking

1. Do you think that what the journalist did was ethical, unethical, or even a computer crime? Justify your choice.

2. What action, if any, do you think the editor of the newspaper should take toward the journalist?

many items to reorder. A business must also know which items are selling well and which are not. Without this information, the inventory might contain items that are not selling well yet are very expensive to maintain.

Because of the large number of items and the high volume of transactions in merchandise inventory, manual record keeping can be a time-consuming, error-prone, and cumbersome process. The computer, on the other hand, lends itself well to the task. The computer can store and retrieve data, make computations quickly and accurately, and sort, organize, and report information.

In a computerized inventory system, the computer stores on disk all relevant data for each stock item, such as stock number, description of the item, unit of measure, reorder point, and retail price. This data file is updated periodically. New stock items are added to the file, data in existing stock items are changed as necessary, and inactive stock items are deleted. Once the stock item file has been maintained (updated), the inventory and accounting system is updated when purchase order, purchase invoice, purchase return, sales, and sales return transactions for the period are entered. Finally, the appropriate accounting and inventory system reports are generated.

Inventory Stock Items Input Form

An **inventory stock items input form** is an input form used to record additions, changes, and deletions to inventory items. Figure 11.1 shows an inventory stock items input form. The first entry is an addition of a new stock item. When a new stock item is added, each of the columns on the input form must be completed. The second entry is a change to an existing stock item. The retail price of stock number 3010 is being changed to $529.95. When recording changes to data fields for an inventory item, you must include the Stock Number field as well as the data fields(s) to be changed. Any data fields that have not changed may

INVENTORY STOCK ITEMS INPUT FORM

Run Date 03/07/--   **Problem No.** Example

Stock Number	Description	Unit of Measure	Reorder Point	Retail Price
3090	Micro Refrig.	EA	10	369.95
3010				529.95
1030	(Delete)			

Figure 11.1
Inventory Stock Items Input Form

be left blank. The third entry shows the deletion of a stock item, number 1030. To delete a stock item, record the Stock Number and the notation (*Delete*) in the description field.

Each field in the form corresponds to a grid cell in the Inventory Account Maintenance window. The field names and a description of each column are illustrated in the Inventory Account Maintenance window shown in Figure 11.2.

Inventory Stock Item Maintenance

When Maintain Accounts is chosen from the Data menu or the Accts. toolbar button is clicked, the Account Maintenance window will appear. Choose the Inventory tab to display the Inventory Maintenance tab shown in Figure 11.2.

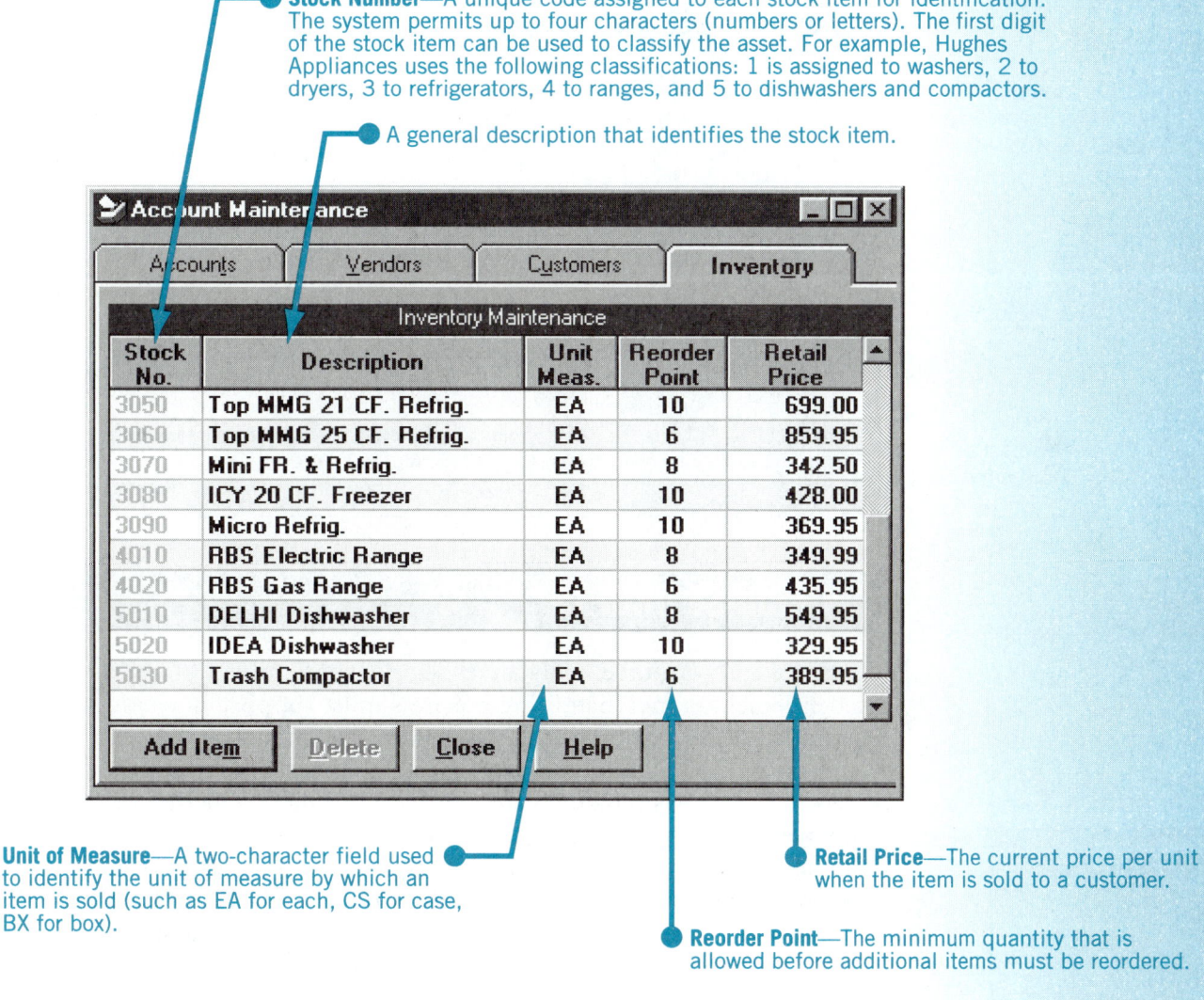

Figure 11.2
Inventory Maintenance Tab

Enter, Change, and Delete Inventory Stock Items

To add a new inventory stock item, simply enter the stock number and the remaining data fields into the grid cell boxes and click the Add Item button. To change existing stock item data, select the stock item by clicking the grid cell containing the data you wish to change. (The Add Item button will change to Change Item when the insertion point is positioned anywhere within an existing stock item.) Enter the correct data for the stock item and click the Change Item button. To delete an inventory stock item, select the stock item to be deleted and click the Delete button.

Table 11.1 contains a description of additional data fields that are stored with each inventory stock item. These fields start out with values of zero. As transactions are entered, these fields are updated.

You will not be allowed to delete a stock item that has current transaction data.

FIELD NAME	DESCRIPTION
Quantity on Hand	This field stores a count of the quantity that is included in the merchandise inventory at the present time.
Quantity on Order	This field contains the quantity that is currently on order but has not yet arrived.
Yearly Quantity Sold	This field stores an accumulation of the number of items sold so far this year.
Yearly Dollars Sold	This field contains an accumulation of the dollar value sold for an item this year.
Last Cost Price	This field contains the price paid per unit for the most recent purchase of this stock item.
Average Cost	This field is used by the computer to maintain a per-unit average cost for this stock item.

Table 11.1 Descriptions of Additional Inventory Data Fields Stored by the Computer

PURCHASE ORDERS

Since cash disbursements are especially susceptible to fraud and embezzlement, a merchandising business must support all claims with valid documents. In addition, the separation of employee duties in the purchase of merchandise and the recording and payment of merchandise received by the business help stem this kind of theft. The degree of employee separation of duties varies, depending on the size and complexities of the business and the products or services provided. Many businesses have turned to the computer to help them control their purchases and cash disbursements due to the large volume of transactions and the complexities of maintaining accurate inventory and accounting records.

In general, a **computerized purchase order processing system** consists of the procedures involved in automatically integrating the purchase order, purchase invoice, and cash disbursement data into the inventory and general ledger. In the purchase order processing system used in this text, the purchasing department issues **purchase requisitions**, which are formal requests for purchases that are entered into the computerized purchase order system. A **purchase order** is a document containing a purchase order number, the vendor name, the quantity and description, the expected price, and the terms of the item(s) ordered. As shown in Figure 11.3, when purchase order information is entered into the computer, the quantity on-order field of the item(s) ordered is increased in the inventory, the data is stored for reference when the merchandise is received by the receiving department, and a purchase order document is generated. The purchase order document is then sent to the vendor for fulfillment of the order.

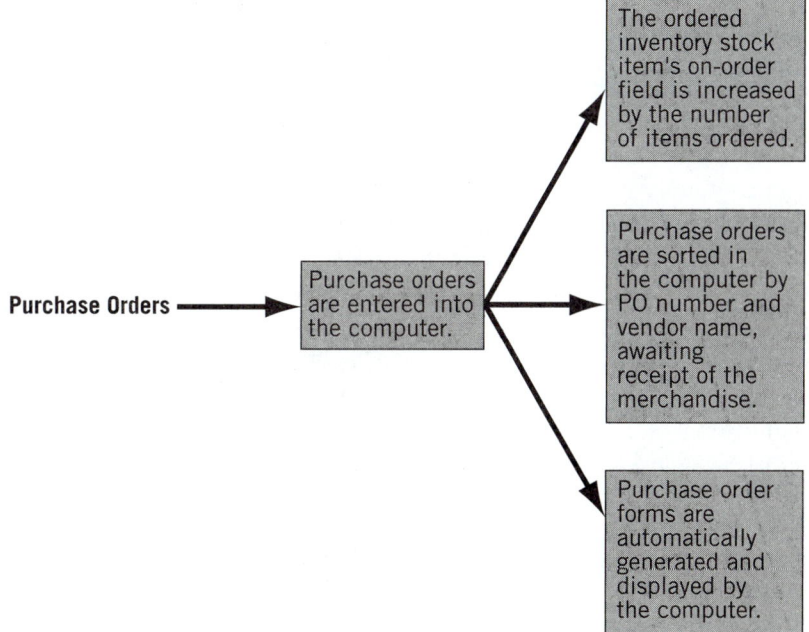

Figure 11.3
Computerized Purchase Order Processing Integration

Purchase Order Input Form

A **purchase order input form** is an input form used to record purchase order transactions when a computerized purchase order processing system is used. The purchase order input form illustrated in Figure 11.4 shows how a purchase order to SIMPCO Mfg., Inc., is recorded.

Purchase order transactions are entered into the computer in the Purchase Order tab in the Other Activities window. Each field on the purchase order input form corresponds to a text box or grid cell in this

PURCHASE ORDER INPUT FORM

Run Date 03/07/--   Problem No. Example

Purch. Ord. #	Date mm/dd/yy	Vendor	Terms	Qty	Inventory Item	Price	GL Account
501	03/01/--	SIMPCO Mfg., Inc.	2/10, n/30	2	SIMPCO Washer	319.00	Purchases

Figure 11.4
Purchase Order Input Form

window. (The explanation provided below detailing how to enter purchase order transactions into the computer is the same for recording them on the input form.)

Purchase Order Transactions

Purchase order transactions that are entered into the software are automatically integrated into the inventory. A purchase order transaction creates a purchase order record containing the purchase order number, date, vendor, terms, and item(s) ordered. In addition, the respective inventory item's on-order field is increased by the number of items ordered.

When the Other toolbar button is clicked or the Other Activities menu item is chosen from the Data menu, the Other Activities window will appear. Click the Purch. Order tab to reveal a Purchase Order window, as shown in Figure 11.5. The data used in Figure 11.5 is from the purchase order input form shown in Figure 11.4.

Enter Purchase Order Transactions

To enter a purchase order transaction, enter the purchase order number, the date, the vendor name, and the terms of the sale. The terms 2/10, n/30 (read as "two ten, net thirty") shown in Figure 11.4 mean that the business can either pay the invoice within ten days of the invoice date and take a 2 percent discount, or the business can pay the full invoice amount within thirty days of the invoice date. Next, enter the number of items ordered in the Quantity field, choose the Inventory item from the Inventory Item drop-down list, and enter the cost in the Price field if it is not the same as that automatically displayed for the item. Repeat this procedure for each item ordered from the vendor.

The computer will multiply the quantity by the price and place the amount in the Item Total column. It will also automatically place the Purchases general ledger account number in the GL Account column.

Chapter 11 Accounts Payable: Purchase Order Processing and Inventory Control

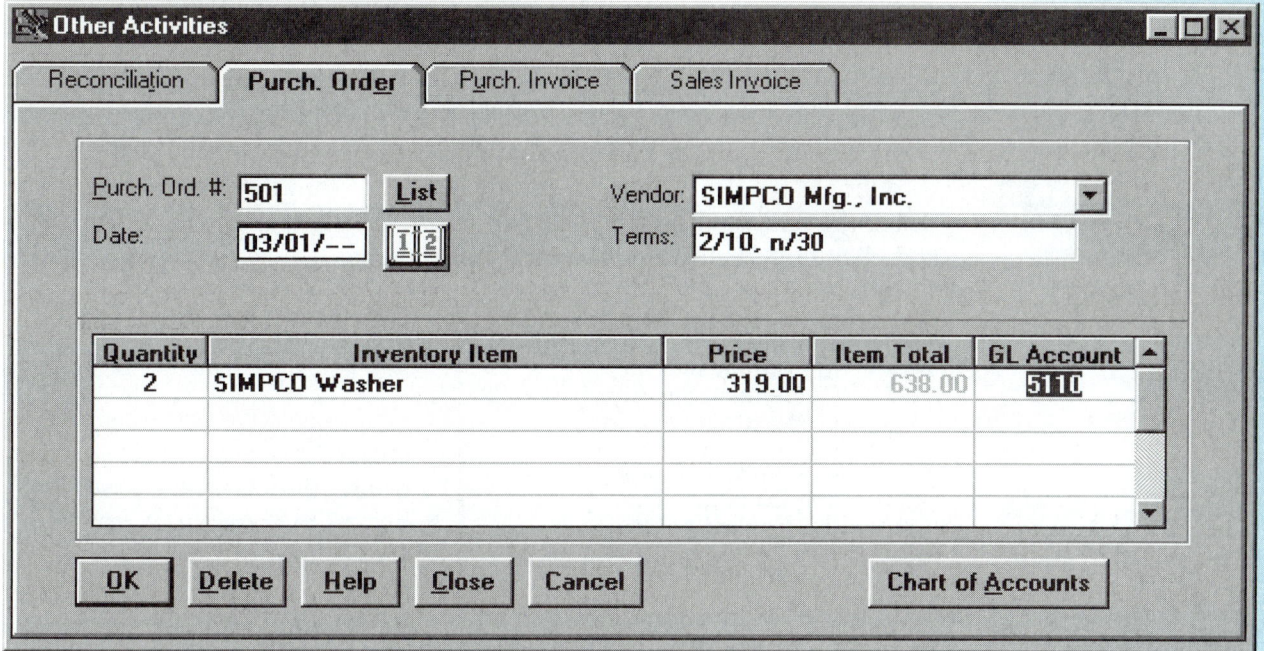

Figure 11.5
Purchase Order Transaction

After the purchase order transaction has been entered and the OK button is clicked, a computer-generated purchase order, similar to the example shown in Figure 11.6, will appear.

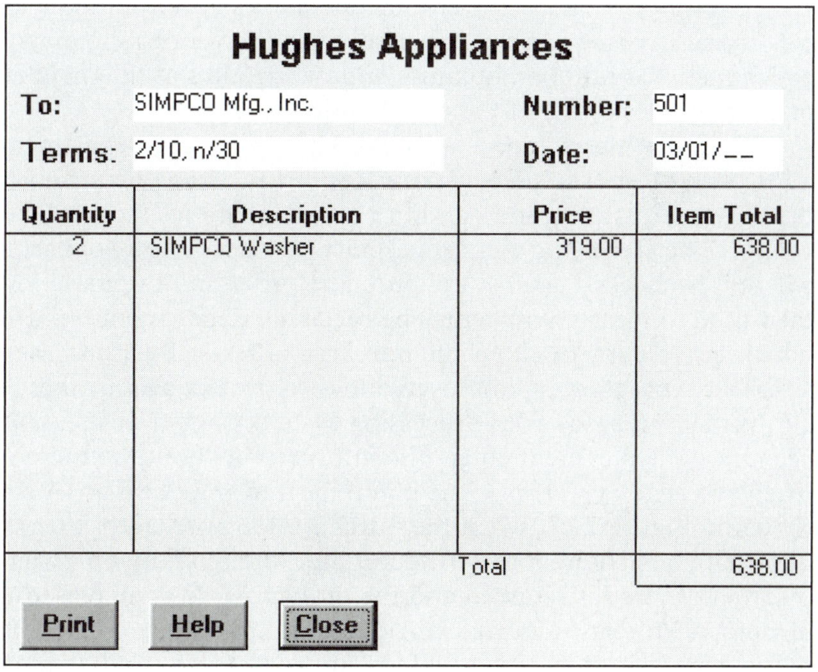

Figure 11.6
Computer-Generated Purchase Order

Change a Purchase Order Transaction

To change a previously entered purchase order transaction, click the List button to the right of the Purch. Ord. # text box to display a list of purchase orders. A sample purchase order list is shown in Figure 11.7.

Choose the purchase order to be changed from the list and click OK. Select the text box for the data you wish to change, enter the correction, and click the OK button to record your change.

Figure 11.7
Purchase Order List

Delete a Purchase Order Transaction

To delete a previously entered purchase order transaction, click the List button to the right of the Purch. Ord. # text box and choose the purchase order to be deleted. Click the Delete button. When the Delete Confirmation dialog box appears, click Yes.

PURCHASE INVOICES AND RECEIVING REPORTS

After receiving a purchase order, the vendor ships the merchandise and sends a purchase invoice to the business's accounting department. A **purchase invoice** is a form that contains the vendor's name, original purchase order number, quantity and description of the merchandise, price, and sales terms of the merchandise sent.

When the merchandise is received, the receiving department prepares a Receiving Report. A **Receiving Report** is a form that shows the description, quantity, and condition of merchandise received from a vendor. The Receiving Report is sent to the accounting department, where it is checked against the purchase order and purchase invoice and then used to initiate payment. The receiving department typically does not receive a copy of either the purchase order or the purchase invoice as a further separation of employee duties to protect against theft.

In the purchase order processing system used in this text, the accounting department enters the information about the merchandise received (or returned) into the computerized purchase order system. As shown in Figure 11.8, when the purchase (or purchase return) information is entered into the computer, the quantity on-order field of the item ordered is reduced and the on-hand field is increased in the inventory. Purchases journal entries are automatically created and posted to the general ledger, and an internal purchase invoice document is

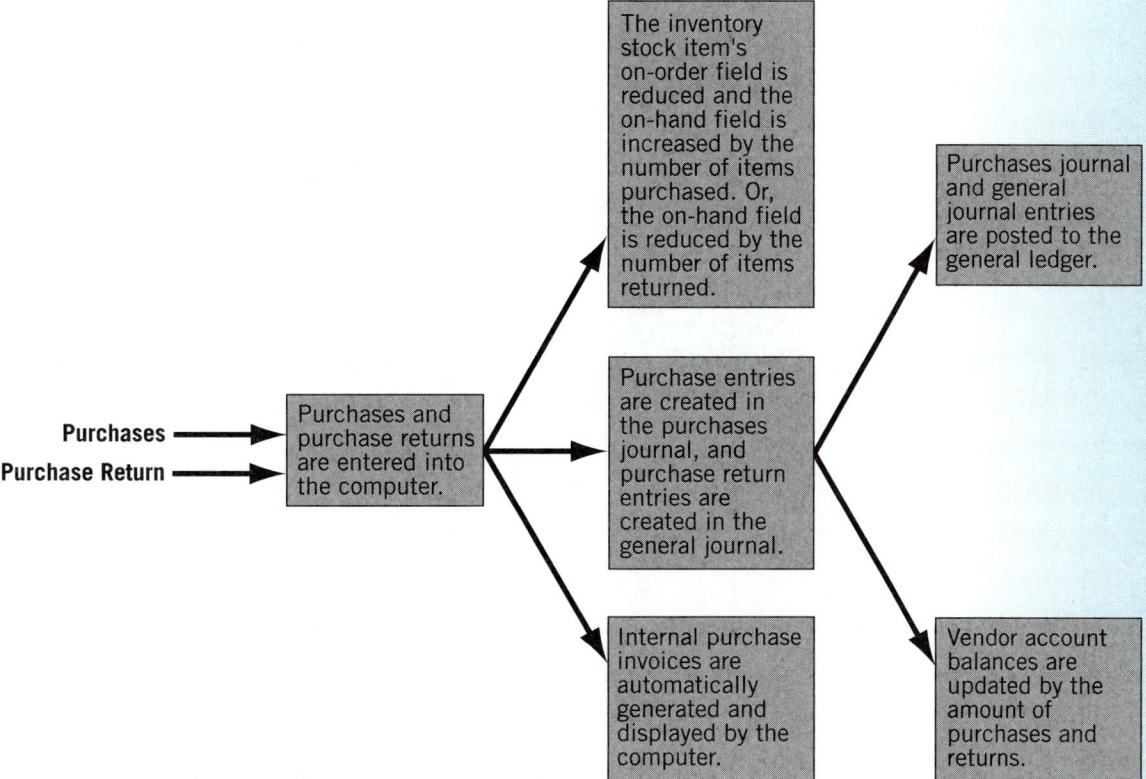

Figure 11.8
Computerized Purchase Invoice/Return Integration

generated. The internal purchase order document is used to authorize cash payment.

PURCHASE INVOICE AND PURCHASE RETURN TRANSACTIONS

A purchase invoice transaction automatically creates and posts the respective journal entry in the purchases journal, updates the vendor account balance, reduces the number of inventory items on order, increases the number of inventory items on hand, and generates an internal purchase invoice document. A purchase return transaction automatically creates and posts the respective journal entry in the general journal and decreases the number of inventory items on hand.

Purchase Invoice Input Form

The **purchase invoice input form** is an input form used to record purchase invoice and purchase return transactions when a computerized purchase order processing system is used. The purchase invoice input form is illustrated in Figure 11.9. The first entry shows how a purchase invoice for merchandise received from RBS Production, Inc., is recorded. The second entry shows how a purchase return from ICY Refrigeration Co. is recorded.

PURCHASE INVOICE INPUT FORM

Run Date 03/07/--   Problem No. Example

Purch. Inv. #	Date mm/dd/yy	Vendor	Purch. Ord. #	Terms	Qty	Inventory Item	Price	GL Account
916	03/02/--	RBS Production, Inc.	474	2/10, n/30	5	Mini Washer & Dryer	540.00	Purchases
R917	03/06/--	ICY Refrigeration Co.			-1	Mini FR. & Refrig.	530.00	Purch. Ret.

Figure 11.9
Purchase Invoice Input Form

Purchase invoice and purchase return transactions are entered into the computer on the Purchase Invoice tab in the Other Activities window. Each field in the purchase invoice input form corresponds to a text box or grid cell in this window. (The explanation provided below, detailing how to enter purchase invoice and purchase return transactions into the computer, is the same for recording them on the input form.)

Enter Purchase Invoice and Purchase Return Transactions

When the Other toolbar button is clicked or the Other Activities menu item is chosen from the Data menu, the Other Activities window will appear. Click the Purch. Invoice tab to reveal the Purchase Invoice Window shown in Figure 11.10. The data shown in Figure 11.10 is from the first entry in the purchase invoice input form shown in Figure 11.9.

To enter a purchase invoice transaction, enter the purchase invoice number, the date, and the vendor name. As soon as the vendor name is entered, a Purch. Ord. # drop-down list box will appear immediately under the vendor name. Select the appropriate purchase order number from the list. The terms and item(s) ordered will appear in the respective grid cells. Enter any changes to the quantity received or price grid cells.

If the transaction is a purchase return, enter the purchase invoice number (with a prefix of *R* to designate *Return*), the date, and the vendor name. Do not enter a purchase order number, but go directly to the Quantity grid cell. Next, enter the quantity returned as a *negative* value, choose the Inventory item from the Inventory Item drop-down list, and enter the cost of the item in Price field if it is not the same as that automatically displayed. Repeat this procedure for each order received from the vendor or each item returned to the vendor.

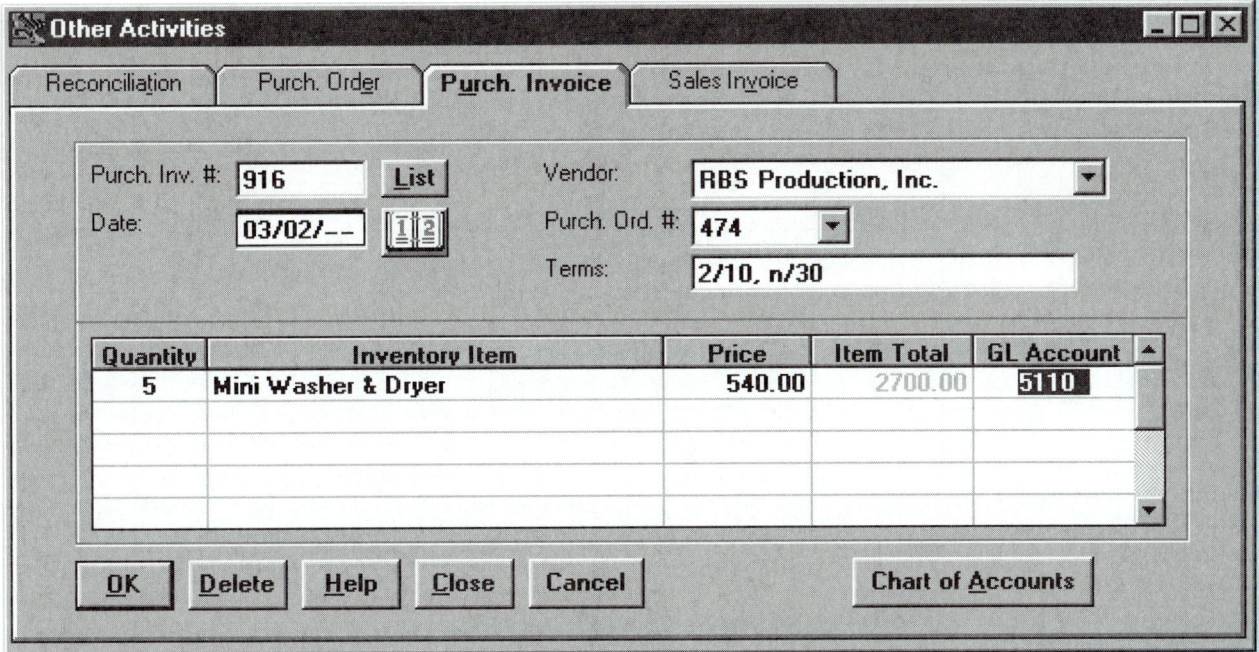

Figure 11.10
Purchase Invoice Transaction

The computer will then multiply the quantity by the price and place the amount in the Item Total column. The computer will also automatically place the Purchases general ledger account number in the GL Account column. (If the quantity is a negative number indicating a purchase return, the computer will insert the Purchases Returns and Allowances account number.)

After the purchase invoice or purchase return transaction has been entered and the OK button has been clicked, a computer-generated internal purchase invoice similar to the example shown in Figure 11.11 will appear.

Change a Purchase Invoice or Purchase Return Transaction

To change a previously entered purchase invoice or purchase return transaction, click the List button to the right of the Purch. Inv. # text box to display a list of purchase invoices. A sample list is shown in Figure 11.12.

Choose the purchase invoice to be changed from the list and click OK. Select the text box for the data you wish to change, enter the correction, and click OK to record your change.

Delete a Purchase Invoice or Purchase Return Transaction

To delete a previously entered purchase invoice or purchase return transaction, click the List button to the right of the Purch. Inv. # text box

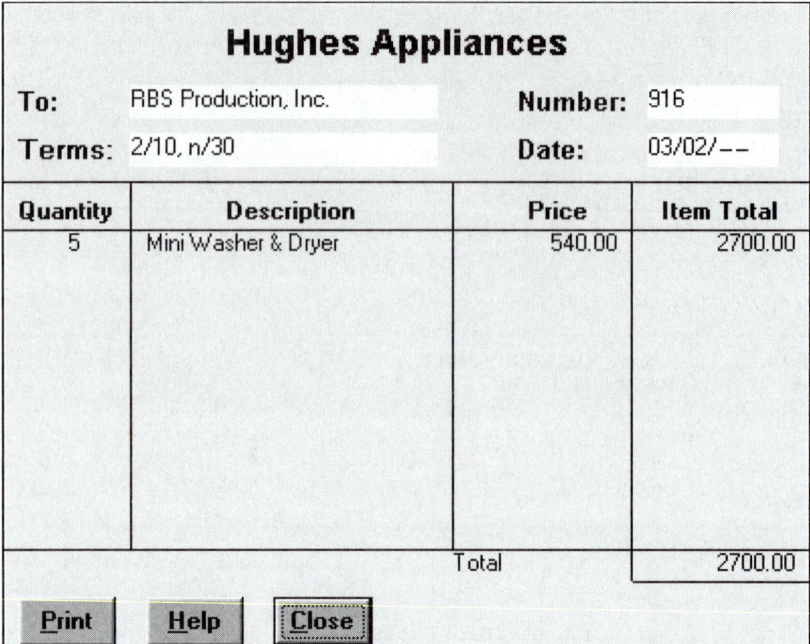

Figure 11.11
Computer-Generated Internal Purchase Invoice

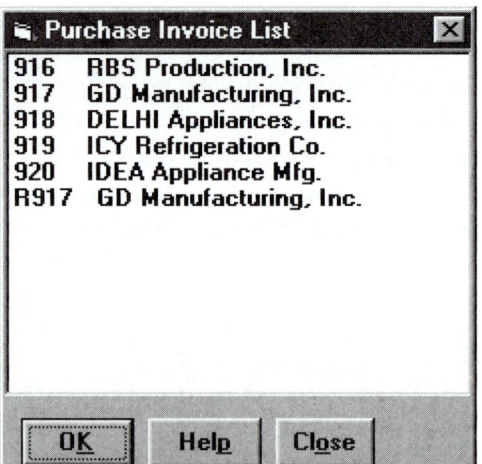

Figure 11.12
Purchase Invoice List

and choose the purchase invoice or purchase return to be deleted. Click the Delete button. When the Delete Confirmation dialog box appears, click Yes.

PURGE INVOICES AND PURCHASE ORDERS

Automated Accounting 8.0 has a capacity of 50 purchase orders and 50 purchase invoice transactions. If either of these capacities is exceeded, an Alert dialog box will appear, informing you of this condition. Before additional purchase orders or purchase invoices can be entered, the previously entered data must be erased by choosing the Purge Invoices and Purchase Orders menu item from the Options menu. A dialog box will appear, asking you to confirm whether you indeed want to purge purchase invoices and purchase orders (in the event you accidentally chose this menu item). Since the purchase orders and purchase invoices previously entered have been automatically integrated into the inventory and general ledger, purging them will not cause information to be lost. A backup file should be made before the purchase orders and purchase invoices are purged. This procedure should not be necessary in this textbook since none of the problems exceeds the system capacity.

REPORTS

The General Journal, Purchases Journal, Cash Payments Journal, Schedule of Accounts Payable, and Accounts Payable Ledger Reports you have already worked with in previous chapters will be used for purchase order reporting. In addition, Purchase Order and Purchase Invoice Registers will be used for purchase order reporting, and the Inventory Items, Inventory Transactions, Inventory Exceptions, and Inventory Valuation (Average Cost, LIFO, and FIFO) Reports will be used for inventory reporting. The procedure to display and print the register and inventory reports is identical to that used in previous chapters.

Purchase Order Register

After purchase order transactions have been entered into the computerized purchase order processing system, a Purchase Order Register should be displayed. A **Purchase Order Register** is a report that lists purchase orders in numerical and date order. Each purchase order is shown with the total amount ordered from each vendor during the processing period. In the example shown in Figure 11.13, the processing period is one week, March 1 through March 7.

```
                      Hughes Appliances
                   Purchase Order Register
                          03/07/--

P.O.       P.O.           Vendor                         P.O.
Number     Date           Name                           Amount

501        03/01/01       SIMPCO Mfg., Inc.                638.00
502        03/02/01       RBS Production, Inc.             930.00
503        03/04/01       MMG Refrigerators, Inc.         3503.50
504        03/07/01       MMG Refrigerators, Inc.          910.00
                                                        ---------
                          Total Amount                   5981.50
                                                        =========
```

Figure 11.13
Purchase Order Register

Purchase Invoice Register

After purchase invoice transactions have been entered into the computerized purchase order processing system, a Purchase Invoice Register should be displayed. A **Purchase Invoice Register** is a report that lists purchase invoices in numerical order with purchase returns listed last. Each purchase invoice is shown with the total amount of expenditure due (or credited) each vendor during the processing period. In the example shown in Figure 11.14, the processing period is one week, March 1 through March 7.

```
                    Hughes Appliances
                  Purchase Invoice Register
                         03/07/--
```

Invoice Number	Invoice Date	Vendor Name	Invoice Amount
916	03/02/01	RBS Production, Inc.	2700.00
917	03/03/01	GD Manufacturing, Inc.	1060.00
918	03/05/01	DELHI Appliances, Inc.	1750.00
919	03/06/01	ICY Refrigeration Co.	2379.50
920	03/07/01	IDEA Appliance Mfg.	710.25
R917	03/06/01	GD Manufacturing, Inc.	-530.00
		Total Amount	8069.75

Figure 11.14
Purchase Invoice Register

Inventory List

The **Inventory List Report** is a report that lists the current status of each inventory item for reference. The report is also useful for verifying the accuracy of inventory maintenance. An example of an inventory list report is shown in Figure 11.15.

Inventory Transactions Report

The **Inventory Transactions Report** is a list of all transactions that have affected inventory items during the processing period. You should display this report whenever you enter, correct, or delete purchase orders, purchase invoices, or purchase return transactions. This will help verify that all data have been recorded and entered correctly in the inventory system. An example of an Inventory Transactions Report is

			Hughes Appliances Inventory List 03/07/--				
Stock No.	Description	Unit Meas.	On Hand	On Order	Reorder Point	Last Cost	Retail Price
1010	GD Washer	EA	19	0	10	241.00	359.95
1020	SIMPCO Washer	EA	13	2	8	319.00	529.95
1040	Mini Washer & Dryer	EA	20	0	10	540.00	798.00
2010	IDEA Electric Dryer	EA	24	0	12	220.00	359.95
2020	IDEA Gas Dryer	EA	9	0	10	305.00	429.95
2030	Mini Electric Dryer	EA	11	0	8	225.00	379.95
3010	1 Door 18 CF. Refrig.	EA	18	0	8	350.00	529.95
3020	1 Door 22 CF. Refrig.	EA	11	3	10	435.00	699.00
3030	S by S 19 CF. Refrig.	EA	14	0	6	530.00	789.00
3040	S by S 29 CF. Refrig.	EA	7	2	6	530.00	1899.00
3050	Top MMG 21 CF. Refrig.	EA	13	2	10	455.00	699.00
3060	Top MMG 25 CF. Refrig.	EA	14	0	6	510.00	859.95
3070	Mini FR. & Refrig.	EA	13	0	8	237.95	342.50
3080	ICY 20 CF. Freezer	EA	6	0	10	285.00	428.00
3090	Micro Refrig.	EA	0	0	10		369.95
4010	RBS Electric Range	EA	21	0	8	216.00	349.99
4020	RBS Gas Range	EA	7	3	6	310.00	435.95
5010	DELHI Dishwasher	EA	15	0	8	350.00	549.95
5020	IDEA Dishwasher	EA	20	0	10	236.75	329.95
5030	Trash Compactor	EA	13	0	6	233.90	389.95

Figure 11.15
Inventory List Report

shown in Figure 11.16. (The item's quantity sold and selling price data will be discussed in the next chapter.)

Inventory Exceptions Report

An **Inventory Exceptions Report** is a report that lists items in the inventory that are out of stock (quantity on hand of zero or less) and items that are at or below the reorder point (quantity on hand less than or equal to the reorder point). This report alerts management to items in the inventory that need attention. An Inventory Exceptions Report is shown in Figure 11.17.

Inventory Valuation Report

An **Inventory Valuation Report** is a report that lists the per-item and total cost and retail prices of all items currently in the inventory. Three Inventory Valuation Reports are provided: Average Cost, LIFO

Hughes Appliances
Inventory Transactions
03/07/--

Date	Description	Inv./P.O.	Quantity Sold	Selling Price	Quan. Ord.	Quan. Recd.	Cost Price
Purchase Orders							
03/01	SIMPCO Washer	501			2		
03/02	RBS Gas Range	502			3		
03/04	1 Door 22 CF. Refrig.	503			3		
	S by S 29 CF. Refrig.				2		
03/07	Top MMG 21 CF. Refrig.	504			2		
Purchase Invoices							
03/02	Mini Washer & Dryer	916				5	540.00
03/03	S by S 19 CF. Refrig.	917				2	530.00
03/05	DELHI Dishwasher	918				5	350.00
03/06	Mini FR. & Refrig.	919				10	237.95
03/07	IDEA Dishwasher	920				3	236.75
03/06	S by S 19 CF. Refrig.	R917				-1	530.00
	Totals				12	24	

Figure 11.16
Inventory Transactions Report

Hughes Appliances
Inventory Exceptions
03/07/--

Stock No.	Description	Unit Meas	On Hand	On Order	Reorder Point	Exception
2020	IDEA Gas Dryer	EA	9		10	At/below reorder point
3080	ICY 20 CF. Freezer	EA	6		10	At/below reorder point
3090	Micro Refrig.	EA	0		10	Out of stock

Figure 11.17
Inventory Exceptions Report

(Last-In, First-Out), and FIFO (First-In, Last-Out). All three Inventory Valuation Reports are identical, with the exception that the Cost and calculated Value at Cost columns are based on the chosen valuation method.

Average Cost Method The **average cost method** is an inventory valuation method that uses an average of the actual costs and quantities to calculate the value of an inventory. The Average Cost option lists each item in the inventory, showing the quantity currently on hand and the weighted average cost for each item.

The following example shows how the computer calculates the weighted average cost. Assume that there is 1 unit of a stock item at $275.00, and 11 units at $300.00 each. The average cost would be calculated as follows:

Quantity		Cost		Total	
1	×	$ 270.00	=	$ 270.00	
11	×	300.00	=	3300.00	
12				$3570.00	($3570.00 ÷ 12 = $297.50 average cost)

If no purchase transactions are available (due to inactivity or purging of the invoices and purchase orders), the computer uses the average cost previously calculated and stored in the inventory stock item's record to value the inventory. An Inventory Valuation (Average Cost) Report is shown in Figure 11.18.

Last-In, First-Out (LIFO) The second type of inventory valuation report is based on the LIFO (last-in, first-out) method. The **LIFO method** is an inventory valuation method that uses the earliest costs to calculate the value of an inventory. The LIFO method makes the assumption that the last items received into inventory are the first to be sold. Therefore, any items remaining in the inventory are the first items received. The computer calculates LIFO on a perpetual basis, according to the order that transactions are entered. The report lists the quantity in inventory for each different cost. The quantity and cost are extended to provide an inventory valuation based on the LIFO valuation method. The Inventory Valuation (LIFO) Report is identical to the Average Valuation Report shown in Figure 11.15 except that the Cost and calculated Value at Cost columns are based on the LIFO method.

First-In, First-Out (FIFO) The last Inventory Valuation Report is based on the FIFO (first-in, first-out) method. The **FIFO method** is an inventory valuation method that uses the latest costs to calculate the value of an inventory. The FIFO method assumes that the first items received into inventory are the first sold. Therefore, any items remaining in inventory are the last items received. The report shows the quantity in inventory for each different cost. The quantity and cost are extended to provide an inventory valuation based on the FIFO valuation method. The Inventory Valuation (FIFO) Report is identical to the Average Valuation Report shown in Figure 11.15 except that the Cost and calculated Value at Cost columns are based on the FIFO method.

```
                        Hughes Appliances
                   Inventory Valuation (Average Cost)
                              03/07/--

Stock                         On              Value        Retail       Value
No.    Description            Hand   Cost     At Cost      Price        At Retail

1010   GD Washer              19     241.00   4579.00      359.95       6839.05
1020   SIMPCO Washer          13     319.08   4148.04      529.95       6889.35
1040   Mini Washer & Dryer    20     540.00   10800.00     798.00       15960.00
2010   IDEA Electric Dryer    24     220.00   5280.00      359.95       8638.80
2020   IDEA Gas Dryer         9      305.00   2745.00      429.95       3869.55
2030   Mini Electric Dryer    11     225.00   2475.00      379.95       4179.45
3010   1 Door 18 CF. Refrig.  18     350.00   6300.00      529.95       9539.10
3020   1 Door 22 CF. Refrig.  11     435.00   4785.00      699.00       7689.00
3030   S by S 19 CF. Refrig.  14     530.00   7420.00      789.00       11046.00
3040   S by S 29 CF. Refrig.  7      1135.00  7945.00      1899.00      13293.00
3050   Top MMG 21 CF. Refrig. 13     455.00   5915.00      699.00       9087.00
3060   Top MMG 25 CF. Refrig. 14     510.00   7140.00      859.95       12039.30
3070   Mini FR. & Refrig.     13     237.95   3093.35      342.50       4452.50
3080   ICY 20 CF. Freezer     6      285.00   1710.00      428.00       2568.00
4010   RBS Electric Range     21     214.50   4504.50      349.99       7349.79
4020   RBS Gas Range          7      310.00   2170.00      435.95       3051.65
5010   DELHI Dishwasher       15     350.00   5250.00      549.95       8249.25
5020   IDEA Dishwasher        20     236.75   4735.00      329.95       6599.00
5030   Trash Compactor        13     233.90   3040.70      389.95       5069.35
                                              --------                  --------
       Total Inventory Value                  94035.59                  146409.14
                                              ========                  ========
```

Figure 11.18
Inventory Valuation (Average Cost) Report

Chapter Review

1. A business's success in controlling merchandise inventory has a direct relationship to profitability. Since the costs associated with merchandise inventory are high, a business must try to keep the stock levels as low as possible yet maintain sufficient inventory to meet customer demand.

2. Inventory stock items can be added, changed, or deleted from the inventory system. The inventory stock item input form can be used to record stock items maintenance.

3. A stock number is a unique, four-character code that is assigned to each inventory item for identification. The unit of measure is a

two-character abbreviation that indicates how the item is sold (i.e., each, by the case, by the box). The minimum quantity that is allowed before additional items must be reordered is referred to as the reorder point. The quantity on hand is a count of the quantity that is included in the merchandise inventory at the present time. The quantity on order is the quantity of additional merchandise that has been ordered but has not yet arrived. The current selling price per unit is called the retail price.

4. A computerized purchase order processing system consists of the procedures involved in automatically integrating the purchase order, purchase invoice, purchase return, and cash disbursement data into the inventory and general ledger.

5. A purchase requisition is a formal request for the purchase of merchandise. A purchase order is a document containing a purchase order number, vendor name, quantity and description, expected price, and terms of the item(s) ordered. Purchase order transactions increase the amount of inventory on order. A purchase order input form may be used to record purchase order transactions.

6. A purchase invoice contains the vendor's name, original purchase order number, quantity and description of the merchandise, price, and terms of the order. A Receiving Report created by the receiving department contains the description, quantity, and condition of the merchandise.

7. A purchase invoice transaction automatically creates and posts the respective journal entry in the purchases journal, updates the vendor account balance, reduces the number of inventory items on order, increases the number of inventory items on hand, and generates an internal purchase invoice document. A purchase return transaction automatically creates and posts the respective journal entry in the general journal and decreases the number of inventory items on hand. A purchase invoice input form may be used to record purchase invoice and purchase return transactions.

8. A Purchase Order Register lists the total amount ordered from each vendor in numerical and date order for the processing period. A Purchase Invoice Register lists the total amount of expenditure due (or credited) each vendor during the processing period.

9. The Inventory Items Report provides the current status of each inventory item for reference and is useful for verifying the accuracy of inventory maintenance.

10. The Inventory Transactions Report lists all the transactions that have affected the inventory items during the processing period.

11. The Inventory Exceptions Report alerts management to items in the inventory that need attention by listing items that are out of stock (quantity on hand of zero or less) and items that are at or below the reorder point (quantity on hand less than or equal to the reorder point).

12. The Average Cost Valuation Report lists each item in the inventory, showing its quantity currently on hand and its average cost. Average cost is a calculated per-unit average of the cost price.

13. The LIFO inventory valuation method is based upon the assumption that the last items received into the inventory are the first to be sold; therefore, any items remaining are valued at the cost of the first items received.

14. The FIFO inventory valuation method is based upon the assumption that the first items received into the inventory are the first to be sold; therefore, any items remaining are valued at the cost of the last items received.

ACCOUNTING CAREERS IN DEPTH

Public Accounting Firms

Public accountants work in partnerships that provide accounting services to individuals, businesses, and governments. This field offers advancement potential to audit manager, tax manager, or partner—positions reached by only 2 to 3 percent of new hires.

A common entry-level strategy is to work for a public accounting firm to obtain broad experience before moving on to government or business. Most accountants at public accounting firms do not become partners, but the experience and training can be excellent.

Firms are implementing new electronic systems for submitting and preparing financial statements. Therefore, it would be advantageous to have computer coursework in addition to some on-the-job experience working with computers.

Most accountants spend several years at public accounting firms and then move on to different industries and put their experience to work. The skills gained in public accounting firms give the accountant a breadth and depth of knowledge and experience within different types of industries. Sometimes, accountants of public accounting firms are later hired by the clients of those firms because the accountants are familiar with the inner workings of the clients' businesses.

Public accounting firms are a great place to start, but they are also very competitive. The firms seek out the best and brightest college students to discuss future employment. Preparation for college-level accounting can begin as early as high school. Now is a good time to start planning to be ready for this kind of opportunity.

TUTORIAL PROBLEM 11-T

In this problem, you will perform the operating procedures necessary to add new inventory stock items, make changes to existing inventory stock items, and delete an inventory stock item. In addition, you will process the purchase orders, purchase invoices, and cash payment transactions for the week of March 1st through March 7th of the current year for Hughes Appliances.

STEP 1: Start up *Automated Accounting 8.0*.

STEP 2: Load the opening balances file named AA8 Problem 11-T.

STEP 3: Enter your name in the User Name text box and click *OK*.

STEP 4: Save the file with a file name of 11-T Your Name.

STEP 5: Enter the inventory stock item maintenance data.
Click the *Accts.* toolbar icon. When the Account Maintenance window appears, click the *Inventory* tab, and enter the following inventory stock item maintenance data:

Add Stock No. 3090; Micro Refrig.; unit of measure, EA; reorder point, 10; retail price, 369.95 to the inventory stock item file.

Change the retail price of 1 Door 18 CF. Refrig (Stock No. 3010) to $529.95.

Change the retail price of Mini FR. & Refrig. (Stock No. 3070) to $342.50.

Change the reorder point of DELHI Dishwasher (Stock No. 5010) to 8.

Delete Mini Washer (Stock No. 1030) from the stock item file.

STEP 6: Enter the purchase order and purchase invoice transactions shown below. The March 01 Purchase Order No. 501 is shown in Figure 11.19a, and the March 02 Purchase Invoice No. 916 is shown in Figure 11.19b.
From the Other Activities window, click the appropriate *Purch. Order* or *Purch. Invoice* tab and enter the March 1 through March 7 transactions. If there is a unit cost difference (e.g., March 04 Purchase Order No. 503), make sure you enter the data shown in the transaction.

Mar. 01 Ordered the following merchandise from SIMPCO Mfg., Inc., terms 2/10, n/30. Purchase Order No. 501. This purchase order is shown in Figure 11.19a.

TUTORIAL PROBLEM 11-T

It is important that you enter the transactions in date sequence; otherwise, your reports will be incorrect because the computer calculates perpetual inventory according to the transactions' dates.

Description	Quantity	Unit Cost
SIMPCO Washer	2	319.00

02 Ordered the following merchandise from RBS Production, Inc., terms 2/10, n/30. Purchase Order No. 502.

Description	Quantity	Unit Cost
RBS Gas Range	3	310.00

02 Received the following merchandise for Purchase Order No. 474 from RBS Production, Inc., terms 2/10, n/30. Purchase Invoice No. 916.

Description	Quantity	Unit Cost
Mini Washer & Dryer	5	540.00

03 Received the following merchandise for Purchase Order No. 480 from GD Manufacturing, Inc., terms 2/10, n/30. Purchase Invoice No. 917.

Description	Quantity	Unit Cost
S by S 19 CF. Refrig.	2	530.00

04 Ordered the following merchandise from MMG Refrigerators, Inc., terms 2/10, n/30. Purchase Order No. 503. (**Note:** Be sure to enter the unit cost difference.)

Description	Quantity	Unit Cost
1 Door 22 CF. Refrig.	3	426.30
S by S 29 CF. Refrig.	2	1112.30

05 Received the following merchandise for Purchase Order No. 486 from DELHI Appliances, Inc., terms 2/10, n/30. Purchase Invoice No. 918.

Description	Quantity	Unit Cost
DELHI Dishwasher	5	350.00

Chapter 11 Accounts Payable: Purchase Order Processing and Inventory Control

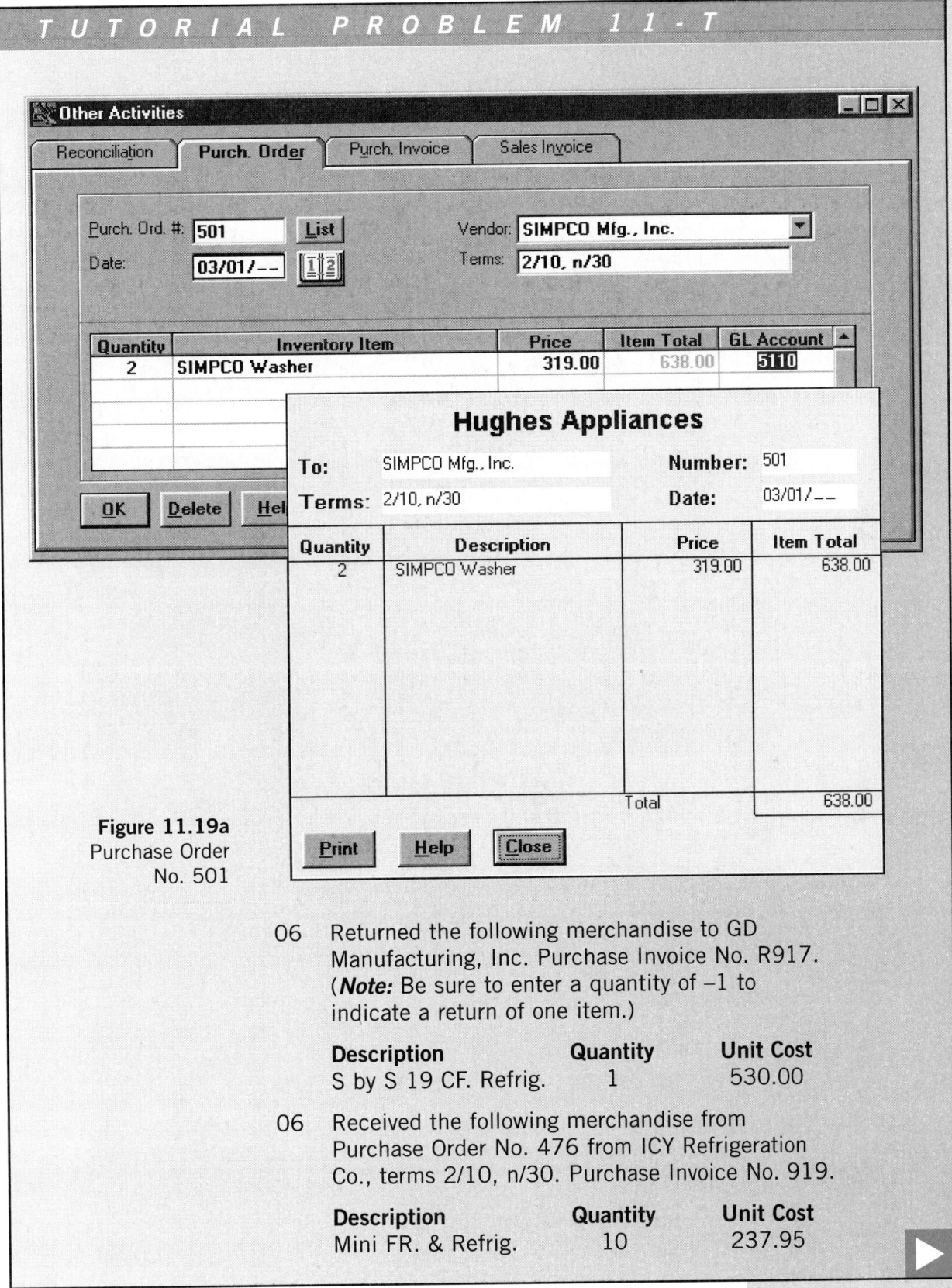

Figure 11.19a
Purchase Order No. 501

06 Returned the following merchandise to GD Manufacturing, Inc. Purchase Invoice No. R917. (*Note:* Be sure to enter a quantity of –1 to indicate a return of one item.)

Description	Quantity	Unit Cost
S by S 19 CF. Refrig.	1	530.00

06 Received the following merchandise from Purchase Order No. 476 from ICY Refrigeration Co., terms 2/10, n/30. Purchase Invoice No. 919.

Description	Quantity	Unit Cost
Mini FR. & Refrig.	10	237.95

TUTORIAL PROBLEM 11-T

07 Received the following merchandise for Purchase Order No. 500 from IDEA Appliance Mfg., terms 2/10, n/30. Purchase Invoice No. 920.

Description	Quantity	Unit Cost
IDEA Dishwasher	3	236.75

07 Ordered the following merchandise from MMG Refrigerators, Inc., terms 2/10, n/30. Purchase Order No. 504.

Description	Quantity	Unit Cost
Top MMG 21 CF. Refrig.	2	455.00

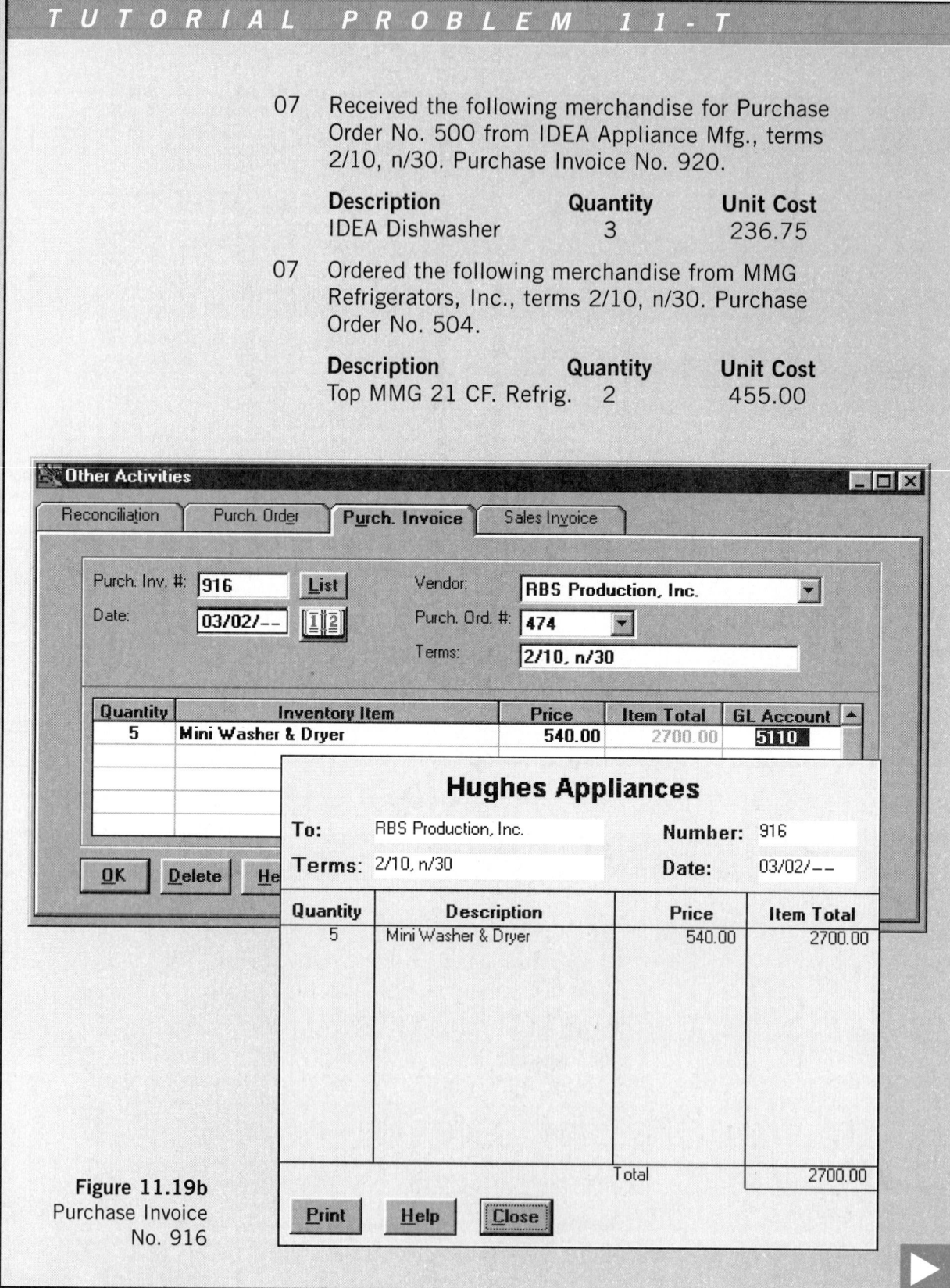

Figure 11.19b
Purchase Invoice No. 916

Chapter 11 Accounts Payable: Purchase Order Processing and Inventory Control

TUTORIAL PROBLEM 11-T

STEP 7: Enter the cash payments journal transactions shown below and illustrated in Figure 11.20.

Mar. 05 Paid Invoice No. 916 to RBS Production, Inc., $2,700.00, no discount. Check No. 4732.

06 Paid Invoice No. 918 to DELHI Appliances, Inc., $1,750.00, less 2% discount, $35.00. Check No. 4733.

07 Paid Invoice No. 919 to ICY Refrigeration Co., $2,379.50, less 2% discount, $47.59. Check No. 4734.

Date	Refer.	A.P. Debit	Purchase Disc Cr	Cash Credit	Vendor
03/05/--	C4732	2700.00		2700.00	RBS Production, Inc.
03/06/--	C4733	1750.00	35.00	1715.00	DELHI Appliances, Inc.
03/07/--	C4734	2379.50	47.59	2331.91	ICY Refrigeration Co.

Figure 11.20
Cash Payments

STEP 8: Display the Purchase Order and Purchase Invoice Registers for the period March 1 through March 7.

Click the *Reports* toolbar button. Choose the *Purchase Orders and Invoices* option button, and then select the *Purchase Orders* and then the *Purchase Invoices* Reports. The reports appear in Figures 11.21a and 11.21b.

```
               Hughes Appliances
              Purchase Order Register
                    03/07/--
---------------------------------------------------------------
P.O.      P.O.          Vendor                      P.O.
Number    Date          Name                        Amount
---------------------------------------------------------------

501       03/01/01      SIMPCO Mfg., Inc.            638.00
502       03/02/01      RBS Production, Inc.         930.00
503       03/04/01      MMG Refrigerators, Inc.     3503.50
504       03/07/01      MMG Refrigerators, Inc.      910.00
                                                   ---------
                        Total Amount                5981.50
                                                   =========
```

Figure 11.21a
Purchase Order Register

TUTORIAL PROBLEM 11-T

```
              Hughes Appliances
           Purchase Invoice Register
                  03/07/--
------------------------------------------------------------
Invoice      Invoice       Vendor                   Invoice
Number       Date          Name                     Amount
------------------------------------------------------------
916          03/02/01      RBS Production, Inc.     2700.00
917          03/03/01      GD Manufacturing, Inc.   1060.00
918          03/05/01      DELHI Appliances, Inc.   1750.00
919          03/06/01      ICY Refrigeration Co.    2379.50
920          03/07/01      IDEA Appliance Mfg.       710.25
R917         03/06/01      GD Manufacturing, Inc.   -530.00
                                                   --------
                           Total Amount             8069.75
                                                   ========
```

Figure 11.21b
Purchase Invoice Register

STEP 9: **Display an Inventory List Report.**
Choose the *Inventory Reports* option button, and then select the *Inventory List* Report. Click *OK*. The report appears in Figure 11.22.

STEP 10: **Display the General Journal for the period March 1 through March 7.**
The report appears in Figure 11.23.

STEP 11: **Display the Purchases Journal for the period March 1 through March 7.**
The report appears in Figure 11.24 (page 388).

STEP 12: **Display the Cash Payments Journal for the period March 1 through March 7.**
The report appears in Figure 11.25 (page 388).

TUTORIAL PROBLEM 11-T

Hughes Appliances
Inventory List
03/07/--

Stock No.	Description	Unit Meas.	On Hand	On Order	Reorder Point	Last Cost	Retail Price
1010	GD Washer	EA	19	0	10	241.00	359.95
1020	SIMPCO Washer	EA	13	2	8	319.00	529.95
1040	Mini Washer & Dryer	EA	20	0	10	540.00	798.00
2010	IDEA Electric Dryer	EA	24	0	12	220.00	359.95
2020	IDEA Gas Dryer	EA	9	0	10	305.00	429.95
2030	Mini Electric Dryer	EA	11	0	8	225.00	379.95
3010	1 Door 18 CF. Refrig.	EA	18	0	8	350.00	529.95
3020	1 Door 22 CF. Refrig.	EA	11	3	10	435.00	699.00
3030	S by S 19 CF. Refrig.	EA	14	0	6	530.00	789.00
3040	S by S 29 CF. Refrig.	EA	7	2	6	530.00	1899.00
3050	Top MMG 21 CF. Refrig.	EA	13	2	10	455.00	699.00
3060	Top MMG 25 CF. Refrig.	EA	14	0	6	510.00	859.95
3070	Mini FR. & Refrig.	EA	13	0	8	237.95	342.50
3080	ICY 20 CF. Freezer	EA	6	0	10	285.00	428.00
3090	Micro Refrig.	EA	0	0	10		369.95
4010	RBS Electric Range	EA	21	0	8	216.00	349.99
4020	RBS Gas Range	EA	7	3	6	310.00	435.95
5010	DELHI Dishwasher	EA	15	0	8	350.00	549.95
5020	IDEA Dishwasher	EA	20	0	10	236.75	329.95
5030	Trash Compactor	EA	13	0	6	233.90	389.95

Figure 11.22
Inventory List Report

Hughes Appliances
General Journal
03/07/--

Date	Refer.	Acct.	Title	Debit	Credit
03/06	R917	2110	AP/GD Manufacturing, Inc.	530.00	
03/06	R917	5120	Purchases Ret. & Allow.		530.00
			Totals	530.00	530.00

Figure 11.23
General Journal

TUTORIAL PROBLEM 11-T

Hughes Appliances
Purchases Journal
03/07/--

Date	Inv. No.	Acct.	Title	Debit	Credit
03/02	916	5110	Purchases	2700.00	
03/02	916	2110	AP/RBS Production, Inc.		2700.00
03/03	917	5110	Purchases	1060.00	
03/03	917	2110	AP/GD Manufacturing, Inc.		1060.00
03/05	918	5110	Purchases	1750.00	
03/05	918	2110	AP/DELHI Appliances, Inc.		1750.00
03/06	919	5110	Purchases	2379.50	
03/06	919	2110	AP/ICY Refrigeration Co.		2379.50
03/07	920	5110	Purchases	710.25	
03/07	920	2110	AP/IDEA Appliance Mfg.		710.25
			Totals	8599.75	8599.75

Figure 11.24 Purchases Journal

Hughes Appliances
Cash Payments Journal
03/07/--

Date	Ck. No.	Acct.	Title	Debit	Credit
03/05	C4732	2110	AP/RBS Production, Inc.	2700.00	
03/05	C4732	1110	Cash		2700.00
03/06	C4733	2110	AP/DELHI Appliances, Inc.	1750.00	
03/06	C4733	1110	Cash		1715.00
03/06	C4733	5130	Purchases Discount		35.00
03/07	C4734	2110	AP/ICY Refrigeration Co.	2379.50	
03/07	C4734	1110	Cash		2331.91
03/07	C4734	5130	Purchases Discount		47.59
			Totals	6829.50	6829.50

Figure 11.25 Cash Payments Journal

TUTORIAL PROBLEM 11-T

STEP 13: **Display a General Ledger Report for the Accounts Payable, Purchases, Purchases Returns and Allowances, and Purchases Discount accounts.**

Choose *Ledger Reports*, select the *General Ledger*, and then click *OK*. Enter the accounts payable account (2110) in both the From and To drop-down text boxes in the Account Range dialog box. To display the Purchases, Purchases Returns and Allowances, and Purchases Discount accounts, enter Purchases (5110) in the From: text box and Purchases Discount (5130) in the To: text box. The reports appear in Figures 11.26a and 11.26b.

Hughes Appliances
General Ledger
03/07/--

Account Journal	Date	Refer.	Debit	Credit	Balance
2110-Accounts Payable					
Balance Forward					24240.00Cr
Purchases	03/02	916		2700.00	26940.00Cr
Purchases	03/03	917		1060.00	28000.00Cr
Purchases	03/05	918		1750.00	29750.00Cr
Cash Payments	03/05	C4732	2700.00		27050.00Cr
General	03/06	R917	530.00		26520.00Cr
Purchases	03/06	919		2379.50	28899.50Cr
Cash Payments	03/06	C4733	1750.00		27149.50Cr
Purchases	03/07	920		710.25	27859.75Cr
Cash Payments	03/07	C4734	2379.50		25480.25Cr

Figure 11.26a
Accounts Payable

On the Internet, fraudulent businesses can appear genuine. Don't assume that a professional-looking web site means that the company is legitimate.

TUTORIAL PROBLEM 11-T

Hughes Appliances
General Ledger
03/07/--

Account Journal	Date	Refer.	Debit	Credit	Balance
5110-Purchases					
Balance Forward					164054.70Dr
Purchases	03/02	916	2700.00		166754.70Dr
Purchases	03/03	917	1060.00		167814.70Dr
Purchases	03/05	918	1750.00		169564.70Dr
Purchases	03/06	919	2379.50		171944.20Dr
Purchases	03/07	920	710.25		172654.45Dr
5120-Purchases Ret. & Allow.					
General	03/06	R917		530.00	530.00Cr
5130-Purchases Discount					
Cash Payments	03/06	C4733		35.00	35.00Cr
Cash Payments	03/07	C4734		47.59	82.59Cr

Figure 11.26b
Purchases, Purchases Returns and Allowances, and Purchases Discount

STEP 14: **Display a Trial Balance Report.**
The Trial Balance Report is shown in Figure 11.27.

STEP 15: **Display a Schedule of Accounts Payable.**
The report is shown in Figure 11.28.

STEP 16: **Display an Accounts Payable Ledger.**
The report is shown in Figure 11.29 (page 392).

STEP 17: **Display the Inventory Transactions Report.**
Select *Inventory Transactions* and click *OK*. The report appears in Figure 11.30 (page 393).

STEP 18: **Display the Inventory Exceptions Report.**
Select *Inventory Exceptions* and click *OK*. The report appears in Figure 11.31 (page 393).

Chapter 11 Accounts Payable: Purchase Order Processing and Inventory Control

TUTORIAL PROBLEM 11-T

Hughes Appliances
Trial Balance
03/07/--

Acct. Number	Account Title	Debit	Credit
1110	Cash	1283.12	
1120	Accounts Receivable	69260.00	
1130	Merchandise Inventory	85965.84	
1140	Supplies	2460.64	
1150	Prepaid Insurance	1546.07	
2110	Accounts Payable		25480.25
3110	Dawn Hughes, Capital		145468.73
3120	Dawn Hughes, Drawing	24000.00	
4110	Sales		206237.99
5110	Purchases	172654.45	
5120	Purchases Ret. & Allow.		530.00
5130	Purchases Discount		82.59
6110	Advertising Expense	1800.00	
6120	Miscellaneous Expense	637.65	
6140	Rent Expense	10000.00	
6160	Telephone Expense	3973.50	
6170	Utilities Expense	4218.29	
	Totals	377799.56	377799.56

Figure 11.27 Trial Balance

Hughes Appliances
Schedule of Accounts Payable
03/07/--

Name	Balance
DELHI Appliances, Inc.	3995.00
GD Manufacturing, Inc.	4700.65
ICY Refrigeration Co.	5485.50
IDEA Appliance Mfg.	4185.25
RBS Production, Inc.	2235.85
SIMPCO Mfg., Inc.	4878.00
Total	25480.25

Figure 11.28 Schedule of Accounts Payable

TUTORIAL PROBLEM 11-T

Hughes Appliances
Accounts Payable Ledger
03/07/--

Account Journal	Date	Refer.	Debit	Credit	Balance
DELHI Appliances, Inc.					
Balance Forward					3995.00Cr
Purchases	03/05	918		1750.00	5745.00Cr
Cash Payments	03/06	C4733	1750.00		3995.00Cr
GD Manufacturing, Inc.					
Balance Forward					4170.65Cr
Purchases	03/03	917		1060.00	5230.65Cr
General	03/06	R917	530.00		4700.65Cr
ICY Refrigeration Co.					
Balance Forward					5485.50Cr
Purchases	03/06	919		2379.50	7865.00Cr
Cash Payments	03/07	C4734	2379.50		5485.50Cr
IDEA Appliance Mfg.					
Balance Forward					3475.00Cr
Purchases	03/07	920		710.25	4185.25Cr
MMG Refrigerators, Inc.					
*** No Activity ***					.00
RBS Production, Inc.					
Balance Forward					2235.85Cr
Purchases	03/02	916		2700.00	4935.85Cr
Cash Payments	03/05	C4732	2700.00		2235.85Cr
SIMPCO Mfg., Inc.					
Balance Forward					4878.00Cr

Figure 11.29
Accounts Payable Ledger

When the messages posted to a discussion group are first read and screened, the group is called a "moderated" group. Discussion groups without moderators are called "unmoderated."

TUTORIAL PROBLEM 11-T

Hughes Appliances
Inventory Transactions
03/07/--

Date	Description	Inv./P.O.	Quantity Sold	Selling Price	Quan. Ord.	Quan. Recd.	Cost Price
Purchase Orders							
03/01	SIMPCO Washer	501			2		
03/02	RBS Gas Range	502			3		
03/04	1 Door 22 CF. Refrig.	503			3		
	S by S 29 CF. Refrig.				2		
03/07	Top MMG 21 CF. Refrig.	504			2		
Purchase Invoices							
03/02	Mini Washer & Dryer	916				5	540.00
03/03	S by S 19 CF. Refrig.	917				2	530.00
03/05	DELHI Dishwasher	918				5	350.00
03/06	Mini FR. & Refrig.	919				10	237.95
03/07	IDEA Dishwasher	920				3	236.75
03/06	S by S 19 CF. Refrig.	R917				-1	530.00
	Totals				12	24	

Figure 11.30
Inventory Transactions Report

Hughes Appliances
Inventory Exceptions
03/07/--

Stock No.	Description	Unit Meas.	On Hand	On Order	Reorder Point	Exception
2020	IDEA Gas Dryer	EA	9		10	At/below reorder point
3080	ICY 20 CF. Freezer	EA	6		10	At/below reorder point
3090	Micro Refrig.	EA	0		10	Out of stock

Figure 11.31
Inventory Exceptions Report

TUTORIAL PROBLEM 11-T

STEP 19: Display the Average Cost Valuation Report.
Select *Valuation (Average Cost)* and click *OK*. The report appears in Figure 11.32.

```
                        Hughes Appliances
                   Inventory Valuation (Average Cost)
                              03/07/--
```

Stock No.	Description	On Hand	Cost	Value At Cost	Retail Price	Value At Retail
1010	GD Washer	19	241.00	4579.00	359.95	6839.05
1020	SIMPCO Washer	13	319.08	4148.04	529.95	6889.35
1040	Mini Washer & Dryer	20	540.00	10800.00	798.00	15960.00
2010	IDEA Electric Dryer	24	220.00	5280.00	359.95	8638.80
2020	IDEA Gas Dryer	9	305.00	2745.00	429.95	3869.55
2030	Mini Electric Dryer	11	225.00	2475.00	379.95	4179.45
3010	1 Door 18 CF. Refrig.	18	350.00	6300.00	529.95	9539.10
3020	1 Door 22 CF. Refrig.	11	435.00	4785.00	699.00	7689.00
3030	S by S 19 CF. Refrig.	14	530.00	7420.00	789.00	11046.00
3040	S by S 29 CF. Refrig.	7	1135.00	7945.00	1899.00	13293.00
3050	Top MMG 21 CF. Refrig.	13	455.00	5915.00	699.00	9087.00
3060	Top MMG 25 CF. Refrig.	14	510.00	7140.00	859.95	12039.30
3070	Mini FR. & Refrig.	13	237.95	3093.35	342.50	4452.50
3080	ICY 20 CF. Freezer	6	285.00	1710.00	428.00	2568.00
4010	RBS Electric Range	21	214.50	4504.50	349.99	7349.79
4020	RBS Gas Range	7	310.00	2170.00	435.95	3051.65
5010	DELHI Dishwasher	15	350.00	5250.00	549.95	8249.25
5020	IDEA Dishwasher	20	236.75	4735.00	329.95	6599.00
5030	Trash Compactor	13	233.90	3040.70	389.95	5069.35
	Total Inventory Value			94035.59		146409.14

Figure 11.32
Inventory Valuation (Average Cost) Report

STEP 20: Generate a most-profitable-inventory-item graph and a least-profitable-inventory-item graph.
The graphs are shown in Figures 11.33a and 11.33b.

Chapter 11 Accounts Payable: Purchase Order Processing and Inventory Control

TUTORIAL PROBLEM 11-T

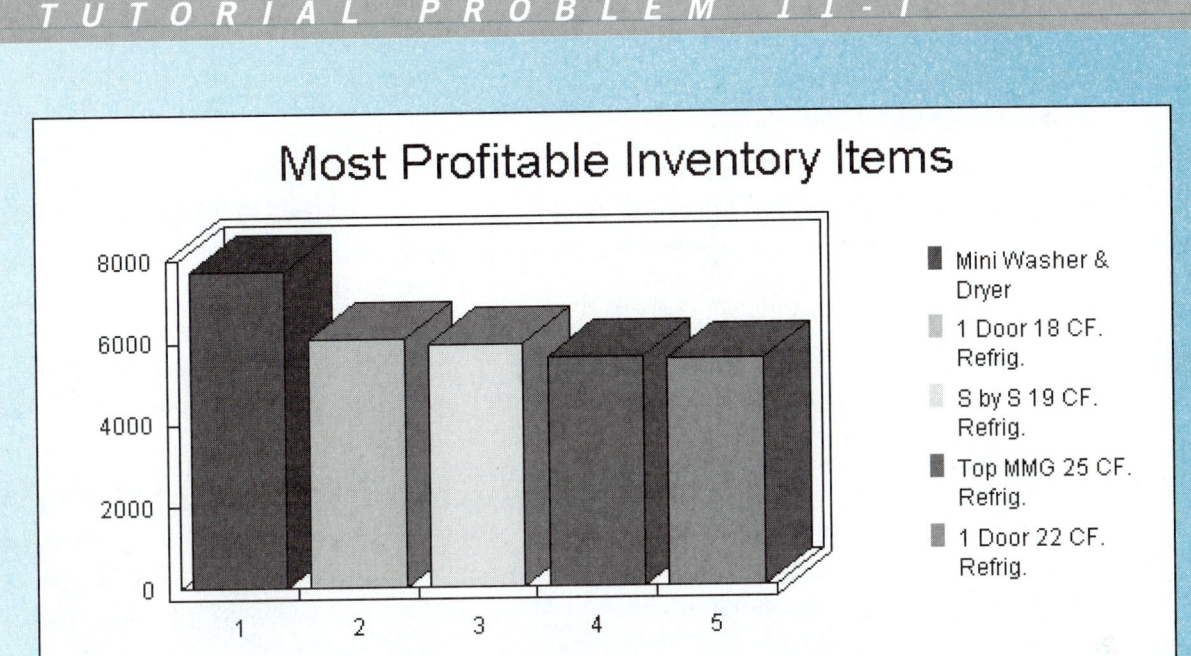

Figure 11.33a
Most-Profitable-Inventory-Item Graph

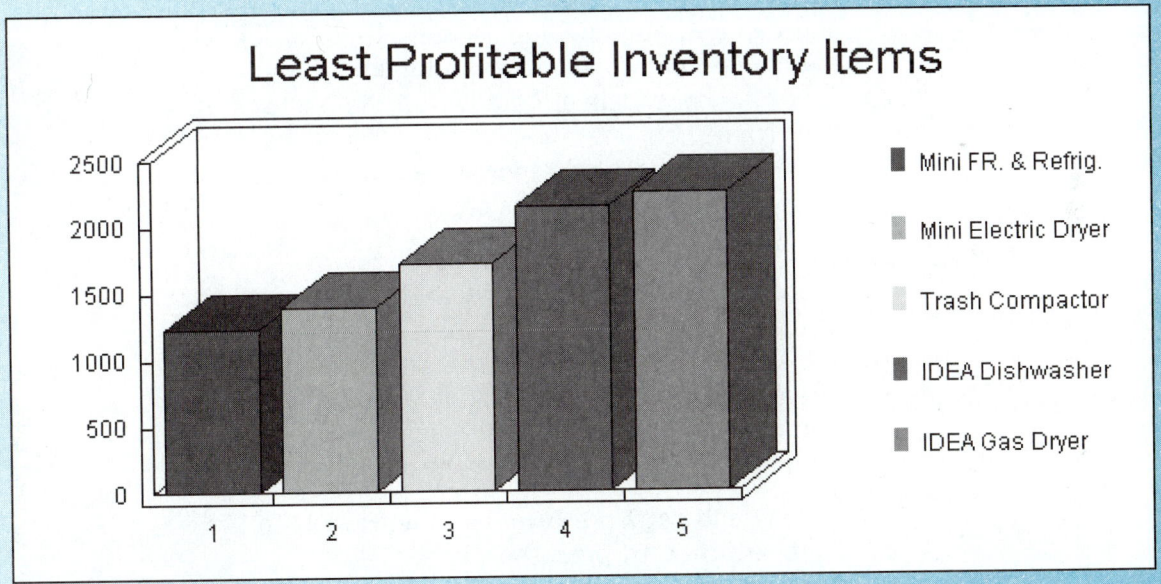

Figure 11.33b
Least-Profitable-Inventory-Item Graph

TUTORIAL PROBLEM 11-T

STEP 21: Save your data.

STEP 22: Optional Spreadsheet Integration Activity.
Hughes Appliances has asked you to use a spreadsheet to calculate the percent of markup for each item in its inventory, based upon the Inventory Valuation (Average Cost) Report. Markup is the amount added to the cost of merchandise to establish the selling (or retail) price.

  a. Display and copy the Inventory Valuation (Average Cost) Report to the clipboard in spreadsheet format.
  b. Start up your spreadsheet software, use the New menu item in the File menu to create a new worksheet, select cell A1 as the current cell, and paste the Inventory Valuation (Average Cost) Report from the clipboard into the spreadsheet.
  c. Enter *Markup* in cell H7 and *Percent* in cell H8. Enter the formula to calculate the Markup Percent in cell H10, and then copy it to cells H11 through H28 and cell H30. Markup Percent = (Value at Retail − Value at Cost) ÷ Value at Cost
  d. Format the report (widen columns, format as currency and percent, align column headings, etc.), similar to the completed report shown in Figure 11.34.
  e. Save your spreadsheet data with a file name of 11-T Your Name.
  f. Print the spreadsheet report.
  g. End your spreadsheet session.

STEP 23: Optional Word Processing Integration Activity.
The manager of the accounting department has asked you to provide a list of all inventory items currently on order. The list should include the average and last cost paid for each item on the list. A memorandum with space left for the inventory on-order information has already been prepared.

  a. Display and copy the Inventory List Report to the clipboard in word processor format.
  b. Start up your word processing software and load the file named AA8 Wordprocessing 11-T as a text file.
  c. Paste the contents of the clipboard into the memorandum at the location specified.

Chapter 11 Accounts Payable: Purchase Order Processing and Inventory Control

TUTORIAL PROBLEM 11-T

d. Enter your name and today's date where indicated.
e. Remove the report headings and align the column headings. Remove all inventory items that do not have on-order quantities and format the information as necessary to match the completed memorandum shown in Figure 11.35.
f. Save the memorandum document with a file name of 11-T Your Name.
g. Print the document.
h. End your word processing session.

Student Name

Hughes Appliances
Inventory Valuation (Average Cost)
As of 03/07/--

Stock No.	Description	On Hand	Cost	Value At Cost	Retail Price	Value At Retail	Markup Percent
1010	GD Washer	19	$241.00	$4,579.00	$359.95	$6,839.05	49.36%
1020	SIMPCO Washer	13	$319.08	$4,148.04	$529.95	$6,889.35	66.09%
1040	Mini Washer & Dryer	20	$540.00	$10,800.00	$798.00	$15,960.00	47.78%
2010	IDEA Electric Dryer	24	$220.00	$5,280.00	$359.95	$8,638.80	63.61%
2020	IDEA Gas Dryer	9	$305.00	$2,745.00	$429.95	$3,869.55	40.97%
2030	Mini Electric Dryer	11	$225.00	$2,475.00	$379.95	$4,179.45	68.87%
3010	1 Door 18 CF. Refrig.	18	$350.00	$6,300.00	$529.95	$9,539.10	51.41%
3020	1 Door 22 CF. Refrig.	11	$435.00	$4,785.00	$699.00	$7,689.00	60.69%
3030	S by S 19 CF. Refrig.	14	$530.00	$7,420.00	$789.00	$11,046.00	48.87%
3040	S by S 29 CF. Refrig.	7	$1,135.00	$7,945.00	$1,899.00	$13,293.00	67.31%
3050	Top MMG 21 CF. Refrig.	13	$455.00	$5,915.00	$699.00	$9,087.00	53.63%
3060	Top MMG 25 CF. Refrig.	14	$510.00	$7,140.00	$859.95	$12,039.30	68.62%
3070	Mini FR. & Refrig.	13	$237.95	$3,093.35	$342.50	$4,452.50	43.94%
3080	ICY 20 CF. Freezer	6	$285.00	$1,710.00	$428.00	$2,568.00	50.18%
4010	RBS Electric Range	21	$214.50	$4,504.50	$349.99	$7,349.79	63.17%
4020	RBS Gas Range	7	$310.00	$2,170.00	$435.95	$3,051.65	40.63%
5010	DELHI Dishwasher	15	$350.00	$5,250.00	$549.95	$8,249.25	57.13%
5020	IDEA Dishwasher	20	$236.75	$4,735.00	$329.95	$6,599.00	39.37%
5030	Trash Compactor	13	$233.90	$3,040.70	$389.95	$5,069.35	66.72%
	Total Inventory Value			$94,035.59		$146,409.14	55.70%

Figure 11.34
Spreadsheet Yearly Sales Report

TUTORIAL PROBLEM 11-T

MEMORANDUM

TO: Hughes Appliances
FROM: Student Name
DATE: (Today's Date)
SUBJECT: Inventory Items that are on Order

As of the end of the current week, Hughes Appliances inventory items that are on order are listed below. I have included the last cost and retail price of each item as well as additional information for your financial planning.

Stock No.	Description	Unit Meas.	On Hand	On Order	Reorder Point	Last Cost	Retail Price
1020	SIMPCO Washer	EA	13	2	8	319.00	529.95
3020	1 Door 22 CF. Refrig.	EA	11	3	10	435.00	699.00
3040	S by S 29 CF. Refrig.	EA	7	2	6	530.00	1899.00
3050	Top MMG 21 CF. Refrig.	EA	13	2	10	455.00	699.00
4020	RBS Gas Range	EA	7	3	6	310.00	435.95

Figure 11.35
Word Processing Memorandum

STEP 24: End the *Automated Accounting* session.

If you are planning your career, searching the Internet using keywords related to your field will provide many new sources of job information. Many job-related web sites allow you to post your resume for employers to see.

E-mail is so easy that people tend to use it too much. Information overload is caused by e-mail boxes full of unnecessary messages.

Chapter 11 Accounts Payable: Purchase Order Processing and Inventory Control

Review and Practice: Applying Your Information Skills

I. MATCHING

Directions: In the *Working Papers*, write the letter of the appropriate term next to each definition.

    a. average cost method
    b. computerized purchase order processing system
    c. FIFO method
    d. Inventory Exceptions Report
    e. Inventory List Report
    f. inventory stock items input form
    g. Inventory Transactions Report
    h. Inventory Valuation Report
    i. LIFO method
    j. purchase invoice
    k. purchase invoice input form
    l. purchase order
    m. purchase order input form
    n. Purchase Order Register
    o. purchase requisition
    p. Purchase Invoice Register
    q. Receiving Report
    r. reorder point
    s. retail price
    t. stock number
    u. unit of measure

1. A two-character field used to identify the unit of measure by which an item is sold (such as EA for each, CS for case, BX for box).

2. An input form used to record additions, changes, and deletions to obsolete inventory items.

3. An input form used to record purchase order transactions when a computerized purchase order processing system is used.

4. A form that shows the description, quantity, and condition of merchandise received from a vendor.

5. A unique code assigned to each stock item for identification.

6. The current price per unit when the item is sold to a customer.

7. The procedures involved in automatically integrating the purchase order, purchase invoice, and cash disbursement data into the inventory and general ledger.

8. An input form used to record purchase invoice and purchase return transactions when a computerized purchase order processing system is used.

9. A report that lists purchase orders in numerical and date order.

10. The minimum quantity that is allowed before additional items must be reordered.

11. A report that lists purchase invoices in numerical order with purchase returns listed last.

12. Formal requests for purchases that are entered into the computerized purchase order system.

13. A report that lists the current status of each inventory item for reference.

14. A document containing a purchase order number, the vendor name, the quantity and description, the expected price, and the terms of the item(s) ordered.

15. A list of all transactions that have affected inventory items during the processing period.

16. A report that lists items in the inventory that are out of stock (quantity on hand of zero or less) and items that are at or below the reorder point (quantity on hand less than or equal to the reorder point).

17. A form that contains the vendor's name, original purchase order number, quantity and description of the merchandise, price, and sales terms of the merchandise sent.

18. An inventory valuation method that uses an average of the actual costs and quantities to calculate the value of an inventory.

19. A report that lists the per-item and total cost and retail prices of all items currently in the inventory.

20. An inventory valuation method that uses the latest costs to calculate the value of an inventory.

21. An inventory valuation method that uses the earliest costs to calculate the value of an inventory.

II. REVIEW QUESTIONS

Directions: Write the answers to each of the following questions in the *Working Papers*.

1. What problem may occur if the merchandise inventory is too low?

2. Why is data not lost when purchase invoices and purchase orders are purged?

3. What information is contained on the Purchase Order Register?
4. What information is contained on the Purchase Invoice Register?
5. What is the purpose of the Inventory List Report?
6. What is the purpose of the Inventory Transactions Report?
7. What is the purpose of the Inventory Exceptions Report?
8. How does the computer determine the value of the inventory based on an average cost as shown in the Valuation (Average Cost) Report?
9. What assumption does the computer make to determine the value of the inventory based on the last-in, first-out method as shown in the Valuation (LIFO) Report?
10. What assumption does the computer make to determine the value of the inventory based on the first-in, first-out method as shown in the Valuation (FIFO) Report?

III. INTERNET ACTIVITY

Directions: If you have access to the Internet, use your browser to find information about international entrepreneur business trends and opportunities. **Hint:** Use *business opportunities* and *entrepreneur* as your search arguments. Report on your findings. Be sure to include the source and the URL (Internet address) of your search.

Independent Practice Problem 11-P

In this problem, you will perform the operating procedures necessary to maintain inventory stock items and process purchase orders, purchase invoices, and cash payment transactions for the week of March 8 through March 14 for Hughes Appliances.

STEP 1: Start up *Automated Accounting 8.0*.

STEP 2: Load the opening balances file named AA8 Problem 11-P.

STEP 3: Enter your name in the User Name text box and click *OK*.

STEP 4: Save the file with a file name of 11-P Your Name.

STEP 5: Enter the following inventory stock item maintenance data:
Add Stock No. 4030; GD Electric Range; unit of measure, EA (Each); reorder point, 5; retail price, $469.95 to the stock item file.

Add Stock No. 4040; GD Gas Range; unit of measure, EA (Each); reorder point, 5; retail price, $539.95 to the stock item file.

Change the retail price of S by S 29 CF. Refrig. (Stock No. 3040) to $1,869.00.

Change the reorder point of GD Washer (Stock No. 1010) to 12 and the retail price to $349.95.

STEP 6: **Enter the following purchase order and purchase invoice transactions:**

Mar. 08 Ordered the following merchandise from ICY Refrigeration Co., terms 2/10, n/30. Purchase Order No. 505.

Description	Quantity	Unit Cost
Micro Refrig.	12	225.00

08 Received the following merchandise for Purchase Order No. 501 from SIMPCO Mfg., Inc., terms 2/10, n/30. Purchase Invoice No. 921.

Description	Quantity	Unit Cost
SIMPCO Washer	2	319.00

08 Ordered the following merchandise from IDEA Appliance Mfg., terms 2/10, n/30. Purchase Order No. 506.

Description	Quantity	Unit Cost
IDEA Gas Dryer	3	305.00

09 Received the following merchandise for Purchase Order No. 503 from MMG Refrigerators, Inc., terms 2/10, n/30. Purchase Invoice No. 922.

Description	Quantity	Unit Cost
1 Door 22 CF. Refrig.	3	426.30
S by S 29 CF. Refrig.	2	1112.30

10 Ordered the following merchandise from RBS Production, Inc., terms 2/10, n/30. Purchase Order No. 507. (**Note:** The Unit Cost is different from the existing unit cost in the inventory records.)

Description	Quantity	Unit Cost
Trash Compactor	1	230.00
Mini Electric Dryer	2	220.00

11 Returned the following merchandise to ICY Refrigeration, Co. Purchase Invoice No. R919.

Description	Quantity	Unit Cost
Mini Fr. & Refrig.	2	237.95

12 Received the following merchandise from Purchase Order No. 502 from RBS Production, Inc., terms 2/10, n/30. Purchase Invoice No. 923.

Description	Quantity	Unit Cost
RBS Gas Range	3	310.00

13 Ordered the following merchandise from ICY Refrigeration, Co., terms 2/10, n/30. Purchase Order No. 508.

Description	Quantity	Unit Cost
ICY 20 CF. Freezer	5	285.00

14 Received the following merchandise for Purchase Order No. 504 from MMG Refrigerators, Inc., terms 2/10, n/30. Purchase Invoice No. 924.

Description	Quantity	Unit Cost
Top MMG 21 CF. Refrig.	2	455.00

STEP 7: Enter the cash payments journal transactions shown below:

Mar. 12 Paid Invoice No. 917 to GD Manufacturing, Inc., $1,060.00, no discount. Check No. 4735.
13 Paid Invoice No. 920 to IDEA Appliance Mfg., $710.25, less 2% discount, $14.21. Check No. 4736.
14 Paid Invoice No. 921 to SIMPCO Mfg., Inc., $638.00, less 2% discount, $12.76. Check No. 4737.

STEP 8: Display the Purchase Order and Purchase Invoice Registers for the period March 8 through March 14.

STEP 9: Display an Inventory List Report.

STEP 10: Display the General, Purchases, and Cash Payments Journals for the period March 8 through March 14.

STEP 11: Display a General Ledger Report for the Accounts Payable, Purchases, Purchases Returns and Allowance, and Purchases Discount accounts.

STEP 12: Display a Trial Balance Report.

STEP 13: Display a Schedule of Accounts Payable.

STEP 14: Display an Accounts Payable Ledger.

STEP 15: Display the Inventory Transactions Report for the period March 8 through March 14.

STEP 16: Display the Inventory Exceptions Report.

STEP 17: Display the LIFO Cost Valuation Report.

STEP 18: Generate the most-profitable-inventory-item graph and the least-profitable-inventory-item graph.

STEP 19: Save your data to disk.

STEP 20: Optional Spreadsheet Integration Activity.
Use a spreadsheet to calculate the percent of markup for each item in Hughes Appliances inventory, based upon the Inventory Valuation (LIFO) Report. Use the optional spreadsheet integration activity in Tutorial Problem 11-T and Figure 11.34 (page 397) as a guide, if necessary.

a. Display and copy the Inventory Valuation (LIFO) Report to the clipboard in spreadsheet format.
b. Start up your spreadsheet software, use the New menu item in the File menu to create a new worksheet, select cell A1 as the current cell, and paste the Inventory Valuation (LIFO) Report from the clipboard into the spreadsheet.
c. Enter *Markup* in cell H7 and *Percent* in cell H8. Enter the formula to calculate the Markup Percent in cell H10, and then copy it to the following cells and the total line.
d. Format the report (widen columns, format as currency and percent, align column headings, etc.).
e. Save your spreadsheet data with a file name of 11-P Your Name.
f. Print the spreadsheet report.
g. End your spreadsheet session.

STEP 21: Optional Word Processing Integration Activity.
You are to complete a memorandum that lists inventory items currently on order. The list should include the last cost and retail price for each item on the list. Refer to Figure 11.35 (page 398) as a guide, if necessary.

a. Display and copy the Inventory List Report to the clipboard in word processor format.
b. Start up your word processing software and load the file named AA8 Wordprocessing 11-T as a text file.
c. Paste the contents of the clipboard into the memorandum at the location specified.
d. Enter your name and today's date where indicated.
e. Remove the report heading and align the column headings. Remove all inventory items that do not have on-order quantities and format the information as necessary.

Chapter 11   Accounts Payable: Purchase Order Processing and Inventory Control   405

      f. Save the memorandum document with a file name of 11-P Your Name.
      g. Print the memorandum.
      h. End your word processing session.

STEP 22: End the *Automated Accounting* session.

Applying Your Technology Skills 11-P

Directions: Using Independent Practice Problem 11-P, write the answers to the following questions in the *Working Papers*.

Register Reports

1. What is the total amount of purchase orders for the period?
2. What is the total amount of purchase invoices for the period?

Inventory List Report

3. What is the last cost for the RBS Electric Range?
4. What is the reorder point for the ICY 20 C.F. Freezer?
5. How many Trash Compactors are on hand?

Journal and Ledger Reports

6. What are the total debits and credits shown in the Purchases Journal?
7. What are the total debits and credits shown in the Cash Payments Journal?
8. From the General Ledger Report, what was the Purchases account balance on March 12?
9. What is the account balance of the following accounts as of March 14?

    (a) Accounts Payable

    (b) Purchases

    (c) Purchases Returns and Allowances

    (d) Purchases Discounts

10. From the Schedule of Accounts Payable, what is the total amount owed?

Inventory Reports and Graphs

11. How many items were ordered during the period?

12. List the item(s) that are out of stock for which there are no items currently on order.

13. What is the inventory LIFO value at cost?

14. From the graphs, what is the most profitable inventory item?

Mastery Problem 11-M

In this problem, you will perform the operating procedures necessary to maintain inventory stock items and process purchase orders, purchase invoices, and cash payment transactions for the week of March 15 through March 21 for Hughes Appliances.

STEP 1: Start up *Automated Accounting 8.0*.

STEP 2: Load the opening balances file named AA8 Problem 11-M.

STEP 3: Enter your name in the User Name text box and click *OK*.

STEP 4: Save the file with a file name of 11-M Your Name.

STEP 5: Enter the following inventory stock item maintenance data:
Add Stock No. 4050; Mini Gas Range; unit of measure, EA (Each); reorder point, 6; retail price, $199.95 to the stock item file.

Add Stock No. 5040; Garbage Disposal; unit of measure, EA (Each); reorder point, 8; retail price, $119.95 to the stock item file.

Change the retail price of DELHI Dishwasher (Stock No. 5010) to $529.95.

Change the reorder point of 1 Door 18CF. Refrig. (Stock No. 3010) to 10 and the retail price to $499.95.

STEP 6: Enter the following purchase order and purchase invoice transactions:
Mar. 15 Ordered the following merchandise from GD Manufacturing, Inc., terms 2/10, n/30. Purchase Order No. 509.

Description	Quantity	Unit Cost
GD Electric Range	8	280.00
GD Gas Range	8	325.00

17 Received the following merchandise for Purchase Order No. 505 from ICY Refrigeration Co., terms 2/10, n/30. Purchase Invoice No. 925.

Description	Quantity	Unit Cost
Micro Refrig	12	225.00

    18   Received the following merchandise for Purchase Order No. 506 from IDEA Appliance Mfg., terms 2/10, n/30. Purchase Invoice No. 926.

Description	Quantity	Unit Cost
IDEA Gas Dryer	3	305.00

    19   Returned the following merchandise to ICY Refrigeration, Co. Purchase Invoice No. R925.

Description	Quantity	Unit Cost
Micro Refrig	1	225.00

    20   Received the following merchandise from Purchase Order No. 507 from RBS Production, Inc., terms 2/10, n/30. Purchase Invoice No. 927.

Description	Quantity	Unit Cost
Trash Compactor	1	230.00
Mini Electric Dryer	2	220.00

    21   Received the following merchandise for Purchase Order No. 509 from GD Manufacturing, Inc., terms 2/10, n/30. Purchase Invoice No. 928.

Description	Quantity	Unit Cost
CD Electric Range	2	280.00
GD Gas Range	1	325.00

STEP 7: Enter the cash payments journal transactions shown below:

    Mar. 19   Paid Invoice No. 922 to MMG Refrigerators, Inc., $3,503.50, less 2% discount, $70.07. Check No. 4738.
          20   Paid Invoice No. 923 to RBS Production, Inc., $930.00, less 2% discount, $18.60. Check No. 4739.
          21   Paid Invoice No. 924 to MMG Refrigerators, Inc., $910.00, less 2% discount, $18.20. Check No. 4740.

STEP 8: Display the Purchase Order and Purchase Invoice Registers for the period March 15 through March 21.

STEP 9: Display an Inventory List Report.

STEP 10: Display the General, Purchases, and Cash Payments Journals for the period March 15 through March 21.

STEP 11: Display a General Ledger Report for the Accounts Payable, Purchases, Purchases Returns and Allowance, and Purchases Discount accounts.

STEP 12: Display a Trial Balance Report.

STEP 13: Display a Schedule of Accounts Payable.

STEP 14: Display an Accounts Payable Ledger.

STEP 15: Display the Inventory Transactions Report for the period March 15 through March 21.

STEP 16: Display the Inventory Exceptions Report.

STEP 17: Display the FIFO Cost Valuation Report.

STEP 18: Generate the most-profitable-inventory-item graph and the least-profitable-inventory-item graph.

STEP 19. Save your data to disk.

STEP 20: Optional Spreadsheet Integration Activity.
Use a spreadsheet to calculate the percent of markup for each item in Hughes Appliances inventory, based upon the Inventory Valuation (FIFO) Report. Use the optional spreadsheet integration activity in Tutorial Problem 11-T and Figure 11.34 (page 397) as a guide, if necessary.

a. Display and copy the Inventory Valuation (FIFO) Report to the clipboard in spreadsheet format.
b. Start up your spreadsheet software, use the New menu item in the File menu to create a new worksheet, select cell A1 as the current cell, and paste the Inventory Valuation (FIFO) Report from the clipboard into the spreadsheet.
c. Enter *Markup* in cell H7 and *Percent* in cell H8. Enter the formula to calculate the Markup Percent in cell H10, and then copy it to the following cells and the total line.
d. Format the report (widen columns, format as currency and percent, align column headings, etc.).
e. Save your spreadsheet data with a file name of 11-M Your Name.
f. Print the spreadsheet report.
g. End your spreadsheet session.

STEP 21: Optional Word Processing Integration Activity.
You are to complete a memorandum that lists inventory items currently on order. The list should include the last cost and retail price for each item on the list. Refer to Figure 11.35 (page 398) as a guide, if necessary.

Chapter 11 Accounts Payable: Purchase Order Processing and Inventory Control

   a. Display and copy the Inventory List Report to the clipboard in word processor format.
   b. Start up your word processing software and load the file named AA8 Wordprocessing 11-T as a text file.
   c. Paste the contents of the clipboard into the memorandum at the location specified.
   d. Enter your name and today's date where indicated.
   e. Remove the report heading and align the column headings. Remove all inventory items that do not have on-order quantities and format the information as necessary.
   f. Save the memorandum document with a file name of 11-M Your Name.
   g. Print the memorandum.
   h. End your word processing session.

STEP 22: End the *Automated Accounting* session.

Applying Your Technology Skills 11-M

Directions: Using Mastery Problem 11-M, write the answers to the following questions in the *Working Papers*.

Register Reports

1. What is the total amount of purchase orders for the period?
2. What is the total amount of purchase invoices for the period?

Inventory List Report

3. What is the last cost for the RBS Gas Range?
4. What is the reorder point for the Mini Washer & Dryer?
5. How many SIMPCO Washers are on hand?

Journal and Ledger Reports

6. What are the total debits and credits shown in the Purchases Journal?
7. What are the total debits and credits shown in the Cash Payments Journal?
8. From the General Ledger Report, what was the Accounts Payable account balance on March 18?

9. What is the account balance of the following accounts as of March 21?

   (a) Accounts Payable

   (b) Purchases

   (c) Purchases Returns and Allowances

   (d) Purchases Discounts

10. From the Schedule of Accounts Payable, what is the total amount owed?

Inventory Reports and Graphs

11. How many items were ordered during the period?

12. List the item(s) that are out of stock for which there are no items currently on order.

13. What is the inventory FIFO value at cost?

14. From the graphs, what is the most profitable inventory item?

Chapter 12

ACCOUNTS RECEIVABLE: SALES ORDER PROCESSING AND INVENTORY CONTROL

KEY TERMS

Sales Order Processing
Computerized Sales Order Processing System
Sales Invoice
Sales Return
Sales Invoices Input Form

LEARNING OBJECTIVES

Upon completion of this chapter, you will be able to:

1. Complete the sales invoices input form.
2. Enter sales and sales return transactions and generate sales invoices.
3. Display reports reflecting sales order processing and inventory integration.

INTRODUCTION

An organization's revenue depends upon its ability to sell its products or services to customers. To accomplish this task, a sales order processing system is used. **Sales order processing** consists of the procedures and controls involved in preparing invoices, updating accounting records, and shipping merchandise.

The complexity of sales order systems and the procedures they use vary greatly depending upon the size of the business and the products or services provided. Many businesses have turned to the computer to help their sales order processing due to the large volume of transactions and the complexities of maintaining accurate inventory and other accounting related records. A **computerized sales order processing system** consists of the procedures involved in preparing a sales invoice and automatically integrating the data it contains into the inventory and general ledger records. A **sales invoice** is a form used to describe the goods sold, the quantity, and the price. It is used as a source document for recording sales-on-account transactions.

Most computerized sales order processing systems enable businesses to prepare the invoice at the time of sale or at the time an order is received. As the sales invoice is prepared, the computer checks the inventory to make sure the goods are available. If any of the goods ordered are out of stock, the computer immediately notifies the user so action can be taken to replenish stock. When the computer finds stock on hand, it updates inventory and other accounting-related records and

ETHICS

Many people believe that industry standards should be imposed to eliminate the incompatibility problems that exist among computer hardware manufacturers and software developers. For example, unless special hardware is added or special software is used, software that is written for an Apple Macintosh computer system will not run on an IBM personal computer. Other people believe that industry standards would inhibit creativity, restrict competition, and hamper product development.

Critical Thinking

1. Do you think the present incompatibility of hardware and software is an ethical issue? Explain.

2. Do you think industry standards should be imposed to make all computer hardware and software compatible? Defend your opinion.

generates a sales invoice. Depending on the type of business and merchandise sold, the sales invoice may be given to the customer at the time of sale. Or, the sales invoice may be included with the merchandise when it is shipped to the customer. The sales invoice may be sent to the warehouse to be used to fill the order and prepare it for shipment. (When a sales invoice is sent to the warehouse to be used to fill an order, it is known as a *pick list* or *picking slip*.)

A computerized sales order processing system should also be able to account for sales return transactions. A **sales return** is a credit allowed a customer for the sales price of returned merchandise, resulting in a decrease in the vendor's accounts receivable. In addition, the inventory records are updated to reflect the return of inventory.

In *Automated Accounting 8.0*, a complete invoice is prepared for each sale on account and each sales return. The sales invoice contains the customer name, credit terms, revenue account, invoice number, date, and sales tax percent, as well as the quantity, description, and selling price of each item from inventory sold. As shown in Figure 12.1, when invoice data are entered, the inventory records are updated. The quantity on hand is reduced by the quantity sold, or increased in the case of a sales return, and other sales information is stored for later reporting purposes. Journal entries resulting from the sale are created and entered into the sales journal and posted to the general ledger. The customer's account in the subsidiary ledger is updated to reflect the amount owed. Finally, a sales invoice is generated. A copy may be given to the customer at the

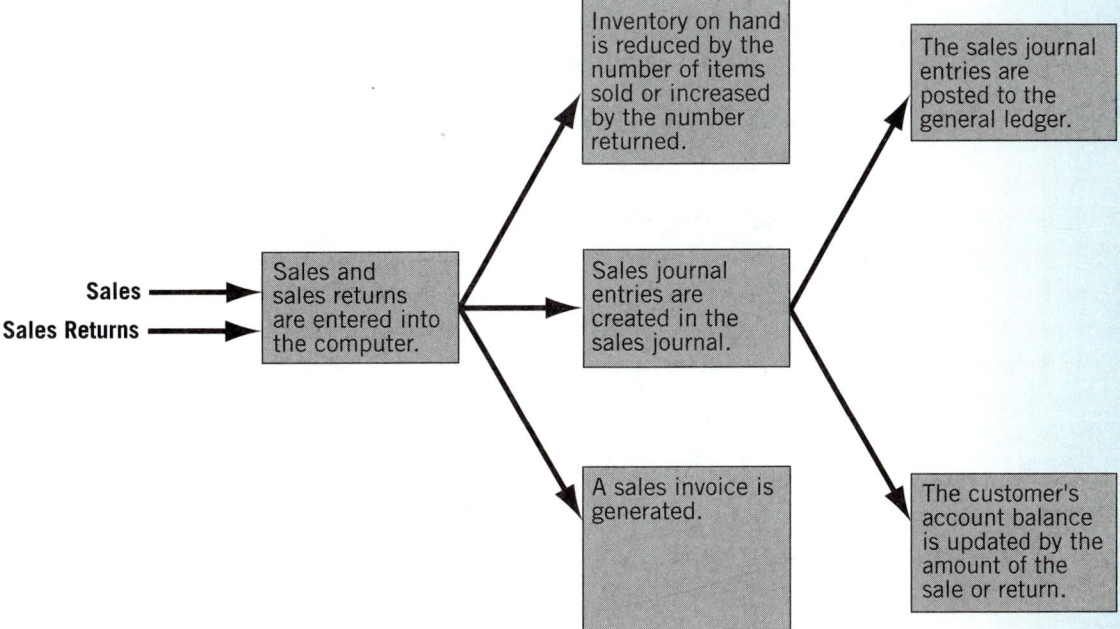

Figure 12.1
Computerized Sales Order Processing Integration

time of the sale, packaged with the merchandise, or mailed after the merchandise is shipped. Sometime during the month, a statement of account that shows all account activity and current account balance is generated and sent to each customer who has an outstanding balance.

The examples used in this chapter are for Park Vacuum Cleaners, a retailing business. The business sells vacuum cleaners, vacuum cleaner supplies, and attachments to local customers. Only information related to sales order processing and related reports will be discussed in this chapter.

SALES INVOICES INPUT FORM

A **sales invoices input form** is an input form used to record sales and sales return transactions when a computerized sales order processing system is used. The sales invoices input form illustrated in Figure 12.2 shows an example of how a sale to Lutz Industries, Inc., and a sales return from Frost Department Stores are recorded.

Sales and sales return transactions are entered in the Other Activities window in the Sales Invoice tab. Each field in the sales invoices input

SALES INVOICES INPUT FORM

Run Date 02/07/-- **Problem No.** Example

Customer	Terms	Revenue Account	Invoice Number	Date mm/dd/yy	Sales Tax %	Qty	Inventory Item	Price
Lutz Industries, Inc.	2/10, n/30	Sales	525	02/02/--	7	1	Kelly Canister Vac	689.95
						4	Canister Cleaner Bag	3.85
						2	Allergenci Bag	8.95
Frost Department Stores		Sales Ret	R511	02/06/--	7	-2	Battery Powered Vac	38.95

- Sales Return—Frost Department Stores returned two Battery Powered Vacs that were originally sold at $38.95 with a 7% sales tax. The number of items returned is recorded in the Qty column as a *negative* number, and the Revenue Account column indicates that the transaction is a sales return. The invoice number begins with an *R* to indicate a return.

- Sale—Sold one Kelly Canister Vac for $689.95, four Canister Cleaner Bags at $3.85 each, and two Allergenci Bags for $8.95 each at 7% sales tax to Lutz Industries, Inc., with terms of 2/10, n/30. If payment is made within 10 days, the customer can take a 2% discount off the merchandise; if not, then payment in full is due in 30 days from the date of the invoice. The sales invoice number is recorded in the Invoice Number column, and the Revenue Account column indicates that the transaction is a sale.

Figure 12.2
Sales Invoices Input Form (Examples)

Chapter 12 Accounts Receivable: Sales Order Processing and Inventory Control

form corresponds to a text box or grid cell in this tab. Therefore, the explanation provided in Figure 12.2 detailing how to record sales and sales return transactions on an input form is the same for entering them into the computer.

SALES AND SALES RETURN TRANSACTIONS

The Sales Invoice tab is used to enter sales and sales return transactions and to generate sales invoices. Sales and sales return transactions entered in this window are automatically integrated into the general ledger and inventory. A sales transaction automatically creates the respective journal entry in the sales journal and then posts the entry to the general ledger. A sales return transaction automatically creates the respective journal entry in the general journal and then posts the entry to the general ledger. Likewise, the transactions are automatically recorded in the Other Activities Inventory window to keep the inventory records up to date.

When the Other toolbar button is clicked or the Other Activities menu item is chosen from the Data menu, the Other Activities window will appear. Click the Sales Invoice tab to activate it, as shown in Figure 12.3. The data shown in the example in Figure 12.3 are for the first transaction recorded on the sales invoices input form in Figure 12.2.

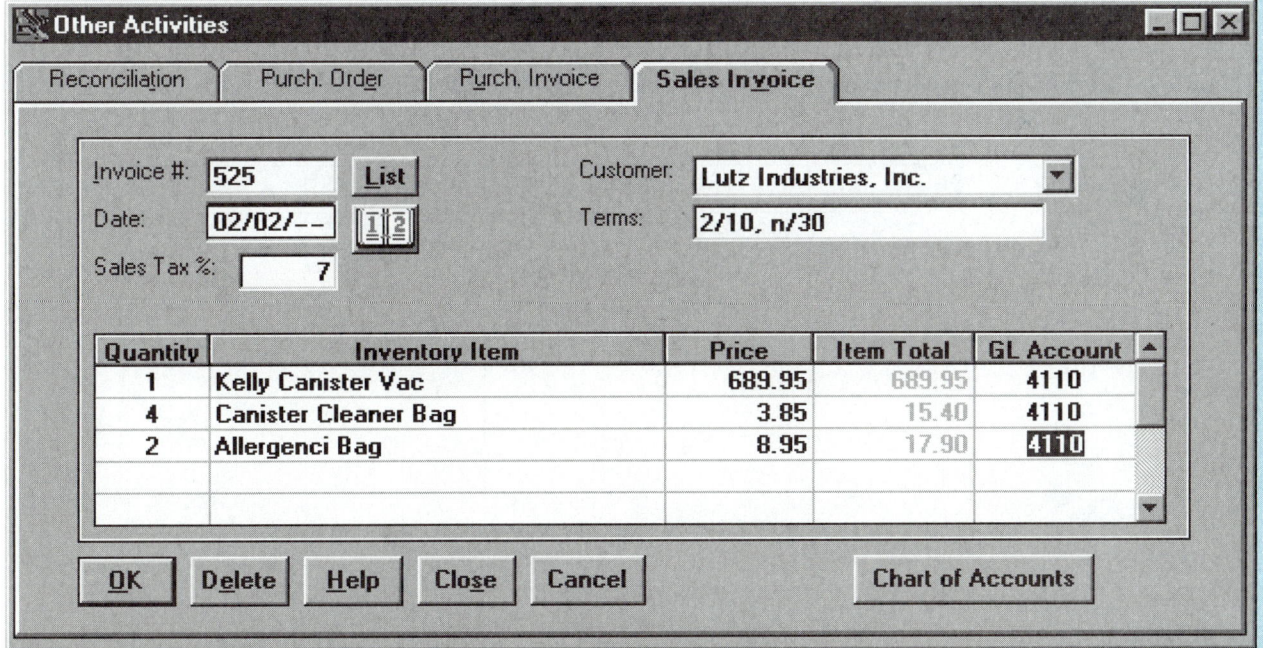

Figure 12.3
Sales Invoice Tab

Entering a Sales or Sales Return Transaction

To enter a sales invoice or sales return transaction, enter the invoice number, date, sales tax percent, customer name, and terms of the sale. Then enter the number of items sold in the Quantity field (*if the item is a sales return, enter the quantity as a negative value*), choose the inventory item from the Inventory Items drop-down list, and enter the selling price in the Price field (if it is not the same as that automatically displayed for the item). Repeat this procedure for each item sold or returned by the customer.

The computer will automatically multiply the quantity by the price and place the amount in the Item Total column. The computer will also automatically place the Sales general ledger account number in the GL Account column. (If the quantity is a negative number, indicating a sales return, the computer will insert the Sales Return and Allowance account number.)

After the sales invoice or sales return transaction has been entered and the OK button clicked, a computer-generated sales invoice, similar to the example shown in Figure 12.4, will appear. Click the Print button to print the invoice to an attached printer, or click the Close button to dismiss the invoice and continue.

fyi...

If the item chosen has an on-hand quantity at or below its reorder point, a warning message will appear within a red bar at the bottom of the window, indicating this condition.

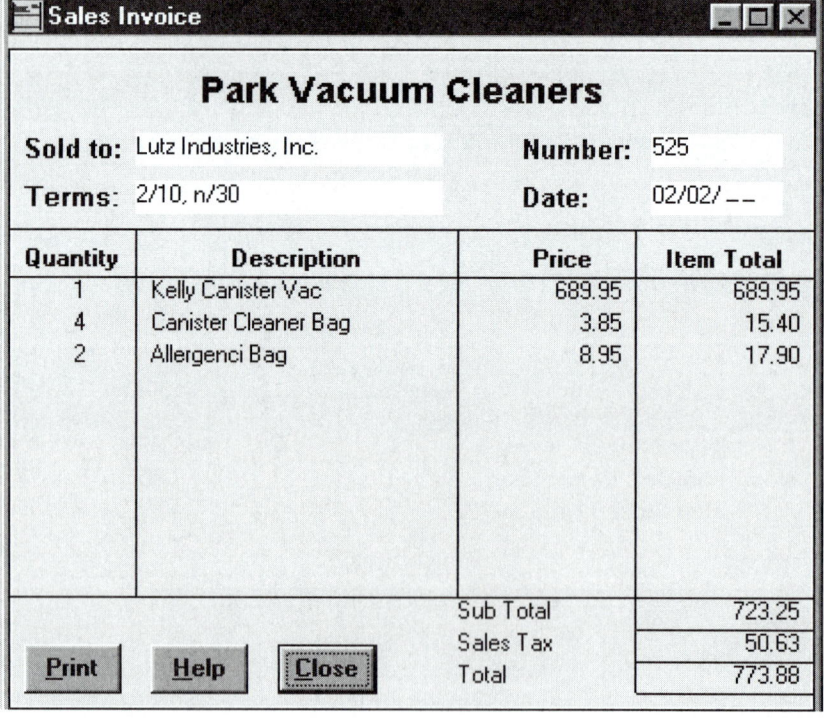

Figure 12.4
Sales Invoice

Chapter 12 Accounts Receivable: Sales Order Processing and Inventory Control

Changing a Sales Transaction

To change a previously entered sales invoice or sales return transaction, click the List button to the right of the Invoice # text box to display a list of invoices. An example sales invoice list is shown in Figure 12.5.

Choose the invoice to be changed from the Sales Invoice list and click OK. Select the text box for the data you wish to change, enter the correction, and click the OK button to record your change.

Figure 12.5
Sales Invoice List

Deleting a Sales Transaction

To delete a previously entered sales invoice or sales return transaction, click the List button to the right of the Invoice # text box and choose the invoice to be deleted. Click the Delete button. When the Delete Confirmation dialog box appears, click Yes.

PURGE SALES INVOICES

Automated Accounting 8.0 has a capacity of 50 sales invoice transactions. If this capacity is exceeded, an alert dialog box will appear, informing you of this condition. Before additional invoices can be entered, previously entered invoices must be erased by choosing the Purge Invoices and Purchase Orders menu item from the Option menu. When this menu item is chosen, a dialog box will appear, asking you to confirm whether you indeed want to purge invoices and purchase orders (in the event you accidentally chose this menu item). Since the sales and purchase invoices and purchase orders previously entered have been automatically integrated into the inventory and general ledger, purging them will not cause any information to be lost. A backup file should be made before the invoices and purchase orders are purged. This condition will not occur with this textbook since none of the problems exceed the system capacity.

Chapter Review

1. A computerized sales order processing system consists of the procedures involved in preparing a sales invoice and automatically integrating the data it contains into the inventory and general ledger. As sales invoice (or sales return) data are entered into the computer: (1) inventory records are updated; (2) journal entries resulting from the sale are created and entered into the sales journal and posted to the general ledger; (3) the customer's account in the customer's file is updated; and (4) a sales invoice is generated.

2. The sales invoices input form may be used to record sales and sales return transactions.

3. Sales and sales return transactions are entered into the computer in the Other Activities Sales Invoice tab. A sales invoice is automatically generated by the computer for sales and sales return transactions entered into the computer.

4. Purging invoices and purchase orders is the process in which previously entered invoices and purchase orders are erased when capacity is reached.

Most financial institutions offer online banking services to their customers. These services give you the ability to access your accounts from a computer, transfer money from one account to another, and pay bills by authorizing the bank to disburse money.

ACCOUNTING CAREERS IN DEPTH

Mortgage Clerk

A mortgage clerk performs any combination of the following duties to process payments and maintain records of mortgage loans:

- Using a computer to type letters, forms, checks, and other documents used for collecting, disbursing, and recording mortgage principal, interest, and escrow account payments.
- Using a computer to answer customer questions regarding mortgage accounts and correcting records.
- Examining documents such as deeds, assignments, and mortgages to ensure compliance with escrow instructions, institution policy, and legal requirements.
- Recording the disbursement of funds to pay insurance and tax.
- Typing notices to the government and specifying changes to loan documents, such as a discharge of mortgage.
- Ordering property insurance policies to ensure protection against loss on mortgaged property.
- Entering data in a computer to generate tax and insurance premium payment notices to customers.
- Reviewing printouts of allocations for interest, principal, insurance, or tax payments to locate errors.
- Using a computer to correct errors.

A mortgage clerk may also be responsible for calling or writing loan applicants to obtain information for bank officials.

Experience with high-school accounting would provide a good background for a job applicant interested in a mortgage clerk position. In addition, attention to detail is an important requirement in this type of job. The ability to effectively deal with the public in answering questions and gathering information would also be necessary.

A mortgage clerk may be designated according to the type of work that has been assigned—for example, Escrow Clerk, Foreclosure Clerk, Insurance Clerk, or Tax Clerk. Because there are so many loan institutions, a job applicant would have a relatively large field in which to search for work. Once a position has been secured, the experience gained on the job would be helpful when looking toward advancement opportunities in the industry.

TUTORIAL PROBLEM 12-T

In this problem, you will process the sales and purchase transactions for the week of February 1 through February 7 of the current year for Park Vacuum Cleaners. You will perform the operating procedures necessary to process sales invoices, sales return, purchase orders, purchase invoices, and purchase return transactions using the sales order and purchase order processing features of *Automated Accounting 8.0*.

STEP 1: Start up *Automated Accounting 8.0*.

STEP 2: Load the opening balances file named AA8 Problem 12-T.

STEP 3: Enter your name in the User Name text box and click *OK*.

STEP 4: Save the file with a file name of 12-T Your Name.

STEP 5: Enter the purchase order, purchase invoice, and sales invoice transactions shown below.

From the Other Activities window, click the appropriate tab and enter the following transactions. Sales Invoice No. 525 with its accompanying sales invoice is shown in Figure 12.6 as a guide.

Feb. 02 Sold the following merchandise to Lutz Industries, Inc., terms 2/10, n/30, 7% sales tax, Sales Invoice No. 525.

Description	Quantity Sold	Selling Price
Kelly Canister Vac	1	689.95
Canister Cleaner Bag	4	3.85
Allergenci Bag	2	8.95

02 Ordered the following merchandise from Heyer Manufacturing, Inc., terms 2/10, n/30. Purchase Order No. 275.

Description	Quantity	Unit Cost
Allergenci Bag	12	5.35

03 Sold the following merchandise to Martin Cramer, terms 30 days, 7% sales tax, Sales Invoice No. 526.

Description	Quantity Sold	Selling Price
Electric Broom	1	99.99

Chapter 12 Accounts Receivable: Sales Order Processing and Inventory Control 421

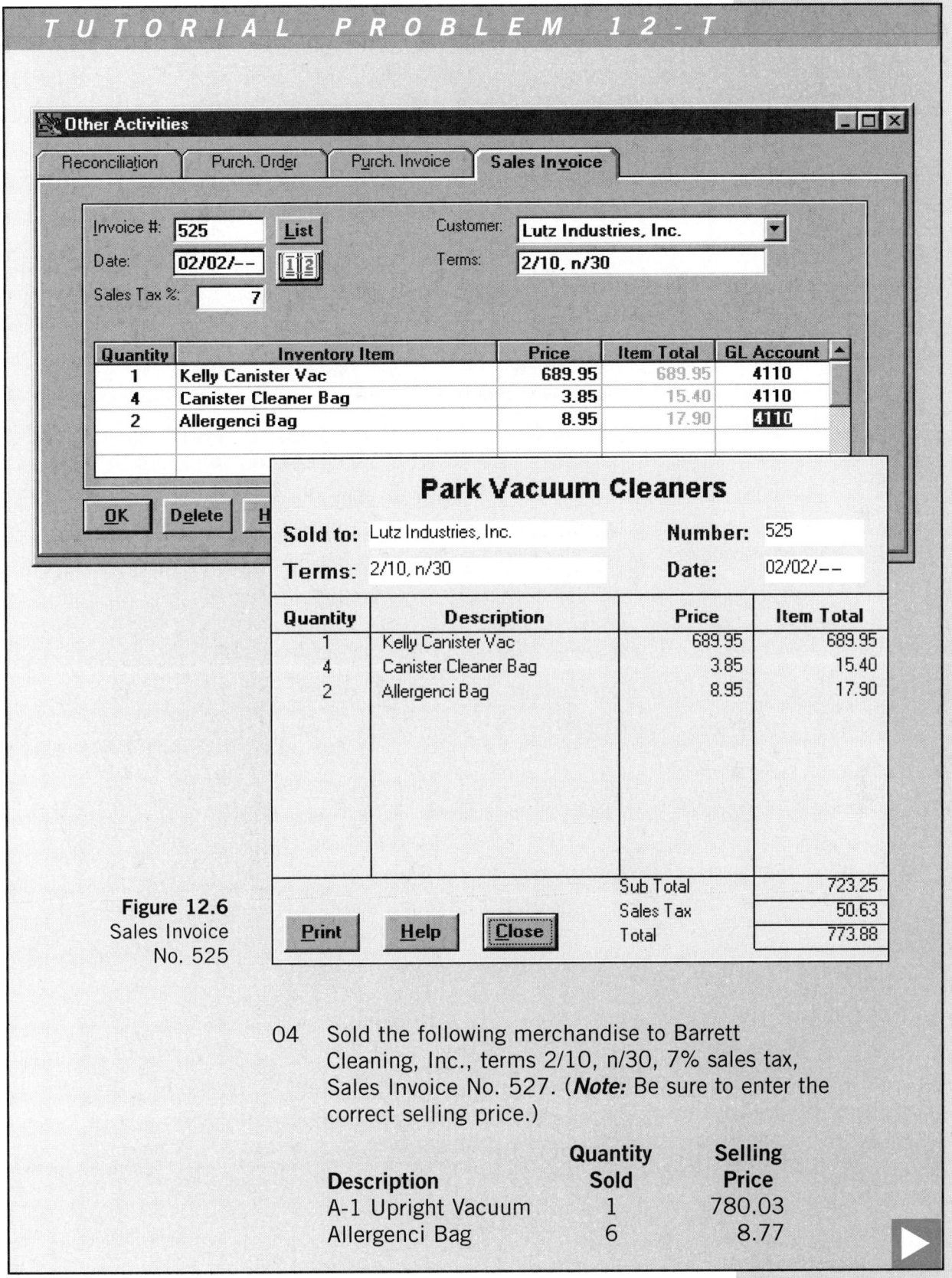

Figure 12.6
Sales Invoice
No. 525

04   Sold the following merchandise to Barrett Cleaning, Inc., terms 2/10, n/30, 7% sales tax, Sales Invoice No. 527. (*Note:* Be sure to enter the correct selling price.)

Description	Quantity Sold	Selling Price
A-1 Upright Vacuum	1	780.03
Allergenci Bag	6	8.77

TUTORIAL PROBLEM 12-T

04 Received the following merchandise for Purchase Order No. 271 from Kelly Vacuum Cleaners, terms 2/10, n/30. Purchase Invoice No. 856.

Description	Quantity	Unit Cost
Kelly Canister Vac	7	405.00

05 Sold the following merchandise to Roger Taylor, terms 30 days, 7% sales tax, Sales Invoice No. 528.

Description	Quantity Sold	Selling Price
Wet & Dry Vacuum	1	325.00

05 Received the following merchandise for Purchase Order No. 272 from Rupp Accessories, Inc., terms 2/10, n/30. Purchase Invoice No. 857.

Description	Quantity	Unit Cost
Canister Cleaner Bag	64	2.30

06 Received the following merchandise for Purchase Order No. 273 from Ness Vacuum Cleaner Co., terms 2/10, n/30. Purchase Invoice No. 858.

Description	Quantity	Unit Cost
Pile Lifter Brush	5	31.50

06 The following merchandise was returned to Park Vacuum Cleaners by Frost Department Stores, 7% sales tax, Sales Return No. R511. (**Note:** Remember to use a minus sign for the quantity on a sales return.)

Description	Quantity Returned	Price
Battery Powered Vac	2	38.95

06 Sold the following merchandise to Braam Company, 2/10, n/30, 7% sales tax, Sales Invoice No. 529.

Description	Quantity Sold	Selling Price
Ness Canister Vacuum	1	369.99
Wet & Dry Vacuum	1	325.00
Steam Cleaner	1	219.00
Canister Cleaner Bag	16	3.85

TUTORIAL PROBLEM 12-T

07   Sold the following merchandise to Wilmes Motel, terms 30 days, 7% sales tax, Sales Invoice No. 530.

Description	Quantity Sold	Selling Price
Heyer Upright Vacuum	1	485.00
Upright Cleaner Bag	6	3.95

07   Ordered the following merchandise from Rupp Accessories, Inc., terms 2/10, n/30. Purchase Order No. 276.

Description	Quantity	Unit Cost
Attachment Kit	2	32.95
Upright Cleaner Bag	12	2.35

STEP 6: Enter the cash-payment and cash-receipt transactions shown below and illustrated in Figures 12.7a and 12.7b.

Feb. 03 Received cash on account from Barrett Cleaning, Inc., covering Sales Invoice No. 518 for $620.35, less 2% discount, $12.40. Receipt No. R518.

05 Received cash on account from Lutz Industries, Inc., covering Sales Invoice No. 514 for $1,247.50, less 2% discount, $24.95. Receipt No. R519.

Date	Refer.	A.P. Debit	Purchase Disc. Cr	Cash Credit	Vendor
02/06/--	C3618	2835.00	56.70	2778.30	Kelly Vacuum Cleaners
02/07/--	C3619	147.20	2.94	144.26	Rupp Accessories, Inc.
02/07/--	C3620	157.50	3.15	154.35	Ness Vacuum Cleaner Co.

Figure 12.7a
Cash Payments

Date	Refer.	A.R. Credit	Sales Credit	Sales Tax Pay. Cr	Sales Disc. Dr	Cash Debit	Customer
02/03/--	R518	620.35			12.40	607.95	Barrett Cleaning, Inc.
02/05/--	R519	1247.50			24.95	1222.55	Lutz Industries, Inc.
02/07/--	R520	3150.00			63.00	3087.00	Frost Department Stores

Figure 12.7b
Cash Receipts

TUTORIAL PROBLEM 12-T

06 Paid Invoice No. 856 to Kelly Vacuum Cleaners, $2,835.00, less 2% discount, $56.70. Check No. 3618.

07 Paid Invoice No. 857 to Rupp Accessories, Inc., $147.20, less 2% discount, $2.94. Check No. 3619.

07 Received cash on account from Frost Department Stores, covering Sales Invoice No. 520 for $3,150.00, less 2% discount, $63.00. Receipt No. R520.

07 Paid Invoice No. 858 to Ness Vacuum Cleaner Co., $157.50, less 2% discount, $3.15. Check No. 3620.

STEP 7: **Display the Purchase Order, Purchase Invoice, and Sales Invoice Registers for the period February 1 through February 7.**

The reports are shown in Figures 12.8a, 12.8b, and 12.8c.

```
                     Park Vacuum Cleaners
                    Purchase Order Register
                           02/07/--
```

P.O. Number	P.O. Date	Vendor Name	P.O. Amount
275	02/02/01	Heyer Manufacturing, Inc.	64.20
276	02/07/01	Rupp Accessories, Inc.	94.10
		Total Amount	158.30

Figure 12.8a
Purchase Order Register

Lurkers are members of newsgroups or e-mail discussion lists who read the postings but do not post messages of their own. Because you never know all the people who will be reading your messages, always use common sense and etiquette.

TUTORIAL PROBLEM 12-T

```
                    Park Vacuum Cleaners
                   Purchase Invoice Register
                          02/07/--

Invoice    Invoice      Vendor                         Invoice
Number     Date         Name                           Amount

856        02/04/01     Kelly Vacuum Cleaners          2835.00
857        02/05/01     Rupp Accessories, Inc.          147.20
858        02/06/01     Ness Vacuum Cleaner Co.         157.50
                                                      --------
                        Total Amount                   3139.70
                                                      ========
```

Figure 12.8b
Purchase Invoice Register

```
                    Park Vacuum Cleaners
                    Sales Invoice Register
                          02/07/--

Invoice    Invoice      Customer                Invoice     Sales
Number     Date         Name                    Amount      Tax

525        02/02/01     Lutz Industries, Inc.    723.25     50.63
526        02/03/01     Martin Cramer             99.99      7.00
527        02/04/01     Barrett Cleaning, Inc.   832.65     58.29
528        02/05/01     Roger Taylor             325.00     22.75
529        02/06/01     Braam Company            975.59     68.29
530        02/07/01     Wilmes Motel             508.70     35.61
R511       02/06/01     Frost Department Stores  -77.90     -5.45
                                                --------   -------
                        Total Amount            3387.28    237.12
                                                ========   =======
```

Figure 12.8c
Sales Invoice Register

TUTORIAL PROBLEM 12-T

STEP 8: **Display the General, Purchases, Cash Payments, Sales, and Cash Receipts Journals for the period February 1 through February 7.**

The journal reports are shown in Figures 12.9a, 12.9b, 12.9c, 12.9d (page 428), and 12.9e (page 428).

Park Vacuum Cleaners
General Journal
02/07/--

Date	Refer.	Acct.	Title	Debit	Credit
02/06	R511	4120	Sales Returns & Allow.	77.90	
02/06	R511	2120	Sales Tax Payable	5.45	
02/06	R511	1130	AR/Frost Department Stores		83.35
			Totals	83.35	83.35

Figure 12.9a
General Journal

Park Vacuum Cleaners
Purchases Journal
02/07/--

Date	Inv. No.	Acct.	Title	Debit	Credit
02/04	856	5110	Purchases	2835.00	
02/04	856	2110	AP/Kelly Vacuum Cleaners		2835.00
02/05	857	5110	Purchases	147.20	
02/05	857	2110	AP/Rupp Accessories, Inc.		147.20
02/06	858	5110	Purchases	157.50	
02/06	858	2110	AP/Ness Vacuum Cleaner Co.		157.50
			Totals	3139.70	3139.70

Figure 12.9b
Purchases Journal

Chapter 12 Accounts Receivable: Sales Order Processing and Inventory Control

TUTORIAL PROBLEM 12-T

```
                    Park Vacuum Cleaners
                    Cash Payments Journal
                          02/07/--

Date    Ck. No.  Acct.   Title                      Debit      Credit

02/06   C3618    2110    AP/Kelly Vacuum Cleaners   2835.00
02/06   C3618    1110    Cash                                  2778.30
02/06   C3618    5130    Purchases Discount                      56.70

02/07   C3619    2110    AP/Rupp Accessories, Inc.   147.20
02/07   C3619    1110    Cash                                   144.26
02/07   C3619    5130    Purchases Discount                       2.94

02/07   C3620    2110    AP/Ness Vacuum Cleaner Co.  157.50
02/07   C3620    1110    Cash                                   154.35
02/07   C3620    5130    Purchases Discount                       3.15
                                                   --------   --------
                        Totals                      3139.70    3139.70
                                                   ========   ========
```

Figure 12.9c
Cash Payments Journal

STEP 9: **Display a General Ledger Report for the Accounts Receivable, Sales, Sales Returns and Allowance, and Sales Discount accounts.**
The general ledger reports appear in Figures 12.10a and 12.10b (page 429).

STEP 10: **Display a Trial Balance Report.**
The trial balance report is shown in Figure 12.11 (page 430).

STEP 11: **Display a Schedule of Accounts Receivable and an Accounts Receivable Ledger Report for all customers.**
The Schedule of Accounts Receivable and Accounts Receivable Ledger Reports are shown in Figures 12.12a (page 430) and 12.12b (page 431).

TUTORIAL PROBLEM 12-T

Park Vacuum Cleaners
Sales Journal
02/07/--

Date	Inv. No.	Acct.	Title	Debit	Credit
02/02	525	1130	AR/Lutz Industries, Inc.	773.88	
02/02	525	4110	Sales		723.25
02/02	525	2120	Sales Tax Payable		50.63
02/03	526	1130	AR/Martin Cramer	106.99	
02/03	526	4110	Sales		99.99
02/03	526	2120	Sales Tax Payable		7.00
02/04	527	1130	AR/Barrett Cleaning, Inc.	890.94	
02/04	527	4110	Sales		832.65
02/04	527	2120	Sales Tax Payable		58.29
02/05	528	1130	AR/Roger Taylor	347.75	
02/05	528	4110	Sales		325.00
02/05	528	2120	Sales Tax Payable		22.75
02/06	529	1130	AR/Braam Company	1043.88	
02/06	529	4110	Sales		975.59
02/06	529	2120	Sales Tax Payable		68.29
02/07	530	1130	AR/Wilmes Motel	544.31	
02/07	530	4110	Sales		508.70
02/07	530	2120	Sales Tax Payable		35.61
			Totals	3707.75	3707.75

Figure 12.9d
Sales Journal

Park Vacuum Cleaners
Cash Receipts Journal
02/07/--

Date	Refer.	Acct.	Title	Debit	Credit
02/03	R518	1110	Cash	607.95	
02/03	R518	4130	Sales Discount	12.40	
02/03	R518	1130	AR/Barrett Cleaning, Inc.		620.35
02/05	R519	1110	Cash	1222.55	
02/05	R519	4130	Sales Discount	24.95	
02/05	R519	1130	AR/Lutz Industries, Inc.		1247.50
02/07	R520	1110	Cash	3087.00	
02/07	R520	4130	Sales Discount	63.00	
02/07	R520	1130	AR/Frost Department Stores		3150.00
			Totals	5017.85	5017.85

Figure 12.9e
Cash Receipts Journal

TUTORIAL PROBLEM 12-T

Park Vacuum Cleaners
General Ledger
02/07/--

Account	Journal	Date	Refer.	Debit	Credit	Balance
1130-Accounts Receivable						
	Balance Forward					14255.52Dr
	Sales	02/02	525	773.88		15029.40Dr
	Sales	02/03	526	106.99		15136.39Dr
	Cash Receipts	02/03	R518		620.35	14516.04Dr
	Sales	02/04	527	890.94		15406.98Dr
	Sales	02/05	528	347.75		15754.73Dr
	Cash Receipts	02/05	R519		1247.50	14507.23Dr
	General	02/06	R511		83.35	14423.88Dr
	Sales	02/06	529	1043.88		15467.76Dr
	Sales	02/07	530	544.31		16012.07Dr
	Cash Receipts	02/07	R520		3150.00	12862.07Dr

Figure 12.10a
Accounts Receivable

Park Vacuum Cleaners
General Ledger
02/07/--

Account	Journal	Date	Refer.	Debit	Credit	Balance
4110-Sales						
	Balance Forward					92717.21Cr
	Sales	02/02	525		723.25	93440.46Cr
	Sales	02/03	526		99.99	93540.45Cr
	Sales	02/04	527		832.65	94373.10Cr
	Sales	02/05	528		325.00	94698.10Cr
	Sales	02/06	529		975.59	95673.69Cr
	Sales	02/07	530		508.70	96182.39Cr
4120-Sales Returns & Allow.						
	General	02/06	R511	77.90		77.90Dr
4130-Sales Discount						
	Cash Receipts	02/03	R518	12.40		12.40Dr
	Cash Receipts	02/05	R519	24.95		37.35Dr
	Cash Receipts	02/07	R520	63.00		100.35Dr

Figure 12.10b
Sales, Sales Returns and Allowances, and Sales Discounts

TUTORIAL PROBLEM 12-T

Park Vacuum Cleaners
Trial Balance
02/07/--

Acct. Number	Account Title	Debit	Credit
1110	Cash	10969.51	
1120	Petty Cash	150.00	
1130	Accounts Receivable	12862.07	
1140	Merchandise Inventory	27426.06	
1150	Supplies	2500.00	
1160	Prepaid Insurance	1500.00	
2110	Accounts Payable		3067.32
2120	Sales Tax Payable		237.12
3110	Sandra Renor, Capital		34592.34
3120	Sandra Renor, Drawing	6000.00	
4110	Sales		96182.39
4120	Sales Returns & Allow.	77.90	
4130	Sales Discount	100.35	
5110	Purchases	70942.30	
5130	Purchases Discount		62.79
6110	Advertising Expense	130.00	
6120	Miscellaneous Expense	105.00	
6130	Rent Expense	850.00	
6140	Telephone Expense	207.60	
6150	Utilities Expense	321.17	
	Totals	134141.96	134141.96

Figure 12.11 Trial Balance

Park Vacuum Cleaners
Schedule of Accounts Receivable
02/07/--

Name	Balance
Barrett Cleaning, Inc.	890.94
Braam Company	1982.48
Frost Department Stores	2374.65
Janice Miner	733.05
Lutz Industries, Inc.	773.88
Martin Cramer	859.87
Roger Taylor	1291.27
Wilmes Motel	3955.93
Total	12862.07

Figure 12.12a Schedule of Accounts Receivable

TUTORIAL PROBLEM 12-T

Park Vacuum Cleaners
Accounts Receivable Ledger
02/07/--

Account	Journal	Date	Refer.	Debit	Credit	Balance
Barrett Cleaning, Inc.						
	Balance Forward					620.35Dr
	Cash Receipts	02/03	R518		620.35	.00
	Sales	02/04	527	890.94		890.94Dr
Braam Company						
	Balance Forward					938.60Dr
	Sales	02/06	529	1043.88		1982.48Dr
Frost Department Stores						
	Balance Forward					5608.00Dr
	General	02/06	R511		83.35	5524.65Dr
	Cash Receipts	02/07	R520		3150.00	2374.65Dr
Janice Miner						
	Balance Forward					733.05Dr
Lutz Industries, Inc.						
	Balance Forward					1247.50Dr
	Sales	02/02	525	773.88		2021.38Dr
	Cash Receipts	02/05	R519		1247.50	773.88Dr
Martin Cramer						
	Balance Forward					752.88Dr
	Sales	02/03	526	106.99		859.87Dr
Roger Taylor						
	Balance Forward					943.52Dr
	Sales	02/05	528	347.75		1291.27Dr
Wilmes Motel						
	Balance Forward					3411.62Dr
	Sales	02/07	530	544.31		3955.93Dr

Figure 12.12b
Accounts Receivable Ledger

TUTORIAL PROBLEM 12-T

STEP 12: **Display a Statement of Account for Frost Department Stores.**
Select the *Statements of Account* and click *OK*. Advance through the statement by clicking the >> button until Frost Department Stores appears, as shown in Figure 12.13.

STATEMENT OF ACCOUNT
Park Vacuum Cleaners

To: Frost Department Stores   Date 02/07/__

Date	Reference	Description	Charges	Credits	Balance
02/01/__		Balance Forward			5608.00
02/06/__	R511	Credit Memo		83.35	5524.65
02/07/__	R520	Payment		3150.00	2374.65

Figure 12.13
Frost Department Stores Statement of Account

STEP 13: **Display an Inventory List Report.**
The report appears in Figure 12.14.

STEP 14: **Display the Inventory Transactions Report for the period February 1 through February 7.**
The report appears in Figure 12.15 (page 434).

STEP 15: **Display the Inventory Exceptions Report.**
The report appears in Figure 12.16 (page 434).

STEP 16: **Display the Yearly Sales Report.**
The report appears in Figure 12.17 (page 435).

STEP 17: **Display the Top Customers graph.**
The Top Customers graph is shown in Figure 12.18 (page 435).

Chapter 12 Accounts Receivable: Sales Order Processing and Inventory Control

TUTORIAL PROBLEM 12-T

Park Vacuum Cleaners
Inventory List
02/07/--

Stock No.	Description	Unit Meas.	On Hand	On Order	Reorder Point	Last Cost	Retail Price
1010	A-1 Upright Vacuum	EA	11	0	6	480.00	795.95
1020	Heyer Upright Vacuum	EA	19	0	8	315.25	485.00
1030	Kelly Canister Vac	EA	11	0	5	405.00	689.95
1040	Ness Canister Vacuum	EA	11	0	8	240.00	369.99
1050	Steam Cleaner	EA	15	0	10	152.00	219.00
1060	Rug Machine	EA	16	0	10	135.00	189.99
1070	Wet & Dry Vacuum	EA	11	0	12	199.00	325.00
1080	Electric Broom	EA	13	10	10	58.00	99.99
1090	Battery Powered Vac	EA	20	0	15	22.80	38.95
1100	Car Vac	EA	27	0	15	20.95	29.95
2010	Upright Cleaner Bag	EA	65	12	32	2.35	3.95
2020	Canister Cleaner Bag	EA	76	0	32	2.30	3.85
2030	Allergenci Bag	EA	8	12	12	5.35	8.95
2040	Pile Lifter Brush	EA	16	0	10	31.50	49.00
2050	Shampoo Attachment	EA	15	0	8	25.70	38.95
2060	Attachment Kit	EA	18	2	10	32.95	49.95

Figure 12.14
Inventory List Report

STEP 18: **Save your data.**

STEP 19: **Optional Spreadsheet Integration Activity.**
Park Vacuum Cleaners has asked you to prepare a spreadsheet, based on the current inventory data, that will provide management with information about items with low gross sales. You are to prepare a list of inventory items that have year-to-date gross sales of less than $1,000.00.

a. Display and copy the Yearly Sales Report to the clipboard in spreadsheet format.
b. Start up your spreadsheet software and load the file named AA8 Spreadsheet 12-T.
c. Select cell A1 as the current cell and paste the Yearly Sales Report into the spreadsheet.

TUTORIAL PROBLEM 12-T

Park Vacuum Cleaners
Inventory Transactions
02/07/--

Date	Description	Inv./P.O.	Quantity Sold	Selling Price	Quan. Ord.	Quan. Recd.	Cost Price
Sales Invoices							
02/02	Kelly Canister Vac	525	1	689.95			
	Canister Cleaner Bag		4	3.85			
	Allergenci Bag		2	8.95			
02/03	Electric Broom	526	1	99.99			
02/04	A-1 Upright Vacuum	527	1	780.03			
	Allergenci Bag		6	8.77			
02/05	Wet & Dry Vacuum	528	1	325.00			
02/06	Ness Canister Vacuum	529	1	369.99			
	Wet & Dry Vacuum		1	325.00			
	Steam Cleaner		1	219.00			
	Canister Cleaner Bag		16	3.85			
02/07	Heyer Upright Vacuum	530	1	485.00			
	Upright Cleaner Bag		6	3.95			
02/06	Battery Powered Vac	R511	-2	38.95			
Purchase Orders							
02/02	Allergenci Bag	275			12		
02/07	Attachment Kit	276			2		
	Upright Cleaner Bag				12		
Purchase Invoices							
02/04	Kelly Canister Vac	856				7	405.00
02/05	Canister Cleaner Bag	857				64	2.30
02/06	Pile Lifter Brush	858				5	31.50
	Totals		40		26	76	

Figure 12.15
Inventory Transactions Report

Park Vacuum Cleaners
Inventory Exceptions
02/07/--

Stock No.	Description	Unit Meas	On Hand	On Order	Reorder Point	Exception
1070	Wet & Dry Vacuum	EA	11		12	At/below reorder point
2030	Allergenci Bag	EA	8	12	12	At/below reorder point

Figure 12.16
Inventory Exceptions Report

Chapter 12 Accounts Receivable: Sales Order Processing and Inventory Control

TUTORIAL PROBLEM 12-T

```
                    Park Vacuum Cleaners
                        Yearly Sales
                         02/07/--
-----------------------------------------------------------------
 Stock                              Unit      Yearly       Yearly
 No.     Description                Meas     Quantity      Amount

 1010    A-1 Upright Vacuum         EA          25       19882.83
 1020    Heyer Upright Vacuum       EA          29       14065.00
 1030    Kelly Canister Vac         EA          42       28977.90
 1040    Ness Canister Vacuum       EA          39       14429.61
 1050    Steam Cleaner              EA          21        4599.00
 1060    Rug Machine                EA          14        2659.86
 1070    Wet & Dry Vacuum           EA          13        4225.00
 1080    Electric Broom             EA          33        3299.67
 1090    Battery Powered Vac        EA          15         584.25
 1100    Car Vac                    EA          23         688.85
 2010    Upright Cleaner Bag        EA          60         237.00
 2020    Canister Cleaner Bag       EA          88         338.80
 2030    Allergenci Bag             EA          32         285.32
 2040    Pile Lifter Brush          EA           7         343.00
 2050    Shampoo Attachment         EA          10         389.50
 2060    Attachment Kit             EA          22        1098.90
                                                -----    --------
                                                 473     96104.49
                                                =====    ========
```

Figure 12.17 Yearly Sales Report

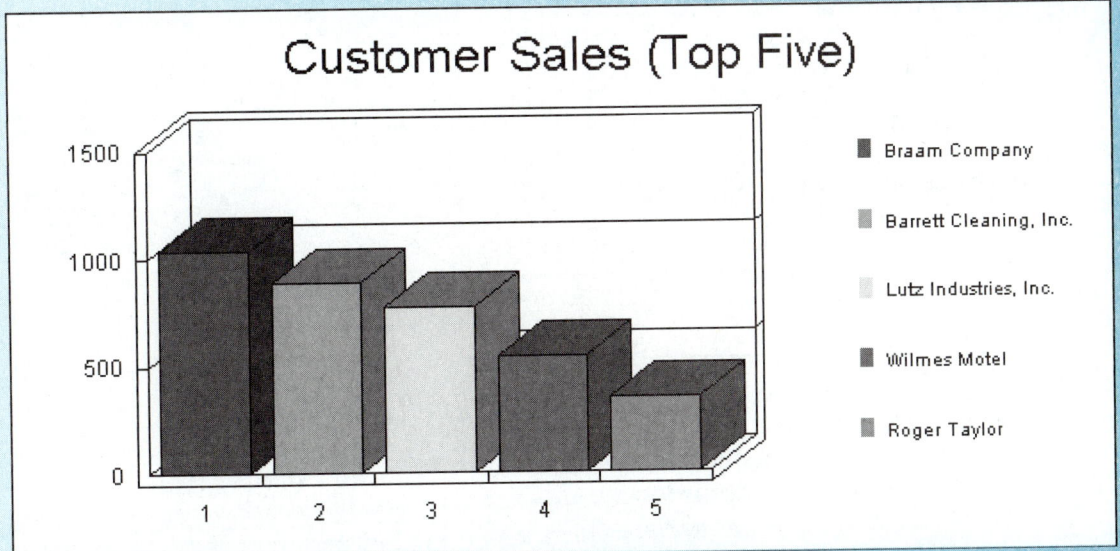

Figure 12.18 Top Customers Graph

TUTORIAL PROBLEM 12-T

d. In cell B35, enter the IF function appropriate for your spreadsheet software to display the description of each inventory item that has a yearly sales less than $1,000.00—if not, display "Delete this row." For example, @IF(E10<1000,B10,"Delete this row"). Copy the formula from cell B35 to cells B36 through B50.

e. In cell C35, enter the IF function appropriate for your spreadsheet software to display the amount of each inventory item that has a yearly sales less than $1,000.00—if not, display a blank. For example, @IF(E10<1000,E10," "). Copy the formula from cell C35 to cells C36 through C50.

f. Delete the rows in cells B35–B50 that contain "Delete this row."

g. Sum the amount (column C) of the items that match the criteria, and use this sum to calculate and display the percent of yearly total sales as shown in Figure 12.19.

h. Save your spreadsheet data with a file name of 12-T Your Name.

i. Print the item list and percentage of total sales. The completed spreadsheet is shown in Figure 12.19.

Battery Powered Vac	$584.25
Car Vac	$688.85
Upright Cleaner Bag	$237.00
Canister Cleaner Bag	$338.80
Allergenci Bag	$285.32
Pile Lifter Brush	$343.00
Shampoo Attachment	$389.50
	2,866.72
Percent of Total Sales	2.98%

Figure 12.19
Inventory Items with Year-to-Date Sales less than $1,000.00

STEP 20: Optional Word Processing Integration Activity.
Prepare a memorandum to the Owner of Park Vacuum Cleaners (Sandra Renor). List the items of inventory that have gross year-to-date sales less than $1,000.00 and their percent of total sales. A memorandum with space left for this information has already been prepared.

TUTORIAL PROBLEM 12-T

a. Copy the list of inventory items with gross sales less than $1,000.00 and the percentage of total sales from the spreadsheet.
b. Start up your word processing software and load the template file named AA8 Wordprocessing 12-T as a text file.
c. Paste the contents of the clipboard into the memorandum at the location specified.
d. Format the document as necessary (i.e., choose smaller font size for spreadsheet pasted data, center data, etc.).
e. Enter your name and today's date where indicated.
f. Save the memorandum document with a file name of 12-T Your Name.
g. Print the memorandum. The completed memorandum is shown in Figure 12.20.

STEP 21: End the *Automated Accounting* session.

MEMORANDUM

TO: Sandra Renor
FROM: Your Name
DATE: (Today's Date)
SUBJECT: Year-to-Date Gross Sales Data

The following inventory items have year-to-date gross sales less than $1,000.00. Note the percent of total sales these items generate.

Battery Powered Vac	$ 584.25
Car Vac	688.85
Upright Cleaner Bag	237.00
Canister Cleaner Bag	338.80
Allergenci Bag	285.32
Pile Lifter Brush	343.00
Shampoo Attachment	389.50
	$2,866.72
Percent of Total Sales	2.98%

Figure 12.20
Word Processing Memorandum

Review and Practice: Applying Your Information Skills

I. MATCHING

Directions: In the *Working Papers*, write the letter of the appropriate term next to each definition.

    a. computerized sales order processing system
    b. sales invoice
    c. sales invoices input form
    d. sales order processing
    e. sales return

1. A form used to describe the goods sold, the quantity, and the price.

2. The procedures and controls involved in preparing invoices, updating accounting records, and shipping merchandise.

3. A credit allowed a customer for the sales price of returned merchandise, resulting in a decrease in the vendor's accounts receivable.

4. The procedures involved in preparing a sales invoice and automatically integrating the data it contains into the inventory and general ledger records.

5. An input form used to record sales and sales return transactions when a computerized sales order processing system is used.

II. REVIEW QUESTIONS

Directions: Write the answers to each of the following questions in the *Working Papers*.

1. Identify the tasks that the computer performs when sales and sales return data are entered.

2. How is the quantity recorded on the sales invoices input form for a sales return transaction?

3. Itemize the steps required to make a change to an existing sales invoice.

4. What totals are contained at the bottom of the computer-generated sales invoice?

5. Why are data not lost when sales invoices are purged?

Chapter 12   Accounts Receivable: Sales Order Processing and Inventory Control

III. INTERNET ACTIVITY

Directions: If you have access to the Internet, use your browser to find information about VAT (value added tax) in another country. *Hint:* Use *International Taxation* as a search argument, and then use search argument *VAT*. Report on your findings. Be sure to include the source and the URL (Internet address) of your search.

Independent Practice Problem 12-P

In this problem, you will process the sales and purchases transactions for the week of February 8 through February 14 for Park Vacuum Cleaners.

STEP 1: Start Automated *Accounting 8.0.*

STEP 2: Load the opening balances file named AA8 Problem 12-P.

STEP 3: Enter your name in the User Name text box and click *OK.*

STEP 4: Save the file with a file name of 12-P Your Name.

STEP 5: Enter the purchase order, purchase invoice, and sales invoice transactions shown below:

Feb. 08   Ordered the following merchandise from Heyer Manufacturing, Inc., terms 2/10, n/30. Purchase Order No. 277.

Description	Quantity	Unit Cost
Wet & Dry Vacuum	6	199.00

08   Sold the following merchandise to Frost Department Stores, terms 2/10, n/30, 7% sales tax, Sales Invoice No. 531.

Description	Quantity Sold	Selling Price
Attachment Kit	1	49.95
Steam Cleaner	1	219.00
A-1 Upright Vacuum	1	795.95
Upright Cleaner Bag	12	3.95

09   Sold the following merchandise to Janice Miner, terms 30 days, 7% sales tax, Sales Invoice No. 532.

Description	Quantity Sold	Selling Price
Rug Machine	1	189.99
Pile Lifter Brush	1	49.00

10   The following merchandise was returned to Park Vacuum Cleaners by Wilmes Motel, 7% sales tax, Sales Return No. R530.

Description	Quantity Returned	Price
Heyer Upright Vacuum	1	485.00

10   Sold the following merchandise to Wilmes Motel, terms 30 days, 7% sales tax, Sales Invoice No. 533.

Description	Quantity Sold	Selling Price
A-1 Upright Vacuum	1	795.95
Electric Broom	2	99.99
Shampoo Attachment	1	38.95

11   Received the following merchandise for Purchase Order No. 275 from Heyer Manufacturing, Inc., terms 2/10, n/30. Purchase Invoice No. 859.

Description	Quantity	Unit Cost
Allergenci Bag	12	5.35

11   Sold the following merchandise to Roger Taylor, terms 30 days, 7% sales tax, Sales Invoice No. 534.

Description	Quantity Sold	Selling Price
Car Vac	1	29.95

12   Received the following merchandise for Purchase Order No. 276 from Rupp Accessories, Inc., terms 2/10, n/30. Purchase Invoice No. 860.

Description	Quantity	Unit Cost
Attachment Kit	2	32.95
Upright Cleaner Bag	12	2.35

12   Sold the following merchandise to Barrett Cleaning, Inc., terms 2/10, n/30, 7% sales tax, Sales Invoice No. 535.

Description	Quantity Sold	Selling Price
Upright Cleaner Bag	5	3.95
Steam Cleaner	2	214.62

13   Sold the following merchandise to Lutz Industries, Inc., terms 2/10, n/30, 7% sales tax, Sales Invoice No. 536.

Chapter 12 Accounts Receivable: Sales Order Processing and Inventory Control

Description	Quantity Sold	Selling Price
Wet & Dry Vacuum	1	325.00
Allergenci Bag	6	8.95
Attachment Kit	1	49.95
Rug Machine	2	189.99

14 Ordered the following merchandise from Ness Vacuum Cleaner Co., terms 2/10, n/30. Purchase Order No. 278.

Description	Quantity	Unit Cost
Ness Canister Vacuum	5	240.00

14 Sold the following merchandise to Martin Cramer, terms 30 days, 7% sales tax, Sales Invoice No. 537.

Description	Quantity Sold	Selling Price
Wet & Dry Vacuum	1	325.00

STEP 6: Enter the cash payment and cash receipt transactions shown below:

Feb. 10 Received cash on account from Lutz Industries, Inc., covering Sales Invoice No. 525 for $773.88, less 2% discount, $15.48. Receipt No. R525.

12 Received cash on account from Barrett Cleaning, Inc., covering Sales Invoice No. 527 for $890.94, less 2% discount, $17.82. Receipt No. R527.

13 Received cash on account from Roger Taylor, covering Sales Invoice No. 528 for $347.75, less 2% discount, $6.95. Receipt No. R528.

13 Paid Invoice No. 859 to Heyer Manufacturing, Inc., $64.20, less 2% discount, $1.28. Check No. 3621.

14 Paid Invoice No. 835 to Ness Vacuum Cleaner Co., $437.50, no discount. Check No. 3622.

STEP 7: Display the Purchase Order, Purchase Invoice, and Sales Invoice Registers for the period February 8 through February 14.

STEP 8: Display the General, Purchases, Cash Payments, Sales, and Cash Receipts Journals for the period February 8 through February 14.

STEP 9: Display a General Ledger Report for the Accounts Receivable, Sales, Sales Returns and Allowance, and Sales Discount accounts.

STEP 10: Display a Trial Balance Report.

STEP 11: Display a Schedule of Accounts Receivable and an Accounts Receivable Ledger Report for all customers.

STEP 12: Display a Statement of Account for Barrett Cleaning, Inc.

STEP 13: Display an Inventory List Report.

STEP 14: Display the Inventory Transactions Report for the period February 8 through February 14.

STEP 15: Display the inventory exceptions report.

STEP 16: Display the Yearly Sales Report.

STEP 17: Display the Top Customers graph.

STEP 18: Save your data to disk.

STEP 19: Optional Spreadsheet Integration Activity.

Use a spreadsheet to prepare a list of inventory items that have year-to-date gross sales greater than $10,000.00. Use Figure 12.19 (page 436) as a guide, if necessary.

a. Display and copy the Yearly Sales Report to the clipboard in spreadsheet format.
b. Start up your spreadsheet software and load the file named AA8 Spreadsheet 12-T.
c. Select cell A1 as the current cell and paste the Yearly Sales report into the spreadsheet.
d. In cell B35, enter the IF function that is appropriate for your spreadsheet software to display the description of each inventory item that has a year-to-date gross sales greater than $10,000.00—if not, display "Delete this row." For example, @IF(E10>10000,B10,"Delete this row"). Copy the formula from cell B35 to cells B36 through B50.
e. In cell C35, enter the IF function that is appropriate for your spreadsheet software to display the amount of each inventory item that has a year-to-date gross sales greater than $10,000.00—if not, display a blank. For example, @IF(E10>10000,E10," "). Copy the formula from cell C35 to cells C36 through C50.
f. Delete the rows in cells B35-B50 that contain "Delete this row."
g. Sum the amount (column C) of the items that match the criteria, and use this sum to calculate and display the percent of yearly total sales.
h. Save your spreadsheet data with a file name of 12-P Your Name.
i. Print the list of items that meet the criteria.

Chapter 12 Accounts Receivable: Sales Order Processing and Inventory Control   443

STEP 20: **Optional Word Processing Integration Activity.**
Prepare a memorandum to the Owner of Park Vacuum Cleaners (Sandra Renor). List the items of inventory that have year-to-date gross sales greater than $10,000.00 and their percent of total sales.

a. Copy the list of inventory items from the spreadsheet.
b. Start up your word processing software and load the template file named AA8 Wordprocessing 12-T as a text file.
c. Paste the contents of the clipboard into the memorandum at the location specified and change the text reference from less than $1,000.00 to greater than $10,000.00.
d. Format the document as necessary.
e. Enter your name and today's date where indicated.
f. Save the memorandum document with a file name of 12-P Your Name.
g. Print the memorandum.

STEP 21: End the *Automated Accounting* session.

Applying Your Technology Skills 12-P

Directions: Using Independent Practice Problem 12-P, write the answers to the following questions in the *Working Papers*.

Register Reports

1. What is the total amount of purchase orders for the period?
2. What is the total amount of purchase invoices for the period?
3. What is the total amount of sales for the period?

Journal and Ledger Reports

4. What are the total debits and credits shown on the Purchases Journal?
5. What are the total debits and credits shown on the Cash Payments Journal?
6. What are the total debits and credits shown on the Sales Journal?
7. What are the total debits and credits shown on the Cash Receipts Journal?
8. From the General Ledger Report, what was the Accounts Receivable account balance on February 14?

9. What is the account balance of the following accounts as of February 14?

   (a) Sales

   (b) Sales Returns and Allowances

   (c) Sales Discounts

10. From the Trial Balance, what is the amount of sales?

11. From the Schedule of Accounts Receivable, what is the total due from all customers as of February 14?

12. From the Statement of Account for Barrett Cleaning, Inc., what is the current account balance?

Inventory Reports and Graph

13. How many items were sold during the period?

14. List the item(s) that are at or below the reorder point.

15. Which item has the greatest sales volume based on the dollar amount?

16. What is the total amount of yearly sales?

17. From the graph, what customer has the greatest amount of sales to date?

Mastery Problem 12-M

In this problem, you will process the sales and purchases transactions for the week of February 15 through February 21 for Park Vacuum Cleaners.

STEP 1: Start *Automated Accounting 8.0*.

STEP 2: Load the opening balances file named AA8 Problem 12-M.

STEP 3: Enter your name in the User Name text box and click *OK*.

STEP 4: Save the file with a file name of 12-M Your Name.

STEP 5: Enter the purchase order, purchase invoice, and sales invoice transactions shown below:

Feb. 15 Ordered the following merchandise from A-1 Vacuum Mfg., Inc., terms 2/10, n/30. Purchase Order No. 279.

Description	Quantity	Unit Cost
A-1 Upright Vacuum	4	480.00

15 Sold the following merchandise to Braam Company, terms 2/10, n/30, 7% sales tax, Sales Invoice No. 538.

Description	Quantity Sold	Selling Price
Kelly Canister Vac	1	689.95
Electric Broom	2	99.99
Canister Cleaner Bag	12	3.85

16 Sold the following merchandise to Martin Cramer, terms 30 days, 7% sales tax, Sales Invoice No. 539.

Description	Quantity Sold	Selling Price
Car Vac	1	29.95

17 The following merchandise was returned to Park Vacuum Cleaners by Barrett Cleaning, Inc., 7% sales tax, Sales Return No. R535.

Description	Quantity Returned	Price
Steam Cleaner	1	214.62

17 Sold the following merchandise to Barrett Cleaning, Inc., terms 2/10, n/30, 7% sales tax, Sales Invoice No. 540.

Description	Quantity Sold	Selling Price
Rug Machine	1	189.99
Attachment Kit	1	49.95
Pile Lifter Brush	1	49.00

18 Received the following merchandise for Purchase Order No. 277 from Heyer Manufacturing, Inc., terms 2/10, n/30. Purchase Invoice No. 861.

Description	Quantity	Unit Cost
Wet & Dry Vacuum	6	199.00

18 Sold the following merchandise to Janice Miner, terms 30 days, 7% sales tax, Sales Invoice No. 541.

Description	Quantity Sold	Selling Price
Steam Cleaner	1	219.00

19 Received the following merchandise for Purchase Order No. 278 from Ness Vacuum Cleaner Co., terms 2/10, n/30. Purchase Invoice No. 862.

Description	Quantity	Unit Cost
Ness Canister Vacuum	5	240.00

20 Sold the following merchandise to Frost Department Stores, terms 2/10, n/30, 7% sales tax, Sales Invoice No. 542.

Description	Quantity Sold	Selling Price
Upright Cleaner Bag	5	3.95
Heyer Upright Vacuum	1	485.00

21 Sold the following merchandise to Lutz Industries, Inc., terms 2/10, n/30, 7% sales tax, Sales Invoice No. 543.

Description	Quantity Sold	Selling Price
Rug Machine	1	189.99
Allergenci Bag	8	8.95
Attachment Kit	1	49.95

21 Ordered the following merchandise from Heyer Manufacturing, Inc., terms 2/10, n/30. Purchase Order No. 280.

Description	Quantity	Unit Cost
Allergenci Bag	26	5.35

STEP 6: Enter the cash payment and cash receipt journal transactions shown below:

Feb. 17 Received cash on account from Martin Cramer, covering Sales Invoice No. 526 for $106.99, no discount. Receipt No. R521.

19 Received cash on account from Braam Company, covering Sales Invoice No. 529 for $1,043.88, less 2% discount, $20.88. Receipt No. R529.

20 Received cash on account from Frost Department Stores, covering Sales Invoice No. 531 for $1,190.16, less 2% discount, $23.80. Receipt No. R531.

20 Paid Invoice No. 860 to Rupp Accessories, Inc., $94.10, less 2% discount, $1.88. Check No. 3623.

21 Paid Invoice No. 837 to A-1 Vacuum Mfg., Inc., $815.00, no discount. Check No. 3624.

Chapter 12 Accounts Receivable: Sales Order Processing and Inventory Control

STEP 7: Display the Purchase Order, Purchase Invoice, and Sales Invoice Registers for the period February 15 through February 21.

STEP 8: Display the General, Purchases, Cash Payments, Sales, and Cash Receipts Journals for the period February 15 through February 21.

STEP 9: Display a General Ledger Report for the Accounts Receivable, Sales, Sales Returns and Allowance, and Sales Discount accounts.

STEP 10: Display a Trial Balance Report.

STEP 11: Display a Schedule of Accounts Receivable and an Accounts Receivable Ledger Report for all customers.

STEP 12: Display a Statement of Account for Frost Department Stores.

STEP 13: Display an Inventory List Report.

STEP 14: Display the Inventory Transactions Report for the period February 15 through February 21.

STEP 15: Display the Inventory Exceptions Report.

STEP 16: Display the Yearly Sales Report.

STEP 17: Display the Top Customers graph.

STEP 18: Save your data to disk.

STEP 19: Optional Spreadsheet Integration Activity.
Use a spreadsheet to prepare a list of inventory items that have year-to-date gross sales greater than $4,000.00. Use Figure 12.19 (page 436) as a guide, if necessary.

a. Display and copy the Yearly Sales Report to the clipboard in spreadsheet format.
b. Start up your spreadsheet software and load the file named AA8 Spreadsheet 12-T.
c. Select cell A1 as the current cell and paste the Yearly Sales Report into the spreadsheet.
d. In cell B35, enter the IF function that is appropriate for your spreadsheet software to display the description of each inventory item that has a year-to-date gross sales greater than $4,000.00—if not, display "Delete this row." For example, @IF(E10>4000,B10,"Delete this row"). Copy the formula from cell B35 to cells B36 through B50.
e. In cell C35, enter the IF function that is appropriate for your spreadsheet software to display the amount of each inventory item that has a year-to-date gross sales greater than $4,000.00—if not, display a blank. For example,

@IF(E10>4000,E10," "). Copy the formula from cell C35 to cells C36 through C50.

f. Delete the rows in cells B35–B50 that contain "Delete this row."

g. Sum the amount (column C) of the items that match the criteria, and use this sum to calculate and display the percent of yearly total sales.

h. Save your spreadsheet data with a file name of 12-M Your Name.

i. Print the list of items that meet the criteria.

STEP 20: **Optional Word Processing Integration Activity.**

Prepare a memorandum to the Owner of Park Vacuum Cleaners (Sandra Renor) listing the items of inventory that have year-to-date gross sales greater than $4,000.00 and their percent of total sales.

a. Copy the list of inventory items from the spreadsheet.
b. Start up your word processing software and load the template file named AA8 Wordprocessing 12-T as a text file.
c. Paste the contents of the clipboard into the memorandum at the location specified and change the text reference from less than $1,000.00 to greater than $4,000.00.
d. Format the document as necessary.
e. Enter your name and today's date where indicated.
f. Save the memorandum document with a file name of 12-M Your Name.
g. Print the memorandum.

STEP 21: **End the *Automated Accounting* session.**

Applying Your Technology Skills 12-M

Directions: Using Mastery Problem 12-M, write the answers to the following questions in the *Working Papers*.

Register Reports

1. What is the total amount of purchase orders for the period?

2. What is the total amount of purchase invoices for the period?

3. What is the total amount of sales for the period?

Chapter 12 Accounts Receivable: Sales Order Processing and Inventory Control

Journal and Ledger Reports

4. What are the total debits and credits shown on the Purchases Journal?

5. What are the total debits and credits shown on the Cash Payments Journal?

6. What are the total debits and credits shown on the Sales Journal?

7. What are the total debits and credits shown on the Cash Receipts Journal?

8. From the General Ledger Report, what was the Accounts Receivable account balance on February 21?

9. What is the account balance of the following accounts as of February 21?

    (a) Sales

    (b) Sales Returns and Allowances

    (c) Sales Discounts

10. From the Trial Balance, what is the amount of sales?

11. From the Schedule of Accounts Receivable, what is the total due from all customers as of February 21?

12. From the Statement of Account for Frost Department Stores, what is the current account balance?

Inventory Reports and Graph

13. How many items were sold during the period?

14. List the item(s) that are at or below the reorder point.

15. Which item has the greatest sales volume based on the dollar amount?

16. What is the total amount of yearly sales?

17. From the graph, what customer has the greatest amount of sales to date?

Chapter 13
ACCOUNTING SYSTEM SETUP

KEY TERMS

New Command
Required Accounts
Journal Wizard
Accounts Pick List

Opening Balances
Budget
Performance Report

LEARNING OBJECTIVES

Upon completion of this chapter, you will be able to:

1. Set up a computerized accounting system.
2. Enter the accounting system setup data.

Chapter 13 Accounting System Setup

INTRODUCTION

Many options are available that allow accounting system software to be tailored to a specific business. Because many software packages are written to handle a wide variety of business processing tasks, it is unlikely that a business user will use all of the capabilities and capacities of a given system. The problems that you have completed up to this point have been set up for you, including opening balances, type of business, etc.

In this chapter, you will learn how to set up a computerized accounting system and enter opening balance data for ABC Corporation, a merchandising business organized as a corporation.

Prior to setting up a computerized accounting system, you must carefully plan, design, and gather data. Account numbers must be assigned to each account to identify it as an asset, liability, equity, revenue, or expense account. Controlling account balances must match the totals of related subsidiary ledgers. Assets, liabilities, and equity account balances must be current. Total debit balances must equal total credit balances.

SYSTEM SETUP SPECIFICATIONS

The tasks that are necessary to set up a computerized accounting system are covered in this chapter. The order in which they must be performed is detailed in the problems at the end of the chapter.

The use of automation in factories and computers in offices has led to the reduction and elimination of many jobs in the work force. Company management argues that the use of computers and automated systems improves efficiency, increases productivity, and helps the business stay competitive. Labor unions argue that companies that install these systems have an obligation to the workers who are replaced.

Critical Thinking

1. What obligation, if any, do you think companies have toward their employees who are replaced?

2. What would you do, if anything, to help replaced workers?

3. What jobs can you think of that computers have created?

New

The **New command** in the File menu is a software feature that clears any existing data from memory in preparation for setting up a new accounting system. If you have data in memory, you should save it before you choose New. You will be asked to enter your name in the User Name text box so that your name can be associated with the newly created file.

Company Information

The Customize Accounting System window is used to provide setup information to *Automated Accounting 8.0*. It can be accessed by choosing Customize Accounting System from the Data menu or by clicking the Custom toolbar button. Figure 13.1 shows the Company Info. tab in the Customize Accounting System window. The setup data for ABC Corporation is shown. The purpose and function of each text box, check box, and option button in the Company Info. tab is described in Table 13.1.

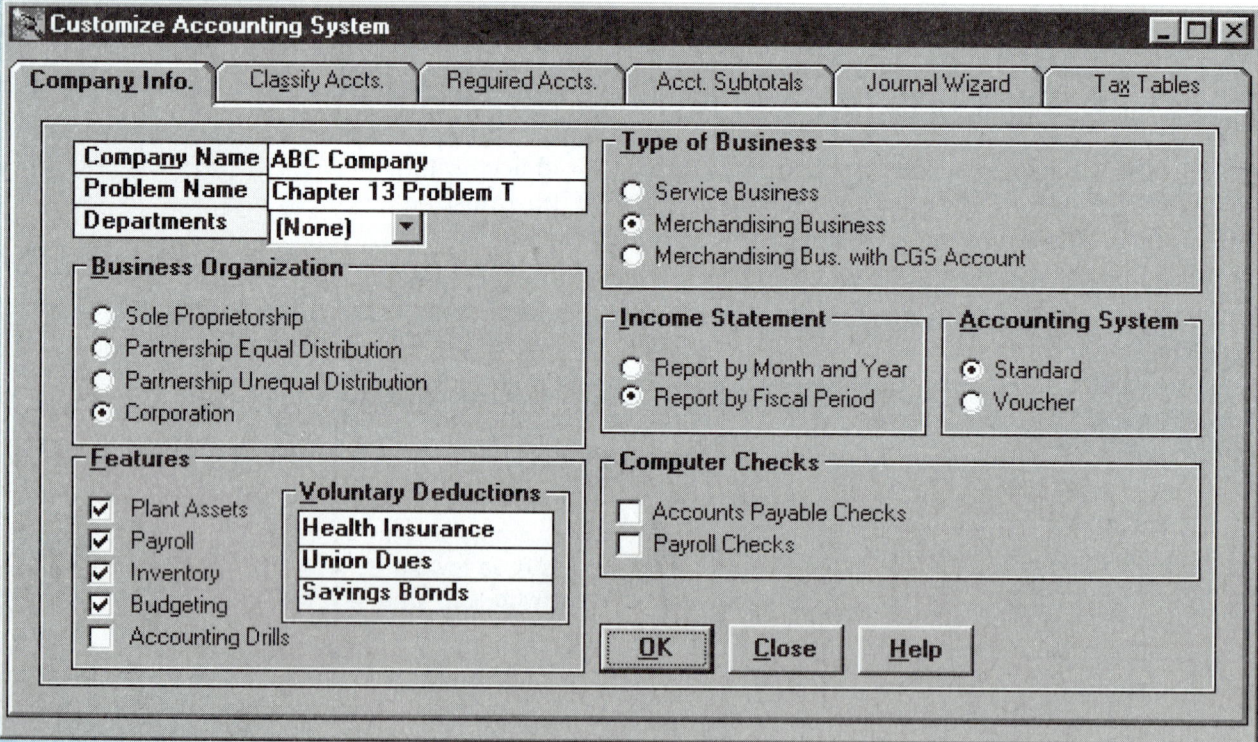

Figure 13.1
Company Information

When the Company Info. tab is active, enter the company name, enter the problem name, and click the Departments drop-down list to select the number of departments (if any). Select the appropriate business organization and click each Features check box to indicate the

Chapter 13   Accounting System Setup

OPTION	DESCRIPTION
Company Name	The company name is entered in this text box. The name of the company is displayed and printed as part of the heading for each report.
Problem Name	The problem name is entered in this text box. The problem name is printed at the top of the report along with the user name. The problem name also appears in parentheses on the title bar of the *Automated Accounting 8.0* main window as a reminder of the problem currently stored in memory.
Departments	This drop-down list allows you to select from three options: None, 2, or 3. Click the radio button of your choice.
Business Organization	The Business Organization option is used by the software during financial statement preparation and period-end closing. Click the radio button of your choice.
Features	A check box is provided for each type of accounting system to be included during setup. Appropriate windows, reports, data entry tabs, etc., are automatically activated based upon the features selected. For example, when the Payroll check box is selected, an Employees tab appears in the Account maintenance window to permit employee maintenance. A Payroll tab appears in the Other Activities window to permit entry of payroll transactions. A Payroll reports option appears in the Report selection window that enables the user to display and print various payroll reports. When the Payroll feature is checked, a Voluntary Deductions group box will appear, permitting the user to enter the names of up to three different voluntary deductions that are to be withheld from the employees' pay. The Accounting Drills feature is used to activate the Drills toolbar button you used in Chapter 1 for basic accounting principles review. Click the check boxes of your choice.
Type of Business	The Type of Business option is used by the software to determine the format of the income statement. Click the radio button of your choice.
Income Statement	This option allows the income statement to be customized. If the option is set to Month and Year, the income statement will include a column for the current month and another column for the current year. Also included for each column is a percentage, indicating the percent each amount is of total operating revenue. If this option is set to Fiscal Period, only the amount column and percent of total operating revenue are included on the income statement representing the current fiscal period. Click the radio button of your choice.
Accounting System	The Standard option is used for all problems in this textbook. The Voucher option is an alternative to an Accounts Payable system.
Computer Checks	If the Accounts Payable Checks option is set On, checks will be created each time a cash payment that involves a vendor is entered into the computer. If the Payroll Checks option is set On, pay checks will be created each time a payroll transaction is entered for an employee. Click the check boxes of your choice.

Table 13.1
Company Information Text Boxes and Option Settings

accounting system setup data that is to be included in setup. If the Payroll feature is selected, the Voluntary Deductions group box will appear. Enter the names of up to three different voluntary deductions that are to be withheld from the employee's pay. Next, select the desired type of business and income statement. Finally, click the appropriate Computer Checks box to indicate whether the computer is to generate payable and/or payroll checks. If neither of the check boxes is checked, the computer assumes that checks are written manually.

Classify Accounts

The Classify Accounts tab allows you to classify the general ledger accounts based on account number ranges. Figure 13.2 contains the account number ranges for ABC Corporation. In order to perform financial statement analysis, the range of account numbers for long-term assets and long-term liabilities must be established. This data is provided in the Extended Classification section of the window.

Figure 13.2
Classify Accounts

From	To	Account Classification
1000	1999	Assets
2000	2999	Liabilities
3000	3999	Equity
4000	4999	Revenue
5000	5999	Cost
6000	6999	Expenses
7000	7999	Other Revenue
8000	8999	Other Expenses
9000	9999	Corporate Income Tax

From	To	Extended Classification
1500	1999	Long-Term Assets
2500	2999	Long-Term Liabilities

The account classification shown in Figure 13.2 is also the default classification used by the *Automated Accounting* system. Unless the account classification-numbering scheme is different, it will not be necessary to change the account ranges as they appear. If they must be changed, do *not* key the actual range of account numbers, but enter the *potential* range. For example, if your chart of accounts currently has five assets ranging from account number 1110 to 1150, you should not specify the actual range, 1110 to 1150. Specify the potential range, such as 1000 to 1999, so that asset accounts added later will be included in the assets classification automatically. If your chart of accounts does not include a certain classification, key the anticipated account number range for that classification. For example, if your chart of accounts does not include Other Expenses, include a range of account numbers that are to be reserved for Other Expenses in the event they need to be added at a later date.

To enter account classifications, click the Classify Accts. tab. If the account classifications are different from those shown, enter the account number range for each of the classes of accounts. You can click the Chart of Accounts button to select an account from the Chart of Accounts list window.

Required Accounts

Because you have a great deal of flexibility in assigning account numbers and titles, you must provide account numbers for certain key accounts. **Required accounts** are the accounts that the software needs in order to prepare financial statements; to carry out integration among the systems, such as payroll and sales order processing; and to complete period-end closing tasks. The required accounts for ABC Corporation are shown in Figure 13.3.

Acct. #	Account Title	Required Account
1105	Cash	Cash
1115	Accounts Receivable	Accounts Receivable
1130	Merchandise Inventory	Merchandise Inventory
2105	Accounts Payable	Accounts Payable
3120	Retained Earnings	Retained Earnings
3130	Cash Dividends	Cash Dividends
3135	Stock Dividends	Stock Dividends
3145	Income Summary	Income Summary
2120	Emp. Inc. Tax Pay.--Fed.	Federal Income Tax Payable
2121	Emp. Inc. Tax Pay.--State	State Income Tax Payable

Figure 13.3
Required Accounts

Based upon the departmentalization, business organization, features, and type of business settings in the Company Info. tab, the computer will automatically determine and list the required accounts. For example, if the type of business is a service business, no merchandise inventory accounts are required. For a merchandising business, a Merchandise Inventory and an Income Summary account are required for each department. For a sole proprietorship and a partnership, capital account(s) are listed. For a corporation, a Stock Dividends account is required. If the corporation does not have stock dividends, the account number for the Cash Dividends account is entered.

To specify the required accounts, click the Required Accts. tab, and then click the Auto Setup button. The computer will search the newly entered chart of accounts and attempt to match the required accounts to the account titles. All matching accounts are displayed. Enter the account number for each of the unmatched accounts. You can click the Chart of Accounts button to select an account from the Chart of Accounts list window.

Account Subtotals

The purpose of the Account Subtotals tab is to allow you to specify and select where subtotals are to be printed on the financial statements. For example, you may wish to tailor the balance sheet so that a subtotal prints after current assets and another after plant assets. To create subtotals, click the Acct. Subtotals tab and key the account number range of the accounts to be included in the subtotal and the title to be printed on the subtotal line. The account number ranges need not reference actual accounts. Instead, the potential range should be entered so that it will not be necessary to modify the account number range as accounts are added to the chart of accounts. The Account Subtotals for ABC Corporation are shown in Figure 13.4.

Figure 13.4 Account Subtotals

Account Range		Subtotal Title
From	To	
1000	1499	Total Current Assets
1500	1999	Total Plant Assets
2000	2499	Total Current Liabilities
2500	2999	Total Long-Term Liabilities

Journal Wizard

The **Journal Wizard**, shown in Figure 13.5, is a software feature that can be used to create special general, purchases, cash payments, sales, and cash receipts journals. Basic default journals are automatically provided when a new business is established. The Journal Wizard can be used to expand these default journals to better meet the needs of the business being established. New journals will be saved along with your data and will be used when entering future transaction data. The Journal

Chapter 13 Accounting System Setup

Wizard can also be used with an ongoing system to create special journals to more efficiently handle data entry activities. The example shown in Figures 13.5 through 13.8 was used to produce the cash payments journal for ABC Corporation shown in Figure 13.9.

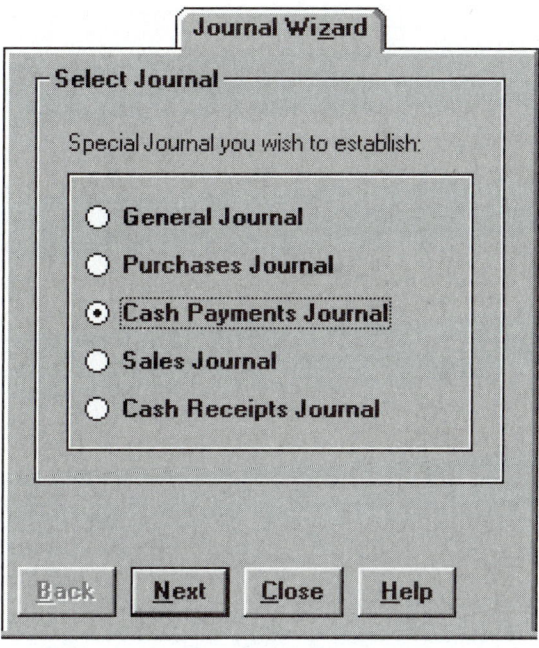

Figure 13.5
Journal Wizard Tab

Click the Journal Wizard tab and select the journal to be created (cash payments). Click the Next button to continue. The dialog box shown in Figure 13.6 will appear.

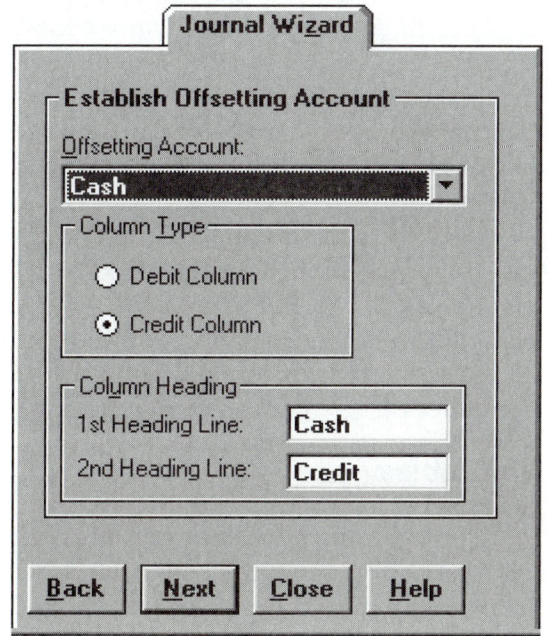

Figure 13.6
Establish Offsetting Account Dialog Box

Click the drop-down text box to select the offsetting account (Cash), and then click either Debit Column or Credit Column. (The offsetting Cash account will be credited.) Enter a one- to two-line heading to identify the offsetting account column on the journal (Cash Credit). Click Next to continue. The dialog box shown in Figure 13.7 will appear.

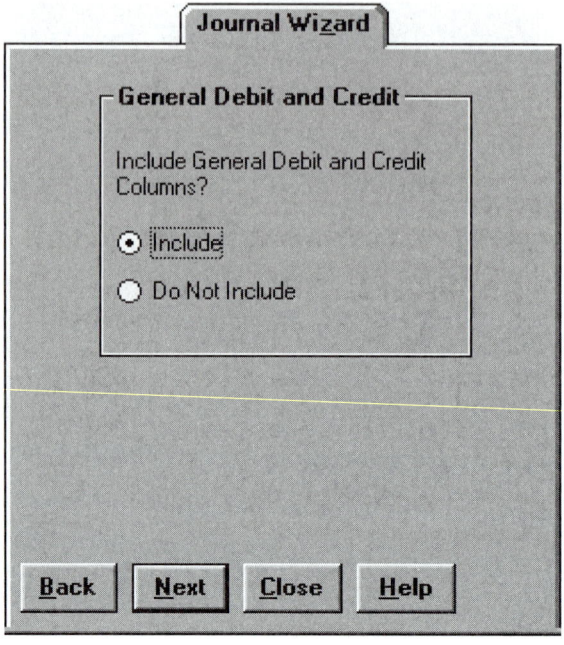

Figure 13.7
General Debit and Credit Column Dialog Box

Click the Include or Do Not Include button to indicate if general debit and credit columns should be on the journal (select Include). Click Next to continue. The dialog box shown in Figure 13.8 will now appear.

Use the Account drop-down list to select the account to be included on the journal, enter the first and second header to identify the account column on the journal, and click the Debit or Credit check box to indicate if the account is to be treated as a debit or credit amount. Repeat this procedure for each column to be added to the journal and then click Finish.

Click the appropriate tab in the Journal Entries window and verify that the newly created journal is correct (see Figure 13.9).

The Date and Refer. columns will also be included as the left-most columns on the journal. A Vendor or Customer column will also be added as the right-most column to the appropriate journal if the computer detects that vendor or customer data exists.

Tax Tables

There are three sections in the Tax Tables tab, as shown in Figure 13.10. The first section, Federal Tax Brackets, contains the federal withholding rates. These rates can be updated at any time by keying in

Chapter 13 Accounting System Setup

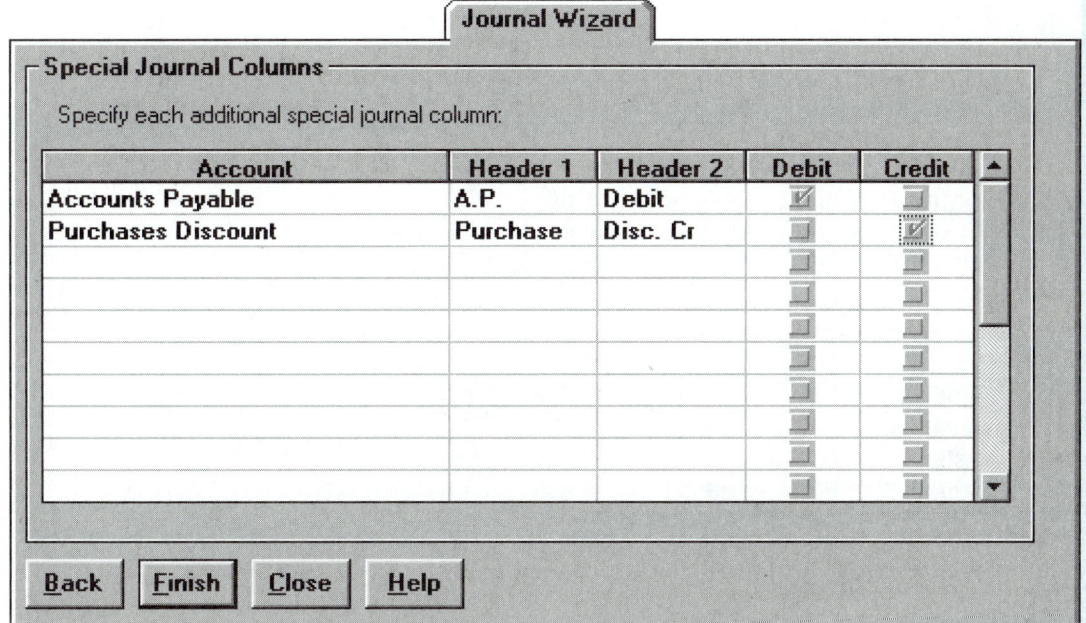

Figure 13.8
Special Journal Columns Dialog Box

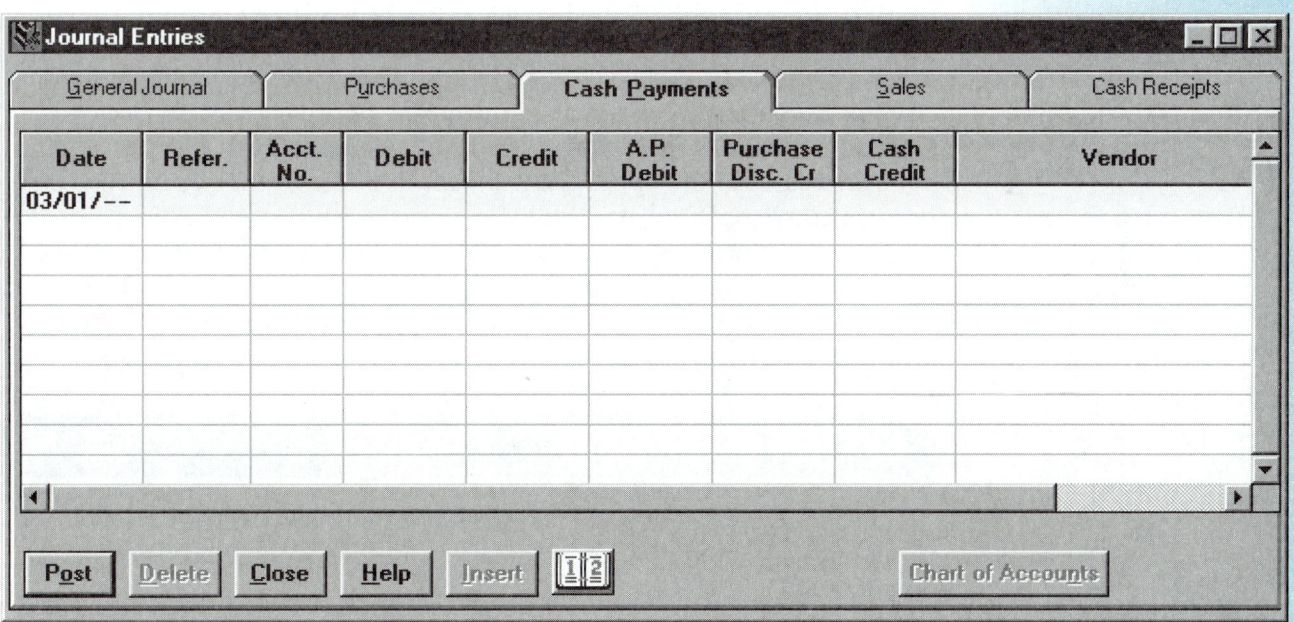

Figure 13.9
Journal-Wizard-Created Cash Payments Journal

corrected rates in the appropriate column. Refer to the IRS Circular E (*Employer's Tax Guide*), Table 7 (*Annual Payroll*) for the most current rates. Section 2, State Tax Brackets, contains the state withholding rates

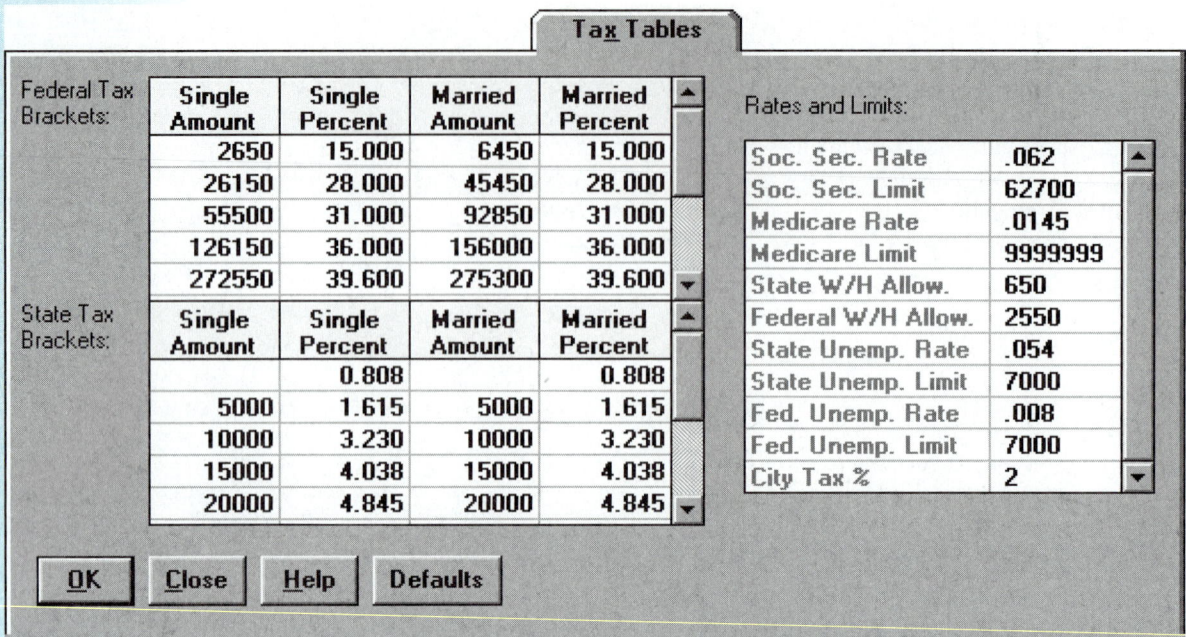

Figure 13.10
Tax Tables

used by the software for the problems in this textbook. Section 3, Rates and Limits, contains the various tax rates, upper limits, and allowance amounts required by the software to calculate employee and employer payroll taxes. Like the Federal Tax Brackets figures, the State Tax Brackets and Rates and Limits figures can be updated by keying corrected rates in the appropriate columns. Refer to the appropriate state or local employer's tax guide for the most current rates.

It is recommended that you *not* change these rates, unless instructed to do so, when working with payroll problems in this textbook. If the brackets, rates, or percentages are changed, the calculated withholding amounts will no longer match the solutions provided to your instructor.

SYSTEM SETUP DATA

Once the company information has been entered, the chart of accounts, vendor, customer, plant assets, payroll, and inventory data can be entered.

Accounts Pick List

An **accounts pick list** is a preset master chart of accounts that can be used when adding to, creating, or updating a chart of accounts. As an alternative to keying the chart of accounts entries, you can use the Pick List button located at the bottom of the Accounts tab in the Account Maintenance window, as shown in Figure 13.11. You should use the

Chapter 13 Accounting System Setup

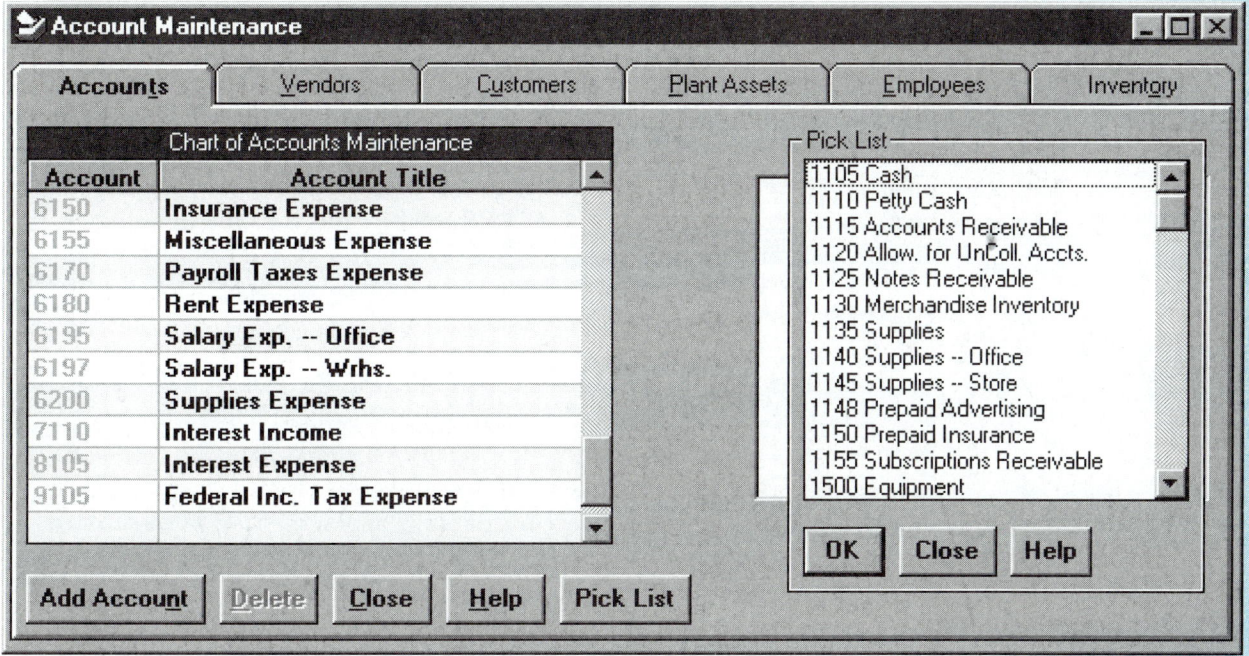

Figure 13.11
Chart of Accounts Maintenance with Pick List

Accounts tab in the Account Maintenance window to enter accounts that do not appear in the pick list or to change the account titles as desired.

Click the Accts. toolbar button, click the Accounts tab, and then click the Pick List button. Select an account from the Accounts Pick List column and click OK. The selected account will be placed in the Chart of Accounts Maintenance list. Click the Add Account button (or press the Enter key) to add the selected account to the chart of accounts. The selected account will be added to the chart of accounts in account number sequence and will appear in the Chart of Accounts column. To remove an account from the chart of accounts, simply select the desired account and click the Delete button.

Opening Balances

Opening balances are the general and subsidiary ledger balances at the beginning of the fiscal period. The account balances must be recorded in the new accounting system before a company can begin recording accounting transactions. General ledger opening balance data is keyed into the general journal, and each opening balance is posted as a separate general journal entry. Likewise, each customer account balance must be keyed as a separate entry. The total of the balances for all the customers will be the balance of the Accounts Receivable general ledger account. Each vendor account balance must also be keyed as a separate entry. The total of the balances for all the vendors will be the balance of the Accounts Payable general ledger account.

Once a general ledger account has been added, its account number cannot be changed. To change the account number of an existing account, first delete the account and then add it back as a new account.

As opening balance data is keyed, the debit and credit totals will not be equal until all transactions have been entered. However, you should post each transaction anyway. When the word *BALANCE* is keyed in the reference grid cells, the software will know that the entry is an opening balance and will not display the warning message that the entry is not in balance. After all data has been entered, you should display a trial balance to verify the accuracy of your keying and that the debit and credit totals are equal.

Budgets

A **budget** is a financial plan for the future. Budgets are developed for a specific period of time, such as a month or a year. While budgets can be developed for many aspects of a business, *Automated Accounting 8.0* uses budgets for income statement accounts only. Once budget data is entered, a Performance Report becomes available. The **Performance Report** is a report that compares actual revenues and expenses with budgeted revenues and expenses in income statement format.

The Budgets tab in the Other Activities window allows you to key the budgeted amounts—a task that is usually performed during accounting system setup if budgets are to be used. A budgeted amount is the estimated balance for that particular account at the end of the fiscal period. The account titles and current budget amounts (if any) are displayed in the window, as illustrated in Figure 13.12, so that you may either key new budget amounts or correct previously keyed budgeted amounts.

Account Title	Budget
Total Revenue	650000.00
Cost of Goods Sold	350000.00
Advertising Expense	3000.00
Depr. Exp. -- Off. Eq.	3600.00
Depr. Exp. -- Wrhs. Eq.	4600.00
Insurance Expense	5800.00
Miscellaneous Expense	1000.00
Payroll Taxes Expense	22000.00
Rent Expense	30000.00
Salary Exp. -- Office	110000.00
Salary Exp. -- Wrhs.	60000.00

Figure 13.12 Budgets Tab

Click the Other toolbar button, and then click the Budgets tab. Enter the budgeted amount for the first account (or enter an amount that you wish to change). Press the Tab key to move to the next account. The accounts are scrollable. When you have entered the amount for the last account shown in the window, the accounts will scroll up so that you can enter the next budget amount. Similarly, if you press the Shift+Tab keys, the accounts will scroll down. When all budget amounts have been entered, click OK.

Plant Assets

If plant assets are going to be part of the new accounting system, each of the plant assets must also be entered in the Plant Assets Account Maintenance window. If you need more information on adding plant assets, refer to Chapter 8.

Payroll

If payroll is going to be part of the new accounting system, each of the employees must be entered in the Employees Account Maintenance window. If you need more information on adding employees, refer to Chapter 10. If the accounting system is being established at a time other than the beginning of a new year, you must establish the quarterly and yearly earnings and withholdings for each employee. Quarterly and yearly balances are established by either of two methods: (1) by running simulated payrolls for each pay period up to the desired date or (2) by keying one payroll transaction for each employee for each quarter that represents the sum of that employee's earnings and withholdings for the quarter. In either case, since the payroll is date sensitive, be sure to use the appropriate pay-period or end-of-quarter dates. Since the accounting system for ABC Corporation is being established on March 1 and each employee is paid once each month, simulated payrolls can be run for the months of January and February to bring the quarterly and yearly balances up to date.

Inventory

Two tasks are required to set up an inventory system: (1) data for each stock item must be entered and (2) purchase order, purchase invoice, and sales invoice historical data must be entered. The procedure to enter stock items was described in Chapter 11. After the company's stock items have been entered, the historical data can be entered.

When purchase orders and purchase invoices historical data are entered, the computer will perform system integration, as explained in Chapter 11. Therefore, the accounts payable, cost, and vendor accounts balance will be updated automatically. Likewise, when the sales invoices historical data are entered, the computer will perform system integrations, as explained in Chapter 12. Thus, the Accounts Receivable, Revenue, and Customer account balances will be updated automatically.

Chapter Review

1. Prior to setting up a computerized accounting system, you must carefully plan, design, and gather data. The New command in the File menu clears any existing data from memory in preparation for setting up a new accounting system. The Customize Accounting System window is used to provide setup information to the *Automated Accounting* software.

2. The Classify Accounts tab allows you to classify the general ledger accounts based on account number ranges. Required accounts are needed by the software to prepare financial statements, carry out integration among the systems (i.e., payroll, sales order processing), and to complete period-end closing tasks. Required accounts are entered in the Required Accts. tab. Account Subtotals can be used to specify and select where subtotals are to be printed on the financial statements. Subtotals are entered in the Acct. Subtotals tab.

3. The Journal Wizard can be used to create special general, purchases, cash payments, sales, and cash receipts journals to improve the efficiency of entering transaction data into the computer.

4. The federal tax brackets, state tax brackets, rates, and limits in the Tax Tables are required by the software to calculate employee and employer payroll taxes. Changes to the default setting can be made in the Tax Tables tab.

5. The Account Maintenance window allows you to create a chart of accounts, vendor list, and customer list. An accounts pick list from a master chart of accounts can be used to help create a chart of accounts.

6. Opening balances are entered in the general journal. If you key the word *BALANCE* in the general journal reference grid cells, the computer will know that the entry is an opening balance and will therefore not display the warning message that the entry is not in balance.

7. A budget is a financial plan for the future. Budget amounts are usually entered during accounting system setup if budgets are to be used in the new accounting system.

8. If payroll is going to be a part of a new accounting system, each of the employees must be entered in the Employees Account Maintenance window. If a payroll is being established at a time other than the beginning of a new year, you must establish the quarterly and yearly earnings and withholdings for each employee.

9. Two tasks are required to set up an inventory system: (1) data for each stock item must be entered and (2) purchase order, purchase invoice, and sales invoice historical data must be entered.

ACCOUNTING CAREERS IN DEPTH

Financial Planner

A financial planner develops and implements financial plans for individuals, businesses, and organizations, utilizing a knowledge of tax and investment strategies, securities, insurance, pension plans, and real estate. A financial planner performs the following duties:

- Interviewing a client to determine the client's assets, liabilities, cash flow, insurance coverage, tax status, and financial objectives.
- Analyzing a client's financial status, developing a financial plan based on the analysis, and discussing financial options with the client.
- Preparing and submitting documents to implement the plan selected by the client.
- Maintaining contact with the client to revise the plan based on modified needs of the client or on changes in the investment market.

A financial planner may also do the following:

- Referring a client to other establishments to obtain services outlined in the financial plan.
- Selling insurance to the client, recommending the amount and type of coverage.
- Buying and selling stocks and bonds for a client.
- Renting, buying, or selling property for a client.

As is apparent from the job duties listed, a financial planner needs to be knowledgeable about a wide range of financial issues. As a result, the educational requirements for a financial planner include a college degree. In addition, a financial planner may be registered with professional self-regulatory associations and be designated as a Certified Financial Planner. In dealing with the public, a planner must be able to prove to potential clients that the planner has the skills and background necessary to wisely deal with the client's financial needs.

Financial planning is a career that can be very interesting to people who enjoy working with a wide variety of clients. It requires good human relations skills in addition to the ability to analyze information and develop a plan on the basis of the client's needs in light of the current and future economic environment.

TUTORIAL PROBLEM 13-T

In this problem, you will set up a complete accounting system. You will complete the processing necessary to set up the general ledger, plant assets, payroll, inventory, and budget data for ABC Corporation as of March 1 of the current year.

STEP 1: **Start up *Automated Accounting 8.0*.**

STEP 2: **Use the New command to erase data in memory and prepare the computer for setup.**
Choose *New* from the File menu.

STEP 3: **Enter your name in the User Name text box and click *OK*.**

STEP 4: **Enter or set the data fields, check boxes, and option buttons in the Customized Accounting Systems' Company Info. window as follows:**
Click the *Custom* toolbar button.

Company Name	ABC Corporation
Problem Name	Chapter 13 Problem T
Departmentalization	Non Departmentalized
Business Organization	Corporation
Features	Plant Assets
	Payroll
	Health Insurance
	Union Dues
	Savings Bonds
	Inventory
	Budgeting
Type of Business	Merchandising Business
Income Statement	Report by Fiscal Period
Accounting System	Standard
Computer Checks	None

STEP 5: **Save your data with a file name of 13-T Your Name.**

STEP 6: **Enter the chart of accounts.**
Click the *Accts.* toolbar button. When the Accounts Maintenance window appears, click the *Accounts* tab and click the *Pick List* button. When the Pick List window appears, select the desired account from the Pick List window, and then click *OK* to place the selected account in the Chart of Accounts Maintenance window. Click *Add Account* to add the account to the chart of accounts.

Chapter 13 Accounting System Setup

TUTORIAL PROBLEM 13-T

Note: Several of the account titles chosen from the pick list should be changed to match ABC Corporation's chart of accounts.

As an alternative, key each of the accounts. The completed chart of accounts is shown in Figure 13.13.

Account	Account Title
1105	Cash
1115	Accounts Receivable
1130	Merchandise Inventory
1135	Supplies
1150	Prepaid Insurance
1520	Equipment—Office
1530	Accum. Dep.—Off. Eq.
1560	Warehouse Equipment
1565	Accum. Dep.—Wrhs. Eq.
2105	Accounts Payable
2113	Salaries Payable
2120	Emp. Inc. Tax Pay.—Fed.
2121	Emp. Inc. Tax Pay.—State
2122	Emp. Inc. Tax Pay.—City
2125	Social Security Tax Pay.
2126	Medicare Tax Payable
2130	Sales Tax Payable
2135	Unemp. Tax Pay.—Fed.
2140	Unemp. Tax Pay.—State
2150	Health Ins. Prem. Pay.
2160	Union Dues Payable
2170	Savings Bonds Payable
2505	Notes Payable
3105	Capital Stock
3120	Retained Earnings
3130	Cash Dividends
3135	Stock Dividends
3145	Income Summary
4105	Sales
4110	Sales Discount
4115	Sales Ret. and Allow.
5105	Purchases
5107	Purchases Discount
5110	Purch. Ret. and Allow.
6105	Advertising Expense
6130	Depr. Exp.—Off. Eq.
6140	Depr. Exp.—Wrhs. Eq.
6150	Insurance Expense
6155	Miscellaneous Expense
6170	Payroll Taxes Expense
6180	Rent Expense
6195	Salary Exp.—Office
6197	Salary Exp.—Wrhs.
6200	Supplies Expense
7110	Interest Income
8105	Interest Expense
9105	Federal Inc. Tax Expense

Figure 13.13
Chart of Accounts

TUTORIAL PROBLEM 13-T

STEP 7: Enter the vendors.
Click the *Vendors* tab in the Account Maintenance window and enter each of the vendors shown in Figure 13.14.

Bruno Insurance Agency
Elam Development Co.
Ellis Power Tools, Inc.
Fotz Manufacturing, Inc.
Long Shore Tool Supplies
Payroll Bank Account
Southern Utilities Co.
Talbot Advertising
West Coast Tool Corp.
Wilke Office Supplies

Figure 13.14
Vendors

STEP 8: Enter the customers.
Click the *Customers* tab in the Account Maintenance window and enter each of the customers shown in Figure 13.15.

Brockert Rentals
C B Industrial Tools
Deters Machinery
Merchant Power Tools
Scholz Hardware
Wilkens Power Machines
Wisdom Industries

Figure 13.15
Customers

STEP 9: Verify account classification and extended account classification data. The software will automatically try to determine account classifications.
Click the *Custom* toolbar button and choose the *Classify Accts.* tab. Verify the appropriate account number ranges, as shown in Figure 13.16.

STEP 10: Enter the required account data shown below.
Click the *Required Accts.* tab, and then click *Auto Setup* to try to match as many required accounts to the chart of account titles as possible. Complete the unmatched required accounts by entering the appropriate account

Chapter 13 Accounting System Setup

TUTORIAL PROBLEM 13-T

From	To	Account Classification
1000	1999	Assets
2000	2999	Liabilities
3000	3999	Equity
4000	4999	Revenue
5000	5999	Cost
6000	6999	Expenses
7000	7999	Other Revenue
8000	8999	Other Expenses
9000	9999	Corporate Income Tax

From	To	Extended Classification
1500	1999	Long-Term Assets
2500	2999	Long-Term Liabilities

Figure 13.16
Account Classification

numbers, or using the Chart of Accounts List box to select the desired accounts. The completed required accounts are shown in Figure 13.17.

Acct. #	Account Title	Required Account
1105	Cash	Cash
1115	Accounts Receivable	Accounts Receivable
1130	Merchandise Inventory	Merchandise Inventory
2105	Accounts Payable	Accounts Payable
3120	Retained Earnings	Retained Earnings
3130	Cash Dividends	Cash Dividends
3135	Stock Dividends	Stock Dividends
3145	Income Summary	Income Summary
2120	Emp. Inc. Tax Pay.--Fed.	Federal Income Tax Payable
2121	Emp. Inc. Tax Pay.--State	State Income Tax Payable
2125	Social Security Tax Pay.	Social Security Tax Payable
2126	Medicare Tax Payable	Medicare Tax Payable
2150	Health Ins. Prem. Pay.	Health Insurance Payable
2160	Union Dues Payable	Union Dues Payable
2170	Savings Bonds Payable	Savings Bonds Payable
6170	Payroll Taxes Expense	Payroll Tax Expense
2140	Unemp. Tax Pay. -- State	Unemployment Tax Payable--State
2135	Unemp. Tax Pay. -- Fed.	Unemployment Tax Payable--Feder.
2113	Salaries Payable	Salaries Payable
2122	Emp. Inc. Tax Pay.--City	City Income Tax Payable

Figure 13.17
Required Accounts

TUTORIAL PROBLEM 13-T

STEP 11: Enter the account subtotals.

Click the *Acct. Subtotals* tab and enter the appropriate account number ranges and subtotal titles, as shown in Figure 13.18.

Account Range		Subtotal Title
From	To	
1000	1499	Total Current Assets
1500	1999	Total Plant Assets
2000	2499	Total Current Liabilities
2500	2999	Total Long-Term Liabilities

Figure 13.18
Account Subtotals

STEP 12: Enter the general ledger opening balances.

Click the *Journal* toolbar button, and then click the *General Journal* tab and enter the data from the completed general journal shown in Figure 13.19. Use March 1 as the date.

Date	Refer.	Account	Debit	Credit	Vendor/Customer
03/01/__	Balance	1105 Cash	21993.03		
03/01/__	Balance	1130 Merchandise Inventory	6585.50		
03/01/__	Balance	1135 Supplies	1913.76		
03/01/__	Balance	1150 Prepaid Insurance	1300.00		
03/01/__	Balance	1520 Equipment -- Office	14091.00		
03/01/__	Balance	1530 Accum. Dep. -- Off. Eq.		2912.91	
03/01/__	Balance	1560 Warehouse Equipment	30351.30		
03/01/__	Balance	1565 Accum. Dep. -- Wrhs. Eq.		5978.60	
03/01/__	Balance	2505 Notes Payable		6100.00	
03/01/__	Balance	3105 Capital Stock		48500.00	
03/01/__	Balance	3120 Retained Earnings		12743.08	

Figure 13.19
General Ledger Opening Balances

STEP 13: Enter budget amounts.

Click the *Other* toolbar button, and then click the *Budgets* tab and enter the budget amounts shown in Figure 13.20.

STEP 14: Display a Chart of Accounts, Vendor List, and Customer List.

Click the *Reports* toolbar button. Select and display the *Chart of Accounts, Vendor List,* and *Customer List.* Set the Run Date to March 1 of the current year. Examine each report in Figure 13.21 and verify that the data you entered is correct.

TUTORIAL PROBLEM 13-T

Account Title	Budget
Total Revenue	650000.00
Cost of Goods Sold	350000.00
Advertising Expense	3000.00
Depr. Exp. -- Off. Eq.	3600.00
Depr. Exp. -- Wrhs. Eq.	4600.00
Insurance Expense	5800.00
Miscellaneous Expense	1000.00
Payroll Taxes Expense	22000.00
Rent Expense	30000.00
Salary Exp. -- Office	110000.00
Salary Exp. -- Wrhs.	60000.00

Supplies Expense	3750.00
Interest Income	2000.00
Interest Expense	3500.00
Federal Inc. Tax Expense	30000.00

Figure 13.20
Budget Amounts

ABC Corporation
Chart of Accounts
03/01/--

Assets

1105 Cash
1115 Accounts Receivable
1130 Merchandise Inventory
1135 Supplies
1150 Prepaid Insurance
1520 Equipment—Office
1530 Accum. Dep.—Off. Eq.
1560 Warehouse Equipment
1565 Accum. Dep.—Wrhs. Eq.

Liabilities

2105 Accounts Payable
2113 Salaries Payable
2120 Emp. Inc. Tax Pay.—Fed.
2121 Emp. Inc. Tax Pay.—State 2122 Emp. Inc. Tax Pay.—City
2125 Social Security Tax Pay.
2126 Medicare Tax Payable
2130 Sales Tax Payable
2135 Unemp. Tax Pay.—Fed.
2140 Unemp. Tax Pay.—State
2150 Health Ins. Prem. Pay.
2160 Union Dues Payable
2170 Savings Bonds Payable
2505 Notes Payable

Stockholders' Equity

3105 Capital Stock
3120 Retained Earnings
3130 Cash Dividends
3135 Stock Dividends
3145 Income Summary

(continued)

Figure 13.21
Chart of Accounts, Vendor List, and Customer List

TUTORIAL PROBLEM 13-T

Revenue
4105 Sales
4110 Sales Discount
4115 Sales Ret. and Allow.

Cost
5105 Purchases
5107 Purchases Discount
5110 Purch. Ret. and Allow.

Expenses
6105 Advertising Expense
6130 Depr. Exp.—Off. Eq.
6140 Depr. Exp.—Wrhs. Eq.
6150 Insurance Expense
6155 Miscellaneous Expense
6170 Payroll Taxes Expense
6180 Rent Expense
6195 Salary Exp.—Office
6197 Salary Exp.—Wrhs.
6200 Supplies Expense

Other Revenue
7110 Interest Income

Other Expense
8105 Interest Expense

Corporate Income Tax
9105 Federal Inc. Tax Expense

ABC Corporation
Vendor List
03/01/--

Vendor Name

Bruno Insurance Agency
Elam Development Co.
Ellis Power Tools, Inc.
Fotz Manufacturing, Inc.
Long Shore Tool Supplies
Payroll Bank Account
Southern Utilities Co.
Talbot Advertising
West Coast Tool Corp.
Wilke Office Supplies

ABC Corporation
Customer List
03/01/--

Customer Name

Brockert Rentals
C B Industrial Tools
Deters Machinery
Merchant Power Tools
Scholz Hardware
Wilkens Power Machines
Wisdom Industries

Figure 13.21
Continued

Chapter 13 Accounting System Setup

TUTORIAL PROBLEM 13-T

STEP 15: **Save the data.**

STEP 16: **Enter the data to set up the plant assets.**
Click the *Accts.* toolbar button. Choose the *Plant Assets* tab, and enter the plant asset data shown in Figure 13.22.
Note: Asset numbers 100–199 are assigned to Office Equipment, and asset numbers 200–299 are assigned to Warehouse Equipment.

No.	Asset Name	Date Acquired	Use. Life	Original Cost	Salvage Value	Accum Depr.	Depr. Exp.	Depr. Meth.
110	Facsimile Machine	06/30/01	5	349.50	50.00	1530	6130	SL
120	File Cabinet	11/30/02	10	625.00	75.00	1530	6130	SL
130	Copy Machine	08/31/02	5	2695.00	250.00	1530	6130	SL
140	Adeo Computer	05/31/01	5	9950.00	375.00	1530	6130	SL
210	Delivery Van	10/01/01	10	8500.00	300.00	1565	6140	SL
220	Yuki Computer	07/02/02	5	3895.00	200.00	1565	6140	SL
230	Shelving	09/01/02	10	16995.00	1250.00	1565	6140	SL

Figure 13.22
Plant Assets

STEP 17: **Display a Plant Assets Report.**
Click the *Reports* toolbar button. Choose the *Plant Assets* option button from the Select a Report Group list and select the *Plant Assets List* Report. Click *OK*. The report is shown in Figure 13.23.

STEP 18: **Save the data.**

STEP 19: **Set the City Tax rate to 2.0% in the Payroll Tax Tables.**
Click the *Custom* toolbar button. Choose the *Tax Tables* tab and enter *2.0* in the City Tax % text box. Click *OK*. The completed tax table is shown in Figure 13.24.

STEP 20: **Enter the employee data.**
Click the *Accts.* toolbar button. Choose the *Employees* tab and enter the employee data shown in Figure 13.25.

STEP 21: **Enter and process the January payroll transactions.**
Click the *Other* toolbar button. Choose the *Payroll* tab, and enter the January payroll transaction data shown in Figure 13.26. Have the computer calculate the withholding taxes.

TUTORIAL PROBLEM 13-T

ABC Corporation
Plant Assets List
03/01/--

Asset		Date Acquired	Depr. Method	Useful Life	Original Cost	Salvage Value	Depr. Accts
110	Facsimile Machine	06/30/01	SL	5	349.50	50.00	1530 6130
120	File Cabinet	11/30/02	SL	10	625.00	75.00	1530 6130
130	Copy Machine	08/31/02	SL	5	2695.00	250.00	1530 6130
140	Adeo Computer	05/31/01	SL	5	9950.00	375.00	1530 6130
210	Delivery Van	10/01/01	SL	10	8500.00	300.00	1565 6140
220	Yuki Computer	07/02/02	SL	5	3895.00	200.00	1565 6140
230	Shelving	09/01/02	SL	10	16995.00	1250.00	1565 6140
	Total Plant Assets				43009.50		

Figure 13.23
Plant Assets Report

Federal Tax Brackets:	Single Amount	Single Percent	Married Amount	Married Percent
	2650	15.000	6450	15.000
	26150	28.000	45450	28.000
	55500	31.000	92850	31.000
	126150	36.000	156000	36.000
	272550	39.600	275300	39.600

State Tax Brackets:	Single Amount	Single Percent	Married Amount	Married Percent
		0.808		0.808
	5000	1.615	5000	1.615
	10000	3.230	10000	3.230
	15000	4.038	15000	4.038
	20000	4.845	20000	4.845

Rates and Limits:	
Soc. Sec. Rate	.062
Soc. Sec. Limit	62700
Medicare Rate	.0145
Medicare Limit	9999999
State W/H Allow.	650
Federal W/H Allow.	2550
State Unemp. Rate	.054
State Unemp. Limit	7000
Fed. Unemp. Rate	.008
Fed. Unemp. Limit	7000
City Tax %	2

Figure 13.24
Tax Tables

TUTORIAL PROBLEM 13-T

No.	Employee Name	Address	City, State, Zip	Social Sec. No.	With. Allow
110	Blades, Charles	3132 Shaw Dr.	Chicago, IL 60634-4030	576-89-3288	3
120	Mendez, Bella	8326 Highland Ave.	Chicago, IL 60636-7812	466-21-8976	1
130	Presnell, Maurice	59 Culver Ct.	Chicago, IL 60656-1916	645-89-1432	3
140	Trimble, Dennis	11682 Oakland Rd.	Chicago, IL 60639-5265	480-31-0415	1

Number Pay Per.	G.L. No.	Salary Amount	Hourly Rate	Piece Rate	Comm. %	Marital Status
12	6195	4575.00				Married
12	6195	4800.00				Single
12	6197		14.25			Married
12	6197		14.25			Single

Figure 13.25
Employees

Note: Be sure to enter the 01/31/-- payroll date when entering the payroll transactions and start check numbering with Check Number 1235.

Date	Employee Name	Check No.	Salary	Reg. Hours	O.T. Hours	Pieces	Comm. Sales	Federal Tax
01/31/--	Blades, Charles	1235	4575.00					529.50
01/31/--	Mendez, Bella	1236	4800.00					968.08
01/31/--	Presnell, Maurice	1237		176.00	2.50			207.97
01/31/--	Trimble, Dennis	1238		176.00				326.32

State Tax	City Tax	Social Security	Medicare	Health Insurance	Union Dues	Savings Bonds	Net Pay
182.13	91.50	283.65	66.34	125.00		200.00	3096.88
200.98	96.00	297.60	69.60	85.00		100.00	2982.74
75.86	51.23	158.81	37.14	125.00	10.00	50.00	1845.43
78.52	50.16	155.50	36.37	85.00	10.00	75.00	1691.13

Figure 13.26
January Payroll Transactions

STEP 22: Generate and post the Current Payroll and Employer's Payroll Taxes journal entries for the month of January.
Choose the *Current Payroll Journal Entry* menu item from the Options menu. Click *Yes* when asked if you want to generate the journal entry. When the entry appears in the Current Payroll Journal Entries dialog box, click *Post*. The journal entry will reappear, posted, in the general journal. Repeat this procedure for the Employer's Payroll Taxes menu item in the Options menu.

TUTORIAL PROBLEM 13-T

STEP 23: **Enter and process the February payroll transactions.**
Enter the February payroll transaction data shown in Figure 13.27. Have the computer calculate the withholding taxes.
Note: Be sure to enter the 02/28/-- payroll date when entering the payroll transactions.

Date	Employee Name	Check No.	Salary	Reg. Hours	O.T. Hours	Pieces	Comm. Sales	Federal Tax
02/28/--	Blades, Charles	1239	4575.00					529.50
02/28/--	Mendez, Bella	1240	4800.00					968.08
02/28/--	Presnell, Maurice	1241		168.00	1.50			187.66
02/28/--	Trimble, Dennis	1242		168.00	3.00			312.36

State Tax	City Tax	Social Security	Medicare	Health Insurance	Union Dues	Savings Bonds	Net Pay
182.13	91.50	283.65	66.34	125.00		200.00	3096.88
200.98	96.00	297.60	69.60	85.00		100.00	2982.74
69.30	48.52	150.42	35.18	125.00	10.00	50.00	1749.98
76.10	49.16	152.40	35.64	85.00	10.00	75.00	1662.47

Figure 13.27
February Payroll Transactions

STEP 24: **Generate and post the Current Payroll and Employer's Payroll Taxes journal entries for the month of February.**

STEP 25: **Display the Employee List.**
Click the *Reports* toolbar button. Choose the *Payroll Reports* option, and select the *Employee List* Report. Click *OK*. The report is shown in Figure 13.28.

STEP 26: **Display the Payroll Report.**
Choose the *Payroll Report,* and then click *OK*. The Payroll Report is shown in Figure 13.29.

In the days before graphical user interfaces, users could communicate only with text. Little pictures called "emoticons" were created that explained emotions better than using words. You may be familiar with the "smiley face" emoticon.

Many companies give you a choice on their Websites as to whether and how your personal information is used. Look for this as part of the company's privacy policy.

Chapter 13 Accounting System Setup

TUTORIAL PROBLEM 13-T

ABC Corporation
Employee List
03/01/--

Emp. No.	Employee Name/Address	Soc. Sec./ Mar. Stat.	# Pay Periods	G.L. Acct.	Salary/ Rate	Piece Rate/ Commission
110	Blades, Charles 3132 Shaw Dr. Chicago, IL 60634-4030	576-89-3288 Married W/H 3	12	6195	4575.00	
120	Mendez, Bella 8326 Highland Ave. Chicago, IL 60636-7812	466-21-8976 Single W/H 1	12	6195	4800.00	
130	Presnell, Maurice 59 Culver Ct. Chicago, IL 60656-1916	645-89-1432 Married W/H 3	12	6197	14.25	
140	Trimble, Dennis 11682 Oakland Rd. Chicago, IL 60639-5265	480-31-0415 Single W/H 1	12	6197	14.25	

Figure 13.28
Employee List

ABC Corporation
Payroll Report
3/01/--

		Current	Quarterly	Yearly
110-Blades, Charles	Gross Pay	4,575.00	9,150.00	9,150.00
6195-Salary	Federal W/H	529.50	1,059.00	1,059.00
Married Acct. 6195	State W/H	182.13	364.26	364.26
W/H 3 576-89-3288	Soc. Sec. W/H	283.65	567.30	567.30
Pay Periods 12	Medicare W/H	66.34	132.68	132.68
Salary 4575.00	City Tax W/H	91.50	183.00	183.00
Hourly Rate	Health Insurance	125.00	250.00	250.00
Piece Rate	Union Dues			
Commission %	Savings Bonds	200.00	400.00	400.00
Check Number 1239				
Check Date 02/28/02	Net Pay	3,096.88	6,193.76	6,193.76
				(continued)

Figure 13.29
Payroll Report

TUTORIAL PROBLEM 13-T

ABC Corporation
Payroll Report
3/01/--

		Current	Quarterly	Yearly
120-Mendez, Bella	Gross Pay	4,800.00	9,600.00	9,600.00
6195-Salary	Federal W/H	968.08	1,936.16	1,936.16
Single Acct. 6195	State W/H	200.98	401.96	401.96
W/H 1 466-21-8976	Soc. Sec. W/H	297.60	595.20	595.20
Pay Periods 12	Medicare W/H	69.60	139.20	139.20
Salary 4800.00	City Tax W/H	96.00	192.00	192.00
Hourly Rate	Health Insurance	85.00	170.00	170.00
Piece Rate	Union Dues			
Commission %	Savings Bonds	100.00	200.00	200.00
Check Number 1240				
Check Date 02/28/02	Net Pay	2,982.74	5,965.48	5,965.48
130-Presnell, Maurice	Gross Pay	2,426.06	4,987.50	4,987.50
6197-Salary	Federal W/H	187.66	395.63	395.63
Married Acct. 6197	State W/H	69.30	145.16	145.16
W/H 3 645-89-1432	Soc. Sec. W/H	150.42	309.23	309.23
Pay Periods 12	Medicare W/H	35.18	72.32	72.32
Salary	City Tax W/H	48.52	99.75	99.75
Hourly Rate 14.25	Health Insurance	125.00	250.00	250.00
Piece Rate	Union Dues	10.00	20.00	20.00
Commission %	Savings Bonds	50.00	100.00	100.00
Check Number 1241				
Check Date 02/28/02	Net Pay	1,749.98	3,595.41	3,595.41
140-Trimble, Dennis	Gross Pay	2,458.13	4,966.13	4,966.13
6197-Salary	Federal W/H	312.36	638.68	638.68
Single Acct. 6197	State W/H	76.10	154.62	154.62
W/H 1 480-31-0415	Soc. Sec. W/H	152.40	307.90	307.90
Pay Periods 12	Medicare W/H	35.64	72.01	72.01
Salary	City Tax W/H	49.16	99.32	99.32
Hourly Rate 14.25	Health Insurance	85.00	170.00	170.00
Piece Rate	Union Dues	10.00	20.00	20.00
Commission %	Savings Bonds	75.00	150.00	150.00
Check Number 1242				
Check Date 02/28/02	Net Pay	1,662.47	3,353.60	3,353.60
Payroll Summary	Gross Pay	14,259.19	28,703.63	28,703.63
	Federal W/H	1,997.60	4,029.47	4,029.47
	State W/H	528.51	1,066.00	1,066.00
	Soc. Sec. W/H	884.07	1,779.63	1,779.63
	Medicare W/H	206.76	416.21	416.21
	City Tax W/H	285.18	574.07	574.07
	Health Insurance	420.00	840.00	840.00
	Union Dues	20.00	40.00	40.00
	Savings Bonds	425.00	850.00	850.00
	Net Pay	9,492.07	19,108.25	19,108.25

Figure 13.29
Continued

Chapter 13 Accounting System Setup

TUTORIAL PROBLEM 13-T

STEP 27: **Save the data.**

STEP 28: **Enter the inventory stock item data.**
Click the *Accts.* toolbar icon. Choose the *Inventory* tab and enter the inventory stock items shown in Figure 13.30.

Stock No.	Description	Unit Meas.	Reorder Point	Retail Price
110	Air Hammer	EA	3	895.00
120	Band Saw	EA	10	39.95
130	Circular Electric Saw	EA	12	45.65
140	Cordless Drill	EA	12	49.95
150	Industrial Stapler	EA	10	39.95
160	M-7 Electric Drill	EA	12	45.00
170	Nail Gun	EA	5	68.75
180	Power Band Saw	EA	4	489.00
190	Table Circular Saw	EA	5	735.00

Figure 13.30 Inventory Stock Items

STEP 29: **Enter the purchase order historical data.**
Click the *Other* toolbar button. Choose the *Purchase Order* tab, and enter the following data:

PO#	Date	Vendor	Terms	Qty	Inventory Item	Price
371	03/01	Ellis Power Tools, Inc.	30 Days	20	Air Hammer	523.00
				16	Power Band Saw	290.00
				22	Table Circular Saw	432.00
372	03/01	Long Shore Tool Supplies	30 Days	40	Band Saw	22.50
				50	Circular Electric Saw	26.00
				65	Cordless Drill	28.50
373	03/01	Fotz Manufacturing, Inc.	30 Days	36	Industrial Stapler	24.00
				35	M-7 Electric Drill	27.00
374	03/01	West Coast Tool Corp.	30 Days	25	Nail Gun	40.50

STEP 30: **Enter the purchase invoice historical data.**
Choose the *Purch. Invoice* tab and enter the data below.
Warning: The average-cost calculations may be affected by the order in which transactions are entered. Therefore, making corrections or changing the sequence in which transactions are entered may distort the average cost. If you must make a correction to opening-balance historical data, it is a good idea to delete all occurrences of the inventory transaction first and then to reenter each occurrence in the order presented.

TUTORIAL PROBLEM 13-T

PI#	Date	Vendor	PO #	Terms	Qty	Inventory Item	Price
571	03/01	Ellis Power Tools, Inc.	371	30 Days	6	Air Hammer	523.00
					12	Air Hammer	535.00
					16	Power Band Saw	290.00
					10	Table Circular Saw	432.00
					12	Table Circular Saw	426.00
572	03/01	Long Shore Tool Supplies	372	30 Days	40	Band Saw	22.50
					25	Circular Saw	26.00
					25	Circular Saw	25.00
					60	Cordless Drill	28.50
573	03/01	Fotz Manufacturing, Inc.	373	30 Days	36	Industrial Stapler	24.00
					35	M-7 Electric Drill	27.00
574	03/01	West Coast Tool Corp.	374	30 Days	12	Nail Gun	40.50
					10	Nail Gun	41.50

STEP 31: Enter the sales invoice historical data.

Choose the *Sales Invoice* tab and enter the following data:

Inv#	Date	Tax	Customer	Terms	Qty	Inventory Item	Price
847	03/01	7%	Brockert Rentals	30 Days	5	Air Hammer	895.00
					6	Cordless Drill	49.95
					4	Industrial Stapler	39.95
					8	Nail Gun	68.75
848	03/01	7%	C B Industrial Tools	30 Days	2	Air Hammer	895.00
					15	Industrial Stapler	39.95
					4	Nail Gun	68.75
					8	Table Circular Saw	735.00
849	03/01	7%	Deters Machinery	30 Days	4	Band Saw	39.95
					10	Circular Electric Saw	45.65
					8	Cordless Drill	49.95
850	03/01	7%	Merchant Power Tools	30 Days	6	Air Hammer	895.00
					4	Nail Gun	68.75
					7	Power Band Saw	489.00
					8	Table Circular Saw	735.00
851	03/01	7%	Scholz Hardware	30 Days	12	Band Saw	39.95
					15	Circular Electric Saw	45.65
					18	Cordless Drill	49.95
					9	M-7 Electric Drill	45.00
852	03/01	7%	Wilkens Powers Tools	30 Days	5	Band Saw	39.95
					8	Circular Electric Saw	45.65
					6	Cordless Drill	49.95
					12	M-7 Electric Drill	45.00
853	03/01	7%	Wisdom Industries	30 Days	3	Air Hammer	895.00
					5	M-7 Electric Drill	45.00
					7	Power Band Saw	489.00

Chapter 13 Accounting System Setup

TUTORIAL PROBLEM 13-T

STEP 32: Display an Inventory List Report.
Click the *Reports* toolbar button. Choose *Inventory Reports* from the Select a Report Group list and select the *Inventory List* Report. Click *OK*. The report appears in Figure 13.31.

ABC Corporation
Inventory List
03/01/--

Stock No.	Description	Unit Meas.	On Hand	On Order	Reorder Point	Last Cost	Retail Price
110	Air Hammer	EA	2	2	3	535.00	895.00
120	Band Saw	EA	19	0	10	22.50	39.95
130	Circular Electric Saw	EA	17	0	12	25.00	45.65
140	Cordless Drill	EA	22	5	12	28.50	49.95
150	Industrial Stapler	EA	17	0	10	24.00	39.95
160	M-7 Electric Drill	EA	9	0	12	27.00	45.00
170	Nail Gun	EA	6	3	5	41.50	68.75
180	Power Band Saw	EA	2	0	4	290.00	489.00
190	Table Circular Saw	EA	6	0	5	426.00	735.00

Figure 13.31
Inventory List Report

STEP 33: Display the Inventory Transactions Report.
Select the *Inventory Transactions* Report from the Choose a Report to Display list and click *OK*. The report appears in Figure 13.32.

STEP 34: Display the Average Cost Valuation Report.
Select the *Valuation (Average Cost)* Report from the Choose a Report to Display list and click *OK*. The report appears in Figure 13.33.

STEP 35: Save your data.

STEP 36: Display a Trial Balance, Schedule of Accounts Payable, and Schedule of Accounts Receivable.
Choose *Ledger* Reports in the Report Selection window, and then select and display the *Trial Balance, Schedule of Accounts Payable,* and *Schedule of Accounts Receivable* Reports. The reports appear in Figure 13.34 (pages 484-485).

TUTORIAL PROBLEM 13-T

ABC Corporation
Inventory Transactions
03/01/--

Date	Description	Inv./P.O.	Quantity Sold	Selling Price	Quan. Ord.	Quan. Recd.	Cost Price
Sales Invoices							
03/01	Air Hammer	847	5	895.00			
	Cordless Drill		6	49.95			
	Industrial Stapler		4	39.95			
	Nail Gun		8	68.75			
03/01	Air Hammer	848	2	895.00			
	Industrial Stapler		15	39.95			
	Nail Gun		4	68.75			
	Table Circular Saw		8	735.00			
03/01	Band Saw	849	4	39.95			
	Circular Electric Saw		10	45.65			
	Cordless Drill		8	49.95			
03/01	Air Hammer	850	6	895.00			
	Nail Gun		4	68.75			
	Power Band Saw		7	489.00			
	Table Circular Saw		8	735.00			
03/01	Band Saw	851	12	39.95			
	Circular Electric Saw		15	45.65			
	Cordless Drill		18	49.95			
	M-7 Electric Drill		9	45.00			
03/01	Band Saw	852	5	39.95			
	Circular Electric Saw		8	45.65			
	Cordless Drill		6	49.95			
	M-7 Electric Drill		12	45.00			
03/01	Air Hammer	853	3	895.00			
	M-7 Electric Drill		5	45.00			
	Power Band Saw		7	489.00			
Purchase Orders							
03/01	Air Hammer	371			20		
	Power Band Saw				16		
	Table Circular Saw				22		
03/01	Band Saw	372			40		
	Circular Electric Saw				50		
	Cordless Drill				65		
03/01	Industrial Stapler	373			36		
	M-7 Electric Drill				35		
03/01	Nail Gun	374			25		
Purchase Invoices							
03/01	Air Hammer	571				6	523.00
	Power Band Saw					16	290.00

(continued)

Figure 13.32
Inventory Transactions Report

Chapter 13 Accounting System Setup

TUTORIAL PROBLEM 13-T

ABC Corporation
Inventory Transactions
03/01/--

Date	Description	Inv./P.O.	Quantity Sold	Selling Price	Quan. Ord.	Quan. Recd.	Cost Price
	Table Circular Saw					10	432.00
	Air Hammer					12	535.00
	Table Circular Saw					12	426.00
03/01	Band Saw	572				40	22.50
	Circular Electric Saw					25	26.00
	Cordless Drill					60	28.50
	Circular Electric Saw					25	25.00
03/01	Industrial Stapler	573				36	24.00
	M-7 Electric Drill					35	27.00
03/01	Nail Gun	574				12	40.50
	Nail Gun					10	41.50
	Totals		199		309	299	

Figure 13.32
Continued

ABC Corporation
Inventory Valuation (Average Cost)
03/01/--

Stock No.	Description	On Hand	Value Cost	At Cost	Retail Price	Value At Retail
110	Air Hammer	2	535.00	1070.00	895.00	1790.00
120	Band Saw	19	22.50	427.50	39.95	759.05
130	Circular Electric Saw	17	25.00	425.00	45.65	776.05
140	Cordless Drill	22	28.50	627.00	49.95	1098.90
150	Industrial Stapler	17	24.00	408.00	39.95	679.15
160	M-7 Electric Drill	9	27.00	243.00	45.00	405.00
170	Nail Gun	6	41.50	249.00	68.75	412.50
180	Power Band Saw	2	290.00	580.00	489.00	978.00
190	Table Circular Saw	6	426.00	2556.00	735.00	4410.00
	Total Inventory Value			6585.50		11308.65

Figure 13.33
Inventory Valuation (Average Cost) Report

TUTORIAL PROBLEM 13-T

ABC Corporation
Trial Balance
03/01/--

Acct. Number	Account Title	Debit	Credit
1105	Cash	21993.03	
1115	Accounts Receivable	43012.46	
1130	Merchandise Inventory	6585.50	
1135	Supplies	1913.76	
1150	Prepaid Insurance	1300.00	
1520	Equipment—Office	14091.00	
1530	Accum. Dep.—Off. Eq.		2912.91
1560	Warehouse Equipment	30351.30	
1565	Accum. Dep.—Wrhs. Eq.		5978.60
2105	Accounts Payable		30225.00
2113	Salaries Payable		19108.25
2120	Emp. Inc. Tax Pay.—Fed.		4029.47
2121	Emp. Inc. Tax Pay.—State		1066.00
2122	Emp. Inc. Tax Pay.—City		574.07
2125	Social Security Tax Pay.		3559.26
2126	Medicare Tax Payable		832.41
2130	Sales Tax Payable		2813.91
2135	Unemp. Tax Pay.—Fed.		191.63
2140	Unemp. Tax Pay.—State		1293.50
2150	Health Ins. Prem. Pay.		840.00
2160	Union Dues Payable		40.00
2170	Savings Bonds Payable		850.00
2505	Notes Payable		6100.00
3105	Capital Stock		48500.00
3120	Retained Earnings		12743.08
4105	Sales		40198.55
5105	Purchases	30225.00	
6170	Payroll Taxes Expense	3680.96	
6195	Salary Exp.—Office	18750.00	
6197	Salary Exp.—Wrhs.	9953.63	
	Totals	181856.64	181856.64

Figure 13.34
Trial Balance, Schedule of Accounts Payable, and Schedule of Accounts Receivable

Chapter 13 Accounting System Setup

TUTORIAL PROBLEM 13-T

ABC Corporation
Schedule of Accounts Payable
03/01/--

Name	Balance
Ellis Power Tools, Inc.	23630.00
Fotz Manufacturing, Inc.	1809.00
Long Shore Tool Supplies	3885.00
West Coast Tool Corp.	901.00
Total	30225.00

ABC Corporation
Schedule of Accounts Receivable
03/01/--

Name	Balance
Brockert Rentals	5868.42
C B Industrial Tools	9142.35
Deters Machinery	1087.01
Merchant Power Tools	15994.36
Scholz Hardware	2641.03
Wilkens Power Machines	1502.98
Wisdom Industries	6776.31
Total	43012.46

Figure 13.34
Continued

Note: Check the debit and credit totals of the Trial Balance Report to make sure they equal. Also, make sure the account balances in the Accounts Receivable and Accounts Payable accounts are equal to the totals shown on the respective schedules. If the Trial Balance is out of balance, or the Accounts Receivable and Accounts Payable account balances are not correct, it can be assumed that a keying error has been made and that corrections are necessary.

TUTORIAL PROBLEM 13-T

STEP 37: Create a special multicolumn journal.

ABC Corporation wants to use a multicolumn journal to enter all their transactions into the computer. (*Note:* Some companies that do not have a large volume of transactions prefer to journalize all transactions in a single journal, called a *combination* or *multicolumn journal*.)

Click the *Custom* toolbar button. Click the *Journal Wizard* tab, and then select the *General Journal* option. Click the *Next* button and create a Sales Credit column, a Cash Debit column, and a Cash Credit column. The completed journal is shown in Figure 13.35. Select the *General Journal* from the Journal Entries window to verify that your new multicolumn journal is correct. Notice that the opening balance data have been automatically placed in the appropriate columns.

Date	Refer.	Account	Debit	Credit	Sales Credit	Cash Debit	Cash Credit	Vendor/Customer
03/01/--	Balance	1130 Merchandise Inventory	6585.50			21993.03		
03/01/--	Balance	1135 Supplies	1913.76					
		1150 Prepaid Insurance	1300.00					
03/01/--	Balance	1520 Equipment -- Office	14091.00					
03/01/--	Balance	1530 Accum. Dep. -- Off. Eq.		2912.91				
03/01/--	Balance	1560 Warehouse Equipment	30351.30					
03/01/--	Balance	1565 Accum. Dep. -- Wrhs. Eq.		5978.60				
03/01/--	Balance	2505 Notes Payable		6100.00				
03/01/--	Balance	3105 Capital Stock		48500.00				
03/01/--	Balance	3120 Retained Earnings		12743.08				

Figure 13.35
Journal-Wizard-Created Multicolumn Journal

STEP 38: Calculate the annual retirement income using the Retirement Planner.

Click the *Tools* toolbar button. When the Planning Tools window appears, click the *Retirement Plan* tab. Click the *Annual Retirement Income* option button. Enter the following retirement data, and display the Retirement Schedule Reports. The Retirement Schedule Reports are shown in Figure 13.36.

Beginning Retirement Savings 5000.00
Annual Yield (Percent) 8.25
Current Age 26
Retirement Age 65
Withdraw Until Age 85
Annual Contribution 2500.00

Chapter 13 Accounting System Setup

TUTORIAL PROBLEM 13-T

Retirement Savings Plan
03/01/--

Schedule of Contributions

Age	Annual Contribution	Annual Yield	Retirement Savings
(Beginning Balance)			5000.00
26	2500.00	412.50	7912.50
27	2500.00	652.78	11065.28
28	2500.00	912.89	14478.17
29	2500.00	1194.45	18172.62
30	2500.00	1499.24	22171.86
/\			
61	2500.00	44192.03	582352.97
62	2500.00	48044.12	632897.09
63	2500.00	52214.01	687611.10
64	2500.00	56727.92	746839.02

Schedule of Retirement Income

Age	Annual Income	Annual Yield	Savings Balance
(Retirement Savings			746839.02
65	71582.26	55708.68	730965.44
66	71582.26	54399.11	713782.29
67	71582.26	52981.50	695181.53
68	71582.26	51446.94	675046.21
69	71582.26	49785.78	653249.73
70	71582.26	47987.57	629655.04
/\			
82	71582.26	10495.20	137709.78
83	71582.26	5455.52	71583.04
84	71583.04	.00	.00

Figure 13.36
Retirement Planner Schedules

STEP 39: Save your data.

STEP 40: End the *Automated Accounting* session.

Review and Practice: Applying Your Information Skills

I. MATCHING

Directions: In the *Working Papers*, write the letter of the appropriate term next to each definition.

    a. accounts pick list
    b. budget
    c. Journal Wizard
    d. New command
    e. opening balances
    f. Performance Report
    g. required accounts

1. Accounts that the software needs in order to prepare financial statements, to carry out integration among the systems, and to complete period-end closing tasks.

2. The general and subsidiary ledger balances at the beginning of the fiscal period.

3. A report that compares actual revenues and expenses with budgeted revenues and expenses in income statement format.

4. A software feature in the File menu that clears any existing data from memory in preparation for setting up a new accounting system.

5. A software feature that can be used to create special general, purchases, cash payments, sales, and cash receipts journals.

6. A financial plan for the future.

7. A pre-set master chart of accounts that can be used when adding to, creating, or updating a chart of accounts.

II. REVIEW QUESTIONS

Directions: Write the answers to the following questions in the *Working Papers*.

1. The Income Statement option on the Company Info. window allows two settings. List the two settings and explain the difference between them.

2. How are the data collected on the Required Accounts window used?

3. What is the purpose of the Account Subtotals window?

Chapter 13 Accounting System Setup

4. What is the purpose of the Classify Accounts window?
5. Briefly describe the two methods that can be used to create quarterly and yearly historical data for payroll setup.
6. What is the purpose of the Journal Wizard?
7. What is the purpose of the Tax Tables window?

III. INTERNET ACTIVITY

Directions: If you have access to the Internet, use your browser to find information about the history, usage, or coding of the Universal Product Code (UPC). Use *Universal Product Code* as your search argument. Report your findings. Be sure to note the source and the URL (Internet address) of your search.

Independent Practice Problem 13-P

In this problem, you will perform the accounting system setup for Spotless Chimney Sweep, a chimney cleaning service owned and operated by Julie Boyd. Spotless Chimney Sweep is a service business, which is organized as a sole proprietorship, is not departmentalized, prepares checks manually, and generates the income statement by fiscal period. The Trial Balance, Schedule of Accounts Payable, and Schedule of Accounts Receivable for Spotless Chimney Sweep as of March 1 of the current year are provided as follows:

General Ledger Account Titles and Balances:

Account Number	Account Title	Debit	Credit
Current Assets			
1105	Cash	2040.96	
1115	Accounts Receivable	6460.00	
1125	Notes Receivable	1200.00	
1135	Supplies	215.00	
1150	Prepaid Insurance	250.00	
Plant Assets			
1500	Equipment—Cleaning	2182.00	
1510	Accum. Dep.—Cln. Eq.		654.60
1520	Equipment—Office	5085.00	
1530	Accum. Dep.—Off. Eq.		1678.05
Current Liabilities			
2105	Accounts Payable	1051.82	
2130	Sales Tax Payable		

Long-Term Liabilities
2505 Notes Payable 4500.00

Capital
3110 Julie Boyd, Capital 9548.49
3120 Julie Boyd, Drawing
3135 Income Summary

Revenue
4105 Sales
4110 Sales Discount

Expenses
6105 Advertising Expense
6120 Depr. Exp.—Cln. Eq.
6130 Depr. Exp.—Off. Eq.
6145 Insurance Expense
6165 Rent Expense
6190 Telephone Expense
6200 Utilities Expense
6210 Vehicle Expense

Other Revenue
7110 Interest Income

Other Expense
8105 Interest Expense

Schedule of Accounts Payable:

Name	Balance
Boone Hardware	135.00
Garcia Auto Center	265.45
Mega Office Supply	151.37
Selak Advertising	500.00
Total	1051.82

Schedule of Accounts Receivable:

Name	Balance
Belle Retirement Center	490.00
Highland Hills Apts.	1950.00
John Maddox	85.00
Ruth Steinfield	85.00
Taylor Condo Assoc.	3850.00
Total	6460.00

Chapter 13 Accounting System Setup

STEP 1: Start up *Automated Accounting 8.0*.

STEP 2: Use the New command from the File menu to prepare the computer for setup.

STEP 3: Enter your name in the User Name text box and click *OK*.

STEP 4: Enter the data fields and set the check boxes and option buttons in **Customized Accounting**.

STEP 5: Save your data with a file name of 13-P Your Name.

STEP 6: Enter the chart of accounts data.

STEP 7: Enter the vendors.

STEP 8: Enter the customers.

STEP 9: Verify account classification and extended account classification account number ranges.

STEP 10: Verify the required accounts data.

STEP 11: Enter the following account subtotals:
Total Current Assets
Total Plant Assets
Total Current Liabilities
Total Long-Term Liabilities

STEP 12: Enter the opening balances from the Trial Balance, Schedule of Accounts Payable, and Schedule of Accounts Receivable (shown at the beginning of this problem) into the general ledger.
Hint: Since this accounting system does not involve an inventory, the vendor and customer account balances shown in the Schedules of Accounts Payable and Accounts Receivable must be entered with the rest of the opening balances in the general journal to establish the Accounts Receivable and Accounts Payable account balances. Figure 13.37 shows how the customer balances are entered. (The same procedure is required to enter the vendor account balances.)

Date	Refer.	Acct. No.	Debit	Credit	Vendor/Customer
03/01/__	Balance	1115	490.00		Belle Retirement Center
03/01/__	Balance	1115	1950.00		Highland Hills Apts.
03/01/__	Balance	1115	85.00		John Maddox
03/01/__	Balance	1115	85.00		Ruth Steinfield
03/01/__	Balance	1115	3850.00		Taylor Condo Assoc.

Figure 13.37
Customer Account Balances Entered into the General Journal

STEP 13: Display a Chart of Accounts, Vendor List, and Customer List. Be certain to set the run date to March 1 of the current year.

STEP 14: Display a Trial Balance, Schedule of Accounts Payable, and Schedule of Accounts Receivable.

STEP 15: Display a Balance Sheet.

STEP 16: Calculate the annual contribution toward retirement using the Retirement Planner.
Select the *Annual Contribution* option in the Calculate section of the window, and then enter the following information:

Beginning Retirement Savings	25000.00
Annual Yield (Percent)	8.50
Current Age	32
Retirement Age	65
Withdraw Until Age	85
Annual Retirement Income	75000.00

STEP 17: Create a special cash receipts journal.
Expand the current cash receipts journal to include Sales, Sales Tax Payable, and Sales Discount (similar to what you used in Chapters 7 and 9). Do not include the General Debit and Credit columns. Use the Cash Receipts Journal option of the Journal Wizard to create the expanded journal.

STEP 18: Save your data.

STEP 19: End your *Automated Accounting* session.

Applying Your Technology Skills 13-P

Directions: Write the answers to the following questions in the *Working Papers*.

1. What is the total of the Credit column in the Trial Balance?
2. What is the balance in the Accounts Receivable account in the Trial Balance?
3. What is the balance in the Accounts Payable account in the Trial Balance?
4. What is the amount owed to Selak Advertising?
5. What is the total owed to all vendors?

Chapter 13 Accounting System Setup

6. What is the amount due from Highland Hills Apts.?
7. What is the amount due from all customers?
8. From the Balance Sheet, what are the total current assets?
9. From the Balance Sheet, what are the total plant assets?
10. From the retirement savings plan, what is the annual contribution required for an annual income of $75,000.00?
11. What is the retirement savings balance at the time of retirement (age 65)?

Mastery Problem 13-M

In this problem, you will set up the accounting, plant assets, payroll, inventory, and budgeting data for Paul's Fan City. Paul's Fan City is a merchandising business organized as a sole proprietorship, is not departmentalized, prepares checks manually, and generates the income statement by fiscal period. The data required to set up the accounting system as of January 1 of the current year are provided as follows:

General Ledger Account Titles and Balances:

Account Number	Account Title	Debit	Credit
Assets			
1105	Cash	10792.84	
1115	Accounts Receivable		
1120	Allow. for Uncoll. Accts.		
1130	Merchandise Inventory	26272.90	
1140	Supplies—Office	1928.50	
1145	Supplies—Wrhs.	3300.00	
1150	Prepaid Insurance		
1520	Equipment—Office	20996.38	
1530	Accum. Dep.—Off. Eq.		9900.48
1560	Equipment—Warehouse	13953.45	
1565	Accum. Dep.—Wrhs. Eq.		8601.97
Liabilities			
2105	Accounts Payable		
2110	Salaries Payable		
2120	Emp. Inc. Tax Pay.—Fed.		
2121	Emp. Inc. Tax Pay.—St.		
2122	Emp. Inc. Tax Pay.—City		
2125	Social Security Tax Pay.		

2126	Medicare Tax Payable
2130	Sales Tax Payable
2135	Unemp. Tax Pay.—Fed.
2140	Unemp. Tax Pay.—State
2150	Health Insurance Payable
2160	Dental Insurance Payable
2170	Credit Union Deduct. Pay.

Owner's Equity

3110	Paul Chesley, Capital	58741.62
3120	Paul Chesley, Drawing	
3135	Income Summary	

Revenue

4105	Sales
4110	Sales Discount
4115	Sales Ret. and Allow.

Cost

5105	Purchases
5110	Purchases Discount
5115	Purch. Ret. and Allow.

Expenses

6105	Advertising Expense
6130	Depr. Exp.—Off. Eq.
6140	Depr. Exp.—Wrhs. Eq.
6150	Insurance Expense
6155	Miscellaneous Expense
6170	Payroll Taxes Expense
6180	Rent Expense
6195	Salary Exp.—Office
6197	Salary Exp.—Wrhs.
6215	Telephone Expense
6225	Utilities Expense

Vendors:
Abbot Exhaust Fan Co.
Air Control Fan Corp.
Decor Ceiling Fans
RC Industrial Fans, Inc.

Customers:
Carmen Lopez
David Gilliam
General Hospital
Marlar Construction Co.
Sagel Valley Motel
Winsor Treatment Center

Chapter 13 Accounting System Setup

Budget Amounts:

Account Title	Budget Amount
Total Revenue	$1,265,000.00
Cost of Goods Sold	925,000.00
Advertising Expense	5,200.00
Depr. Exp.—Off. Eq.	4,050.00
Depr. Exp.—Wrhs. Eq.	5,750.00
Insurance Expense	12,500.00
Miscellaneous Expense	2,500.00
Payroll Taxes Expense	22,000.00
Rent Expense	36,000.00
Salary Exp.—Office	52,000.00
Salary Exp.—Wrhs.	42,000.00
Telephone Expense	6,000.00
Utilities Expense	15,500.00

Plant Assets:

Asset No.	Asset Name	Date Acquired	Useful Life	Original Cost	Salvage Value	Accum. Deprec.	Deprec. Exp.	Deprec. Method
Office Equipment								
110	Copy Machine	03/21/00	6	2895.00	220.00	1530	6130	SL
120	Facsimile Machine	01/28/01	5	875.00	75.00	1530	6130	SL
130	File Cabinet	04/20/01	10	760.00	50.00	1530	6130	SL
140	Computer System	02/24/02	5	2695.00	250.00	1530	6130	SL
Warehouse Equipment								
210	Fork Lift	10/31/02	8	3895.00	450.00	1565	6140	SL
220	Shelving	09/30/01	10	11985.00	850.00	1565	6140	SL
230	Hydraulic Hoist	02/20/01	10	2145.00	200.00	1565	6140	SL

Employees:

No.	Name Address, City/State	SS No.	W/H Allow.	No. Pay Periods	G.L. Acct.	Salary/ Rate	Mar. Stat.
210	Apland, Velma 5573 Beverly Dr. Newark, NJ 07112-2100	435-24-5449	3	26	6195	2300.00	Mar.
220	Brantley, James 7718 Western Dr. Newark, NJ 07106-5618	767-33-8092	1	26	6197	2250.00	Single
230	Lenox, Timothy 749 East Sharon Ave. Newark, NJ 07108-7335	587-45-4204	1	26	6197	12.25	Single
240	Maddux, Joyce 95 Fox Chase Ct. Newark, NJ 07107-4550	495-30-9083	2	26	6195	11.85	Mar.

Note: Because the payroll system is being established on the first day of a new calendar year, it is not necessary to establish current, quarter-to-date, or year-to-date opening balance data.

Inventory:

Stock Items

Stock No.	Description	Unit of Measure	Reorder Point	Retail Price
1010	Abbot Exhaust Fan	EA	30	185.00
1020	DX-10 Exhaust Fan	EA	35	99.99
2010	Air Control Fan	EA	28	318.00
2020	RC Attic Fan	EA	25	145.00
3010	Decor Ceiling Fan	EA	25	395.00
3020	Remote Control Fan	EA	18	229.00
3030	TWD Ceiling Fan	EA	30	185.00

Purchase Order Historical Data

PO#	Date	Vendor	Terms	Qty	Inventory Item	Price
416	01/01	Abbot Exhaust Fan Co.	30 Days	85	Abbot Exhaust Fan	105.00
				110	DX-10 Exhaust Fan	58.95
417	01/01	Air Control Fan Corp.	30 Days	70	Air Control Fan	185.00
				60	Remote Control Fan	135.00
418	01/01	RC Industrial Fans, Inc.	30 Days	75	RC Attic Fan	85.95
419	01/01	Décor Ceiling Fans	30 Days	80	Décor Ceiling Fan	232.50
				100	TWD Ceiling Fan	109.00

Purchase Invoice Historical Data

PI#	Date	Vendor	PO #	Terms	Qty	Inventory Item	Price
632	01/01	Abbot Exhaust Fan Co.	416	30 Days	80	Abbot Exhaust Fan	105.00
					110	DX-10 Exhaust Fan	58.95
633	01/01	Air Control Fan Corp.	417	30 Days	70	Air Control Fan	185.00
					60	Remote Control Fan	135.00
634	01/01	RC Industrial Fans, Inc.	418	30 Days	75	RC Attic Fan	85.95
635	01/01	Décor Ceiling Fans	419	30 Days	80	Décor Ceiling Fan	232.50
					100	TWD Ceiling Fan	109.00

Sales Invoice Historical Data

Inv#	Date	Tax	Customer	Terms	Qty	Inventory Item	Price
812	01/01	7%	Carmen Lopez	30 Days	3	Air Control Fan	318.00
					4	Décor Ceiling Fan	395.00
					2	TWD Ceiling Fan	185.00
813	01/01	7%	David Gilliam	30 Days	3	Air Control Fan	318.00
					5	Décor Ceiling Fan	395.00
					2	TWD Ceiling Fan	185.00
814	01/01	7%	General Hospital	30 Days	26	Abbot Exhaust Fan	185.00
					20	Air Control Fan	318.00
					35	Décor Ceiling Fan	395.00
					18	TWD Ceiling Fan	185.00
815	01/01	7%	Marlar Construction Co.	30 Days	40	DX-10 Exhaust Fan	99.99
					46	RC Attic Fan	145.00
					18	Remote Control Fan	229.00
					24	TWD Ceiling Fan	185.00

Chapter 13 Accounting System Setup

816	01/01	7%	Sagel Valley Motel	30 Days	10	Abbot Exhaust Fan	185.00
					27	DX-10 Exhaust Fan	99.99
					9	Décor Ceiling Fan	395.00
817	01/01	7%	Winsor Treatment Center	30 Days	22	Abbot Exhaust Fan	185.00
					20	Air Control Fan	318.00
					11	Remote Control Fan	229.00
					17	TWD Ceiling Fan	185.00

STEP 1: Start up *Automated Accounting 8.0*.

STEP 2: Use the New command from the File menu to prepare the computer for setup.

STEP 3: Enter your name in the User Name text box.

STEP 4: Enter the data fields, and set the check boxes and option buttons in Customize Accounting.

STEP 5: Save your data with a file name of 13-M Your Name.

STEP 6: Enter the chart of accounts data.

STEP 7: Enter the vendors.

STEP 8: Enter the customers.

STEP 9: Verify account classification and extended account classification number ranges.

STEP 10: Complete the required accounts.

STEP 11: Enter the account subtotals data to provide the following subtotals:
Total Current Assets
Total Plant Assets
Total Current Liabilities
Total Long-Term Liabilities

STEP 12: Enter the general ledger opening balances.

STEP 13: Create a special cash payments journal.
Expand the current cash payments journal to include Purchases Discount (credit). Use the Cash Payments Journal option of the Journal Wizard to create the expanded journal. Include General Debit and Credit columns.

STEP 14: Enter budget amounts.

STEP 15: Display a Chart of Accounts, Vendor List, and Customer List.

STEP 16: Save the data to disk.

STEP 17: Enter the plant assets.

STEP 18: Display the Plant Assets List Report.

STEP 19: Save the data to disk.

STEP 20: Enter the employee data.

STEP 21: Display the Employee List.

STEP 22: Enter a 1.5% City Tax Rate in the Payroll Tax Tables.

STEP 23: Save the data to disk.

STEP 24: Enter the inventory stock items.

STEP 25: Enter the purchase order historical data.

STEP 26: Enter the purchase invoice historical data.

STEP 27: Enter the sales invoice historical data.

STEP 28: Display an Inventory Transactions Report.

STEP 29: Display the Average Cost Valuation Report.

STEP 30: Display a Trial Balance, Schedule of Accounts Payable, and Schedule of Accounts Receivable.

STEP 31: Use the following data to calculate annual retirement income:

Beginning Retirement Savings	3000.00
Annual Yield (Percent)	7.50
Current Age	22
Retirement Age	65
Withdraw Until Age	85
Annual Contribution	2400.00

STEP 32: Save your data to disk.

STEP 33: End the *Automated Accounting* session.

Applying Your Technology Skills 13-M

Directions: Using Mastery Problem 13-M, write the answers to the following questions in the *Working Papers*.

Plant Assets

1. What is the salvage value of Asset Number 120 (Facsimile Machine)?

2. On what date was Asset Number 230 (Hydraulic Hoist) acquired?

3. What is the total original cost of all assets?

Chapter 13 Accounting System Setup

Payroll

4. What is the salary amount for James Brantley?
5. What is Timothy Lenox's hourly pay rate?
6. What is Joyce Maddux's address?

Inventory

7. What is the total number of items sold?
8. What is the total inventory value at cost?
9. What is the total inventory value at retail?

Retirement Planner

10. What is the amount of the annual retirement income?
11. What is the retirement savings balance at the time of retirement (age 65)?

General Ledger

12. What is the total of the Credit column in the Trial Balance?
13. What is the balance in the Accounts Receivable account in the Trial Balance?
14. What is the balance in the Accounts Payable account in the Trial Balance?
15. What is the amount owed to Air Control Fan Corp.?
16. What is the total owed to all vendors?
17. What is the amount due from Marlar Construction Co.?
18. What is the amount due from all customers?
19. List the column headings on the new cash payments journal.

If you're planning a vacation, you can book your flights and accommodations online by going to the Websites of specific airlines, hotels, car rental agencies, and entertainment centers, or make all the reservations through a full-service travel site.

The primary reasons consumers report that they do not shop online are security concerns, difficulty in making purchases using the Internet, and a belief that they will receive poor customer service if there are problems with the order or the product.

Glossary

Access Key
Allows quick access to the menu item.

Account Maintenance
The process of keeping a business's chart of accounts up to date by adding new accounts, changing titles of existing accounts, and deleting inactive accounts.

Accounts Payable Ledger Report
A report that shows detailed journal entry activity by vendor.

Accounts Pick List
A preset master chart of accounts that can be used when adding to, creating, or updating a chart of accounts.

Accounts Receivable Ledger Report
A report that shows detailed journal entry activity by customer.

Adjusting Entries
Journal entries recorded to update general ledger accounts at the end of a fiscal period.

Asset Disposition
Removing an asset from use in a business.

Average Cost Method
An inventory valuation method that uses an average of the actual costs and quantities to calculate the value of an inventory.

Balance Sheet
A financial statement that reports assets, liabilities, and owner's equities on a specific date.

Bank Reconciliation
The process of verifying that the bank statement and the checkbook balance are in agreement.

Board of Directors
A group elected by shareholders to manage a corporation.

Budget
A financial plan for the future, developed for a specific period of time, such as a month or a year.

Capital Stock
The total shares of ownership in a corporation.

Cash Payment
Any type of transaction involving the payment of cash.

Cash Payment on Account
A cash disbursement that *does* affect Accounts Payable.

Cash Payments Journal
The special journal used to record all payments of cash.

Cash Payments Journal Input Form
An input form on which all cash payments can be recorded.

Cash Receipt
Any type of transaction involving the receipt of cash.

Glossary

Cash Receipt on Account
A cash-receipt transaction that *does* affect Accounts Receivable.

Cash Receipts Journal
A special journal used to enter all cash-receipt transactions.

Cash Receipts Journal Input Form
An input form used to record all cash receipts.

Clipboard
A temporary storage area.

Component Percentage
Shows the percentage relationship between one financial statement item and the total that includes that item.

Computerized Purchase Order Processing System
The procedures involved in automatically integrating the purchase order, purchase invoice, and cash disbursement data into the inventory and general ledger.

Computerized Sales Order Processing System
The procedures involved in preparing a sales invoice and automatically integrating the data it contains into the inventory and general ledger records.

Corporate Income Tax
The tax that corporations are required to pay on their earnings.

Corporation
An organization that has many of the legal rights of an individual but is typically owned by many people.

Credit Memorandum
The form prepared by the vendor showing the amount deducted for returns and allowances.

Current User Name and File Name
Area of the Title Bar where information will appear when a file is opened and loaded into memory and the user name is entered.

Customer
A business or individual to whom merchandise or services are sold.

Debit Memorandum
The form prepared by the customer showing the price deduction for returns and allowances.

Declaring a Dividend
The decision by a board of directors to distribute earnings to shareholders.

Depreciation
The portion of a plant asset's cost that is transferred to an expense account in each fiscal period during its useful life.

Depreciation Adjusting Entries
The journal entries recorded to update the Depreciation Expense and Accumulated Depreciation accounts at the end of a fiscal period.

Depreciation Schedule
A report that provides annual depreciation for each year for the life of a plant asset.

Direct Payment
A cash disbursement that does *not* affect Accounts Payable.

Direct Receipt
A cash-receipt transaction that does *not* affect Accounts Receivable.

Discount Period
The specified time period within which a deduction from an invoice amount may be taken.

Dividends
Earnings a corporation distributes to shareholders.

Employee List Report
A complete listing of the employee payroll information.

Explore Accounting System
Used to access data stored by the software in order to perform audit checks, check account activity, isolate errors, and perform other tasks that are helpful to managing account information.

FIFO Method
An inventory valuation method that uses the latest costs to calculate the value of an inventory.

Focus
The part of the window that will receive input.

General Journal Input Form
A form with two amount columns that is used to organize and record accounting transaction data before entering data at the computer.

General Journal Report
A display or printout of the general journal that is useful in detecting errors and verifying the equality of debits and credits.

General Journal Tab
A set of grid cells within the Journal Entries window that is used to enter and post general journal entries and to make corrections to or delete existing journal entries.

General Ledger Report
A report that shows detailed journal entry activity by account.

Graph
A pictorial representation of data that can be depicted on a computer screen or printed.

Grid Cells
Arrangements of rows and columns that, like text boxes, are used to enter, edit, or delete data and text.

Help System
Offers a quick way to find information about operating the software.

Hourly Rate
The amount paid an employee for each hour worked.

Income Statement
A financial statement that provides information about the net income or net loss of a business over a specific period of time.

Income Summary Account
An account used to summarize the closing entries for the revenue and expense accounts.

Input Form
A form used to organize and record accounting transaction data before entering the data at the computer.

Insertion Point
A character that is positioned in a text box to indicate where data will be entered or edited.

Inventory Exceptions Report
A report that lists items in the inventory that are out of stock (quantity on hand of zero or less) and items that are at or below the reorder point (quantity on hand less than or equal to the reorder point).

Inventory List Report
A report that lists the current status of each inventory item for reference.

Inventory Stock Items Input Form
An input form used to record additions, changes, and deletions to inventory items.

Inventory Transactions Report
A list of all transactions that have affected inventory items during the processing period.

Inventory Valuation Report
A report that lists the per-item and total cost and retail prices of all items currently in the inventory.

Journal
A record of the debit and credit parts of each transaction recorded in date sequence.

Journal Wizard
A software feature that can be used to create special general, purchases, cash payments, sales, and cash receipts journals.

LIFO Method
An inventory valuation method that uses the earliest costs to calculate the value of an inventory.

Glossary

Management Information System (MIS)
Consists of several computer-integrated systems that supply all the informational needs of a business.

Marital Status
Single or married status for tax purposes.

Menu Bar
Shows titles of menus available.

Menu Item
A command that directs the computer to execute a particular action.

Menu Title
The name of the drop-down menu.

Merchandise
Goods purchased for resale.

Merchandise Inventory Account
An asset account that shows the value of goods on hand for sale to customers.

Merchandising Business
A business that purchases and resells goods.

New Command
A software feature in the File menu that clears any existing data from memory in preparation for setting up a new accounting system.

Number of Pay Periods
The number of times an employee is paid per year.

Opening Balances
The general and subsidiary ledger balances at the beginning of the fiscal period.

Original Cost
All costs paid to make a plant asset usable to a business.

Partnership
A business that is owned by two or more persons.

Payroll Report
A list of earnings and withholding information for the month, quarter, and year.

Performance Report
A report that compares actual revenues and expenses with budgeted revenues and expenses in income statement format.

Period-End Closing
The process of recording and posting closing entries to the general ledger to prepare temporary accounts for a new fiscal period.

Planning Tools
Convenient, fast, easy-to-use ways of producing results for commonly used applications.

Plant Asset Maintenance
The process of adding, changing, and deleting plant assets.

Plant Assets
Assets used for a number of years in the operation of a business.

Plant Assets Input Form
An input form used to record additions, changes, and deletions to plant assets.

Plant Assets List Report
A report that provides a detailed list of all plant assets owned.

Post-Closing Trial Balance
A trial balance that verifies that debits equal credits in the general ledger accounts after closing entries have been posted.

Posting
The process of updating the ledger account balances with all debits and credits affecting each account.

Purchase Invoice
A form that contains the vendor's name, original purchase order number, quantity and description of the merchandise, price, and sales terms of the merchandise sent.

Purchase Invoice Input Form
An input form used to record purchase invoice and purchase return transactions when a computerized purchase order processing system is used.

Purchase Invoice Register
A report that lists purchase invoices in numerical order with purchase returns listed last.

Purchase on Account
A transaction in which merchandise that is purchased is paid for at a later date.

Purchase Order
A document containing a purchase order number, the vendor name, the quantity and description, the expected price, and the terms of the item(s) ordered.

Purchase Order Input Form
An input form used to record purchase order transactions when a computerized purchase order processing system is used.

Purchase Order Register
A report that lists purchase orders in numerical and date order.

Purchase Requisitions
Formal requests for purchases that are entered into the computerized purchase order system.

Purchases Account
An account used to record the cost of the merchandise purchased for resale.

Purchases Discount
From the buyer's point of view, a deduction for early payment of an invoice.

Purchases Journal
The special journal used to record the purchase of merchandise on account.

Purchases Journal Input Form
An input form used to record only purchases of merchandise on account.

Quarterly Report
A report used to disclose Social Security and Medicare taxable wages to the Internal Revenue Service.

Receiving Report
A form that shows the description, quantity, and condition of merchandise received from a vendor.

Reorder Point
The minimum quantity that is allowed before additional items must be reordered.

Required Accounts
The accounts the software needs in order to prepare financial statements, to carry out integration among the systems, such as payroll and sales order processing, and to complete period-end closing tasks.

Retail Price
The current price per unit when the item is sold to a customer.

Retained Earnings
Earnings not yet distributed to shareholders.

Salary Amount
The gross amount paid for an employee's service each pay period.

Sales Discount
From the seller's point of view, a deduction for early payment of an invoice.

Sales Invoice
A form used to describe the goods sold, the quantity, and the price.

Sales Invoices Input Form
An input form used to record sales and sales return transactions when a computerized sales order processing system is used.

Sales Journal
A special journal used to enter only sales-of-merchandise-on-account transactions.

Sales Journal Input Form
An input form used to record only sales-on-account transactions.

Sales Order Processing
The procedures and controls involved in preparing invoices, updating accounting records, and shipping merchandise.

Sales Return
A credit allowed a customer for the sales price of returned merchandise, resulting in a decrease in the vendor's accounts receivable.

Glossary

Sales Transaction
A transaction in which merchandise is sold in exchange for another asset, usually money.

Salvage Value
The amount an owner expects to receive when a plant asset is removed from use.

Schedule of Accounts Payable Report
A report that lists each vendor account balance and the total balance due all vendors.

Schedule of Accounts Receivable Report
A report that lists each customer account balance and the total due from all customers.

Shareholders
Owners of the stock of a corporation.

Shares of Stock
Units that represent ownership in a corporation.

Shortcut Key
Allows a menu item to be selected directly without accessing the drop-down menu.

Sole Proprietorship
A business owned by one person.

Statement of Account
A report that shows the customer name and date, description and amount of each sales invoice, payments on account, and total amount due for that customer.

Statement of Owner's Equity
A financial statement that shows the changes to owner's equity during the fiscal period.

Stock Number
A unique code assigned to each stock item for identification.

Tab Sequence
The logical sequence in which the computer is expecting each grid cell, text box, button, and/or command to be accessed.

Temporary Accounts
Accounts that accumulate information until it is transferred to the owner's capital account.

Title Bar
Identifies contents of a window.

Toolbar Buttons
Provide a shortcut method of accessing the most commonly used menu items.

Tooltips
Brief informational messages that automatically appear when the pointer is positioned on a toolbar button.

Unit of Measure
A two-character field used to identify the unit of measure by which an item is sold (such as EA for each, CS for case, BX for box).

Useful Life
The estimated amount of time an asset can be used in a business.

User Interface
The way the user communicates with the software through images on the monitor.

Vendor
A business from which merchandise is purchased or supplies and other assets are bought.

Voluntary Deductions
Employee-authorized withholdings from earnings for such options as health insurance, dental insurance, savings plans, and charitable contributions.

W-2 Statement
A report that summarizes an employee's taxable wages and various withholdings.

Withholding Allowances
The number of deductions from total earnings for each person legally supported by a taxpayer for tax purposes.

Index

Account classification, 22
Account Column (General Journal Input Form), 48
Account Maintenance, 44–45
Account Maintenance Window tab, 8
Account option (General Journal tab), 48
Account Range dialog box, 123
Account Subtotals, 456
Accountants, functions of, 2
Accounting Careers
   Accounting Clerks, 29
   Audit Clerks, 221
   Auditor, 189
   Budget Accountant, 252
   Cost Accountants, 277
   CPA's, self-employed, 84
   Financial Planners, 465
   Investment Analyst, 335
   Mortgage Clerk, 419
   Payroll Clerk, 112
   skill levels, 29
   Tax Accountant, 160
   Tellers, 126
Accounting Clerk, responsibilities of, 55
Accounting Equation Report, 19–21
Accounting System, setup of
   Setup Data
      accounts pick list, 460–461
      budgets, 462
      inventory, 463
      opening balances, 461–462
      Payroll, 463
      performance report, 462
      Plant Assets, 463
   Setup Specifications
      account subtotals, 456
      classify accounts, 454–455
      company information, 452–453
      Customize Accounting System Window, 452–453
      journal wizard, 456–458
      required accounts, 455–456
      tax tables, 458–460
Accounting System field (Company Information Text Box), 453
Accounts
   Add Account button, 45
   Balances, rule of, 23–24
   Expense accounts, 22
   General Ledger, 24
   Income Summary, 80
      partnerships and, 186–187
   Merchandise Inventory, 114
   Purchases, 114
   Revenue accounts, 22
   T account, 22–23
   Temporary, 80
Accounts Payable Debit text box column, 120
Accounts Payable Ledger, 122
Accounts Payable Ledger Report, 124
Accounts Pick List, 460–461
Accounts Receivable Debit field, 151
Accounts Receivable Ledger Report, 157
Add Account button, 45
Add Asset button, 247
Add Customer button, 149
Add Item Button, 364
Add Vendor button, 115
Adding
   Inventory Stock Items, 364
   lines to transactions, 49
   Plant Assets, 247
Adjusting Entries, 74
   defined, 73, 183
   General Journal, 185
   Trial Balance Before example, 184
Adjusting Entries command (Options menu), 250
Administrators, Network Administrators, 146
Alt Key, 6
Application Window, 5
Asset Disposition, 244
Assets
   adding new, 247
   defined, 19
   deleting, 247
   editing, 247
Audit Clerks, 221
Auditors, 189
Automated Accounting Application Window, 5
Automated Accounting Startup, 4–5
Average Cost Method, 377

Balance, opening balance files, 3–4
Balance Sheet, 77
Bank Reconciliation
   Bank Reconciliation Report, 79–80
   Checkbook Balance text box, 78
   defined, 78
Board of Directors, 270
Bookkeepers, function of, 2

Index

Bookmark, 63
Browser windows, 26–27
Budget Accountants, 252
Budgets, 462–463
Bulletin Boards, Internet, 293
Business, defined, 2
Business Organization field (Company Information Text Box), 453
Buttons
    Add Account, 45
    Add Asset, 247
    Add Customer, 149
    Add Item, 364
    Add Vendor, 115
    Calculate Taxes, 327
    Change Asset, 247
    Change Customer, 149
    Change Employee, 325
    Change Item, 364
    Change Vendor, 115
    Command Buttons, 11–12
    Delete, 45, 115, 149
    Help, 16
    Option Buttons, 11
    Pick List, 460–461
    Post, 251

C

Calculate Taxes Button, 327
Calculator, on-screen, 17–18
Calendar icon, 51
Capital Stock, 270
Careers. *See* Accounting Careers
Cash Payments
    Cash Payments Journal
        defined, 114
        Payment of Quarterly Estimated Income Tax, 274
    Cash Payments Journal Input Form, 118
    Cash Payments on Account, 119–120
    defined, 118
    Direct Payment, 119
    Posting, 272
Cash Receipts
    Cash Receipt on Account, 154–155
    Cash Receipts Journal, 152
        Receipt on Account, 155
    Cash Receipts Journal Input Form, 152
    defined, 152
    Direct Receipts, 154
Certified Public Accountant (CPA), 84
Change Asset button, 247
Change Customer button, 149
Change Employee Button, 325
Change Item Button, 364
Change Print Font menu item (File menu), 13
Change Vendor button, 115
Chart of Accounts
    Account Maintenance, 44–45
    Corporations, 271
    defined, 18
    Delete button, 45
Check Boxes, 11
Checkbook Balance text box, 78
Checks
    Payroll, Sample of, 328
    sample of, 275
Classify Accounts, 454–455
Clerks
    Accounting Clerks, 55
    Audit Clerks, 221
    Mortgage Clerk, 419
    Payroll Clerks, 112
    responsibilities of, 55
Clipboard, 14
Close menu item (File menu), 12–13
College Planner (Planning Tools), 18
Command Buttons, 11–12
commands
    Data menu
        Customize Accounting System, 452
        Journal Entries, 117
        Maintain Accounts, 115, 149, 324
        Other Activities, 78, 366, 415
    Edit menu
        Copy, 14
        Cut, 14
        Find, 49
        Find Next, 49
        Paste, 14
    File menu
        Change Printer Font, 13
        Close, 12
        Exit, 13
        New, 452
        Open, 12
        Print, 13
        Print Setup, 13
        Save, 13
        Save As, 13
    Help menu, 15
    Options menu
        Adjusting Entries, 250
        Current Payroll Journal Entry, 328
        Employer's Payroll Taxes, 329
        Generate Closing Journal Entries, 81, 187
        Purge Invoices and Purchase Orders, 372–373, 417
    Reports menu
        Graph Selection, 52
        Payroll Reports, 330
        Report Selection, 50, 75
Company Info tab (Customize Accounting System Window), 452
Company Name field (Company Information Text Box), 453
Component Percentage, 76–77
Computer Checks field (Company Information Text Box), 453
Computerized Purchase Order Processing System, 365
Computerized Sales Order Processing System, 412
Cookies, 289
Copy command (Edit menu), 14
Copyright law, 72
Corporate Income Tax
    defined, 273
    recording, 274
Corporations
    Board Of Directors, 270
    Capital Stock, 270
    Cash Payments, Posting, 272
    Chart Of Accounts, 271
    defined, 270
    Shareholders, 270
    Shares Of Stock, 270
Cost Accountants, 277
CPA (Certified Public Accountant), 84
Credit
    Credit Entries, 23
    Credit Memorandum
        defined, 218
        General Journal example, 220
    Credit option (General Journal tab), 48
Current Payroll Journal Entry command (Options menu), 328
Customers
    Add Customer button, 149
    Change Customer button, 149

Customers *(continued)*
  Customer Maintenance Window, 149
  Customer Range dialog box, 157
  defined, 149
  Delete button, 149
Customize Accounting System command (Data menu), 452
Customize Accounting System Window, 452–453
Customize Journal Report dialog box, 51
Customize Journal Report option (Journal Report Selection dialog box), 50
Cut command (Edit menu), 14
Cyberspace, 63

D

Data Column (General Journal Input Form), 47
Data menu commands
  Customize Accounting System, 452
  Journal Entries, 117
  Maintain Accounts, 115, 149, 324
  Other Activities, 78, 366, 415
Date Column (General Journal Input Form), 48
Debit
  Debit Entries, 23
  Debit Memorandum
    defined, 218
    General Journal example, 220
  Debit option (General Journal tab), 48
Declaring Dividends, 272–273
Decryption, 148
Delete button, 45, 115, 149, 247
Deleting
  Inventory Stock Items, 364
  Plant Assets, 247
  Purchase Invoice and Return Transactions, 371–372
  Purchase Order Transactions, 368
  Sales Return Transaction, 417
  Transactions from General Journal, 49
Departments Drop-Down List (Company Info Tab), 452
Departments field (Company Information Text Box), 453

Depreciation, 244
  Depreciation Adjusting Dialog Box, 250
  Depreciation Schedule, 249
Dialog Boxes
  Account Range, 123
  Current Payroll Journal Entry Confirmation, 329
  Customer Range, 157
  Customize Journal Report, 51
  Depreciation Adjusting, 250
  Employer's Payroll Taxes Confirmation, 330
  Establish Offsetting Account, 457
  Find Journal Entry, 49
  General Debit and Credit Column, 458
  Graph Selection, 53
  Journal Report, 50
  Journal Report Selection, 50, 121, 156
  Report Selection, 50, 75, 121, 155
  Vendor Range, 124
Direct Payments, 119
Direct Receipts, 154
Discount Period, 218
Discussion Groups, Internet, 392
Displaying
  Financial Statements, 75
  General Journal Report, 50
Dividends, 270
  declaring, 272–273
  paying, 273
Domain Name, 200
Dot-Com Businesses, 200
Down Arrow key, 10
Drop-Down Lists, 10
Drop-Down Menu, 6

E

Edit menu commands
  Copy, 14
  Cut, 14
  Find, 49
  Find Next, 49
  Paste, 14
Editing
  Inventory Stock Items, 364
  Plant Assets, 247
  Sales Return Transactions, 417
Emoticons, 476
Employees
  Employee Input Form, 322

Employee List Report, 331
Employee Maintenance Window, 323–324
Employees Account Maintenance Window, 323
Employer's Payroll Taxes command (Options menu), 329
Encryption, 148
Entering Sales Return Transactions, 416
Equity, Owner's Equity, 19
Establish Offsetting Account Dialog Box, 457
Ethical Issues
  automation, 451
  communication, 217
  copyright law, 72, 114
  encryption, 148
  hacking, 2
  industry standards, 412
  self-employed programmers, 270
  Shareware, 44
  workplace and, 183
Exit menu item (File menu), 13
Expense accounts, 22
Explore Accounting System Window, 25–26

F

Features field (Company Information Text Box), 453
Federal Tax Brackets, 458
FIFO (First-In, First-Out) method, 377
File menu commands
  Change Printer Font, 13
  Close, 12
  Exit, 13
  New, 452
  Open, 12
  Print, 13
  Print Setup, 13
  Save, 13
  Save As, 13
File Transfer Protocol (FTP), 146
Files
  saving, 16
  user data files, 4
Financial Planners, 465
Financial Statements, 185–186
  Balance Sheet, 77
  displaying, 75
  Income Statements, 76
  Owner's Equity Statement, 78

Index

Find command (Edit menu), 49
Find Journal Entry dialog box, 49
Find Next command (Edit menu), 49
Firewalls, 146
First-In, First-Out (FIFO) method, 377
Focus, 7
FTP (File Transfer Protocol), 146

General Debit and Credit Column Dialog Box, 458
General Journal
    Credit Memorandum, 220
    Debit Memorandum, 220
    Depreciation Adjusting Entries, 251
    Federal Income Tax Adjusting Entry, 274
    General Journal Input Form, 46–47
    General Journal Report, 120
        Calendar icon, 51
        defined, 49
        displaying, 50
        example of, 52
        function of, 49
    General Journal tab
        Account option, 48
        Credit option, 48
        Date option, 48
        Debit option, 48
        defined, 47
        Post option, 48–49
        Reference option, 48
    General Journal Transactions
        adding lines to transactions, 49
        changing general journal transactions, 49
        deleting general journal transactions, 49
        finding journal entry, 49
        general journal input form, 46
        general journal tab, 47
        posting, 45
    Transactions
        adding lines to, 49
        deleting, 49
        editing, 49
General Ledger
    defined, 18
    General Ledger Accounts, 24
    General Ledger Report, 122–123

Generate Closing Journal Entries command (Options menu), 81, 187
Graph Selection command (Reports menu), 52
Graph Selection Dialog Box, 53
Graphing, 52–53
Grid Cells, 9

Hacking, 2
Help Contents and Index menu, 15
Help menu commands, 15
Help System
    accessing, 15
    Help window, 15–16
Hits (Internet Hits), 146
Host, 36
Hotlist, 63
Hourly Rate field, 324

Income Statements
    by fiscal period, 76
    Income Statement field (Company Information Text Box), 453
    by Month and Year, 275
Income Summary account
    defined, 80
    partnerships and, 186–187
Income Tax, Corporate Income Tax, 273–274
Index and Search Tab, 16
Index tab, 16
Input Forms, 44
Insertion Point, 7
Installation Requirements, 4
Interface, User, 3
Internet
    addresses, 36
    bookmark, 63
    Bulletin Boards, 293
    Cookies, 289
    Cyberspace, 63
    defined, 146
    discussion groups, 392
    domain name, 200
    dot-com business, 200
    E-commerce, 233
    Emoticons, 476
    fraudulent businesses, 389
    hits, 146
    host, 36
    hotlist, 63
    humor on, 233
    job search info, 398
    modem, 111
    online banking services, 418
    search engines, 193
    security, 173
    servers, 36
    shopping on, 223
    telephone *versus*, 292
    URL (uniform resource locator), 63
    Web Browser, 26–27
    Web-hosting service, 111
    Web Pages, Secure, 349
    Webmasters, 173
Internet Service Provider (ISP), 26
Inventory
    accounting system setup, 463
    Inventory Exceptions Report, 375
    Inventory List Report, 374
    Inventory Maintenance Tab, 363
    Inventory Stock Items Input Form, 362
    Inventory Transactions Report, 374–375
    Inventory Valuation Report, 375–376
    Merchandise, 361
    Stock Items, 364
Investment Analyst, 335
Invoices
    Purchase Invoice, 368
    Purge Invoices, 417
    purging, 372–373
    Sales Invoice, 150, 412–413
ISP (Internet Service Provider), 26

Journal, defined, 45
Journal Entries command (Data menu), 117
Journal Report Selection dialog box, 50, 121, 156
Journal Wizard
    defined, 456
    Establish Offsetting Account Dialog Box, 457
    General Debit and Credit Column Dialog Box, 458

LAN (local area network), 26
Last-In, First-Out (LIFO) method, 377
Ledger Reports, 122–123, 156
    Accounts Payable Ledger Report, 124
    Accounts Receivable Ledger Report, 157
    General Ledger Report, 122–123
    Schedule of Accounts Receivable Report, 123, 157
Liabilities, 19
LIFO (Last-In, First-Out) method, 377
List Boxes
    defined, 9
    example of, 10
    selecting items from, 9
Listserv, 146
Local Area Network (LAN), 26
Lurkers, 424

Maintain Accounts command (Data menu), 115, 149, 324
Management Information System (MIS), 2
Marital Status field, 324
Memory Requirements, 4
Menu Bar
    drop-down menu, 6
    illustration of, 5
    menu titles, list of, 5–6
Menu Items, selecting, 6
Merchandise Inventory account, 114
Merchandising Business, 114
MIS (Management Information System), 2
Modem, 111
Mortgage Clerk, 419
Moving Windows, 7

Navigation, 14
Network Administrators, 146
New command (File menu), 452
Newsgroups, Lurkers, 424
Number of Pay Periods field, 324

On-Screen Calculator, 17–18
Online Banking Services, 418
Open menu item (File menu), 12–13
Opening Balances, 461–462
    Opening Balance Files, 3–4
    Opening Balances Data, 3–4
Operating Procedures
    Change Printer Font, 13
    Check Boxes, 11
    Close Menu, 12
    Command Buttons, 11–12
    Drop-Down List, 10
    Edit Menu, 14
    Exit Menu, 13
    Grid Cells, 9
    List Boxes, 9
    Menu Bar, 5–6
    Menu Items, Selecting, 6
    Navigation, 14
    Open Menu, 12
    Option Buttons, 11
    Print menu, 13
    Print Setup Menu, 13
    Save As Menu, 13
    Save Menu, 13
    Tab Sequence, 14
    Tabs, 7
    Text Boxes, 7–8
    Window Controls, 6–7
Option Buttons, 11
Options menu commands
    Adjusting Entries, 250
    Current Payroll Journal Entry, 328
    Employer's Payroll Taxes, 329
    Generate Closing Journal Entries, 81, 187
    Purge Invoices and Purchase Orders, 372–373, 417
Original Cost, of Asset, 245
Other Activities command (Data menu), 78, 366, 415
Owner's Equity, 19
Owner's Equity Statement, 78

Partnerships
    defined, 114
    Period-End Closing for, 186–187
Paste command (Edit menu), 14
Paying Dividends, 273

Payroll
    Accounting System Setup, 463
    Employee Input Form, 321–323
    Employee Maintenance, 324–325
    Employer's Payroll Taxes, 329
    Journal Entries, Generating, 328–329
    Payroll Check, sample of, 328
    Payroll Clerks, 112
    Payroll Reports
        accessing, 330
        Employee List Report, 331
        W-2 Statements, 332
    Payroll Reports command (Reports menu), 330
    Payroll Transactions Input Form, 325
    Payroll Transactions Window, 326–327
    Quarterly Reports, 332
Performance Report, 462
Period-End Closing
    defined, 80
    for partnerships, 186–187
Picking Slip, 413
Planning Tools
    College Planner example, 18
    overview, 17
    types of, 17
Plant Assets
    Accounting System Setup, 463
    Asset Disposition, 244
    defined, 244
    Depreciation, 244
    Depreciation Schedule, 249
    Original Cost, 245
    Plant Asset Maintenance, 247
    Plant Assets Input Form, 245
    Plant Assets List Report, 248
    Plant Assets Maintenance Window, 246
Post Button, 251
Post-Closing Trial Balance, 81–82
Post option (General Journal tab), 48–49
Posting, defined, 45
Posting Column (General Journal Input Form), 48
Price field (Purchase Order Input Form), 366
Print menu item (File menu), 13
Print Setup menu item (File menu), 13
Problem Name field (Company Information Text Box), 453
Public Accountants, 380

Index

Purchase Invoice, 368
Purchase Invoice Input Form, 369–370
Purchase Invoice Register Report, 374
Purchase on Account, 115–116
Purchase Orders, 364
    defined, 365
    Invoice and Return Transactions
        deleting, 371–372
        editing, 371
        entering, 370–371
    Purchase Order Input Form, 365–366
    Purchase Order Report, 373
    purging, 372–373
    transactions
        accessing, 366
        deleting, 368
        editing, 368
        entering, 366–367
Purchase Requisitions, 365
Purchases Account, 114
Purchases Discount, 218
Purchases Journal, 114–116
Purchases Journal Input Form, 115–116
Purchases On Account, 115–116
Purge Invoices and Purchase Orders command (Option menu), 372–373, 417

Quantity Field (Purchase Order Input Form), 366
Quarterly Reports, 332

Rates and Limits fields, 460
Receiving Report, 368
Reconciliation. *See* Bank Reconciliation
Reference Column (General Journal Input Form), 47–48
Reference option (General Journal tab), 48
Reference text box (Customize Journal Report dialog box), 51
Report by Fiscal Period option, 76

Report Selection dialog box, 50, 75, 121, 155
Report Selection (Reports menu), 50
Reports
    Accounting Equation Report, 21
    Accounts Payable Ledger, 124
    Accounts Receivable Ledger Report, 157
    Average Cost Method, 377
    Bank Reconciliation, 79–80
    Depreciation Schedule, 249
    Employee List Report, 331
    First-In, First-Out (FIFO), 377
    General Journal, 120
        Calendar icon, 51
        defined, 49
        displaying, 50
        example of, 52
        function of, 49
    General Ledger, 122–123
    Inventory Exceptions, 375
    Inventory List, 374
    Inventory Transactions, 374–375
    Inventory Valuation, 375–376
    Last-In, First-Out (LIFO), 377
    Payroll Reports, 331
    Performance Report, 462
    Plant Asset List Report, 247
    Purchase Invoice Register, 374
    Purchase Order, 373
    Quarterly, 332
    Receiving, 368
    Schedule of Accounts Payable, 123
    Schedule of Accounts Receivable Report, 157
    W-2 Statements, 332
Reports menu commands
    Graph Selection, 52
    Payroll Reports, 330
    Report Selection, 50, 75
Required Accounts, 455
Retained Earnings, 270
Revenue accounts, 22

Salary Amount field, 324
Sales Discount
    Cash Receipt example, 219
    defined, 218
Sales Invoice
    defined, 150
    Sales Invoice Input Form, 414–415
    Sales Invoice Tab, 415

Sales Journal
    defined, 150
    example of, 151
    Sales Journal Input Form, 150
    Transactions, entering, 151
Sales Order Processing
    Computerized Sales Order Processing System, 412
    defined, 412
    Purge Invoices, 417
    Sales Invoice, 412–413
    Sales Return, 413, 415
        transactions, deleting, 417
        transactions, editing, 417
        transactions, entering, 416
Sales Transaction, 150
Save As menu item (File menu), 13
Save menu item (File menu), 13
Saving Files, 16
Schedule of Accounts Payable Report, 123
Schedule of Accounts Receivable Report, 157
Search Engines, 193
Search tab, 16
Selecting
    Items
        from drop-down lists, 10
        from list boxes, 9
        for Open menu, 12
    Menu Items, 6
Servers, 36
Shareholders, 270
Shares of Stock, 270
Shareware, 44
Shortcut Keys, 6
Sole Proprietorship, 44
Spam, 63
State Tax Brackets, 459
Statement of Account, 158
Stock
    Capital Stock, 270
    Shares of Stock, 270

T Account, 22–23
Tab Sequence, 14
Tabs, 7
    Account Maintenance Window, 8
    General Journal, 47
        Account option, 48
        Credit option, 48
        Debit option, 48

Tabs *(continued)*
    Post option, 48–49
    Reference option, 48
Index, 16
Index and Search, 16
operating procedure, 7
Search, 16
tab sequence, 14
Tax Accountants, 160
Tax Tables
    Federal Tax Brackets option, 458
    Rates and Limits fields, 460
    State Tax Brackets option, 459
Taxes
    Corporate Income Tab, 273–274
    Employer's Payroll, 329
    Payroll Taxes, 325
Tellers, 126
Telnet, 172
Temporary Accounts, 80
Text Boxes
    defined, 7
    text within, selecting, 8
Title Bar, 5
Tooltips, 5
Type of Business field (Company Information Text Box), 453

Uniform Resource Locator (URL), 63
Up Arrow key, 10
URL (Uniform Resource Locator), 63
Useful Life, of Asset, 245
User Data Files, 4
User Interface, 3

Vendors
    Add Vendor button, 115
    Change Vendor button, 115
    defined, 115
    Delete button, 115
    Vendor/Customer Column (General Journal Input Form), 46
    Vendor Maintenance List, 115
    Vendor Range dialog box, 124
Voluntary Deductions, 325, 453

W-2 Statements, 332
Web Browser, 26–27
Web-Hosting Service, 111
Web Pages, Secure, 349
Webmasters, 173
Windows
    Application, 5
    Automated Accounting Application, 5
    Browser, 26–27
    Customers Maintenance, 149
    Customize Accounting System, 452–453
    defined, 6–7
    Employee Account Maintenance, 323
    Employee Maintenance, 323–324
    Explore Accounting System, 25–26
    Help, 15–16
    Moving, 7
    Payroll Transactions, 326–327
    Plant Assets Maintenance, 246
Withholding Allowances field, 324